FAMILY LAW FOR THE HONG KONG SAR

FAMILY LAW
FOR THE
HONG KONG SAR

ATHENA NGA CHEE LIU

HONG KONG UNIVERSITY PRESS

Hong Kong University Press
14/F Hing Wai Centre
7 Tin Wan Praya Road
Aberdeen, Hong Kong

© Hong Kong University Press 1999
First published 1999
Reprinted 2000, 2003

ISBN 962 209 492 9

All rights reserved. No portion of this publication may be reproduced or transmitted in any form or by any means, electronic or mechanical, including photocopy, recording, or any information storage or retrieval system, without permission in writing from the publisher.

Secure On-line Ordering
http://www.hkupress.org

Cover designed by Lea & Ink Design
Printed in Hong Kong by Caritas Printing Training Centre

Contents

Preface   vii

Table of Cases   xi

Table of Legislation   xxxvii

Part I: Marriage and Its Termination   1

1   Customary Marriage, Union of Concubinage and Modern Marriage   3
2   Dissolution under the Marriage Reform Ordinance   55
3   Marriage under the Marriage Ordinance   73
4   Divorce under the Matrimonial Causes Ordinance   99
5   Nullity and Judicial Separation   141

Part II: Children   177

6   Status   179
7   Parentage   193

8	Parental Rights and Authority	211
9	Welfare of the Child	245
10	Children on Family Breakdown	275
11	Adoption	291
12	Wardship	321
13	International Child Abduction	333

Part III: Financial Provision for Family Members	349
14 Maintenance Obligations during Marriage	351
15 Money and Property on Divorce	363
16 Financial Provision for Children	413
17 Settlement, Consent Order and Variation	421

Part IV: Protection	437
18 Child Protection	439
19 Protection against Domestic Violence	459

Index	477

Preface

'Oh, East is East, and West is West, and never shall the twain meet.'[1] This is true, to some extent, with Hong Kong family law. For reasons which can only be explained by reference to history, 'customary marriage', 'union of concubinage' and 'modern marriage', on the one hand, and 'Christian marriage', on the other, the two cultural marriage systems, were strolling hand in hand like a loving couple. But this was not a love affair without problems. 7 October 1971 spelt the demise of one; yet her presence is still undeniable. Only recently the High Court has to consider the validity of a union of concubinage contracted in the mainland China.[2] In fact, judgment of *Re Ng Kwok-hing* on the validity of a purported customary marriage was delivered for the first time in Chinese.[3]

1 July 1997 heralds a historical moment for Hong Kong. The Hong Kong Special Administrative Region, an autonomous region of the Peoples' Republic of China, retains its own legal system. Article 8 of the Basic Law provides that:

> The laws previously in force in Hong Kong, that is, the common law, rules of equity, ordinance, subordinate legislation and customary law shall be maintained, except for any that contravene this Law, and subject to any amendment by the legislature of the Hong Kong Special Administration Region.

---

[1] R Kipling, 'The Ballad of East and West'.
[2] *Chan Chiu-lam v Yau Yee-ping* [1998] HKLRD 716.
[3] High Court, Miscellaneous Proceedings No 2564 of 1994 (1996).

The impact of the Basic Law is immediately tested in two family-related cases, first, the right of abode of person born in the mainland China. The Immigration (Amendment) (No 2) Ordinance came into effect on 1 July 1997 and limits the right of abode of persons born in mainland China to a parent who had the right of abode in Hong Kong at the time of their birth. It was held in *Chan Kam-nga v the Director of Immigration*[4] that the Immigration (Amendment) (No 2) Ordinance contravened Article 24(3) of the Basic Law. As Keith J rightly pointed out, one of the anomalies which the Ordinance created was that:

> Not only could parents be separated from their children, but children could be separated from their younger brothers and sisters. That could happen if their brothers and sisters, unlike them, were born after their mother or father had acquired the right of abode in Kong Kong . . .

Secondly, the conduct of complex litigation on financial matters is expansive. In *Y v Y*,[5] the wife who was unable to finance the litigation sought a capital sum to be released from the family assets, using the principle of Roman-Dutch law which had long been accepted in South Africa, a common law jurisdiction. Deputy Judge Hartmann held that although Article 8 of the Basic Law stated that the laws previously in force in Hong Kong shall be maintained, this meant the 'Common Law of England' and not the rules of all common law jurisdictions. Consequently, the Roman-Dutch principle arising from community of property and the husband's duty of support did not apply in Hong Kong, enabling the wife to seek a contribution towards costs in matrimonial litigation.

Although the impact of the change of sovereignty remains to be unfolded,[6] English case law on family law, particular on some areas, remains an important reference point and its influence is unlikely to diminish in the near future. Thus, in *C v C*,[7] Hunter J said that Hong Kong courts 'can and should derive considerable help from the much wider experience of the English courts in this field'.[8] A good example of this historical linkage can be seen in the law on nullity, and more particularly, the prohibited degrees of consanguinity and affinity, where Hong Kong law is tied to English law. The trend, however, is to move away from the unquestioning acceptance of both English law and case law interpretation for Hong Kong. For instance,

---

[4] 1997 AL No 104 (1998).
[5] [1997] 3 HKC 43.
[6] Bart Rwezaura, 'Hong Kong Family Law and the 1997 Countdown', The International Survey of Family Law (1996) 189–213.
[7] [1990] 2 HKLR 183.
[8] Ibid. at p. 187.

divorce by mutual consent was introduced by Matrimonial Causes (Amendments) Ordinance (No 29 of 1995) at a time when England was debating her own reform direction. Similarly, local decisions governing custody of children reflect Hong Kong's culture specific emphasis and the approach to financial provision and property adjustment on divorce reflect a preference of the parties for a clean break. In the course of writing this book, I have been conscious to cite as many Hong Kong cases as possible to demonstrate the trend and development of local jurisprudence in family law. Attempts have also been made to ensure that those unreported judgments which have now been reported are cited with reference to the Hong Kong Law Reports (HKLR), Hong Kong District Court Law Reports (HKDCLR), Hong Kong Cases (HKC) or Hong Kong Law Yearbook (HKLY), or Hong Kong Law Reports and Digest (HKLRD). However, cases which remain unreported are cited in their usual manner, that is, the court and the filling number to be followed by the year when the action is filed. In most cases, this is followed with the judgment year in brackets.

Children have been a major concern of the law. This book thus includes a chapter on the Protection of Children and Juveniles Ordinance, and the recently enacted Child Abduction and Custody Ordinance which introduces the Hague Convention into Hong Kong.

The last concerted effort to reform family law was in 1971. The time has come for another major effort of law reform. The Hong Kong Law Reform Commission sub-committee on Guardianship and Custody of Minors will initiate its public consultation and so will a judicial Working Group to consider the introduction of a pilot court-annexed mediation. Family law will prove to be a fast changing area of law and practice.

This book is principally a student text. Practitioners, however, may find it a useful resource book, providing ideas, commentaries, important references, and update on current law. In the course of writing this book, it became clear that many family law judgments are still unreported, and thus not easily accessible to the public. It is hoped that a greater degree of transparency could be provided on written judgments.

Lastly, I would like to thank a lot of people for their kind support without which this book would not have been possible. First, my thanks to my colleagues at the Faculty of Law, Professor Albert Chen, and Ms Jill Cottrell, and Ms Sharon Ser, a partner at Hampton, Winter and Glynn for their moral support throughout the gestation period of this work. Enormous thanks are also due to Professor Julien Payne who commented on some draft chapters, Ms Erica Chan who assisted in checking case references, Ms Ivy Man Yuk-sim who, during her summer holiday, diligently checked all case references, produced the table of cases and assisted in indexing. My gratitude is also due to Ms Anne Storey and Ms Frances Irving who read my draft chapters. I owe my biggest debt to Mr Robin Corcos who read the bulk of the book and made it read well. Lastly, my thanks to my husband, Soo-lik, and Emma, our daughter, who has been such a wonderful baby, allowing me the luxury to work long hours — time which I would have otherwise spent with them.

The remaining errors are mine. The law stated is up to date as of July 1998.

Athena Nga Chee Liu
The University of Hong Kong
July 1998

Note on this reprint edition

My colleague, Bart Rwezuara, has helpfully identified a number of corrections to be made for the first reprint. I am most grateful for his kind advice.

Table of Cases

Hong Kong Cases

Adoption Application, Re [1958] HKLR 150   296–297
Agell v Agell, High Court, Action No 4 of 1977 (1977)   362
An Infant, Re [1962] HKLR 167   297
An Infant, Re, [1985] HKLY 512   300

Baillieu v Baillieu, Court of Appeal, Civil Appeal Action No 149 of 1995 (1995)   381, 390, 399
Baring v Baring [1992] HKLY 526   461
Beynon v Beynon, District Court, Divorce Jurisdiction, Action No 614 of 1975 (1977)   382, 383
Boulter v Boulter [1977–1979] HKC 282   278, 279, 286

C (a minor) (wardship: medical treatment), Re [1994] 1 HKLR 60   224, 225, 328
C (a minor), Re [1989] 2 HKLR 652   331
C v C, Court of Appeal, Civil Appeal Action No 44 of 1988 (1988)   252
C v C [1971] HKLR 56   158
C v C [1990] 2 HKLR 183   viii, 364, 380, 385, 402
C v C, [1977–1979] HKC 363   262, 383, 385, 402
CCCY v CWL [1980] HKC 522   158, 159
Chan Cheung-hing v Chan Tang-lan [1985] 2 HKC 316   370
Chan Chiu-lam v Yau Yee-ping [1998] HKLRD 716   vii, 31, 37

Chan Chuck-wai v Chan Chan Yin-kwan, District Court, Divorce Jurisdiction, Action No 245 of 1979 (1981)   382, 408
Chan Chung-hing v Wong Kim-wah [1986] HKLR 715   7, 11, 12, 13, 18, 19, 21, 23, 67, 77
Chan Chun-hon v Chan Lam Lai-bing, Court of Appeal, Civil Appeal Action No 43 of 1994 (1994)   466, 467, 468
Chan Heung (an infant), Re, High Court, Miscellaneous Proceedings No 349 of 1983 (1983)   251
Chan Kam-nga v Director of Immigration, 1997 AL No 104 (1998)   viii
Chan Lee-kuen v Chan Sui-fai [1966] HKLR 796   12, 80
Chan Shin Sui-ping v Chan Din-tsang [1958] HKLR 283   79, 80
Chan Tse-shi, Re [1954] HKLR 9   291
Chan Wei-yin v Cheong Shun-chiu [1993] 2 HKLR 485   368
Chan Wing-ming v Chan Li-li [1957] HKLR 474   126
Chan Yu Wai-ming v Chan Cheak-wing, Court of Appeal, Civil Appeal Action No 123 of 1985 (1986)   128
Chan Yue v Henry Leong Estate Ltd [1953] HKLR 66   291
Chau Ming-cheong v R [1983] HKLR 187   442
Cheung Lai-wah v The Director of Immigration [1997] 3 HKC 64   188
Cheung Wong Kim-ching v Cheung Chai-kong [1991] 1 HKLR 698   362, 370, 385, 386, 392, 395, 396, 404, 405
Cheung Yee-mong v So Kwok-yan [1996] 2 HKC 360   220
Cheung Yuk-lin v Hui Shiu-wing (No 4) [1970] HKLR 119   382, 396, 397
Chiu Kwai-fun v Lam Hing-keung, High Court, Miscellaneous Proceedings No 968 of 1985 (1985)   326, 333
Cho Fok Bo-ying v Cho Chi-biu [1990] 2 HKC 269   422
Chong Chui Yuk-ching v Chong Pui-cheong [1983] HKDCLR 1   22, 42, 77
Chow Cheung Suk-king v Chow Yan-piu, Court of Appeal, Civil Appeal Action No 180 of 1984 (1984)   255, 256, 257, 259, 260
Choy Kin-choy v Choy Chan Kai-ngar, Court of Appeal, Civil Appeal Action No 47 of 1993 (1993)   370, 371, 383, 409, 412
Chung Kai-fun v Lau Wai-king [1966] HKLR 881   79

D (an infant), Re [1962] HKLR 431   294, 295
Director of Social Welfare v Lam Kwok-wah [1988] 1 HKLR 206   224, 329
Director of Social Welfare v Tam [1987] HKLR 66   224, 328

Fei Tai-chung v Gloria Fei, Court of Appeal, Civil Appeal Action No 170 of 1994 (1995)   380, 383, 398, 411

Fong Pak-kai v Fong Chue Yiu-ling [1995] 2 HKC 518   153
Fung Ling Pui-sim v Fung Ning-sam, District Court, Divorce Jurisdiction, Action No 69 of 1981 (1982)   410

Gensburger v Gensburger [1968] HKLR 403   108
Griggs v Griggs [1971] HKLR 299   104

H v H [1981] HKLR 376   388
Hamlett v Hamlett [1996] 1 HKC 61   380, 382, 393, 405, 411, 470
Ho Har-chun v Yiu Hon-ming, District Court, Action No 2381 of 1970   12, 19, 22, 23
Ho Lee Kam-wan v Ho Man, Court of Appeal, Civil Appeal Action No 78 of 1988 (1988)   269
Ho Tsz-tsun v Ho Au-shi (1915) 10 HKLR 69   30
Ho Yiu-chuen Fong v Ho Wei-yiu [1986] HKLR 99   417
Hon To Lai-chu v Hon Wing-chun [1985] HKLR 490   385
Horton v Horton, High Court, Divorce Jurisdiction, Action No 19 of 1983 (1984)   362
Hudson v Hudson, District Court, Divorce Jurisdiction, Action No 1223 of 1980   385
Huen Sook Jong Miller v Stephen Henry Miller, High Court, Divorce Jurisdiction, Action No 6 of 1985 (1985)   362
Hui I-mei v Cheng Yau-shing, Court of Appeal, Civil Appeal Action No 157 of 1996 (1996)   369, 381, 383, 385, 395, 402, 408, 411
Hui Shiu-wing v Cheung Yuk-lin [1968] HKLR 501   121
Huthart (infants), Re, High Court, Miscellaneous Proceedings No 1037 of 1981 (1984)   247, 251, 253, 262, 267

Ives v Ives [1967] HKLR 423   83

Julie Ong, Re, High Court, Miscellaneous Proceedings No 1895 of 1988 (1989)   252, 260

K v W [1998] 1 HKLRD 402   363, 419
Kam Leung Kit-yee v Kam Ying-fai, Court of Appeal, Civil Appeal Action No 194 of 1996 (1997)   368
Kao Yeung Lun-kuk v Kao Cho [1975] HKLR 449   83
Keiko Maruko v Yoshio Maruko, Court of Appeal, Civil Appeal Action No 32 of 1995 (1995)   367
Kishen Das, Re (1933) 26 HKLR 42   5, 82
Kwan Bui-lock v Isabella Stamm Lock, District Court, Miscellaneous Proceedings No 106 of 1979   125

Kwan Chui Kwok-ying v Tao Wai-chun [1995] 1 HKC 374   19, 22, 26, 36, 37
Kwan Kai-ming, Re, High Court, Miscellaneous Proceedings No 2996 of 1990 (1994)   199
Kwok Micah (a minor), Re, High Court, Miscellaneous Proceedings No 3040 of 1984 (1985)   251, 253, 326

L (an infant), Re [1989] 1 HKLR 614   299
L v C, High Court, Miscellaneous Proceedings No 4167 of 1993 (1994)   191, 198
L v L [1970] HKLR 556   251
Lai Kin-fung (an infant), Re, District Court, Miscellaneous Proceedings No 401 of 1979 (1980)   259, 262
Lai Lai-hing v Lai Kwai-ping [1995] 1 HKC 654   368, 380, 383, 411
Lau Chu v Lau Tang Su-ping [1989] 2 HKLR 470   131, 421
Lau Lap-che v Wong Sut-fan [1996] 1 HKC 165   411
Law Lo Shiu-chun v Law Wing-chee, Court of Appeal, Civil Appeal Action No 130 of 1993 (1994)   388, 389
Law Shi-ying v Law Kam-tai, Court of Appeal, Civil Appeal Action No 45 of 1994 (1994)   389
Lee Cheuh-wah (an infant), Re, High Court, Miscellaneous Proceedings No 2678 of 1983 (1984)   252, 255, 261, 262
Lee Ka-ming, Re, Court of Appeal, Civil Appeal Action Nos 162 & 163 of 1990 (1991)   187
Lee Lan v Henry Ho, High Court, Miscellaneous Proceedings No 3441 of 1978 (1980)   19, 40, 42, 43
Lee Wai-chu v Lee Yim-chuen, High Court, Miscellaneous Proceedings No 2678 of 1983 (1984)   277, 326
Lee Yuen-sam v Lee Tang Hop-wo, High Court, Divorce Jurisdiction, Action No 14 of 1978 (1979)   111
Leung May-ling v Leung Sai-lun [1997] HKLRD 12   26
Leung Yuet-ming v Hui Hon-kit, Court of Appeal, Civil Appeal Action No 63 of 1994 (1994)   361
Li Kao Feng-ning v Li Hung-lit, Court of Appeal, Civil Appeal Action No 58 of 1983 (1983)   110
Li Wang-fat v R [1982] HKLR 133   441
Lily Li v Patrick Wu [1956] HKLR 363   106
Lindsay v Lindsay [1983] 2 HKC 302   109
Liu Lau Oi-yuk v Liu Chian-hsiong, Court of Appeal, Civil Appeal Action No 126 of 1997 (1997)   255, 261, 263
Lo Chun Wing-yee v Lo Pong-hing [1985] 2 HKC 647   277, 278, 279
Lui Kit-chiu v Lui Kwok Hin-chau [1976] HKDCLR 51   42, 43

TABLE OF CASES xv

Lui Sik-kuen v Lee Suk-ling [1992] 2 HKLR 371   433
Lui Yuk-ping v Chow To [1962] HKLR 515   12, 28, 32, 245, 247, 262
LYC (an infant), Re [1961] HKLR 491   297

M, Re [1989] 2 HKLR 117   468
Mark Leung, Re, High Court, Miscellaneous Proceedings No 142 of 1985 (1985)   255, 259, 261, 327
Melwani v Melwani, Court of Appeal, Civil Appeal Action No 39 of 1986 (1986)   288
Mok Po-sing v Lie Lie-khim [1996] 3 HKC 330   160, 172
Mong Ka-hung (a minor), High Court, Miscellaneous Proceedings No 1908 of 1982 (1983)   253
Moss v Moss, Court of Appeal, Civil Appeal Action No 145 of 1992 (1993)   382, 385, 393, 395
Mr and Mrs C v Mr D, Guardian ad litem [1993] 2 HKLR 385   299, 311–312
Murphy v Murphy, Court of Appeal, Civil Appeal Action No 56 of 1992 (1992)   366, 367, 374, 381, 390

Ng Cheei-fai v Ng Han Lai-wah, Court of Appeal, Civil Appeal Action No 28 of 1980 (1980)   257
Ng Kwok-hing, Re, High Court, Miscellaneous Proceedings No 2564 of 1994 (1996)   vii, 22, 26
Ng Shum (No 2), Re [1990] 1 HKLR 67   12, 18, 19, 24, 31, 46, 47
Ng Ying-ho v Tam Suen-yu [1963] HKLR 923   13, 35
Ngai Wong Yun ping v Ngai Yun-lung, Court of Appeal, Civil Appeal Action No 50 of 1996 (1996)   368, 370, 371, 401, 410
Ngao Tang Yau-lin v Ngao Kai-suen [1984] HKLR 310   380
Nguyen Dang Vu v AG, High Court, Miscellaneous Proceedings No 4257 of 1993 (1994)   322, 323, 331
NTH (an infant), Re [1996] 1 HKC 93   296

Partridge v R [1977] HKLR 89   153
Phillips, Re, High Court Adoption Nos 2 & 3 of 1985 (1986)   308

R v Cheung King-po [1927] HKLR 104   291
R v Sze Tin-sin [1987] 3 HKC 333   153
R v Wong Tin Kau, 28 March 1996, *South China Morning Post*   220
Ryker (infants), Re, High Court, Miscellaneous Proceedings No 1184 of 1980 (1982)   258, 277

S v S, High Court, Miscellaneous Proceedings No 364 of 1998 (1998)   340, 341

Savournin v Lau [1971] HKLR 180   104
Seghin v Seghin, Court of Appeal, Civil Appeal Action No 274 of 1995 (1996)   258
Shu Wing-li v Yeung Siu-ling, Court of Appeal, Civil Appeal Action No 42 of 1994 (1994)   161
Sit Woo-tung [1990] 2 HKLR 410   187
So Mei-chu v Wong Wai-anucha, High Court, Miscellaneous Proceedings No 3360 of 1990 (1991)   324

T.M.H. an infant, Re (No 2) [1962] HKLR 316   327
Ta Tran Thi Thanh v Ta Van Hung and other [1981] HKDCLR 37   104
Tang Lai Sau-kiu v Tang Loi [1987] HKLR 85   12, 79
Tang Lau Wai-chun v Tang Fung-fat [1986] HKLR 907   264, 265
Tang Yung Wai-han v Kwing Pui-yung, Civil Appeal, Civil Appeal Action No 201 of 1985 (1986)   362
Tao Chen Pi-o v Tai Hsiuo-ming, Court of Appeal, Civil Appeal Action Nos 37 and 38 of 1993 (1993)   388, 389
Thomson v Thomson, Court of Appeal, Civil Appeal Action No 52 of 1991 (1991)   365, 380
Trance v Walli, High Court, Miscellaneous Proceedings No 905 of 1988 (1988)   260, 322, 327

V (infant), Re, Miscellaneous Proceedings No 477 of 1979 (1979)   326, 344
V v V, Court of Appeal, Civil Appeal Action No 200 of 1980 (1981)   362

W (an infant), Re [1971] HKLR 219   307
W v W [1970] HKLR 4   106, 158
W v W [1981] HKC 466   258
Wong Che-wa v Wong Chung Yee-fong, High Court, Divorce Jurisdiction, Action No 64 of 1981 (1983)   362
Wong Chiu Ngar-chi v Wong Hon-wai [1987] HKLR 179   252, 277, 278, 324, 326
Wong Choi-ho, Re [1969] HKLR 391   10, 13, 14, 25, 31, 32
Wong Kam-ying v Man Chi-tai [1967] HKLR 201   6, 11, 13, 21, 33, 34, 37
Wong Leung-see v Wong Lo Lung-kwan [1985] 2 HKC 228   130
Wong Sin-yee v Cheung Si-yan, Court of Appeal, Civil Appeal Action No 222 of 1996 (1997)   391–392, 395, 411
Wong Tai-hing v Wong Lau Yuk-ling, District Court, Divorce Jurisdiction, Action No 776 of 1983 (1984)   368
Wong Tat-lun v Wong Chan Siu-ping, Court of Appeal, Civil Appeal Action No 111 of 1987 (1987)   133

TABLE OF CASES   xvii

Wong Wong, Re, High Court, Probate Jurisdiction No 1797 of 1998 (1998)   26
Wong Yee-ling v Ng Tung-hoi [1970] HKLR 183   245, 247, 262
Wong Yip Yuk-ping v Wong Sze-sang, Court of Appeal, Civil Appeal Action No 116 of 1985 (1985)   251, 256, 257
Wong Yiu-lan v Wong Yuen-ting [1995] 1 HKLR 411   389, 395, 397, 410

Y (minors), Re [1984] HKLR 204   257, 262, 321, 324, 325
Y v Y [1997] 3 HKC 43   viii
Y, Re [1946–1972] HKC 378   251
Yau Tin-sung v Yau Wan-loi [1983] 2 HKC 647   291
Yeung Chung-ping v Yeung Wan Yuet-kuen [1987] 1 HKC 206   202
Yeung Leung Yau-lin v Yeung Kam-wah [1977–1979] HKC 328   109
Yeung Yeu-kong v Yeung Fung Lai-mui [1971] HKLR 13   26, 30, 32
Yue Chen Kuei-mei v Yue Kwok-kee, Court of Appeal, Civil Appeal Action No 19 of 1993 (1993)   376
Yuen Yu-biu v Yuen Nip [1977–1979] HKC 453   114, 133

Other Cases

A (a minor) (abduction), Re [1988] 1 FLR 365   340
A (a minor) (adoption: access), Re (1991) Fam Law 360   315
A (a minor) (paternity: refusal of blood test), Re [1994] 2 FLR 463   204
A (minors) (wardship: children in care), Re [1980] 1 FLR 100   267
A (minors: disclosure of material), Re [1991] 2 FLR 473   325
A (section 8 order: grandparent application), Re [1995] 2 FLR 153   289
A v A (a minor: financial provision) [1994] 1 FLR 657   363, 366, 419
A v A (children: arrangements) [1979] 1 WLR 533   129
A v A (family: unborn child) [1974] 2 WLR 106   415
A v A (minors) (shared residence order) [1994] 1 FLR 669   279
A v DPP, (1996) The Times Law Report 18 April   219
A v J (nullity) (1989) Fam Law 63   160
A v Liverpool City Council [1982] AC 363   331
AB (adoption: joint residence), Re [1996] 1 FLR 27   295
Adeoso v Adeoso [1981] 1 All ER 107   117, 461
Adoption Application (non-patrial: breach of procedures), Re (1993) Fam Law 275   310
Adoption Application (payment for adoption), Re [1987] Fam 81   311
Adoption Application, Re [1992] 1 FLR 341   311
Agar-Ellis, Re (1878) 10 Ch. D 49; (1883) 24 Ch D 318   218
Ah Chuck v Needham [1931] NZLR 559   197

Ainsbury v Millington [1986] 1 All ER 73   471, 472
Aldrich v AG [1968] P. 281   198, 199
Allsop v Allsop (1981) Fam Law 18   433
Amey v Amey [1992] 2 FLR 89   434
Ampthill Peerage Case, The [1977] AC 547   179, 194, 199
An infant, Re, [1963] 6 FLR 12 (Supreme Court of Victoria, Australia)   152
Ansah v Ansah [1977] 2 All ER 638   468
Archard v Archard (1972) The Times 20 April   108
Armstrong v Armstrong (1974) 118 SJ 579   406
Ash v Ash [1972] 1 All ER 582   108
Associated Provincial Picture Houses Ltd. Wednesbury Corporation [1948] 1 KB 223   444
Atkinson v Atkinson [1988] FLR 353   393
Attar v Attar (No 2) [1985] FLR 653   380, 382, 389, 398
AW (adoption application), Re [1993] 1 FLR 62   311
AZ (a minor) (abduction: acquiescence), Re [1993] 1 FLR 682   339

B (a minor) (abduction), Re [1994] 2 FLR 249   336
B (a minor) (access), Re [1984] FLR 648   287
B (a minor) (adoption: jurisdiction), Re [1975] 2 All ER 449   308
B (a minor) (adoption: parental agreement), Re [1990] 2 FLR 383   307
B (a minor) (disclosure of evidence), Re [1993] 1 FLR 191   270
B (a minor) (wardship: medical treatment), Re [1981] 1 WLR 1421   224
B (a minor) (wardship: sterilisation), Re [1987] 2 All ER 206   223
B (adoption: child's welfare), Re [1995] 1 FLR 895   300, 306
B (JA) (an infant), Re [1965] Ch 1112   325
B (minors)(abduction) (No 2), Re [1993] 1 FLR 993   336, 337, 339
B (parentage), Re [1996] 2 FLR 15   207
B and G (minors) (custody), Re [1985] FLR 134   254
B and G (minors) (custody), Re [1985] FLR 493   254
B v AG (B and others intervening) [1966] 2 All ER 145   199
B v B (abduction) [1993] 1 FLR 238   340
B v B (consent order: variation) [1995] 1 FLR 9   424, 432
B v B (custody of children) [1985] FLR 166   254, 263
B v B (discovery: financial provision) [1990] 2 FLR 180   389
B v B (financial provision) [1982] 3 FLR 298   385, 391
B v B (financial provision) [1990] 1 FLR 20   387
B v B (minors) (interviews and listing arrangements) [1994] 2 FLR 489   251, 252, 268
B (otherwise S) v B [1958] 1 WLR 619   159
B v C (enforcement: arrears) [1995] 1 FLR 467   366
B v K (child abduction) (1993) Fam Law 17   341

TABLE OF CASES

B v Miller & Co [1996] 2 FLR 23   422
Baby M 109 NJ 396; 537 A 2d 1227 (1988)   206
Banbury Peerage Case, The (1811) 1 Sim. & St. 153   197
Bannister v Bannister (1980) 10 Fam Law 240   109
Barder v Barder (Caluori Intervening) [1987] 2 FLR 480   433
Barnado v McHugh [1891] AC 388   229
Barrett v Barrett [1988] 2 FLR 516   378, 382
Baxter v Baxter [1948] AC 274   158
BC (a minor) (access), Re [1985] FLR 639   287
Beach v Beach [1995] 2 FLR 160   424
Beeken v Beeken [1948] P. 302   118
Bennett v Bennett [1969] 1 All ER 539   168
Bennett v Bennett (1979) 9 Fam Law 19   391
Benson v Benson (deceased) [1996] 1 FLR 692   434
Bernstein v Bernstein [1892] P. 375   356
Birchall, Re (1880) 16 Ch D 41   222
Blower v Blower (1986) 16 Fam Law 56   396
Bolsom v Bolsom [1983] 4 FLR 21   266, 382
Bowman v Bowman [1949] P. 353   124
Boylan v Boylan [1988] 1 FLR 282   382
Bradley v Bradley [1973] 1 WLR 1291   113
Bradshaw v Bradshaw [1956] P. 274   82
Brickell v Brickell [1974] Fam 31   134
Brockwell v Brockwell (1976) 6 Fam Law 46   423
Brooks v Brooks [1995] 2 FLR 13   370
Brown v Brown [1959] P. 86   369
Brown v Brown [1994] 1 FLR 233   468
Brown v Matthews [1990] 2 All ER 155   266, 267
Browning v Browning [1911] P. 161   353
BT v BT (divorce: procedure) [1990] 2 FLR 1   433
Buchler v Buchler [1947] 1 All ER 319   121
Buckland v Buckland [1968] P. 296   163
Buffery v Buffery [1988] 2 FLR 365   105
Burbury v Jackson [1917] 1 KB 16   191
Burgess v Burgess [1996] 2 FLR 34   385, 402
Burke v Burke [1987] 2 FLR 71   468
Burnett v George [1992] 1 FLR 525   474
Burris v Azadani [1996] 1 FLR 266   473
Burton v Burton [1986] 2 FLR 419   370

C (a minor) (abduction), Re [1989] 1 FLR 403   340
C (a minor) (adoption application), Re [1993] 1 FLR 87   311

C (a minor) (adoption order: conditions), Re [1989] AC 1   314
C (a minor) (adoption: parental agreement: contact), Re [1993] 2 FLR 260   302, 306
C (a minor) (irregularity of practice), Re [1991] 2 FLR 438   270
C (a minor) (wardship: medical treatment), Re [1989] 3 WLR 240   224, 328
C (a minor) (wardship: surrogacy), Re (1985) 15 Fam Law 191   330
C (a minor), Re (1979) Fam Law 50   266
C (an infant), Re (1956) Times, 14 December   323
C (minors) (wardship: adoption), Re [1989] 1 FLR 222   296
C (minors) (wardship: jurisdiction) [1977] 3 WLR 561   326, 344
C (minors) (parental rights) [1992] 1 FLR 1   233
C v C (1981) 11 Fam Law 147   268
C v C (divorce: exceptional hardship) [1980] Fam 23   125, 126
C v C (financial provision: non-disclosure) [1994] 2 FLR 272   433
C v C (financial provision: personal damages) [1995] 2 FLR 171   391
C v C (financial relief: short marriage) [1997] 2 FLR 26   366, 383, 399
C v C (minors: custody) [1988] 2 FLR 291   257
C v C [1942] NZLR 356   165, 166
C v K (inherent powers: exclusion order) [1996] 2 FLR 506   472
C, Re (financial provision: leave to appeal) [1993] 2 FLR 799   433
C, Re [1978] Fam 105   237
Cackett v Cackett [1950] P. 233   158
Cadman v Cadman [1982] 3 FLR 275   264, 266
Calderbank v Calderbank [1976] Fam 93   364, 385, 396, 397
Camm v Camm [1983] 4 FLR 577   416, 424
Campbell v Campbell [1977] 1 All ER 1   400
Campbell v Tameside Metropolitan BC [1982] 2 All ER 791   266
Carpenter v Carpenter [988] 1 FLR 121   469
Carr v Carr [1974] 1 WLR 1534   107
Carson v Carson [1983] 1 All ER 478   429
Cassidy v Cassidy [1959] 3 All ER 187   353
CB (a minor)(blood tests) [1994] 2 FLR 762   203
CH (contact: parentage), Re [1996] 1 FLR 569   289
Chamberlain v Chamberlain [1974] 1 All ER 33   417
Chard v Chard [1956] P. 259   83
Chatterton v Gerson [1981] 1 Q.B. 432   222
Chaudhuri v Chaudhuri [1992] 2 FLR 73   434
Cheang Thye Phin v Tan Ah Loy [1920] AC 369   35
Choo Eng-neo v Neo Chan-neo (1908) 12 SSLR 120   29
Churchman v Churchman [1945] P. 44   356
Clark v Clark (1970) 114 SJ 318   266

TABLE OF CASES xxi

Clarke-Hunt v Newcombe [1983] 4 FLR 482   268
Cleary v Cleary [1974] 1 All ER 498   106, 107
Clutton v Clutton [1991] 1 FLR 242   382
Coleman v Coleman [1972] 3 All ER 886   366
Collett v Collett [1968] P. 482   76
Cook v Cook [1988] 1 FLR 521   434
Cooper v Crane [1891] P. 369   162
Corbett v Corbett [1971] P. 83   155, 156, 158
Cornick v Cornick [1994] 2 FLR 530   434
Cossey v UK (1990) 13 EHRR 622   157
Council of Civil Service Unions v Minister of the Civil Service [1985] AC 374   444
Court v Court [1982] 3 WLR 199   124
Crabtree v Crabtree [1953] 2 All ER 56   119
Crowther v Crowther [1951] AC 723   119
Crozier v Crozier [1994] 1 FLR 126   434
Cumbers v Cumbers [1975] 1 All ER 1   131, 383

D (a minor) (abduction), Re [1989] 1 FLR 403   335
D (a minor) (adoption: freeing order), Re [1991] 1 FLR 48   301, 306
D (a minor) (contact: mother's hostility), Re [1993] 2 FLR 1   287
D (a minor) (wardship: sterilisation), Re [1976] 1 All ER 326   223, 322, 324, 325
D (a minor), Re [1987] 1 AC 317   449, 450, 451
D (adoption reports: confidentiality), Re [1995] 1 FLR 631   313
D (adoption: parents consent), Re [1977] AC 602   308
D (minors) (adoption by step-parent), Re [1981] 2 FLR 102   307, 308
D (minors) (conciliation: privilege), Re [1993] 1 FLR 932   265
D (minors) (wardship: jurisdiction), Re [1973] 2 All ER 993   247, 282
D v A (1845) 1 Rob Eccl 279   158
D v D (custody of child) [1981] 2 FLR 74   267
D v D (nullity) [1979] 3 All ER 337   144
D v D [1979] 3 WLR 185   170
D v Hereford and Worcester County Council [1991] 1 FLR 205   233
D v National Society for the Prevention of Cruelty to Children [1978] AC 171   266, 442
D v Registrar General [1996] 1 FLR 707   317
D.J.M.S. (a minor), Re [1977] 3 All ER 582   219
Dart v Dart [1996] 2 FLR 286   389, 395
Daubney v Daubney [1976] 2 All ER 453   391
Davis v Johnson [1979] AC 264   459, 461, 462, 464
De Lasala v De Lasala [1980] AC 546   423, 433, 435

De Reneville v De Reneville [1948] P. 100   142
Deacock v Deacock [1958] P. 230   153
Dean v Dean [1923] P. 172   397
Dennis v Dennis (1955) P. 153   106
Dennis v Dennis (1976) 6 Fam Law 54   391
Des Salles d'Epinoix v Des Salles d'Epinoix [1967] 1 WLR 553   470
Dickson v Dickson (1983) 13 Fam Law 174   268
Dicocco v Milne [1983] 4 FLR 247   254
Dinch v Dinch [1987] 2 FLR 162   429
Dipper v Dipper [1980] 2 All ER 722   277, 278
Dodds v AG (1880) The Law Times 22 May   198
Dorin v Dorin (1875) LR 7   188
Douglas v Douglas [1951] P. 85   357
Drew v Drew (1888) 13 PD 97   118
Dunford v Dunford [1980] 1 All ER 122   410
Dunn v Dunn [1965] 1 All ER 1043   119, 121
Durham v Durham (1885) 10 PD 80   166
Duxbury v Duxbury [1987] 1 FLR 7   387, 394

E (a minor) (child support: blood test), Re [1994] 2 FLR 548   203
E (a minor) (wardship: court's duty), Re [1984] 1 WLR 156   325
Edgar v Edgar [1980] 3 All ER 887   423, 424, 427, 432
Edmonds v Edmonds [1990] 2 FLR 202   434
Edwards v Edwards [1986] 1 FLR 187   265
EH and MH (step-parent adoption), Re (1993) Fam Law 187   307, 308
Elder v Elder [1986] 1 FLR 610   267
EL-G (minors) (wardship and adoption), Re [1983] 4 FLR 421   301, 305
Essex County Council v R [1993] 2 FLR 826   271
Essex County Council v T.L.R. and K.B.R. (1979) 9 Fam Law 15   451
Ette v Ette [1964] 1 WLR 1433   389
Ettenfield v Ettenfield [1940] P. 96   195
Eve, Re [1909] 1 Ch. 796   188
Ewart v Ewart [1959] P. 23   425

F (a minor), Re [1989] 1 All ER 1155   331
F (an infant), Re [1969] 2 Ch. 238   251
F (an infant), Re [1970] 1 QB 385   300
F (an infant), Re [1988] 2 Ch. 238   263
F (child abduction: risk if returned), Re [1995] 2 FLR 31   335, 340
F (in utero), Re [1988] 2 All ER 193   332, 451
F (minor: paternity tests), Re [1993] 1 FLR 225   203
F (minors) (police investigation), Re [1989] Fam 18   266

F v AG (1980) Fam Law 60   182
F v F (Duxbury calculation: rate of return) [1996] 1 FLR 833   387
F v F (Maintenance Pending Suit) (1982) Fam Law 16   362
F v F (protection from violence: continuing cohabitation) [1989] 2 FLR 451   462, 463
F v F [1902] 1 Ch. 688   240
F v Metropolitan Borough of Wirral District Council [1991] 2 FLR 114   216
F v S (adoption: ward) [1973] Fam 203   324
F v Suffolk County Council [1981] 2 FLR 208   450
F v West Berkshire Health Authority [1989] 2 All ER 545   222
Fay v Fay [1982] AC 835   125
Fisher v Fisher [1948] P. 263   125
Foley v Foley [1981] Fam 160   400
Ford v Ford (1987) Fam Law 232   160
Fowke v Fowke [1983] 1 Ch. 774   144
Fowler v Fowler [1963] P. 311   269
Francis v Francis [1960] P. 17   197
Freeman-Thomas v Freeman-Thomas [1963] 1 All ER 17   430
Fuller v Fuller [1973] 1 WLR 730   113, 114
Furniss v Furniss [1982] 3 FLR 46   385
Fynn, Re (1848) 2 De G & SM 457   248

G (a minor) (abduction), Re [1989] 2 FLR 475   340
G (adoption: freeing order), Re [1997] 2 FLR 202   305
G (minors) (welfare report: disclosure), Re [1993] 2 FLR 293   265
G (parentage: blood sample), Re [1997] 1 FLR 360   205
G v G (1871) LR 2 P & D 287   159
G v G (minors) (abduction) [1991] 2 FLR 506   343
G v G (minors: custody appeal) [1985] FLR 894   268
G v G [1924] AC 349   159
G v J (ouster order) [1993] 1 FLR 1008   465, 466, 467, 468
Galan v Galan [1985] FLR 905   464, 468
Gallagher v Gallagher [1965] 1 WLR 1110   119, 120
Gardner v Gardner (1877) 4 R. (HL) 56   184, 196
Garner v Garner [1992] 1 FLR 573   432
Gaskin v Liverpool City Council [1980] 1 WLR 1549   266
Gengler v Gengler [1976] 2 All ER 81   398
George v George [1986] 2 FLR 347   462
Gereis v Yagoub [1997] 1 FLR 854   152
Gillick v West Norfolk and Wisbech Area Health Authority [1985] 3 All ER 402   216, 218, 226
Gipps v Gipps (1864) 11 HL Cas 1   356, 357

Godfrey v Godfrey [1965] AC 444   357
Goertz v Gordon unreported, (May 2 , 1996) (Supreme Court of Canada)   278
Gojkovic v Gojkovic [1990] 1 FLR 140   383, 387, 403
Gollins v Gollins [1963] 2 All ER 966   121
Goodfield v Goodfield (1975) 5 Fam Law 197   409
Goodrich v Goodrich [1971] 1 WLR 1142   107
Gorman v Gorman [1964] 3 All ER 739   427
Gorst v Gorst [1952] P. 94   356
Goshawk v Goshawk (1965) 109 SJ 290   106
Griffiths v Griffiths (1944) 1R 35   164
Griffiths v Griffiths [1974] 1 All ER 932   385
Griffiths v Griffiths [1984] 2 All ER 626   417
Grigson v Grigson [1974] 1 All ER 478   131

H (a minor) (contact), Re [1994] 2 FLR 776   289
H (a minor) (parental responsibility), Re [1993] 1 FLR 484   234, 287, 288
H (abduction: acquiescence), Re [1997] 1 FLR 872   335, 337, 339
H (abduction: custody rights) [1991] 2 FLR 262   335, 338
H (adoption: disclosure of information), Re [1995] 1 FLR 236   317
H (an infant), Re [1959] 3 All ER 746   238
H (conciliation: welfare reports), Re [1986] 1 FLR 476   265
H (illegitimate children: father: parental rights (No 2)), Re [1991] 1 FLR 214   231, 233
H (infants) (adoption: parental consent), Re [1977] 1 WLR 471   301
H (minors) (access), Re [1992] 1 FLR 148   286
H (minors) (sexual abuse: standard of proof), Re [1996] 2 WLR 8   106, 449, 451
H (orse. D) v H [1953] 2 All ER 1229   161, 164
H (paternity: blood test), Re [1996] 2 FLR 65   203
H v H (child abuse: access) [1989] 1 FLR 212   288
H v H (child: judicial interview) [1974] 1 All ER 1145   267
H v H (financial provision: conduct) [1994] 2 FLR 801   407
H v H (financial provision: remarriage) [1975] 1 All ER 367   375, 394, 401
H v H (financial provision: short marriage) [1981] 2 FLR 392   399
H v H (Kent County Council intervening) (child abuse: evidence) [1989] 3 All ER 740   449, 450, 452
H v H (minors) (forum conveniens) [1993] 1 FLR 958   345
H v H (residence order: leave to remove from jurisdiction) [1995] 1 FLR 529   250
H v H [1969] 1 All ER 262   256
H v H (1982) The Times Law Report 1 April   269

H's Settlement, Re [1909] 2 Ch. 260   324, 328
Haines v Jeffreys (1696) 92 ER 929   148
Hale v Hale [1975] 2 All ER 1090   367, 368
Hall v Hall (1749) 3 Atk. 719   218
Hall v Hall [1960] 1 WLR 52   120
Hall v Hollander (1825) 4 B & C 660   215
Hanlon v Hanlon [1978] 2 All ER 889   410
Hanlon v Law Society [1981] AC 124   372
Harnett v Harnett [1973] 3 WLR 1   373, 406
Haroutunian v Jennings [1980] 1 FLR 62   419
Harris v Manahan [1997] 1 FLR 205   424, 435
Harrison v Lewis [1988] 2 FLR 339   461, 462
Hartford v Morris (1776) 2 Hag Con 423   162
Harthan v Harthan [1948] 2 All ER 639   160
Harvey v Harvey [1982] 1 All ER 693
Hawkins v AG [1966] 1 All ER 392   183
HB (abduction: children's objections), Re [1997] 1 FLR 392   339, 340, 341
Healey v Healey [1984] 3 All ER 1040   129
Heath, Re [1945] 1 Ch. 417   195
Hennie v Hennie [1993] 2 FLR 351   471
Hepworth, Re [1936] 1 Ch. 750   184
Hewer v Bryant [1970] 1 QB 357   212, 213, 217, 279
Hewitson v Hewitson [1995] 1 FLR 241   435
Hill v Hill [1997] 1 FLR 730   366, 400, 432, 435
Hillier v Hillier [1958] P. 186   124
Hirani v Hirani [1983] 4 FLR 232   161, 163
Hitchcock v WB [1952] 2 All ER 119   306
Hopes v Hopes [1948] 2 All ER 920   113, 117
Hope-Smith v Hope-Smith [1989] 2 FLR 56   434
Horner v Horner [1982] 2 WLR 914   462, 469
Horton v Horton [1947] 2 All ER 871   159
Hunt v Hunt (1884) 28 Ch. D 606   278
Hunter v Canary Wharf Ltd [1997] 2 All ER 426   473
Hyde v Hyde (1866) LR 1 P & D 130   73, 154
Hyman v Hyman [1929] AC 601   421

In the Goods of Lao Leong An [1893] 1 SSLR 1   29
In the marriage of C and D [1979] 35 FLR 304   156
Inglis v Inglis [1967] 2 All ER 71   356
Inze v Republic of Austria (1987) 10 EHRR 394   180
Iredell v Iredell (1885) 1 TLR 260   326

J (a minor) (abduction), Re [1990] 1 FLR 276   336
J (a minor) (abduction: custody rights), Re [1990] 2 AC 562   335, 336, 337
J (a minor) (interim custody: appeal), Re [1989] 2 FLR 304   255
J (a minor) (wardship), Re [1988] 1 FLR 65   203
J (a minor) (wardship: medical treatment), Re [1990] 3 All ER 930   224
J (adoption order: conditions), Re [1973] Fam 106   315
J (H.D.) v J (A.M.) [1980] 1 WLR 124   430
J v C [1969] 1 All ER 788   246, 259
J v J (C intervening) [1989] 1 FLR 453   416
J v S-T (formerly J) (transsexual-ancillary relief) [1997] 1 FLR 402   154
J.-P.C. v J.-A.F. [1955] P. 215   390
Jackson v Jackson [1964] P. 25   196
Jackson v Jackson [1973] Fam 99   396
James & Son Ltd v Smee [1955] 1 QB 78   76, 152
James v McLennan 1971 SLT 162   184
Jane v Jane [1983] 4 FLR 712   277, 279
Janvier v Sweeney [1919] 2 KB 316   474
Jenkins v Hargood [1978] 3 All ER 1001   396
Jessel v Jessel [1979] 3 All ER 645   429
Jodla v Jodla [1960] 1 WLR 236   159
Johnson v Calvert (1993) 5 Cal. 4th 84   193, 206
Johnson v Johnson (1981) 12 Fam Law 116   132
Johnson v Walton [1990] 1 FLR 350   462
Jones v Jones [1971] 2 All ER 737   470
Jones v Jones [1975] 2 All ER 12   407
Jones v Jones [1976] Fam 8   396
JS (a minor) (declaration of paternity), Re [1981] 2 FLR 146   198, 199, 203
Julian v Julian (1972) 116 SJ 763   132
Jussa v Jussa [1972] 2 All ER 600   280

K (a minor) (wardship: adoption), Re [1991] 1 FLR 57   260
K (abduction: child's objections), Re [1995] 1 FLR 977   341
K (abduction: consent: forum conveniens), Re [1995] 2 FLR 211   344
K (minors) (children: care and control), Re [1977] Fam 179   262
K v K (financial relief: widow's pension) [1997] 1 FLR 35   133, 404
K v K (minors: property transfer) [1992] 2 FLR 220   418
K v K [1961] 2 All ER 266   426
KD (a minor) (access: principle), Re [1988] 2 FLR 139   260, 285
Kaczmarz v Kaczmarz [1967] 1 WLR 317   119
Kane v Littlefair [1985] FLR 859   191
Kaur v Singh [1972] 1 WLR 105   159
Kendricks v Kendricks [1990] 2 FLR 107   469

TABLE OF CASES xxvii

Khoo Hooi Leong v Khoo Hean Kwee [1926] AC 529   35
Khorasandjian v Bush [1993] 3 All ER 669   473
Kinnear v DHSS (1989) 19 Fam Law 146   222
Knowles v Knowles [1962] P. 161   196
Kokosinski v Kokosinski [1980] 1 All ER 1106   400, 406
Krystman v Krystman [1973] 1 WLR 927   400
Kyte v Kyte [1987] 3 All ER 1041   407

L (an infant), Re [1968] P. 119   285
L (child abduction) (psychological harm), Re [1993] 2 FLR 401   340
L (minors) (wardship: jurisdiction), Re [1974] 1 WLR 250   255, 326, 342, 344
L (police investigation: privileged), Re [1996] 1 FLR 731   457
L v L (child abuse: access) [1989] 2 FLR 16   258, 288
L v L [1962] P. 101   379
Lang v Lang [1955] AC 402   121
Le Marchant v Le Marchant [1977] 1 WLR 559   132, 404
Leadbeater v Leadbeater [1985] FLR 789   382, 398, 406
Lee Gee-chong (deceased) (1965) 31 MLJ 102   35, 68
Lee v Lau [1967] P. 14   61, 81
Lee v Lee (1975) 5 Fam Law 48   133
Lee v Lee [1984] FLR 243   467
Lewis (AH) v Lewis (RWF) [1978] 1 All ER 729   469
Lewis v Lewis [1977] 3 All ER 992   432
Lilford (Lord) v Glynn [1979] 1 WLR 78   417
Livesey v Jenkins [1985] 1 All ER 106   422, 435
Livingstone-Stallard v Livingstone-Stallard [1974] 2 All ER 766   108, 109
London Borough of Sutton v Davis [1994] 1 FLR 737   220
Lort-Williams v Lort-Williams [1951] P. 395   370
Loseby v Newman [1995] 2 FLR 754   468
Lough v Ward [1945] 2 All ER 338   215
Lucas v Lucas [1992] 2 F.L.R 53   471

M (a minor) (care order: threshold conditions), Re [1994] 3 All ER 298   453
M (a minor: custody appeal) [1990] 1 FLR 291   306
M (child support act: parentage), Re [1997] 2 FLR 90   206
M (contact: welfare test), Re [1995] 1 FLR 274   284, 286, 288
M v M (child of the family) [1981] 2 FLR 39   415
M v M (child: access) [1973] 2 All ER 81   285, 286
M v M (custody application) [1988] 1 FLR 225   472
M v M (financial provision) [1987] 2 FLR 1   381
M v M (sale of property) [1988] FLR 389   409

Macey v Macey [1982] 3 FLR 7   393
MacLennan v MacLennan [1958] SC 105   106
Mahadervan v Mahadervan [1964] P. 233   81, 82
Manser v Manser [1940] P. 224   153
Marckx v Kingdom of Belgium [1979–1980] 2 EHRR 330   180
Marsden v Marsden [1967] 3 WLR 230   120, 121
Marsden v Marsden [1973] 2 All ER 851   394
Martin (BH) v Martin (D) [1978] Fam 12   374, 375, 395
Martin v Martin [1976] 3 All ER 625   407, 408
Mary Ng v Ooi Gim-teong [1972] 2 MLJ 18   61
Mason v Mason [1972] 3 WLR 405   115
Mathias v Mathias [1972] 3 WLR 201   134
McEwan v McEwan [1972] 1 WLR 1217   390
McGill v Robson [1972] 1 WLR 237   115
McGrath (infants), Re [1893] 1 Ch. 143   240, 248
Mckee v Mckee [1951] 1 All ER 942   344
McLean v Nugent [1980] FLR 26   461
McVeigh v Beattie [1988] 2 All ER 500   191, 204
Mehta v Mehta [1945] 2 All ER 690   166
Mesher v Mesher [1980] 1 All ER 126   395, 411
Messina v Smith [1971] P. 322   165, 166
Michael v Michael [1986] 2 FLR 389   392
Militante v Ogunwomoju (1994) Fam Law 17   165
Milligan v Milligan [1941] 2 All ER 62   117
Milne v Milne [1981] 2 FLR 286   391
Minton v Minton [1979] 1 All ER 79   379, 421
Moge v Moge [1992] 2 SCR 813   377
Montgomery v Montgomery [1964] 2 All ER 22   470, 471
Mordaunt v Mordaunt (1870) LR 2 P & D 109   73
Morgan v Morgan [1959] 1 All ER 539   164
Morgan v Morgan [1977] 2 All ER 515   392
Moss v Moss [1897] P. 263   165, 166
Mouncer v Mouncer [1972] 1 All ER 289   113, 114
M.T. v J.T. 355 A. 2d 204 (1976)   155
MT v MT (financial provision: lump sum) [1992] 1 FLR 362   392
Mullard v Mullard [1983] 2 FLR 330   370
Mummery v Mummery [1942] P. 107   122
MW (adoption: surrogacy), Re [1995] 2 FLR 759   304, 311

N (minors) (abduction), Re, [1991] 1 F.LR. 413   341
N (minors) (parental rights-acquisition.), Re [1974] Fam 93   239
N v N (abduction: article 13 defence) [1995] 1 FLR 107   340

TABLE OF CASES

N v N (consent order: variation) [1993] 2 FLR 868   431
Naylor v Naylor [1961] 2 WLR 751   117
Newham London Borough Council v AG [1993] 1 FLR 281   451
Nicholas v Nicholas [1984] FLR 285   369
Norman v Norman [1983] 1 All ER 486   429
Nota v Nota [1984] FLR 573   125
Nutley v Nutley [1970] 1 WLR 217   120
NW (a minor) (medical reports), Re [1993] 2 FLR 591   270

O (a minor) (abduction: habitual residence), Re [1993] 2 FLR 594   336
O (a minor) (custody: adoption), Re [1992] 1 FLR 77   306
O (abduction: consent and acquiescence), Re [1997] 1 FLR 924   339
O (contact: imposition of conditions), Re [1995] 2 FLR 124   284, 285, 286, 287, 288
O'Donnell v O'Donnell [1975] 2 All ER 993   383
O'Neill v O'Neill [1975] 3 All ER 289   109
O'Neill v Williams [1984] FLR 1   461–462
Official Solicitor v K [1965] AC 201   270, 325
Overbury, Re [1955] 1 Ch. 122   195
Oxfordshire County Council v P [1995] 1 FLR 552   271, 456

P (a minor) (parental responsibility order), Re [1994] 1 FLR 578   235
P (abduction: non-convention country), Re [1997] 1 FLR 780   343
P (GE) (an infant), Re [1965] Ch. 568   322, 323
P (infants), Re [1967] 2 All ER 229   257
P v P (financial provision: lump sum) [1978] 3 All ER 70   385
P v P (ouster) (1993) Fam Law 283   471, 472
P v P (ouster: decree nisi of nullity) [1994] 2 FLR 400   144
Page v Page [1981] 2 FLR 198   382, 385, 395, 408
Pardy v Pardy [1939] 3 All ER 779   118
Park Estate, Re [1954] P. 112   167
Parker v Parker [1972] Fam 116   404
Parkinson v Parkinson [1939] P. 346   153
Parojcic v Parojcic [1959] 1 All ER 1   163
Patel v Patel [1988] 2 FLR 179   460, 472
Paton v British Pregnancy Advisory Service Trustees [1979] QB 276   332
Payne v Payne [1968] 1 WLR 390   389, 432
Peete, Re [1952] 2 All ER 599   83
Pelech v Pelech [1987] 1 SCR 801 (Supreme Court of Canada)   431
Penrose v Penrose [1994] 2 FLR 621   434
Perry v Perry [1963] 3 All ER 766   118
Pheasant v Pheasant [1972] 1 All ER 587   103, 108

Pidduck v Molloy [1992] 2 FLR 202   460, 474
Piers v Piers (1849) 2 HL Cas 331   82
Piper v Piper (1978) 8 Fam Law 243   114
Potter v Potter (1975) 5 Fam Law 161   160
Pound v Pound [1994] 1 FLR 775   422, 424
Practice Direction (injunction: domestic violence) [1978] 1 WLR 1123   464
Practice Direction [1984] 1 All ER 187   266
Pratt v Pratt [1939] AC 417   122
Preston v Preston [1982] Fam 17   366, 367, 375, 395, 397, 402
Preston-Jones v Preston-Jones [1951] AC 391   197
Priest v Priest [1979] 9 FLR 252   391
Pritchard v Cobden [1987] 2 FLR 56   391
Prow v Brown [1983] 4 FLR 352   436
Pulford v Pulford [1923] P. 18   117
Puttick v AG [1980] Fam 1   76, 152, 165

Q (parental order), Re [1996] 1 FLR 369   207, 208, 209
Quinn v Quinn [1983] FLR 394   472
Quoraishi v Quoraishi [1985] FLR 780   121

R (a minor) (child abuse: access), Re [1988] 1 FLR 206   258, 288
R (a minor) (wardship: medical treatment), Re [1991] 4 All ER 177   227
R (a minor: abduction), Re [1992] 1 FLR 105   340
R (adoption), Re [1967] 1 WLR 34   300
R (child abduction: acquiescence), Re [1995] 1 FLR 716   341
R (minors: child abduction), Re, (1994) The Times Law Report December 5   338
Re R (minors) (wardship: jurisdiction) [1981] 2 FLR 416   343
R (MJ) (an infant) (proceedings transcript: publication), Re [1975] 2 All ER 749   266
R (wardship: child abduction), Re [1992] 2 FLR 481   335, 337
R v Ahluwalia [1992] 4 All ER 889   460
R v Brighton Inhabitants (1861) 1 B & S 447   148
R v D [1984] 1 AC 778   218, 333
R v Derriviere (1969) 53 Cr App R 637   219
R v Devon County Council, ex parte L [1991] 2 FLR 541   443, 444
R v Gyngall (1893) 2 QB 232   325
R v Hatton [1925] 2 KB 322   448
R v Holmes [1979] Crim LR 52   449
R v Hopley (1860) 2 F & F 202   219
R v Human Fertilisation and Embryology Authority ex parte Blood [1997] 2 All ER 687   208

TABLE OF CASES xxxi

R v Ireland [1997] 1 All ER 112   473
R v Jenkins [1949] VLR 277   194
R v Lewisham London Borough Council ex parte P [1991] 2 FLR 185   444
R v London Borough of Harrow ex parte Deal (1990) Fam Law 18   443
R v Nash (1883) 10 QBD 454   228
R v Norfolk County Council ex parte X [1989] 2 FLR 120   444
R v R (rape: marital exemption) [1991] 2 All ER 257   460
R v Registrar-General, ex parte Smith [1990] 2 QB 253   316
R v Rushmoor Borough Council ex parte Barrett [1988] 2 FLR 252   370
R v Senior [1899] 1 QB 283   76, 152
R v Sheppard [1981] AC 394   441, 448, 449
R v Tan [1983] 2 All ER 12   155
R v Thornton [1992] 1 All ER 306   460
Radziej v Radziej [1967] 1 All ER 944   369
Ratcliffe v Ratcliffe [1962] 3 All ER 993   426, 427
Re Roberts (deceased) [1978] 3 All ER 225   144
Redpath v Redpath [1950] 1 All ER 600   106
Rees v United Kingdom, The [1987] 2 FLR 111   156
Reiterbund v Reiterbund [1975] Fam 99   132
Richards v Richards [1972] 3 All ER 695   111
Richards v Richards [1983] 2 All ER 807   465, 467, 470
Richardson v Richardson (No 2) [1996] 2 FLR 617   431
Rigby v Rigby [1944] P. 33   353
Ritchie v Ritchie [1996] 1 FLR 898   434
Roberts v Roberts [1970] P. 1   396
Roberts v Roberts [1986] 2 All ER 483   391, 393
Roberts v Roberts [1991] 1 FLR 294   469
Robinson v Robinson (disclosure) [1983] 4 FLR 102   433
Robinson v Robinson [1965] P. 39   470, 471
Robinson v Robinson [1983] 1 All ER 391   406
Rogers v Rogers (1830) 162 ER 1079   357
Rukat v Rukat [1975] 1 All ER 343   133
Rumbelow v Rumbelow [1965] P. 207   356
Russell v AG [1949] P. 391   81
Rutherford v Richardson [1923] AC 1   73

S (a minor) (adoption or custodianship), Re [1987] 2 FLR 331   309, 315
S (a minor) (adoption order: access), Re [1976] Fam 1   315
S (a minor) (blood transfusion: adoption order condition), Re [1994] 2 FLR 416   314
S (a minor) (custody), Re [1991] 2 FLR 388   257
S (contact: grandparents), Re [1996] 1 FLR 158   286

S (infants), Re [1967] 1 All ER 202   252, 324
S (minors) (access: religious upbringing), Re [1992] 2 FLR 313   252, 288
S (parental responsibility), Re [1995] 2 FLR 648   233
S v H (abduction: access rights) [1997] 1 FLR 971   336
S v McC [1972] AC 24   197, 200, 202, 203, 204, 210
S v S (child abduction) (child's view) [1992] 2 FLR 492   338, 340, 341
S v S (child abuse: access) [1988] 1 FLR 213   258, 288
S v S (financial provision) (post divorce cohabitation) [1994] 2 FLR 228   435
S v S [1961] 1 WLR 445   285
S v S [1976] Fam 18   396
S v S [1977] 1 All ER 56   399
S.Y. v S.Y. (orse. W) [1962] P. 37   155, 158
Sandford v Sandford [1986] 1 FLR 412   430
Samson v Samson [1982] 1 WLR 252   467
Santos v Santos [1972] 2 All ER 246   113, 115
Savage v Savage [1982] 3 WLR 199   124
Schuller v Schuller [1990] 2 FLR 193   392
Scott v Scott [1959] 1 All ER 531   169
Scott v Scott [1992] 1 FLR 529   465, 468
Scott v Sebright (1886) 12 PD 21   162
Serio v Serio [1983] 4 FLR 756   106, 198
Sheward v AG [1964] 2 All ER 324   183
Silver v Silver [1955] 2 All ER 614   164
Sim Siew-guan Deceased, Re (1932) MLJ 95   58, 59
Simister v Simister [1987] 1 All ER 233   427
Singh v Singh [1971] 2 WLR 963   159, 161, 163
Slater v Slater [1982] 3 FLR 364   385, 386, 393
Slawson v Slawson [1942] 2 All ER 527   122
SM (a minor) (natural father: access), Re [1991] 2 FLR 333   287
Smith v McInerney [1994] 2 FLR 1077   424
Smith v Smith [1991] 2 All ER 306   403, 434
SN v ST (maintenance order: enforcement) [1995] 1 FLR 868   366
Spence, Re [1990] 1 Ch. 652   183
Spencer v Camacho [1983] 4 FLR 662   462, 464
Spindlow v Spindlow [1978] 3 WLR 777   468
Starkowski v AG [1954] AC 155   41
Stephenson v Stephenson [1985] F.L.R 1140   266
Stockford v Stockford [1982] 3 FLR 58   385, 386
Stringfellow v Stringfellow [1976] 2 All ER 539   110
Sullivan v Sullivan 2 Hag Con 237   76, 152
Surtees v Kingston-upon-Thames BC [1991] 2 FLR 559   216
Suter v Suter [1987] 2 All ER 336   382, 393

TABLE OF CASES

SW (a minor) (wardship: jurisdiction), Re (1985) 15 Fam Law 322   328
SY v SY [1963] P. 37   158
Sydall v Castings Ltd [1967] 1 QB 302   188
Szechter v Szechter [1970] 3 All ER 905   161, 162

T (a minor) (parental responsibility: contact), Re [1993] 2 FLR 450   233
T (a minor), Re (welfare report recommendation) [1980] 1 FLR 59   266
T (adoption: contact), Re [1995] 2 FLR 251   315
T (infants), Re [1968] Ch. 704   344
T (wardship: medical treatment), Re [1997] 1 FLR 502   225, 329
T v S (financial provision for children) [1994] 2 FLR 883   419
T v T (consent order: procedure to set aside) [1996] 2 FLR 640   436
Talbot v Talbot (1967) 111 SJ 213   154
Talbot v Talbot (1971) 115 SJ 870   132
Talyor v Talyor [1967] P. 25   84
Taylor v Taylor (1974) 119 SJ 30   400
Taylor, Re [1961] 1 All ER 55   81
Taylor's Application, Re [1972] 2 QB 769   222
Thain, Re [1926] Ch. 676   248, 254
Thomas v Thomas [1948] 2 KB 294   117
Thompson v Thompson [1985] FLR 863   370, 429
Thompson v Thompson [1986] 1 FLR 212   265, 266
Thompson v Thompson [1991] 2 FLR 530   434
Thurlow v Thurlow [1975] 2 All ER 979   111, 112
Thwaite v Thwaite [1982] Fam 1   435
Thyssen-Bornemisza v Thyssen-Bornemisza (No 2) [1985] FLR 1069   375, 389
Tinsley v Milligan [1993] 2 FLR 963   154
Tommey v Tommey [1982] 3 All ER 385   422
Townson v Mahon [1984] FLR 690   255
Tremain's case (1721) 1 Strange 168   218
Trippas v Trippas [1973] Fam 134   394
Tuck v Nicholls [1989] 1 FLR 283   462
Turner v Blunden [1986] 2 All ER 75   191
Tweney v Tweney [1946] P. 180   83

Ulrich v Ulrich [1968] 1 All ER 67   369

V (a minor) (adoption: dispensing with agreement), Re [1987] 2 FLR 89   303
Van G v Van G (financial provision: millionaire's defence) [1995] 1 FLR 328   389
Vaughan v Vaughan [1973] 3 All ER 449   462

Vervaeke v Smith [1982] 2 All ER 144   165
Vicary v Vicary [1992] 2 FLR 272   408
V-P v V-P (access to child) [1980] FLR 336   286

W (a minor) (adoption by grandparents), Re [1981] 2 FLR 161   310
W (a minor) (adoption: custodianship), Re (1992) Fam Law 64   310
W (a minor) (adoption: custodianship: access), Re [1988] 1 FLR 175   310
W (a minor) (contact), Re [1994] 2 FLR 441   286, 287
W (a minor) (custody), Re [1983] 4 FLR 492   256, 265
W (a minor) (medical treatment), Re [1992] 4 All ER 627   227, 228
W (a minor) (residence order), Re [1992] 2 FLR 332   254, 256
W (a minor) (residence order), Re [1993] 2 FLR 625   260
W (adoption: homosexual adopter), Re [1997] 2 FLR 406   294, 305
W (an infant), Re [1971] AC 682   300
W (infants), Re [1965] 3 All ER 231   248
W (otherwise K) v W [1967] 3 All ER 178   158
W v D [1980] 1 FLR 393   255
W v Ealing London Borough Council [1993] 2 FLR 788   233
W(C) v W (R) [1968] 3 All ER 608   281
W (otherwise K) v W [1967] 3 All ER 178   158
Wachtel v Wachtel [1973] Fam 72   372, 373, 384, 385, 386, 391, 394, 401, 405, 406
Wagstaff v Wagstaff [1992] 1 FLR 333   391
Ward v Secretary of State for Social Services [1990] 1 FLR 119   144
Warden v Warden [1981] 3 WLR 435   428
Waterman v Waterman [1989] 1 FLR 380   383
Watson v Watson [1954] P. 48   197
Way v Way [1950] P. 71   166
Webb v Webb [1986] 1 FLR 541   471
Wells v Wells [1954] 3 All ER 491   356
Wells v Wells [1992] 2 FLR 66   434
West v West [1978] Fam 1   406
Westminister City Council v Croyalgrange Ltd [1986] 2 All ER 353   76, 152
Whiston v Whiston [1995] 2 FLR 268   153, 154
White v British Sugar Corporation [1977] IRLR 121   155
White v White [1983] 4 FLR 696   461, 469
Whitfield v Whitfield [1985] FLR 955   429
Whiting v Whiting [1988] 1 WLR 565   374
Wilde v Wilde [1988] 2 FLR 83   471
Wilkinson v Downton [1897] 2 QB 57   474
Willett v Wells [1985] FLR 514   190

Williams v Williams [1939] P. 365   122
Williams v Williams [1963] 2 All ER 994   121
Wilson v Wilson [1973] 2 All ER 17   131
Wiseman v Simpson [1988] 1 FLR 490   465, 468
Woodbury v Woodbury [1949] P. 154   356
Woolf v Pemberton (1877) 6 Ch D 19   222
Wooton v Wooton [1984] FLR 871   463, 464
Worlock v Worlock [1994] 2 FLR 689   434
Wright v Wright [1960] P. 85   353
Wright v Wright [1970] 3 All ER 209   423

X (a minor) (wardship: injunction), Re [1984] 1 WLR 1422   325, 330
X (a minor) (wardship: jurisdiction), Re [1975] Fam 47   322, 330, 332
X (minors) v Bedfordshire County Council [1995] 2 FLR 276   442
X, Y, Z (wardship: disclosure of materials), Re (1991) Fam Law 318   266

Y (minors) (adoption: jurisdiction), Re (1986) 16 Fam Law 26   296
Young v Young [1962] 3 All ER 120   121
Young v Young (1973) 117 SJ 204   425

ZHH (adoption application), Re [1993] 1 FLR 83   311

Table of Legislation

Hong Kong Legislation

Adaptation of Laws (Courts and Tribunals) Ordinance 1998   222

Adoption Ordinance (No 22 of 1956)   217, 247, 291, 318,
  s2   294, 296, 298
  s4   294
  s4(1)   292, 294
  s4(2)   293, 295
  s4(3)   294, 295
  s4A(1)   292
  s4A(2)   293
  s5   295
  s5(3)   294
  s5(4)   295
  s5(5)a   298
  s5(5)b   295
  s5(5A)   298
  s5(5B)   299
  s5(5C)   299
  s5(5D)   299
  s5(5F)   299, 311
  s5(6)   296
  s5(7)   297
  s5(7)(a)(aa)   297
  s5(7)(b)   297
  s5(8)   297
  s5A   304
  s5A(1)   304
  s5A(3)   305
  s5A(4)   305
  s6(1)   300
  s6(2)   295
  s7(3)   298
  s8(1)   298
  s8(1)(b)   305, 307
  s8(1)(c)   310
  s8(1A)   315
  s8(2)   314
  s12   310
  s12(3)   312
  s13(1)   185, 313
  s13(3)   148, 313
  s15   313
  s18(1)   316
  s18(4)   316

s19(3)   316
s19(4)   316
s22   310
s25   291

Adoption Rules
　Form 4   298
　Form 4a   298
　r6   316
　r9   311
　r13   313
　r14   313
　Second Schedule   313

Affiliation Proceedings Ordinance (Cap 14)   190, 191, 197

Age of Majority (Related Provisions) Ordinance (Cap 410)   226
　s6   282

Basic Law
　Article 8   vii
　Article 24   187
　Article 24(3)   viii, 188

Births and Deaths Registration Ordinance (Cap 174)
　s7   191
　s12   191, 196, 197
　s12B   199
　s24(2)   196

Child Abduction and Custody Ordinance (No 49 of 1997)   ix, 327, 334, 342
　s3   334
　s4   334, 346
　s4(2)(b)   335
　s5   335
　s6   335

Corporal Punishment (Repeal) Ordinance (No 72 of 1990)   220

Crimes Ordinance (Cap 200)
　ss47–51   150, 441

Detention Centres Ordinance (Cap 239)   220

District Court Ordinance (Cap 336)
　s48(1)   470

Divorce Ordinance No 35 of 1932   99

Divorce (Amendment) Ordinance (No 44 of 1956)   99

Domestic Violence Ordinance (Cap 189)   247, 463, 470, 474
　s2(2)   461
　s3   461, 468
　s3(1)   460, 462
　s3(2)   464, 467
　s4   460, 461
　s5(1)   469
　s5(2)   469
　s5(3)   469
　s6(1)   464
　s6(3)   461
　s7   464

Domestic Violence Rules
　r5   469
　r6   469

Education Ordinance (Cap 297)
　s74   219
　s74(2A)   219
　s74(2B)   219
　s78   219
　s87(3A)   219

TABLE OF LEGISLATION

Education Regulations
   r58   220

Evidence (Amendment) Ordinance (No 70 of 1995)   440

Fatal Accidents Ordinance (Cap 22)   185

Guardianship of Minors Ordinance (Cap 13)   191, 192, 211, 213, 215, 241, 413
   Part III   236
   Part VI   213
   s2   236, 282
   s3   211, 264, 275, 282, 285
   s3(1)   216, 220, 245, 247, 251
   s3(1)(a)   230
   s3(1)(b)   229
   s3(1)(c)   190, 230
   s3(1)(d)   232, 298
   s3(a)(ii)   229
   s3(2)   233
   s4(1)   235
   s4(2)   229, 235
   s5   236, 237, 238
   s5(b)   238
   s6(1)   237
   s6(2)   237
   s6(3)   238
   s7   239
   s8   239
   s9   240
   s10   236, 284, 326
   s10(1)   247, 282
   s10(2)   283, 418
   s11   238
   s12(a)   238, 240
   s13(1)(a)   283
   s13(1)(b)   283
   s13(2)   284
   s14(1)   283
   s15(1)   284
   s17   265, 284
   s17(1)   284
   s18(1)   235
   s18(2)   240
   s20   420
   s21   189, 234, 236

High Court Ordinance (Cap 4)
   s21L(1)   470
   s26   324

Hong Kong Bill of Rights Ordinance (Cap 383)
   Article 14   157
   Article 19   157
   Article 20   180
   Article 22   180

Hong Kong Reunification Ordinance (No 110 of 1997)
   s8   293
   s24(2)   321

Housing Ordinance (Cap 283)
   Schedule   368

Immigration Ordinance (Cap 115)
   s19(1)(b)   331

Immigration (Amendment) (No 2) Ordinance (No 122 of 1997)   viii
   s5   187

Infants Custody Ordinance (No 48 of 1935)
   s2(1)   245

Inheritance (Provision for Family and Dependants) Ordinance (Cap 481)   48
   s2   186
   s4   428, 433

Inland Revenue Ordinance (Cap 112)
  s8(2)(i) 386

Intestates' Estates Ordinance (Cap 73)
  s2 186
  s3A 186
  s4A(1) 174
  s4A(2) 354
  s13 48
  s13(2) 37
  Schedule 1 48

Juvenile Offenders Ordinance (Cap 226)
  s10 219

Law Amendment and Reform (Consolidation) Ordinance (Cap 23)
  s20B 215

Law Reform (Miscellaneous Provisions and Minor Amendments) Ordinance (No 80 of 1997) 75, 217
  s26 296
  s28 151, 192
  s31 151
  s78 191
  s79 191

Legal Practitioner Ordinance (Cap 159) 310

Legitimacy Ordinance (Cap 184)
  Schedule 1 184
  s2 183
  s3(1) 184
  s4(1) 184, 185
  s4(4) 185
  s5 185
  s6 185
  ss4–9 184
  s10 186
  s11 143, 183, 184
  s11(1) 182
  s11(3) 182
  s11(4) 182
  s11(5) 182
  s12 143, 183
  s14 181, 352
  s14(2) 37, 181
  s14(3) 181

Mandatory Provident Fund Schemes Ordinance (Cap 485) 405

Marriage and Children (Miscellaneous Amendments) Ordinance (No 69 of 1997) 352, 358, 370, 417, 463
  s4 283
  s11 354
  s20 280
  s25 358
  s26 276
  s30 366

Marriage Ordinance (Cap 181) 3, 4, 7, 16, 33, 181, 217, 352
  s6 74
  s7 74
  s9 75
  s11 76
  s12 75
  s13 75, 151
  s14 151, 192
  s15 151
  s16(1) 151
  s18A 151
  s19 75
  s21 75, 152
  s24 77

TABLE OF LEGISLATION

s27(1)   147
s27(2)   76
s39   76
s40   74

Marriage Reform (Amendment) Ordinance (No 62 of 1979)   67

Marriage Reform Ordinance (Cap 178)   3, 15, 35, 55, 62, 64, 139, 181, 184, 352
  Part V   65, 67
  s2   17, 40, 69
  s4   16, 74
  s5(2)(b)   36
  s6   47
  s7   25, 106
  s7(1)   17
  s7(2)   17, 18, 19, 23, 24
  s7(2)(a)   19
  s7(2)(b)   19
  s8   40, 41, 43
  s9   26, 41, 45
  s9(3)   45
  s9(5)   44
  s9(7)   44
  s10   44
  s11   26, 45
  s14   62, 68
  s15   64, 67, 68
  s16(1)   65
  s16(2)   65
  s17(1)   65
  s18   65
  s19(1)   65
  s20   65
  s22A   63

Matrimonial Causes Ordinance (Cap 179)   26, 64, 68, 99, 172
  s2   26, 45, 78, 106, 145
  s3   103
  s5   173
  s6(1)   153
  s7A(1)   66
  s7A(2)   66
  s9   26, 45, 67, 104, 145
  s11   103, 136
  s11A   103, 105
  s11A(1)   101
  s11A(2)   105, 119, 123, 124, 173
  s11A(2)(c)   136, 137
  s11A(2)(e)   110
  s11A(3)   113
  s11B   135
  s11B(2)   105
  s11C   136
  s11C(1)   113
  s12   124
  s12(1)   124
  s13(1)   123
  s14   108
  s15   105
  s15(1)   144
  s15A   173
  s15A(1)   128
  s15A(3)(a)   107
  s15A(3)(b)   107, 123
  s15A(4)   113
  s15A(5)   123, 136
  s15B   132, 133, 173, 404
  s15C(1)   115, 173
  s15C(2)   137
  s17(2)   123, 137
  s17A   137, 173
  s17A(2)   130
  s17A(3)   130, 131
  s17A(3)(b)   131
  s17A(4)   131, 132
  s18A   355
  s18(B)(b)   127
  s20(1)   145
  s20(1)(a)(iii)   152
  s20(B)   143

s20(d) 168
s20(2) 157
s20(2)(c) 167
s20(2)(d) 167
s20(3) 169
s20(3)(b) 170
s20(4) 170
s20(5) 170
s20(6) 170
s22 144
s24 77, 173
s24(1A) 173
s24(2) 174
s24(3) 174
s26 153
s32(2) 174
s38 26
s48A(1) 280, 281
s48A(2) 280
s48A(3) 280
s48A(4) 280

Matrimonial Causes (Amendment) (No 2) Ordinance (No 33 of 1972) 100, 101

Matrimonial Causes (Amendment) Ordinance (No 29 of 1995) ix, 102, 107, 119, 124, 138
  s7 104
  s14 174

Matrimonial Causes Rules
  Form 2C 136
  Form 2E 137
  r5 125
  r13 108
  r15A 115
  r33 134
  r33(2B) 137
  r40(1) 77
  r47A 135

r47(1A) 137
r73(2) 387, 388, 389
rr86–91 366
r95(1) 264
r95(2) 264
r107 166, 167
r108 325

Matrimonial Proceedings and Property Ordinance (Cap 192) 131, 173, 275, 351, 352, 355, 358, 363, 375, 380, 435
  s2 124, 213, 276, 414, 419
  s3 174, 351, 361
  s4 365, 370, 371
  s4(2)(b) 367
  s5 351, 361, 370, 415
  s5(1) 413, 414
  s5(2) 413
  s5(3) 414
  s5(4) 414
  s5(5) 414
  s6 365, 370, 371, 391, 414, 415, 430
  s6(1)(a)–(b) 408
  s6A 365, 408, 409
  s6A(1) 370
  s6A(2) 370
  s7 376
  s7(1) 361, 371, 373, 374, 387, 388, 389, 391, 405, 412, 422, 430
  s7(1)(a)–(g) 405
  s7(1)(g) 404
  s7(1)(h) 370
  s7(2) 416, 417, 419, 428
  s7(2)(a) 416
  s7(3) 359, 415, 416, 426, 427
  s8 351, 358, 396, 413, 414, 418
  s8(1) 358, 359
  s8(2) 358
  s8(5) 360

TABLE OF LEGISLATION

s8(6)   359
s8(7)(a)   359
s8(7)(b)   360
s9(1)(2)   366
s9(4)   396
s10   360, 417
s10(2)   419
s10(2)(b)–(c)   420
s10(3)   360
s11   380, 423, 425, 428
s11(1)   430
s11(2)   429
s11(4)   429
s11(5)   430
s11(6)   432, 433
s11(7)   430
s12A   420
s14   424, 425
s14(1)(b)   425
s14(2)   425
s15   423
s15(1)   426
s15(2)   425, 426, 427
s16(1)   428
s16(2)   428
s18   134, 173
s18(1)   128, 129
s18(1)(b)   129
s18(1)(c)   129
s18(2)   129
s18(3)   129
s18(6)   128
s19   276
s19(1)   281
s19(7)   281
s20   428, 433
s26   409
s28   360
s28A   360

Mental Health Ordinance (Cap 136)   157, 201

s2   167

Offences Against the Person Ordinance (Cap 212)
   s27   218, 441, 448
   s43   218
   s45   153

Official Solicitor Ordinance (Cap 416)   325

Parent and Child Ordinance (Cap 429)   180, 230
   Part III   194
   Part IV   192
   Part V   206
   s2   201
   s3   188
   s3(1)   189
   s3(2)   189
   s5(1)   194
   s5(1)(b)   196, 199
   s5(2)   197
   s5(3)   196
   s6   191
   s6(1)   198
   s6(1)(a)   199
   s6(1)(b)   199
   s6(2)   198
   s6(3)   199
   s6(4)   199
   s6(5)   199
   s6(6)   199
   s6(7)   199
   s6(8)   199
   s7   199
   s9(1)   206, 208
   s10   207
   s10(2)   208
   s10(3)   207, 208
   s10(4)   208
   s10(5)   207

s10(6)   208
s10(6)(b)   208
s12   208, 247, 310
s12(5)   209
s12(6)   209
s12(9)   209
s13   204, 247
s13(1)   201
s14(1)   201
s14(2)   201
s14(3)   201
s14(4)   201
s15(1)   204

Pensions Benefits Ordinance (Cap 99)   185–186

Pensions Benefits Ordinance (Judicial Officers) (Cap 401)   186

Pensions Regulations   186

Protection of Children and Juvenile Ordinance (Cap 213)   ix
s2   446
s8   446
s26   218
s34   220
s34(1)   247, 447, 448
s34(1)(d)   455
s34(1AA)   455
s34(2)   445, 448, 449, 451, 454
s34(4)(a)   454
s34(5)   454
s34(6)   454
s34E(1)   446
s34E(2)   447
s34E(5)   447
s34E(6)(7)   447
s34F(1)(2)   447
s34F(4)   447
s45A   447

s45A(1)   445, 446
s45A(1)(a)   447
s45A(2)   446
s45A(5)   446
s45A(6)   446
s45A(8)   446
s45A(9)   446

Reformatory Schools Ordinance (Cap 225)   220

Royal Hong Kong Auxiliary Police Force Ordinance (Cap 233)   186

Rules of the High Court
O15 r16   45, 199
O80 r2   222

Separation and Maintenance Orders Ordinance (Cap 16)   48, 275, 351, 359, 413, 418
s2   352, 353
s3   354
s3(1)   353
s3(2)   353
s5   281, 357, 359
s5(1)   354
s5(3)   355
s5(b)(d)   353
s6(1)   282, 355
s6(2)   357
s6A   282, 356
s9A(1)   357
s9A(2)   358
s12   355

Supreme Court Ordinance (No of 1873)
s3   293
s5   5

Surviving Spouses' and Children's Pensions Ordinance (Cap 79)   185

Training Centre Ordinance (Cap 280) 220

Widows and Orphans Ordinance (Cap 94) 186

Australian Legislation

Adoption Act 1984 (Vic) 316

Adoption Act 1988 (SA) 316

Adoption Act 1988 (Tas) 316

Adoption Act 1991 (ACT) 316

Adoption Information Act 1990 (NSW) 316

Adoption Legislation Amendment Act 1991 (Qld) 316

Adoption of Children Act 1986–1991 (WA) 316

Adoption of Children Amendment Act 1990 (NT) 316

Children (Equality of Status) Act 1976 (NSW) 195

Family Law Act 1975 100, 272–273

Marriage Act 1961 (Commonwealth of Australia) 150

Canadian Legislation

Divorce Act 1985 100

Marriage (Prohibited Degrees) Act 1990 150

Ontario Family Law Act 1986
   s5(1) 372

Chinese/PRC Legislation

Ta Tsing Leu Lee 7–10, 30, 31, 47, 57
   Article 90 25
   Article 101 8
   Article 102 33
   Article 103 27
   Article 105 26
   Article 116 34, 58, 59, 60, 61, 68

Chinese Civil Code 1930 5, 40, 56, 68, 78, 79, 80
   Article 972 38, 43
   Article 980 39, 49–53
   Article 982 39, 49–53
   Article 983 39, 49–53
   Article 985 38, 40, 49–53
   Article 986 39, 49–53
   Article 988 39, 49–53
   Article 993 39, 49–53
   Article 997 43
   Article 1049–1058 71–72
   Book IV 14, 38

Marriage Law of 1950 78, 79, 83, 85–91
   Article 1 80
   Article 6 79

Marriage Law of 1980 78, 81, 91–98, 100, 180
   Article 2 80
   Article 3 80

Article 5   80
Article 6   80, 150
Article 7   81

Marriage Registration Regulations (1 February 1994)   80

New Zealand Legislation

Family Proceedings Act 1980   100, 171
  s31   150
  s64(1)   372

Marriage Act 1955
  s15   150

Matrimonial Property Act 1976   372

Status of Children Act 1969   180

Singaporean Legislation

Maintenance of Parents Ordinance   396

UK Legislation

Abduction and Custody Act 1985   334

Adoption Act 1976   30, 318
  s6   305
  s16   318
  s47(1)
  s50(1)   317
  s51   316
  s51A   317

British Nationality Act 1981
  s15   186
  s16   187
  s50(9)   187

Children Act 1975   214, 309

Children Act 1989
  s1   247
  s1(3)   249
  s2(4)   242
  s2(9)   241
  s3(1)   214
  s3(2)   221
  s3(2)(3)   242
  s3(3)   221
  s4   232
  s5(5)   242
  s5(6)   242
  s5(7)   243
  s5(7)(a)   243
  s5(8)   243
  s5(9)   243
  s6(5)   243
  s8(1)   284
  s11(7)   284
  s44   447
  s85   214
  s86   281
  s88   317
  Schedule 10   317

Children (Scotland) Act 1995   231
  s1(1)   214
  s2(1)   214

Custody of Infants Act 1839 (Talfourd's Act)   228

Deceased Brother's Widow's Marriage Act 1921   147

Deceased Wife's Sister's Marriage Act 1907   147

Divorce and Matrimonial Causes Act 1857   142

Divorce Reform Act 1969   101, 172

Domestic Proceedings and Magistrates' Courts Act 1976
  s2   469

Domestic Proceedings and Magistrates' Courts Act 1978
  s1   354

Domestic Violence and Matrimonial Proceedings Act 1976   460

Family Law Act 1996   138, 460

Family Law Reform Act 1969
  s8   226

Family Law Reform Act 1987   180
  s1(1)   179
  s4   232

Family Law Act 1996   100

Guardianship of Minors Act 1971
  s5(1)   239

Law Reform (Parent and Child) (Scotland) Act 1986   195

Marriage (Enabling) Act 1960   148

Marriage (Prohibited Degrees of Relationship) Act 1931   147

Marriage (Prohibited Degrees of Relationship) Act 1986   148

Marriage Act 1949
  s78(1)

Matrimonial Act 1983
  s1(3)   467

Matrimonial and Family Proceedings Act 1984   372, 375, 379, 407

Matrimonial Causes Act 1973
  s23(6)   367
  s25   372, 374, 375, 407
  s33A(1)   422

Pension Act 1995   405

Summary Jurisdiction (Married Women) Act 1895   352

International Conventions

European Convention on Human Rights
  Article 8   156
  Article 12   156–157

The Hague Convention on Civil Aspects of International Child Abduction 1980   334, 337, 344
  Article 3   335
  Article 4   335
  Article 12   337, 338, 341
  Article 13   338

UN Convention on the Rights of the Child   216, 305
  Article 2   180

Article 3(1) 455
Article 9 439
Article 9(2) 251
Article 9(3) 285
Article 12(1) 251, 455
Article 12(2) 456
Article 19(1) 439
Article 21

Part I

Marriage and Its Termination

1

Customary Marriage, Union of Concubinage and Modern Marriage

INTRODUCTION

7 October 1971 was a watershed date for Hong Kong marriage law. This was because prior to that date there was in operation a dual marriage system. One of the marriage systems was peculiarly 'Chinese', and it consisted of 'customary marriages', 'unions of concubinage' and 'modern marriages'. The other system was 'Western' or Christian in nature and origin. It was and is commonly referred to as 'marriage under the Marriage Ordinance' or 'registry marriage'.

As from 7 October 1971, the Chinese system was abolished by the Marriage Reform Ordinance (MRO), and since then only marriage under the Marriage Ordinance has been recognised. This institution will be examined in greater detail in Chapter 3. Suffice to say here that one of the distinguishing features of a marriage under the Marriage Ordinance is monogamy, that is, the voluntary union of one man and one woman to the exclusion of all others.

This chapter is concerned with the Chinese marriage system. The need to study this system, abolished almost three decades ago, is not, as some may assume, merely a matter of historical interest. As can be seen from Table 1.1, there are 2582 Chinese marriages registered under the MRO. This system of registration was introduced on 7 October 1971 and one of the consequences of registration is that evidence of a marriage is provided. However, outside this system of registration, there are no statistics indicating how many customary marriages, unions of concubinage and modern

Table 1.1 'Chinese' marriages registered under the Marriage Reform Ordinance (figures extracted from Hong Kong: Yearbook, Hong Kong Government Press, an annual publication, from the period 1973–97)

	Customary	*Modern*
1972	181	21
1973	45	8
1974	25	4
1975	52	19
1976	124	39
1977	80	27
1978	66	25
1979	44	20
1980	43	21
1981	53	17
1982	54	20
1983	71	26
1984	72	15
1985	97	19
1986	98	27
1987	85	34
1988	53	60
1989	136*	140*
1990	78	136
1991	49	113
1992	17	60
1993	25	42
1994	24	32
1995	23	22
1996	15	25
sub-total	1610	972
Total		2582

* This sharp increase in numbers was probably because of Tiananmen Square and registration for immigration purposes.

marriages still exist today. More importantly the status of parties who have entered into these marriages, and of children born as a result, hinges on the validity of these marriages. Often, the issue of validity, unquestioned during the lifetime of the parties concerned, arises when one of them dies and succession is at stake. With the passing of time, all these marriages will become extinct. To that extent, the Chinese system of marriage is of transitional interest only since marriage under the Marriage Ordinance will eventually become the sole marriage system relevant in Hong Kong family law.

The marriages which are of transitional interest are:
(1) Customary marriage: this refers to a marriage contracted in accordance with 'Chinese law and custom'. The parties to such a marriage are a husband and wife. The wife is sometimes called the prinicipal wife or *t'sai* (妻). In addition, Chinese law and custom permitted a husband to take secondary wives. These secondary wives are sometimes referred to as concubines or *t'sip* (妾). The union between a husband and a secondary wife being referred to as a union of concubinage.
(2) Modern Marriage: this refers to a marriage contracted in accordance with certain requirements of the Chinese Civil Code of the Republic of China, 1930.

We will first consider customary marriage and this will be followed by an examination of union of concubinage which are an integral part of customary marriages. Both customary marriages and unions of concubinage are steeped in Chinese legal and social history. Modern marriages, however, are of more recent origin and will be examined in the latter part of this chapter.

CUSTOMARY MARRIAGE

Prior to 1843, and before Hong Kong became a British colony, it was the practice of the Chinese inhabitants to marry in accordance with 'Chinese law and custom'. This type of marriage is sometimes referred to as 'Chinese customary marriage'. Consistent with the terminology of the MRO, the term 'customary marriage' (舊式婚姻) will be adopted. There is no real difference between the two; customary marriage in Hong Kong refers only to Chinese custom, and to no other.[1]

The legal basis for customary marriages has been the subject of much debate[2] and it can be traced back to s5 of the Supreme Court Ordinance which stated that:

> Such of the laws of England as existed when the Colony obtained a local legislature, that is to say, on the 5th day of April, 1843, shall be in force

---

[1] See *Re Kishen Das* (1933) 26 HKLR 42.
[2] Greenfield, 'Marriage by Chinese Law and Custom in Hongkong', 7 ICLQ (1958) 437 (hereafter referred to as Greenfield); Haydon, 'The Choice of Chinese Customary Law in Hong Kong' 11 ICLQ (1962) 231 (hereafter referred to as Haydon); D Lewis, 'A Requiem for Chinese Customary Law in Hong Kong' 32 ICLQ (1983) 347.

within the Colony . . . except so far as the said laws shall be inapplicable to the local circumstances of the Colony or of its inhabitants.[3]

This was almost universally interpreted[4] as the legal basis for the preservation of customary marriages, as practised in 1843, up to 7 October 1971.[5]

Nature and Function of Marriage

Customary marriage in dynastic Qing China was a product of centuries of development and evolution from earlier customs and practices.[6] Chu Tung-tsu,[7] a well respected scholar on Qing law and customs, described customary marriage as follows:

> The ceremony of "marriage is a bond of affection between two surnames. It serves the ancestral temple on the one hand and continues the family line on the other," says the Hun-i (The meaning of marriage), a chapter in the Li Chi. From this ancient and most authoritative definition, it can be seen that it was the family that was the greatest concern, not the individual. Perpetuation of the family and ancestor worship were closely linked, and the latter seems to be the more decisive. It may be said that the family had to be maintained so that the ancestors could be sacrificed to. Ancestor worship was then the first and the last purpose of marriage. It is therefore not difficult to understand why a bachelor or a married man without a son was considered unfilial. Says Mencius, "There are three unfilial acts, the most serious of which is to be without descendants." Without a

---

[3] Ordinance No 3 of 1873.
[4] See n. 2.
[5] See for example *Wong Kam-ying v Man Chi-tai* [1967] HKLR 201.
[6] Vermier Chiu, *Marriage Laws and Customs of China,* Chinese University Press, Hong Kong, 1966, p. 1 (hereafter referred to as Vermier Chiu). See also J Dull, 'Marriages and Divorce in Han China: A Glimpse at "Pre-Confucian" Society' in *Chinese Family Law and Social Changes,* ed by D Buxbaum, University of Washington Press, Hong Kong, 1978 (hereafter referred to as J Dull); 陳顧遠《中國婚姻史》商務印書館, 上海, 1936 (Chen Ku-yuan, *A History of Marriage in China,* hereafter referred to as Chen Ku-yuan); 趙鳳喈《中國婦女在法律上之地位》食貨月刊社, 台北, (Chao Feng-chieh, *The Legal Status of Women in China,* hereafter referred to as Zhao Fung-Zia); A Wolf & Chieh Shan-huang, *Marriage and Adoption in China, 1845–1945,* Stanford University Press, Stanford, 1980; 馬之驌《中國的婚俗》經世書局, 台北, 1981. (Ma Chih-su, *Chinese Marriage Customs*).
[7] 瞿同祖《中國法律與中國社會》商務, 1947 (中華書局 1996 年第二次印刷) translated into English, Chu Tung-tsu, *'Law and Society in Traditional China',* Westport, Connecticut, Hyperion Press, reprinted edition, 1980 (hereafter referred to as Chu Tung-tsu).

descendant, the ancestors would become unworshipped ghosts. Many ancient peoples believed that ghosts must have sacrifices.[8]

Unlike a marriage contracted under the Marriage Ordinance[9] with which we are familiar today, customary marriage was a union between two families as opposed to a union of two individuals. The purpose of such a union was not the pursuit of individual happiness, rather it was the procreation of male descendants.[10] The consent of the prospective groom and bride to their union was therefore unnecessary, nor was there a requirement for a minimum age of marriage.[11] Indeed, the contract of marriage was made between the heads of two families, usually the father or an agnatic senior of the family of the prospective groom and bride.[12] The head of the prospective groom's family selected a prospective bride, engaged a go-between[13] to negotiate a betrothal contract, and the heads of the families concluded the nuptial agreement.[14]

Customary marriage, important as it undoubtedly was to the family, was based on traditional customs and rites. According to the *Li Chi* or the Book of Rites (禮記), the ceremonials for a valid customary marriage consisted of what was known as the 'Three Covenants and Six Rites' (三書六禮). Their observance was crucial to the validity of a customary marriage.[15] On the other hand, Qing Law or the *Ta Tsing Leu Lee* (大清律例),[16] penal

---

[8] Chu Tung-tsu, p. 91; see n. 7.
[9] See Chapter 3.
[10] Vermier Chiu, p. 4; see n. 6.
[11] See *Chan Chung-hing v Wong Kim-wah* [1986] HKLR 715; cf. Chao Feng-chieh p. 39; see n. 6.
[12] For the parties who might contract a marriage for a family member, see G Jamieson, *Chinese Family and Commercial Law,* Vetch & Lee Ltd., Hong Kong, 1970 (original edition by Kelly & Walsh Ltd., Shanghai, 1921, hereafter referred to as Jamieson) p. 46. The order of the ranking of these parties were: (1) parents and paternal grandparents; (2) paternal uncles and their wives; (3) paternal aunts; (4) elder brothers and elder sisters; (5) maternal grandparents. See also Vermier Chiu, p. 99; n. 6.
[13] Such a person was also called a marriage broker, messenger, match-maker, introducer, *chieh shao jen* (介紹人) or *mei jen* (媒人); see also Chen Ku-yuan; n. 6.
[14] For detailed rules governing who the Master of Matrimony or *chu hun* (主婚) was, see Vermier Chiu, p. 15; n. 6.
[15] Vermier Chiu, p. 4; n. 6.
[16] The entire body of traditional Qing law was the product of over two thousand years of development in the work of codification. This was embodied in the *Ta Tsing Leu Lee*. Its first edition was promulgated by Emperor Yung Chen in 1728. The final edition was promulgated in 1908. Reference here to the *Ta Tsing Leu Lee* is that translated by George Thomas Staunton, Cheng Wen Publishing Co., Taipei, 1966 (hereafter referred to as Staunton). The *Ta Tsing Leu Lee* consists of seven parts. The first is called 'Names and General Rules', the other parts are named to correspond to the six departments or ministries of the central government. They were: 'Personnel/Civil Service', 'Revenue/Hu Pu', 'Rites',

in nature, did not prescribe the forms and procedures to be followed to contract a valid customary marriage.[17] The relationship between Qing law on one hand and custom on the other was not always an easy one, and what impact this had on customary marriages in Hong Kong will be considered later.

Early Formalities: The Three Covenants and Six Rites

The Six Rites, according to Vermier Chiu, an authority on customary marriage, consisted of the following, and it is useful to quote him here:[18]

1. *Na T'sai* (納采) – the procedure of sending a messenger, usually a go-between . . . to offer a present to the girl-elect in an attempt to find out whether or not she is marriageable. If she is not already betrothed or married and if the offer of marriage is acceptable, the girl's family will accept the present . . .
2. *Wen Ming* (問名) – the procedure of enquiring as to the name and date of birth of the girl-elect. After the girl's family has accepted the present which represents an offer of marriage, the same messenger is sent by the boy's family with a formal letter asking for the full name and date of birth of the girl-elect. In reply thereto the girl's family writes back, also formally, giving the year, month, date and hour of her birth besides her full name.
3. *Na Chi* (納吉) – the procedure of finding out whether or not the match would be suitable or felicitous. This is done by matching the girl's horoscope . . . with that of the boy. If they harmonise with one another, the match will be deemed favourable . . . the eight characters of nativity of the intended bride are written on a piece of red paper and placed underneath the incense burner in front of the ancestral tablets for three days. If during that period nothing infelicitous has happened, such as quarrelling in the family, breaking of earthenware or glassware, burning of the rice pan, etc., then the match will be deemed suitable and a messenger will be sent to the intended bride's family notifying her paterfamilias that the match is hereby approved . . .

'War', 'Punishments' and 'Works'. Hu Pu referred to 'family' or 'household'. The department was equivalent to revenue as taxes in China were levied on the family. The section on Hu Pu thus contained laws pertaining to family relations such as marriages, succession and inheritance. For further details on the *Ta Tsing Leu Lee*, see Tsao Wen-yen, 'The Chinese Family Law from Customary Law to Positive Law', [1966] 17 Hastings Law Journal 727 (hereafter referred to as Tsao Wen-yen); *The Great Qing Code*, (William C Jones tr) Oxford, Clarendon Press, 1994 (hereafter referred to as William Jones).

[17] Except Article 101 of the *Ta Tsing Leu Lee* which dealt with betrothal, Staunton; see n. 16.
[18] Vermier Chiu, p. 5; see n. 6; see also J Dull; Chen Ku-yuan; n. 6.

4. *Na Cheng* (納徵) – the procedure of paying money in settlement of the marriage. This is done by sending a messenger to the intended bride's family with the sum of money previously agreed upon. This is the final step in the betrothal.
5. *Ch'ing Ch'i* (請期) – the procedure of requesting the fixing of the date of the wedding. The literal meaning of these characters is: request made by the intended bridegroom's family to the intended bride's family for a day to be fixed for the wedding; but in actual practice the fixing of the wedding day rests with the intended bridegroom's family. The procedure generally adopted is this: the paterfamilias of the boy's family selects a lucky day, then he writes a formal letter to the paterfamilias of the girl's family informing him that the day of the wedding has been decided on, and finally he sends a messenger to deliver the letter to the paterfamilias of the girl's family who invariably declares in his reply thereto that such and such a day . . . shall be the wedding day . . . In this way, the letter and spirit of 'ching chi' are harmonized.
6. *Ch'in Ying* (親迎) – the procedure of the bride being welcomed by the bridegroom at his home. A commoner needed not welcome his bride to his home in person, but a person of position, especially in the days of yore, must proceed in person to the bride's home – usually on horseback – to escort her to his home.

The Six Rites are sometimes summarised as follows:[19]
(1) Initiating the proposal;
(2) Asking the name of the girl;
(3) Reporting the results of the divination before the shrine in the groom's ancestral temple;
(4) Such divination being propitious, the presenting of the betrothal gift;
(5) Asking for the wedding date, and
(6) Welcoming the bride.

Two additional rites were also performed by the bride, one called 'rites for becoming a wife', the other, 'rites for becoming a woman'.

> The former is consummated by sexual intercourse on the night of the wedding . . . The latter is completed by paying respect to the bridegroom's parents by kowtowing and serving tea to them on the day after the wedding . . . the latter is more important than the former because consummation of the marriage by sexual intercourse is a matter concerning only the parties to the marriage, whilst completion of the latter is indispensable to becoming

---

[19] See Leonard Pegg, *Family Law in Hong Kong*, 3rd edition, Butterworths Asia, Hong Kong, 1994, p. 6 (hereafter referred to as Pegg).
[20] Vermier Chiu, p. 6; see n. 6.

a member of the husband's clan — a matter of no small concern for both the parties to the marriage and the whole clan.[20]

In the course of these Six Rites three documents might be exchanged, comprising the so-called 'Three Covenants'. The first document (聘書) which formed part of the betrothal and emanated from the prospective groom's family contained the prospective groom's pedigree. This would be reciprocated by the prospective bride's family, returning details of her pedigree. The second document (禮書), also forming part of the betrothal, consisted of a list of gifts presented to the girl's family.[21] The final document was the marriage document (迎書), written by the bride's family on the day of the wedding.[22]

Evolving customs: From 1843–1971

By the very nature of human society, the customs of 1843 had to adapt to suit changing times and circumstances, and Hong Kong society in the 1950s and 1960s was vastly different from Hong Kong in 1843, not least in terms of demographics. In 1843, Hong Kong had a population of 5000, and by the 1950s, it was nearly three million. Thus, Haydon wrote in 1962:

> Prima facie it is remarkable that many of the Chinese in Hong Kong at the present day, who comprise some of the most cultured people to be found in the Far East, should be at law subject in their domestic affairs, matters which are all important in Chinese eyes, to theoretical concepts of the customs of a riff-raff living in this same region of Kwangtung Province a hundred and twenty years ago.[23]

Fortunately, the courts did not consider customs ossified as at 1843. Thus, in 1969, in the case of *Re Wong Choi-ho* (which concerned the position of a concubine), Briggs J said that the correct law to apply was:

> . . . the Ch'ing law and custom as it existed in 1843 with such modifications in custom and in the interpretation of the law as have taken place in Hong Kong since that period.[24]

---

[21] Sometimes also called 'the Passing of the Big Gift' (過大禮).
[22] Vermier Chiu, p. 76; see n. 6; see *Local Traditional Chinese Weddings*, Hong Kong Urban Council, Hong Kong, 1987, pp. 17 and 48, where this was described as a deed for the delivery of the bride, registering permission to take the bride.
[23] See Haydon; n. 2.
[24] [1969] HKLR 391 at 394.

The courts recognised that Chinese law and custom had evolved and developed to meet new circumstances. It was for the courts to decide how, and to what extent, it had developed.[25] Thus, Huggins J said that the applicable customary law was to be derived from a process which he described as follows:

> ... one merely looks to 1843 to ascertain the applicability of the customary law and the basic rules as they then existed and thereafter one applies those rules subject to such developments as may have taken place since that date.[26]

Customary law, then, was seen by the courts as a 'living and developing organ' and it was not static.[27] Writing in the 1960s, Vermier Chiu was of the view that the Six Rites had been reduced to three essentials, even as early as the Sung Dynasty (960–1279 AD).

> *na ts'ai* and *wen ming* were combined and the new combination was called *ts'ai tse* (采擇) or select. *Na chi*, *na cheng* and *ch'ing ch'i* were amalgamated and became *na pi* (納幣) or payment of money. Only *ch'in ying* was left intact.[28]

Similarly, Leonard Pegg takes the view that the Six Rites had three dominant features:[29] betrothal through the go-between;[30] transfer of the bride to the bridegroom's home; reception of the bride into the bridegroom's family and giving her the status of daughter-in-law who then became responsible for the ancestral worship. The nature of these three dominant features for constituting a valid customary marriage will be considered later.

The role of expert witnesses and authoritative writings

Although customs evolved in line with social change, how were these modifications to customs to be ascertained? The problem became acute with the mass influx of immigrants from different parts of China in the 1950s and 1960s. It was exacerbated by the fact that Chinese customs varied among the inhabitants of different districts and clans; the customs of the boat people differed from those of shore dwellers and among different

---

[25] *Wong Kam-ying v Man Chi-tai* [1967] HKLR 201 at p. 211.
[26] Ibid.
[27] See also Saied J in *Chan Chung-hing v Wong Kim-wah* [1986] HKLR 715 at p. 724.
[28] Vermier Chiu, see p. 7; n. 6.
[29] Pegg, p. 6; see n. 19; see also Jamieson, p. 45; n. 6.
[30] See also Chen Ku-yuan; n. 6.

linguistic and regional groups such as the Cantonese, Hakka, Chiu Chow, Fukienese, Shanghainese or Pekinese.[31]

By the 1950s, extensive efforts had been made by the government to study the institution of customary marriage in Hong Kong. The Strickland Report,[32] in 1948, was followed by the White Paper on Chinese Marriages in Hong Kong in 1960.[33] Further studies were published in the McDouall-Heenan Report in 1965[34] and then in the White Paper on Chinese Marriages in Hong Kong in 1967.[35]

It thus became clear that there could be no single authoritative account of the relevant customs in 1843 and the modifications to them which had occurred; yet important matters concerning the status of the parties to the marriage, the legitimacy of children, succession,[36] and the jurisdiction of the courts to entertain matrimonial applications,[37] all hinged on establishing the validity of a marriage.

The difficulty in ascertaining what constituted a valid customary marriage was daunting and this finally surfaced in 1962 in the Court of Appeal case of *Lui Yuk-ping v Chow To*,[38] where Macfee J observed that the practice of using expert witnesses to assist the court in ascertaining what constituted a valid customary marriage was effectively treating Chinese law and custom as foreign law. He remarked that:

> If Chinese law and custom is to be accepted as part of the law of Hong Kong then surely its existence is a matter of which judicial notice is to be taken, and if the court should require any assistance on points of this, or any other law of this Colony, then surely the proper procedure is to consult written authorities on the subject, if necessary with the assistance of learned counsel and translators?

---

[31] Chinese Marriages in Hong Kong, Hong Kong Government Printer, Hong Kong, 1965 (hereafter referred to as the McDouall-Heenan Report 1965), para 15.

[32] Also called the Report on Chinese Law and Customs in Hong Kong (chaired by the then Solicitor General, Mr G Strickland), Hong Kong Government Printer, Hong Kong, 1948 (hereafter referred to as the Strickland Report 1948).

[33] White Paper on Chinese Marriages in Hong Kong, Hong Kong Government Printer, Hong Kong, 1960 (hereafter referred to as White Paper 1960).

[34] Chinese Marriages in Hong Kong, Hong Kong Government Printer, Hong Kong, 1965 (hereafter referred to as the McDouall-Heenan Report 1965).

[35] The 1967 White Paper on Chinese Marriages in Hong Kong, Hong Kong Government Printer, Hong Kong, 1967 (hereinafter referred to as the White Paper 1967).

[36] *Chan Chung-hing v Wong Kim-wah* [1986] HKLR 715; *Re Ng Shum (No 2)* [1990] 1 HKLR 67.

[37] *Tang Lai Sau-kiu v Tang Loi* [1987] HKLR 85; *Chan Lee-kuen v Chan Sui-fai* [1966] HKLR 796; *Ho Har-chun v Yiu Hon-ming*, District Court, Action No 2381 of 1970 (judgment date unknown).

[38] [1962] HKLR 515.

Macfee J doubted the propriety of using expert witnesses:

> Here in Hong Kong, or anywhere else, there is obviously nobody now living who has had any practical experience of the Chinese law of 1843, and there must be comparatively few who have had practical experience of it immediately prior to the Revolution of 1911, yet the practice prevails in our courts of calling as witnesses learned *"experts"* in such law; it may well be that such practice originated in by-gone days when lawyers experienced in Chinese law of 1843 were available, at all events it obviously has not stopped when, in the course of time, they ceased to become available .... For my part I have doubted as to the propriety in any witness coming forward and, in effect, saying to a court *"I have studied such and such a branch of the law of this Colony and I now tell you on oath that the answer to the legal problem now propounded is so and so."*[39]

Despite this, the practice of calling expert evidence continued. Thus, one year later, in 1963, in the case of *Ng Ying-ho v Tam Suen-yu* (which concerned the position of a concubine), Huggins J allowed expert evidence to be given by a solicitor of the Supreme Court, whom he was satisfied was 'well-qualified' to speak as to Chinese law on the basis that 'there are no books of Chinese law' to which he (the judge) might refer.[40] However, in 1967, in *Wong Kam-ying v Man Chi-tai* (a case again concerning a concubine), there was no expert witness before Huggins J and he had to rely for guidance upon 'such writings as are available'.[41] Yet, in 1969, in *Re Wong Choi-ho*,[42] Briggs J allowed expert evidence to be tendered. Since then, and up until today, expert evidence has been accepted by the courts. However, the evidence of an expert is not conclusive, the final decision resting with the court, which is not bound to accept such evidence.[43]

'Chinese law and custom' not modified by events outside Hong Kong

Although the 'Chinese law and custom' preserved in Hong Kong was the Qing law and custom, the marriage law in China had undergone fundamental changes since 1843. Most notably, early twentieth-century China had

---

[39] Ibid., at pp. 531–2. Italic original. It is worth noting that in *Re Wong Choi-ho* [1969] HKLR 391 which was lengthy litigation, two expert witnesses died before the litigation concluded.
[40] [1963] HKLR 923.
[41] [1967] HKLR 201 at p. 212.
[42] [1969] HKLR 391.
[43] Saied Deputy High Court Judge in *Chan Chung-hing v Wong Kim-wah* [1986] HKLR 715 at p. 728.

witnessed much effort at modernisation, and, concerning marriage, there had been a move away from customary marriage rituals towards a more simplified form.[44] In furtherance of this trend, after the Qing Dynasty had been overthrown by the Republican Revolution in 1911 and the Nationalist government established in 1928, in 1930 the Nationalists promulgated Book IV (entitled 'Family') of the Chinese Civil Code.[45] The Chinese Civil Code 1930 adopted a simpler form of marriage which was modelled on Japanese, German and Swiss law. It recognised, *inter alia*, an individual's freedom to contract a marriage without the consent of the head of the family (thus freeing the prospective bride and groom from the control of their families) and removed the need to follow ceremonials of customary practice for contracting a valid marriage. As will be seen later in the section on modern marriages, all that was required in terms of formalities was that a marriage be celebrated in an 'open' ceremony in the presence of two witnesses.[46]

Many of the inhabitants in Hong Kong embraced this simplified form for marriage.[47] Arguably, it could be considered as an evolved form of customary marriage,[48] a product of changing times and social circumstances. This view, if accepted, would mean that customary marriage had simply evolved to become the kind of marriage characterised in the Chinese Civil Code. This view, however, was not accepted by the courts, which took the view that modifications to customs were relevant only if they had developed in Hong Kong. Thus, it was held in *Re Wong Choi-ho,* in 1969, that such changes in the customs and in the law made in 'another country' were irrelevant. They could not be regarded as a part of the evolution of customary marriages in Hong Kong. Evolution relevant to customary marriages meant evolution that had taken place in Hong Kong alone and therefore modifications of Chinese custom in Chinese communities in other jurisdictions, such as Singapore and Malaysia, were also irrelevant. As Briggs J said:

> We must . . . keep our eyes in the boat; and the boat is Hong Kong. What happened outside Hong Kong must be ignored.[49]

---

[44] For a history of law reform, see Van der Valk, *An Outline of Modern Chinese Family Law,* Henri Vetch, Peking, 1939 (hereafter referred to as Van der Valk).

[45] See Annex I of this chapter.

[46] See pp. 37–43.

[47] See the McDouall-Heenan Report 1965; n. 31.

[48] See also Greenfield at p. 449; n. 2, where it was remarked that the 'modern' form of marriage was neither a simplified version nor a development of customary marriage; Leonard Pegg, 'Chinese Marriage and Divorce under British Colonial Law: The Hong Kong Experience' (1974; M Phil. Thesis; HKU Library).

[49] [1969] HKLR 391 at p. 395.

From 1971 Onwards: The Marriage Reform Ordinance

As mentioned earlier, customs change in step with a changing society and Hong Kong society was changing at a rapid pace. Apart from local variations, the practices of different clans, and the difficulty in ascertaining the relevant customs, the reality was that by the late 1960s and early 1970s, customary marriages were considered distinctly feudal and anachronistic. Some of the characteristics of a customary marriage, for instance, a husband's prerogative to unilaterally repudiate the marriage,[50] and his freedom to take concubines,[51] were clearly incompatible with women's role in society.

> So far as United Nations standards are concerned, Chinese customary marriages leave a good deal to be desired, in that they are not registered or registrable, they are not celebrated before an official, they are not monogamous. Furthermore since such marriages can be unilaterally dissolved by the husband they are not consistent with Article 16 of the United Nations Universal Declaration of Human Rights which proclaimed that men and women are entitled to equal rights to marriage, during marriage and at its dissolution.[52]

This provided the final impetus for reform, the main aim of which was the abolition of customary marriages prospectively. Abolition served the function of capping the numbers of customary marriages and the epoch within which they have to be assessed as to their validity. Law reform was effected by the MRO.[53]

Abolition of customary marriage

During the second reading of the Marriage Reform Bill on 3 June 1970, abolition of customary marriage was regarded as long overdue. Mr P C Woo said:

> ... the main provisions of this bill are based on the recommendations of the Committee on Chinese Law and Custom in Hong Kong made in February 1953 but it took 17 years before this matter comes to this Council for debate, and during these 17 years as the mover of the bill rightly pointed out, "that public attitudes and preferences and practice have been undergoing changes", which behoves us to review the antiquated Chinese

---

[50] See Chapter 2.
[51] See pp. 27–37.
[52] White Paper 1967, para 15; see n. 35.
[53] For some of the debates for and against law reform prior to the introduction of the MRO, see *Ming Pao,* 9 April 1958, 20 October 1958, *South China Morning Post,* 7 October 1962, 27 November 1964, 14 July 1967, *Sing Pao,* 23 August 1968.

law of marriages and to reform the same so as to suit the present condition in Hong Kong.[54]

The passage of the Bill was uncontroversial; four legislators spoke, three of whom were in favour and only one against. Mr Oswald Cheung made a last appeal to save customary marriages. He remarked that customary marriage, together with the institution of concubinage, was not an inferior institution to that of monogamy. Consequently, the law should not deprive a man of his right to contract a customary marriage. He argued as follows:

> ... is monogamy so manifestly a superior institution to the traditional Chinese institution of marriage that we should completely deny the right to people to opt out of it if they so wish? Are we right to force this institution upon the people who do not believe in it and who do not want it?
>
> I regret I am completely unable to draw the conclusion from the historical or the present day evidence which is available to me that monogamy is so successful, so obviously superior and so more conducive to the public good and to the individual happiness of men and women, that I am prepared to say that this — and this only — shall be the way men and women shall regulate their lives. Let me next observe that the institution of monogamy, which is in force in Hong kong ... is at best a compromise between polygamy and the teachings of the Christian church. The Church decrees that a man shall have only one wife in his life. Our system of monogamy says a man shall have one wife at one time. It does permit him to have different wives at different times. Equally the Chinese customary marriage is a compromise.[55]

The main aim of the MRO was to abolish, inter alia, customary marriages prospectively. As Mr Holmes, the then Secretary for Home Affairs, who moved the second reading of the Marriage Reform Bill, stated:

> all the connected matters fell into place more or less as transitional provisions ... [and] as time goes on fewer and fewer [customary marriages] will exist and in due course the provisions I have described will become entirely spent.[56]

S4 of the MRO thus provides that marriages contracted in Hong Kong on or after the 7 October 1971 shall imply the voluntary union for life of one man and one woman to the exclusion of all others, and may be contracted only in accordance with the Marriage Ordinance. This thereby abolished customary marriage as of 7 October 1971.

---

[54] HK Hansard, 3 June 1970, p. 728.
[55] Ibid., pp. 735–6.
[56] Ibid., pp. 677–8.

Customary marriage defined

The prospective abolition of customary marriage as of 7 October 1971 did not deal with the questions of validity of those which had already been contracted prior to that date. To remedy the lack of a definition as to what constituted a valid customary marriage, the MRO defined it as:

> a marriage celebrated in Hong Kong in accordance with section 7.[57]

S7(1) of the MRO provides that:

> For the purposes of this Ordinance, a marriage shall constitute a customary marriage if it was or is celebrated in Hong Kong before the [7 October 1971] in accordance with Chinese law and custom.

'Chinese law and custom' means:

> such of the laws and customs of China as would immediately prior to 5 April 1843 have been applicable to Chinese inhabitants of the Colony[58]

S7(2) further provides that a marriage 'shall be deemed' to accord with Chinese law and custom if it was celebrated in accordance with the

> ... traditional Chinese customs accepted at the time of the marriage as appropriate for the celebration of marriage either
> (a) in the part of Hong Kong where the marriage took place; or
> (b) in the place recognised by the family of either party to the marriage as their family place of origin.

Customs of when

S7(2) of the MRO focuses on 'traditional Chinese customs' for the celebration of a marriage, not those of 1843, but those at the time of the marriage. Its intention is to avoid disputes concerning what the customs were in 1843. For example, if a customary marriage was alleged to have taken place in 1940, all the court has to ask is: 'was the ceremony accepted as appropriate for the celebration of a customary marriage in 1940?' This is consistent with the notion that customary law is a living creature, evolving with changing social conditions. As has been mentioned earlier, this, indeed, has been the approach of the courts. What appears to be new, however, is

---

[57] S2.
[58] S2.

that the customs adopted need not be the local (or Hong Kong) customs, but could be those imported from other parts of China, being the customs of the place of origin of either party to the marriage.[59]

Customs of where

The relevant customs could be those 'in that part of Hong Kong where the marriage took place'. For example, a customary marriage involving two families, one from Shandong, Guangdong (山東, 廣東) and one from Changsha, Hunan (長沙, 湖南), and celebrated in Kowloon Walled City, would be valid if the parties adopted the customs of Kowloon Walled City, as opposed to say the customs of a Hakka Village in the New Territories.

The customs could be that of the 'place recognised by the family of either party to the marriage as their family place of origin'. This envisages inter-marriage between families which have adopted different customs and rites.[60] Again, using the above example, it would suffice if the ceremony was in accordance with either the customs of Shandong or Changsha. But if the parties adopted a mixture of both Shandong and Changsha customs, the marriage would not be a valid customary marriage. It is also worth mentioning that as the customs of the place of origin of either party to the marriage could be used, there would be a valid customary marriage even if the customs of the wife's family, as opposed to that of the husband's family were adopted. This appears to recognise an element of equality between the families as to whose customs were to be adopted for the celebration of the marriage.[61]

Customs accepted by whom

S7(2) of the MRO is silent on this. If the parties adopted the customs of the place of origin of the husband's family, it would be difficult to envisage that, after many years of marriage, its validity would be questioned either by the wife, an interested relative, a guest who had attended the wedding ceremony, or even by a local inhabitant of the place where the marriage took place. The McDouall-Heenan Report 1965 suggested that acceptance by the parties to the marriage was the relevant test:

---

[59] See Greenfield; n. 2; *Re Ng Shum (No 2)* [1990] 1 HKLR 67; *Chan Chung-hing v Wong Kim-wah* [1986] HKLR 715.
[60] C Osgood, *The Chinese: A Study of a Hong Kong Community,* University of Arizona Press, Tucson, 1975.
[61] See Greenfield; n. 2; *Re Ng Shum (No 2)* [1990] 1 HKLR 67; see also G MacCormack, *The Spirit of Traditional Chinese Law,* University of Georgia Press, Athens, 1996, Ch. 5.

> All genuine customary marriages have at least one identifiable factor in common: they must be celebrated according to the accepted rites and ceremonies of the parties' families, in conformity with traditions which go back beyond their living memory.[62]

This must be correct as it is consistent with the approach hitherto taken by the courts. Although sections S7(2)(a) and (b) of the MRO refer to the practices of a certain area, and arguably this relates to the customs practised by the people of a particular locality,[63] however, in *Chan Chung-hing v Wong Kim-wah*,[64] Judge Saied took the view that the appropriateness of the traditional Chinese custom was not to be judged from ascertaining from 'each resident what that traditional custom' might be. He was of the view that it had to be judged only by those who were actually present at the wedding ceremony. However, this view would seem to carry the unfortunate consequence that the more people who attended, the more likely it would be that disagreements could arise.

The role of expert witnesses

S7(2) does not set out in concrete terms the requirements of a valid customary marriage. It is therefore left to the court to ascertain whether a custom adopted in a particular case was capable of constituting such a marriage. Expert evidence, however, may continue to assist the court.[65]

Judicial interpretation

For nearly three decades, the courts have entertained a large degree of laxity in interpreting the customs required for a valid customary marriage. The cardinal rules are: that each case is to be considered in the light of its own facts; the ceremonies must be viewed as a whole, taking into account changing social circumstances in Hong Kong, and; strict adherence to formality is not as important as the intention of the parties to proceed in accordance with customary rites.

Thus, it has been held that the first two of the Six Rites were obsolete by the 1970s.[66] It has also been held, in *Kwan Chui Kwok-ying v Tao Wai-*

---

[62] McDouall-Heenan Report 1965, para 16; see n. 31.
[63] See Pegg, p. 10; n. 19.
[64] [1986] HKLR 715.
[65] See *Lee Lan v Henry Ho*, High Court, Miscellaneous Proceedings No 3441 of 1978 (1980); *Chan Chung-hing v Wong Kim-wah* [1986] HKLR 715, *Re Ng Shum (No 2)* [1990] 1 HKLR 67, *Kwan Chui Kwok-ying v Tao Wai-chun* [1995] 1 HKC 374.
[66] *Ho Har-chun v Yiu Hon-ming*, District Court, Action No 2381 of 1970 (judgment date unknown).

chun,[67] (concerning a marriage which took place in 1960), that documentary evidence of the 'three covenants' was not necessary, nor was it necessary that the bridegroom fetch the bride on the wedding day personally, nor would it be fatal if the marriage took place on an inauspicious day or that it was within one year of mourning the death of a parent.

As was said earlier, of the Six Rites, there remained three which were crucial. They were: betrothal through a go-between, transfer of the bride to the bridegroom's home, and accepting the bride into the family as the daughter-in-law. As will be seen from cases decided since 1971, the role parents played in betrothal has been much reduced. The courts have been inclined to consider customary marriages as *affaires de coeur* as opposed to contracts between parents. However, the betrothal gift cementing the union could not be omitted. Finally, the rites for accepting the bride into the groom's family need not be exact and the parents welcoming of the bride some months after the marriage has been accepted as sufficient, either because it was taken as a form of *ex post facto* acceptance (and therefore still crucial) or because it was regarded as largely symbolic.

Affaires de coeur

By the late 1960s and early 1970s, customary marriages were no longer 'arranged marriages' but *affaires de coeur,* the role which heads of the families played having been seriously eroded, particularly when circumstances rendered it difficult, if not impossible, for them to participate. In *Ho Har-chun v Yiu Hon-ming*,[68] the marriage took place in 1970. The husband was a seaman, and through the medium of friends, he exchanged photographs and corresponded with the wife. Their first meeting was arranged by a go-between who acted on behalf of the wife's family and other members of the wife's family also attended. After a short period of courtship, the wife accepted the husband's suggestion of marriage. He fixed the wedding by agreement with his own family and communicated the arrangement to his prospective wife. Gifts were then exchanged. On the wedding day, the wife was fetched from her mother's home by the husband and was taken to the husband's home. Photographs were taken. An evening dinner of 18 tables was provided in a restaurant, at which the parties served tea to their mothers and the two go-betweens. There was also 'some form of worshipping of the gods'.

A fundamental challenge to the validity of the marriage was that the betrothal was at the instance of the parties themselves; it was not concluded

---

[67] [1995] 1 HKC 374.
[68] District Court, Action No 2381 of 1970 (date of judgment unknown).

between the heads of the families and so was contrary to the spirit of a customary marriage. However, Cons J in the District Court held that tradition was by no means inflexible, particularly in circumstances where it was difficult, if not impossible, for the heads of the family to participate. In this case, the husband's father was in mainland China, and 'there was no mention in the evidence of any senior male member of the wife's family'. Nevertheless, betrothal was clearly with the consent of 'the close members of the respective families' and was 'cemented by the exchange of gifts'. It was a valid customary marriage.

Indeed, in 1967, Huggins J said (obiter) in *Wong Kam-ying v Man Chi-tai,* that customary marriages

> ... are now usually *affaires de coeur* rather than contracts between parents[69]

In other words, so long as a customary marriage was concluded with the consent (explicit or implicit) of close members of the respective families and was cemented by the exchange of gifts, it was a valid customary marriage.

This view of the diminished role which parents (or agnatic seniors of the families) played in a customary marriage was also accepted in the case of a marriage which took place during the Japanese Occupation, reflecting the circumstances of those whose families had been displaced by the social and political upheaval of the time. Thus, in *Chan Chung-hing v Wong Kim-wah,*[70] it was alleged (in a probate action) that a valid customary marriage was contracted between the plaintiff-woman and the deceased. The plaintiff and her widowed mother had come to Hong Kong from Chiu Chow in 1936 and they had no relatives in Hong Kong. The deceased also had no relatives in Hong Kong, although he had an elder brother and a mother in his native village in China. It was argued that a betrothal was not an agreement between the prospective bridegroom and the mother of the prospective bride. The court, accepting without much difficulty that a widowed mother had the exclusive right to consent to the marriage of her daughter, focused on the question of the capacity of a 'solo' man in Hong Kong to contract his own customary marriage. Deputy High Court Judge Saied was unwilling to deny to such a man 'his right to procreate' and be condemned to 'a life of bachelorhood'. He remarked:

> I doubt very much that in a situation where ethnic communities leave the shores of their native countries and settle in foreign lands, it could ever be said that a young person, living alone without his parents or another senior male relative, would be denied the natural rights of procreation

---

[69] [1967] HKLR 201 at p. 213, italics original.
[70] [1986] HKLR 715.

through the sanctity of marriage on the argument of lack of the requisite consent to marry. Such rigidity would surely condemn such a person to the status of permanent bachelorhood or spinsterhood which cannot be in accord with the traditional customs with which we are concerned.[71]

He held that Chinese customary law permitted a junior member of the family, such as the deceased, living away from home and earning his own livelihood, if his betrothal had not already been arranged by his senior relatives, to arrange his own marriage without reference to them.[72]

Betrothal gift

There is no customary marriage unless there has been a betrothal, signified by the passing of the 'Big Gift' or betrothal gift. So far, the courts have not considered the nature and value of the gift to be important.[73] For example, in *Chan Chung-hing v Wong Kim-wah*,[74] the gift of '4 silver coins of mainland China' was considered to be sufficient. In *Ho Har-chun v Yiu Hon-ming*, it was said that 'gifts were exchanged' and 'jewellery, wine and food were conveyed to the wife and her family'.[75] In *Chong Chui Yuk-ching v Chong Pui-cheong*, 'cash and 200 catties of wedding cakes' were involved.[76] However, the lack of any betrothal gift was fatal. Thus, in the recent case of *Re Ng Kwok-hing*,[77] the parties met, fell in love, and they decided to marry with the approval of their families. As it was during the Japanese occupation, they held a small dinner at the home of the parents of the 'husband', followed by the 'wife' serving tea to the parents-in-law. It was held, however, that a crucial element to a customary marriage — betrothal gift signifying the union between the two families — was missing. It was not a valid customary marriage.

Accepting the bride into the groom's family

The customs and rites signifying acceptance of the bride into the bridegroom's family were not exact. Indeed, cases suggest that these might consist of the couple 'serving tea to the parents' and 'kowtowing to them',

---

71 Ibid., at p. 725, cf. Pegg's commentary on the case in 17 (1987) HKLJ 237.
72 See also *Kwan Chui Kwok-ying v Tao Wai-chun* [1995] 1 HKC 374.
73 Chen Ku-yuan; see n. 6.
74 [1986] HKLR 715; see also Pegg's commentary in (1987) 17 HKLJ 237.
75 District Court, Action No 2381 of 1970 (unreported, date of judgment unknown).
76 [1983] HKDCLR 1.
77 High Court, Miscellaneous Proceedings No 2564 of 1994 (1996), judgment in Chinese only.

'worshipping heaven and earth' or the 'ancestral tablets' if they were available. For instance, in *Ho Har-chun v Yiu Hon-ming,* the couple offered tea 'to their mothers' and there was also 'some form of worshipping of the gods'.[78] In *Chan Chung-hing v Wong Kim-wah,* the husband did not have his ancestors' shrine so the couple worshipped 'heaven and earth'.[79]

Furthermore, if the prospective groom was living in the same premises as the prospective bride, conveyance of the bride to the bridegroom's house would be unnecessary, and the rites for the acceptance of the bride could be condensed into one place with the bride being 'accepted' in her own home. Thus, in *Chan Chung-hing v Wong Kim-wah* (above), the deceased lived with the plaintiff and her mother. He occupied a canvas bed just outside the room which the mother and daughter occupied in a premises in Second Street, Sai Ying Pun, Hong Kong. The ceremony took place at the premises following Chiu Chow customs. On the wedding day, the plaintiff wore a wedding gown and another tenant of the premises acted as a go-between, escorting her into the room of the deceased[80] where he received her. They 'worshipped heaven and earth' in the sitting room.

Where the father or an agnatic senior of the family of the groom could not be involved in the betrothal or the marriage ceremony, acceptance of the bride subsequently (i.e. after the marriage) has been recognised by the court as sufficient acceptance of the daughter-in-law into the groom's family. Thus, in *Chan Chung-hing v Wong Kim-wah* (above), the defendant took the plaintiff back to his native village to visit his mother after the marriage. The plaintiff 'served tea to her' and received a *laisee* packet. The High Court held that the marriage ceremony was to be considered as a whole in order to decide if traditional customs had been complied with. There was evidence that the defendant received her in his room (which was probably so designated on that occasion), they later worshipped heaven and earth, and the deceased took her to meet his mother after the wedding. There had accordingly been sufficient compliance with the traditional customs.

Chinese 'law' prevails over 'custom'

So far, we have focused on s7(2) — the customs required to contract a valid customary marriage. However, compliance with customs alone has not been accepted by the courts as satisfying the statutory requirement that customary marriage was a marriage in accordance with 'Chinese law and

---

[78] Ibid.
[79] Ibid.
[80] Probably so designated on that occasion.

custom'. Indeed, conflicts between Chinese 'law' and 'custom' were noted by McAleavy in 1963 when he observed that:

> In the Chinese law and custom of 1843 . . . there are a number of these topics, where the statute law, applied by the Chinese courts, laid down one rule, and custom, followed by the great mass of the people, persisted in another. Which of the two, custom or statute, ought to be recognised by the Hong Kong courts?[81]

This conflict has now been resolved in favour of Chinese law in the case of *Re Ng Shum (No 2)*,[82] where Benjamin Liu J held in the High Court that although s7(2) provided that a marriage be deemed to accord with 'Chinese law and custom' if it was celebrated in conformity with s7(2), such compliance created only a rebuttable presumption that a marriage was in compliance with custom, and hence a presumption that there was a valid customary marriage.[83] A party disputing the marriage may rebut such a presumption by showing that the alleged marriage was contrary to Chinese law.

In *Re Ng Shum (No 2)*,[84] the deceased died intestate. The plaintiff was the deceased's lawful *tin fong* (填房) wife.[85] Problems arose when the first defendant also claimed to be a wife of equal standing to the plaintiff or *ping t'sai* (平妻).[86] The plaintiff had married the deceased in 1942 in accordance with traditional customs and rites. In 1944, the deceased went through a form of marriage ceremony with the first defendant and the marriage ceremony followed the same rites as those befitting a wife. Indeed, the ceremony followed the same rites as those performed by the deceased and the plaintiff, and furthermore, both ceremonies were conducted by the same person, Mr Lai Chow-kwong, an old friend of the deceased. Betrothal was completed with the passing of the 'Big Gift' (過大禮), and on the wedding day, the first defendant wore a red wedding gown and was conveyed by a horse-drawn carriage to the deceased's home. The deceased and the first defendant worshipped ancestors and the gods and tea was offered to the father-in-law and other relatives. After the marriage, the deceased regarded both the plaintiff and the first defendant as his equal wives, and they were treated as such on both formal and informal occasions.

---

[81] McAleavy, 'Chinese Law in Hong Kong: The Choice of Sources' in Anderson (ed), *Changing Law in Developing Countries*, George Allen & Unwin Ltd., London, 1963 (hereafter referred to as McAleavy).
[82] [1990] 1 HKLR 67.
[83] Compare the deeming provision in s8.
[84] Ibid.
[85] See below on *tin fong*, p. 31.
[86] See below on *kim tiu*, pp. 46–7.

Benjamin Liu J held that the defendant's ceremonials had been shown to be in conformity with Chinese customs, which allowed equal wives or *ping t'sai*. However, compliance with customs only raised a rebuttable presumption that there was a valid customary marriage. In this case, the presumption was rebutted by the plaintiff proving that the marriage was contrary to the *Ta Tsing Leu Lee* (大清律例), which prohibited the taking of two wives:

> Whoever, having a first wife living, enters into marriage with another female as a first wife, shall likewise be punished with 90 blows, and the marriage being considered null and void, the parties shall be separated, and the woman returned to her parents.[87]

A marriage which contravened the Qing law was not a customary marriage under s7 of the MRO. Consequently, the first defendant was not a wife. It appeared that she was not a concubine either because she had 'categorically denied ever offering tea or kow-towing to the plaintiff as a sign of obeisance',[88] and according to Benjamin Liu J, '[t]here was nothing to even remotely suggest a union with a "Tsip"'.[89]

This was a case where the woman was caught between Chinese 'law' and 'custom'. Benjamin Liu J noted this unfortunate outcome and he offered to address it thus:

> ... I derive much comfort from the thought that there can be little doubt of the first defendant continuing to be respected by members of her family and in society as the widowed "Ping Tsai" of the deceased. That is the understanding of Mr Lai Chow-kwong, the elderly scholar, and there is every reason to believe that no right-thinking members of our community would wish to take issue with that common sense notion.[90]

However, in the eyes of the law, the first defendant was not a wife, nor was she a concubine. She was a mistress, albeit not a clandestine one.[91] The decision has the effect of rendering any customary marriage invalid should it be found to be in contravention of the Qing law.

Interestingly, non-compliance with the Qing law was also raised as an issue in *Re Wong Choi-ho*, where the question was whether a son or grandson who assaulted a parent or grandparent was to be disinherited.[92] It

---

[87] See Article 90 of Staunton, *Ta Tsing Leu Lee*; n. 16.
[88] [1990] 1 HKLR 67 at p. 75, see later on concubinage.
[89] Ibid., at p. 81.
[90] Ibid., at p. 84.
[91] See below, pp. 27–37.
[92] [1969] HKLR 391.

was argued that under the Qing law, it was a crime which attracted the death penalty. However, Briggs J said (obiter) that contravention of the Qing law could not affect the status of a person.

> In my view the relevant provision in Ching [Qing] law is of a penal nature pure and simple. I do not think that the correct inference to draw is that if a man commits an offence and renders himself liable to punishment his status is thereby altered.[93]

Similarly, it was held in *Re Ng Kwok-hing* that the fact that a marriage was held within one year of mourning the death of the woman's father (although it was contrary to the Qing law),[94] it did not render the marriage invalid.

Post-Registration

A customary marriage contracted prior to 7 October 1971 was not registrable but s9 of the MRO provides for their post-registration.[95] As mentioned earlier, registration and the certificate issued provide evidence of the marriage.[96] Further, registration provides the court with matrimonial jurisdiction under the Matrimonial Causes Ordinance (MCO).[97] Another means whereby the court would have matrimonial jurisdiction under the Matrimonial Causes Ordinance is where the parties to a monogamous customary marriage[98] contract a marriage with each other in accordance with s38 of the Marriage Ordinance. Such marriage has the effect of superseding the original, potentially polygamous union by a monogamous union, thus giving the court jurisdiction to dissolve the marriage.[99] The procedure for post-registration will be considered later.

---

[93] Ibid., at p. 402.
[94] See Article 105 of Staunton, *Ta Tsing Leu Lee;* n. 16; see also William Jones; n. 16 and Vermier Chiu; n. 6.
[95] See below, pp. 43–5.
[96] S11 MRO.
[97] S9 MCO; s2 MCO. S2 of the MCO defines a 'monogamous marriage' being one celebrated in Hong Kong (i) in accordance with the MO; (ii) being a validated marriage registered under the MRO or (iii) if it took place outside Hong Kong a marriage in accordance with the law of the *lex loci celebrationis* and recognised by that law as a monogamous marriage.
[98] That is, where there is no concubine.
[99] *Yeung Yeu-kong v Yeung Fung Lai-mui* [1971] HKLR 13; *Kwan Chui Kwok-ying v Tao Wai-chun* [1995] 1 HKC 374; *Leung May-ling v Leung Sai-lun* [1997] HKLRD 12. However, a monogamous marriage could not be converted to a potentially polygamous one, see *In the estate of Wong Wong,* High Court, Probate Jurisdiction No 1797 of 1998 (1998).

UNIONS OF CONCUBINAGE

Union of concubinage was part of the institution of customary marriage.[100] Together with customary marriages, it was abolished on 7 October 1971. Today, no man can contract a union of concubinage, and no woman can become a concubine.

Terminology

> The feminine noun concubine has two meanings according to the Oxford English Dictionary: either a mistress whose relationship has no lawful standing, or a secondary wife who though inferior to the principal wife has definite marital and economic rights.[101]

A concubine added to a customary marriage becomes a secondary wife and is sometimes called an inferior wife or a *t'sip*,[102] while the principal wife is sometimes known as the first wife or *t'sai*. Under Chinese law and custom and as the nomenclature indicates, a concubine occupied a status below that of a wife, but she was not a mistress in the Western sense of the word.

The *Ta Tsing Leu Lee*, apart from prohibiting the taking of two wives, distinguished the position or ranking of a wife and a concubine:

> Whoever degrades his first or principal wife to the condition of an inferior wife or concubine, shall be punished with 100 blows. Whoever, during the lifetime of his first wife raises an inferior wife to the rank and condition of a first wife, shall be punished with 90 blows, and in both cases, each of the several wives shall be replaced in the rank to which she was originally entitled upon her marriage.[103]

Who Might Have Concubines (and How Many)

Vermier Chiu describes the origin of concubinage, who might have concubines, and how many:

> The origin of concubinage may be traced to the time when feudalism flourished in China. Under the feudal system a king was entitled to marry one wife and eight concubines, a feudal lord was given the right to wed one wife and six concubines, a 'ta fu' (an official from the first rank to the

---

[100] For history, see Vermier Chiu, p. 22; n. 6.
[101] McDouall-Heenan Report 1965, para 28; see n. 31.
[102] But not a concubine added to a modern marriage who is a mistress only, see below.
[103] Article 103 of Staunton, *Ta Tsing Leu Lee;* see n. 16.

fifth rank) could have one wife and two concubines, a 'shih' (an official from the sixth rank to the ninth or lowest rank) could take one wife and one concubine and a commoner could marry one wife only — no concubine for a commoner.'[104]

Despite this ancient custom, the taking of one or more concubines by a Chinese man in Hong Kong was rarely so restricted and was common in wealthy families:

> Originally, therefore, the taking of concubines was a privilege belonging exclusively to the ruling class and commoners were not given such special rights. But after feudalism had fallen into disintegration, gradually it became quite a common occurrence for the rich to take as many concubines as they could afford until in the course of time a man's wealth and social prestige were measured by the number of concubines and slaves he possessed.[105]

How Many Concubines in Hong Kong

Exactly how many unions of concubinage were contracted in Hong Kong prior to the 7 October 1971 is unclear. In 1962, it was said that there was 'a large number of highly respectable Chinese ladies who are concubines'.[106] A system of registration of such unions was suggested but was rejected.[107]

Monogamy or Polygamy

The fact that a Chinese man could take a wife and an unlimited number of concubines, with all of whom he could have marital relations raised the question of whether customary marriage was monogamous or polygamous in nature. The courts (the judicial personnel of which consisted mainly of non-Chinese) have classified customary marriage as polygamous, or at least, potentially so.

---

[104] Vermier Chu, p. 22; see n. 6.
[105] Vermier Chu, p. 23; see n. 6.
[106] Macfee J in *Lui Yuk-ping v Chow To* [1962] HKLR 515 at p. 523; see also M Jaschok, *Concubines and Bondservants: A Social History*, Oxford University Press, Hong Kong, 1988.
[107] See Mrs Ellen Li, who spoke during the second reading of the Marriage Reform Bill to the effect that 'I myself am of the opinion that such registration is unnecessary and would even bring embarrassment to many self-respecting and self-righteous men who would prefer to keep their private affairs private.' HK Hansard, 3 June 1970, p. 733.

This conclusion appears natural if a marriage is seen in simple polar terms either monogamous or polygamous. In a registry marriage, a man and a woman are united to the exclusion of all others. In other words, a husband is not permitted to marry another woman during the subsistence of the first marriage. To do so is to commit the crime of bigamy, and the second 'marriage' is null and void. A husband in a customary marriage, however, was permitted to take at least one concubine. Thus, a customary marriage must be polygamous.

This was the view of the courts in Singapore. Thus, in 1867, in the Singaporean case of *in the Goods of Lao Leong An*,[108] (concerning what share a concubine was to have in intestate succession) Sir Benson Maxwell, having acknowledged that under Qing law a concubine had no share, equated her to that of a wife. He said:

> Our law, to which polygamy is not only foreign but repugnant, furnishes no rule for determining in what proportion wives of higher or lower ranking shall share the widow's share, and I am unable to see any adequate grounds for any other division than an equal one.[109]

Similarly, in another Singaporean case, *Choo Eng Neo v Neo Chan-neo* (better known as the Six Widows Case),[110] Law Ag CJ, in classifying customary marriage as polygamous, said:

> I think that in regard to these secondary or inferior wives (or concubines as they have been called), though socially their position is no doubt very inferior to that of a first wife, yet legally their position more nearly resembles that of a wife where polygamy is allowed than it resembles anything else; and I think myself, though I do not think the matter is free from doubt, that Chinese marriages must be regarded as polygamous as Sir Benson Maxwell held.[111]

In Hong Kong, the dichotomy appeared equally stark. As the Strickland Report 1948 said:

> It seems strange to the Westerner at first sight that a Chinese can even according to Chinese law be guilty of bigamy and strange to the Chinese to be called polygamous.[112]

---

[108] [1893] 1 SSLR 1 (Ch. 1).
[109] Ibid., at p. 3.
[110] (1908) 12 SSLR 120.
[111] See section on *Promotion: fu ching* below, p. 32.
[112] Para 49.

Indeed, if a man could have one or more concubines, why would he risk contravening the *Ta Tsing Leu Lee* deliberately by taking a second principal wife whilst the first principal wife was still living? Even if he was ignorant of the law, the need to do so was not obvious.[113]

The Hong Kong courts have concluded that customary marriage, together with the incidence of concubinage, was potentially polygamous.[114] In 1915, President Havilland de Sausmarez of the Court of Appeal in *Ho Tsz-tsun v Ho Au-shi*, remarked that:

> Shortly stated, it is clear . . . that China is a polygamous country; that the first wife has precedence, but that the other wives are wives and not merely concubines . . .[115]

Similarly, Rees-Davies CJ said:

> Interestingly evidence has been laid before me by gentlemen who may fitly claim to have expert knowledge of Chinese law and customs, which demonstrates, what is in fact a matter of common knowledge, that polygamy is expressly recognised by Chinese law, that the children of the principal wife ('Tsai') and those of the secondary wife or concubine ('Tsip') are treated alike as the lawful children . . .[116]

From this point of view, when a husband exercised his right to take a concubine his customary marriage became actually polygamous.

However, as Vermier Chiu points out, the Qing law equally prohibited a husband from taking a second principal wife whilst the first wife was alive. Indeed, any later 'marriage' was treated as null and void, the offending parties were to be separated and the woman was to be returned to her parents. He, thus, concluded that the Chinese were neither polygamous or monogamous. What pertained was a 'system of one wife among many concubines'.[117] More recently, Keith J shrewdly observed that whether a customary marriage was monogamous or potentially polygamous depended on whether:

---

[113] For example, to produce male descendants for two branches of the family, see *kim tiu* below, pp. 46–7.
[114] This is the same as that of the English Courts, see *Lee v Lau* [1967] P. 14.
[115] (1915) 10 HKLR 69 at p. 73; see also *Yeung Yeu-kong v Yeung Fung Lai-mui* [1971] HKLR 13.
[116] Ibid., at pp. 79–80.
[117] Vermier Chiu, p. 82; see n. 6; see also Chu Tung-tsu, n. 7; Leong Wai Kum, 'Common Law and Chinese Marriage Custom in Singapore'; Carol Tan, 'The Twilight of Chinese Customary Law Relating to Marriage in Malaysia' (1993) 42 ICLQ 147.

a concubine is to be regarded as a wife (albeit a secondary one) or a person enjoying some intermediate status between a wife and a mistress.[118]

One principal wife: kit fat (結髮) *or* tin fong (填房)

The prohibition by the *Ta Tsing Leu Lee* on a husband taking more than one principal wife was at times difficult to understand when such a husband could have a *kit fat* wife and a *tin fong* wife. These terms require some explanation.

As has been seen, Qing law allowed the taking of only one principal wife in a customary marriage and no more.[119] Consequently, even if a woman went through the rituals of marriage as a principal wife, she could not be one if the man's undivorced principal wife was still alive. At best, she could only be a concubine who was in an inferior position to that of the principal wife.[120] However, on the death of the principal wife, a husband might take a 'replacement'/'substitute' principal wife to fill the place of the deceased wife.[121] *Kit fat* refers to marriages between spinsters and bachelors in their first marriage. Thus, a widower's first deceased principal wife is called a *kit fat* wife (literally meaning 'to tie up hair'),[122] and a woman who marries a widower, in substitution of his deceased *kit fat,* is called a *tin fong* (literally meaning to fill a room). Both *kit fat* and *tin fong* are wives; neither is a concubine.

According to this arrangement, a man could not have a *kit fat* and a *tin fong* simultaneously. Thus, in *Re Wong Choi-ho,*[123] the woman entered the husband's household whilst the *kit fat* wife was alive, albeit dying, and she claimed to be a *ting fong*. It was held that as a man could not have a *kit fat* wife and a *tin fong* simultaneously,[124] she was only a concubine. The counsel in this case used an ingenious argument for the *tin fong* claimant: as the principal wife was dying and she had already moved out of her room, the woman who filled the room of the *kit fat* in effect became the *tin fong*. But status acquisition by literal construction was, it is submitted, rightly rejected.

---

[118] *Chan Chiu-lam v Yau Yee-ping* [1998] HKLDR 716 at p. 723.
[119] See below on concubinage, pp. 33–5.
[120] See *Re Ng Shum (No 2)* [1990] HKLR 67.
[121] There could be only one *tin fong* at a time but a man could, due to misfortunes, have more than one *tin fong* in his lifetime, see McAleavy; n. 81.
[122] The use of the two words had its origin in the custom of a married woman tying up the hair into a bun at the back of the head, signifying marriage. See Vermier Chiu, p. 28; n. 6.
[123] [1969] HKLR 391.
[124] And since there had been no elevation of her, or *fu ching* (扶正), since the death of the *kit fat*.

Promotion: fu ching (扶正)

It was argued in *Re Wong Choi-ho* that if the woman was a concubine when she entered the household, then on the death of the *kit fat*, she was elevated to the status of a *tin fong*. This is also known as *fu ching* (literally meaning lifting to be a principal).[125] As to the requirements of such elevation or promotion, Briggs J said (obiter) that some sort of ceremony or pronouncement to the family was required:

> And that as in all changes of status within a family it was usual at least in old times to effect this by some ceremony. When such a change in status is made there must be a degree of publicity. Some announcement by the husband that he will from henceforth consider his concubine to be his Tin Fong wife or some dinner to celebrate that event. The authorities are agreed that there was no established customary ceremony to achieve this, that it was up to the husband to devise his own method of effecting and making known the change. In China in later times it appears that no ceremony was required: mere tacit recognition by the husband being considered enough . . . . I think that in the circumstances of the case that there would have been some sort of ceremony or pronouncement to the family in accordance with custom. There is no evidence that mere recognition is sufficient for a change of status in Hong Kong. And I think the old custom prevails.[126]

Judicial Attitude towards Unions of Concubinage

Given that customary marriage was regarded as potentially polygamous, the attitude of the courts towards concubinage was ambivalent at times. Thus, Macfee J in *Lui Yuk-ping v Chow To*,[127] (which concerned a custody dispute between a husband and his concubine) said that he did not wish to cast any doubt on the 'respectability of the state of concubinage'. However, when a registry (monogamous) marriage was juxtaposed with a union of concubinage, the latter was morally less desirable. Thus, in 1971, in the case of *Yeung Yeu-kong v Yeung Fung Lai-mui,* Huggins J, in comparing a registry marriage with a customary marriage which allowed a husband to take concubines, remarked that:

> Our law, for better or for worse, regards the estate of matrimony to which monogamy is incident as a more honourable and therefore a greater

---

[125] Vermier Chiu, p. 28; see n. 6.
[126] [1969] HKLR 391 at p. 397.
[127] [1962] HKLR 515 at p. 523.
[128] [1971] HKLR 13 at p. 32.

estate than the estate of matrimony to which potential polygamy is incident.[128]

Apart from the questionable nature of this value judgment, the result of comparing concubinage with a monogamous union in a registry marriage produced inconsistent outcomes even within the facts of one case. Thus, in *Wong Kam-ying v Man Chi-tai*, where a man married under the Marriage Ordinance and subsequently purported to take a concubine, the latter 'union' was held to be void and bigamous, but the children born were held to be legitimate.[129]

Position of Concubines in Family under Chinese Law and Custom

As will be seen later, a wife in a customary marriage was expected to serve and submit to her husband,[130] her authority in the management of household affairs being limited to routine household matters. With regard to family property, the final authority rested with her husband. She had no property of her own, and as a daughter, she inherited none.[131] Furthermore, following the death of her husband, she had no right to inheritance, being permitted to only manage the family property until her son reached majority. If a wife's status was subordinate to that of her husband, a concubine's position in the family was one tier below that of the wife.

This three tier descending hierarchical position of husband, wife and concubine can be seen in the *Ta Tsing Leu Lee* which sometimes offered a wife and a concubine equal protection as against the husband, but sometimes attenuated the inferior status of a concubine *vis-à-vis* the wife as against the superior position of the husband. For example, the *Ta Tsing Leu Lee* prohibited the selling or hiring of wives, no distinction was made between *t'sip* and *t'sai*. Article 102 provided that he who put his wife or *t'sip* in pawn for the purpose of becoming another man's wife or *t'sip* should receive 80 strokes.[132] Article 102 further provided that he who fraudulently married his wife or *t'sip* to another man as his sister should receive 100 strokes.[133] Elsewhere, however, the hierarchy between a wife and a concubine

---

[129] [1967] HKLR 201.
[130] Chapter 2.
[131] Chu Tung-tsu, see n. 6; Chao Feng-chieh, see n. 6; Tsao Wen-yen, see n. 16.
[132] See Staunton, *Ta Tsing Leu Lee*; n. 16; see also Jamieson, p. 35; n. 12 and William Jones; n. 16.
[133] Ibid.

was apparent; if a husband beat his wife, the punishment was two degrees less those of an ordinary case. Where a husband beat his concubine, the punishment was two degrees less than that for the beating of a wife, that is, four degrees less than that in an ordinary case. Similarly, a wife who turned her back on her husband and ran away would be punished with 100 strokes. If she was a concubine, however, the punishment would be reduced by two degrees.[134] This differential treatment also pertained to divorce; a concubine, like a wife, could be unilaterally divorced by the husband although the grounds for divorcing a concubine, once again, highlighted her inferior position as compared to that of a wife.[135] Furthermore, unlike a wife, who upon marriage joined her husband's *tsu* (祖),[136] a concubine was not included among her husband's relatives and kin; thus no terms fixed their relationship to her nor hers to them.[137] In sum, a concubine clearly occupied a lower position than a wife.

> as a concubine she occupies a lower position in the family than the wife, her rival in love, whom she is obliged to serve, obey and respect — a position not much better than that of a menial . . . Children born by a concubine, for instance, owed their filial duty to the wife and not to the concubine. They become the legitimate children of the wife whom they call 'mother', while the concubine (their own mother) is addressed by them as well as by the wife's children as *'chieh'* or sister.[138]

Requirements of a Union of Concubinage

As in the case of customary marriages, the *Ta Tsing Leu Lee* did not prescribe any forms or procedures to be followed for a union of concubinage. It is therefore not surprising that, prior to 7 October 1971, there were conflicting judicial views in Hong Kong as to the requirements for taking a concubine. In *Wong Kam-yin v Man Chi-tai*,[139] Huggins J said (obiter) that the lack of any ceremony was not crucial.[140] He stressed the elements of common intention of the parties to form a permanent union as husband and concubine, the husband having treated the woman as a

---

[134] Article 116 of Staunton, *Ta Tsing Leu Lee;* see n. 16.
[135] See Chapter 2.
[136] Thereby becoming a member of her husband's kinship group.
[137] Chu Tung-tsu, Chapter 2; see n. 6.
[138] Vermier Chiu, p. 22; see n. 6.
[139] [1967] HKLR 201.
[140] See also Jameison, p. 45; see n. 12.

concubine, and the principal wife having accepted her as a *t'sip*.[141] Another view was that, apart from an intention on the part of the man to take the woman as a concubine, some ceremony was essential to introduce the concubine to the other members of the family. Additionally, what was required was a public holding out of the woman by the man as his concubine. Thus, in *Ng Ying-ho v Tam Suen-yu*,[142] the expert witness was of the view that:

> '... there are two essentials for the taking of a t'sip. One is an intention on the part of the man to take the woman as a t'sip and the other is the public holding out of the woman as his t'sip: it is customary to introduce the woman to the family and to have the family recognise her as a t'sip but the recognition by the family appears not to be an essential so long as the public in general recognise the relationship between the man and the woman.'[143]

A union of concubinage has to be distinguished from a clandestine relationship between a man and his mistress. In *Ng Ying-ho v Tam Suen-yu* (above), the defendant claimed to be a concubine of the deceased. She and the deceased cohabited for some years but no ceremony was held for taking her as a concubine, she was never introduced to members of the deceased's family as a concubine, she never worshipped the ancestral tablets of the deceased family, nor did she serve tea to the principal wife. The family of the deceased disapproved of the defendant and there was no evidence from parties unconnected with the family as to the relationship between the deceased and the defendant. She was held not to be a concubine.[144]

Abolition of Concubinage by the Marriage Reform Ordinance

No concubines could be taken after 7 October 1971, but the status or rights of concubines lawfully taken before that date are not affected, nor

---

[141] See also *Cheang Thye Phin v Tan Ah Loy* [1920] AC 369 affirming decision of the Supreme Court of the Straits Settlements that no form of marriage ceremony was necessary for creating the position of a *t'sip* and *Khoo Hooi Leong v Khoo Hean Kwee* [1926] AC 529.
[142] [1963] HKLR 923.
[143] Ibid., at p. 926 per Huggins J.
[144] Compare this with the approach of the Federal Court of Malaysia in the case of *Re Lee Gee-chong Deceased* (1965) 31 MLJ 102 where the requirements for taking a concubine were less stringent and the relationship between the man and concubine was discreet.

are the status or rights of their children, whether born before, or after that date.[145]

The MRO differs from its treatment of customary marriages in that it provides no definition to resolve the conflicting requirements in case law for the taking of a concubine. Further, the Ordinance does not define the status and rights of existing concubines and their children. During the passage of the Marriage Reform Bill, this approach was justified by the then Secretary for Home Affairs, Mr Holmes. He remarked that since the people of Hong Kong:

> have managed for 130 years without these definitions . . . it would be quite incongruous to attempt to introduce them in the present bill, of which the main purpose . . . is to abolish the institution as soon as this can be done without causing distress or hardship.[146]

The requirements for the taking of a concubine were recently considered by Patrick Chan J in *Kwan Chui Kwok-ying v Tao Wai-chun*.[147] In that case, it was held that the union of concubinage which took place in 1964 was valid. Patrick Chan J held that there had to be both an intention on the part of the man to take the woman and recognition of her status by the wife and the family. Resolving the conflicting views, he took the line that in almost all cases the intention to take a concubine would be evident by a *yap kung* (入宮)[148] ceremony. He said:

> . . . to contract a lawful union of concubinage, there must first be an intention on the part of the man to take the woman into the family as his concubine. His intention would normally be manifested by taking the woman back to his home and introducing her to his family members and friends. Apart from that, there must also be an acceptance or recognition by both the wife and the family. I think it is important that the wife's acceptance must be present. This is because a concubine is supposed to be junior or subservient to the wife who has the status and authority as the female head of the family. Hence in almost all cases except where there is no principal wife, there would be a yap kung ceremony which includes the concubine serving tea to the wife. This is a symbol of subservience . . . I would also think that the acceptance or at least recognition by the family generally is necessary. It is immaterial or indeed inevitable that there may be individual members who are not friendly to her.

---

[145] See S5(2)(b) MRO.
[146] HK Hansard, 3 June 1970, p. 679.
[147] [1995] 1 HKC 374.
[148] Literally meaning 'entering the household', or ceremonies of initiating the concubine into the family, see Vermier Chiu, p. 25; see n. 6.

Indeed, s14(2) of the Legitimacy Ordinance provides that, for the purposes of the Ordinance, a 'union of concubinage' means:

> a union of concubinage, entered into by a male partner and a female partner before 7 October 1971, under which union the female partner has, during the lifetime of the male partner, been accepted by his wife as his concubine and recognised as such by his family generally.[149]

A Concubine without a Principal Wife

A similar definition to that in the Legitimacy Ordinance is provided by s13(2) of the Intestates' Estates Ordinance. These definitions appear to rule out the possibility of a man taking a *t'sip* without a principal wife. However, in *Kwan Chiu Kwok-ying v Tao Wai-chun*,[150] Patrick Chan J said (obiter) that the existence of a principal wife was not strictly necessary.[151]

MODERN MARRIAGE

Although customary marriage, together with its companion union of concubinage, was popular in Hong Kong prior to 7 October 1971, 'modern marriage' (新式婚姻) was also popular with the Chinese inhabitants of Hong Kong. This form of marriage was sometimes called *man ming kit fan* (文明結婚).[152] Before explaining what 'modern marriage' is, it is necessary to examine its origin and derivation.

Origin and Basis

Unlike customary marriage, modern marriage was of more recent origin. As mentioned earlier, it could be traced back to the early part of the

---

[149] A 'union of concubinage' means a union of concubinage *de jure*. Where the law of a jurisdiction has already abolished the status of concubinage, a union of concubinage *de facto* would not be sufficient. See *Chan Chiu-lam v Yau Yee-ping* [1998] HKLRD 716.
[150] [1995] 1 HKC 374.
[151] S13(2) of the Intestates' Estates Ordinance was a transition provision enacted as a safety net for concubines and their issue, and a more liberal interpretation might be applied to achieve that objective. S13(2) thus could be construed as acceptance by the wife, if any. See also *Wong Kam-ying v Man Chi-tai* [1967] HKLR 201.
[152] Literally meaning 'modern marriage' — a phrase used in the late 1920s to describe a simplified form of marriage as compared to a customary marriage.

twentieth century when the people of China felt that the Qing law was too far behind the times, so serious efforts were made to effect law reform. However, before new law could be adopted and promulgated, the Qing Dynasty was overthrown and a republic was established in 1911. Later, civil wars threw China into chaos and the relevant law governing domestic relations was not promulgated as Book IV of the Chinese Civil Code until 26 December 1930.[153]

Modern marriages in Hong Kong were, to some extent, modelled on Book IV, entitled 'Family' of the Civil Code of the Republic of China, 1930 (hereafter referred to as the Chinese Civil Code).[154] Book IV came into force on 5 May 1931, governing marriages which took place on or after that date in the Republic of China. One of the aims of Book IV was to introduce a fundamental reform of the marriage law, replacing customary marriage with a new kind of marriage. Just as the people discarded the decadent rule of the Qing government in 1911, the marriage institution was throwing off the shackles of feudal traditions and customs.

Book IV on 'Family' was divided into seven Chapters; these were 'General Provisions', 'Marriage', 'Parents and Children', 'Guardianship', 'Maintenance', 'House' and 'Family Council'. For ease of reference, Chapter I on 'General Provisions' and Chapter II on 'Marriage' are reproduced in Annex I.

Characteristics

The main characteristics of a marriage under the Chinese Civil Code, as compared to customary marriage, were, firstly, that young people chose their own partners. Thus, Article 972 of the Chinese Civil Code provided that:

> An agreement to marry shall be made by the male and the female parties of their own accord.[155]

Secondly, equality between husband and wife was provided for and a husband was not permitted to take concubines. In other words, monogamy was adopted. Thus, Article 985 of the Chinese Civil Code provided that:

---

[153] See Vermier Chiu, p. 108; n. 6; Van der Valk; see n. 44.
[154] The Chinese Civil Code 1930 consisted of five Books, Book I on 'General Principles', Book II on 'Obligations', Book III on 'Rights over Things'; and Book IV on 'Family' and Book V on 'Succession'.
[155] Interestingly, although Article 972 provided that an agreement to marry had to be made by a man and a woman 'of their own accord', there was no such provision on the conclusion of the marriage itself.

A person who has a spouse may not contract another marriage.

Thirdly, the formalities required to contract a valid marriage were greatly simplified. Article 982 of the Chinese Civil Code provided that:

> A marriage must be celebrated by open ceremony and in the presence of two or more witnesses.[156]

Fourthly, minimum ages were stipulated for the parties to a marriage. Article 980 of the Chinese Civil Code provided that:

> A man who has not completed his eighteenth year of age and a woman her sixteenth may not conclude a marriage.

These requirements constituted the spirit of a marriage under the Chinese Civil Code. Additionally, the Chinese Civil Code stipulated other requirements; for example, Article 983 prohibited marriages between certain relatives, such marriages being null and void,[157] and Article 986 prohibited marriage between an adulterer and adulteress, such a marriage being voidable.[158] However, there was no requirement that a marriage be registered.

Hong Kong Inhabitants' Version of Marriage under the Chinese Civil Code

Despite the fact that the Chinese Civil Code, promulgated by the Nationalist Government, was not part of Hong Kong law, marriages in accordance with its spirit were, nonetheless, purportedly celebrated in Hong Kong prior to 7 October 1971. By popular consent of those who embraced this form of marriage, modern marriage was interpreted as requiring an open, but otherwise undefined, ceremony in the presence of at least two unspecified witnesses. This reflected the requirements in Article 982 of the Chinese Civil Code. However, it was doubtful whether, and how far, other requirements stipulated in the Chinese Civil Code had been complied with.[159]

Although all such marriages, therefore, were technically invalid,[160] nevertheless, the practice of the Hong Kong government was to accept these

---

[156] There is no provision that the marriage be celebrated in the presence of the parties themselves. This suggested that it might be possible to contract a marriage by proxy.
[157] Article 988, see Annex I of this chapter, pp. 49–53.
[158] Article 993, see Annex I of this chapter, pp. 49–53.
[159] White Paper 1967, para 21; see n. 35.
[160] HK Hansard, 3 June 1970, p. 677.

marriages as valid in many aspects of civil administration.[161] Consequently, their validity has never been tested in the Hong Kong courts.[162]

These marriages were not registrable in Hong Kong. They were not celebrated before an official and did not have any requirements of due publicity. Although the Chinese Civil Code envisaged that such marriages be monogamous in nature,[163] given that a husband in a customary marriage was permitted to take concubines, the male partners to marriages purportedly celebrated in accordance with the Chinese Civil Code also added concubines to their 'marriage'. The McDouall-Heenan Report 1965 characterised this unsatisfactory state of affairs as follows:

> Women who in Hong Kong have been tricked by men, and those who have tricked men, into being taken on as alleged concubines attached to a Chinese Modern Marriage are legally, and often socially and economically, nothing more nor less than mistresses.[164]

The Marriage Reform Ordinance's Version: Modern Marriage

In the light of these problems, and with a view to ameliorating any possible hardship arising from the technical invalidity of these marriages, s2 of the Marriage Reform Ordinance (MRO) retroactively validated all these marriages, calling them 'modern marriages'.

In defining this term the MRO adopted the popular version of a marriage under the Chinese Civil Code and provided that a 'modern marriage' means:

> a marriage celebrated in Hong Kong before [7 October 1971] by open ceremony as a modern marriage and in the presence of two or more witnesses.

Other requirements for a modern marriage included the provision that the minimum age of the parties at the time of the marriage be 16, and that the marriage be monogamous in nature.[165]

S8 of the MRO provides for retrospective validation of a modern marriage. It stipulates that:

---

[161] For example, for the purposes of calculating the salary of civil servants, liabilities of taxpayers, etc. It has been recognised as valid by inferior courts dealing with domestic litigation and by the Registrar of the Supreme Court in its probate jurisdiction.
[162] White Paper 1967, para 22; see n. 35.
[163] Article 985, see Annex I, and see *Lee Lan v Henry Ho*, High Court, Miscellaneous Proceedings No 3441 of 1978 (1980).
[164] Para 12.
[165] *Lee Lan v Henry Ho*, see n. 163.

> ... every marriage celebrated in Hong Kong before [7 October 1971] as a modern marriage by a man and a woman each of whom, at the time of the marriage, was not less than 16 years of age and was not married to any other person shall be a valid marriage, and shall be deemed to have been valid since the time of celebration ...

The effect of s8 is to validate all modern marriages contracted in Hong Kong before 7 October 1971 provided that at the time of the marriage the parties had attained the age of 16,[166] and were not married to another person. The time of validation was from the date of the celebration of the modern marriage. Where a modern marriage is so validated, the MRO referred to it as a 'validated marriage'.[167]

Where either party to a modern marriage was already married to another person at the time of the marriage, s8 would not operate. However, where the parties to a modern marriage had terminated their marriage before the coming into force of the MRO, the intention of s8 was to provide retrospective validation but limiting such validation to the period during which the modern marriage subsisted.[168] However, an unforeseen problem may arise in cases where a party had contracted a modern marriage, and then, believing that it was invalid, had contracted another marriage either prior to, or after, the MRO. Would s8 of the MRO operate to validate such modern marriage retrospectively, thus rendering the subsequent marriage void?[169] What is unusual about s8 of the MRO is that remedial legislation only came after a long lapse of time from the discovery of the invalidity of modern marriage, and much could have happened in the interim. It is submitted that where a subsequent marriage was contracted after the MRO, the post-MRO marriage having had the benefit of clarifying any uncertainty regarding the validity of the first marriage under the MRO itself,[170] as such it would not be unjust to render the post-MRO marriage void. Hardship, however, remains in a small number of cases where the subsequent marriage was contracted prior to the MRO.[171]

Open ceremony

Hong Kong courts have since provided an interpretation as to the meaning of an 'open' ceremony. An 'open' ceremony has a public element, meaning

---

[166] Although Article 980 provided that the minimum age for a man was 18, see Annex I of this chapter, pp. 49–53.
[167] S9.
[168] See White Paper 1967, p. 28; n. 35.
[169] See Pegg, p. 16; n. 19.
[170] See below.
[171] See *Starkowski v AG* [1954] AC 155 concerning Austrian law operating with retroactive effect.

that it is 'so held that it is known and can be seen by all those who are not particularly invited to participate.'[172] Such public element could be satisfied even if the ceremony were held in a private place. Thus, in *Lui Kit-chiu v Lui Kwok Hin-chau*,[173] a wedding banquet was hosted by the parties for about eighty guests at premises occupied by the relative of one of the parties. Traditional red invitation cards were sent out, which announced the parties' date of marriage and that there was to be a wedding dinner. Scrolls were placed at the entrance to the premises and the door was left open. The bride wore a Chinese wedding gown and a name tag marked 'bride', and the groom wore a European style suit and a name tag marked 'groom'. During the wedding feast, they toasted the guests table by table. 'Official witnesses' were the groom's aunt and another woman guest. After the dinner the groom took the bride home and they lived together as husband and wife. It was held that as the ceremony took place in private premises adjoining the street, and the door was left ajar, it was an open ceremony. However, had the ceremony been held behind closed doors and had it been known by and visible to only those who were invited, it would not have been an open ceremony.[174]

A ceremony which involved only relatives and friends of one of the parties to the marriage would be discreet and not 'open'. Thus, in *Lee Lan v Henry Ho*,[175] the 'wedding ceremony' consisted of the parties worshipping ancestors at the home of the man in the presence of the woman's sister, her children from her former marriage, and her friend. This was done whilst the front door was left wide open, but the iron grille locked. After the ceremony, the man proclaimed that they were married. In the evening, a dinner was hosted for the woman's friends and relatives. The parties then lived together for ten years but the 'husband' stayed in the 'matrimonial home' only four nights a week. It was held that there was no modern marriage as there was no intention to bind each other in matrimony. The parties had been deliberately discreet about their relationship, the wedding 'ceremony' and the dinner having been held without announcement or notification to the man's own circle of friends and relatives. The 'marriage' was thus no more than an extra-marital relationship which had been concealed with the acquiescence of the female party.

The 'ceremony' need not be in any particular form. A wedding feast

---

[172] *Lui Kit-chiu v Lui Kwok Hin-hau* [1976] HKDCLR 51 (see also HKLJ (1977) 270).
[173] [1976] HKDCLR 51.
[174] Cf. *Chong Chui Yuk-ching v Chong Pui-cheong* [1983] HKDCLR 1.
[175] High Court, Miscellaneous Proceedings No 3441 of 1978 (1980).

was held to be a ceremony,[176] even though it did not involve the parties publicly expressing their intention to marry each other.[177]

Most marriages in Hong Kong would meet these requirements for an 'open' ceremony. For instance, in a customary marriage, the conveyance of the bride to the groom's home and the welcoming of the bride into the groom's family would rarely be a private affair. If the door was left ajar and the proceedings were known and could be seen by all those who were not invited, this would satisfy the requirement of an 'open' ceremony.

Consent of the parties

Although there is no requirement in the MRO that a modern marriage be entered by consent of the parties, Article 972 provided that betrothal should be made by the parties to the marriage themselves, and not at the dictate of parents. Furthermore, Article 997 allowed a marriage to be annulled on the grounds of duress. Consent of the parties could, therefore, be taken as essential by implication.

Post-Registration of Validated Marriage

As mentioned above, where a modern marriage is validated by s8 of the MRO, the MRO refers to it as a 'validated' marriage. Like a customary marriage, a validated marriage can then be registered under the MRO.

POST-REGISTRATION OF CUSTOMARY MARRIAGE AND VALIDATED MARRIAGE

As can be seen from the above sections, neither customary marriages nor modern marriages are registrable prior to 7 October 1971. However, s9 of the MRO provides a mechanism for their post-registration. A party to a customary marriage or a validated marriage may with the consent in writing of the other party, or a court declaration, apply to the Registrar of Marriages for the registration of the marriage.

---

[176] *Lui Kit-chiu v Lui Kwok Hin-chau* [1976] HKDCLR 51.

[177] The parties to a marriage expressing their intention to marry each other at the ceremony was not required by the Chinese Civil Code, see Annex I. Compare the views of the expert witness in *Lee Lan v Henry Ho,* High Court, Miscellaneous Proceedings No 3441 of 1978 (1980).

Requirements for Post-Registration

S9(5) of the MRO provides that:

> Where the registrar is satisfied that-
> (a) the particulars contained in any application under this section are true; and
> (b) the form of marriage did take place between the parties named at the time and place and before the witnesses specified in the application; and
> (c) the marriage constitutes a valid customary marriage or a validated marriage, he shall prepare a certificate of marriage . . . and the Registrar, and the applicants, or applicant as the case may be, and 2 witnesses to the marriage, shall thereby sign duplicate certificates . . . .

A certificate, however, is not invalidated by the absence of the signature of one of the witnesses or both witnesses if the Registrar is satisfied that the witnesses or either of them is unable and cannot reasonably be made available to sign the certificate, and the Registrar records that he is so satisfied on the certificate itself.[178]

Application to the Registrar of Marriage

Upon the receipt of an application under s9, the Registrar may summon any applicant, any alleged party to the marriage and any person alleged to have been present at the marriage and may require such person to answer such questions as the Registrar may ask for the purpose of determining the application before him. The Registrar may also require any applicant to furnish such further information either by statutory declaration or otherwise as he may reasonably require.[179]

Judicial Declaration

S9(7) of the MRO provides that where, on an application to the Registrar, the Registrar is not satisfied with the particulars furnished relating to the marriage, a party to the marriage may apply to the District Court for a declaration that a customary marriage or validated marriage, as the case may be, subsists between the parties.

---

[178] S9(5).
[179] S10.

Where a person alleges that a validated marriage or a customary marriage subsists between him and the other party, but the other party disputes the existence of the marriage, or is unwilling to join in the application for the registration, or his or her whereabouts cannot be ascertained after careful and reasonable inquiry, or it is impracticable for that party to be apprised of the application for registration, that person may apply to the District Court for a declaration that a customary marriage or a validated marriage subsists between them.[180]

Resisting an Application for Registration

A party who disputes the existence of a customary or modern marriage is given no remedy by the MRO. He could, however, seek a general declaration from the court as to the parties' marital status.[181] The other possible alternative is to petition for a decree of nullity. The problem with the latter course of action is that in order for the courts to have matrimonial jurisdiction, the marriage must be monogamous. However, such a marriage cannot be treated as monogamous unless and until it has been validated and registered under s9 of the MRO.[182]

Effect of Certificate of Marriage

A certificate under s9 of a customary marriage or a validated marriage shall be admissible as evidence of the marriage to which it relates in any court and before any person having by law or by consent of the parties authority to hear, receive, and examine evidence.[183]

CONCLUSION

The Marriage Reform Ordinance was enacted with a view to closing the 'Chinese' chapter of the marriage system in Hong Kong but the actual demise of customary marriages, unions of concubinage and modern marriages has yet to come about. At the moment, the courts are dealing

---
[180] S9(3).
[181] See r16 O15 Rules of the High Court.
[182] See s2 and s9 MCO.
[183] S11.

with various aspects of customary marriages contracted in the second half of this century. However, as people's life expectancy increases, 'Chinese' marriages contracted just before their abolition may continue to be litigated decades into the twenty-first century.

Where a customary marriage does not meet with the liberal requirements of the customs and rites hitherto sanctioned by the courts, it could still be considered to be a modern marriage as most genuine 'Chinese' marriages would have the necessary publicity to amount to an 'open' ceremony. A marriage, however, may fail to constitute either a customary marriage or a modern marriage if two wives are allegedly involved, as in the case of *Re Ng Shum (No 2)*.[184] Here, one little known topic called *kim tiu* may be relevant. In the Strickland Report 1948, Vermier Chiu explained what these words mean:

> As regards "kim t'iu", "kim" (兼) means concurrent and "t'iu" (祧) means ancestral temple. The two words combined together mean a man responsible for the worship of two ancestral temples as well as for the propagation of the future generations of the two branches of the family. Three qualifications should be considered: (1) The man must be an adopted son. (2) He must be an adopted son of his paternal uncle. (3) He must be an only son. A and B are brothers. A has no son whilst B has an only son named X. Now X is adopted by A. A is a "kim t'iu" son. The privileges X enjoys are: (a) He inherits the estates of both A and B. (B) He may marry 2 wives, one for A and one for B. (C) He is responsible for the propagation of the future generations of both A and B and for their ancestral worship. And X's two wives are 'ping chai' or wives of equal standing. ("Ping Chai" means wives of equal standing and no more. It does not necessarily apply exclusively to "kim t'iu"). The law of "kim t'iu" was made by Emperor Chien Lung in the 18th century and was in force in 1843 throughout China, including of course Kwangtung.[185]

According to Vermier Chiu, the number of wives a *kim tiu* son is entitled to marry depended on the number of the branches of the family such a son represented. The minimum was two, but he reports a case of nine wives.[186] He was of the view that this was the only practice which bore any resemblance to polygamy.[187]

---

[184] See p. 12.
[185] Pp. 201–2; compare his book where he said that 'ping tsai' is a term used only in the *kim tiu* system; see Vermier Chiu, p. 35; n. 6.
[186] Vermier Chiu, pp. 32–40; see n. 6; yet if sterility afflicted a *tim kiu* son, all was not lost; a last and desperate remedy called *kai hou men fang feng* (開後門放風) (literally meaning: open the back door to let wind in) could be resorted to. This referred to getting a male servant of the household in through the backdoor to visit the wives' bedchambers. Such a person acted as the human studhorse and when his mission was completed, he would be

Reference to the practice of *kim tiu* can be found also in Van der Valk[188] and in Chu Tung-tsu.[189] According to Chu Tung-tsu, only 'ignorant' people believed that they might take more than one principal wife. The severe penalty of the *Ta Tsing Leu Lee*, however, was not insisted upon in this instance, where custom conflicted with the law. He said:

> It is human nature to be protective of daughters, so it would be rare for someone to be betrothed to a man who was clearly known to have a principal wife. As for the man who is the successor to two branches of a family, ignorant people often make the mistake and think that they may take a principal wife for each branch, and for this reason daughters are betrothed to them. After discussing the correct rites, we must distinguish the title of the principal and not confuse the legal wife with the concubine. As the law of the land takes account of human nature, we are lenient and there is no need to order that they be separated; the one who has violated this rule shall be treated as a concubine, and nature and the law should be in balance.[190]

The conflict between the *Ta Tsing Leu Lee*, prohibiting the taking of another wife whilst the first wife was alive, was resolved in practice by treating the second wife as a concubine. Thus, Qing law, instead of insisting that the parties be separated and the woman be returned to her family, accorded an inferior status to the second wife but allowed the marital relationship to continue. This, according to Chu Tung-tsu, was a balance which needed to be struck between custom and the law.

The decision of *Re Ng Shum (No 2)* appears to suggest that *kim tiu* marriages would be treated in the same way as 'Ping Tsai'.[191] This is not necessarily inconsistent with references to *kim tiu* in the MRO, s6 of which provides that no person shall contract a *kim tiu* marriage after 7 October 1971. However, the status and rights of a party to a *kim tiu* marriage lawfully contracted before its abolition and the status and rights of a child born to parties to a *kim tiu* marriage are unaffected.

---

paid and sent away to a distant place. The modern version of this remedy is donor insemination, see Chapter 7 below.

[187] Vermier Chiu, p. 33; see n. 6; compare McAleavy's ingenious argument of simultaneous marriages; see n. 81; see also Decisions of the Chinese Supreme Court, 1917-No 1167; 1981-No 1036; 1918-No 84; 1919-No 1197; 1919-No 177 (郭衛編《大理院判決例全書》成文出版社，台北, 1961).

[188] Van der Valk, *Conservatism in Modern Chinese Family Law*, E J Brill, Leiden, 1956, p. 42.

[189] See n. 7.

[190] Note that this passage was quoted in *Re Ng Shum (No 2)* [1990] 1 HKLR 67, but it does not appear in Chu Tung-tsu's English translated text.

[191] Cf. Liu J in *Lee Lan v Henry Ho,* High Court, Miscellaneous Proceedings No 3441 of 1978 (1980).

As for concubines, the McDouall-Heenan Report 1965 recommended that,[192] *inter alia,* concubines be offered protection under the law in the following ways:

(1) a concubine to a customary marriage should be given a statutory right to dissolve her marriage at will (with or without reason), and ancillary matters post-divorce should be determined by mutual agreement or by the courts.

(2) a concubine to a customary marriage, and her children, should be endowed with the same right as a principal wife to seek maintenance against the husband;

(3) a concubine added to a modern marriage[193] prior to 7 October 1971 should have the right to apply for maintenance for herself and her children from the husband and from his estate.

Legislation does not provide for these rights, except that a concubine is included in the Separation and Maintenance Orders Ordinance[194] as a 'married woman', enabling her to apply for maintenance. She is also entitled to protection under the Intestates' Estates Ordinance (s13 and Schedule 1) and the Inheritance (Provision for Family and Dependants) Ordinance. However, as will be seen in Chapter 2, she has no right to dissolve her marriage, nor is her position recognised in a modern marriage. Dissolution of customary marriages, modern marriages and unions of concubinage will be examined in Chapter 2.

---

[192] See para 40.
[193] See above, pp. 27–37.
[194] See Chapter 10.

Annex I

THE CHINESE CIVIL CODE 1930, BOOK IV — FAMILY (From The Civil Code of the Republic of China, translated into English by Ching-lin Hsia, James Chow, Liu Chieh and Yukon Chang, Kelly & Walsh Limited, Shanghai, 1931)

CHAPTER I

GENERAL PROVISIONS

Article 967. – Lineal relatives (of a person) by blood are his relatives by blood from whom he is descended or those that are descended from him.

Collateral relatives (of a person) by blood are his non-lineal relatives that are descended from the same common ancestor as the person himself.

Article 968. – The degree of relationship by blood between a person and his lineal relative by blood is determined by counting the number of generations upwards or downwards from himself (as the case may be), one generation being taken as one degree. As between the person and his collateral relative, the degree of relationship is determined by the total number of generations counting upwards from himself to the common lineal ancestor and then from such common ancestor downwards to the relative by blood with whom the degree of relationship is to be determined.

Article 969. – Relatives by marriage (of a person) are the spouse of his relative by blood, the relative by blood of his spouse and the person who is married to the relative by blood of his spouse.

Article 970. – The line and the degree of relationship between relatives by marriage is determined in the following ways:–
1. As regards the spouse of a relative by blood, by the line and the degree of relationship of the person who is married to the said spouse;
2. As regards a relative by blood of a spouse, by the line and the degree of relationship between such relative by blood and the said spouse;
3. As regards the person to whom a relative by blood of a spouse is married, by the line and the degree of relationship between such person and the said spouse.

Article 971. – Relationship by marriage is extinguished by divorce. The same rule applies when a wife remarries after the death of the husband, or a 'chui-fu'* remarries after the death of the wife.

---

* Chui-fu (贅夫) is a man who is married into the house of his wife.

CHAPTER II

MARRIAGE

TITLE I. – BETROTHAL

Article 972. – An agreement to marry shall be made by the male and the female parties of their own accord.

Article 973. – A man who has not completed his seventeenth year of age and a woman her fifteenth may not make an agreement to marry.

Article 974. – Where a minor makes an agreement to marry, the consent of his statutory agent must be obtained.

Article 975. – No demand may be made for the specific performance of an agreement to marry.

Article 976. – Where one of the betrothed parties is found in one of the following conditions, the other party may dissolve the agreement to marry:–
1. Where, having made an agreement to marry, the party makes another agreement or concludes a marriage with another person;
2. Where the party wilfully fails to observe the appointed date of marriage;
3. Where it has been uncertain for over a year whether the party is alive or dead;
4. Where the party has a serious disease which is incurable;
5. Where the party has venereal or other loathsome disease;
6. Where, having made the agreement to marry, the party becomes permanently disabled;
7. Where, having made the agreement to marry, the party has sexual intercourse with a third person;
8. Where, having made the agreement to marry, the party is sentenced to imprisonment;
9. Where other grave reasons exist.

In the case where a person intends to dissolve an agreement to marry in accordance with the provisions of the preceding paragraph, if circumstances do not enable him to declare such intention to the other party, it is not necessary for him to do so, and he is no longer bound by the agreement as from the time when its dissolution may be effected.

Article 977. – Where an agreement to marry is dissolved in accordance with the provisions of the preceding article, the innocent party may claim compensation from the other party who is at fault for damage thus sustained.

Article 978. – A party to an agreement to marry, who breaks it without any of the grounds provided in Article 976, shall be liable to compensate the other party for any damage thus sustained.

Article 979. – In the case provided in the preceding article, even where the damage is not a pecuniary loss, the injured party, provided that he is not at fault, may also claim an equitable compensation in money.

The aforementioned claim is not transferable and may not pass to heirs, unless it has been acknowledged by contract or unless an action has been commenced.

TITLE II. – CONCLUSION OF MARRIAGE

Article 980. – A man who has not completed his eighteenth year of age and a woman her sixteenth may not conclude a marriage.

Article 981. – A minor must have the consent of his statutory agent for concluding a marriage.

Article 982. – A marriage must be celebrated by open ceremony and in the presence of two or more witnesses.

Article 983. – A person may not marry any of the following relatives:–
1. A lineal relative by blood or by marriage;
2. A collateral relative by blood or by marriage of a different rank,** except where the former is beyond the eighth degree of relationship and the latter beyond the fifth;
3. A collateral relative by blood who is of the same rank and within the eighth degree of relationship; but this provision does not apply to 'piao cousins.'***

The marriage prohibitions between relatives by marriage provided in the preceding paragraph shall continue to apply even after the dissolution of the marriage which has created the relationship.

Article 984. – A guardian may not marry his ward during the continuance of guardianship, unless the consent of the ward's parents has been obtained.

** "Rank" (輩分) meaning persons of the same generation.
*** By "piao cousins" (表兄弟姊妹) are meant all the collaterals of the same generation other than those to whom one is related exclusively through males.
  In the case of Article 983 No 3 the "piao cousins" of a person include all his collaterals of the same rank of the fourth, sixth, and eighth degree, except:
  (a) the children of the brothers of his father,
  (b) the children born from sons of brothers of his paternal grandfather,
  (c) the children descending through males from the brothers of the father of his paternal grandfather.

Article 985. – A person who has a spouse may not contract another marriage.

Article 986. – A person who, on account of adultery, has been divorced or sentenced to criminal penalty may not marry the other party to the adultery.

Article 987. – A woman may not re-marry until six months have elapsed after the dissolution of her first marriage, unless within the six months she has given birth to a child.

Article 988. – A marriage is void in any of the following cases:–
1. Where it does not conform to the form provided by Article 982;
2. Where it violates the marriage prohibition between relatives as provided in Article 983.

Article 989. – Where a marriage is concluded contrary to the provision of Article 980, the party concerned or his statutory agent may apply to the Court for its annulment; but such application may not be made, where the party concerned has attained the age specified in the said article or where the woman has become pregnant.

Article 990. – Where a marriage is concluded contrary to the provision of Article 981, the statutory agent may apply to the Court for its annulment; but such application may not be made where six months have elapsed after the discovery of the fact or one year has elapsed after the conclusion of the marriage, or where the woman has become pregnant.

Article 991. – Where a marriage is concluded contrary to the provision of Article 984, the ward or his nearest relative may apply to the Court for its annulment; but such application may not be made where one year has elapsed after the conclusion of the marriage.

Article 992. – Where a marriage is concluded contrary to the provision of Article 985, an interested party may apply to the Court for its annulment; but such application may not be made after the dissolution of the former marriage.

Article 993. – Where a marriage is concluded contrary to the provision of Article 986, the former spouse may apply to the Court for its annulment; but such application may not be made where one year has elapsed after the conclusion of the marriage.

Article 994. – Where a marriage is concluded contrary to the provision of Article 987, the ex-husband or his lineal relatives by blood may apply to the Court for its annulment; but such application may not be made where six months have elapsed after the dissolution of the former marriage, or where the woman has become pregnant after the latter marriage.

Article 995. – Where one of the parties is incapable of marital intercourse at the time of marriage and such incapacity is incurable, the other party may apply to the Court for the annulment of the marriage; but such application may not be made after three years from the time of the discovery of such incurability.

Article 996. – Where, at the time of the marriage, one of the parties is in a condition of absence of discernment or mental disorder, such party may within six months after he is restored to normal condition apply to the Court for its annulment.

Article 997. – A person who has been induced by fraud or by duress to conclude a marriage may apply to the Court for its annulment within six months after the discovery of the fraud or after the cessation of the duress.

Article 998. – The effect of an annulment of marriage is not retroactive.

Article 999. – A party to a marriage who has sustained damage through the nullity or the annulment of the marriage may claim compensation from the other party. This, however, does not apply where the other party is not at fault.

In the case mentioned in the preceding paragraph, the injured party, if he is not at fault, may also claim an equitable compensation in money even where the injury is not a pecuniary loss.

The claim mentioned in the preceding paragraph is not transferable and does not pass to heirs, unless it has been acknowledged by contract or an action has been commenced.

Article 1000. – Unless otherwise agreed upon by the parties, a wife shall prefix to her surname that of the husband, and a 'chui-fu' shall prefix to his surname that of the wife.

Article 1001. – Husband and wife are under mutual obligation to live together, unless for good reason they cannot live together.

Article 1002. – A wife takes the domicile of the husband as her domicile; a 'chui-fu' takes the domicile of the wife as his domicile.

Article 1003. – In daily household matters, the husband and the wife act as agents for each other.

Where one of the parties abuses the aforesaid right of agency, the other party may restrict it, but such restriction cannot be set up against bona fide third parties.

2

Dissolution under the Marriage Reform Ordinance

INTRODUCTION

The institutions of customary marriage and modern marriage were discussed in Chapter 1. We are here concerned with the dissolution of these marriages which is now partly governed by the Marriage Reform Ordinance (MRO). As such, it is important to consider dissolutions falling within two distinct periods: (i) the period prior to 7 October 1971, and (ii) the period after 7 October 1971. Dissolution of a union of concubinage will be considered at the end of this chapter.

THE POSITION PRIOR TO 7 OCTOBER 1971

As was seen in Chapter 1, just as the law had difficulty with 'Chinese' marriages — customary and modern — the law confronted similar difficulties when it came to the 'Chinese' methods of dissolution.

Prior to 7 October 1971, the dissolution of these marriages was beset by difficulties. The 1967 White Paper characterised the problem as follows:

> There is no provision in Hong Kong law whereby parties to marriages celebrated in Hong Kong otherwise than in accordance with the Marriage Ordinance . . . can be divorced. The fact remains however that Chinese Customary Marriages and Chinese Modern Marriages are generally

regarded in Hong Kong as terminable by mutual consent; this practice rests in the former case on long-standing tradition going back at least to the Han Dynasty, and in the latter case on the 1930 Civil Code, which specifically provided for such dissolution ... It should additionally be noted that, apart from divorce by mutual consent, the husband in a Chinese Customary Marriage traditionally has the right to dissolve the marriage unilaterally in certain circumstances.[1]

Dissolution of Customary Marriage under Qing Law

Under Qing law, a wife's position was subservient to that of her husband and appreciating the degree of subjugation assists in understanding the divorce law.

As mentioned in Chapter 1, the purpose of a customary marriage was to serve the ancestral temple and continue the family line. Thus, marriage was not a matter between the prospective bride or groom but was rather a union between the heads of the two families so the consent of the prospective marriage partners was unnecessary. The conclusion of a marriage contract was often based on a consideration of the need to match the families' socio-economic position, rather than on the compatibility of personality, temperament or characteristics of the prospective bride and groom. This is in line with the popular Chinese saying that 'wooden doors match wooden doors and bamboo doors to bamboo doors', or the importance of *men dang hu dui* (門當互對).

Position of a wife vis-à-vis *the husband*

Although both men and women in marriage were to serve the family, according to Confucius' five classifications of human relationships, like a minister to the sovereign and like a son to the father, a wife was to be subordinated to her husband.[2] Such subordination was reflected in the Chinese saying that:

> Married to a chicken the woman follows the chicken; married to a dog, the woman follows the dog.

A wife, thus, was destined to obey the men in her family. This was the

---

[1] White Paper on Chinese Marriage in Hong Kong, Hong Kong Government Printer, Hong Kong, 1967, para 31 (hereafter referred to as the White Paper 1967).
[2] G MacCormack, *The Spirit of Traditional Chinese Law,* The University of Georgia Press, Athens, 1996, Chapter 5; see also 陳東原《中國婦女生活史》上海商務印書館, 上海, 1928 (Chen Dong-yuan, *The Story of the Chinese Women*).

so-called *san tsung* or three obediences (三重) — before marriage, a woman obeyed her father; after marriage, her husband; widowed, her son. Chu Tung-tsu explained the position of a wife *vis-à-vis* her husband:

> In the family the division of labor between the sexes also rested on man's recognised superiority to woman. It had long been orthodox for man to rule outside the household, woman within it. Care of the children, cooking, washing, sewing, cleaning, and directing the maid servants were all inside tasks — in their final analysis services for the husband. Such expression, "to stand by with towels and combs (*shih chin chieh* 侍巾櫛), and "to hold a broom" (*chi chi chou* 侍巾櫛) were commonly used by the wife to underline her humble position *vis-à-vis* her husband. The story of Huai-ying (懷嬴) who held a basin for Prince Chung-erh (重耳) reveals that even in a princely family, humble labors of this kind were performed by the wife and not by domestics.
>
> The character fu (婦), "woman", is a combination of nu, "female" and Chou, "broom". It has the meaning "to serve" and "to submit".[3]

The three obediences were further buttressed by the four virtues of womanhood (四德),[4] and the divorce law can be seen in the context of a wife's subjugation to her husband and the standard of behaviour which could be expected of her.

Qing law or the *Ta Tsing Leu Lee* (大清律例)[5] recognised four types of divorce.[6] (1) A husband could unilaterally dissolve his marriage, (2) A wife

---

[3] 瞿同祖《中國法律與中國社會》商務, 1947, (中華書局 1996 第二次印刷) Chu Tung-tsu, '*Law and Society in Traditional China*', Westport, Connecticut, Hyperion Press, reprinted edition 1980 (hereafter referred to as Chu Tung-tsu), p. 103.

[4] (即婦德、婦言、婦容、婦功) see《中國婦女法律實用全書》中華全國婦女聯合會編, 法律出版社, 北京, 1993 Chapter 7. 'By means of four virtues a woman is made to preserve her feminine qualities, to be gentle in disposition and pleasing in appearance, to be chary of speech, and to be assiduous in the performance of her domestic duties.' See Vermier Chiu, *Marriage Laws and Customs of China*, Chinese University Press, Hong Kong, 1966, p. 1 (hereafter referred to as Vermier Chiu); p. 20; see also Chu Tung-tsu; 陳顧遠《中國婚姻史》商務印書館, 上海, 1936, (Chen Ku-yuan, *A History of Marriage in China* hereafter referred to as Chen Ku-yuan); 趙鳳喈《中國婦女在法律上之地位》食貨月刊社, 台北, (Chao Feng-chieh, *The Legal Status of Women in China*, hereafter referred to as Chao Feng-chieh).

[5] Reference here to the *Ta Tsing Leu Lee* is that translated by George Thomas Staunton, Cheng Wen Publishing Co., Taipei, 1966 (hereafter referred to as Staunton).

[6] See J Dull, 'Marriages and Divorce in Han China: A Glimpse at "Pre-Confucian" Society' and Tai Yen-hui, 'Divorce in Traditional China', both in *Chinese Family Law and Social Changes*, ed by D Buxbaum, University of Washington Press, Hong Kong, 1978 (hereafter cited as J Dull and Tai Yen-hui respectively); 譚紉就《中國婚姻的研究》中華基督教女青年會全國協會, 上海, 1932. Bernhardt, 'Divorce in the Republican Period' in *Civil Law in Qing and Republican China* ed by K Bernhardt & P Huang, Stanford University Press, Standford, 1994; Chu Tung-tsu, n. 3; Chen Ku-yuan; Chao Feng-chieh; see n. 4.

could divorce her husband under very limited circumstances, (3) A divorce could be affected by mutual consent, and (4) under certain circumstances, the parties were obliged to divorce.

Husband's unilateral repudiation

A husband could unilaterally dissolve his marriage with the principal wife[7] on any of the following grounds. These were known as the *ch'u ch'i* (七出) or 'seven ousts' which were restricted by the *san pu ch'u* (三不出) or 'three non-ousts'.[8] The *ch'u ch'i* referred to:[9]

(1) Failure to serve the husband's parents and disobedience to them
(2) Failure to give birth to a son
(3) Adultery
(4) Jealousy
(5) Malignant disease
(6) Loquacity (talkativeness)
(7) Larceny of the husband's goods

These 'seven ousts' may appear quaint to women of the modern era. Apart from larceny which pertained to a wife's personal integrity, the other six ousts were focused on maintaining the well-being of the family. Chu Tung-tsu explained how arbitrarily some of the other six ousts could operate and what they meant.

> Barrenness nullified the most important and sacred purpose of marriage — the continuation of the family line and the worship of the ancestors . . . Actually very few cases can be documented in which a husband divorced his wife solely on the ground of barrenness . . . the law held that a man could only divorce his wife on the ground of barrenness if she was over fifty years of age — that is, at the time of menopause . . . barrenness presented no serious problem so long as concubinage was institutionally and legally recognised. . . .The situation became difficult only when the wife was both barren and so jealous that she would not permit her husband to take a concubine. Jealousy, therefore, was another of the seven reasons for divorce.
> Since adultery in the event of offspring led to the introduction of strange blood into the family line and since it was a common belief amongst the ancients that a ghost would not accept a sacrifice by anyone not of the same blood as the husband, adultery could not be tolerated and divorce was justified. . . .

---

[7] For concubine, see *Re Sim Siew-guan Deceased* (1932) MLJ 95.
[8] See Article 116 of *Ta Tsing Leu Lee*, Staunton; n. 5.
[9] For a more detailed explanation of these grounds for divorce, see Vermier Chiu, p. 63; n. 4.

> The ancients held that a woman with an incurable disease could not be tolerated since a person so afflicted could not prepare a sacrifice. . . .
> To serve her husband's parents was the duty of a daughter-in-law. Failure to do so properly put an end to the parent-in-law – daughter-in-law relationship and usually to the marriage as well . . . Tseng Shen, a disciple of Confucius, divorced his wife because she undercooked a pear for his parents. Pao Yung (end of the 1st century BC) divorced his wife because she shouted at a dog in her mother-in-law's presence. Chiang Shih (1st century AD) divorced his wife because she took too long to fetch water from the river for her mother-in-law who was thirsty . . . What was entailed in not serving one's parents-in-law "well" or in not being in accord with them depended more on the attitude of the parents-in-law than on the behaviour of the daughter-in-law. The Li Chi clarifies the point. It states that a son should divorce his wife, even when he is fond of her, if she is disliked by his parents; and that he should treat her as his wife during his lifetime, even when he is not fond of her, but when his parents say, "She serves us well.". . .
> The inclusion of loquacity among the causes for divorce is also understandable from the standpoint of familism. Naturally it was important to maintain order within the family and prevent quarrels between its members . . .[10]

Although a wife could be divorced by reason of any one of the seven ousts, the husband could not divorce her if one of the *san pu ch'u* applied. They were:[11]
(1) if she had participated, in lieu of her husband, in the three-year mourning of either of her husband's parents,
(2) if her husband's family was poor before the marriage but had become rich after the marriage, or
(3) if, after the divorce, she had no home to return to.

Apart from the three non-ousts, the wife was not well protected,[12] and, on her part, could not divorce her husband except in very limited circumstances. As will be seen, divorce by mutual consent was possible, but if a husband refused to consent to a divorce and she deserted her husband, she became subject to a punishment of 100 blows and her husband was entitled to sell her in marriage.[13] If she married before later returning to her deserted husband's home, the punishment was death by strangling.[14] Those who harboured a fugitive wife were also punished.

---

[10] Chu Tung-tsu at p. 119–121; n. 3.
[11] Vermier Chiu p. 69; see n. 4; G Jamieson, *Family Law and Commercial Law*, Vetch & Lee Ltd., Hong Kong, 1970, p. 53.
[12] See Chen Ku-yuan, Chao Feng-chieh; n. 4.
[13] Article 116 of the *Ta Tsing Leu Lee*, Staunton; see n. 5.
[14] Article 116 of the *Ta Tsing Leu Lee*, Staunton; see n. 5.

> Whoever harbours a fugitive wife or slave, or marries them knowing them to be fugitives, shall participate equally in their punishment, except in capital cases, when the punishment shall be reduced one degree . . .[15]

Divorce at wife's suit

There appeared to be one situation where a wife could divorce her husband, and this was where the husband had deserted the wife for 3 years. However, in Article 116 of the *Ta Tsing Leu Lee*, it was provided that:

> If, previous to the expiration of a period of three years after a husband had deserted and been no more heard of by his wife, such wife, without notice at a tribunal of government, should likewise quit her home and abscond, she shall be punished with 80 blows . . .[16]

Mutual consent

Apart from unilateral dissolution by a husband, a customary marriage could also be dissolved by mutual consent. Thus the *Ta Tsing Leu Lee* provided that:

> When the husband and wife do not agree, and both parties are desirous of separation, the law limiting the right of divorce shall not be enforced to prevent it.[17]

Breaking of the Bond of Matrimonial Relations

According to Chu Tung-tsu, divorce was required by law, and therefore obligatory for the parties under certain circumstances.[18] Thus, although the seven ousts could be invoked by the husband alone, breaking of the bond of matrimonial relations or *I Chueh* (義絕), might be invoked against both parties to a marriage.

Criminal conduct was the basis for *I Chueh*. This included acts on the part of a husband, wife or certain of their relatives. Criminal acts by a husband were considered to be less severe than those committed by the wife. Criminal acts on the part of a husband were:

---

[15] Article 116 of the *Ta Tsing Leu Lee*, Staunton; see n. 5.
[16] Staunton; see n. 5.
[17] Article 116 of the *Ta Tsing Leu Lee*, Staunton; see n. 5.
[18] Chu Tung-tsu, pp. 122–3; n. 3; Chao Feng-chieh; Chen Ku-yuan; see n. 4; Tai Yen-hui; J Dull; see n. 6; see also Interpretation of the Chinese Supreme Court, 813, 10 July 1918 (郭衛編《大理院解釋例全書》成文出版社, 台北, 1961).

(1) Beating of the wife's grandparents or parents;
(2) Killing of the wife's maternal grandparents, paternal uncles and their wives, brothers, paternal aunts and sister;
(3) Adultery with the wife's mother.

Criminal acts on the part of a wife were:
(1) Beating or cursing of the husband's grandparents or parents;
(2) Killing or injuring of the husband's maternal grandparents, paternal uncles and their wives; brothers, paternal aunts and sister;
(3) Adultery with the husband's relatives within the five ranks of mourning;
(4) Attempting to harm or kill the husband.

Divorce is also required for killing committed by relatives of either spouse against the relatives of the other in the following categories: paternal grandparents, parents, maternal grandparents, paternal uncles and their wives, brothers, paternal aunts and sister.

Where divorce was required by law, a party who failed to do so was subject to a punishment of 80 blows.[19]

Formalities

Whether a customary marriage was dissolved unilaterally or by mutual consent, there was no prescribed form or procedure to be followed,[20] but it was not uncommon for there to be a divorce letter or a divorce document which might be used as evidence of divorce.[21] The validity of a unilateral divorce or divorce by mutual consent has, however, not been judicially considered by the Hong Kong courts although the issue arose in 1972, in the Malaysian case of *Mary Ng v Ooi Gim Teong*.[22] In that case, the question was whether the husband had divorced his principal wife. The husband alleged that the wife was guilty of disrespectful and disobedient behaviour towards him and his mother. He announced the wife's various acts of misconduct in the presence of his mother, grandmother, two uncles and an old family friend of his intention to divorce her. It was held that under Chinese customary law a divorce must be made publicly known, and that what had been done was sufficient. Mohamed Azmi J commented on

---

[19] Article 116 of *Ta Tsing Leu Lee*, Staunton; see n. 5; see also other grounds cited by Tai Yen-hui; n. 6.
[20] Vermier Chiu; see n. 6; Decisions of the Chinese Supreme Court, 1914-No 1115 & 1919-No 460 (郭衞編《大理院判決例全書》成文出版社, 台北, 1961).
[21] See *Lee v Lau* [1967] P. 14.
[22] [1972] 2 MLJ 18.

the injustice to a wife of being divorced on any such pretext as 'talkativeness' or 'disobedience' in this modern age. It was, he said, equivalent to giving 'thousands of Chinese husbands a gun in their hands'. As will be seen later, this position was ameliorated, to a certain extent, by the MRO which offered some protection against the vagaries of the Qing law.

Dissolution of a Modern Marriage by Mutual Consent Under the Chinese Civil Code

In Chapter 1, we discussed the relevance of the Chinese Civil Code to the marriage law of Hong Kong. It was also remarked that the Chinese Civil Code modernised marriage law by conferring on individuals the right to choose their own partners and that the Code had made marriage a monogamous institution. In addition to these changes, the Code introduced equality between husband and wife into the law on divorce. Thus, unlike customary marriages where a husband could unilaterally repudiate his marriage, the Chinese Civil Code provided that both husband and wife enjoyed equally the right to bring a marriage to an end.[23] It permitted the parties to terminate a marriage themselves by mutual consent effected in writing, signed by the parties and two witnesses.[24] Alternatively, either spouse might apply to the court for a divorce provided certain conditions could be satisfied, which included, for instance, a respondent spouse having committed bigamy or adultery, or having ill-treated the petitioner.[25]

Remedial Provisions: Validation of Dissolution of Modern Marriage before 7 October 1971

As was mentioned in Chapter 1, a modern marriage contracted in Hong Kong was technically invalid so any purported dissolution of such a marriage under the Chinese Civil Code would be similarly invalid.

The Marriage Reform Ordinance (MRO) retrospectively validated modern marriages contracted in Hong Kong prior to 7 October 1971. As these marriages might have been purportedly terminated by mutual consent in accordance with the Chinese Civil Code, s14 of the MRO also retrospectively recognised this method of dissolution. S14 thus provides that dissolution of a validated marriage, at any time prior to 7 October

---

[23] See Annex I of this chapter, pp. 71–2.
[24] See Article 1049, Annex I of this chapter, p. 71.
[25] See Article 1052, Annex I of this chapter, p. 71.

1971, by mutual consent of the parties to the marriage signified by their signatures in the presence of two attesting witnesses to an agreement or memorandum in writing setting out unequivocally the dissolution of the marriage shall be deemed to have been valid. Validity dates back to the execution of the agreement.

Remedial Provisions: Validation of Dissolution in Hong Kong of Marriages Celebrated in China under the Chinese Civil Code

So far, we have considered dissolution of 'Chinese' marriages in Hong Kong. One peculiar ancillary problem which has surfaced in Hong Kong concerns marriages celebrated in China after 4 May 1931 but before 1 May 1950, under the law then in force in China, that is the Chinese Civil Code. Such marriages were valid foreign marriages and had always been recognised as such by Hong Kong courts. Consequently, these marriages could only be properly dissolved by a decree of a competent court.

Unfortunately, many parties to such marriages purported to have dissolved their marriages in Hong Kong prior to 7 October 1971 by mutual consent as if the Chinese Civil Code had been in force in Hong Kong. Strangely enough:

> Some of these consensual dissolutions were entered into in the presence of officers of the Secretariat of Home Affairs and were widely regarded as valid. This belief was supported by the fact that the government itself recognised them to the extent that persons whose marriages were dissolved in this manner were permitted to re-marry under the Marriage Ordinance and [such dissolutions] were accepted for various purposes under the Widows and Orphans Pensions Ordinance and the Establishment Regulations.[26]

These dissolutions were, in fact, invalid as would be any subsequent marriages. *A fortiori,* any children born to such latter union would be illegitimate. Given this unsatisfactory state of affairs, the MRO validated all such dissolutions effected in Hong Kong prior to the 7 October 1971. This was effected by s22A of the MRO which provides that where the parties to such marriages signified by signature of each of the parties, in the presence of two attesting witnesses, to an agreement in writing which sets forth unequivocally the final and complete dissolution of the marriage,

---

[26] HK Hansard, 1 December 1971, p. 249.

such dissolution shall be valid for all purposes from the time of the execution of the agreement. It included the important condition that at the date of the agreement (i) both parties must have been domiciled in Hong Kong or (ii) either party must have had a substantial connection with Hong Kong.

However, dissolution of such a marriage after 7 October 1971 by mutual consent would be invalid. Such a marriage could only be dissolved under the Matrimonial Causes Ordinance. It should be added here that the Matrimonial Causes Ordinance also governs the dissolution in Hong Kong of marriages celebrated in China after 1 May 1950.[27]

THE POSITION AFTER 7 OCTOBER 1971

Dissolution of Customary Marriage or Validated Marriage under the MRO

It has already been mentioned that one of the methods for dissolving both customary marriages and modern marriages was by mutual consent, a method which has since 7 October 1971 been preserved by the MRO. However, the MRO introduced further means of dissolution — dissolution under the Matrimonial Causes Ordinance (MCO).

Essential Requirements

Today, under s15 of the Marriage Reform Ordinance, a customary marriage or a validated marriage, subsisting on 7 October 1971, can be dissolved either by mutual consent or under the MCO. The essential requirement here is that such a marriage has been registered under the MRO and that either party to the marriage has a substantial connection with Hong Kong.

Thus, s15 of the MRO provides that:

> a customary marriage, [or a validated marriage] subsisting on [7 October 1971] and registered in accordance with Part IV may, where at least one party to the marriage has a substantial connection with Hong Kong, be dissolved on or after [7 October 1971] . . .
> (a) in accordance with the Matrimonial Causes Ordinance; or
> (b) in accordance with this Part [Part V of the MRO].

---

[27] See Chapter 3.

Consensual divorce: Procedures

Part V of the MRO provides for consensual divorce and stipulates the procedures to be followed:

(1) The parties to the marriage may give notice of their intention to dissolve the marriage to a designated public officer.[28] Such notice must be signed by both parties. A person who has given notice may cancel such notice.[29]

(2) Not less than one month after the giving of the notice, the parties may appear before the designated officer to whom notice was given for the purpose of satisfying him that both parties wish to voluntarily and freely dissolve his or her marriage to the other.[30]

(3) The designated officer shall interview the parties in the presence of each other and in the absence of each other[31] for the purposes of satisfying himself that the notice of intention to dissolve the marriage has not been cancelled, that the parties understand that the effect of the dissolution is to put an end to the marriage, and the parties freely and voluntarily desire to dissolve the marriage. Where he is so satisfied, he shall sign a prescribed form to this effect and deliver one copy to each of the parties.

(4) The parties may within one month of the delivery of this form, sign in Hong Kong, in the presence of both parties and two attesting adult witnesses, an agreement or memorandum in writing for the dissolution of the marriage unequivocally.

(5) An agreement or memorandum for dissolution of marriage shall have effect as from registration.[32]

(6) The parties shall register particulars of the agreement or memorandum for the dissolution of marriage within 14 days with the designated officer.[33]

From Table 2.1, it can been seen that the number of divorces under Part V remains small and that there has been none since 1991.

Effect of dissolution

Dissolution in accordance with Part V shall be deemed to be a final decree of divorce granted by the court, and the court shall have the same jurisdiction

---

[28] S16(1).
[29] S16(2).
[30] S17(1).
[31] S18.
[32] S19(1).
[33] S20.

Table 2.1 Dissolution of Marriages under Part V of the Marriage Reform Ordinance

Year	Cases Completed
1971	0
1972	2
1973	2
1974	4
1975	7
1976	12
1977	23
1978	17
1979	7
1980	7
1981	9
1982	10
1983	9
1984	6
1985	7
1986	3
1987	7
1988	2
1989	0
1990	1
1991	1
1992–Present	0
Total:	136

Source: Home Affairs Department

and powers in respect of ancillary relief and the protection of children as it would have had if the court had granted a final decree of divorce.[34]

Ancillary matters

Where the parties have agreed as to the amount of maintenance payable by one of the parties to the other after the dissolution of the marriage and have recorded the terms of that agreement as part of the agreement or memorandum dissolving the marriage, the court shall not have jurisdiction in respect of maintenance for either of the parties to the former marriage.[35]

---

[34] See s7A(1) MCO.
[35] S7A(2) MCO.

Divorce under the Matrimonial Causes Ordinance

The second method of dissolving a validated marriage or a customary marriage is under the Matrimonial Causes Ordinance (MCO).[36]

This confers on a wife in a customary marriage the right to divorce her husband against his will, a right which was previously unknown to her.[37] Indeed, s9 of the MCO goes further. It introduces nullity and judicial separation to both customary marriages and validated marriages by providing that:

> [n]othing in this Ordinance shall authorize the court to pronounce a decree of divorce, nullity, judicial separation or presumption of death and dissolution of marriage or to make any other order unless the decree or order relates to a customary marriage or validated marriage registered under the MRO.

The effect of s9 of the MCO is to allow the grounds for divorce, nullity and judicial separation under the MCO to be applied to both customary marriages and validated marriages.[38] For instance, a wife in a customary marriage may divorce her husband on the grounds that he has behaved in such a way that she cannot reasonably be expected to live with him. However, it is doubtful if there could be a decree of nullity if she had married him when she was under the age of 16.[39]

Dissolution in Accordance with Qing Law

Although Part V of the MRO provides for the dissolution of a customary marriage after 7 October 1971 by mutual consent, the question remains as to whether such a marriage could still be dissolved today under Chinese law and custom and thus outside the ambit of s15 of the MRO.

The recommendation of the White Paper 1967[40] was that after 7 October 1971, dissolution of a customary marriage should be either (i) by mutual consent subject to certain safeguards (which would have removed the right

---

[36] In the case of a customary marriage, this was made possible as a result of the Marriage Reform (Amendment) Ordinance (No 62 of 1979).
[37] Debates to the Marriage Reform (Amendment) Bill 1979, HK Hansard, 18 July 1979, p. 991; see also Chapter 4.
[38] Leonard Pegg, *Family Law in Hong Kong*, 3rd edition, Butterworths Asia, Hong Kong, 1994, pp. 73–75 (hereafter referred to as Pegg).
[39] See *Chan Chung-hing v Wong Kim-wah* [1986] HKLR 715.
[40] Para 34.

of a husband to divorce his wife by unilateral act) or (ii) under the MCO. However, there is no provision to this effect in the MRO. Therefore, given that registration of customary marriages is not compulsory and there is no specific provision for the dissolution of an unregistered customary marriage, it seems that a husband's right to divorce his wife unilaterally remains. More importantly, where a customary marriage is registered, s15 appears to be directory only, but not mandatory.[41]

Although s15 is merely directory in relation to a customary marriage, it is mandatory in relation to a validated marriage. This is because divorce under the Chinese Civil Code 1930 was technically invalid. S14 MRO was remedial in nature and it retrospectively validated such method of dissolution. S15 now provides for the dissolution of a validated marriage after 7 October 1971. Apart from dissolution under the MCO, the only other method is under Part V of the MRO.

DISSOLUTION OF UNION OF CONCUBINAGE

There is very little material to be found on this subject. As we have seen, under Qing law a concubine's status was more humble than that of a wife. The husband was not restricted by the 'seven ousts' and could thus divorce her arbitrarily. Furthermore, in relation to the breaking of the bond of matrimonial relations, the beating or killing of a concubine's relative did not constitute a breaking of the bond by the husband. However, an offence committed by a wife against a husband, should it be committed by a concubine (whose status was lower than a wife) would be considered to be more serious.[42]

There is no Hong Kong case on this point. In the Singaporean case of *Re Lee Gee-chong Deceased*,[43] it was held that a concubine could be divorced at the will of the husband if she was disobedient to him or to his principal wife, if she did not conform to the household rules, or was guilty of immoral conduct.

As to the procedure for effecting such a divorce, a husband's notification to either his near relatives or clansmen sufficed. Thus in another Singaporean

---

[41] Pegg, pp. 118–9; n. 38.
[42] See Tai Yen-hui; n. 6 and Chao Feng-chieh; n. 4; Article 116 of *Ta Tsing Leu Lee*, Staunton; n. 5; K Bernhardt; Decisions of the Chinese Supreme Court 1919-No 177; 1920-No 1124; 1923-No 1170.
[43] (1965) 31 MLJ 102.

case, *Re Sim Siew-guan Deceased*,[44] the deceased had a principal wife and a concubine. Prior to his death, the concubine had been accused of improper conduct and was turned out of the house. In the probate action, the question was whether the concubine had been divorced by the deceased. The Court noted that there were no law reports or textbooks as to what constituted divorce under Chinese custom. Having heard expert evidence, the court held that a husband could divorce his concubine by notifying either his near relatives or his clansmen, no actual ceremony being needed. Indeed, it would be enough if the husband merely communicated his intention to his relations in the course of a casual conversation, and that such communication need not necessarily be made in the presence of the concubine, nor before she left the house.

The MRO made no provision regarding the dissolution of unions of concubinage.[45] Consequently, a concubine has no legal protection from repudiation of the union by the husband at will[46] even though the McDouall-Heenan Report 1965 recommended that,[47] *inter alia*, a concubine should be given a statutory right to dissolve her marriage at will (with or without reason).

CONCLUSION

The law on divorce governing customary marriage or validated marriage can now be summarised in the following charts.

---

[44] (1932) MLJ 95.
[45] See s2 MRO which excludes a concubine as a party to a marriage for the purposes of the Ordinance.
[46] See Vermier Chiu; n. 4, see also *Re Sim Siew-guan* [1932] MLJ 95.
[47] See para 40.

Customary Marriage

Pre-7 October 1971	Post-7 October 1971	
	Unregistered	Registered
Husband's unilateral repudiation	Husband's unilateral repudiation	
Mutual consent	Mutual consent	Mutual consent
Breaking of the bond	Breaking of the bond	
		MCO

Modern Marriage

Pre-7 October 1971	Post-7 October 1971	
	Unregistered	Registered
Mutual consent, retrospectively validated		Mutual consent
		MCO

Annex I

THE CHINESE CIVIL CODE 1930, BOOK IV — FAMILY (From The Civil Code of the Republic of China, translated into English by Ching-lin Hsia, James Chow, Liu Chieh and Yukon Chang, Kelly & Walsh Limited, Shanghai, 1931)

CHAPTER II
TITLE IV. – DIVORCE

Article 1049. – Husband and wife may effect a divorce themselves where they mutually consent to it; but in the case of a minor, the consent of his or her statutory agent must be obtained.

Article 1050. – Divorce by mutual consent is effected in writing and requires the signatures of at least two witnesses.

Article 1051. – After divorce by mutual consent, the guardianship of the children rests with the husband; but where it has been otherwise agreed upon, such agreement shall be followed.

Article 1052. – Either spouse may apply to the Court for a divorce provided that one of the following conditions exists:–
1. Where the other spouse has committed bigamy;
2. Where the other spouse has had sexual intercourse with another person;
3. Where the spouse receives such ill-treatment from the other spouse as to render it intolerable to live together;
4. Where the wife has so ill-treated the lineal ascendants of the husband, or has been so ill-treated by them that life in common becomes intolerable;
5. Where the other party has deserted the spouse in bad faith and such desertion still continues;
6. Where the other party has made an attempt on the life of the spouse;
7. Where the other party has a loathsome disease which is incurable;
8. Where the other party has a serious mental disease which is incurable;
9. Where it has been uncertain for over three years whether the other party is alive or dead;
10. Where the other party has been sentenced to not less than three years' imprisonment or has been sentenced to imprisonment for an infamous crime.

Article 1053. – In the cases specified in Sections 1 and 2 of the preceding article, the party who has the right of action may not apply for a divorce, where he previously consented to the act or has since condoned it or has had cognizance of it for over six months, or where two years have elapsed after the occurrence of the act.

Article 1054. – In the cases specified in Sections 6 and 10 of Article 1052, the party who has the right of action may not apply for a divorce where one year has elapsed after he had cognizance of the act or where five years have elapsed after the act occurred.

Article 1055. – In the case of a divorce by judicial decree, the provisions of Article 1051 shall apply in regard to guardianship of the children. But the Court may, in the interest of the children, appoint a guardian.

Article 1056. – Where one of the spouses has suffered damage from a judicial divorce, he may claim compensation from the party at fault.

In the case provided in the preceding paragraph, the injured party, provided he is not at fault, may also claim an equitable compensation in money even where the damage is not a pecuniary loss.

The claim mentioned in the preceding paragraph is not transferable and may not pass to heirs unless it has been acknowledged by contract or an action has been commenced.

Article 1057. – Where an innocent spouse is reduced to difficulties in livelihood on account of a judicial divorce, the other spouse, even if he be also innocent, shall pay an equitable sum for maintenance.

Article 1058. – On divorce each spouse recovers his or her own property whatever was their matrimonial property regime. If there is any deficit, it is borne by the husband, unless such deficit arises from circumstances for which he is not responsible.

3

Marriage under the Marriage Ordinance

DEFINITION

In 1866, Lord Penzance, in *Hyde v Hyde*[1] offered the classic judicial definition of a 'Christian' marriage. He said that such a marriage was the 'voluntary union for life of one man and woman to the exclusion of all others'. Furthermore, a marriage is not just a simple contract between two individuals. In 1870, Lord Penzance, again remarked that:

> Marriage is an institution. It confers a status on the parties to it, and upon the children that issue from it. Though entered into by individuals, it has a public character. It is the basis upon which the framework of civilised society is built: and, as such, is subject in all countries to general laws which dictate and control its obligations and incidents, independently of the volition of those who enter upon it.[2]

Similarly, in 1923, Viscount Birkenhead LC, stated:

> Marriage is more than a simple contract between spouses, or a thing which they can dissolve by their own acts or choice, even consensually. It is a status, involving other and more important interests.'[3]

---

[1] (1866) LR 1 P & D 130, at p. 133.
[2] *Mordaunt v Mordaunt* (1870) LR 2 P & D 109 at 126.
[3] *Rutherford v Richardson* [1923] AC 1 at p. 7.

The importance of marriage will be seen in later chapters. Lord Penzance's definition of a 'Christian' marriage has now been adopted by s40 of the Marriage Ordinance (MO) which provides that:

(1) Every marriage under this Ordinance shall be a Christian marriage or the civil equivalent of a Christian marriage.
(2) The expression "Christian marriage or the civil equivalent of a Christian marriage" implies a formal ceremony recognised by the law as involving the voluntary union for life of one man and one woman to the exclusion of all others.

What this means is that parties to a marriage must voluntarily enter into a union for life to the exclusion of all others. The formal ceremony recognised by law today is one of two types: (i) religious or (ii) civil. The parties may adopt either a Christian, Hindu, Taoist or Islamic ceremony or a civil ceremony devoid of any religious elements. But in either case, a marriage under the MO is monogamous and heterosexual in nature. Provisions thus are made under the MO for the celebration of a marriage:
(i) in a licensed place of worship by a competent minister,
(ii) in a marriage registry officiated by a marriage registrar.

Prior to 7 October 1971, customary marriage, modern marriage and union of concubinage were part of the marriage law.[4] The Marriage Reform Ordinance abolished these forms of marriage on or after 7 October 1971. Today, a marriage under the MO is the only form of marriage that a person can enter into in Hong Kong.[5]

FORMALITIES

Notice of Marriage

The MO provides that any party who intends to marry shall give notice to the Registrar in the prescribed form.[6] The Registrar shall exhibit a copy of such notice at the office of the Registrar.[7] At any time not more than three months or less than 15 days after the giving of such notice, the Registrar

---

[4] See Chapter 1.
[5] See s4 MRO.
[6] S6.
[7] S7.

shall, on the request of a party issue a certificate (Certificate of Registrar of Marriages).[8] Prior to the issue of the certificate, one of the parties to the intended marriage shall appear personally before the Registrar and make affidavit that he or she 'believes that there is not any impediment of kindred or alliance, or any other lawful hindrance to the marriage,' and that consent to the marriage has either been obtained, or is not required by law.[9] If a marriage does not take place within three months after the giving of the notice, the notice and all proceedings thereupon shall be utterly void, and fresh notice will be required before any marriage can be celebrated between the parties.[10]

Celebration of Marriage in a Registry or Licensed Place of Worship

A marriage may take place in the office of the Registrar (and before the Registrar or any deputy registrar), or a licensed place of worship.[11] A marriage in a licensed place of worship may be celebrated by any competent minister of the church, denomination or body to which such place of worship belongs. The ceremony may adopt such rites or usages of marriage observed in such licensed place of worship provided that the marriage is celebrated with open doors between 7 am and 7 pm in the presence of two witnesses besides the officiating minister. No minister however shall celebrate any marriage until the parties deliver to him the Certificate of Registrar of Marriages.[12] A licensed place of worship is given books of marriage certificates by the Registrar. After the marriage, duplicate certificates are signed by the officiating minister, the parties and the witnesses, one certificate the minister gives to the parties and the other he transmits to the Registrar.

Marriage by Special Licence/Marriage of a Dying Person[13]

The Marriage Ordinance provides that the Chief Executive of the Hong Kong Special Administrative Region (Chief Executive) may, when he sees

---

[8] S9.
[9] S12.
[10] S13.
[11] S19, s21.
[12] Or a special licence, as the case may be, s19.
[13] See Law Reform (Miscellaneous Provisions and Minor Amendments) Ordinance (No 80 of 1997).

fit, grant a special licence dispensing with notice or with the Certificate of the Registrar of Marriages, or with both, and authorising the celebration of a marriage between the parties named at a place and at a time specified in the licence.[14]

Marriage of a dying person requires minimal formalities.[15] Such a marriage may be celebrated notwithstanding that no Certificate of the Registrar of Marriages has been issued and no special licence has been granted by the Chief Executive. S39 of the Marriage Ordinance provides that where two persons who have lived in unlawful concubinage desire to marry and one of them is dying, the Registrar or any competent minister may celebrate the marriage at any place and at any time notwithstanding that the Registrar has not issued his certificate and that the Chief Executive has not granted a special licence. But no such marriage shall be valid unless the conditions in s39 have been complied with. They relate to consent of the parties, witnesses, the prohibited degrees of consanguinity and affinity, etc.

Defective Formalities and Void Marriages

Not every failure to observe the formalities in the MO renders a marriage void. The MO provides that no marriage shall, after celebration, be deemed to be invalid by reason that the provisions relating to formalities have not been complied with[16] except where the parties 'knowingly and wilfully acquiesce'[17] to the celebration of a marriage:
- in any place other than the office of the Registrar or a licensed place of worship,[18] or
- under a false name,[19] or
- without a certificate of notice or licence duly issued, or
- by a person not being a competent minister or a Registrar or his deputy.

---

[14] S11.
[15] S39.
[16] Section 27(3); *Collett v Collett* [1968] P. 482.
[17] See *James & Son Ltd v Smee* [1955] 1 QB 78 at p. 91; *Westminister City Council v Croyalgrange Ltd* [1986] 2 All ER 353; *R v Senior* [1899] 1 QB 283 at pp. 290–1.
[18] For exceptions, see s27(2).
[19] *Sullivan v Sullivan* 2 Hag Con 237; cf. marriage by special licence *Puttick v AG* [1980] Fam 1.

CAPACITY

A person lacks the capacity to enter into a valid marriage which takes place after 30 June 1972 if:
(a) the parties are within the prohibited degrees of consanguinity or affinity; or
(b) either party is under the age of 16; or
(c) at the time of the marriage, either party was already lawfully married; or
(d) the parties are not respectively male and female.

These are provided in s20 of the Matrimonial Causes Ordinance and will be considered in Chapter 5.

PROOF OF MARRIAGE UNDER THE MARRIAGE ORDINANCE

S24 of the MO provides that a marriage certificate shall be admissible as evidence of the marriage to which the same relates in any court or before any person having by law or by consent of parties authority to hear, receive and examine evidence. It is *prima facie* evidence of the validity of the marriage (that the marriage was duly solemnised and registered), but it cannot be evidence that no valid earlier marriage subsisted.[20]

FOREIGN/PRC MARRIAGE

Formal requirements of a marriage contracted outside Hong Kong are governed by the law of the place of celebration, the *lex loci celebrationis*. Capacity of the parties to marry is governed by the parties' law of domicile at the time of the marriage. These are the basic rules of private international law.[21]

R40(1) of the Matrimonial Causes Rules provides that a marriage celebrated outside Hong Kong and its validity is not disputed may be proved by the evidence of one of the parties to the marriage by the production of a document purporting to be (i) a marriage certificate or

---
[20] See *Chong Chui Yuk-ching v Chong Pui-cheong* [1983] HKDCLR 1.
[21] *Chan Chung-hing v Wong Kim-wah* [1986] HKLR 715.

similar document issued under the law of the place where the marriage was celebrated or (ii) a certified copy of an entry in a register of marriages kept under the law in that country. Where the document produced is not in English it shall be accompanied by a translation certified by a notary public or authenticated by affidavit or affirmation.

Hong Kong, being so close to mainland China, has had to consider marriages contracted in the PRC under the different marriage law of the PRC. Detailed examination of the marriage law in the PRC is outside the scope of this text and standard texts on this subject should be consulted.[22] For the purposes of Hong Kong law, apart from proving the existence and validity of these marriages, the main question has been centred upon the nature of these marriages, that is, whether they were monogamous or polygamous. If it were the latter, the Hong Kong courts have no matrimonial jurisdiction. This is so because s2 of the Matrimonial Causes Ordinance provides that a 'monogamous marriage' means:

> if it took place outside Hong Kong, celebrated or contracted in accordance with the law in force at the time and in the place where the marriage was performed and recognised by such law as involving the voluntary union for life of one man and one woman to the exclusion of all others.

Most marriages contracted in mainland China fall under three periods:
(1) Under the Chinese Civil Code 1930 which was in force from 5 May 1931.
(2) Under the Marriage Law of 1950 which came into force on 1 May 1950.
(3) Under the Marriage Law of 1980 which came into force on 1 January 1981.

Marriages under the Chinese Civil Code

Provisions governing marriages under the Chinese Civil Code can be seen in Annex I to Chapter 1. These were not registrable and the form they took often resembled that of customary marriages discussed in Chapter 1. Consequently, Hong Kong courts had to consider if they had matrimonial jurisdiction over such marriages. Thus, in 1958, in the case of *Chan Shin*

---

[22] 林蔭茂《婚姻家庭法比較研究》澳門基金會, 澳門, 1997 (Lin Yin-mao, *Marriage and Family Law Comparative Studies*); 張賢鈺編《婚姻家庭法教程》法律出版社, 北京, 1995 (Zhang Xian-yu, *Marriage and Family Law*).
[23] [1958] HKLR 283.

Sui-ping v Chan Din-tsang,[23] the marriage was said to have taken place in 1939 in the Toi Shan [Taishan] District of China. The petitioner wife claimed that she was

> carried in a bridal chair from her village to her husband's village and on arrival at her husband' home was assisted by two women to leave the chair and fire-crackers were ignited. She then changed into an embroidered robe, red skirt and bridal hat and with her husband worshipped before his ancestral tablets. This was followed by fire-crackers. She then knelt before her husband's parents and offered tea to them and the other relatives. In the evening there was a wedding feast.

The District Court, having heard expert evidence that marriages under the Chinese Civil Code 1930 were monogamous in nature, held that it had the jurisdiction to grant a divorce.

Similarly, in *Tang Lai Sau-kiu v Tang Loi*,[24] the parties were married in Canton [Guangdong] Province in China in 1940 according to customary rites. The judge at first instance accepted expert evidence that Chinese customary marriages were not voluntary unions between the parties because (i) only the respective families needed to give their consent and (ii) they were potentially polygamous. The Court of Appeal disagreed and held that the mere fact that the marriage was arranged for the parties did not negate consent. If the parties played their appropriate roles in the ceremony, in the absence of duress, their consent would be inferred. Further, although the marriage partook the form of customary marriage, it was not a customary marriage because the incidence attached to it was prescribed by the Chinese Civil Code, but not by custom. The Chinese Civil Code prohibited polygamy, the marriage was thus monogamous in nature.[25]

Marriages under the Marriage Law of 1950

Marriages contracted under the Marriage Law of 1950 were registrable. Indeed, registration was the only formal requirement for a valid marriage.[26] Article 6 provides that:

> In order to contract a marriage, both the man and the woman should register in person with the people's government of the district or township in which they reside. If the proposed marriage is found to be in conformity

---

[24] [1987] HKLR 85.
[25] See also *Chung Kai-fun v Lau Wai-king* [1966] HKLR 881.
[26] See Annex I of this chapter, pp. 85–91.

with the provisions of this Law, the local people's government should, without delay, issue marriage certificates. If the proposed marriage is not found to be in conformity with the provisions of this Law, registration should not be granted.

Further, Article 1 of the Marriage Law of 1950[27] provided that the marriage system was based on 'monogamy'. Despite the fact that a marriage under the Marriage Law of 1950 might retain many of the features of a customary marriage, it was held to be monogamous. Thus, in *Chan Lee-kuen v Chan Sui-fai*,[28] the marriage took place on 3 January 1951 in China. The parties followed customary rites. Again, similar to the rites in *Chan Shin Siu-ping v Chan Din-tsang,* the prospective husband sent 'wedding gifts, consisting of a cake and a roast pig'. On the wedding day, the wife was 'carried in a sedan chair' to the husband's house, she 'kow-towed to her intended husband's parents', 'worshipped his ancestors' and this was followed by a large 'wedding party'. Expert evidence was that any marriage in China, validly concluded on or after 1 May 1950, between members of the Han race was monogamous. The certificate produced of the registration of the marriage was *prima facie* evidence of the registration of the marriage. The legal effect of the certificate was that the marriage had taken place from the date of its registration (not from the date of its actual celebration). Consequently, the court had the jurisdiction to entertain a divorce petition.

Marriages under the Marriage Law of 1980

Marriages under the Marriage Law of 1980[29] have not been confronted with the same problems associated with marriages under the Chinese Civil Code or the Marriage Law of 1950. Marriages under the Marriage Law 1980 are based on monogamy,[30] bigamy is prohibited.[31] No marriage can be contracted before a man has reached 22 years of age and a woman 20 years of age.[32] Marriages between close relatives are prohibited.[33] Lastly, and as with marriages under the Marriage Law of 1950, registration is the only formal requirement. Upon the issuing of the marriage certificate, the

---

[27] Van der Valk, *Conservatism in Modern Family Law*, 1956; M J Meijier, *Marriage Law and Policy in the Chinese Peoples' Republic*, HKUP, HK, 1971.
[28] [1966] HKLR 796.
[29] See Annex II of this chapter, pp. 91–8; see also texts; Marriage Registration Regulations 1 February 1994.
[30] Article 2.
[31] Article 3.
[32] Article 5.
[33] Article 6.

relationship of husband and wife is acquired.[34] Although a marriage under the Marriage Law of 1980 is a foreign marriage, a certificate of marriage is regarded as *prima facie* proof and no expert evidence is required to assist the courts on proof of validity or its nature before the courts accede jurisdiction.[35]

PRESUMPTION OF MARRIAGE

The presumption of marriage may arise in various ways: it may arise if a marriage has been proved to have been celebrated, i.e. where the parties have gone through a form of ceremony followed by cohabitation;[36] it may arise from the parties having cohabited and had the reputation in the community of being married;[37] and it may arise simply because of the nature of the proceedings, e.g. in divorce[38] or nullity proceedings, the court assumes that a valid marriage subsists until proven otherwise. The presumption is a rebuttable presumption of law, and the standard of proving to the contrary depends on the nature of the defect which a party seeks to establish. Today, registration of marriages is common in most countries, and the likelihood of the inability to find a record of a marriage is much reduced.[39]

Formal Validity

Where there is evidence of a ceremony of marriage having been performed, everything necessary for the validity of the marriage will be presumed in the absence of decisive evidence to the contrary. The burden to disprove is on those denying the validity of the marriage. This presumption is an application of the maxim *omnia praesumuntur rite et solemnitur esse acta*,

---

[34] Article 7.
[35] See M Palmer, 'The Re-emergence of Family Law in Post Mao China: Marriage, Divorce and Reproduction', The China Quarterly; 'Ideas and Conceptions for Revision of Marriage Law in China' The China Quarterly (1997) 72.
[36] '... where there is evidence of a ceremony of marriage having been performed, followed by a cohabitation of the parties, the validity of the marriage will be presumed, in the absence of decisive evidence to the contrary.' Per Barnard J in *Russell v AG* [1949] P. 391 at 394; *Mahadervan v Mahadervan* [1964] P. 233.
[37] Halsbury's Laws of England, 4th edition, Vol 22, para 992.
[38] *Lee v Lau* [1967] P. 14.
[39] *Re Taylor* [1961] 1 All ER 55.

that is, all acts are presumed to have been done rightly and regularly. It applies where persons are found to have set out with the intention of complying with the law. The maxim operates in aid of the proof that everything was in fact done in a proper manner unless decisive evidence to the contrary proves otherwise.

The operation of this presumption as to formal validity can be seen in *Mahadervan v Mahadervan*.[40] The marriage in question was contracted in Ceylon (today the Republic of Sri Lanka). The Marriage General Ordinance required compliance with certain forms: that the marriage should be solemnised by a registrar in his office, and that the registrar should address the parties as to the monogamous nature of the union. The certificate of marriage showed that the marriage had been solemnised by the registrar at his office. After the ceremony of marriage, the parties cohabited as husband and wife. Subsequently, the husband went through a marriage ceremony with an English woman. The wife to the first union complained of the husband's adultery, and the husband claimed that the marriage was invalid because it was in fact celebrated in the wife's house and the registrar made no address to them as to the nature of the union. The Privy Council held that where a ceremony of marriage was proved, followed by cohabitation as husband and wife, a strong presumption was raised which could only be rebutted by evidence satisfying the court beyond reasonable doubt that there was no valid marriage.[41]

Essential Validity

If there is some evidence that either party to the marriage lacked the capacity to contract a marriage, the presumption of marriage disappears, and the validity of the marriage is left to be decided on the balance of probabilities. A common problem in relation to capacity is where H married W2; and W2 later discovers that at the time of her marriage, H was married to W1. The validity of the marriage of H and W2 depends on whether W1's marriage terminated. Another situation is where H married W2, believing that W1 was dead. Is the marriage of W2 valid? This depends on whether W1 was in fact dead at the time of W2's marriage.

Thus, in *Bradshaw v Bradshaw*,[42] H2 challenged the validity of a maintenance order on the grounds that his marriage in 1940 was null and

---

[40] [1964] P. 233.
[41] *Piers v Piers* (1849) 2 HL Cas 331 applied; but compare *Re Kishen Das* (1933) 26 HKLR 42.
[42] [1956] P. 274.

void in that the wife was married to another person at the relevant time. The wife was married to H1 in 1916, H1 was then 22 years old. It was held that as there was no divorce and the presumption of death did not apply, the maintenance order could be discharged.[43] Similarly in *Re Peete*[44] the 'wife' at the time of the marriage had previously gone through a ceremony of marriage with another person and there was no evidence that he was dead at the relevant time. It was held that the presumption of essential validity was rebutted by proof that the wife was already married to another person.

However, a doubtful previous marriage could not displace a presumption in favour of the latter marriage. In *Ives v Ives*,[45] H2 and W (a Christian) went through a form of marriage ceremony, in Karachi, in 1955. A certificate of marriage was produced to the court. The marriage was followed by cohabitation for four years. W sued for arrears under a deed of separation signed between hers and H2. H2 claimed that the marriage was invalid as W was at all material times married to H1 (a Moslem). That 'marriage' was alleged to have taken place in Karachi in 1930 in accordance with Moslem rites. However, there was no evidence that the law of India recognised a marriage between a Moslem and a Christian celebrated in accordance with Moslem rites. It was held by the Court of Appeal that the latter marriage was presumed to be valid in the absence of decisive evidence to the contrary. A doubtful previous marriage could not displace a presumption in favour of the latter marriage between H2 and W. Similarly in *Kao Yeung Lun-yuk v Kao Cho*,[46] the wife petitioned to dissolve her marriage contracted at a Hong Kong Registry office in 1966. After the marriage, the parties cohabited for seven years and the petitioner bore him a child. The respondent alleged that at the time of the Registry marriage, the petitioner was married to one Mr Chan in China. Evidence was given that, although no ceremony was performed, the parties cohabited between 1956 and 1962 and the petitioner bore Mr Chan two children before coming to Hong Kong. There was also evidence that Mr Chan addressed her as his wife, and they were treated as husband and wife by their families. It was held that evidence in the form of a Hong Kong marriage certificate must be accepted until there was decisive evidence to the contrary. The relationship between the petitioner and Mr Chan was no more than a doubtful marriage; it did not comply with the requirement of the Marriage Law of 1950 which

---

[43] *Chard v Chard* [1956] P. 259; *Tweney v Tweney* [1946] P. 180.
[44] [1952] 2 All ER 599.
[45] [1967] HKLR 423.
[46] [1975] HKLR 449.

provided that registration was essential to a contract of marriage. A doubtful earlier marriage could not displace the presumption of validity of a later marriage.[47]

---

[47] See *Taylor v Taylor* [1967] P. 25 at p. 39. See criticisms of P M Bromley, *Family Law*, 7th edition, Butterworths, London, 1987, p. 66.

Annex I

THE MARRIAGE LAW OF THE PEOPLE'S REPUBLIC OF CHINA

(Adopted by the Central People's Government Council at its 7th Meeting on 13 April 1950. Promulgated on 1 May 1950 by order of the Chairman of the Central People's Government on 30 April 1950)

GENERAL PRINCIPLES

ARTICLE 1

The feudal marriage system based on arbitrary and compulsory arrangements and the supremacy of man over woman, and in disregard of the interests of the children, is abolished.

The New-Democratic marriage system, which is based on the free choice of partners, on monogamy, on equal rights for both sexes, and on the protection of the lawful interests of women and children, is put into effect.

ARTICLE 2

Bigamy, concubinage, child betrothal, interference in the remarriage of widows, and the exaction of money or gifts in connection with marriages, are prohibited.

CHAPTER II
THE MARRIAGE CONTRACT

ARTICLE 3

Marriage is based upon the complete willingness of the two parties. Neither party shall use compulsion and no third party is allowed to interfere.

ARTICLE 4

A marriage can be contracted only after the man has reached 20 years of age and the woman 18 years of age.

ARTICLE 5

No man or woman is allowed to marry in any of the following instances:
a) Where the man and woman are lineal relatives by blood or where the

man and woman are brother and sister born of the same parents or where the man and woman are half-brother and half-sister. The question of prohibiting marriage between collateral relatives by blood (up to the fifth degree of relationship) is determined by custom.
b) Where one party, because of certain physical defects, is sexually impotent.
c) Where one party is suffering from venereal disease, mental disorder, leprosy or any other disease which is regarded by medical science as rendering a person unfit for marriage.

ARTICLE 6

In order to contract a marriage, both the man and the woman should register in person with the people's government of the district or township in which they reside. If the proposed marriage is found to be in conformity with the provisions of this Law, the local people's government should, without delay, issue marriage certificates.

If the proposed marriage is not found to be in conformity with the provisions of this Law, registration should not be granted.

CHAPTER III
RIGHTS AND DUTIES OF HUSBAND AND WIFE

ARTICLE 7

Husband and wife are companions living together and enjoy equal status in the home.

ARTICLE 8

Husband and wife are in duty bound to love, respect, assist and look after each other, to live in harmony, to engage in productive work, to care for their children and to strive jointly for the welfare of the family and for the building up of the new society.

ARTICLE 9

Both husband and wife have the right to free choice of occupation and free participation in work or in social activities.

ARTICLE 10

Husband and wife have equal rights in the possession and management of family property.

ARTICLE 11

Husband and wife have the right to use his or her own family name.

ARTICLE 12

Husband and wife have the right to inherit each other's property.

CHAPTER IV
RELATIONS BETWEEN PARENTS AND CHILDREN

ARTICLE 13

Parents have the duty to rear and to educate their children; the children have the duty to support and to assist their parents. Neither the parents nor the children shall maltreat or desert one another. The foregoing provision also applies to foster-parents and foster-children. Infanticide by drowning and similar criminal acts are strictly prohibited.

ARTICLE 14

Parents and children have the right to inherit one another's property.

ARTICLE 15

Children born out of wedlock enjoy the same rights as children born in lawful wedlock. No person is allowed to harm them or discriminate against them.

Where the paternity of a child born out of wedlock is legally established by the mother of the child or by other witnesses or material evidence, the identified father must bear the whole or part of the cost of maintenance and education of the child until the age of 18.

With the consent of the mother, the natural father may have custody of the child.

With regard to the maintenance of a child born out of wedlock, if its mother marries, the provisions of Article 22 apply.

ARTICLE 16

Neither husband nor wife may maltreat or discriminate against children born of a previous marriage by either party and in that party's custody.

CHAPTER V
DIVORCE

ARTICLE 17

Divorce is granted when husband and wife both desire it. In the event of either the husband or the wife alone insisting upon divorce, it may be granted only when mediation by the district people's government and the judicial organ has failed to bring about a reconciliation.

In cases where divorce is desired by both husband and wife, both parties should register with the district people's government in order to obtain divorce certificates. The district people's government, after establishing that divorce is desired by both parties and that appropriate measures have been taken for the care of children and property, should issue the divorce certificates without delay.

When one party insists on divorce, the district people's government may try to effect a reconciliation. If such mediation fails, it should, without delay, refer the case to the country or municipal people's court for decision, the district people's government should not attempt to prevent or obstruct either party from appealing to the country or municipal people's court. In dealing with a divorce case, the country or municipal people's court should, in the first instance, try to bring about a reconciliation between the parties. In case such mediation fails, the court should render a decision without delay.

After divorce, if both husband and wife desire the resumption of marriage relations, they should apply to the district people's government for a registration of remarriage. The district people's government should accept such a registration and issue certificates of remarriage.

ARTICLE 18

The husband is not allowed to apply for a divorce when his wife is pregnant, and may apply for divorce only one year after the birth of the child. In the case of a woman applying for divorce, this restriction does not apply.

ARTICLE 19

In the case of a member of the revolutionary army on active service who maintains correspondence with his or her family, that army member's consent must be obtained before his or her spouse can apply for divorce.

Divorce may be granted to the spouse of a member of the revolutionary army who does not correspond with his or her family for a period of two years subsequent to the date of the promulgation of this Law. Divorce may also be granted to the spouse of a member of the revolutionary army, who had not maintained correspondence with his or her family for over two years prior to the promulgation of this Law, and who fails to correspond with his or her family for a further period of one year subsequent to the promulgation of the present Law.

CHAPTER VI
MAINTENANCE AND EDUCATION CHILDREN AFTER DIVORCE

ARTICLE 20

The blood ties between parents and children are not ended by the divorce of the parents. No matter whether the father or the mother has the custody of the children, they remain the children of both parties.

After divorce, both parents continue to have the duty to support and educate their children.

After divorce, the guiding principle is to allow the mother to have the custody of a breast-fed infant. After the weaning of the child, if a dispute arises between the two parties over the guardianship and an agreement cannot be reached, the people's court should render a decision in accordance with the interests of the child.

ARTICLE 21

If, after divorce, the mother is given custody of a child, the father is responsible for the whole or part of the necessary cost of the maintenance and education of the child, both parties should reach an agreement regarding the amount and the duration of such maintenance and education. Lacking such an agreement, the people's court should render a decision.

Payment may be made in cash, in kind or by tilling land allocated to the child.

An agreement reached between parents or a decision rendered by the people's court in connection with the maintenance and education of a child does not obstruct the child from requesting either parent to increase the amount decided upon by agreement or by judicial decision.

ARTICLE 22

In the case where a divorced woman remarries and her husband is willing to pay the whole or part of the cost of maintaining and educating the child or children by her former husband, the father of the child or children is entitled to have such cost of maintenance and education reduced or to be exempted from bearing such cost in accordance with the circumstances.

CHAPTER VII
PROPERTY AND MAINTENANCE AFTER DIVORCE

ARTICLE 23

In case of divorce, the wife retains such property as belonged to her prior to her marriage. The disposal of other family property is subject to agreement between the two parties. In cases where agreement cannot be reached, the people's court should render a decision after taking into consideration the actual state of the family property, the interests of the wife and the child or children, and the principle of benefiting the development of production.

In cases where the property allocated to the wife and her child or children is sufficient for the maintenance and education of the child or children, the husband may be exempted from bearing further maintenance and education costs.

ARTICLE 24

In case of divorce, debts incurred jointly by husband and wife during the period of their married life should be paid out of the property jointly acquired by them during this period. In cases where no such property has been acquired or in cases where such property has been acquired or in cases where such property is insufficient to pay off such debts, the husband is held responsible for paying them. Debts incurred separately by the husband or wife should be paid off by the party responsible.

ARTICLE 25

After divorce, if one party has not remarried and has maintenance difficulties, the other party should render assistance. Both parties should work out an agreement with regard to the method and duration of such assistance; in case an agreement cannot be reached, the people's court should render a decision.

CHAPTER VIII
BY-LAWS

ARTICLE 26

Persons violating this Law will be punished in accordance with law. In cases where interference with the freedom of marriage has caused death or injury to one or both parties, persons guilty of such interference will bear responsiblility for the crime before the law.

ARTICLE 27

This Law comes into force from the date of its promulgation.

In regions inhabited by minority nationalities in compact communities, the people's government (or the Military and Administrative Committee) of the Greater Administrative Area or the provincial people's government may enact certain modifications or supplementary articles in conformity with the actual conditions prevailing among minority nationalities in regard to marriage. But such measures must be submitted to the Government Administration Council for ratification before enforcement.

Annex II

MARRIAGE LAW OF THE PEOPLE'S REPUBLIC OF CHINA 1981

(Adopted by the Fifth National People's Congress at its Third Session on 10 September 1980, and put into Effect from 1 January 1981)

CHAPTER I
GENERAL PRINCIPLES

ARTICLE 1

This Law is the fundamental code governing marriage and family relations.

ARTICLE 2

The marriage system based on the free choice of partners on monogamy and on equal rights for the sexes is put into effect.

The lawful rights and interests of women, children and the aged are protected.

Family planning is practised.

ARTICLE 3

Marriage upon arbitrary decision by any third party, mercenary marriage and any other acts of interference in the freedom of marriage are prohibited. The exaction of money or gifts in connection with marriage is prohibited. Bigamy is prohibited. Within the family mal-treatment and desertion are prohibited.

CHAPTER II
MARRIAGE CONTRACT

ARTICLE 4

Marriage must be based upon the complete willingness of the two parties. Neither party shall use compulsion and no third party is allowed to interfere.

ARTICLE 5

No marriage shall be contracted before the man has reached 22 years of age and the woman 20 years of age. Late marriage and late childbirth should be encouraged.

ARTICLE 6

Marriage is not permitted in any of the following circumstances:
1. Where the man and woman are lineal relatives by blood or collateral relatives by blood (up to the third degree of relationship); and
2. Where one party is suffering from leprosy, a cure not having been effected, or from any other disease which is regarded by medical science as rendering a person unfit for marriage.

ARTICLE 7

Both the man and the woman desiring to contract a marriage shall register in person with the marriage registration office. If the proposed marriage is found to be in conformity with the provisions of this Law, registration shall be granted and a marriage certificate be issued. The relationship of husband and wife is established when a marriage certificate is acquired.

ARTICLE 8

After a marriage has been registered, the woman may become a member of the man's family, or the man may become a member of the woman's family, according to the agreed wishes of the two parties.

CHAPTER III
FAMILY RELATIONS

ARTICLE 9

Husband and wife enjoy equal status in the family.

ARTICLE 10

Husband and wife each has the right to use his or her family name.

ARTICLE 11

Both husband and wife have the freedom to engage in production, to work, to study and to participate in social activities; neither party is allowed to restrain or interfere with the other.

ARTICLE 12

Husband and wife are duty bound to practise family planning.

ARTICLE 13

The property acquired during the period in which husband and wife are under contract of marriage is in the joint possession of the two parties unless they have agreed otherwise.

ARTICLE 14

Husband and wife have the duty to support and assist each other.

When one party fails to perform this duty, the party in need of support and assistance has the right to demand that the other party pay the cost of support and assistance.

ARTICLE 15

Parents have the duty to rear and educate their children; children have the duty to support and assist their parents.

When parents fail to perform this duty, their children who are minors or who are not capable of living on their own have the right to demand that their parents pay for their care.

When children fail to perform the duty of supporting their parents, parents who have lost the ability to work or have difficulties in providing for themselves have the right to demand that their children pay for their support.

Infanticide by drowning and any other acts causing serious harm to infants are prohibited.

ARTICLE 16

Children may adopt either their father's or their mother's family name.

ARTICLE 17

Parents have the right and duty to subject their children who are minors to discipline and to protect them. When children who are minors have done harm to the state, to the collective, or to any other person, their parents are in duty bound to compensate for any economic loss.

ARTICLE 18

Husband and wife have the right to inherit each other's property.
Parents and children have the right to inherit each other's property.

ARTICLE 19

Children born out of wedlock enjoy the same rights as children born in lawful wedlock. No person shall harm or discriminate against them.

The father of a child born out of wedlock must bear part or the whole of the cost of maintenance and education of the child until he or she can live on his or her own.

ARTICLE 20

The state protects lawful adoption. The relevant provisions in the Law governing the right and duties between parents and children are applicable to foster-parents and their foster-children.

The rights and duties in the relations between foster-children and their natural parents are terminated on the establishment of relationship of adoption.

ARTICLE 21

No maltreatment or discrimination is allowed between step-parents and their step-children.

The relevant provisions in this Law governing the relations between parents and children are applicable to the rights and duties in the relations between step-fathers or step-mothers and their step-children who receive care and education from their step-parents.

ARTICLE 22

Grandparents or maternal grandparents who have the capacity to bear the relevant costs have the duty to rear their grandchildren or maternal grandchildren who are minors and whose parents are deceased. Grandchildren or maternal grandchildren who have the capacity to bear the relevant costs have the duty to support and assist their grandparents or maternal grandparents whose children are deceased.

ARTICLE 23

Elder brothers or elder sisters who have the capacity to bear the relevant costs have the duty to rear their minor younger brothers or sisters whose parents either are deceased or have no capacity to rear them.

CHAPTER IV
DIVORCE

ARTICLE 24

Divorce is granted when husband and wife both desire it. Both parties should apply for divorce to the marriage registration office. The marriage registration office, after clearly establishing that divorce is desired by both parties and that appropriate measures have been taken for the care of any children and property, should issue the divorce certificate without delay.

ARTICLE 25

When one party insists on divorce, the organizations concerned may try to effect a reconciliation, or the party may appeal directly to the people's court for divorce.

In dealing with a divorce case, the people's court should try to bring about a reconciliation between the parties. In cases of complete alienation of mutual affection, and when mediation has failed, divorce should be granted.

ARTICLE 26

If the spouse of a member of the armed forces on active service insists on divorce, consent must be obtained from the member concerned.

ARTICLE 27

The husband is not allowed to apply for a divorce when his wife is pregnant or within one year after the birth of a child. This restriction does not apply in the case of the wife applying for divorce, or when the people's court deems it absolutely necessary to agree to deal with a divorce application by the husband.

ARTICLE 28

After divorce, if both parties desire to resume husband-and-wife relations, they should apply to the marriage registration office for a registration of remarriage. The marriage registration office should accept such a registration.

ARTICLE 29

The blood ties between parents and children are not ended by the divorce of the parents. Whether the father or the mother has the custody of the children, they remain the children of both parties.

After divorce, both parents continue to have the right and duty to rear and educate their children.

The guiding principle after divorce is to allow the mother to have the custody of a breast-fed infant. If a dispute arises between the two parties over the guardianship of a child after weaning and agreement cannot be reached, the people's court should make a judgment in accordance with the rights and interests of the child and the circumstances of both parties.

ARTICLE 30

If, after divorce, one party is given custody of a child, the other party is responsible for part or all of the necessary cost of the maintenance and education of the child. The two parties should reach an agreement regarding the amount of the cost and the duration of its payment for such maintenance and education. If such an agreement is lacking, the people's court should make a judgment.

An agreement reached between parents or a judgment made by the people's court in connection with the cost of the maintenance and education of a child does not preclude the child from making a reasonable request where necessary for either parent to increase the amount decided upon by agreement or by judicial decision.

ARTICLE 31

In case of divorce, the disposal of the property in the joint possession of husband and wife is subject to agreement between the two parties. In cases where agreement cannot be reached, the people's court should make a judgment after taking into consideration the actual state of the family property and the rights and interests of the wife and the child or children.

ARTICLE 32

In case of divorce, debts incurred jointly by husband and wife during the period of their married life should be paid off out of their joint property. In cases where such property is insufficient to pay off such debts, the two parties should work out an agreement with regard to the payment; if an agreement cannot be reached, the people's court should make a judgment. Debts incurred separately by the husband or wife should be paid off by the party responsible.

ARTICLE 33

In case of divorce, if one party has maintenance difficulties the other party should render appropriate financial assistance. Both parties should work out an agreement with regard to the details; in case an agreement cannot be reached, the people's court should make a judgment.

CHAPTER V
BY-LAWS

ARTICLE 34

Persons violating this Law shall be subject to administrative disciplinary measures or legal sanctions according to law and the circumstances.

ARTICLE 35

In cases where the relevant party refuses to execute judgments or rulings regarding maintenance, costs of upbringing or support, or regarding the division or inheritance of property, the people's court has the power to enforce their execution in accordance with the law. The organizations concerned have the duty to assist such execution.

ARTICLE 36

The people's congresses and their standing committees in national autonomous areas may enact certain modifications or supplementary articles in keeping with the principles of this Law and in conformity with the actual conditions prevailing among the minority nationalities of the locality in regard to marriage and family relations. Both such provisions enacted by autonomous prefectures and autonomous counties must be submitted to the standing committee of the provincial or autonomous regional people's congress for ratification. Provisions enacted by autonomous regions must be submitted to the Standing Committee of the National People's Congress for the record.

ARTICLE 37

This Law comes into force from 1 January 1981.

The Marriage Law of the People's Republic of China promulgated on 1 May 1950 shall be repealed as of the date of the coming into force of this Law.

4

Divorce under the Matrimonial Causes Ordinance

INTRODUCTION

Marriage is a voluntary union of a man and a woman. Parties can freely enter into a marriage with few preconditions, but this may not always be so with a divorce. Indeed, divorce prior to 1972 under the Matrimonial Causes Ordinance[1] was difficult as it required proof of matrimonial fault. The idea of fault was said to provide a moral framework for marriage and to act as a restraint on the parties' behaviour. These may have been important functions of the law but realising them was always problematic. The emphasis on fault required the court to act as an arbiter, making value judgments about family life and assessing the relative blameworthiness of the parties.

An inquest into who was responsible for the demise of any marriage may be difficult, costly and time-consuming. This may be the cost of enforcing acceptable marital behaviour, but can the law, by requiring an inquest on the parties' relative moral blameworthiness after marriage breakdown effectively provide a moral framework for marriage?

> . . . restricting divorce to matrimonial fault is an illogical and ineffective means of trying to achieve acceptable standards of marital behaviour, because the sanction cannot work. Logically, of course, where both parties

---

[1] See for example, the Divorce Ordinance (No 35 of 1932); Divorce (Amendment) Ordinance (No 44 of 1956).

are equally guilty, it denies them *both* a divorce, but the law recognised some time ago that that was absurd. If only one is "guilty", but divorce is what he wants, then it is scarcely acting as a restraint on behaviour or providing a sound moral framework to give him just that. Allowing the innocent party to punish the guilty by refusing the divorce is unlikely in today's society to change that behaviour. If divorce is *not* what the guilty party wants, then the important sanction is not so much the public marking of his or her guilt but the breakdown of the marriage itself. The fact that adultery or violence or other bad behaviour may lead to an unwanted break up of the marriage is the real deterrent — and long may it remain so.[2]

The law in many jurisdictions has doubted the efficacy of a post-mortem in many cases, and moved away from a wholly fault-based divorce law.[3] It has been recognised that such a system denies a divorce to couples who both want one but who have not behaved badly, or who do not want to blame each other. It would also keep many dead marriages 'alive'.

Given these disadvantages of a fault-based system, many countries have adopted the principle of irretrievable breakdown of marriage as a basis for divorce. But this approach also raises the difficult problems of how to determine whether a marriage has irretrievably broken down or whether it could be saved and the parties reconciled, and whether this determination should be made by way of a judicial inquiry.

Since the Matrimonial Causes (Amendment) (No 2) Ordinance 1972, Hong Kong has adopted the principle of irretrievable breakdown of marriage. As will be seen, it embodies a mixture of fault- and non-fault-based divorce. In practice, very few divorces entail a judicial enquiry as to who was responsible for the marriage breakdown and in the majority of cases divorce involves no more than an administrative or quasi-judicial process.[4] The trend indeed is to move away from fault towards non-adversarial and consensual divorce and this can be seen in divorce by joint application, which will be examined later.

---

[2] English Law Commission Report, 'The Grounds for Divorce', No 192, HMSO, London, 1990, para 3.7, emphasis original.

[3] For Australia, see the Family Law Act 1975 (one-year separation); for England, see the Family Law Act 1996 (period of notice); for New Zealand, see the Family Proceedings Act 1980 (one-year separation); for Canada, see the Divorce Act 1985; for PRC, see the Marriage Law of 1980.

[4] B Rwezaura, 'Recent Developments in the Divorce Law of Hong Kong: Towards Minimal Adjudication and Consensual Divorce', 26 (1996) HKLJ 81 (hereafter cited as B Rwezaura).

The Divorce Law Pre-24 June 1996

In 1972, following the English Divorce Reform Act 1969, the Matrimonial Causes Ordinance[5] provided that the sole ground for divorce was the irretrievable breakdown of marriage. However, the court should not hold the marriage to have broken down irretrievably unless the petitioner satisfied the court of one of five 'facts'. These five facts were deemed to be evidence of irretrievable breakdown of a marriage. They were 'adultery', 'unreasonable behaviour', 'two-year desertion', 'two-year separation with consent' and 'five-year separation without consent'. The first three of these were fault-based and the latter two separation 'facts' were non-fault-based. Thus, s11A(1) of the Matrimonial Causes Ordinance provided that the court should not hold a marriage to have broken down irretrievably unless the petitioner satisfied the court of one of the following facts:–

(a) the respondent has committed adultery and the petitioner finds it intolerable to live with the respondent;
(b) that the respondent has behaved in such a way that the petitioner cannot reasonably be expected to live with the respondent;
(c) that the respondent has deserted the petitioner for a continuous period of at least 2 years immediately preceding the presentation of the petition;
(d) that the parties to the marriage have lived apart for a continuous period of at least 2 years immediately preceding the presentation of the petition and the respondent consents to a decree being granted;
(e) that the parties to the marriage have lived apart for a continuous period of at least 5 years immediately preceding the presentation of the petition.

As can be seen from Table 4.1, divorce since 1972 has been on the increase. In 1992, the Hong Kong Law Reform Commission recommended the following changes to the divorce law:[6]
(i) reduction in the period required for separation,
(ii) abolition of desertion,
(iii) introduction of joint application, and
(iv) reduction of the three-year time bar to present a petition for divorce.

---

[5] Matrimonial Causes (Amendment) (No 2) Ordinance (No 33 of 1972).
[6] Hong Kong Law Reform Commission, Report on Grounds for Divorce and Time Restriction on Petitions for Divorce Within Three Years of Marriage (Topic 29), Hong Kong, The Law Reform Commission, 1992, Appendix A1 (thereafter cited as HKLRC).

Table 4.1 Hong Kong and Divorce Statistics

Year	Divorce Petitions Filed	Joint Application	Divorce Decrees Absolute
1972	532	–	354
1973	793	–	493
1974	789	–	714
1975	893	–	668
1976	1054	–	809
1977	1372	–	955
1978	1728	–	1420
1979	2018	–	1520
1980	2421	–	2087
1981	2811	–	2060
1982	3120	–	2673
1983	3734	–	2750
1984	4764	–	4086
1985	5047	–	4313
1986	5339	–	4257
1987	5747	–	5055
1988	5893	–	5098
1989	6275	–	5507
1990	6767	–	5551
1991	7287	–	6295
1992	8067	–	5650
1993	8626	–	7454
1994	9272	–	7735
1995	10 292	–	9404
1996	12 834	203	9473
1997	15 037	710	10 492

Source: Information extracted from Hong Kong Law Reform Commission, *Report on Grounds for Divorce and Time Restriction on Petitions for Divorce Within Three Years* Topic 29, 1992, Appendix A1, 1992. The updated figures are taken from the Judiciary Annual Reports 1992–1997.

In order to implement these recommendations, the Matrimonial Causes (Amendment) Ordinance[7] was enacted on 18 March 1995. The amendments came into force on 24 June 1996.[8]

---

[7] No 29 of 1995.
[8] Matrimonial Causes (Amendment) Ordinance (No 29 of 1995) (Commencement) Notice 1996.

DIVORCE POST-24 JUNE 1996: BY PETITION OR BY JOINT APPLICATION

The law governing divorce is now to be found in s11 of the Matrimonial Causes Ordinance (MCO). S11 provides two separate and distinct routes to obtaining a decree of divorce: by way of petition or by joint application.

S11 of the MCO provides:

> The sole ground for presenting or making a petition or application for divorce shall be that the marriage has broken down irretrievably and proceedings for divorce shall be instituted either–
> (a) by a petition for divorce; or
> (b) by an application for divorce.[9]

Divorce by joint application is new and this procedure will be examined towards the end of this chapter. We shall first examine grounds for a petition.

Grounds for a Petition

The grounds for petition today are 'adultery', 'unreasonable behaviour', 'one-year separation with consent', 'two-year separation without consent', and 'one-year desertion'.

S11A of the MCO provides:

> (1) A petition for divorce may be presented to the court by either party to a marriage.
> (2) The Court hearing a petition for divorce shall not hold the marriage to have broken down irretrievably unless the petitioner satisfies the court of one or more of the following facts–
> (a) the respondent has committed adultery and the petitioner finds it intolerable to live with the respondent;
> (b) that the respondent has behaved in such a way that the petitioner cannot reasonably be expected to live with the respondent;
> (c) that the parties to the marriage have lived apart for a continuous period of at least 1 year immediately preceding the presentation of the petition and the respondent consents to a decree being granted;
> (d) that the parties to the marriage have lived apart for a continuous period of at least 2 years immediately preceding the presentation of the petition;

---

[9] Irretrievable breakdown has to be proved at the time of the hearing, see *Pheasant v Pheasant* [1972] 1 All ER 587.

(e) that the respondent has deserted the petitioner for a continuous period of at least 1 year immediately preceding the presentation of the petition.

DIVORCE LAW: OBJECTIVES

The objects of the divorce law remain twofold:

> ... (i) to buttress, rather than to undermine the stability of marriage; and (ii) when, regrettably, a marriage has irretrievably broken down, to enable the empty legal shell to be destroyed with the maximum fairness, and the minimum bitterness, distress and humiliation.[10]

JURISDICTION TO ENTERTAIN A PETITION OR APPLICATION FOR DIVORCE

S3 of the MCO provides that the court has jurisdiction to entertain a petition or application for divorce if:

(a) either of the parties to the marriage was domiciled in Hong Kong at the date of the petition or application;
(b) either of the parties to the marriage was habitually resident in Hong Kong throughout the period of 3 years immediately preceding the date of the petition or application; or
(c) either of the parties to the marriage had a substantial connexion[11] with Hong Kong at the date of the petition or application.[12]

With respect to a married woman, she may now acquire a domicile independent of that of her husband.[13]

---

[10] English Law Commission Report, Reform of the Grounds of Divorce, The Field of Choice, No 192, HMSO, London, 1996, (Cmnd 3123), para 15.

[11] A Vietnamese refugee who was in Hong Kong for 12 months, awaiting resettlement was held to have a 'substantial connexion' with Hong Kong, *Ta Tran Thi Thanh v Ta Van Hung and another* [1981] HKDCLR 37; *Griggs v Griggs* [1971] HKLR 299; *Savournin v Lau* [1971] HKLR 180.

[12] See also ss2 and 9 MCO, Chapter 2.

[13] S11C MCO, as amended by s7 of the Matrimonial Causes (Amendment) Ordinance (No 29 of 1995).

DUTY OF THE COURT TO ENQUIRE

S15 of the MCO provides that in any proceedings for divorce it shall be the duty of the court to enquire, in so far as it reasonably can, into any facts alleged by any party to the proceedings. If the court is satisfied on the evidence of any such fact as is mentioned in section 11A(2) or 11B(2),[14] then unless it is satisfied on all the evidence that the marriage has not broken down irretrievably, it shall grant a decree nisi of divorce.

GROUNDS FOR A PETITION FOR DIVORCE

Although s11 of the MCO stipulates that the sole ground for presenting a petition for divorce shall be that the marriage has broken down irretrievably, s11A(1) requires the court not to hold the marriage to have broken down irretrievably unless the petitioner proves one of the 'facts'. Thus, in *Buffery v Buffery*,[15] the parties had been married for 20 years, they had grown apart, had nothing in common and could no longer communicate. The court accepted that the marriage had irretrievably broken down but could not grant a decree because none of the facts was established. Conversely, even if one of the facts is proved, the court may refuse to grant a decree on the ground that irretrievable breakdown of the marriage has not been proved. This, however, is unlikely to happen.

> The true position in most cases is that however relenting and desirous of reconciliation the respondent spouse may be, the marriage cannot be said to have not irretrievably broken down when the petitioner is not prepared to continue cohabitation.[16]

As is stands, s11A means that divorce is available if, and only if, the marriage has irretrievably broken down and it is also accompanied by one of the five facts. We shall now turn to examine what each of these five facts means.

Adultery

Adultery refers to 'consensual sexual intercourse between a married person and a person of the opposite sex, not being the other spouse, during the

---

[14] See below.
[15] [1988] 2 FLR 365.
[16] Leonard Pegg, *Family Law in Hong Kong*, 3rd edition, Butterworths Asia, Hong Kong, 1994, p. 81.

subsistence of the marriage.'[17] Thus, an act of adultery may involve a married and an unmarried person; it is not necessary that both parties be married. This definition of adultery is modified to take into account the existence of concubines in customary marriages. Thus, s2 of the MCO states that 'adultery' does not include intercourse between a man and his *t'sip*, both being parties to a customary marriage in accordance with s7 of the Marriage Reform Ordinance.

Sexual intercourse is required for adultery. Therefore, indecent familiarity or an attempt at sexual intercourse is insufficient. However, it is not necessary to prove a complete act of sexual intercourse of the kind which is needed for consummation of a marriage,[18] and as in the case of rape, some degree of penetration suffices. Intercourse must be voluntary and rape is a good defence to an allegation of adultery, the burden of proving non-consensual intercourse lying on the party who alleges it.[19]

Petitioner finds it intolerable to live with the respondent

Although adultery strikes at the heart of a marital relationship and may signify irretrievable marriage breakdown, it need not be the reason why the petitioner finds it intolerable to live with the respondent. In other words, a petitioner is not required to prove that the respondent has committed adultery and 'in consequence of the adultery' he finds it intolerable to live with the respondent. In *Cleary v Cleary,*[20] the wife had committed adultery and the husband forgave her. She then had correspondence with men and went out alone at night. Finally she left the husband and children. The marriage broke down irretrievably, but it was her conduct subsequent to the adultery (and not the act of adultery) that the husband found intolerable to live with. The Court of Appeal held that the two facts should be treated separately and independently. A petitioner did not have to show that he found the respondent intolerable to live with because of her adultery. Indeed, the test as to whether the petitioner finds it intolerable to live with the

---

[17] Rayden and Jackon's *Law & Practice in Divorce & Family,* 16th edition, Butterworths, London, 1991, p. 197 (hereafter Rayden and Jackson on Divorce).

[18] *Dennis v Dennis* (1955) P. 153; *Lily Li v Patrick Wu* [1956] HKLR 363. Donor insemination which resulted in a wife giving birth to a child of the semen donor is not adultery, *MacLennan v MacLennan* [1958] SC 105.

[19] *Redpath v Redpath* [1950] 1 All ER 600; *Goshawk v Goshawk* (1965) 109 SJ 290. For standard of proof, see *W v W* [1970] HKLR 4; in *Serio v Serio* [1983] 4 FLR 756 it was held that the burden of proof must be commensurate with the seriousness of the issue involved; see also *Re H (minors) (sexual abuse: standard of proof)* [1996] 2 WLR 8 per Lord Nicholls at p. 23.

[20] [1974] 1 All ER 498.

respondent is subjective.[21] In practice, however, most cases proceed either undefended or under the special procedure,[22] the need for judicial interpretation on this point remaining remote.

Infidelity may be blameworthy but an adulterer may be the petitioner. For instance:

> H is a playboy and W, who is aware of his sexual exploits, is content to put up with his conduct. On rare occasions she commits adultery to get her own back. H is aware of this but is not jealous either. They continue to live together. Recently, W has been converted to Christianity and believes that adultery is immoral. She hopes her own good conduct may influence H and that he may mend his ways. H, however, is so offended by W's beliefs and new life style that he finds living with W intolerable. Relying on W's adultery, H is entitled to a divorce.[23]

Effect of continuing cohabitation

Where a respondent's adultery has become known to the petitioner and the parties have thereafter lived together for a period of six months or less, that period of cohabitation shall be disregarded in determining whether the petitioner finds it intolerable to live with the respondent.[24] In other words, a lengthy period of cohabitation following knowledge of an adulterous liaison is taken as indicating that the petitioner, in spite of the adultery, finds it tolerable to live with the respondent. But this is inconsistent with the decision in *Cleary v Cleary* where it was held that adultery and intolerability are not co-dependent. Where the period of cohabitation exceeds six months, the petitioner cannot rely on that adultery.[25]

Damages for adultery or criminal conversation

Prior to the Matrimonial Causes (Amendment) Ordinance 1995, a petitioner might, on a petition for divorce (or for judicial separation) claim damages from any person on the ground of adultery with the wife or husband of the petitioner. This action has now been abolished.[26] So is the common law

---

[21] *Goodrich v Goodrich* [1971] 1 WLR 1142.
[22] See pp. 134–5.
[23] See similar example in S Cretney, *Principles of Family Law*, 5th edition, Sweet & Maxwell, London, 1990, p. 105.
[24] S15A(3)(a) MCO.
[25] S15A(3)(b). See *Carr v Carr* [1974] 1 WLR 1534.
[26] See the Matrimonial Causes (Amendment) Ordinance (No 29 of 1995).

action of criminal conversation.[27] Where a petitioner alleges that the respondent has committed adultery, the petitioner shall make the alleged adulterer or adulteress a party to the proceedings unless that person is not named in the petition or the court otherwise directs.[28]

Behaviour

This ground for divorce is often abbreviated to 'unreasonable behaviour'. However, this term is misleading as it tends to suggest that only blameworthy behaviour is relevant.[29] In fact, the behaviour needs to be neither unreasonable nor blameworthy. What the law requires the petitioner to prove is that the respondent has behaved in such a way that the expectation that the petitioner continue to live with the respondent be unreasonable.

The test

The test is stated by Dunn J, in *Livingstone-Stallard v Livingstone-Stallard*.[30]

> Would any right-thinking person come to the conclusion that this husband has behaved in such a way that this wife cannot reasonably be expected to live with him, taking into account the whole of the circumstances and the characters and the personalities of the parties.

The words 'petitioner/respondent' refer to the particular petitioner/respondent in question, not a hypothetical reasonable spouse.[31] 'Reasonably be expected' is not to be taken as meaning in an anticipatory sense, ie whether there is a reasonable prospect of the petitioner continuing to live with the respondent.[32] Rather, it means 'reasonably required', and the court needs to consider whether it is reasonable to require the petitioner to continue living with the respondent, having regard to the respondent's behaviour.

---

[27] *Gensburger v Gensburger* [1968] HKLR 403; the Matrimonial Causes (Amendment) Ordinance (No 29 of 1995).
[28] S14 of the MCO, see r13 MCR.
[29] *Archard v Archard* (1972) The Times 20 April; *Pheasant v Pheasant* [1972] 1 All ER 587.
[30] [1974] 2 All ER 766 at p. 771.
[31] *Ash v Ash* [1972] 1 All ER 582.
[32] *Pheasant v Pheasant* [1972] 1 All ER 587, Ormrod J at p. 590.

Positive and negative behaviour

Behaviour covers both acts and omissions, but is not the same as a state of mind or a feeling. Acts include violent conduct, abusive manner, and omissions include neglect, indifference and failure to provide maintenance. In deciding whether these militate against continued cohabitation, the court needs to look at the petitioner's personality and his ability to endure the behaviour complained of. A violent petitioner can reasonably be expected to live with a respondent similarly addicted; a taciturn and morose spouse can reasonably be expected to live with a partner with the same characteristics; a flirtatious husband can reasonably be expected to live with a wife who is equally susceptible to the attractions of the opposite sex.[33]

The behaviour fact seems to suggest a requirement for incompatibility in personality and attitudes and to that extent that this is so, divorce is not necessarily granted on the basis of fault. In *Livingstone Stallard v Livingstone-Stallard*[34] the court granted a divorce in favour of the wife whose husband was selfish, unloving and who continually subjected her to petty criticisms about her way of life and behaviour.[35] In *O'Neill v O'Neill*,[36] the wife complained that the husband embarked on renovation work lasting for two years, involving mixing cement in the living room, raising floorboards, and that for some eight months, there was no lavatory door and no curtains in the bedrooms. The decree was granted. In *Bannister v Bannister*,[37] the wife complained that the husband had not taken her out for two years, did not speak to her except when it was unavoidable, stayed away for nights at a time, giving her no idea where he was going, and had been living an entirely independent life, ignoring her completely. It was held that the husband's behaviour was such that it was unreasonable to expect the wife to live with him. In *Lindsay v Lindsay*,[38] the wife married at the age of 27 and wanted to have children. Due to the husband's unwillingness to cooperate, she was deprived of the joy of motherhood for nine years. A divorce was granted.

There is no requirement that behaviour be the cause of marriage breakdown. However, in *Yeung Leung Yau-lin v Yeung Kam-wah*,[39] the unhappy marriage was marred by the parties' quarrels and fights, and the

---

[33] *Ash v Ash* [1972] 1 All ER 582 Bagnall J at p. 585.
[34] [1974] 2 All ER 766.
[35] *Birch v Birch* [1992] 1 FLR 564.
[36] [1975] 3 All ER 289.
[37] (1980) 10 Fam Law 240.
[38] [1983] 2 HKC 302.
[39] [1977–1979] HKC 328.

wife left after one year of marriage. She sought a decree on the grounds of the husband's behaviour. The court found that the wife was neurotic, violent in temper, and demanded her rights but was none too eager to carry out her duties. The husband, however, was a rough person who was not able to handle her. Although this would suggest that neither spouse could reasonably be expected to live with the other, a decree was nonetheless refused on the ground that the irretrievable breakdown of the marriage was not due to the conduct of the husband.

Simple desertion not included

What if a respondent spouse simply leaves the petitioner and does not return? It has been held that 'behaviour' goes beyond simple desertion or steps leading up to desertion, otherwise s11A(2)(e) would be rendered redundant. Thus, in *Stringfellow v Stringfellow*,[40] the parties were married for six years, the husband told the wife that he no longer loved her and that she should go and stay with her parents temporarily. When she returned, the husband had not changed his mind and he left the matrimonial home. The wife petitioned on the ground that the husband had behaved in such a way that she could not reasonably be expected to live with him. The Court of Appeal held that the husband's conduct amounted to desertion or behaviour leading up to desertion, and that was insufficient.

Isolated incident

A petitioner can rely on an isolated instance of conduct, as well as a culmination of conduct as 'unreasonable behaviour'. This is so even though the conduct in question was precipitated by the petitioner's own wrongdoing. Thus, in *Li Kao Feng-ning v Li Hung-lit*,[41] the petitioner wife's adultery and her expressed desire to marry her lover brought about a violent and frightening response from her husband, who subjected her and the son to a terrifying ordeal lasting for five hours. This was held to be so grave that the petitioner could not reasonably be expected to continue to live with the respondent.

Physical/mental illness

Cases involving illness present particular difficulties to the court. The issue

---

[40] [1976] 2 All ER 539.
[41] Court of Appeal, Civil Appeal Action No 58 of 1983 (1983).

here is whether a decree be granted against a respondent who is not morally responsible for his behaviour. Despite the marriage vow of 'for better or for worse; in sickness and in health', behaviour resulting from the mental or physical illness of a spouse, although involuntary, is capable of constituting 'behaviour'. The circumstances of the case must be looked at as a whole, Rees J remarking:

> all the circumstances including the disabilities and temperaments of both parties, the causes of the behaviour and whether the causes were or were not known to the petitioner, the presence or absence of intention, the impact of it on the petitioner and the family unit, its duration, and the prospect of cure or improvement in the future.[42]

Where the behaviour stems from misfortune, the court must take full account of the obligations of married partners, including the duty to accept normal burdens caused by the respondent's illness and misfortune, the likely length of such burden, and its effect on the petitioner's health and his capacity to endure it. In *Richards v Richards*,[43] it was held that a wife could not rely on this fact where the husband's illness made him moody and taciturn and he disturbed her at night because of his insomnia.

A case which falls on the other side of the line is *Thurlow v Thurlow*.[44] Here the wife suffered epilepsy and severe neurological disorders. She was confined to bed and was incapable of performing household tasks. She was violent and attempted to burn the house down. The stress and strain resulting from looking after her led the husband to petition for divorce. It was held that he was entitled to a divorce. Similarly, in *Lee Yuen-sam v Lee Tang Hop-wo*,[45] the respondent wife's 'strange' behaviour included nocturnal activities such as using a hard object to knock against the bed at 20 to 30 minute intervals and rearranging objects in a cupboard until dawn. Other behaviour included locking the husband out of the home, burning the father-in-law's photograph and fighting with neighbours. The husband could not stand such conditions. Although there was no medical evidence as to the wife's mental health nor was there medical evidence of any prognosis, it was held that conduct consequent upon mental illness could come within 'behaviour'. The cumulative conduct of the wife was such as the husband ought not to be called upon to endure.

What if a spouse is rendered a human vegetable after an accident?

---

[42] [1975] 2 All ER 979 at p. 988.
[43] [1972] 3 All ER 695.
[44] [1975] 2 All ER 979.
[45] High Court, Divorce Jurisdiction, Action No 14 of 1978 (1979).

Could it be said that that spouse has 'behaved' in such a way that the petitioner could not reasonably be expected to live with him or her? This question was left undecided in *Thurlow v Thurlow*. Rees J seemed to think that it would be difficult to establish that there was behaviour towards the petitioner, or that such behaviour was sufficient to justify the conclusion that the petitioner could not reasonably be expected to live with the respondent.[46]

However, the biggest of all difficulties with 'unreasonable behaviour' is that a petition usually contains a catalogue of incidents. In order to ensure that a decree is granted, there is a tendency to dredge up as many incidents as possible, which tends to exacerbate the parties' bitterness.

> Respondents to behaviour petitions seem to fall into three board categories: first, those who have agreed with the petitioner that the marriage has broken down and have allowed this fact to be used as a contrivance for obtaining a speedy divorce; secondly, those who had no idea that anything was wrong and for whom the petition had arrived "out of the blue"; thirdly, those who have been guilty of violence or other forms of serious misconduct. For those in the first two categories, unnecessary hostility and conflict may well be generated by the very use of the behaviour fact. The effect of requiring the petitioner to produce "behaviour" allegations is to encourage her to dwell on everything in the marriage and about the respondent which is bad and therefore to encourage a resentful and uncompromising attitude. A respondent in the second category is likely to react bitterly and antagonistically to the surprise petition and this will reduce the chances of saving the marriage even if he denies that it has broken down. A respondent in the first category may not be able to view the allegations against him with indifference despite his consent to the use of the behaviour fact. Where the respondent is in the third category, and undeserving of sympathy, the behaviour allegations may not exacerbate conflict but will certainly not reduce it. In all cases the seeds of post-divorce ill-feeling and difficulties have been sown by what has been called "ritualized hostility".[47]

Effect of continuing cohabitation

Where a petitioner alleges that the respondent has behaved in a way that he or she cannot reasonably be expected to live with the latter, and the parties have lived together for not more than six months since the incidents relied on by the petitioner, this fact will be disregarded for the purposes of determining whether the petitioner can reasonably be expected to live with

---

[46] [1975] 2 All ER 979.
[47] English Law Reform Commission, Facing the Future: A Discussion Paper on the Ground for Divorce, No 170, HMSO, London, 1988, para 3.27.

the respondent.[48] However, a petitioner (for instance, a wife) who continues to live with the husband for more than six months because she has no other alternative accommodation, is not debarred from petitioning for a divorce and adducing evidence to show that she could not reasonably be expected to live with him.[49]

One-Year Living Apart with Consent

Living apart usually involves the parties living physically apart as separate individuals. Problems arise when the parties, despite the deterioration in their marital relationship, continue to live under one roof, the lack of alternative accommodation often being responsible for this compromise.[50] In such cases, the law adopts the two-household test and asks, whether the parties share a communal life? What then is the nature of this communal life?

Living with each other in the same household

The parties may 'live apart' even if they continue to live under one roof. S11C(1) of the MCO states that:

> a husband and wife shall be treated as living apart unless they are living with each other in the same household.

'Living with each other' means living with each other as husband and wife.[51] 'In the same household' are words of limitation, qualifying 'living with each other'.[52] 'Household' is an abstract concept. It does not mean a place or address, but refers to people held together by a particular tie, even if temporarily separated.[53]

Where the parties cease marital intercourse, but continue to live under one roof, the question is whether they continue to share any communal life. In *Hopes v Hopes*,[54] there were frequent quarrels between the parties

---

[48] S15A(4).
[49] *Bradley v Bradley* [1973] 1 WLR 1291.
[50] HKLRC; see n. 6.
[51] *Fuller v Fuller* [1973] 1 WLR 730.
[52] 'Living with each other' and 'living in the same household' do not impose two separate requirements; s11A(3), however, does not envisage a couple living in the same household but not living with each other, see *Mouncer v Mouncer* [1972] 1 All ER 289.
[53] *Santos v Santos* [1972] 2 All ER 246.
[54] [1948] 2 All ER 920.

who slept in separate bedrooms and abstained from marital intercourse. The wife refused to do the husband's household chores. The parties, nonetheless, ate as a family and shared the common parts of the house. The Court of Appeal held that this was not a case where the parties were living as two separate households but rather a case of a couple living under the same roof in dissension. Similarly, in *Yuen Yu-biu v Yuen Nip*,[55] the parties lived in the same apartment (although in separate bedrooms), and the wife occasionally cooked meals and washed for the husband. The husband had also visited the wife every day for ten days in hospital when she was ill. It was held that the marital relationship had not come to an end and the parties were not living apart.

Where the parties live under one roof for the sake of the children, the requirement of two separate households is difficult, if not impossible, to achieve. In *Mouncer v Mouncer*, the parties continued to live under one roof because the husband wanted to help out with caring for the children. They slept in separate bedrooms, but continued to take their meals, cooked by the wife, together with the children. They also shared the cleaning of the house, making no distinction between one part of the house and another, but the wife no longer did any washing for the husband. Because of the communal life they shared together, it was held that the parties were living with each other in the same household.

The two household test, however, was satisfied in the unusual case of *Fuller v Fuller*.[56] The parties had been physically separated for four years and the wife lived with her lover. When the husband suffered from ill-health, he moved in with the wife and her lover. He stayed in his own bedroom, and the wife provided domestic services such as laundry and catering in return for a fee. The Court of Appeal held that the parties were not living with each other as husband and wife, but rather that they lived with each other as landlady and lodger. Similarly, in *Piper v Piper*,[57] the parties lived in their own apartments. The husband visited the wife frequently, spending weekends and sometimes several nights during working days with her. On one occasion, the husband spent four-and-a-half months continuously with the wife. The Court of Appeal held that the parties were not living with each other in the same household. Their relationship was one of the husband visiting the wife as an intimate friend, and they had not re-established the relationship of husband and wife.

---

[55] [1977–1979] HKC 453.
[56] [1973] 1 WLR 730.
[57] (1978) 8 Fam Law 243.

Physical separation insufficient: mental element required

'Living apart', however, must mean more than simply physical separation,[58] otherwise absurdities and injustices might result. One such scenario might be that of a prisoner whose wife has, with his encouragement, stood by him for one year, only to find on his release that he files a petition for divorce. Similarly, injustice may be suffered, for example, by a wife who lives apart from her husband because he is on an overseas posting or attending to business overseas.

'Living apart' requires an attitude of mind such that one party recognises that the marriage has come to an end.[59] A unilateral recognition not communicated to the other party is sufficient. The degree of proof required to establish 'living apart' depends on the circumstances of each case. In some cases, there will be evidence, such as a letter, a cessation of visits to a spouse or cohabitation with a third party. However, where only one spouse's oral evidence is available, the court will treat that with caution. On the other hand, where resumption of married life is plainly impossible, very little evidence is needed to establish 'living apart'.[60]

Consent

There is no requirement that the parties consented to the separation, consent being needed only to the decree being granted. The respondent's consent is indicated in the acknowledgment of the service stating that he consents to the decree.[61] Consent, however, may be withdrawn. Where this happens, and the petition relies only on one-year separation with consent, the proceedings on the petition shall be stayed.[62]

Once the decree nisi has been granted, the power of the respondent to prevent the decree absolute is limited to one situation. S15C(1) of the MCO states that the court may rescind a decree nisi any time before it is made absolute if the petitioner has misled the respondent, whether intentionally or unintentionally, about any matter which the respondent has taken into account in deciding whether to consent to the granting of the decree.

---

[58] *Santos v Santos* [1972] 2 All ER 246.
[59] Ibid.
[60] Ibid.
[61] *McGill v Robson* [1972] 1 WLR 237; *Mason v Mason* [1972] 3 WLR 405.
[62] R15A MCR.

Two-Year Separation

This is the same as (c) above, but the period of separation required is two years. After two-year separation, the respondent's consent to the decree being granted is not needed, and the petitioner can divorce the respondent against his or her will.

One-Year Desertion

Table 4.2 shows that desertion is rarely used and thus the Hong Kong Law Reform Commission recommended that it be abolished. An amendment at the committee stage of the Matrimonial Causes (Amendment) Bill, however, resulted in it being retained as a ground for divorce. Consequently, despite the relatively archaic and insignificant use of desertion, discussion of this complex topic is still necessary as it may still be of importance if:
(i) the parties have lived apart for one year and the respondent has refused to consent to a divorce on the basis of one year separation, or
(ii) the parties have lived apart for two years but the petitioner may not wish to rely on that fact which entitles the respondent to certain protection.[63]

Table 4.2 Divorce Facts Cited in Petition

Year	Adultery	Behaviour	Desertion	Separation 2 years	Separation 5 years	Other Misc.
1980	142 (6%)	496 (20%)	148 (6%)	1247 (51%)	384 (16%)	48 (2%)
1982	138 (5%)	474 (17%)	174 (6%)	1544 (54%)	463 (16%)	68 (2%)
1988	218 (4%)	1267 (24%)	164 (3%)	2551 (49%)	851 (16%)	143 (3%)
1990	202 (3%)	1633 (24%)	206 (3%)	3485 (51%)	1151 (17%)	99 (2%)

Showing breakdown of the facts cited in petitions in the years 1980, 1982, 1988, 1990. This table is extracted from the HKLRC.

---

[63] See below.

Desertion means separation which is against the will of one spouse, and is accompanied by an intention on the part of the deserting spouse to end married life permanently without just cause.[64] A simple case of desertion (simple desertion) involves one party abandoning the other, leaving the home with the intention of permanent separation. Two elements are required on the part of the deserting spouse, i.e. the fact of separation (*factum*) and the intention to live apart (*animus deserendi*). On the part of the deserted spouse, it must be shown that the separation was non-consensual, and absence of conduct which would justify the deserting spouse's withdrawal from cohabitation.

The fact of separation

The fact of separation is the same as 'living apart', Sir Henry Duke P explaining desertion in these terms:

> Desertion is not the withdrawal from a place, but from a state of things. . . . The law does not deal with the mere matter of place. What it seeks to enforce is the recognition and discharge of the common obligations of the married state. If one party does not acknowledge them, the party who has so offended cannot be heard to say that he or she is not guilty of desertion on the ground that there has been no desertion from a place.[65]

In other words, an innocent spouse can establish *de facto* separation even though the parties continue to live under the same roof. For instance, a husband who shuts himself up in one or two rooms of his house, and ceases to have anything to do with his wife, is living separately and apart from her as effectively as if they were living in two separate flats. However, there is no *de facto* separation if the facts show only a case of gross neglect or chronic discord. Thus, in *Hopes v Hopes*,[66] a case which was discussed earlier, the parties had frequent quarrels. The husband, seeking peace and quiet, often retired to his own bedroom. The parties slept in separate bedrooms and the wife refused to do the husband's household chores. They nonetheless ate as a family and shared the common parts of the house. The Court of Appeal held that there was insufficient separation to amount to desertion.[67] This case is to be contrasted with *Naylor v Naylor*[68] where the wife cast off her wedding ring in front of the husband, indicating

---

[64] Rayden and Jackson on Divorce, see n. 17.
[65] *Pulford v Pulford* [1923] P. 18 at p. 21; *Milligan v Milligan* [1941] 2 All ER 62.
[66] [1948] 2 All ER 920.
[67] See also *Thomas v Thomas* [1948] 2 KB 294; cf. *Adeoso v Adeoso* [1981] 1 All ER 107.
[68] [1961] 2 WLR 751.

her intention of no longer being his wife. Thereafter, the parties slept separately, the wife performed no wifely services and there was a complete absence of any family life. It was held that the wife was in desertion.

The intention to live apart or animus deserendi

A *de facto* separation may take place without there being an *animus deserendi*, for instance if the parties agree to live apart, or if the husband has to travel overseas for work. Where *de facto* separation is coupled with *animus*, or if *animus* supervenes, desertion will begin from that moment.[69] Further, once desertion commences, it is not necessarily interrupted by enforced separation which prevents cohabitation. Thus, in *Drew v Drew*,[70] the husband told the wife that he was going to Ireland for a week's shooting. In fact he went to Australia to escape arrest on a charge of embezzlement. Up to the time of his flight, he had an adulterous relationship with a woman with whom he had made arrangements to go away, and he was found living in adultery with another woman in Sydney. When arrested and brought back to England, he was tried and sentenced to ten year's penal servitude. It was held that the circumstances in which he left his wife constituted desertion, and the desertion continued notwithstanding that he was prevented by imprisonment from returning to his wife.

Where the separation is involuntary (for instance, a husband being posted overseas with the armed forces), there is *prima facie* no intention. However, a demonstration of intention to abandon the matrimonial relationship may intervene (e.g. if there is a letter from the deserting spouse that he intends to leave the other permanently). In *Beeken v Beeken*,[71] the parties were captured by the Japanese during the war and were interned in a camp in Amoy, China. They were subsequently moved to Shanghai and were each interned in different camps. When the wife visited the husband in his camp, she asked if he would agree to divorce and she told him that she intended to marry someone else. On release they went their separate ways. It was held that the wife deserted the husband at the time when they were involuntarily separated, during which time she formed her intention to remarry.

Mental illness may prevent a party from forming the necessary *animus deserendi*. Thus, in *Perry v Perry*,[72] the wife suffered from paranoid psychosis and accused her husband of attempting to murder her. She left the

---

[69] *Pardy v Pardy* [1939] 3 All ER 779.
[70] (1888) 13 PD 97.
[71] [1948] P. 302.
[72] [1963] 3 All ER 766.

matrimonial home and never returned. Medical evidence showed she knew what she was doing and her convictions were strongly held. It was held that she had left the matrimonial home under the force of delusions as a fugitive from apprehended danger. Consequently, she did not have the mental capacity to form an intention to desert.[73]

The old rule was that *animus deserendi* might be terminated by the onset of the deserting spouse's insanity. This was the rule in *Crowther v Crowther*,[74] which stated that there was a presumption that intention did not continue, and it was for the petitioner to prove that it did so continue. Prior to the Matrimonial Causes (Amendment) Ordinance 1995, s11A(2) provided that the court might treat a period of desertion as having continued and not terminated by the onset of insanity of the deserting spouse. This has now been deleted from s11, probably unintentionally.

Absence of consent

Consensual separation is not desertion. Whether separation is consensual depends on the facts of the case.[75] A separation agreement which recites that the parties agree to live separate and apart converts desertion into a consensual separation. But an agreement which merely defines the duration of financial payments, and does not amount to a bargain binding the parties to live separate and apart will not prevent desertion from running. Thus, in *Crabtree v Crabtree*,[76] there was an agreement which stated that the parties had lived separate and apart, and the husband agreed that he would, for so long as they lived separate and apart, pay maintenance. It was held that the words 'if they shall so long live separate and apart' simply defined the duration of the payment. The phrase did not bind them to live separate and apart so the agreement did not prevent desertion from running.

Desertion must be shown to have occurred for a continuous period of not less than one year immediately before the presentation of the petition and it may be brought to an end before the one year if the deserting spouse makes a genuine offer of return. A deserted spouse, however, is entitled to reject an offer to return if it is not bona fide and genuine.[77] A spouse to whom a genuine offer is addressed is not bound to accept it but he is

---

[73] Compare *Kaczmarz v Kaczmarz* [1967] 1 WLR 317. The wife was suffering from chronic schizophrenia. She wrote several letters to the husband showing her intention to remain permanently apart from him. It was held that on the evidence of the letters and her conduct, she was capable of forming *animus deserendi*.
[74] [1951] AC 723.
[75] *Gallagher v Gallagher* [1965] 1 WLR 1110.
[76] [1953] 2 All ER 56.
[77] *Dunn v Dunn* [1965] 1 All ER 1043.

bound to consider it. Thus, in *Gallagher v Gallagher*,[78] the parties agreed to live apart. Subsequently the husband wrote to the wife stating that he had purchased a bungalow which would be large enough for them and asked her to join him. It was held that the husband's proposal for the resumption of cohabitation had been bona fide and genuine. It was an offer which ought to have been considered. The wife must at least have been willing to resume cohabitation, though not necessarily on the terms proposed. As she was unwilling to do so, she was in desertion.

Just as a consensual separation may develop into desertion, so may a desertion be converted into a separation by consent. An agreement to live apart for an indefinite period is terminable at the will of either party.[79] Where one party to a consensual separation has made it clear that he is putting an end to the agreement to live apart, e.g. by making a bona fide and genuine offer to resume married life, and the other party refuses to accept such an offer of reconciliation, the latter is the deserting spouse.[80]

The absence of just and reasonable cause for the separation

Usually, separation takes the form of one spouse leaving the matrimonial home. But who is the deserting spouse? Again, this depends on the facts of the case. In a case of simple desertion (as opposed to constructive desertion), the spouse who leaves may be in desertion. However, a spouse who leaves the matrimonial home with a just and reasonable excuse is not. In *Marsden v Marsden*,[81] the husband suspected that the wife had committed adultery with a lodger who was the fiancé of their daughter. At no time did he reveal his suspicion or ask the wife for an explanation. He became reserved and withdrawn and the atmosphere in the house became unbearable. After a quarrel between the husband and the lodger in which he hinted at his suspicion, he ordered the lodger to leave. The lodger, the daughter and the wife all left. It was held, however, that it was incumbent upon the husband to give the wife an opportunity to explain the suspected adultery. As the husband did not do so and his attitude made the wife's life miserable, she was entitled to treat herself as dismissed from the matrimonial home and to have left with just and reasonable excuse.[82]

---

[78] [1965] 1 WLR 1110.
[79] *Nutley v Nutley* [1970] 1 WLR 217, see also P M Bromley, *Family Law*, 5th edition, Butterworths, London, 1976, p. 192 (hereafter referred to as Bromley).
[80] *Hall v Hall* [1960] 1 WLR 52.
[81] [1967] 3 WLR 230.
[82] To furnish a good excuse for withdrawal from cohabitation, a bona fide belief that the other has committed adultery must be induced by his or her conduct and not merely from extraneous circumstances. If evidence comes into the possession of a spouse which

Constructive desertion

Where the conduct of one spouse is such that the other is compelled to withdraw from cohabitation, the former is the deserter, and the case is one of constructive desertion. The same elements must be proved in a case of constructive desertion as in simple desertion. The only difference is that in a case of constructive desertion, the *factum* of desertion lies in the deserting spouse's expulsive conduct.[83] A man may wish that his wife would leave him, but such a wish, unless accompanied by expulsive conduct driving the other spouse away, can have no effect whatsoever.[84] Where the expulsive conduct is established, the necessary intention is readily inferred, since one cannot be heard to say that he did not intend the natural and probable consequences of his acts.[85]

Expulsive conduct, in order to constitute constructive desertion, must be of such grave and weighty nature as to make cohabitation impossible, or it must exceed behaviour which every spouse bargains to endure when accepting the other 'for better or worse'. Thus, in *Buchler v Buchler*,[86] the husband formed an association with a male friend. The relationship persisted to the exclusion of the wife. This caused her great distress and aroused comments among friends and neighbours who believed the relationship was homosexual in nature. The wife continually objected to the husband's conduct and threatened to leave unless it ceased. The husband replied that if she did not like it, she could 'clear out'. The Court of Appeal held that the husband's conduct caused the wife intense unhappiness, but it did not justify her leaving the matrimonial home.

> Where the gravity of the conduct itself is in question, the standard is the same both for good cause for separation and for cruelty; in both cases it must amount to such a grave and weighty matter as renders the continuance of the matrimonial cohabitation virtually impossible.[87]

---

raises a suspicion of adultery, unless the evidence points to adultery beyond reasonable doubt, it is incumbent on the spouse in possession of that evidence to give the other an opportunity to explain it, and if the former does not do so within a reasonable time, he or she cannot thereafter claim that the belief in adultery was unreasonable, *Marsden v Marsden* [1967] 3 WLR 230.

[83] *Hui Shiu-wing v Cheung Yuk-lin* [1968] HKLR 501; *Marsden v Marsden* [1967] 3 WLR 230; *Buchler v Buchler* [1947] 1 All ER 319; *Quoraishi v Quoraishi* [1985] FLR 780; *Dunn v Dunn* [1965] 1 All ER 1043.
[84] *Buchler v Buchler* [1947] 1 All ER 319.
[85] *Lang v Lang* [1955] AC 402; *Gollins v Gollins* [1963] 2 All ER 966; *Williams v Williams* [1963] 2 All ER 994.
[86] [1947] 1 All ER 319.
[87] *Young v Young* [1962] 3 All ER 120 at p. 124.

A spouse now can petition for a divorce on the grounds that the partner has behaved in such a way that he cannot reasonably be expected to continue cohabitation. As the test for just and reasonable cause for separation is more onerous than that required for the behaviour 'fact', a spouse petitioning for divorce will rarely rely on constructive desertion.[88]

Termination of desertion

If one of the four elements necessary for desertion is negated, there is no desertion. Thus, where the spouse resumes cohabitation, this will bring desertion to an end. However, one or more acts of sexual intercourse does not put an end to the continuance of desertion where the sexual relationship falls short of an actual resumption of cohabitation.[89]

Desertion will come to an end if the deserter loses the *animus deserendi*. In such a case he must communicate his intention to resume cohabitation by offering to return.[90] An offer to return, however, will not terminate desertion if it is conditional on there being no resumption of marital intercourse, as it would not be an honest proposal to live together as man and wife.[91]

What amounts to an genuine offer to return depends on the facts of each case. In a case of simple desertion, all that is necessary is for the guilty spouse to ask for an opportunity to discuss the situation, and there is a duty on the other party at least to see that spouse and give him an opportunity to say what he wishes to say. If the innocent spouse fails to do so, she will be in desertion.[92] In other cases, e.g. where the deserting spouse has been guilty of adultery, the deserted spouse is not obliged to take him back unless the offending spouse gives the other a credible assurance that the conduct complained of will not be repeated in the future.

Counting the Period

The period required for 'separation' and 'desertion' must be continuous and separate periods cannot be added together to make up the required one or two years. For example, one cannot add six months desertion, followed by seven months cohabitation, to another six months of desertion to produce

---

[88] Bromley, p. 196; see n. 79.
[89] *Mummery v Mummery* [1942] P. 107.
[90] *Williams v Williams* [1939] P. 365.
[91] *Slawson v Slawson* [1942] 2 All ER 527.
[92] *Pratt v Pratt* [1939] AC 417.

the required period of one-year desertion. There is, however, one exception. S15A(5) provides that in considering whether the period during which the parties have lived apart has been continuous, no account shall be taken of any period or periods of cohabitation not exceeding six months. Further, no such period or periods of cohabitation shall be counted as part of the required period. For instance, it would be possible for the court to grant a decree of divorce on the basis of one-year separation if the parties have lived apart from each other for four months, followed by resumption of cohabitation for a period of five months, and then separation for another eight months. Similarly, it would be possible for the court to grant a decree of divorce on the basis of two-year separation if the parties have lived apart for six months, cohabitation for three months, separation for another ten months, followed by cohabitation for another two months, and by another eight months' separation.

The period required in s11A(2) must immediately precede the presentation of the petition for divorce. In other words, the desertion or separation must be running when the proceedings are commenced. The one exception to this rule is where a deserted spouse has obtained a judicial separation or a separation order which relieves her from the duty to cohabit with the respondent (or the deserting spouse). In such a case, it could not be said that there is desertion immediately prior to the presentation of the petition. Thus, s13(1) provides that a person shall not be prevented from presenting a petition for divorce on the ground that the petitioner has at any time been granted a decree of judicial separation or a separation order, providing that there was a continuous period of one-year desertion immediately prior to the institution of the earlier proceedings, and that the order is still in force, and that the parties have not resumed cohabitation at the date of the presentation of the divorce.

Cohabitation after Decree Nisi

A decree of divorce is granted in two stages: decree nisi and absolute.[93] The two stages are treated as a single decree so cohabitation between decree nisi and absolute would be treated as cohabitation before nisi. Thus the cohabitation bar in s15A(3)(b) operates if the parties resume cohabitation for over six months after the decree nisi has been pronounced. In the case of unreasonable behaviour, the court has acknowledged that there might be reasons why a woman continues to live with an ill-behaved husband.

---

[93] S17(2) MCO.

Nonetheless, continuing cohabitation with the respondent may indicate that the petitioner can reasonably be expected to live with the other spouse.[94]

In the case of desertion and separation, cohabitation after decree nisi would preclude the granting of a decree absolute because a petitioner is not permitted to continue to live with the respondent while at the same time treating the marriage as having broken down when it clearly has not. However, s11A(2) only requires separation for a period immediately prior to the presentation of the petition.

BUTTRESSING MARRIAGE

The MCO contains three provisions designed to buttress the stability of marriages. They are (i) the one-year discretionary bar, (ii) certification of reconciliation and (iii) adjournment for reconciliation.

One-Year Discretionary Bar

S12(1) of the MCO provides that no petition shall be made for divorce within one year from the date of the marriage. This is only a discretionary bar in that the court may grant leave for the presentation of a petition within one year of marriage if the case is one of exceptional hardship suffered by the petitioner, or exceptional depravity on the part of the respondent. The court, in considering whether to allow the presentation of a petition, shall have regard to the interests of any child of the family[95] and to the probability of a reconciliation between the parties.[96]

The purpose of the discretionary bar is to safeguard against irresponsible or trial marriages and to buttress the stability of marriages during the difficult early years.[97] Prior to the Matrimonial Causes (Amendment) Ordinance, s12 of the MCO provided for a three-year discretionary bar. However, the HKLRC concluded that three years was too long a period and, following its recommendation, it was reduced to one year.

---

[94] *Court v Court* [1982] 3 WLR 199; *Savage v Savage* [1982] 3 WLR 199.
[95] As defined by s2 MPPO.
[96] *Hillier v Hillier* [1958] P. 186; *Bowman v Bowman* [1949] P. 353.
[97] HKLRC, para 4.5; see n. 6.

Exceptional hardship

'Hardship' itself would not be sufficient to lift the bar and it must be of an exceptional nature. In *Fay v Fay*, the court took the view that any attempt to define 'exceptional' would be 'a betrayal of the deliberate imprecision favoured by Parliament in entrusting the court with the power to grant leave to present an early petition.'[98] 'Exceptional hardship' refers to 'something out of the ordinary'. There must be evidence of ill-health, nervous sensitivity or tension resulting in severe emotional or mental stress or breakdown.[99] This includes exceptional hardship in the past and the probability of it being endured in the future if the applicant is not permitted to present the petition within the barred period.[100] Detailed evidence as to the nature and extent of an applicant's suffering is needed[101] with assessment on the basis of the subjective reaction of the petitioner, taking into account her particular situation and disposition.[102] In *Kwan Bui-lock v Isabella Stamm Lock*,[103] the husband became extremely distressed and his speech problem deteriorated following the wife's adultery. Medical evidence suggested that the husband's condition was likely to be exacerbated so long as the marriage subsisted. Leave was granted for the presentation of the petition for divorce. Again, in *C v C (divorce: exceptional hardship)*,[104] a wife who was deeply hurt and distressed on discovering the husband's homosexual practices was granted leave. However, it is doubtful whether anything less would suffice. One might, for instance, consider as hardship a situation where, shortly after the marriage, one party decides that it was a mistake and begins an adulterous relationship; but this probably would not be taken as amounting to exceptional hardship.[105] Exceptional hardship is a matter best left to judges of first instance and appellate courts would be reluctant to intervene the lower court's decision unless it could be shown to be clearly wrong.[106]

Exceptional depravity

Depravity is an outmoded concept. Thus, Ormrod LJ said:

---

[98] *Fay v Fay* [1982] AC 835 at p. 844.
[99] Ibid., p. 842.
[100] This is so despite the word 'suffered', see ibid., p. 843.
[101] R5 MCR.
[102] *Nota v Nota* [1984] FLR 573; *C v C (divorce: exceptional hardship)* [1980] Fam 23 at p. 26.
[103] District Court, Miscellaneous Proceedings No 106 of 1979 (1979).
[104] [1980] Fam 23.
[105] *Fisher v Fisher* [1948] P. 263 at p. 266.
[106] *Fay v Fay* [1982] AC 835.

The word 'depravity' has fallen out of general use — it is not included in Fowler's Modern English Usage — so that it now conveys only a vague idea of very unpleasant conduct. In 1937 it may have carried to contemporary minds a much more specific meaning, but norms of behaviour, particularly in the sexual sense have changed greatly in the last 40 years.[107]

Depravity is not confined to perverse sexual conduct but is often associated with it. However, there are no reported cases where this has been successfully argued. Thus, in *Chan Wing-ming v Chan Li-li*,[108] it was held that alleged adultery by the wife with two European men was not exceptional depravity. In *C v C (divorce: exceptional hardship)*,[109] the husband's homosexual activity was not regarded as falling within the category of exceptional depravity.

Probability of reconciliation

If exceptional hardship or depravity has been made out, the court may exercise its discretion and grant leave having regard to the interests of children of the family and to whether there is a reasonable probability of reconciliation prior to the first anniversary of the marriage. In reality, reconciliation is impossible when exceptional hardship or depravity is alleged or has been proved and it is difficult to see how the interests of children may play a part in the court's decision of granting leave. However, it was held in 1957 that an application would be dismissed if one party was willing to reconcile and the other party had not done anything to promote reconciliation. In *Chan Wing-wing v Chan Li-li*,[110] it was alleged the wife had committed adultery with two men. The wife was willing to reconcile, but the husband's view was that he would lose face if he were to attempt reconciliation. The court was not satisfied that the husband had done nothing to promote reconciliation and his application was dismissed.

As has already been mentioned, prior to 24 June 1996, the discretionary bar was three years. This was felt to be too long and the period was reduced to one year. Apart from being too long, the discretionary bar was also unsatisfactory in that it required a petitioner to make extremely damaging allegations against the respondent. This was inconsistent with the goal of divorce law which is to destroy empty legal shells with maximum

---

[107] *C v C (divorce: exceptional hardship)* [1980] Fam 23 at p. 97.
[108] [1957] HKLR 474.
[109] [1980] Fam 23.
[110] [1957] HKLR 474.

fairness and minimum bitterness, distress and humiliation, a view succinctly put thus:

> If two married people have parted with a settled intention never to resume cohabitation, it is difficult to see how a rule restricting the right to file a divorce petition can be justified on the basis that it will keep them "together". All it can do is keep them married in a technical sense when the marriage is no more than an empty shell. A time restriction on the filing of a petition cannot preserve a marriage which has irretrievably broken down any more than the postponement of an application for a death certificate can alter the fact of death.[111]

More importantly, the deterrent effect of this time restriction depends on knowledge of its existence. Yet few people are actually aware of it when they enter into a marriage.[112] Given that a divorce can be obtained after two-year separation, the one-year discretionary bar serves little, except symbolic, purpose.

Certificate of reconciliation

S18(B)(b) provides that a solicitor must certify whether or not he has discussed the possibility of reconciliation with the petitioner. In practice, most solicitors certify that they have not discussed the matter of reconciliation with their clients.[113] The certification, therefore, is largely a formality and it serves little practical purpose. In 1996, the Report of the Working Group to Review Practices and Procedures Relating to Matrimonial Proceedings (the Hartmann Report)[114] agreed to amend Form 2A to require a solicitor to confirm that services available for reconciliation and mediation have been discussed and the names and addresses of persons qualified to help to effect a reconciliation and mediation have been given to the client.

Adjournment to Enable Reconciliation

The court, if it appears that there is a reasonable possibility of a reconciliation, may adjourn the proceedings for divorce to enable attempts

---

[111] HKLRC, para 5.18; see n. 6.
[112] HKLRC, para 5.19; see n. 6.
[113] HKLRC, paras 3.7–3.8; see n. 6.
[114] See Report of the Working Group to Review Practices and Procedures Relating to Matrimonial Proceedings (the Hartmann Report), 1996, p. 2, unpublished.

at reconciliation to be made.[115] This provision is unlikely to be of much practical use because by the time the parties come before the court, there is little chance for reconciliation.[116]

PROTECTION OF CHILDREN AND DEPENDANT SPOUSE

The MCO offers some measure of financial protection to a spouse who is divorced against her wishes. As for children, the law attempts to provide protection by ensuring, in so far as is practicable, that arrangements for their post-divorce welfare are satisfactory.

Declaration of Satisfaction

Family breakdown can have seriously adverse consequences for children. In contested custody proceedings, the court, before determining what are the best interests of a child, would almost invariably call for a social welfare report. However, where custody is not disputed, the courts also have a duty to consider children's welfare.[117]

This role is made possible by s18(1) of the Matrimonial Proceedings and Property Ordinance (MPPO), which directs that a court shall not to make absolute[118] a decree of nullity or divorce unless it has made a declaration to the effect that it is satisfied:

> (a) that for the purposes of this section there are no children of the family to whom this section applies; or
> (b) that the only children who are or may be children of the family to whom this section applies are the children named in the order and that
> (i) arrangements for the welfare of every child so named have been made and are satisfactory or are the best that can be devised in the circumstances; or
> (ii) it is impracticable for the party or parties appearing before the court to make any such arrangements; or

---

[115] See s15A(1).
[116] HKLRC, para 3.9; see n. 6.
[117] This includes custody, education and financial provision; see s18(6) MPPO.
[118] *Chan Yu Wai-ming v Chan Cheak-wing*, Court of Appeal, Civil Appeal Action No 123 of 1985 (1986).

(c) that there are circumstances making it desirable that the decree should be made absolute without delay notwithstanding that there are or may be children of the family to whom this section applies and that the court is unable to make a declaration in accordance with paragraph (b).

S18(2) of the MPPO further provides that, in the case of s18(1)(c) applying, the court shall not make a decree absolute unless it has obtained a satisfactory undertaking from either or both parties to bring the question of arrangements for the children before the court within a specified time.

In practice, a judge may have insufficient time or information to enable him to identify any problems likely to arise with proposed future arrangements for the children. Where he is unhappy with the proposal, he may still accept it because the alternative may be even more unsatisfactory (e.g. committing the child to the care of the Director of Social Welfare, or forcing an unwilling parent to have custody of the children). In such a case, the court may be ready and willing to make a declaration of satisfaction under s18(1)(b) of the MPPO.

In many cases, long-term arrangements for children are contingent upon decree absolute, remarriage and reallocation of housing, and where this is the case, the matter may be dealt with under s18(1)(c). Where custody is in dispute, the courts are generally reluctant to declare that arrangements 'have been made and are satisfactory'. In such cases, a decree absolute needs to be deferred. If custody is not to be heard within a fairly short period of time, consideration may be given to the existing *de facto* arrangements. If these appear satisfactory, though not necessarily the best that can be made, a declaration in the form of s18 (1)(b)(i) or s18(1)(c) can be made unless there is some positive advantage to be gained for the children in deferring the decree absolute.[119]

S18(3) of the MPPO further provides that if the court makes absolute a decree nisi of divorce without having made a declaration under s18(1), the decree shall be void. Where a declaration of satisfaction has been made, no person shall be entitled to challenge the validity of the decree on the grounds that the conditions prescribed by subs (1) and (2) have not been not fulfilled.[120]

S18 applies to certain children of the family,[121] they are:[122]

---

[119] See *A v A (children: arrangements)* [1979] 1 WLR 533, Ormrod LJ at pp. 535–6.
[120] *Healey v Healey* [1984] 3 All ER 1040.
[121] See s2 for a definition; see also Chapter 16.
[122] See s18(5).

(a) any minor child of the family who at the date of the order under subsection (1) is–
   (i) under the age of sixteen, or
   (ii) who is receiving instruction at an educational establishment, or undergoing training for a trade, profession or vocation, whether or not he is also in gainful employment; and
(b) any other child of the family to whom the court by an order under that subsection directs that this section shall apply;
and the court may give such a direction if it is of the opinion that there are special circumstances which make it desirable in the interests of the child that this section should apply to it.

'Special circumstances' may include children requiring special care, for instance, a handicapped child who is over 16.

Protecting the Respondent's Financial Position in All Separation Cases

Where a decree nisi has been granted on a petition based on one-year separation with consent or two-year separation, and the respondent has applied to the court for it to consider her post-divorce financial position, s17A(2) of the MCO provides that the court shall consider:

(a) all the circumstances, including the age, health, conduct, earning capacity, financial resources and financial obligations of each of the parties; and
(b) the financial position of the respondent as, having regard to the divorce, it is likely to be after the death of the petitioner should the petitioner die first.

According to s17A(3), the court shall not grant the decree absolute unless it is satisfied that:[123]

(a) the petitioner should not be required to make any financial provision; or
(b) the financial provisions made by the petitioner to the respondent is reasonable and fair or the best that can be made in the circumstances,

---

[123] Where the court has overlooked an application under s17A(2) and granted a decree absolute, it was held in *Wong Leung-see v Wong Lo Lung-kwan* [1985] 2 HKC 228, Court of Appeal, Civil Appeal Action No 121 of 1985 (1985) that the decree is only voidable and not void.

Notwithstanding s17A(3), s17A(4) provides the court may grant a decree absolute if

> (a) it appears that there are circumstances making it desirable that the decree should be made absolute without delay; and
> (b) the court has *obtained a satisfactory undertaking* from the petitioner that he *will* make such financial provision for the respondent as the court *may approve*.[124]

S17A(3)(b) enjoins the court not to make a decree absolute unless it is satisfied that financial provision made by the petitioner is reasonable and fair. In *Wilson v Wilson*,[125] the English Court of Appeal held that financial provision must have been made. Mere proposals by the petitioner as to what he would do were insufficient. In that case, it was held that no decree absolute could be made until the matrimonial home had been sold and the proceeds divided between the parties.

S17A(4) and its English equivalent have presented some difficulties in interpretation. In *Grigson v Grigson*,[126] the English Court of Appeal held that before a court could grant leave to make a decree nisi absolute, a petitioner had to formulate proposals in outline as to the future provision he intended to make for the respondent. The court had to be satisfied that those proposals were reasonable and fair or the best that could be made in the circumstances.[127] An undertaking to make such financial provision for the respondent as the court might approve was insufficient.

Grigson v Grigson was distinguished in the Court of Appeal in *Lau Chu v Lau Tang Su-ping*.[128] There, the husband, a man worth $175 million, was anxious to obtain a decree absolute. He undertook to comply with any order that the court might make for ancillary relief to the respondent, fortified by undertakings not to remove assets out of the jurisdiction. The Court of Appeal by a majority held that the purpose of s17A(4) was to protect the reasonable financial claims of a wife under the Matrimonial Proceedings and Property Ordinance. 'Will make' referred to the future and that provision could only be assessed and approved after full enquiry had been made but not at the time of the permission to make a decree absolute. Given the husband's assets and his undertaking, the wife's position was well protected even though the actual amount had not been fixed.

---

[124] Author's italics.
[125] [1973] 2 All ER 17.
[126] [1974] 1 All ER 478.
[127] *Grigson v Grigson* followed in *Cumbers v Cumbers* [1975] 1 All ER 1.
[128] [1989] 2 HKLR 470.

Fuad, V-P dissenting noted the inherent difficulties with a husband's undertaking:

> If it merely means that he will obey the order of the Court, it says nothing, for he is bound to do so. If he failed to obey the order . . . would enforcement proceedings be founded upon the breach of the earlier undertaking or upon the breach of the later order? If he were legitimately dissatisfied with the order for financial relief made by the Court, could it be said, that by the form of his undertaking, he had deprived himself of his rights of appeal?

Given the majority's view on the interpretation of s17A(4), the protection of s17A(4) is now *de minimis*. As Hunter JA said:

> I can therefore find . . . no hint of support for the suggestion that such approval, when embodied in an undertaking, become irrevocable, and fixes the wife's minimum provision however erroneous and unreasonable it might prove upon full enquiry to be . . . I have no doubt that the legislative intent behind the while of s17A is to give the wife protection, and within the limits of the practical, to ensure that she receives then or thereafter fair and reasonable financial provision. The purpose of the section is defensive not offensive: it is a shield and not a sword.[129]

Grave financial or other hardship

A spouse who is being divorced against her wishes after two-year separation may oppose the granting of a decree nisi under s15B of the MCO. Where the respondent opposes the granting of a decree nisi, the court shall dismiss the petition, if it is of the opinion that, having considered all the circumstances (including the conduct of the parties, the interest of the parties, and any children concerned) the dissolution of the marriage will result in grave financial or other hardship to the respondent, and that it would in all the circumstances be wrong to dissolve the marriage. This is a defence of last resort, and it is for the respondent to show that the requirements of s15B are satisfied.

In practice, the only significant 'grave financial hardship' which may flow from a divorce is the loss of a widow's pension which a husband is unable to make up to the wife by way of periodical payments, lump sum, or property adjustment. However, in England, this protective formula has rarely been successfully invoked[130] except in the recent case of *K v K*

---

[129] P. 491.
[130] *Talbot v Talbot* (1971) 115 SJ 870; *Julian v Julian* (1972) 116 SJ 763; *Johnson v Johnson* (1981) 12 Fam Law 116; see *Le Marchant v Le Marchant* [1977] 1 WLR 559; *Reiterbund v Reiterbund* [1975] Fam 99.

(financial relief: widow's pension).[131] The husband and wife were 47 and 50 respectively. The wife opposed the husband's divorce petition on the ground that she would lose the substantial widow's pension (£5800 pa) she would enjoy if her husband predeceased her. She was earning £9408 pa and if she worked until 65 her own retirement pension would only be £3388 pa. The husband would retire at 50 with a pension of £15 674 pa. The husband offered to pay her periodical payment, and on retirement, he would pay her a proportion of his pension. He would take out a death in service insurance policy, nominating her as the beneficiary. He would also take out a policy on the parties joint lives, covering the period until he reached the age of 65. It was held that the husband's offer was wholly inadequate. The periodical payment and pension was no more than what the wife would get on divorce after the husband's retirement. As to the death in service insurance, it provided no protection to the wife if the husband were to die after retirement, leaving the wife with the possibility of financial stringency for many years. The joint life insurance until the husband reached 65 provided insufficient protection to the wife whose life expectancy was in the region of a further 33 years. Consequently, decree nisi was not granted.

In Hong Kong, there is no reported case where this defence has succeeded.[132]

S15B is not confined to financial hardship; other grave hardship of a non-financial kind is also included but, even so, there have been no reported Hong Kong cases where this defence has succeeded. The fact that the respondent will be unhappy would not suffice. However, if divorce results in a respondent being ostracised by her community, or excluded from religious and social life, this may amount to hardship. This defence, however, failed in *Rukat v Rukat*.[133] The wife was a Sicilian who married in England. One year after the marriage, she returned with her child to Sicily where she lived as a separated woman for 25 years. It was alleged that a divorce would result in her being rejected by her community. However, on the facts of the case, she failed to show grave hardship; nobody would know that there had been a divorce and there had not been shown any adverse consequences which would flow from a divorce as opposed to the separation, a fact which she had lived with for 25 years.

---

[131] [1997] 1 FLR 35.

[132] *Wong Tat-lun v Wong Chan Siu-ping,* Court of Appeal, Civil Appeal Action No 111 of 1987 (1987); *Yuen Yu-biu v Yuen Nip* [1977–1979] HKC 453.

[133] [1975] 1 All ER 343; in *Lee v Lee* (1975) 5 Fam Law 48. A decree was refused because the dissolution of the marriage and the sale of the matrimonial home would have made it difficult for the wife to take care of a chronically ill son. On appeal, the decree was granted because of a change of circumstances.

The test for hardship is a subjective one. The court will act as a bystander, looking at the situation through the eyes of the respondent in considering whether a reasonable man would agree that a particular wife would suffer grave hardship. The court is thus not obliged to accept the situation as portrayed by the respondent. Where a woman has already lived apart from her husband for a long period, hardship may be difficult to prove, unless she could show consequential hardship would result from divorce.

Wrong to dissolve the marriage: factors to consider

It is difficult to envisage circumstances in which it could be said to be wrong to dissolve a marriage. In *Mathias v Mathias*,[134] the court held that in considering whether it would be 'wrong' to dissolve the marriage, there had to be due regard to the circumstances of the persons involved, including children, but also to the balance between upholding the sanctity of marriage and the desirability of ending 'empty' ties. In *Mathias v Mathias*, the parties were young and had lived apart for many years. It was held that it would not be wrong to bring to an end an 'empty' shell and to allow the parties to settle down to a happier life. The court therefore took into account the fact that one spouse might have a cohabiting partner with whom they had children and that they might wish to marry. In *Brickell v Brickell*,[135] the respondent wife stood to lose a widow's pension of £200, but in view of the fact that she was in desertion herself, it would not be wrong to dissolve the marriage.

SPECIAL PROCEDURE

Where an undefended petition for divorce is based on s11A(2)(a), (c), (d) or (e), there are no children of the family under s18 of the MPPO, it will be dealt with by way of the special procedure.[136] This is sometimes referred to as divorce by administrative process.[137] This means that the Registrar will consider the evidence filed by the petitioner and if he is satisfied that the petitioner has sufficiently proved the contents of the petition, a day will be fixed for the pronouncement of the decree by a judge in open court, there

---

[134] [1972] 3 WLR 201.
[135] [1974] Fam 31.
[136] R33 MCR.
[137] See B Rwezaura; n. 4.

being no need for any party to appear on that day.[138] The exact number of petitions dealt with by special procedure is unclear; an unofficial estimate by the Divorce Registry has indicated that about 95 percent of all petitions are undefended. Of those 95 percent, about 30 to 35 percent are dealt with by the special procedure.

Recently, it has been recommended that the special procedure should apply to all uncontested divorces, whether or not there are children of the family. When implemented, the special procedure will become the norm and will thus no longer be 'special'.

The advantages of the special procedure are that it would:

(a) do away with the essentially ceremonial but public incantation in respect of uncontested divorces;
(b) reduce the time it takes for a litigant to obtain his or her divorce when the dissolution of the marriage is not a contested issue; and
(c) allow the court . . . , to focus on the substantive issue of the children's welfare by having a private hearing, during which that issue can be canvassed in a more informal and relaxed atmosphere.[139]

JOINT APPLICATION FOR DIVORCE

From Table 4.2, it can been seen that the majority of the petitions have been based on two-year separation with consent.[140] The HKLRC felt that the present mix of fault- and non-fault-based divorce required minimal change, but was conscious of the trend towards a neutral and non-adversarial system of divorce. As a result, it recommended a new divorce process known as joint application. S11B of the MCO now provides that:

(1) An application for divorce shall be made to the court jointly by both parties to the marriage.
(2) The court hearing an application for divorce shall not hold the marriage to have broken down irretrievably unless it is satisfied as regards either or both of the following facts
    (a) that the parties to the marriage have lived apart for a continuous period of at least one year immediately preceding the making of the application; and

---

[138] R47A MCR.
[139] Report of the Working Group to Review Practices and Procedures Relating to Matrimonial Proceedings, 1996, p. 2, unpublished.
[140] See above, p. 116.

(b) that not less than one year prior to the making of the application a notice under subsection (3), signed by each of such parties was given to the court and that the notice was not subsequently withdrawn.

(3) (a) The parties to a marriage may at any time give the court a written notice signed by each of them of their intention to apply to the court to dissolve their marriage.

(b) A notice under this subsection shall be in such form as is for the time being specified in rules made under s54.

Unlike the grounds for divorce in a petition, divorce by application is a joint and consensual process. The court, however, must still be satisfied that the marriage has broken down irretrievably.[141] The evidence required to prove irretrievable breakdown of marriage can be satisfied by (a) the parties have lived apart for a continuous period of one year, or (b) one year prior to the making of the application, a notice in the prescribed form, signed by both parties, was given to the court, and that the notice has not been withdrawn.

Living Apart for One Year[142]

The parties may rely on the fact that they have lived apart for a continuous period of one year. 'Living apart' has the same meaning as in other parts of the MCO.[143] The difference between this and s11A(2)(c) of the MCO is both in form and substance. Firstly, a joint application makes no reference to the 'petitioner' or 'respondent'. The parties in a joint application are referred to as the 'first applicant' and the 'second applicant'.[144] Secondly, a petition is subject to the one-year discretionary bar, and if leave has been granted for a petition to be presented before the expiration of one year, it is possible for a divorce petition to be presented before the first anniversary of a marriage. In the case of a joint application, there is no time bar. In other words, the parties may separate a day after their marriage and file a joint application one year after marriage. Another important difference between a joint application and s11A(2)(c) of the MCO is that in the case of the latter, a petitioner may avail herself to the protection of s17A of the MCO, which does not apply to a joint application.

---

[141] S11 MCO.
[142] For the calculation of the period, see s15A(5).
[143] 'A husband and wife shall be treated as living apart unless they are living with each other in the same household', s11C MCO.
[144] See Form 2C, MCR.

Divorce by Mutual Consent

An alternative to a one-year separation is divorce by mutual consent. Here the parties are not required to 'live apart' but they are required to give the court a written notice of their intention to apply to the court to dissolve their marriage.[145] The reason for dispensing with the requirement of separation is the housing situation in Hong Kong.

> ... the majority of families in Hong Kong are obliged to live in relatively cramped conditions in any event, physical realities may necessitate such a liberal interpretation of "separation under one roof" as to render any such limitation meaningless. Rather than use strained and artificial logic in order to hold that a separation had occurred, it might be preferable to do away with this requirement altogether and to simply opt for "giving notice" ...[146]

The notice of intention to dissolve a marriage must be filed not less than one year prior to the making of the joint application.

Table 4.1 shows that the number of joint applications was 203 in 1996 and 710 as of September 1997.[147] There is as yet no breakdown of the numbers of joint applications by way of notice as opposed to one-year separation. As joint application becomes more widely known, we may see a shift from petition to joint application.

Disposal of a Joint Application and Ancillary Matters

Unlike a petition for divorce, all joint applications will be dealt with by way of special procedure.[148] An application for divorce is processed in two stages; decree nisi and decree absolute.[149] The court has the power to rescind a decree nisi if it is satisfied that one party has misled the other about any matter which the former takes into account when deciding to make the application for divorce.[150]

Ancillary matters in a joint application, i.e. financial matters and custody, are dealt with in the same way as in a petition. Unlike the English Family Law Act 1996, the Hong Kong courts have no jurisdiction to deal with

---

[145] Form 2E MCR.
[146] HKLRC, para 6.22; see n. 6.
[147] See above, p. 102.
[148] R33(2B), r47A(1A) MCR.
[149] S17(2) MCO.
[150] S15C(2).

ancillary matters during the notice period, nor is the one-year period a period of consideration and reflection.[151]

FUTURE DEVELOPMENTS

Divorce by joint application, introduced by the Matrimonial Causes (Amendment) Ordinance, is based to some extent on the idea of 'process over time', a scheme which has been adopted by the English Family Law Act 1996.

'Process over time' means that a divorce is obtainable if the marriage has irretrievably broken down. The test for irretrievable breakdown of marriage is that one or both parties consider that the marriage is at an end. The advantages of the process over time approach was summarised as follows:

> ... two aspects of the criteria of a good divorce law have been particularly emphasised in recent years. These are, first, the importance of promoting co-operation between the parties and, secondly, the fact that divorce must be seen as a process rather than a single event. Most of the options discussed above treat the actual divorce as separate from its consequences, whereas it would seem preferable to treat the process of divorce with all its repercussions as a whole. This would enable appropriate legal and other support to be given to the parties during the transition from married to non-married life ... These aims could be achieved by providing a period of time (referred to as the transition period) in which this transition can take place and during which the parties would be given every encouragement to reach agreement on all aspects of the divorce, failing which these would be decided judicially. The divorce would not be available until the end of the period. Thus, during the whole transition period the parties would have the opportunity to reflect on whether they really wanted a divorce. This would be particularly valuable as they would be able to reassess their decision as all the repercussions of divorce became clear to them. Under the present system, it is often too late to go back by the time that the full implications have become apparent; issues relating to the children are often resolved, and issues of finance and property can only be resolved, after the divorce nisi has been obtained ... The underlying principle, which could be stated in the legislation, would remain the irretrievable breakdown of the marriage, but there would be no need to establish any particular basis for the divorce, which would be available as of right at the end of the transition period ... all negotiations about

---

[151] See below.

children, finance and property could take place without concern as to whether the ground could be made out . . . The main advantage of such a scheme is that it combines the logical position that the only true test of breakdown is that one or both parties consider the marriage at an end, with the need to provide a period of reflection and transition . . . Attention throughout the process would be focused on the continuing obligations of the parties in respect of their children and financial arrangements. The object would be to enable both parties to maintain their relationship with the children, while making the necessary arrangements for the future in as civilised a manner and timespan as can be achieved.[152]

In a joint application, there is no requirement, nor is there any mechanism, for ensuring that the parties treat the one-year separation or notice period as a transitional period during which they resolve issues relating to children and finance.[153] Recent suggestions to introduce mediation to assist the parties to settle custody and financial matters, if implemented, will be crucial to divorce law and practice. Consensual divorce is consistent with divorce under customary marriage as recognised in the Marriage Reform Ordinance.[154] The divorce law, Western-style, may soon come full circle to meet divorce Chinese-style.

---

[152] English Law Reform Commission, Facing the Future: A Discussion Paper on the Ground for Divorce, No 170, HMSO, London, 1988, paras 5.22–5.23.
[153] HKLRC, paras 8.33–8.41; see n. 6.
[154] See Chapter 2.

5

Nullity and Judicial Separation

INTRODUCTION

Capacity and the observance of certain formalities are essential for a marriage to be validly constituted. Nullity of marriage defines the circumstances under which a marriage may be void. However, a 'void marriage' is a tautology for if there is no marriage, it requires no designation. An ostensible marriage, for instance where a man performs a bungy-jumping ceremony with his girlfriend, 'officiated' by a priest, is just as ineffective a marriage as a man merely cohabiting with a woman. In both cases, there is no marriage. Why, then, is it necessary to classify the former as a 'void marriage' whereas, in the latter, the parties are unmarried cohabitants? As Bromley puts it,[1] the term a 'void marriage' distinguishes between a case where the parties have been through a ceremony of marriage but have never acquired the status of husband and wife owing to the presence of some impediments or defects, from all other types of domestic relationships which do not constitute marriage. The distinction is important in that the law prescribes legal consequences to a void marriage.[2] In this chapter, we shall focus mainly on nullity, and judicial separation will be considered at the end.

---

[1] P M Bromley, *Family Law*, 7th edition, Butterworths, London, 1987, p. 77 (hereafter referred to as Bromley).

[2] For powers of the court to make ancillary relief orders, see Chapter 15 below; a decree of nullity is a judgment *in rem* binding upon the world, whereas a declaration of status binds the parties only.

VOID AND VOIDABLE MARRIAGE: THE HISTORICAL DISTINCTION

For reasons which can only be understood by reference to English legal history, the law draws a distinction between a void and voidable marriage.[3] Until the English Divorce and Matrimonial Causes Act 1857, matrimonial jurisdiction was vested in the Ecclesiastical Courts which administered the Canon law. The Canon law adhered to the principle of the indissolubility of marriage so that divorce was not possible. It did, however, recognise some impediments to marriage. In such cases, the court granted a divorce *a vinculo matrimonii* (from the bonds of marriage, which is today's nullity) or a divorce *a mensa et thoro* (from board and bed, which is today's judicial separation). In the case of nullity, the Ecclesiastical Courts recognised certain nullifying impediments such as prior marriage, pre-contract, impotence, lack of consent, or prohibited degrees. In these cases, the Ecclesiastical Courts would grant a divorce *a vinculo matrimonii*, the marriage then being regarded as void *ab initio*. Such a marriage could be attacked at any time, even after the death of one or both parties, by any interested parties. The effect of such a successful attack was to bastardise children born to the couple.

The drastic effect of a decree of nullity attracted the intervention of the common law courts which started to draw a distinction between impediments and remedies. As a result of this distinction, certain impediments could not be challenged after the death of one party (and by the other spouse). The marriage, therefore, was regarded as valid unless it was annulled during the lifetime of either party to the marriage. This introduced the concept of a 'voidable' marriage. Lord Green MR has described the distinction thus:

> A void marriage is one that will be regarded by every court in any case in which the existence of the marriage is in issue as never having taken place and can be so treated by both parties to it without the necessity of any decree annulling it; a voidable marriage is one that will be regarded by every court as a valid subsisting marriage until a decree annulling it has been pronounced by a court of competent jurisdiction.[4]

---

[3] J Jackson, *The Formation and Annulment of Marriage*, 2nd edition, Butterworths, London, 1969.
[4] *De Reneville v De Reneville* [1948] P. 100 at 111.

VOID AND VOIDABLE MARRIAGE: TODAY'S DISTINCTIONS

Today, a void marriage means a marriage which is so fundamentally defective that it does not exist at all. It is void *ab initio*. This is so even though the parties may wish or intend otherwise. Strictly speaking, there is no need for a decree of nullity in such cases, and either party is free to marry another person. A decree, however, is necessary if a party seeks ancillary relief.[5] Moreover, an interested third party can challenge a marriage as being void, even after the death of one or both of the parties, and unlike a voidable marriage, there is no defence to such a challenge. As for children, in the past a void marriage would render them illegitimate. To mitigate this drastic effect, it is now provided that children of a void marriage are legitimate if either or both parents reasonably believed,[6] at the time of the conception (or at the time of the celebration of the marriage if later), that the marriage was valid.[7] Furthermore, the presumption is that one of the parties reasonably believed that the marriage was valid.

In contrast, a voidable marriage refers to a defective marriage which could be avoided only at the instance of a party to a marriage during the joint lives of both parties. It is valid until avoided, and a decree is necessary to set it aside. Until avoided, the parties are not at liberty to marry and, unlike a void marriage, defences are available.

The common law rule concerning a voidable marriage was that a decree of nullity operated with retrospective effect, annulling a marriage from the beginning. This had serious implications for the status of children and for the parties. The harshness of this rule has now been modified by s12 of the Legitimacy Ordinance. This provides that where a decree of nullity is granted in respect of a voidable marriage, any child who would have been the legitimate child of the parties to the marriage if it had been dissolved rather than annulled shall, at the date of the decree, be deemed to be the legitimate child of the parties in spite of the annulment.

As regards the status of the parties, the old common law rule has now been modified by s20B of the Matrimonial Causes Ordinance (MCO). This provides that a nullity decree (granted after 30 June 1972) does not have retrospective effect. Thus, it operates to annul a marriage only from the time of the decree absolute. In other words, the marriage, notwithstanding the decree, is to be treated as if it had existed up to the date of the decree. The effect of a decree of nullity in the case of a voidable

---

[5] See Chapter 15 below.
[6] Even the belief is due to a mistake of the law; see s11 of the Legitimacy Ordinance.
[7] S11 of the Legitimacy Ordinance.

marriage can be seen in *Re Roberts (deceased)*.[8] The deceased, having made a will leaving property to the defendant, married the plaintiff. The marriage, if valid, would have had the effect of revoking the will. On the death of the deceased, the plaintiff sought a grant of letters of administration and the defendant contested this on the ground that the marriage was voidable because the deceased lacked mental capacity. The Court of Appeal held that a voidable marriage was not retrospective in effect and, for the purposes of determining whether any prior will had been revoked, the marriage was valid.[9]

DUTY OF THE COURT

In cases of divorce, it is the duty of the court to inquire, in so far as it reasonably can, into any facts alleged by any party to the proceedings.[10] Although there is no similar provision for nullity proceedings, s22 of the MCO provides that in any proceedings for nullity, the court may direct all necessary papers in the matter to be sent to the Proctor, who is required to instruct counsel to argue before the court any question in relation to the matter which the court deems it necessary or expedient to have fully argued, and it has been held that the court has a duty to enquire into the facts as well as to satisfy itself as to the law.[11]

JURISDICTION OF THE COURT

The court will have jurisdiction in proceedings for nullity under the MCO if:

> (a) either of the parties to the marriage was domiciled in or had a substantial connection with Hong Kong at the date of the petition;

---

[8] [1978] 3 All ER 225; see also *Fowke v Fowke* [1938] 1 Ch. 774.
[9] The inevitable anomaly arising from this decision is that a party who was coerced into a marriage (e.g. by duress) and died before having had any reasonable opportunity to seek its annulment would have his earlier will revoked by the marriage. The other party to the marriage, who could be the offending party, would benefit under the consequent intestacy. See also *Ward v Secretary of State for Social Services* [1990] 1 FLR 119; *P v P (ouster: decree nisi of nullity)* [1994] 2 FLR 400.
[10] S15(1) MCO.
[11] *D v D (nullity)* [1979] 3 All ER 337.

(b) either of the parties to the marriage was habitually resident in Hong Kong throughout the period of 3 years immediately preceding the date of the petition;
(c) both parties to the marriage were resident in Hong Kong at the date of the petition;
(d) the respondent in the proceedings was resident in Hong Kong at the date of the petition; or
(e) the marriage was celebrated in Hong Kong.[12]

VOID MARRIAGES

S20(1) of the MCO provides that a marriage which takes place after 30 June 1972 shall be void on any of the following grounds:

(a) that it is not a valid marriage under section 27 of the Marriage Ordinance, that is to say–
   (i) the parties to the marriage are within the prohibited degrees of kindred or affinity; or
   (ii) either party is under the age of 16; or
   (iii) the parties have intermarried in disregard of certain requirements as to the formation of marriage;
(b) that the marriage is otherwise invalid by the law of Hong Kong;
(c) that at the time of the marriage either party was already married;
(d) that the parties are not respectively male and female.

Parties Are within the Prohibited Degrees of Kindred and Affinity

Kindred refers to blood relations, i.e. persons descended from the same stock or common ancestor,[13] such as parent and child, or brother and sister. These relationships are also known as consanguinity. Affinity refers to a relationship created by marriage. Relatives by affinity are called 'affines' and they include e.g. the spouse of one's own relative, and relatives of one's spouse (e.g. in-laws and step-relations). Should a man be permitted to marry his deceased wife's sister? Or a man marry the daughter of his former wife?

---

[12] See also s9 and s2 MCO, Chapter 2.
[13] *Black's Law Dictionary*, 5th edition, St. Paul, West Pub. Co., 1979.

Rationales for prohibitions on marriage between relatives

Genetic/eugenic considerations

The reasons for the prohibition of marriages between blood relations is that there is a higher chance of mutant genes being present in common in two persons with a common ancestor. Marriage between close relatives increases the chance of passing the defective genes to the offspring.[14] Prohibition based on consanguinity thus can be justified by genetic/eugenic considerations. The proportion of genes which blood relatives have in common can be seen in the following table:[15]

Relationship	*The proportion of genes in common*
father and daughter brother and sister	1/2 or 50%
grandparent and grandchild uncle and niece half brother and sister	1/4 or 25%
first cousins great-uncle and grandniece	1/8 or 12.5%
second cousins	1/32 or 3.1%

Religion

Biological and genetic considerations relating to marriage between close blood relations do not apply to marriage between affines. Prohibition on marriage between affines can be traced to the Christian doctrine that husband and wife was one flesh; if it was wrong for a person to marry his sister, it was also wrong for him to marry his wife's sister.

Social policy

Apart from the above considerations, marriages between close relatives can cause confusion as to family relationships. A marriage between a man and

---

[14] Cf. incest, see below, p. 150. See Chris Barton, 'Incest and the Prohibited Degrees' NLJ (1987) 502.
[15] From S Cretney and J Masson, *Principles of Family Law*, 5th edition, Sweet & Maxwell, London, 1990, p. 34.

his stepdaughter for example, would alter the existing family structure. In such a case, the relationship between the parties, which used to be that of stepfather/stepchild is now transformed to that of husband/wife; the wife's siblings and the husband would now become in-laws.

Another important consideration is the need to preserve harmonious family relationships. If a man could marry his stepchild, such a possibility might be a source of rivalries and jealousies. A related consideration is society's abhorrence of inter-generational sex and the need to prevent a person who is *in loco parentis* from abusing that relationship. For example, the possibility of sexual exploitation and abuse by a stepfather who is in *loco parentis vis-à-vis* his stepdaughter may be real if he is permitted to marry his stepchild.

Most societies have addressed the moral issue of how extensive should be the list those whom one is not permitted to marry on the grounds of consanguinity or affinity, and Hong Kong Law, which is the same as the English law, is no different. S27(1) of the Marriage Ordinance states that:

> no marriage shall be valid which would be null and void on the ground of kindred or affinity in England and Wales.

Until recently, the English rule on prohibited degrees was extensive.[16] However, developments this century have removed a number of prohibitions on grounds of affinity. For instance, the Deceased Wife's Sister's Marriage Act 1907 removed the prohibition on marriage between a man and his deceased wife's sister. Gender symmetry was achieved by the Deceased Brother's Widow's Marriage Act 1921, which removed the embargo on a union between a widow and her deceased husband's brother. The Marriage (Prohibited Degrees of Relationship) Act 1931 further reduced the list of relationships which fell within the prohibited degrees of affinity. As a result, a valid marriage could be contracted between a man and any of the following persons:

his deceased wife's brother's daughter,
his deceased wife's sister's daughter,
his father's deceased brother's widow,
his mother's deceased brother's widow,
his deceased wife's father's sister,
his deceased wife's mother's sister,
his brother's deceased son's widow, and
his sister's deceased son's widow.

---

[16] See W Blackstone, *Commentaries on the Laws of England*, Vol. 2, 1766, pp. 202–7.

The category of prohibited degrees of affinity was further narrowed by the Marriage (Enabling) Act 1960. Its effect was that a man could marry the sister, aunt, or niece of his former wife while the wife was still alive; and a man could marry the former wife of a brother, uncle or nephew whilst that person was still alive. Today, the prohibited degrees of affinity in Hong Kong are restricted to those in the Marriage (Prohibited Degrees of Relationship) Act 1986 which will be considered later.[17]

The law today: prohibited degrees of consanguinity

Today, a man may not marry his mother, daughter, grandmother, granddaughter, sister, aunt or niece, and corresponding prohibitions apply to women.[18] The prohibition includes a relationship traced through whole blood or through half blood,[19] legitimate or otherwise.[20] There is no prohibition on marriages between cousins. However, an adopted person remains within the prohibited degree of consanguinity with his natural parents and his other relatives as if he had not been adopted.[21] In addition, an adopted person and his adoptive parents are within the prohibited degree of consanguinity, and they remain so even if the adopted person is subsequently readopted.[22] Apart from these, there are no other prohibitions arising from adoption. This means that an adopted person may marry a natural child of the adoptors.[23]

The law today: prohibited degrees of affinity

The Marriage (Prohibited Degrees of Relationship) Act 1986 reduces the number of all the prohibited degrees of affinity except for the two categories below.

The first category concerns a marriage between a man and his step-relations (such as a stepdaughter, stepmother, step-grandmother, or stepgranddaughter). Such marriages are valid if both parties have attained the age of 21, and the intended wife has not been related to the other party (as a child of the family) at any time whilst she was under 18.

---

[17] See below.
[18] See Annex I of this chapter, pp. 175–6; the Marriage Acts 1949 to 1986.
[19] See s78(1) Marriage Act 1949.
[20] *Haines v Jeffreys* (1696) 92 ER 929 where a marriage between a man and his sister's illegitimate daughter was held to be barred; *R v Brighton Inhabitants* (1861) 1 B & S 447.
[21] S13(3) Adoption Ordinance.
[22] See n. 21.
[23] See Adoption Act 1976, s47(1).

The second category deals with a marriage between a man and his daughter-in-law, or mother-in-law. Such a marriage is valid if (i) both parties have attained the age of 21 and (ii) in the case of a daughter-in-law, the marriage is solemnised after both the son and the son's mother have died. In the case of a marriage between a man and his mother-in-law, the marriage is solemnized after both the man's former wife and the former wife's father have died (the law thereby appearing to supply a motive for double murder!).

These restrictions may seem odd and unreasonable.[24] Example 1:

> A woman divorces her husband and obtains custody of the children. She is supported by her former husband's father and mother in raising the children. Some years later, the husband's mother dies through ill-health and the woman decides to marry her former husband's father. They cannot do so until the woman's former husband dies.

Example 2:

> A man aged 40 marries a woman aged 25 who has never known her father. The wife is killed in a traffic accident and some years later, the man and his former wife's mother want to get married. They cannot do so until the former wife's father dies.

Example 3:

> A man divorces his wife, and she remarries, taking her son of the marriage to live with her. The son has had very little contact with his father. The son later marries and divorces. The son's former wife begins to see her former father-in-law and eventually decides to marry him. However, they cannot do so and must wait until their respective former spouses are dead.

The restriction is based on the argument that the law should not condone sexual rivalry between close family members. The restriction thus provides a child-in-law a safe place in the new family in which she is exempted from sexual expectations.[25] Here the law serves its symbolic function; sexual intercourse between a person and the parent of his or her former spouses does not amount to incest and the parties in all the examples above would be able to cohabit as husband and wife without committing any offence.

---

[24] Scottish Law Reform Commission, Report on Family Law, No 135, HMSO, Edinburgh, 1992, para 8.8.
[25] Ibid., para 8.12.

Consequences of a Purported marriage within prohibited degrees and the criminal law

A marriage of persons within the prohibited degrees of consanguinity or affinity is void *ab initio*. Knowledge of the nature of the relationship is not relevant. Knowledge, however, must be established in the case of the crime of incest (which requires sexual intercourse), although there need be no marriage. The categories of relationship defined for incest are narrower than the prohibited degrees of consanguinity. It is a criminal offence for a man to have sexual intercourse with a woman, who is, to his knowledge, his daughter, granddaughter, mother or sister[26] but it is not a crime of incest for a man to have sexual intercourse with his aunt or niece.

Other jurisdictions

Other jurisdictions have simplified the prohibition on consanguinity and affinity. Australia, for instance, has removed the prohibited degrees of affinity altogether.[27] The prohibited degree of consanguinity is restricted only to one's ancestor or descendant, or a brother or sister of the whole-blood or half-blood. Thus, a man cannot marry his grandmother, mother, sister, daughter or granddaughter while there is no prohibition on marriage between uncle and niece, or aunt and nephew.[28] Again, in Canada the Marriage (Prohibited Degrees) Act 1990 has also removed all prohibition of marriages between affines.[29] In New Zealand, s31 of the Family Proceedings Act 1980 and s15 of the Marriage Act 1955 provide that any persons who are within the prescribed degrees of affinity may apply to the High Court for its consent to their marriage and the Court, if it is satisfied that neither party to the intended marriage has by his or her conduct caused or contributed to the cause of the termination of any previous marriage of the other party, may make an order dispensing with the prohibition of marriage. In the PRC, Article 6 of the Marriage Law 1980 only prohibits marriage between a man and woman who are lineal relatives by blood or collateral relatives by blood up to the third degree of relationship.

---

[26] Ss47–51 Crimes Ordinance.
[27] See s23(2) of the Marriage Act 1961 (Commonwealth of Australia); see also *Antony Dickey, Family Law,* 2nd edition, Law Book Co., Sydney, 1990, p. 110.
[28] See s23B of the Marriage Act 1961 (Commonwealth of Australia); see also *Antony Dickey, Family Law,* 2nd edition, Law Book Co., Sydney, 1990, p. 110.
[29] See *Annual Review of Population Law,* Vol. 17, p. 48.

Age

A marriage is void if either party is under 16. No certificate (of the Registrar of Marriages) shall be issued if either party to a intended marriage is under 16.[30]

Prior to the Law Reform (Miscellaneous Provisions and Minor Amendments) Ordinance 1997, if either party to an intended marriage, not being a widower or a widow, was over 16 and under 21, the written consent of the father was needed. If he was dead or *non compos mentis,* the mother, or, if both were dead or *non compos mentis,* the lawful guardian of such party, had to be produced before the Registrar could issue a certificate.[31] If there was no parent or lawful guardian residing in Hong Kong and capable of consenting, or if the Registrar was satisfied that after diligent inquiry such person could not be traced, the Registrar might give consent in writing to the marriage.[32]

S28 of the Law Reform (Miscellaneous Provisions and Minor Amendments) Ordinance 1997 makes detailed provisions regarding whose written consent is required for the marriage of a person aged between 16 and 21. As a general rule, where both parents are alive and their marriage is still subsisting, either parent may give consent. Where the parents are divorced or separated by order of any court or by agreement, consent is required from the parent who has custody by order of the court or by agreement.

A person whose consent is required may forbid the issue of the certificate by writing the word 'Forbidden'.[33] Where a person whose consent is required refuses to give his consent, or has written the word 'Forbidden' with respect to a party to an intended marriage, a District Court judge may, on an application being made, consent to the marriage.[34] Consent given by a District Court judge will have the same effect as if it had been given by the person whose consent has been refused, or as if the forbiddance had been withdrawn. There is, as yet, no local reported case of the court overriding a parent's refusal to consent. What if a parent thinks that his daughter is still too young and immature to take on the responsibilities of married life? What if a parent considers that his daughter, innocent and naive, has chosen an inappropriate partner? To the extent that the law

---

[30] S13 Marriage Ordinance.
[31] S14 Marriage Ordinance.
[32] S15 Marriage Ordinance.
[33] S16(1) Marriage Ordinance.
[34] S18A Marriage Ordinance as amended by s31 of the Law Reform (Miscellaneous Provisions and Minor Amendments) Ordinance (No 80 of 1997).

requires parental consent, and has entrusted a parent with the right to refuse to consent to a child's marriage, it may be difficult for the court to override parental assessment.[35] However, a marriage celebrated without the requisite 'parental' consent will not be invalid.[36]

Defective Formalities

S20(1)(a)(iii) of the MCO covers defective formalities, and s20(b) appears to be redundant. The Marriage Ordinance provides that a person who intends to marry shall give notice to the Registrar and, subject to certain requirements, a marriage may take place within three months of the giving of the notice. The Marriage Ordinance provides for other formalities, such as the time and place where a marriage may be celebrated, the requirement, of the presence of two or more witnesses, and the formal wording the marriage ceremony must adopt.[37] Failure to comply with these requirements, however, does not render a marriage void.[38] The Marriage Ordinance lists the circumstances where a marriage will be void on the grounds of defective formalities and this will be so only where the parties 'knowingly and wilfully acquiesce'[39] in the defective formalities. The defects involved relate to the celebration of a marriage:

- in any place other than the office of the Registrar or a licenced place of worship or
- under a false name,[40] or
- without a certificate of notice or licence duly issued, or
- by a person not being a competent minister or a Registrar or his deputy.

In *Gereis v Yagoub*,[41] the parties purported to go through a ceremony of marriage in a Coptic Orthodox church which was not licensed for marriages under English law. The ceremony was, furthermore, performed by a Coptic Orthodox priest who was not licensed to conduct marriages. Following the ceremony the parties lived together. However, the relationship

---

[35] See *Re An infant* [1963] 6 FLR 12 (Supreme Court of Victoria, Australia) in F Bates and N Turner, *The Family Law Casebook,* Law Book Company Ltd., Sydney, 1985, p. 73.
[36] S27(2).
[37] S21.
[38] S27(2).
[39] See *James & Son Ltd v Smee* [1955] 1 QB 78 at p. 91; *Westminster City Council v Croyalgrange Ltd* [1986] 2 All ER 353; *R v Senior* [1899] 1 QB 283 at pp. 290–1.
[40] *Sullivan v Sullivan* 2 Hag Con 237; cf. marriage by special licence *Puttick v AG* [1980] Fam 1.
[41] [1997] 1 FLR 854.

broke down quickly and the woman petitioned for a decree of nullity. It was held that the marriage was void because the parties knowingly went through the ceremony of marriage without having given due notice to the Superintendent Registrar. This was so despite the ceremony in the Coptic church bore all the hallmarks of an ordinary Christian marriage and was treated as such both by the parties and those who attended the ceremony.

Bigamy

A marriage is void if, at the time of the marriage, either party was already lawfully married to a third party.[42] It is irrelevant that the party who was already married reasonably thought that the spouse was dead.[43] In *Whiston v Whiston*,[44] the parties went through a marriage ceremony, and lived together for 15 years and had two children. Although the wife had represented herself as free to marry, she was at all material times married to a third party. In nullity proceedings, the wife admitted that the marriage was bigamous. In ancillary relief proceedings at first instance in the Family Division, it was argued that she was not entitled to benefit from her own wrongdoing. This view was not accepted by Thorpe J who held that a bigamist was not debarred from putting forward a claim for financial relief. However, the wife's behaviour in deceiving the husband, was such as to reduce her entitlement. This was followed in the Hong Kong case of *Fong Pak-kai v Fong Chue Yin-ling*,[45] where the 'husband' had married his Hong Kong wife whilst at all times being lawfully married in the PRC and was consequently convicted of bigamy. The Hong Kong 'marriage' lasted for 20 years, during which time, it was claimed by the husband, he and his wife had acquired several properties, all in the name of the 'wife'. He sought a declaration of nullity with a view to applying for ancillary relief.

---

[42] The criminal offence of bigamy, see s45 of the Offences Against the Person Ordinance, see also *Partridge v R* [1977] HKLR 89; *R v Sze Tin-sin* [1987] 3 HKC 333.

[43] S6(1) and s26 MCO provides that a court may, if it is satisfied that such reasonable grounds exit for supposing that the other party to the marriage is dead, make a decree of presumption of death and dissolution of the marriage. The fact that for a period of seven years or more the other party to the marriage had been continuously absent from the petitioner and the petitioner has no reason to believe that the other party had been living within that time will be evidence that the other party is dead until the contrary is proved, *Parkinson v Parkinson* [1939] P. 346; *Manser v Manser* [1940] P. 224; *Deacock v Deacock* [1958] P. 230 .

[44] [1995] 2 FLR 268.

[45] [1995] 2 HKC 518 (decided before the Court of Appeal's decision in *Whiston v Whiston* was reported).

The Hong Kong Court of Appeal, following the decision of Thorpe J, held that the husband had a right *ex debito justitiae* to a decree of nullity.

Whether a bigamous husband's financial relief is to be reduced or would be extinguished remains to be decided. The English Court of Appeal in *Whiston v Whiston*,[46] disagreed with Thorpe J's decision. It held that had the wife not committed bigamy, she would have had no claim for financial relief. As a matter of public policy, and applying the maxim *ex turpi causa non oritur actio*, the court would not lend its aid to someone who found her claim on a criminal offence.[47]

The Parties Are Not Respectively Male or Female

In *Hyde v Hyde*, Lord Penzance defined marriage as 'the voluntary union for life of one man and one woman'.[48] A 'marriage' between persons of the same sex would therefore be a nullity. In *Talbot v Talbot*,[49] a woman went through a marriage ceremony with a person whom she believed was a man but who turned out to be a woman masquerading as a man. It was held that there was no marriage.

One issue which the courts in different jurisdictions have had to confront is who is a 'man' and who is a 'woman' for the purposes of marriage. The problem arises in two situations: with transsexuals and hermaphrodites (individuals of congenitally intermediate gender). A transsexual is someone who physically belongs to one sex (either male or female) but psychologically feels to be another. This gives rise to a conflict between the biological and the psychological component of gender identification. Advances in medicine now mean that such persons can undergo a 'sex-change operation' or 'gender reassignment surgery'. The effect of such an operation is to render the person's physical appearance compatible with his or her psychological orientation. However, this raises the question of whether a post-operative male-to-female transsexual is a man or a woman. A hermaphrodite poses a slightly different problem; a hermaphrodite is someone who possesses both male and female sexual organs. Is such a person both male and female, or neither?

---

[46] [1995] 2 FLR 268; compare *J v S-T (formerly J) (transsexual-ancillary relief)* [1997] 1 FLR 402.
[47] See also *Tinsley v Milligan* [1993] 2 FLR 963.
[48] (1866) LR 1 P & D 130 at p. 133.
[49] (1967) 111 SJ 213.

English law does not regard a 'sex-change operation' as being capable of altering the sex of a person for the purposes of marriage.[50] In *Corbett v Corbett*,[51] the respondent was born a male but desired to be a female. A 'sex change operation' removed his testicles and scrotum. This was followed by the construction of an artificial vagina and the use of oestrogen to enlarge the breasts. After the operation, the respondent adopted a female name, living and working as a successful female model. The respondent went through a marriage ceremony with the appellant who knew of these facts. On the appellant's petition for a decree of nullity, Ormrod J held that a marriage was essentially heterosexual in nature. There were at least four criteria for establishing the sex of a person, i.e. chromosomal, gonadal,[52] genital and psychological. Despite the sex reassignment operation, the respondent was a male person according to the first three criteria, and the marriage was thus void:[53]

> the biological sexual constitution of an individual is fixed at birth (at the least), and cannot be changed, either by the natural development of organs of the opposite sex, or by medical or surgical means. The respondent's operation, therefore cannot affect her true sex.[54]

The decision of the American Superior Court of New Jersey in the case of *M.T. v J.T.*[55] adopts a very different approach. The case concerned a male-to-female transsexual and the court was willing to give legal effect to the 'sex-change operation':

---

[50] How far can a person be regarded as a man for one purpose, and a woman for another? A male–female transsexual is to be treated as a male for the purposes of offences relating to prostitution, *R v Tan* [1983] 2 All ER 12, for the offence of rape, for the purposes of retirement age, or for the purposes of the Sex Discrimination Ordinance, *White v British Sugar Corporation* [1977] IRLR 121.

[51] [1971] P. 83.

[52] Organs which produce sex cells, i.e. testes or ovaries.

[53] It was said obiter by Ormrod J that the respondent was physically incapable of consummating the marriage as intercourse with a person with an artificially constructed cavity could never constitute true intercourse (at p. 107); cf. *S.Y. v S.Y. (orse. W)* [1963] P. 37 where a wife's defect was one of vaginal astresia, i.e. she had no more than an incipient vagina in the form of a cul-de-sac. It was held that an operation could enlarge it so as to enable consummation. Willmer LJ said that even if the wife had no natural vagina, she could be given an artificial vagina by means of plastic surgery and coitus through such an artificial vagina would constitute *vera copula* so as to consummate a marriage.

[54] [1971] P. 83 at p. 104 per Ormrod LJ.

[55] 355 A. 2d 204 (1976).

In this case the transsexual's gender and genitalia are no longer discordant; they have been harmonised through medical treatment. Plaintiff has become physically and psychologically unified and fully capable of sexual activity consistent with her reconciled sexual attributes of gender and anatomy. Consequently, plaintiff should be considered a member of the female sex for marital purposes. It follows that such an individual should have capacity to enter into a valid marriage relationship with a person of the opposite sex and did do so here ... Such recognition will promote the individual's quest for inner peace and personal happiness, while in no way disserving any societal interest, principle of public order or precept of morality.

In the case of a hermaphrodite, where the biological criteria (chromosomal, gonadal and genital) of a person are not congruent, Ormrod J in *Corbett v Corbett* said obiter that greater weight must be placed on the genital criterion than on the gonadal and chromosomal criteria.[56] The position of a hermaphrodite was considered in the Australian case of *In the Marriage of C and D*.[57] In that case, the respondent was brought up as a male person. Following surgery, he possessed the gonadal and genital features of a male person and the chromosomal gender of a female. The wife petitioned for a decree of nullity on the grounds of mistaken identity. It was held that the marriage was void because of mistaken identity and, in addition, her consent was not real. However, the judge (Bell J) went on to say that the marriage was also void in that the respondent was neither a man nor a woman but a combination of both.[58]

The sexual identity of post-operative transsexuals has also been considered by the European Court of Human Rights. In *Rees v United Kingdom*,[59] the applicant was born with all the physical characteristics of a normal female, but subsequently exhibited masculine behaviour. The applicant underwent a gender-reassignment operation, adopted a masculine name, and lived as a male person. All the identity documents showed him to be a male person, except for the birth certificate which the government refused to change. The applicant alleged that such refusal was a breach of Articles 8 and 12 of the European Convention on Human Rights which guaranteed, *inter alia*, the right to 'respect for private and family life' and the right 'to marry and to found a family' respectively. However, the action failed, the court holding that there was no breach of Article 8 as the entry in a birth certificate was a record of facts at the time of birth and the birth

---

[56] [1971] P. 83 at p. 106.
[57] [1979] 35 FLR 340 (Family Court of Australia); see Rebecca J Bailey, 52 (1979) Australia Law Journal, p. 659.
[58] This meant that such a person could never marry.
[59] [1987] 2 FLR 111.

certificate was a document revealing not current identity but historical facts.[60] The court further held that Article 12 referred only to traditional marriages between persons of opposite biological sex.

Similar questions may arise under the Hong Kong Bill of Rights Ordinance (Articles 14 and 19) and it remains to be seen if Hong Kong courts will be willing to recognise the new sexual identity of a person who has undergone a gender-reassignment operation. In the meantime, the definition of marriage (as interpreted by Ormrod J and the European Court of Human Rights) is slowly being tested. As of 1989, Danish law has permitted persons of the same sex to register their partnership and they are treated almost in the same way as persons in heterosexual partnerships with respect to marriage, divorce, succession and tax laws.[61]

VOIDABLE MARRIAGE

S20(2) of the MCO provides that a marriage which takes place after 30 June 1972 is voidable on the following grounds:

(a) that the marriage has not been consummated owing to the incapacity of either party to consummate it;
(b) that the marriage has not been consummated owing to the wilful refusal of the respondent to consummate it;
(c) that either party to the marriage did not validly consent to it, whether in consequence of duress, mistake, unsoundness of mind or otherwise;
(d) that at the time of the marriage either party to the marriage, though capable of giving a valid consent, was suffering, whether continuously or intermittently, from mental disorder within the meaning of the Mental Health Ordinance (Cap. 136) of such a kind or to such an extent as to be unfitted for marriage;
(e) that at the time of the marriage the respondent was suffering from venereal disease in a communicable form;
(f) that at the time of the marriage the respondent was pregnant by some person other than the petitioner.

---

[60] See also the case of *Cossey v UK* (1990) 13 EHRR 622 (ECt HR) which involved a post-operative male-to-female transsexual.
[61] Same-sex partnerships are not treated in the same way as heterosexual partnerships with respect to the adoption of children and the right to obtain a religious celebration of their partnership, *Annual Review of Population Law*, Vol. 16, p. 56. See also Marianne Hojgaard Pedersen, 'Denmark: Homosexual Marriages and New Rules Regarding Separation and Divorce', 30 (1991–92) Journal of Family Law 289.

Non-Consummation Due to Incapacity of Either Party

Consummation means the first act of sexual intercourse after marriage, which is 'ordinary and complete' and not 'partial and imperfect'.[62] A marriage is consummated once sexual intercourse has taken place and subsequent refusal to have sexual intercourse cannot negate prior consummation.[63] Mere incapacity of conception (sterility or barrenness) is not a ground for a decree of nullity.[64] Moreover, sexual satisfaction or emission of seed[65] is irrelevant and the use of a contraceptive device, such as a sheath, or the practice of coitus interruptus does not prevent consummation.[66]

Either party may petition and a petitioner can rely on his own impotence. Incapacity may relate to the petitioner only or to all the world.[67] Where incapacity is due to a physical/structural defect, the defect causing incapacity must be incurable. Thus, in *S.Y. v S.Y. (orse. W)*,[68] the wife had a malformed vagina which was too short for full penetration. Medical evidence suggested that an operation could be performed and that there was an 89% chance that the operation, if performed, would render the wife capable of sexual intercourse. The wife was willing to undergo the operation. It was held that the wife's incapacity was curable so the husband's petition for a decree of nullity was refused.[69]

Where the condition causing the incapacity could be remedied by an operation attended by danger, or if the spouse refuses to submit to the operation, the incapacity is regarded as incurable and consummation becomes impracticable.[70] Thus, in *CCCY v CWL*,[71] where the parties had been married for six years and the husband had not been able to consummate the marriage, one possible cure for his impotence would have been a change of partner, but that was impractical. It was held that the incapacity was therefore incurable.

For a marriage to be voidable, it is not necessary to prove a physical/structural defect so long as it is shown that connection was practically

---

[62] Dr Lushington in *D v A* (1845) 1 Rob Eccl 279. Penetration which is transient does not amount to consummation, see *W (otherwise K) v W* [1967] 3 All ER 178.
[63] See *C v C* [1971] HKLR 56 for refusal of sexual intercourse and divorce.
[64] Ibid.
[65] *W (otherwise K) v W* [1967] 3 All ER 178; *Cackett v Cackett* [1950] P. 233.
[66] *Baxter v Baxter* [1948] AC 274; *Cackett v Cackett* [1950] P. 233.
[67] *W v W* [1970] HKLR 4.
[68] [1963] P. 37.
[69] Cf. *Corbett v Corbett* [1971] P. 83.
[70] *S.Y. v S.Y. (orse. W)* [1962] P. 37.
[71] [1980] HKC 522.

impossible.[72] It was held in *CCCY v CWL* that where a couple had cohabited for a long period and the wife was still a virgin, the onus was on the husband either to disprove the facts or to prove by clear and satisfactory evidence that non-consummation was attributable to causes other than his impotence.[73]

Incapacity is to be distinguished from mere unwillingness to have intercourse as opposed to impediment stemming from some medical condition. In *Singh v Singh*,[74] it was an arranged marriage between two Sikhs, and the wife had not met her husband before the marriage. After the marriage, the wife decided that she did not like the husband and she never lived with him. She petitioned for a decree of nullity and it was held that her reluctance to have sexual intercourse with him was not due to invincible repugnance. She was not suffering from any sexual aversion or psychiatric condition rendering her unable to have sexual intercourse. A decree of nullity was therefore not granted.

Non-Consummation Due to Wilful Refusal of the Respondent[75]

Wilful refusal means 'a settled and definite decision come to without just excuse'.[76] In determining whether there has been such a refusal the judge will have regard to the whole history of the marriage,[77] and this includes refusal to complete whatever religious formalities are needed to effect a marriage. In *Jodla v Jodla*,[78] the parties were Roman Catholics who went through a civil ceremony of marriage. Prior to the marriage, they agreed that they would not have sexual intercourse until after a church ceremony. The wife requested her husband to arrange one, but he refused. It was held that the wife's request was an implied request for intercourse and his refusal to arrange for the religious ceremony was wilful refusal without just excuse. Similarly, in *Kaur v Singh*,[79] the parties were Sikhs and they went through a civil marriage. Prior to the marriage, they agreed that a Sikh religious

---

[72] *CCCY v CWL*; *G v G* (1871) LR 2 P & D 287; *B (otherwise S) v B* [1958] 1 WLR 619.
[73] *CCCY v CWL* [1980] HKC 522.
[74] [1971] 2 WLR 963 ; *G v G* [1924] AC 349.
[75] See Andrew Borkowski, 'Wilful Refusal to Consummate: "Just Excuse"' (1994) Fam Law 684.
[76] *Horton v Horton* [1947] 2 All ER 871 per Lord Jowitt LC at p. 874.
[77] Ibid.
[78] [1960] 1 WLR 236.
[79] [1972] 1 WLR 105.

ceremony in a Sikh temple would be sufficient ceremony to implement the marriage. The husband procrastinated and eventually stated that he had no intention of arranging such a ceremony. It was held that the husband had wilfully refused to consummate the marriage.[80] In Hong Kong, many couples may defer the performance of customary rites and the holding of a Chinese wedding banquet until some time after their marriage. If the parties have agreed, prior to their marriage, that they would not have sexual intercourse until a wedding banquet has been held, it could be argued that refusal to arrange one would be tantamount to wilful refusal.

Wilful refusal implies a conscious act of volition, which is to be distinguished from neglect, failure to act, omission, or loss of sexual interest.[81] In *Potter v Potter*,[82] the wife was physically incapable of consummating the marriage so she underwent an operation to cure the defect. After the operation, an attempt by the husband to consummate the marriage failed. Thereafter, the husband persistently refused to make another attempt whereupon the wife petitioned for a decree of nullity. This was refused, it being held that the husband's refusal resulted from his loss of sexual interest and thus it was impossible to say that he had come to a deliberate decision to refuse to have sexual intercourse with his wife.[83]

In the recent case of *Mok Po-sing v Lie Lie-khim*,[84] the husband was not impotent but he was not able to consummate his marriage after learning that his wife had previously become pregnant by another man and had had an abortion. It was held by the Court of Appeal that the petitioner was not entitled to a decree of nullity upon his own wilful refusal.

It is acceptable for a petition for nullity to contain alternative pleadings. It can, therefore, be pleaded that the respondent is incapable of consummating or that he has wilfully refused to consummate the marriage. However, a petitioner should not plead incapacity on his own part and wilful refusal to consummate on the part of the respondent at the same time. These are mutually inconsistent allegations for, if the petitioner was not capable of consummating the marriage, it could not be said that other party had wilfully refused to do so.[85]

---

[80] See also *A v J (nullity)* (1989) Fam Law 63.
[81] 'Refusal' already refers to a conscious act of volition, does it render 'wilful' redundant?
[82] (1975) 5 Fam Law 161.
[83] See *Ford v Ford* (1987) Fam Law 232 (no conjugal visits in prison, H could not be said to have wilfully refused to consummate. Decree of nullity granted, however, because his conduct showed a determination not to consummate the marriage in the future).
[84] [1996] 3 HKC 330.
[85] *Harthan v Harthan* [1948] 2 All ER 639.

Lack of Valid Consent

The valid consent of the parties is essential to a marriage. Here, the law is concerned with a real, genuine, or voluntary consent which may be vitiated by duress, mistake, unsoundness of mind, or other causes. What is it that a person must validly consent to? Interestingly, the absence of a valid consent does not render a marriage void but only voidable. This implies, therefore, that a person who has not validly consented to a marriage may subsequently ratify the marriage and cure the defect.

Duress

Duress is capable of nullifying what would otherwise be a valid consent. To prove duress, it must be shown that there existed fear of a sufficient degree as to vitiate consent. It is insufficient for a petitioner to show that he entered into the marriage in order to escape from a disagreeable situation, such as penury or social degradation,[86] or loss of face. In a rather bizarre Hong Kong case,[87] the petitioner went to Canada to see his girlfriend with a view to informing her that he could not marry her. When he arrived at her house, he found that she had already organised a marriage ceremony with a registrar. In order to avoid causing a loss of face to the respondent, the petitioner participated in the ceremony. It was held that the petitioner had consented to the marriage.

Duress, whatever form it takes, is coercion of the will such as to vitiate consent.[88] The threat, or the source of the threat, need not necessarily emanate from the respondent or his agents, but may come, for instance from the petitioner's parents.[89]

The test

In *Szechter v Szechter*,[90] Sir Jocelyn Simon P said:

---

[86] See *Szechter v Szechter* [1970] 3 All ER 905 per Sir Jocelyn Simon at p. 915.
[87] *Shu Wing-li v Yeung Siu-ling* Court of Appeal, Civil Appeal Action No 42 of 1994 (1994).
[88] *Hirani v Hirani* [1983] 4 FLR 232.
[89] See *Hirani v Hirani* [1983] 4 FLR 232; *Singh v Singh* [1971] 2 WLR 963; *H (orse. D) v H* [1953] 2 All ER 1229. The petitioner, a Hungarian citizen, married a Frenchman in order to escape from Hungary. Her fear was that she would be sent to a concentration camp when the Russians occupied Hungary.
[90] [1970] 3 All ER 905.

> In order for the impediment of duress to vitiate an otherwise valid marriage, it must, in my judgment, be proved that the will of one of the parties thereto has been overborne by genuine and reasonably held fear caused by a threat of immediate danger, for which the party is not responsible, to life, limb or liberty, so that the constraint destroys the reality of consent to ordinary wedlock.[91]

The test in *Szechter* is an objective one. That is, the fear must be one which was reasonably entertained. However, in *Scott v Sebright*, it was said that:

> whenever from natural weakness of intellect or from fear — whether reasonably entertained or not — either party is actually in a state of mental incompetence to resist pressure improperly brought to bear, there is no more consent than in the case of a person of stronger intellect and more robust courage yielding to a more serious danger.[92]

This suggests that the test for duress is a subjective one and the English Law Reform Commission[93] has taken the view that this should be so. Thus if a party marries out of fear, reasonable or not, consent to marriage cannot be genuine.

Immediate danger to life, limb or liberty

There are some old English cases where it was held that the threat or the force exerted need not put the petitioner in fear for his or her own well-being.[94] However, *Szechter v Szechter* suggests otherwise. In *Szechter v Szechter*,[95] the petitioner was arrested by the Polish security police for 'anti-state activities'. She was detained in appalling conditions and interrogated. Sentenced to three-year imprisonment and in a poor state of health, she believed that she might die in prison, or if released, might be re-arrested. The respondent was a distinguished Polish historian of Jewish origin whose presence in Poland presented an embarrassment to the

---

[91] Ibid., at p. 915.
[92] (1886) 12 PD 21, at p. 24.
[93] English Law Commission Report on Nullity of Marriage, No 33, HMSO, London, 1970, para 62(b).
[94] E.g. *Hartford v Morris* (1776) 2 Hag Con 423 where the defendant man threatened to kill himself unless the plaintiff married him; *Cooper v Crane* [1891] P. 369 where the respondent threatened to kill himself if the petitioner did not marry him, decree granted; *Scott v Sebright* (1886) 12 PD 21 where a woman married under the threat of being made bankrupt, being accused in every drawing-room in London of having been seduced by the respondent.
[95] [1970] 3 All ER 905.

authorities. In order to effect the petitioner's release and emigration to England, the respondent divorced his wife and married the petitioner in prison. The petitioner sought a decree of nullity. Was this a case where the petitioner's will was overborne by fear for her own life? Or was it a case where the petitioner married with the ulterior motive of being enabled to emigrate to another country? The court held that the marriage was not entered into freely and there was thus no true consent.

In *Szechter*, the fear was caused by a threat of immediate danger to life, limb or liberty. But in *Singh v Singh*,[96] the Court of Appeal refused to grant, a decree of nullity where a Sikh woman contracted a marriage out of respect for her parents. It was held that there was no duress. However, in *Hirani v Hirani*,[97] the petitioner, a 19-year-old Indian Hindu living with her parents, formed an association with an Indian Muslim. Her parents disapproved of the association and they arranged for her to marry the respondent who was a Hindu. The petitioner was wholly dependent on her parents and they threatened to turn her out of the home if she refused to marry as arranged. The trial judge held that as there had been no threat to the petitioner's life, limb or liberty, there was no duress. However, in the Court of Appeal it was held that duress, whatever form it took, was coercion of the will so as to vitiate consent. As the petitioner had no means of supporting herself, she was forced to comply with her parents' wishes. The threats or pressure were such as to overbear the will of the individual and destroy the reality of the consent.[98]

Respondent not responsible for the threat or circumstances giving rise to the threat

The threat of immediate danger must arise from circumstances for which the petitioner is not responsible. In *Buckland v Buckland*,[99] the petitioner, whilst stationed in Malta, was falsely accused by the respondent's father of having had unlawful sexual intercourse with his daughter. His solicitor advised him that he was likely to be convicted and sentenced to imprisonment and that there was only one choice; marry the girl or go to prison. The petitioner chose marriage. It was held that the petitioner's fear was brought about by an unjust charge preferred against him by the

---

[96] [1971] 2 WLR 963.
[97] [1983] 4 FLR 232.
[98] *Parojcic v Parojcic* [1959] 1 All ER 1. Petitioner was threatened by her father that if she did not marry the defendant, she would be sent back to Yugoslavia where she had suffered considerable hardship. She was found to have been terrorised into obedience, decree granted.
[99] [1968] P. 296.

respondent's father. This was aggravated by the legal advice he received. His fear of incarceration vitiated his consent to marriage and he was entitled to a nullity decree.[100]

Where the petitioner has actually done something to elicit the threats (unlike in *Buckland*, who was in no way culpable), it could be argued that there is some justification for the threat. If this is so, the marriage cannot be annulled on the ground of duress. Thus, in *Griffiths v Griffiths*,[101] Haugh J said that 'but if the fear is justly imposed, the resulting marriage, when contracted, is valid and binding.' Here there are two relevant issues: (i) a value judgment as to whether the respondent should be responsible for what he did, and (ii) whether he validly consented to the marriage. Bromley[102] took the view that a threat justly imposed did not necessarily mean that consent was not given under duress. For instance, a father might threaten to shoot the man who was responsible for his daughter's pregnancy. Bromley believed that the test should not be whether the respondent was responsible for the threat or the circumstances giving rise to the threat, rather it should be whether 'it is reasonable to face him with the choice between marriage and the implementation of the threat.'[103] Thus, it is unlikely that the court would hold that it is a legitimate threat, and therefore not capable of vitiating consent, if an employer were to intimate to his office boy who had robbed the till that unless he married the employer's mistress, he would inform the police of his crime.[104]

Marriage of convenience/sham marriage

In the absence of fear or coercion, a marriage is not voidable simply because the parties entered into the marriage with no intention of living together, or for convenience.[105] Marriage for an ulterior motive, e.g. to circumvent immigration requirements, is not sufficient for a decree of nullity. In *Silver v Silver*,[106] a German woman (the petitioner) lived outside the UK with E, an Englishman, as his wife. She later discovered that E was already married. Six years later, E returned to England. In order to be able to live in England with E, the petitioner married E's brother, but they never lived together.

---

[100] *H (orse. D) v H* [1953] 2 All ER 1229.
[101] (1944) IR 35.
[102] Bromley, p. 91; see n. 1.
[103] Ibid., p. 92; see also Terence Ingman and Bruce Grant, 'Duress in the Law of Nullity', 14 Fam Law 92.
[104] See n. 93, para 65.
[105] *Morgan v Morgan* [1959] 1 All ER 539.
[106] [1955] 2 All ER 614.

After the marriage, the petitioner and E lived together for 23 years. E died and the petitioner wished to remarry so she petitioned for a decree of nullity. It was held that there had been no duress, and her ulterior motive in marrying the brother was insufficient for a decree of nullity.[107]

> Where a man and woman consent to marry one another in a formal ceremony conducted in accordance with the formalities required by law, knowing that it is a marriage ceremony, it is immaterial that they do not intend to live together as man and wife...[108]

The law recognises no room for mental reservations or private arrangements regarding the parties' personal relationships. Once it is established that they were free to marry one another, consented to the marriage, and observed the necessary formalities, the marriage cannot be challenged.[109]

Mistake

Not all mistakes are capable of nullifying consent; only mistakes sufficiently fundamental will have this effect. Mistake can be as to the identity of the other party.[110] If the mistake results in the petitioner failing to marry the intended partner, it is a ground for nullifying the marriage. However, mistake as to a person's wealth, family fortune, character or personality will not render a marriage voidable, the maxim *caveat emptor* applying.[111] In the New Zealand case of *C v C*,[112] W married H in the mistaken belief that he was a famous boxer called Miller. It was held that the marriage was not invalidated by the mistake as W had married the very man she meant to marry, that is, H. The fact that she was induced by H's fraudulent misrepresentation that he was Miller or as to his family fortune, age, and habits of life would not nullify consent to marriage.

Fraud itself does not invalidate a marriage.[113] However, if the fraud

---

[107] *Puttick v AG* [1980] Fam 1.
[108] *Vervaeke v Smith* [1982] 2 All ER 144, at p. 148 Lord Hailsham, quoting Ormrod J in *Messina v Smith* [1971] P. 322; marriage to obtain British Nationality and avoid deportation.
[109] *Vervaeke v Smith* [1982] 2 All ER 144, at p. 149 Lord Hailsham.
[110] *Militante v Ogunwomoju* (1994) Fam Law 17.
[111] *Moss v Moss* [1897] P. 263.
[112] [1942] NZLR 356.
[113] 'The strongest case you could establish of the most deliberate plot, leading to a marriage the most unseemly in all disproportions of rank, of fortune, of habits of life, and even of age itself, would not enable this court to release [a suitor] from chains which, though forged by others, he had riveted on himself. If he is capable of consent, and has consented, the law does not ask how the consent has been induced.' Quoted in *Moss v Moss* [1897] P. 263 at p. 270.

procures the appearance of consent without the reality, the marriage may be annulled not because of the fraud but because of the lack of consent.[114] Thus, if A proposes to marry B by correspondence, never having seen B before the marriage (or having last seen B many years previously), and C successfully impersonates B, this would be a case where there is no true consent.[115]

Mistake may be as to the nature of the ceremony, e.g. an engagement ceremony as opposed to a marriage ceremony. If one party does not understand the nature of the ceremony or what was going on, no valid marriage can be contracted. In *Mehta v Mehta*,[116] an English woman agreed to become a Hindu so that she could marry a Hindu, X. In what she thought to be a conversion ceremony she was married to X. It was held that a decree of nullity would be granted to the wife as she did not intend to marry X at that ceremony.

Mistake as to the nature of the marriage has to be distinguished from mistake as to the legal consequences following the ceremony. In *Way v Way*,[117] a petition failed where the husband mistakenly thought that marriage would enable his Russian wife to leave the USSR and live with him. In *Messina v Smith*,[118] a wife (knowingly) went through a marriage ceremony so as to obtain British nationality and avoid deportation. A petition to annul the marriage failed as both parties intended to acquire the status of married persons and it was immaterial that one party was mistaken as to the incidence of that status.

Unsoundness of mind or otherwise

Unsoundness of mind is another factor capable of vitiating consent.[119] A person is presumed to be of sound mind unless proven otherwise. Soundness of mind means the possession of sufficient mental capacity to understand the nature of the marriage ceremony. This is a question of degree which has to be determined according to the facts of each case. What degree of soundness of mind is required? It is insufficient to show that the person is merely aware of what is going on, or that he comprehends the promises exchanged.[120] He needs to understand the nature of the marriage ceremony. This, then, raises the question of what is required to be understood. *Re*

---

[114] *Moss v Moss* [1897] P. 263.
[115] See *C v C* [1942] NZLR 356.
[116] [1945] 2 All ER 690.
[117] [1950] p. 71.
[118] [1971] P. 322.
[119] See r107 MCR.
[120] *Durham v Durham* (1885) 10 PD 80.

Park Estate,[121] a wealthy, 78-year-old widower, who was senile, made a will. He subsequently married the plaintiff. Four days after the marriage, he purported to execute a new will, leaving property to his wife. He died 18 days later. It was argued that the second will and the marriage were void on the ground that the deceased lacked the required mental capacity. It was held by the Court of Appeal that the deceased was of unsound mind at the time when he purported to execute the second will and it was declared invalid. It was held, however, that, notwithstanding his mental state, the deceased did understand the nature of the marriage contract which was a simple one and not requiring a high degree of intelligence. The test adopted by the court was stated thus:

> In order to ascertain the nature of the contract of marriage, a man must be mentally capable of appreciating that it involves the responsibility normally attaching to marriage.[122]

The court went on to describe this responsibility: the commitment between a man and a woman to live together, and to love each other as husband and wife to the exclusion of all others.[123]

Either Party Suffers From Mental Disorder Rendering That Party Unfit for Marriage

This ground for avoiding a marriage has to be distinguished from s20(2)(c) of the MCO which deals with either party to the marriage not having validly consented to the marriage. S20(2)(d) is concerned with the situation where at the time of the marriage, either party was capable of giving a valid consent but was suffering from a mental disorder (whether continuous or intermittent) of such a kind or to such an extent as to render him unfit for marriage.[124]

Mental disorder means 'mental illness, arrested or incomplete development of mind, psychopathic disorder or any disorder or disability of mind.'[125] But the mental illness must be of such a kind or to such an extent as to make a party unfit for marriage. 'Unfit for marriage' means being

---

[121] [1954] P. 112.
[122] Ibid., at p. 127.
[123] Ibid., at p. 123.
[124] See r107 MCR.
[125] S2 of the Mental Health Ordinance: '"Psychopathic disorder" means a persistent disorder or disability of mind (whether or not including significant impairment of intelligence) which results in abnormally aggressive or seriously irresponsible conduct on the part of the person concerned.'

incapable of living in a married state, and of carrying out the ordinary duties and obligations of marriage.[126] Thus, in *Bennett v Bennett*,[127] it was held that a wife who suffered from a hysterical neurosis and behaved strangely, having a tendency to overactivity, occasionally acting in a violent yet harmless manner by way of throwing ashtrays about, was not unfit for marriage.

S20(d) of the MCO permits either party to a marriage to petition for a decree of nullity so a mentally ill person can rely on his own mental disorder as long as it existed at the time of the marriage.

At the Time of the Marriage the Respondent Was Suffering from Venereal Disease in a Communicable Form

As has been seen, although a person is capable of giving a valid consent, a marriage will be voidable if one of the parties suffers from a mental disorder rendering him unfit for marriage. In terms of physical condition, old age *per se* is not a problem unless it negates a person's capacity to give a valid consent. However, if a respondent suffers from venereal disease in a communicable form at the time of the marriage, this will constitute a ground for avoiding the marriage. At one time the Venereal Diseases Ordinance (now repealed) defined venereal diseases as, *inter alia,* gonorrhoea and syphilis. Gonorrhoea was undoubtedly unpleasant and in serious cases could render a woman infertile, while syphilis could be fatal. Nowadays, effective treatments for these diseases mean that they no longer carry such serious long-term risks for the sexual partner of the sufferer. However, certain sexually transmitted diseases for instance, AIDS and hepatitis B, may carry fatal consequences. If a person marries knowing that he has AIDS and conceals it from his partner, should the marriage be voidable at the instance of the 'victim'? More interestingly, could a partner who tests HIV positive but does not yet have the full-blown AIDS be said to be suffering from 'venereal disease'?

At the Time of the Marriage, the Respondent Was Pregnant by Someone Other Than the Petitioner

A marriage is voidable if, at the time of the marriage, the female party was pregnant by someone other than the petitioner. The basis for this ground for avoiding a marriage appears to be:

---

[126] *Bennett v Bennett* [1969] 1 All ER 539.
[127] [1969] 1 All ER 539.

(i) a man marries a woman believing that she is carrying his child but had he known that he was not the father, he would not have married her; this is a case of mistaken paternity and deception may be involved;
(ii) a man marries a woman believing that she was chaste but it transpires that he was mistaken. Again, deception may be involved.

It is questionable whether mistake, deception or otherwise, as to a woman's attributes is a ground for avoiding a marriage. Where duress is pleaded, e.g. a man believes that he is responsible for the woman's pregnancy and her father threatens to shoot him unless he marries her, the case can be considered under the heading of duress.

If it is thought that bringing a child, who is not the child of the parties to the marriage, into the marriage strikes at its heart, such a ground for avoiding the marriage should be available to both the wife as well as to the husband. This means that a wife should be able to petition for a decree of nullity on the ground that at the time of the marriage, the respondent has impregnated another woman.

BARS TO NULLITY

Where a marriage is void, no defence is available. Where a marriage is voidable, there are three defences, the first of which is a general equitable defence. S20(3) of the MCO provides that the court shall not grant a decree of nullity if the respondent satisfies the court that:

> (a) the petitioner, with the knowledge that it was open to him to have the marriage avoided, so conducted himself in relation to the respondent as to lead the respondent to believe that he would not seek to do so; and
> (b) that it would be unjust to the respondent to grant the decree.

This derives from the equitable doctrine of approbation, i.e. approving and sanctioning the marriage. Thus, where a petitioner, knowing the remedy open to him, so conducted himself in relation to the respondent as to lead the respondent to reasonably believe that he would not seek to annul the marriage, he will be considered to have approved the marriage with all its defects. Consequently, equity will not allow him to argue that no marriage exists between the parties. In *Scott v Scott*,[128] the wife, prior to the marriage,

---
[128] [1959] 1 All ER 531.

expressed her distaste for sexual intercourse and the husband agreed not to have sexual intercourse against her wishes. For four years the parties were happily married without having sexual intercourse. However, when the husband became friendly with another woman, he petitioned for nullity. It was held that the decree would be refused because he had accepted the marriage despite the absence of sexual intercourse.[129]

The defence is an absolute bar. It replaces the old common law rule on approbation, ratification or lack of sincerity.[130] Apart from requiring the petitioner to sanction the marriage with its defects, s20(3)(b) of the MCO requires also that the court be satisfied that it would be unjust to grant a decree. This is the most difficult aspect of the defence. Thus, in *D v D*,[131] the wife refused to undergo an operation which would cure a physical impediment to intercourse as a consequence of which the marriage was never consummated. The husband, who knew of his remedy in nullity, agreed to adopt two children. It was held that in agreeing to adopt, the husband led the wife into believing that he would not seek to avoid the marriage. However, it would not be unjust to grant a decree of nullity because the wife would have the same rights to apply for custody and financial relief as she would have had on a decree of divorce. The defence of approbation thus appears to be of little value today.

S20(4) of the MCO provides that nullity proceedings must be instituted within three years of the date of the marriage where a marriage is voidable on grounds other than incapacity to consummate or wilful refusal to consummate. Additionally, s20(5) of the MCO provides that a decree of nullity on the grounds of venereal disease or pregnancy by another man at the time of the marriage is not to be granted unless the petitioner was ignorant of the facts at the time of the marriage.

REFORMING NULLITY

One major issue that needs consideration is whether the law should continue to distinguish between void and voidable marriages. A void marriage is void *ab initio*, whereas a voidable marriage is treated as valid until it is annulled, and the annulment is effective from the date of the decree. Is

---

[129] It is not necessary to prove all the elements of estoppel. In this case, the husband's conduct (i.e. accepting the marriage despite the absence of sexual intercourse) would only have the effect of making the wife not want to change her position.
[130] S20(6); *W v W* [1970] HKLR 4.
[131] [1979] 3 WLR 185.

there, however, any valid reason why some, if not all, of the grounds for a voidable marriage should not be assimilated into divorce? This has been the approach taken in Australia and New Zealand,[132] where the law makes no distinction between void and voidable marriage.

Some twenty years ago, the English Law Reform Commission[133] examined this area of the law and concluded that the distinction should continue. The Commission argued that:

> (a) It is not true to say that the difference between a nullity decree of a voidable marriage and a decree of divorce is a mere matter of form. It may be that the consequences of the two decrees are substantially similar, but the concepts giving rise to the two decrees are quite different: the decree of nullity recognises the existence of an impediment which prevents the marriage from initially becoming effective, while the decree of divorce records that some cause for terminating the marriage has arisen since the marriage. This distinction may be of little weight to the lawyer, but is a matter of essence in the jurisprudence of the Christian Church.[134]

Apart from the religious argument, the grounds for a voidable marriage, incapacity to consummate, whether because of the respondent's inability or wilful refusal, arguably strike at the heart of a marriage. It is just and reasonable that the law should provide a remedy to an aggrieved party. However, such remedy can already be found in divorce given that consensual divorce is obtainable after one-year separation or filing of notice, or alternatively, divorce is available after two year separation.[135] But a more serious challenge to maintaining the notion of voidability is why should the law single out sexual inadequacies as a factor for bringing a marriage to an end? Should it not also recognise other serious personal inadequacies, such as drug addiction, alcoholism, gambling and so on?

Consent is arguably at the centre of what is generally regarded as crucial to a valid marriage and a strong case could be made that lack of consent should be a ground for rendering a marriage void, as opposed to be voidable only. The English Law Reform Commission took the view that as consent or the lack of it may be disputed, it would be preferable for it to remain a ground for rendering a marriage voidable.[136]

---

[132] Family Proceedings Act 1980.
[133] See n. 93.
[134] Ibid., para 24.
[135] See Chapter 4.
[136] See n. 134, paras 11–13.

Mental disorder can easily be incorporated into divorce. Nullity on the grounds that the respondent was suffering from venereal diseases is arguably not needed while a person who suffers from AIDS or other medical condition should be able to contract a valid marriage just as any other person. Nullity on the grounds that the woman was pregnant by a man other than her prospective husband is discriminatory and should be abolished.

There are no judicial statistics on how often nullity is used. In the recent but rare case of *Mok Po-sing v Lie Lie-khim*,[137] the Court of Appeal took the view that a husband who was not impotent but who wilfully refused to consummate the marriage, should find his way out of the marriage by divorce rather than by means of a declaration of nullity.

JUDICIAL SEPARATION

As has been seen in Chapter 4, divorce brings a marriage to an end. However, not all marriages which have irretrievably broken down result in divorce. Judicial separation and separation orders[138] terminate a spouse's obligation to live together.

In England, judicial separation replaced divorce *a mensa et thoro* (meaning from bed and board) which prior to 1875 was granted by the Ecclesiastical courts. In the days when divorce required proof of matrimonial offences, judicial separation was often used by wives who wanted to obtain financial provision from their recalcitrant husbands whilst denying them the right to remarry. After the Divorce Reform Act 1969, judicial separation was widely used as a short-term substitute for divorce because the three-year discretionary bar did not apply to judicial separation. However, it was not possible to deny a party a decree of divorce as five years separation would suffice as evidence of irretrievable breakdown of marriage, entitling even a recalcitrant husband divorce without the wife's consent.

Today, the Matrimonial Causes Ordinance provides for a one-year discretionary bar to divorce but it does not apply to judicial separation. In theory, a spouse can apply for judicial separation after the wedding. Such short-term remedy may be of little importance in view of the fact that consensual divorce is available after one-year separation or filing of notice, or alternatively, after two-year separation without the other spouse's consent. Judicial separation, however, remains an alternative to those with religious objections to divorce.

---

[137] [1996] 3 HKC 330.
[138] See Chapter 14.

Jurisdiction of the Court

S5 of the MCO provides that the court has jurisdiction in proceedings for judicial separation if:
(a) either of the parties to the marriage was domiciled in Hong Kong at the date of the petition;
(b) both parties to the marriage were resident in Hong Kong at the date of the petition;
(c) either of the parties to the marriage had a substantial connection with Hong Kong at the date of the petition.

Grounds for Judicial Separation

A petition for judicial separation may be presented at any time by either party to the marriage on the grounds stipulated in s11A(2) of the MCO.[139] They are one of the five facts required for petitioning a divorce.[140] However, a petition for judicial separation does not have to show that the marriage has irretrievably broken down.

Unlike a decree of divorce, a decree of judicial separation is granted in the form of a single decree (i.e. decree absolute). On hearing a petition for judicial separation, the court, if it is satisfied of any such fact mentioned in s11A(2) of the MCO, shall grant a decree. As in the case of divorce, a decree of judicial separation is only granted if the court is satisfied with the proposed arrangements regarding children,[141] and provisions which encourage reconciliation in s15A of the MCO also apply.[142] But unlike divorce, a respondent cannot defend the proceedings on the basis that a decree would result in grave financial or other hardship.[143] Unlike divorce, a decree for judicial separation cannot be rescinded on the basis that the petitioner has misled the respondent into giving his consent;[144] nor can the respondent delay the decree by applying to the court for it to consider his/her financial position.[145]

---

[139] S24 MCO.
[140] See Chapter 4.
[141] S18 Matrimonial Proceedings and Property Ordinance; s24(1A) MCO.
[142] See above.
[143] See s15B MCO.
[144] S15C(1) MCO.
[145] S17A MCO.

Effect of a Decree of Judicial Separation

A decree of judicial separation brings to an end the parties' obligation to cohabit with one another.[146] This means that if one spouse deserts the other prior to the decree, the decree will bring desertion to an end. Whilst the decree is in force, and the party continues to live separate and apart, the property of a party who dies intestate shall devolve as if the other party to the marriage had been dead.[147] In contrast with divorce, the operation of a will is not effected by a decree of judicial separation. On granting a decree of judicial separation, the court has the power to make financial provision and property adjustment, as well as custody orders, under the Matrimonial Proceedings and Property Ordinance.[148]

Rescission of a Decree of Judicial Separation

S24(3) of the MCO provides that the court may, on an application by a spouse against whom a decree has been made, rescind the decree on the ground that it was obtained in the absence of the applicant. Prior to the Matrimonial Causes (Amendment) Ordinance,[149] it was also possible for the court to rescind a decree, if it was obtained on the ground of desertion, if there was reasonable cause for the alleged desertion. However, this was removed by s14 of the Matrimonial Causes (Amendment) Ordinance. This was probably an oversight; the Matrimonial Causes (Amendment) Bill had intended to remove desertion as a ground for divorce. But when desertion was retained for divorce, the reference to desertion was not reintroduced.

Divorce after Judicial Separation

Judicial separation may be seen by some as a halfway house between marriage and its termination by divorce. It has all the advantages in terms of powers of the court to make financial provision and property adjustment, as well as custody orders. It is less drastic than divorce itself. Divorce after judicial separation may be presented by a spouse who petitioned for judicial separation, and the court may treat the decree of judicial separation as sufficient proof of the fact required for divorce.

---

[146] S24(2) MCO.
[147] S4A(1) Intestates' Estates Ordinance and s32(2) MCO; compare a separation order, see below, pp. 352–8.
[148] Including Maintenance Pending Suit under s3 MPPO.
[149] No 29 of 1995.

Annex I

Today, the law* provides that a marriage between a woman and any of the following persons in the left hand column below, and a marriage between a man and any of the following persons in the right hand column below, is void:

Prohibited degrees of consanguinity

mother	father
adoptive mother or former adoptive mother	adoptive father or former adoptive father
daughter	son
adoptive daughter or former adoptive daughter	adoptive son or former adoptive son
father's mother	father's father
mother's mother	mother's father
son's daughter	son's son
daughter's daughter	daughter's son
sister	brother
father's sister	father's brother
mother's sister	mother's brother
brother's daughter	brother's son
sister's daughter	sister's son

Prohibited degrees of affinity

A marriage between a man and any of the following persons in the left hand column below, and a marriage between a woman and any of the following persons in the right hand column below, is void except where both parties to the marriage have attained the age of 21 and the younger party has not at any time before attaining the age of 18 been a child of the family in relation to the other party.

daughter of former wife	son of former husband
former wife of father	former husband of mother
former wife of father's father	former husband of father's mother
former wife of mother's father	former husband of mother's mother

---

* These are laid down in the Marriage Act 1949, first schedule as amended by the Marriage (Enabling) Act 1960, The Children Act 1975 and the Marriage (Prohibited Degrees of Relationship) Act 1986.

daughter of son of former wife	son of son of former husband
daughter of daughter of former wife	son of daughter of former husband

A marriage between a man and any of the following persons in the left hand column below, and a marriage between a woman and any of the following persons in the right hand column below, is void except if both parties have attained the age of 21 and

(a) in the case of a marriage between a man and the mother of a former wife of his, after the death of both the former wife and the father of the former wife;

(b) in the case of a marriage between a man and the former wife of his son, after the death of both his son, and the mother of his son;

(c) in the case of a marriage between a woman and the father of a former husband of hers, after the death of both the former husband and mother of the former husband;

(d) in the case of a marriage between a woman and a former husband of her daughter, after the death of both her daughter and the father of her daughter.

mother of former wife	father of former husband
former wife of son	fomer husband of daughter

PART II
Children

6

Status

INTRODUCTION

> Status means the condition of belonging to a class in society to which the law ascribes peculiar rights and duties, capacities and incapacities. Such, for example, are the status of married person or of minority. Legitimacy is a status: it is the condition of belonging to a class in society the members of which are regarded as having been begotten in lawful matrimony by the men whom the law regards as their fathers.[1]

Many legal systems distinguish the position of a child born in, and born out of, a legally recognised union. Children born out of wedlock (sometimes called illegitimate children) are commonly accorded an inferior status and have fewer rights than those born in wedlock (sometimes called legitimate children). However, there is nothing 'illegitimate' about being a child. Consequently, less derogatory labels have come into use, e.g. 'ex-nuptial child', 'non-marital child' or 'a child born out of wedlock', and some legislation have avoided labelling the child altogether by referring to the marriage status, or the lack thereof, of the parents rather than to the status of the child.[2]

Labelling apart, the trend nowadays is to accord all children equal

---

[1] *The Ampthill Peerage Case* [1977] AC 547, at p. 577 per Lord Simon.
[2] For instance, s1(1) of the English Family Law Reform Act 1987 refers to a person whose father and mother were married (or not married) to each other at the time of his birth.

rights and protection. Thus, Article 20 of the Hong Kong Bill of Rights Ordinance 1991 provides that:

> Every child shall have, without discrimination as to ... birth, the right to such measures of protection as are required by his status as a minor, on the part of his family, society and the State.

Article 22 of the same provides that:

> All persons are equal before the law and are entitled without discrimination to the equal protection of the law. In this respect, the law should prohibit any discrimination and guarantee to all persons equal and effective protection against discrimination on any ground such as race, colour ... birth or other status.[3]

Similarly, Article 2 of the UN Convention on the Rights of the Child provides that:

> (1) States parties shall respect and ensure the rights set forth in the present Convention to each child within their jurisdiction without discrimination of any kind, irrespective of the child's ... birth or other status.

Some jurisdictions indeed have abolished the distinctions between legitimacy and illegitmacy,[4] and others have reduced the disabilities associated with being illegitimate.[5] In Hong Kong, the Law Reform Commission recommended removing most of the legal disabilities attached to illegitimacy[6] and their proposals were implemented through the Parent and Child Ordinance enacted in 1993. Consequently, the status of legitimacy or illegitimacy, though still relevant, is of lesser importance today.

---

[3] For decisions on legal discrimination against children born out of wedlock in the context of the European Convention on Fundamental Rights and Freedoms, see *Marckx v Kingdom of Belgium* [1979–1980] 2 EHRR 330; *Inze v Republic of Austria* (1987) 10 EHRR 394.
[4] The Marriage Law 1980 (the People's Republic of China); the Status of Children Act 1969 (New Zealand).
[5] The English Family Law Reform Act 1987.
[6] Hong Kong Law Reform Commission, Report on Illegitimacy, (Topic 28), October 1991. Hong Kong Law Reform Commission, Consultation Paper on Illegitimacy, July 1990 (hereafter cited as LRCR).

LEGITIMACY AND ILLEGITIMACY AT COMMON LAW

At common law, a child was a legitimate child if his parents were married at the time of his conception or at the time of his birth. Therefore, a child conceived within his parents' marriage, even though born after his father's death or the parents' divorce, would be legitimate. A child conceived before his parents' marriage, but born after they had married, would also be a legitimate child.[7] An illegitimate child, however, was deemed to be *filius nullius* (nobody's child) and as such he or she had no ancestral or kinship relations.

The common law concept of legitimacy applies to children born to marriages contracted under the Marriage Ordinance as well as to other marriages. Thus, s14 of the Legitimacy Ordinance states that, for the avoidance of doubt, any person who is a child of:

(a) a modern marriage validated by the Marriage Reform Ordinance
(b) a customary marriage declared to be valid by the Marriage Reform Ordinance
(c) a union of concubinage[8] or
(d) a *kim tiu*[9] marriage

shall be a legitimate child of the marriage or union and shall be deemed always to have been so legitimate for all purposes.

STATUTORY MODIFICATIONS

Given the harshness of the common law rules, it is perhaps not surprising that statutes have mitigated their effect.

---

[7] What if a child is conceived by pre-marital intercourse and his parents then marry, but the father dies before the child's birth? 'A bastard, by our English law, is one that is not only begotten, but born, out of lawful matrimony.' Sir William Blackstone, *Commentary on the Laws of England*, Vol. 1, 1765, p. 434.

[8] A union of concubinage is defined by s14(2) of the Legitimacy Ordinance as one 'entered by a male partner and a female partner before 7 October 1971, under which union the female partner has, during the lifetime of the male partner, been accepted by his wife as his concubine and recognized as such by his family generally.' S14(3) of the Legitimacy Ordinance now provides added protection to a child by creating a presumption of acceptance by the wife of a concubine and recognition as such by the male partner's family.

[9] See Chapter 1.

Children of Void Marriage

At common law, a void marriage meant that there had never been a marriage.[10] Children born to such a marriage were thus illegitimate. S11(1) of the Legitimacy Ordinance[11] now provides that a child of a void marriage, whenever born,[12] shall be treated as a legitimate child, if at the time of the conception of the child (or at the time of the celebration of the marriage if later) both or either of the parties reasonably believed that the marriage was valid.[13]

> Example 1, H and W married and A was born to W. H reasonably believed that W was 16 at the time of the marriage, but it turned out that she was only 15. The marriage would be void but A would be treated as a legitimate child.

> Example 2, H, in the reasonable belief that his former wife (W1) had died, married W2. Unbeknown to him, W1 was still alive at the date of H and W2's marriage. Their marriage would be void but any children born to the union would be treated as legitimate.

S11(1) of the Legitimacy Ordinance applies if the father is domiciled in Hong Kong or has substantial connection with Hong Kong at the time of the child's birth, or, if he died before that time, had been so domiciled or had had such connection immediately prior to his death.

Today, one of the parties to the void marriage shall be presumed to have reasonably believed the marriage was valid, unless the contrary is shown.[14] Furthermore, the belief that the marriage was valid could be due to mistake of the law.[15] These provisions strengthen the protection afforded to a child, which is further fortified by the burden of proof being placed on the person claiming that a party to a marriage did not reasonably believe that the marriage was valid. Nonetheless, the legal status of a child depends on the reasonable belief of one of its parents so a child will be illegitimate if both of his parents are shown not to have reasonably believed that the

---

[10] S11(3) Legitimacy Ordinance states that a 'void marriage' means a marriage, not being voidable only, in respect of which the court has or had jurisdiction to grant a decree of nullity, or would have or would have had such jurisdiction if the parties were domiciled in or had a substantial connection with Hong Kong.
[11] Cap 184, LHK 1984 ed.
[12] Whether before or after the commencement of the Ordinance.
[13] See *F v AG* (1980) Fam Law 60.
[14] S11(5) of the Legitimacy Ordinance.
[15] S11(4) of the Legitimacy Ordinance.

marriage was valid. Thus, in *Hawkins v AG*,[16] the husband left the matrimonial home and told the wife that he would divorce her. After the wife received the divorce petition, she told her prospective second husband about her situation and he told her that they could get married even though the divorce had not been finalised. Relying on this, the wife, without enquiring whether the decree absolute had been granted, went through a form of marriage ceremony with her 'second husband'. The petitioner was a child of this 'second marriage' and she sought a declaration of legitimacy on the ground that either her father or mother reasonably believed that the marriage was valid. It was held that the test was an objective one, and reasonable grounds for the belief must be shown. In the circumstances, there were no reasonable grounds for either of her parents to believe that the mother was free to remarry. A declaration of legitimacy was refused.

S11 of the Legitimacy Ordinance applies only to a 'child of a void marriage' but not to a child born before the parents' void marriage. Thus, if the children were born to an unmarried couple who subsequently contracted a void marriage, this section would not apply.[17]

Children of Voidable Marriage

At common law, a decree of nullity had retrospective effect and this meant that a decree of nullity rendered the marriage void *ab initio* thereby making children born to such a marriage illegitimate. The harshness of this rule has now been mitigated by s12 of the Legitimacy Ordinance which provides that where a decree of nullity is granted in respect of a voidable marriage, any child who would have been a legitimate child to the parties of the marriage if it had been dissolved, will be deemed to be legitimate notwithstanding the annulment.

Legitimation by Subsequent Marriage of Parents

Legitimation is a process whereby a person who is born illegitimate is subsequently made legitimate upon the marriage of his or her parents.[18] For instance:

---

[16] [1966] 1 All ER 392; *Sheward v AG* [1964] 2 All ER 324.
[17] *Re Spence* [1990] 1 Ch. 652; but if the marriage was valid, the children would be legitimated by the parents' subsequent marriage. Unlike legitimation by the parents' subsequent marriage, when s11 of the Legitimacy Ordinance applies, a child is treated as having been legitimate as from birth.
[18] S2 of the Legitimacy Ordinance defines marriage as one contracted in accordance with

F and M have a child (A) and, following A's birth, they marry each other. Although A was born an illegitimate child, the marriage of F and M renders A a legitimated person.

S3(1) of the Legitimacy Ordinance applies if the father at the date of the marriage was domiciled in Hong Kong or has a substantial connection with Hong Kong.

The date of legitimation is the date of the marriage or the date of the commencement of the Legitimacy Ordinance (i.e. 7 October 1971) whichever happened last. In other words, a person cannot be considered legitimate prior to 7 October 1971 even though the marriage took place prior to it.[19]

For example, if A was born in 1969, and his parents married in 1970, his date of legitimation would be 7 October 1971 when s11 came into force. If A was born in 1990, and his parents were married in 1992, his date of legitimation would be the date of his parents' marriage.

Whether the parties to a marriage are the parents of the child must be decided on the balance of probabilities.[20] Where a person is legitimated by the parents' subsequent marriage, the Registrar of Births and Deaths may, on production of such evidence as appears to him to be satisfactory, authorise at any time the re-registration of the birth of a legitimated person.[21]

Effect of legitimation

The right of a legitimated person, his spouse, children or remoter issue to take property is provided for in ss4–9 of the Legitimacy Ordinance.

Rights of a legitimated person to take interests in property

According to s4(1) of the Legitimacy Ordinance, a legitimated person, his spouse, children and remoter issue are entitled to take any interest in the estate of a person dying intestate after the date of legitimation, or under

---

the Marriage Ordinance, modern marriage validated by the Marriage Reform Ordinance, customary marriage declared to be valid by the Marriage Reform Ordinance, and foreign marriages celebrated in accordance with the law in force at the time and in the place where the marriage was performed.

[19] *Re Hepworth* [1936] 1 Ch. 750.
[20] See Chapter 7; see also *James v McLennan* 1971 SLT 162; see also *Gardner v Gardner* (1877) 4 R (HL) 56.
[21] See Schedule 1 of the Legitimacy Ordinance.

any disposition coming into operation after the date of legitimation, as if he had been born legitimate.[22] The right to take any interest under any disposition, however, is subject to contrary intention expressed in the disposition.[23]

Succession on intestacy of legitimated persons

Where a legitimated person or a child or remoter issue of a legitimated person dies intestate in respect of all or any of his property, those who would have been entitled to take by way of succession if the legitimated person had been born legitimate shall be so entitled.[24]

Entitlement where an illegitimate person dies before legitimation

Where an illegitimate person dies before the marriage of his parents, leaving any spouse, children or remoter issue living at the date of such marriage, then if the person would, if living at the time of his parents' marriage, have become legitimated, s4 applies. The date of legitimation shall be that of the parents' date of marriage.[25]

Adopted Children

Apart from the situations of a void and voidable marriage, and legitimation by subsequent marriage of parents, where an illegitimate child has been adopted, the effect of an adoption order is to render such a child the legitimate child of the adopters. The adopted infant stands to the adopter in the same position as 'a child born to the adopter in lawful wedlock'.[26]

Fatal Accidents and Pension Claims

An illegitimate child can claim under the Fatal Accidents Ordinance. Additionally, a number of Ordinances governing civil service and judicial pensions have now been amended to cover an illegitimate child, for instance the Surviving Spouses' and Children's Pensions Ordinance, the Pension

---

[22] S4(1).
[23] S4(4).
[24] S5.
[25] S6 of the Legitimacy Ordinance.
[26] S13(1) of the Adoption Ordinance.

Benefits Ordinance, the Pension Benefits (Judicial Officers) Ordinance, and the Widows and Orphans Pension Ordinance .[27]

Inheritance (Provision For Family and Dependants) Ordinance

The Inheritance (Provision for Family and Dependants) Ordinance[28] includes a child as a 'dependant' whose father and mother were not married to each other at the time of its birth.

Intestate Succession

S10 of the Legitimacy Ordinance provided that where the mother of an illegitimate person died intestate and did not leave any legitimate issue, the illegitimate person (or, if he was dead, his issue) was entitled to take any interest therein as if he had been born legitimate. The mother had the same reciprocal right *vis-à-vis* her illegitimate child. This has now been repealed by the Parent and Child Ordinance. Today, any rights under intestacy include both legitimate and illegitimate children or issue.[29] An illegitimate child can therefore participate in the intestacy of his parents on the same terms as he could were he legitimate. However, an illegitimate person is presumed not to have been survived by his father or any person related to him only through his father unless the contrary is shown.[30]

Permanent Residence in Hong Kong

Prior to 1 July 1997, a child born in Hong Kong (or a dependent territory of the United Kingdom) after 1 January 1983 and before 1 July 1997 acquired the right of abode in Hong Kong if at the time of the birth, his father or mother was a BDTC or was settled in a dependent territory.[31] A child born

---

[27] However, see the Pensions Regulations made under the Royal Hong Kong Auxiliary Police Force Ordinance.
[28] S2. The Ordinance, replacing the Deceased Family Maintenance Ordinance, empowers the court, on the application of 'dependants', to make orders for the payment, out of the deceased's estate, of reasonable provision for the maintenance of the dependants.
[29] See s2 Intestates' Estates Ordinance.
[30] S3A of the Intestates' Estates Ordinance.
[31] S15 of the British Nationality Act 1981.

outside Hong Kong (or a dependent territory) was a BDTC if at the time of birth his father or mother was a BDTC otherwise than by descent;[32] or his father or mother was a BDTC and was serving outside a dependent territory in service designated by the Secretary of State.

The ability of a child to acquire BDTC via either his father or mother, however, applied only to a legitimate child. This was because s50(9) of the British Nationality Act 1981 stated that the relationship between a father and child existed only if the child was legitimate. In other words, an illegitimate child born in Hong Kong would not be entitled to BDTC status if his mother was not a BDTC or settled in a dependent territory. The discriminatory nature of s50(9) of the British Nationality Act 1981 was highlighted in two celebrated cases involving illegitimate children born in Hong Kong of illegal immigrant mothers from mainland China.[33]

Today, the position of a child acquiring permanent residence status and a right of abode in the HKSAR is provided for in the Basic Law. Article 24 of the Basic Law provides that permanent residents shall have the right of abode in the HKSAR. Permanent residents of the HKSAR shall be:

(1) Chinese citizens born in Hong Kong before or after the establishment of the HKSAR;
(2) Chinese citizens who have ordinarily resided in Hong Kong for a continuous period of not less than seven years before or after the establishment of the HKSAR;
(3) Persons of Chinese nationality born outside Hong Kong of those residents listed in categories (1) and (2) . . .

S50(9) of the British Nationality Act is now replaced by s5 of the Immigration (Amendment) (No 2) Ordinance[34] which provides that:

The relationship of parent and child is taken to exist as follows:–
(a) of a mother and child, between a woman and a child born to the mother in or out of wedlock;
(b) of a father and child, between a man and a child born to him in wedlock or, if out of wedlock, between a father and a child subsequently legitimated by the marriage of his parents;

---

[32] S16 of the British Nationality Act 1981.
[33] See *Re Lee Ka-ming*, Court of Appeal, Civil Appeal Action Nos 162 & 163 of 1990 (1991) and *Sit Woo-tung* [1990] 2 HKLR 410; Athena Liu, 'The Child's Right of Abode and the Immigration Ordinance', 22 HKLJ (1992) pp. 88–98.
[34] No 122 of 1997.

In relation to children born in mainland China claiming the right of abode in Hong Kong by descent, Keith J held in *Cheung Lai-wah v The Director of Immigration*[35] that the definition of the relationship between parent and child was incompatible with Article 24(3) of the Basic Law which focused on birth but not status. A24(3) of the Basic Law thus equalised the position of all Mainland-born children claiming right of abode in Hong Kong through descent, irrespective of whether or not the parents are married.

Rules of Construction of Relationship

Apart from the above improvements in the position of an illegitimate person, the legal disabilities of illegitimacy have been further reduced by a new general statutory rule of construction of relationship.

The common law rule of construction was that words of relationship, such as 'children' or 'issue' in a will or disposition, referred *prima facie* to a legitimate relationship and excluded illegitimate children or persons. To rebut this presumption, it must be proved that the testator or donor intended to benefit illegitimate children. This might be established if there was a clear expression to the contrary, or if there was evidence showing that at the time the will was executed, it was only possible for illegitimate children to take under it. This rule of construction brought about harsh results which were apparent in the case of *Dorin v Dorin*.[36] The testator married the mother of his two illegitimate children and on the same day he made a will giving his wife a power of appointment in favour of 'our children'. The parties did not have further children of their own. The law as it was did not provide for legitimation by the parents' subsequent marriage. It was held that the two illegitimate children could not take under the will because, *prima facie*, the testator only intended to benefit children born after the marriage and not the illegitimate children.[37]

Now s3 of the Parent and Child Ordinance provides that:

(1) In any–
    (a) Ordinance or publication of the Government in the Gazette having

---

[35] [1997] 3 HKC 64.
[36] (1875) LR 7 (Ch. 6); *Sydall v Castings Ltd* [1967] 1 QB 302.
[37] Cf. *Re Eve* [1909] 1 Ch. 796 residuary estate to 'children' of a widow aged 68 at the date of the will. The widow had only two children, both of whom were illegitimate. Held, the two children took under the will as there were not, and never could be, any legitimate children who could fit the description of the beneficiaries in the will.

legal effect (whenever enacted or published); or
(b) other instrument or document, made after the commencement of this section [i.e. 19 June 1993],
references (whether express or implied) to any relationship between two persons shall, unless the contrary intention appears, be construed without regard to whether or not either of them, or any person through whom the relationship is deduced, is or was at any time an illegitimate person.

The effect of s3(1) of the Parent and Child Ordinance is that in any wills where reference is made to parent-child, grandparent-grandchild or other relationship, the fact that a person is born out of wedlock will not be relevant in construing that relationship.

For example, if a gift is made to the 'children of X', where X has one legitimate and one illegitimate child, the gift will be construed to benefit both children.

The use of the word 'heir' or 'heirs' does not of itself show contrary intention.[38] Similarly, in any future enactments reference to a person's child, parent or other relative are to be construed without regard to whether these relationships arise within or outside marriage.

LEGAL CONSEQUENCES OF ILLEGITIMACY

Although the law has removed some of the more invidious discrimination against an illegitimate child, there are some remaining differences between a legitimate and an illegitimate child.

Guardianship

One important distinction between a legitimate and an illegitimate child is that an unmarried father is not entitled to become his child's guardian on the mother's death, nor can he appoint a testamentary guardian.[39]

---

[38] S3(2) Parent and Child Ordinance.
[39] S21 of the Guardianship of Minors Ordinance, unless he has been awarded custody of the child by the court, see Chapter 8.

Conferral of Parental Rights and Authority

Another major distinction between legitimate and illegitimate children is that parental rights and authority are not automatically conferred on an unmarried father. One of the arguments against conferring automatic parental rights on unmarried fathers is based on the varying circumstances in which illegitimate children come into being. For instance, the child may be born as a result of a casual liaison or a rape, or to an unmarried couple who had no intention of establishing or continuing a stable relationship. In these circumstances, it would be undesirable to confer parental rights and authority on the unmarried father.[40]

S3(1)(c) of the Guardianship of Minors Ordinance provides that where the minor is illegitimate, a mother shall have parental rights and authority, and the father shall only have such rights and authority, if any, as may be ordered by a court.

Financial Provision

Financial provision for a child is governed by several statutes. Until recently, the way in which an illegitimate child could obtain maintenance from his natural father (or putative father)[41] was to seek an affiliation order under the Affiliation Proceedings Ordinance. The Affiliation Proceedings Ordinance provided that the mother of an illegitimate child might apply to the court for an affiliation order and if the respondent was adjudicated to be the father, he could be ordered to pay maintenance. There were, however, two restrictive requirements. Firstly, the mother had to make an application within a time limit,[42] and secondly, the mother's evidence alone as to the

---

[40] See Chapter 8.
[41] 'Putative' means supposed, reputed or commonly supposed to be. For a long time, the term has been used to refer to the natural father of a child born outside marriage but the term is used because of the difficulty frequently encountered in establishing paternity as there was no presumption at common law to establish the paternity of a child born outside a marriage. In the absence of any presumption and firm proof, a man can, at most, be only the 'supposed' or 'putative' father of an illegitimate child.
[42] In *Willett v Wells* [1985] FLR 514, the mother applied for a maintenance order against the respondent man more than three years after the birth of the child and the question was whether within three years of the child's birth he paid money for the child's maintenance. The magistrates found that the respondent was the father but that he had paid no maintenance for the child since its birth save that he had given a birthday present of clothing. It was held that where there was no evidence as to whether the respondent had purchased the clothes or had been given them by someone else, the proper inference to be drawn was that he had paid for them himself.

identity of the child's father had to be accompanied by 'other evidence capable of corroborating the mother's evidence in a material particular'.[43] Even if paternity was not disputed, the range of orders which the court could make, unlike maintenance provisions which applied in cases of children born within wedlock, was very limited.

The Law Reform Commission recommended that

> the Guardianship of Minors Ordinance (Cap 13), the Separation and Maintenance Orders Ordinance (Cap 16), the Affiliation Proceedings Ordinance (Cap 183) and the Matrimonial Proceedings and Property Ordinance (Cap 192) should be amended to ensure that illegitimate children enjoy the **same rights** to financial provision as legitimate children . . .[44]

The Affiliation Proceedings Ordinance has now been repealed.[45] An illegitimate child can now seek a declaration of parentage under s6 of the Parent and Child Ordinance and seek financial provision under the Guardianship of Minors Ordinance. The range of orders under the Guardianship of Minors Ordinance has also been enlarged.[46]

Birth Registration

S7 of the Births and Deaths Registration Ordinance provides that the father of every child born alive in Hong Kong, or, in the case of death, illness, absence, or inability of the father, the mother of such child, shall within 42 days after the day of such birth, give information of the birth to the registrar. S12 further provides that in the case of an illegitimate child, no person shall, as the father of the child, be registered as such except

(a) at the joint request of the mother and the person stating himself to be the father of the child; or
(b) at the request of the mother on production of–
  (i) a declaration made by the mother stating that that person is the father of the child; and

---

[43] *Burbury v Jackson* [1917] 1 KB 16; *Turner v Blunden* [1986] 2 All ER 75; *McVeigh v Beattie* [1988] 2 All ER 500; *Kane v Littlefair* [1985] FLR 859.
[44] LRCR, paras 5.28–5.29 (author's emphasis); see n. 6.
[45] See s79 of the Law Reform (Miscellaneous Provisions and Minor Amendments) Ordinance (No 80 of 1997), see also *L v C*, High Court, Miscellaneous Proceedings No 4167 of 1993 (1994).
[46] See s78 of the Law Reform (Miscellaneous Provisions and Minor Amendments) Ordinance (No 80 of 1997), and Marriage and Children (Miscellaneous Amendments) Ordinance (No 69 of 1997), respectively.

(ii) a statutory declaration made by that person stating himself to be the father of the child; or
(c) at the request of that person on production of–
 (i) a declaration by that person stating himself to be the father of the child; and
 (ii) a statutory declaration made by the mother stating that that person is the father of the child; or
(d) at the request of the mother or that person on production of–
 (i) a certified copy of the relevant order; and
 (ii) if the child has attained the age of 16 of years, the written consent of the child to the registration of that person as his father.

The relevant order refers to a declaration of a court under Part IV of the Parent and Child Ordinance, an order under Guardianship of Minors Ordinance granting a person any right or authority in relation to the child or requiring that person to make any lump sum or periodical payment in respect of the child.

Consent to Marriage

Where a party to a prospective marriage is an illegitimate person, being over 16 but under the age of 21, the written consent of the mother is required. Where the mother is dead or if she has by order of any court been deprived of the custody of the person, the consent of the guardian is required.[47]

CONCLUSION

Most of the distinctions between a child born within marriage and outside marriage relate the to position of the unmarried father, for instance guardianship, conferral of automatic parental rights and authority, consent to marriage, birth registration and financial provision. The means by which the father–child relationship can be established will be examined next.

---

[47] See s14 of the Marriage Ordinance as amended by s28 of the Law Reform (Miscellaneous Provisions and Minor Amendments) Ordinance (No 80 of 1997).

7

Parentage

INTRODUCTION

'Parent' (mother or father) is a term which can have at least 3 meanings: a progenitor (an ancestor), a social/rearing parent (as in *de facto* parent, i.e. someone who stands *in loco parentis vis-à-vis* a child), or legal parent. Parentage in the legal sense is a status. In this chapter, we examine the ways in which the law assigns the legal status of parenthood.

In one sense, legal parentage has not always been commensurate with biological parentage. Until the advent of DNA fingerprinting, biological parentage could not be proved in a rational and scientific manner so the courts had to rely on presumptions to resolve disputes over fatherhood.

Today DNA fingerprinting can prove biological parentage beyond reasonable doubt. However, assisted human reproductive techniques have added a new complication to the question of parentage. For instance, a wife who is unable to carry a child may have her own ovum fertilised extra-corporeally by her husband's sperm. The resultant embryo may then be placed in a surrogate who carries the child to term. The surrogate may also agree to surrender all rights and duties relating to the child, and to have the resultant child raised by the couple. But who is the legal mother of the child? In the Californian case of *Johnson v Calvert*,[1] the husband and wife intended to become parents and it was said that this should be a sufficient basis for parentage.

---
[1] (1993) 5 Cal. 4th 84 (Supreme Court of California, Lexus).

[they] are a couple who desired to have a child of their own genes but are physically unable to do so without the help of reproductive technology. They affirmatively intended the birth of the child, and took the steps necessary . . . But for their having acted on their intention, the child would not exist . . . We conclude that although [the law] recognises both genetic consanguinity and giving birth as means of establishing a mother and child relationship, when the two means do not coincide in one woman, she who intended to procreate the child — that is, she who intended to bring about the birth of a child that she intended to raise as her own — is the natural mother under Californian law.

Generally, a parent is vested with parental rights and authority. The criteria upon which the law allocates parental rights and authority, and how they may be transferred are separate from the question of who in law is a parent.[2] In this chapter, we shall first look at the way in which the law ascribes the status of parentage in natural reproduction; artificial reproduction is governed by separate rules which will be considered in the second half.

PARENTS IN NATURAL CONCEPTION

'One's mother is always certain but one's father is not' is the meaning of the maxim 'mater semper certa est, pater incertus est'. Motherhood is based on the fact of parturition, i.e. delivery of the child from the mother's womb, thus the Latin maxim of 'mater est quam gestatio demonstrat'. Consequently, disputes as to motherhood rarely occur.[3] Paternity, on the other hand, has for many years been proved by presumptions. This is still frequently the case.

> Motherhood . . . is based on fact, being proved demonstrably by parturition. Fatherhood, by contrast, is a presumption.[4]

Establishing Paternity: Presumptions

Presumption of paternity arising from marriage

Part III of the Parent and Child Ordinance s5(1) now states that:

---

[2] See Chapters 8 and 11.
[3] For the problems of babies mistakenly switched in a maternity ward, see *R v Jenkins* [1949] VLR 277; *South China Morning Post*, 7 August 1998.
[4] *The Ampthill Peerage Case* [1977] AC 547 at p. 577 per Lord Simon.

a man shall be presumed to be the father of a child–
(a) if he was married to the mother of the child at any time and if there arises by virtue of that marriage a presumption of law that the child is the legitimate child of that man.[5]

This provision codifies the common law presumption of legitimacy. At common law a child is legitimate if, and only if, he is born or conceived during his parents' marriage. In order to ameliorate the difficulty involved in proving that the husband is the father, and the serious consequences of illegitimacy, the law presumes the mother's husband to be the father of any child born during marriage.[6] This is sometimes called the presumption of legitimacy. The presumption of legitimacy applies to the following three situations:

(1) where the parties were married both at the date of the conception and birth of the child.[7]

For example, H and W marry. A year later, W gives birth to C. H is presumed to be C's father.

(2) the parties were married at the date of the conception but not at the date of the birth of the child.[8]

For example, H and W marry. Six months later, H dies or the parties divorce. C is born five months after that.

(3) the parties were not married at the date of the conception of the child but were married at the date of the birth.

---

[5] This adopts the Scottish provision in the Law Reform (Parent and Child) (Scotland) Act 1986, but cf. the different wording used in the 1986 Act.

[6] *Pater est quem nuptiae demonstrant*, which literally means 'the father is he whom marriage shows to be such'.

[7] The presumption does not apply if the parties have been separated by a decree of judicial separation, but it applies where the spouses were living apart by agreement. See *Ettenfield v Ettenfield* [1940] P. 96.

[8] What if the child is born within a normal period of gestation but after the death of the mother's husband and after the mother's second marriage? In *Re Overbury* [1955] 1 Ch. 122, the husband died after six months of marriage. Seven months later the widow remarried and she gave birth to a child two months later after a normal period of gestation. It was held that there were two conflicting presumptions but it would not be assumed that the mother had ceased to have sexual intercourse with her first husband and was cohabiting with her lover in the shape of her second husband within six months of marriage. See also *Re Heath* [1945] 1 Ch. 417 and s18(3) of the Australian Children (Equality of Status) Act 1976 (NSW).

For example, six months after H and W's marriage, W gives birth to C.[9]

The presumption of legitimacy applies also after the decree nisi for divorce or nullity. In *Knowles v Knowles*,[10] the husband was granted a decree nisi, and a child was born to the wife after a normal period of gestation (270 to 280 days). On the application of the wife for maintenance for herself and the child, the husband denied paternity. It was held that the presumption of legitimacy applied to a child conceived after a decree nisi, the rationale being that

> ... the basis of the presumption is that the law contemplates spouses as fulfilling their marital duties to each other unless there has been an actual order of the court dispensing with the performance of such marital duties.[11]

Since there was no evidence to rebut the presumption of legitimacy, the husband was declared to be the father.[12]

Presumption arising from birth registration

Where there is no presumption of paternity arising from marriage, for instance where a couple cohabits, s5(1)(b) of the Parent and Child Ordinance provides that a man shall be presumed to be the father of a child if he has been registered as the father of the child by an entry made after 19 June 1993 in any register of births kept by the Registrar of Births and Deaths.[13]

This presumption of paternity arises through an entry in the child's birth certificate. Prior to 19 June 1993 the father of an illegitimate child could not enter his name on his child's birth certificate except at the joint request of both father and mother, in which event both had to sign the register.[14] In the absence of such a joint request by the mother and the father, the entry in a child's birth certificate would be left blank. This was

---

[9] See *Gardner v Gardner* (1877) 4 R (HL) 56.
[10] [1962] P. 161.
[11] *Knowles v Knowles* [1962] P. 161 at p. 166 per Wrangham J.
[12] The judge went on to hold that the presumption applied not only as to paternity but also to the date of conception, which meant that the child was conceived prior to the decree absolute. This presumption may now be rebutted on the balance of probabilities, s5(3) of the Parent and Child Ordinance.
[13] See also s24(2) of the Births and Deaths Registration Ordinance; *Jackson v Jackson* [1964] P. 25.
[14] See s12 of the Births and Deaths Registration Ordinance, repealed by the Parent and Child Ordinance.

so even if the mother requested the father's name be entered and even if he had made a statutory declaration acknowledging himself as the father. The entry in the birth certificate was also left blank even if the mother requested that the father's name be entered and there was a copy of an affiliation order,[15] or he had been awarded custody or access of the child, or he had been made liable for the child's maintenance.

Since 19 June 1993, the law has expanded the range of situations in which a father or mother or the child may enter the father's name on the birth certificate, thereby facilitating the recording of paternity and the operation of the presumption.[16]

Rebutting the presumptions

At common law, rebutting the presumption of legitimacy was no easy task.[17] The standard of proof was 'beyond reasonable doubt'.[18] Thus, the presumption was not rebutted by the fact that the husband was using condoms, or that the wife was committing adultery.[19] This heavy onus of proof has resulted in some rather absurd decisions. For example, in *Ah Chuck v Needham*,[20] the wife gave birth to a child with Chinese features. Both the mother and her husband were Europeans, but, at the time of the child's conception, the wife was having an affair with a Chinese man. It was held that the extra-marital relationship was insufficient to rebut the presumption that the husband could have had intercourse with his wife at the material time. The husband would be the father of the child even if the wife had committed adultery with one, two, or twenty men. It was said that, 'there is no accounting for the vagaries of nature.'[21]

S5(2) of the Parent and Child Ordinance now provides that both the presumptions of legitimacy (paternity) and the presumption arising from birth registration can be rebutted on the balance of probabilities. In *S v McC*,[22] Lord Reid stated that the presumption of legitimacy:

---

[15] Under the Affiliation Proceedings Ordinance, now repealed.
[16] See Chapter 6, s12 Births and Deaths Registration Ordinance.
[17] Lord Mansfield's rule in *The Banbury Peerage Case* (1811) 1 Sim. & St. 153 HL in which the House of Lords held that the presumption of legitimacy could be rebutted by evidence of non-access. See PB Carter, *Cases and Statutes on Evidence*, Sweet & Maxwell, London, 1981, p. 100.
[18] See *Preston-Jones v Preston-Jones* [1951] AC 391.
[19] See *Watson v Watson* [1954] P. 48; *Francis v Francis* [1960] P. 17.
[20] [1931] NZLR 559.
[21] Ibid., at p. 564.
[22] [1972] AC 24.

... now merely determines the onus of proof. Once evidence has been led it must be weighed without using the presumption as a make-weight in the scale for legitimacy. So even weak evidence against legitimacy must prevail if there is not other evidence to counterbalance it. The presumption will only come in at that stage in the very rare case of the evidence being so evenly balanced that the court is unable to reach a decision on it.[23]

Today, in any civil proceedings where the paternity of a person is in issue, the court may direct the use of scientific tests to determine whether a party to the proceedings is or is not the father or mother of that person, and the importance of the presumption of legitimacy needs to be examined in this context.[24]

Declaration of Status: Parentage, Legitimacy or Legitimation

Under s6(1) of the Parent and Child Ordinance, any person may apply to the court for a declaration of status. The orders which the court can make are that:

(a) a person named in the application is or was in law his parent;
(b) he is the legitimate child of his parents; or
(c) he has become, or has not become, a legitimate person.[25]

S6(1) does not allow one person to obtain a declaration of status of another. Thus, a mother cannot obtain a declaration that her child is the child of a particular man, or that the child is legitimate.[26] However, the child himself can, through his next friend, obtain a declaration that a person is his parent, and that he is the legitimate child of his parents.[27]

The standard of proof required, it seems, is heavier than 'on the balance of probabilities'. The court will only make a declaration if it is satisfied

---

[23] Ibid., at p. 41. See *Re JS (a minor) (declaration of paternity)* [1981] 2 FLR 146; *Serio v Serio* [1983] 4 FLR 756.
[24] See below.
[25] The jurisdiction of the court to entertain an application for a declaration is limited by S6(2).
[26] *Aldrich v AG* [1968] P. 281 where it was held that the court had no jurisdiction to grant a father a declaration that a deceased woman was his legitimate daughter; see also *Dodds v AG* (1880) The Law Times 22 May.
[27] *L v C,* High Court, Miscellaneous Proceedings No 4167 of 1993 (1994).

PARENTAGE 199

with the truth of the proposition,[28] and that to make such declaration would not be contrary to public policy.[29] Several consequences flow from the making of a declaration under s6; first, where a declaration is made under subsection s6(1)(a) or (b), the court shall notify the Registrar of Births and Deaths.[30] A declaration made under s6 is binding on the Crown and on all other persons.[31] A person who is so registered or re-registered as the father of a child pursuant to such a declaration will be the parent and not simply presumed to be the parent.[32]

There are, however, limits on the power of the court. They are: (1) On the dismissal of an application for a declaration, the court will have no power to make any alternative declaration for which application has not been made.[33] (2) No declaration which may be applied for under s6 may be made otherwise than under s6 by any court.[34] (3) The court cannot make a declaration that a person is or was illegitimate.[35] To safeguard against potential abuse of the power of the court to make declaration of parentage, for instance where the application is not opposed by anyone,[36] provisions have been made in s7 for the intervention of the Attorney-General.

The Use of Scientific Tests to Ascertain Parentage

Until the mid-1980s, the best physical evidence concerning parentage was blood group (serological) evidence. Blood group evidence is based on the genetic principle that a child derives half of its genetic material from its mother and the other half from its father. Thus, if a child is blood type AB, and its mother's blood type AB, then its father's must be either A or B or

---

[28] A declaration ought not to be granted if the evidence in support of it cannot be properly investigated, *Aldrich v AG* [1968] P. 281 at p. 291; *Re JS (a minor) (declaration of paternity)* [1981] 2 FLR 146, where Ormrod LJ said (obiter) that the court should not exercise its discretion to make a declaration of paternity unless the evidence is conclusive or very nearly so, at p. 151; see also *Re Kwan Kai-ming*, High Court, Miscellaneous Proceedings No 2996 of 1990 (1994).
[29] S6(3).
[30] S6(4). S12B of the Births and Deaths Registration Ordinance provides for re-registration of the birth register.
[31] S6(5), see *The Ampthill Peerage* Case [1977] AC 547.
[32] S5(1)(b), see above, pp. 196–7.
[33] S6(6).
[34] S6(7). This is to preclude the use of the court's inherent jurisdiction to make a declaration of status under O15 r16, Rules of the High Court, the effect of which would be to circumvent the procedural safeguard in s6.
[35] S6(8). See *B v AG (B and others intervening)* [1966] 2 All ER 145.
[36] A man thus could be declared to be a father without his knowledge.

AB.[37] Thus, a man alleged to be the child's father cannot in fact be so if he is found to be of blood type O. However, blood group evidence is exclusionary only. If the alleged father has a blood type A or B or AB, this only shows that he may be, but not that he is, the father.

Although a blood test cannot show directly whether an alleged man is the father, it may show indirectly that he is the father. For instance, where the wife had sexual relations only with the husband and another man at the material time, if the husband is excluded, then the other man must be the father. Blood group evidence may suffice in some cases to prove that a man is probably the father of the child. This hinges on the statistical incidence of certain blood types in the general population. If the characteristics of a child's blood are relatively uncommon and these are shared by the alleged father, this may establish the latter's paternity on the balance of probabilities.

> . . . if it were to appear from a blood test that the characteristics common to father and child could have been supplied by, say, any one of half the men in this country then the test would be of no value at all in helping to prove that the husband was the father. But, on the other hand, if these characteristics were so uncommon that if they were not derived from the husband they could only have been derived from one man in a thousand, then the result of the test would go a long way towards proving (in the sense of making it more probable than not) that the husband was in fact the father because it would be very unlikely that the wife had happened to commit adultery with the one man in a thousand who could have supplied this uncommon characteristic. And if it appeared that only one man in a hundred or one man in ten could have been the father, if the husband was not, that might go some way towards making it probable that the husband was the father.[38]

The advent of DNA fingerprinting — a scientific procedure which decodes the chemical 'signals' in human cells into a series of bar bands (similar to commercial bar codes) — allows parentage to be determined with little doubt. Where a child and the mother are tested, the mother's codes can be eliminated from the child's codes and the remaining codes must derive from the father. It has been said that the accuracy of the test is such that the chance of two persons having all the remaining bands are some 30 000 million to one.[39]

---

[37] In Hong Kong, about 40% of the population has blood type 'O', approximately 25% has 'A', 25% has 'B' and another 10% has 'AB'.
[38] See *S v McC* [1972] AC 24 at pp. 41–2 per Lord Reid.
[39] Except for identical twins who share the same DNA bands, see Antony Dickey, *op. cit.*, p. 272.

The use of scientific tests can assist the court in determining disputed parentage. S13(1) of the Parent and Child Ordinance provides that:

> In any civil proceedings in which the parentage of any person falls to be determined, the court may, either of its own motion or on an application by any party to the proceedings, give a direction–
> (a) for the use of scientific tests showing whether a party to the proceedings is or is not the father or mother of that person; and
> (b) for the taking of bodily samples from that person or any party to the proceedings...

'Scientific tests' means scientific tests carried out with the object of ascertaining the inheritable characteristics of bodily fluids or bodily tissues, and 'bodily sample' refers to 'bodily fluid or bodily tissue'.[40]

Consent to the taking of bodily sample

The court may direct that scientific tests be used to determine parentage but it cannot compel a party to provide a bodily sample — consent is required.[41] A person who has attained the age of 16 is competent to give a valid consent,[42] but in the case of a child under 16, a sample can be taken only if a person who has care and control of the child consents.[43] A bodily sample may be taken from a person who suffers from a mental disorder[44] and is incapable of understanding the nature and purpose of the scientific tests, provided that the person who has care and control of that person consents and the scientific test is not prejudicial to the proper care and treatment of the mental-health patient.[45]

Exercising the discretion to direct the use of scientific tests

S13(1) provides no guidance as to the circumstances under which the court may direct the use of scientific tests. Assuming that all the relevant adults are cooperative, an important consideration must be whether the use of scientific tests would expose the child, who would otherwise be protected by legitimacy, to the status of illegitimacy and hence be against the interests of that child. In recent cases, the courts have expressed doubts as to whether

---

[40] S2.
[41] S14(1).
[42] S14(2).
[43] S14(3).
[44] See the Mental Health Ordinance, LHK.
[45] S14(4).

exposing the child to illegitimacy always operates to the disadvantage of the child. In *S v McC*,[46] the husband alleged on divorce that the child born to the wife was not his. The court directed that the couple, the child and the alleged adulterer provided blood samples for testing. The guardian *ad litem* objected on the ground that it had not been shown that a blood test would be for the benefit of the child. The child had been born within marriage and was presumed to be legitimate so a blood test could prove only that he was born out of wedlock. On the risk of harm to a child being rendered illegitimate by the result of such a test, Lord Reid said:

> In former times it was plainly in the child's interest to have a finding of legitimacy ... An illegitimate child was not only deprived of the financial advantage of legitimacy but in most circles of society ... it carried throughout its life a stigma which made it a second class citizen. But now modern legislation has removed almost all the financial disadvantages of illegitimacy and it has become difficult to foretell how grave a handicap the stigma of illegitimacy will prove to be in later life. There are two aspects to this: how far will its neighbours look down on the child by reason of its illegitimacy and how far will the child itself feel a sense of inferiority. Doubtless there are still many circles where an illegitimate person is not well received. But there are many others, particularly in large towns, where nobody knows and nobody cares whether a newcomer is legitimate or illegitimate ... one cannot say whether any particular child will grow up to be sensitive or resentful at having been born illegitimate ... Nor can one foretell what view the child will take about evidence having been suppressed. Some will resent that. Others will accept the decision at its face value.[47]

Lord Hudson was doubtful if the truth would operate to the disadvantage of a child.

> Who is to say what is in the interests of the child and whether knowledge of true paternity would or would not favour his or her future prospects in life? How are these interests to be assessed? I find these questions especially difficult to answer in view of the fact that it must surely be in the best interests of the child in most cases that paternity doubts should be resolved on the best evidence ...[48]

The House of Lords held that while the court had to protect the best interests of the child, justice required that available evidence should not be

---

[46] [1972] AC 24; applied in *Yeung Chung-ping v Yeung Wan Yuet-kuen* [1987] 1 HKC 206.
[47] Ibid., at p. 43.
[48] Ibid., at p. 59.

suppressed. The person most affected by the refusal was the husband who denied paternity, the court ought to permit a blood test of a child unless it was satisfied that to do so would be against the child's interest. The welfare of the child was not the paramount consideration.[49]

There are now two lines of decisions. One prefers that the biological truth be ascertained by available evidence and the other continues to recognise some residual value of legitimacy and the advantage of avoiding the possibility of a 'stranger' disrupting existing family relationships.

S v McC was distinguished in 1993 in *Re F (minor: paternity tests)*[50] and it represents the latter view where the court was unwilling to remove the protection which the presumption of legitimacy offered to the child. In that case, the wife (W) had an affair outside marriage with C whilst her relationship with the husband (H) continued. W ended her relationship with C as soon as she discovered that she was pregnant. Both W and H maintained that the child was theirs and wished to bring the child up as a child of their family. C applied for a direction for blood tests with a view to bring proceedings to establish paternity and made an application for contact with the child. Both W and H refused to give blood samples. The Court of Appeal held that where a child was conceived and brought up in an existing marriage as a child of the family, and the association of the mother with the alleged father had terminated well before the birth of the child, and such association coexisted with sexual relations with the husband, the court should decline to exercise its discretion to order a blood test for DNA profiling. It was unfair to expose the child to the risk of losing the presumption of legitimacy when the applicant was unlikely to be successful in obtaining a contact order.[51]

However, in *Re H (paternity) (blood test)*,[52] the Court of Appeal held that the child had a right to know his biological father. In *Re H (paternity: blood test)*, the husband (H) underwent a vasectomy operation in 1990 and in 1994 the wife became pregnant. The wife and her lover, B, reached an understanding that they would live together when H left the matrimonial home. The wife later changed her mind and she reconciled with H, who had taken up the role as the father of the child. The mother opposed B's

---

[49] *Re H (paternity: blood test)* [1996] 2 FLR 65.
[50] [1993] 1 FLR 225; see also *Re CB (a minor) (blood tests)* [1994] 2 FLR 762; cf. *Re E (a minor) (child support: blood test)* [1994] 2 FLR 548 applying *S v McC* [1972] AC 24.
[51] See also *Re JS (a minor) (declaration of paternity)* [1981] 2 FLR 146; Cf. *Re J (a minor) (wardship)* [1988] 1 FLR 65 where DNA fingerprinting was upheld. There the mother was unable to care for the child and the putative father sought care and control. See also 'Truth and the interests of the child: *Re F (a minor: paternity tests)* [1993] Journal of Child Law 138.
[52] [1996] 2 FLR 65.

application for a contact order whereupon B sought directions for a blood test. It was held that every child had a right to know the truth about his parentage unless his welfare justified a cover-up. If the child had a right to know, then the sooner he was told the better. The issue of biological parentage should be divorced from psychological parentage. If the child grew up knowing the truth, that would not undermine his attachment to his father figure. He would cope with knowing that he had two fathers and this was better than hiding the truth which would be like a time-bomb ticking away. The court directed the taking of blood samples for scientific testing.

Refusal to comply with direction of the court

Where a court gives a direction under s13 for the use of scientific tests and for the taking of bodily sample from a person, consent of the person is required for the taking of the bodily sample. This protects a person from interference with his personal liberty.[53] The court has no power to order a blood test to be carried out against the will of the person. Thus, a non-cooperative person may flout a court's direction. The court is not provided with any power to enforce its direction, but s15(1) provides that where a person fails to comply with a court direction, the court may draw such inferences as appear proper in the circumstances.

Thus, in *Re A (a minor) (paternity: refusal of blood test)*,[54] the mother had sexual intercourse with three men at the relevant time. One of these, the defendant, was unsure about whether he was the father of the child. However, he failed to comply with a blood test direction. It was held by the Court of Appeal held that the inference that he was the father was virtually inescapable.[55]

> Against the background of law and scientific advance, it seems to me to follow, both in justice and in common sense, that if a mother makes a claim against one of the possible fathers, and he chooses to exercise his right not to submit to be tested, the inference that he is the father of the child should be virtually inescapable. He would certainly have to advance very clear and cogent reasons for his refusal to be tested — reasons which it would be just and fair and reasonable for him to be allowed to maintain.[56]

---

[53] *S v McC* [1972] AC 24 at p. 43.
[54] [1994] 2 FLR 463.
[55] [1994] 2 FLR 463; *McVeigh v Beattie* [1988] 2 All ER 500.
[56] P. 473.

Similarly, in *Re G (parentage: blood sample)*,[57] the husband initiated proceedings, after divorce, to determine the level of contact with a seven-year-old child born to his wife prior to their marriage. The mother disputed that the husband was the father and applied for DNA testing. Despite a court direction that blood samples be taken, the husband refused to allow this on the basis that he was virtually certain that he was the father, and if tests showed that he was not, the mother would use that fact to break the bond between himself and the child. The Court of Appeal held that the proper inference was a forensic inference, and since the forensic process was advanced by presenting the truth to the court, he who obstructed the truth would have the inference drawn against him. On the facts, the mother was willing to have her belief tested and the petitioner was not. The only inference that could properly be drawn was that the petitioner was not in fact the father.

PARENTS OF CHILDREN BORN AS A RESULT OF REPRODUCTIVE TECHNOLOGY

Medical technology has overcome many causes of subfertility but it also brings along legal, social, and ethical problems. Where gamete donation is not involved, for instance, in artificial insemination using the sperm cells of the husband (AIH), or in vitro fertilization and embryo transfer (IVF and ET), the only difference between a child born as a result of these procedures and any other children born in wedlock is the method of conception.

Where donated gametes are used, the question of parenthood arises. For instance, donor insemination or DI (that is, where a wife is artificially inseminated using sperm from an anonymous donor) raises the question of parentage. Who is the father of a child born as a result of DI? Is it the sperm donor or the husband? Similarly, in the case of a donated ovum, who is the mother? Is it the ovum donor or the wife?

The matter may be further complicated by a surrogacy agreement.[58] In general, there are two types of surrogacy agreement. A full surrogacy agreement is where a commissioning husband and wife agree with a surrogate that the latter will carry an embryo, derived from the couples' own gametes (i.e. the husband's sperm and the wife's ovum) to term and after parturition,

---

[57] [1997] 1 FLR 360.
[58] See Athena Liu, *Artificial Reproduction and Reproductive Rights,* Aldershot, Dartmouth Publishing Company, 1991; see also G Douglas and N Lowe, 'Becoming a Parent in English Law', 108 LQR (1992), 414.

the surrogate will hand the child over to the couple. A variation on this is sometimes referred to as partial surrogacy, where the surrogate is artificially inseminated using the sperm from the commissioning husband. The difficulties created by such agreements can be seen in the celebrated *Baby M* case.[59] There, a professional couple employed the services of a surrogate mother. The surrogate conceived using the semen of the husband. After she gave birth to the child, she changed her mind and refused to hand the child over to the commissioning husband and wife. The New Jersey Supreme court held that surrogacy contract was invalid and against public policy. Such an agreement was no different from 'baby-selling'. However in the best interests of the child, the court ordered that the husband was to have custody and the surrogate was granted visitation rights.

Apart from the question of custody disputes, the parenthood of surrogate-born children has proved to be a fertile field for legal theorists. In the Californian case of *Johnson v Calvert*,[60] the wife had a hysterectomy and could not bear a child. The couple employed the services of a single black woman. A child was born following IVF & ET and it therefore had no genetic link with the surrogate. The surrogate changed her mind several months into her pregnancy. The California Supreme Court adopted a novel legal theory that the intention of individuals should play a key role in deciding whom the law recognised as parents. It was held that as the couple intended to be the parents, they would be treated as such.

Part V of the Parent and Child Ordinance deals with both the question of parenthood where birth or pregnancy results from medical treatment.[61]

Mother

S9(1) provides that a woman who carries or has carried a child, as a result of the 'placing in her of an embryo or of sperm and eggs' is to be regarded as the mother.[62] Motherhood, thus, is now based on gestation and it is not dependant on one's marital status or genetic connection with the child.[63]

---

[59] 109 NJ 396; 537 A 2d 1227 (1988).
[60] (1993) 5 Cal. 4th 84 (Supreme Court of California, Lexus).
[61] Provisions regarding parentage has no retrospective effect, see *Re M (child support act: parentage)* [1997] 2 FLR 90.
[62] S9.
[63] See Code of Practice to Human Reproductive Technology Bill on selection criteria of patients/clients.

Father

S10 provides that:

> (1) This section applies in the case of a child who is being or has been carried by a woman as the result of placing in her of an embryo or of sperm and eggs or her artificial insemination.
> (2) If–
> (a) at the time of the placing in her of the embryo or the sperm and eggs or her insemination, the woman was a party to a marriage; and
> (b) the creation of the embryo carried by her was not brought about with the sperm of the other party to the marriage,
> then . . . the other party to the marriage shall be regarded as the father of the child unless it is shown that he did not consent to the placing in her of an embryo or of sperm and eggs or to her insemination (as the case may be).

In other words, where a wife has conceived as a result of the 'placing in her of an embryo or of sperm and eggs or her artificial insemination', the husband, whose sperm was not used to bring about the resultant pregnancy, will be regarded as the father, unless he can show that he did not consent to the reproductive procedure.

S10(5) preserves the common law presumption of legitimacy arising from marriage. Thus, in a case where a wife is a recipient of DI, the child born as a result will be protected by the presumption of legitimacy. If the presumption of legitimacy is rebutted, the husband will still be regarded as the father, unless he can show that he did not consent to the wife receiving DI. This, to a large extent, protects a child from illegitimacy. It also confers fatherhood on the husband. But if the husband can prove that he did not consent, the child would be fatherless.

In the case of an unmarried woman using DI, s10(3) broke new legal ground. It provides that where an unmarried woman and her male partner:

> (a) together obtained treatment[64] services in the course of which the embryo or the sperm and eggs were placed in the woman or she was artificially inseminated and
> (b) the creation of the embryo carried by her was not brought about with the sperm of that man

then, that man shall be regarded as the father of the child.

The innovative aspect of s10(3) is that it does not require that the male partner be cohabiting with the woman. 'Treatment services' is defined in s2

---

[64] See *Re B (parentage)* [1996] 2 FLR 15 and cf. *Re Q (parental order)* [1996] 1 FLR 369.

as meaning 'medical, surgical or obstetric services administered for the purpose of assisting a woman to carry a child'. Presumably this would exclude 'do it yourself' (or DIY) by a woman who has a male partner. Where a man answers the description of a 'partner' in s10(3), he will be regarded as the father and the sperm donor will not.[65] If no man answers the description in s10(3), the child would be fatherless.[66]

Posthumous Child

S10(7) provides that:

> For the purposes of the law of succession, where–
> (a) the sperm of a man was used after his death; or
> (b) any embryo was used after the death of the man with whose sperm the embryo was created,
> that man is not to be regarded as the father of the child.

Thus, where a husband who had his semen frozen dies, and his wife uses it to have a child after his death, the deceased husband will not, for the purposes of succession, be regarded as the father of the posthumous child.[67] This provision ensures that the estate of a deceased person can be administered without delay and with some degree of finality.

Surrogacy and Parental Order

The question of legal father and mother is more complex when surrogacy is involved. Assuming that the surrogate is married, and the pregnancy is achieved by insemination using sperm from the commissioning husband, according to s9(1) and s10(2), the surrogate will be regarded as the mother and her husband will be regarded as the father unless it is shown that he did not consent to the surrogacy. In a case where both the commissioning couple are the progenitors, again, the same rules apply. In either of these cases, the relationship between the child and the commissioning couple may be regularised by a parental order, which is a short form of adoption.

S12 of the Parent and Child Ordinance now provides that where a married couple employ the services of a surrogate mother, and where at least one of them is the genetic parent of the resulting child, they may

---

[65] S10(4).
[66] S10(6)(b); *Re Q (parental order)* [1996] 1 FLR 369.
[67] *R v Human Fertilisation and Embryology Authority ex parte Blood* [1997] 2 All ER 687.

apply, within six months of the birth of the child, to the court for a parental order, the effect of which is that the child will be treated in law as the child of the parties to the marriage.[68]

Before the court can make a parental order, it must be satisfied that at the time of the application:–
(i) the child has its home with the applicants, or either of them;
(ii) that the parties satisfy the residence requirement;
(iii) the applicants have attained the age of 18.

The court has also to be satisfied that no money has been given by the married couple in consideration of the making of the parental order, except expenses reasonably incurred.[69] Finally, consent of the surrogate (and the father) to the making of the order is needed. Consent must be been given freely and with full understanding of what is involved, and it is ineffective if given by the surrogate less than six weeks after the child's birth.[70]

Where a parental order is made, the Registrar of the court shall notify the Registrar of Births and Deaths, in such a manner as may be prescribed, of the making of that order. This envisages the re-registering of the child after a parental order is made.[71]

In *Re Q (parental order)*[72] an unmarried woman acted as a surrogate for a married couple, carried and gave birth to a child created from the egg of the wife fertilised by sperm donated by a man who was not the husband. When the couple applied for a parental order, the question arose as to who was the father whose consent was required. It was held that as the surrogate was an unmarried woman, the only provision which was relevant was that of a woman obtaining treatment services together with her male partner. However, the husband could not be said to be the male partner together with whom treatment services were provided. There was no man who was to be treated as the father and whose consent was necessary.

CONCLUSION

In natural reproduction where paternity is disputed, the trend is increasingly

---

[68] See the Human Reproductive Technology Bill, 3 January 1997. Consultation Paper on the Draft Reproductive Technology Bill, Hong Kong Government Printer, Hong Kong, 1996.
[69] *Re Q (parental order)* [1996] 1 FLR 369.
[70] Ss12(5) and (6).
[71] S12(9).
[72] [1996] 1 FLR 369.

that of using scientific tests to ascertain the truth. Lord Hudson thus remarked:

> The interests of justice in the abstract are best served by the ascertainment of the truth and there must be few cases where the interests of children can be shown to be served by the suppression of truth.[73]

At one time, the opportunity to ascertain the truth concerning one's person's parentage may be lost with the passage of time. However, science may overcome this obstacle and the dead may be exhumed and remains provide evidence in paternity disputes.

The irony, however, is that in cases of assisted human reproduction, the legal fiction of parentage ensures that a sperm donor remains anonymous. As adopted children are beginning to be provided with more information about their biological background,[74] children born as a result of assisted human reproduction may arguably request similar information.[75]

---

[73] *S v McC* at p. 59.
[74] See Chapter 11.
[75] See s31 of the Human Reproductive Technology Bill; n. 68.

8

Parental Rights and Authority

INTRODUCTION

Children's well-being depends on their care-givers who normally are the parents. 'Parental rights and authority' is the central concept in s3 of the Guardianship of Minors Ordinance (GMO) governing the parent–child relationship. A person with parental rights and authority has the right to control almost every aspect of a child's upbringing. However, a rebellious teenager may assert his or her own autonomy by acting contrary to parental decisions. Whose wishes prevail depends on the duration and extent of parental rights and authority. With the emergence of children rights, it is clear that parental rights and authority are not absolute and their exercise is limited by the best interests of the child and by the concept of the mature minor. Before we examine the legal incidents which attach to parenthood, who has parental rights and authority, and what happens on the death of a parent, there are two important points to note. First, the terms used, and second, the diminished nature of parental rights and authority.

TERMINOLOGY

'Guardianship' at Common Law

Parental rights and authority have been expressed through a confusing array of terms in both statutes and cases. These expressions include 'guardianship', 'custody', 'legal custody', 'care and control', and 'access'.

> In the end, so far as comprehensibility on these matters is concerned, one finds that this voluminous and well-intentioned legislation has created a bureaucrat's paradise and a citizen's nightmare.[1]

Guardianship is an old concept which needs to be reviewed and updated so that it can fit into today's notion of the parent–child relationship. At common law, the principal concept which governed the parent–child relationship was guardianship. Guardianship was deeply rooted in medieval landholding and there were as many as thirteen different kinds of guardianship.[2] Over the last century, these different types of guardianship fell into disuse so that by the 1970s, only four species of guardianship survived. These were guardianship by nature, by nurture, by testamentary disposition, or by court order.[3] The English Law Commission in their Report on Child Law: Guardianship and Custody, succinctly summarised the historical position of guardianship and its interplay with the modern notion of parenthood as follows:

> Our present law has no coherent legal concept of parenthood as such. Historically, guardianship came first. It developed as a means of safeguarding a family's property and, later, became an instrument for maintaining the authority of the father over his legitimate minor children. Hence he was recognised as their "natural" guardian. While he was alive the mother had no claims as natural guardian and was originally in no better position than a stranger. Nineteenth century legislation gave her limited rights to apply to the courts for custody and access and, in 1886, made her automatically guardian after the father's death. The Guardianship of Infants Act 1925 provided that the father should be guardian on the mother's death. It also gave the mother "like powers" to those of the father to apply to the court in any matter affecting the child but deliberately stopped short of making her a joint guardian during his lifetime. The Guardianship Act 1973 now states that the mother's rights and authority are the same as the law allows the father, but nowhere does statute equate her position to the natural guardianship of the father, which has never

---

[1] *Hewer v Bryant* [1970] 1 QB 357 at p. 371 per Sach LJ.
[2] S Cretney, *Principles of Family Law*, 2nd edition, Sweet & Maxwell, London, 1976, p. 320; see also English Law Commission Working Paper, Review of Child Law: Guardianship, No 91, HMSO, London, 1985, paras 2.1–2.35 (hereafter referred to as English Law Commission Working Paper, No 91, 1985); English Law Commission Working Paper, Review of Child Law: Custody, No 96, HMSO, London, 1986 (hereafter referred to as English Law Commission Working Paper, No 96, 1986).
[3] *Hewer v Bryant*, see n. 1 at p. 373.

been expressly abolished . . . we suggested that these archaic and confusing rules, under which parents who for all practical purposes have the same rights and authority are sometimes guardians and sometimes not, should be abolished.[4]

Today, 'guardian' is a term which is sometimes used synonymously with 'parent'. More often, it refers to non-parental testamentary guardianship or guardianship by court appointment.[5] The general understanding is that such a person acts as a parent-substitute in the event of the death of a parent, and arguably should have the same rights and authority as a parent.

'Custody', 'Care and Control' and 'Access' at Common Law

As guardianship has fallen into disuse, 'custody' has become an important concept in the parent–child relationship. Custody has a wide and a narrow meaning.[6] In its broadest sense, it is synonymous with all rights and authority which a parent has in relation to a child. There is no exhaustive list of what these rights and authority entail, but they embrace a bundle of powers, for example, to control the child's day-to-day upbringing, to control the child's education and religion, to administer moderate punishment, to administer the child's property, or to consent to the child's medical treatment.[7] 'Custody', however, is capable of bearing a more restrictive meaning; in particular the right to physical possession and control of the infant's movement. This is sometimes referred to as actual or physical custody or 'care and control'. The terms 'custody', 'care and control' and 'access' are used in Ordinances[8] by the divorce courts in an undefined fashion.[9]

'Parental Rights and Authority' in the Guardianship of Minors Ordinance

The GMO uses 'parental rights and authority' to denote the parent–child relationship. However, it provides no definition of these important concepts.

---

[4] English Law Commission, Family Law: Review of Child Law, Guardianship & Custody No 172, HMSO, London, 1988, paras 2.2–2.3 (hereafter referred to as English Law Commission Report, No 172, 1988).
[5] See Part VI of GMO below.
[6] *Hewer v Bryant*, see n. 1 at p. 372.
[7] *Hewer v Bryant*, see n. 1 at p. 373.
[8] S2 Matrimonial Proceedings and Property Ordinance provides that 'custody' includes access.
[9] See below.

This omission may be compared with s85 of the English Children Act 1975 which used the term 'parental rights and duties', which was defined as:

> as respects a particular child ... all the rights and duties which by law the mother and father have in relation to a legitimate child and his property; and references to a parental right or duty shall be construed accordingly and shall include a right of access and any other element included in a right or duty.

S3(1) of the English Children Act 1989 has adopted the term 'parental responsibility'. This reflects society's perception that children are individual persons in their own right, and that the parent–child relationship is one of responsibility on the part of parent rather than right. S3(1) of the English Children Act 1989 defines 'parental responsibility' as:

> All the rights, duties, powers, responsibilities and authority which by law a parent of a child has in relation to the child and his property.

Interestingly, none of these statutes explains exactly what rights, duties, powers, responsibilities and authority a parent has in relation to his child.

If we look at the law in Scotland by way of comparison, the Children (Scotland) Act 1995 provides substance by expanding on the notions of both 'parental rights' and 'parental responsibility'. S1(1) provides that:

> ... a parent has in relation to his child a responsibility–
> (a) to safeguard and promote the child's health, development and welfare;
> (b) to provide, in a manner appropriate to the stage of development of the child–
>   (i) direction;
>   (ii) guidance,
> to the child;
> (c) if the child is not living with the parent, to maintain personal relations and direct contact with the child on a regular basis; and
> (d) to act as the child's legal representative,
> but only in so far as compliance with this section is practicable and in the interests of the child.[10]

As for 'parental rights', s2(1) provides that:

> ... a parent, in order to enable him to fulfil his parental responsibilities in relation to his child, has the right,

---

[10] See also Scottish Law Commission Report on Family Law, No 135, HMSO, Edinburgh, 1992, para. 2.6 (hereafter referred to as Scottish Law Commission Report, No 135, 1992).

(a) to have the child living with him or otherwise to regulate the child's residence;
(b) to control, direct or guide, in a manner appropriate to the stage of development of the child, the child's upbringing;
(c) if the child is not living with the him, to maintain personal relations and direct contact with the child on a regular basis; and
(d) to act as the child's legal representative.[11]

Given the confusing array of terminology at common law and under the GMO, it is necessary to standardise the use of these terms and strengthen the clarity of their meanings. The Hong Kong Law Reform Subgroup on Guardianship and Custody of Minors is currently examining reform proposals in this area and one of their recommendations is to adopt the English Children Act 1989 and shift the emphasis from 'parental rights' to 'parental responsibilities'. This would be more than a merely cosmetic change as society is increasingly coming to see children as individual persons in their own right and the parent–child relationship as one of responsibility rather than one of rights. However, for the sake of consistency, this chapter continues to use the existing terminology adopted by the GMO.

DIMINISHING NATURE OF PARENTAL RIGHTS AND AUTHORITY

Before we examine what parental rights and authority are, it is useful to note that the law (both statutes and decisional law) has, over the last four decades, made inroads into the parent–child relationship.[12] For instance, at common law, parents had the right to the services of their child, just as a master had to those of his servant.[13] Although it was not possible to enforce this right directly, it had indirect practical importance in so far as it was an actionable tort to do an act wrongfully depriving a parent of his child's services[14] — an action now abolished by s20B of the Law Amendment and Reform (Consolidation) Ordinance.

---

[11] Ibid., para 2.35.
[12] B Dickens, 'The Modern Function and Limits of Parental Rights' 97 (1981) LQR 462; Susan Maidment, 'The Fragmentation of Parental Rights', 40 (1981) Cam LR 135; John Eekelaar, 'The Emergence of Children's Rights', 6 (1986) Oxford Journal of Legal Studies 161; J Montgomery, 'Children As Property', 51 (1988) MLR 323.
[13] See *Lough v Ward* [1945] 2 All ER 338.
[14] But not where the child was too young to be capable of performing any service, see *Hall v Hollander* (1825) 4B & C 660, where the child was two-and-a-half years old.

Additionally, parental rights and authority are limited or qualified by the welfare of the child principle.[15] This rests on the recognition that a child is a separate entity, having interests distinct from those of the parents and requiring the protection of the law. Thus, s3(1) of the GMO provides that, in relation to the custody or upbringing of a minor, the court shall regard the welfare of the minor as the first and paramount consideration. Consequently, a parent may not be permitted to act in a manner adverse to the interests of a child.

> In the great majority of cases in which there are legal proceedings concerning the upbringing of a child, the child's own welfare will be the first and paramount consideration. The parent will not, therefore, be permitted to insist upon action which is contrary to that welfare or to resist action which will promote it.[16]

Indeed, parental 'rights' reflects a misconception of the nature of the parent–child relationship.[17] To the extent that the law enables parents to decide how to bring up their children without interference from others, it does so primarily because this is a necessary part of the parents' responsibility for that upbringing and in order thus to promote the welfare of their children.[18] Lord Scarman in *Gillick v West Norfolk and Wisbech Area Health Authority*[19] said that:

> The principle of law ... is that parental rights are derived from parental duty and exist only so long as they are needed for the protection of the person and property of the child.[20]

In many cases, 'parental rights and authority' terminate well before the child reaches the age of majority, in effect diminishing as the child grows older. In 1994, the UN Convention on the Rights of the Child was extended to Hong Kong.[21] As a result, there is an increasing emphasis on the rights

---

[15] See below, pp. 217–228.
[16] English Law Commission Working Paper, No 91, 1985, para 1.11; see n. 2.
[17] A Bainham, *Children, Parents and the State*, Chapter 3.
[18] English Law Commission Working Paper, No 91, 1985, para 1.11; see n. 2. There is no separate tort of interference with parental rights, *F v Metropolitan Borough of Wirral DC* [1991] 2 FLR 114. The court would also be wary of holding parents in breach of a duty of care owed to their children, see *Surtees v Kingston-upon-Thames BC* [1991] 2 FLR 559.
[19] [1985] 3 All ER 402.
[20] [1985] 3 All ER 402 at p. 420.
[21] B Rwezaura, 'The Legal and Cultural Context of Children's Rights in Hong Kong', 24 (1994) HKLJ 276.

of the child as opposed to parents' rights. Lord Denning in *Hewer v Bryant* eloquently described the right of a parent as:

> ... a dwindling right which the court will hesitate to enforce against the wishes of the child, the older he is. It starts with the right of control and ends with little more than advice.[22]

WHAT CONSTITUTES 'PARENTAL RIGHTS AND AUTHORITY'

Despite the diminishing nature of parental rights and authority, the powers of parents to control various aspects of a child's life cannot be underestimated. They include the regulation of routine matters such as when the child should get up in the morning, what comprises the child's diet, with whom the child may associate, what time the child goes to bed, what clothes he may wear, and what TV programmes can be watched. Apart from statutory provisions,[23] the common law manifestations of parental rights and authority include the following:
- the right to live with the child and control the child's day-to-day upbringing
- the right to decide on the child's education and religion
- the right to inflict moderate punishment
- the right to administer the child's property
- the right to act for the child in legal proceedings
- the right to consent to medical treatment

The Right to Live With the Child and Control the Child's Day-to-Day Upbringing

The right of a parent to live with the child is a salient feature of parental rights and authority.[24] As between a parent and child, this means that the parent determines how a child's physical needs, such as the provision of food, clothing and shelter are to be met. Parents can also determine the

---

[22] See n. 1 at p. 369.
[23] Consent to the child's marriage, see Marriage Ordinance as amended by the Law Reform (Miscellaneous Provisions and Minor Amendments) Ordinance (No 80 of 1997); Consent to the child's adoption, see the Adoption Ordinance; surname of the child is governed by usage rather than common law or statutes.
[24] *Hewer v Bryant,* see n. 1.

manner and place in which the child is to spend his time although their claim to control the child's day-to-day upbringing is coupled with a responsibility for providing proper care. Indeed, it is an offence to ill-treat, neglect, abandon or expose a child in a manner likely to cause the child unnecessary suffering or injury to his health.[25] However, as will be seen later, the extent to which a parent can control a child's upbringing diminishes as the child grows older.[26] For instance, if a 17-year-old boy refuses to return home, it is unlikely that the parent's claim could be enforced.

A parent's claim to possession of his child *vis-à-vis* a third party is protected by s26 of the Protection of Children and Juvenile Ordinance, which provides for the offence of abduction of a child. Any person who unlawfully takes a child (under the age of 18) out of the possession and against the will of its parent or lawful guardian commits an offence.[27] Indeed, as against a person who has no right to detain a child, the parent can simply take the child back.

The Right to Decide on the Child's Secular and Religious Education

At common law, a guardian could determine what secular and religious education a child was to receive. In *Hall v Hall*,[28] for example, a 16-year-old lad refused to attend Eton school. It was held that the guardian was a proper judge as to what school his ward should be placed in and the court would take proper course to compel the child to attend. Similarly, in *Tremain's case*,[29] an infant went to Oxford University against the wishes of his guardian. A court messenger removed the child from Oxford and transported him to Cambridge, where his guardian wished him to attend. In *Re Agar-Ellis*,[30] it was held that a father had the right 'as master of his own house, as king and ruler in his own family'[31] to determine the children's religious education. In that case, the father was a Protestant and the mother a Roman Catholic. The mother was restrained from taking the children to confession without the father's consent, or to any church, or places of

---

[25] See s27 of the Offences Against the Person Ordinance.
[26] *Gillick v West Norfolk and Wisbech Area Health Authority*, see n. 19.
[27] See also s43 Offences Against the Person Ordinance for the offence of stealing a child under the age of 14; and *R v D* [1984] 1 AC 778.
[28] (1749) 3 Atk. 719.
[29] (1721) 1 Strange 168.
[30] (1878) 10 Ch. D 49; (1883) 24 Ch D 318 disapproved in *Gillick*, see n. 26.
[31] Ibid., at p. 75 per James LJ.

PARENTAL RIGHTS AND AUTHORITY 219

worship where worship was performed otherwise than in accordance with the rites of the Church of England.

Today, parents may still decide a child's secular and religious education as such decisions fall within the child's day-to-day upbringing. Parents, however, have no legal duty to provide either secular or religious education as every child is entitled to nine years of free education provided by the government. However, s74 of the Education Ordinance[32] provides that the Director of Education, where it appears to him that a child is not attending primary or secondary school without reasonable excuse, can make reasonable inquiries and serve an attendance order on a parent requiring him to cause the child to attend school regularly. Any parent who, without reasonable excuse, fails to comply with an attendance order will be guilty of an offence.[33] The Director of Education also may require the management committee of a primary or secondary school named in an attendance order to admit the pupil named,[34] and no person shall expel the pupil without the permission of the Director of Education.[35] However, where a child fails to attend, there appears to be little practical value in punishing the parents.[36]

The Right to Inflict Moderate Punishment

Parents may prescribe and maintain reasonable boundaries for a child's behaviour as this is part of the child's upbringing.[37] In prescribing standards of behaviour and in attempting to secure obedience to them, parents may administer reasonable punishment.[38] However, where the punishment is disproportionate to a child's 'offence', parents may incur civil liability for assault or criminal liability for ill-treatment.[39] The concept of reasonableness must be judged against the standards prevailing in contemporary society with regard to physical punishment, taking into account the nature and the context of the punishment, the manner and method of execution, its

---

[32] Cap 297.
[33] S78.
[34] S74(2A) Education Ordinance. It is an offence to contravene this provision, see s87(3A).
[35] S74(2B) Education Ordinance. It is an offence to contravene this provision, see s87(3A).
[36] *Re D.J.M.S. (a minor)* [1977] 3 All ER 582.
[37] A parent may even be held accountable for a child's criminal behaviour. S10 of the Juvenile Offenders Ordinance provides that where a child or young person is charged with any offence for the commission of which a fine, damages or costs may be imposed, the court may order that the fine, damages, or costs awarded be paid by the parent. See *A v DPP* (1996), The Times Law Report 18 April.
[38] *R v Hopley* (1860) 2 F & F 202.
[39] *R v Derriviere* (1969) 53 Cr App R 637.

duration, and its physical and mental effects on the child. The child's sex, age and state of health are also relevant considerations. Strictly speaking, striking a child with a hand, a bamboo stick, a belt or some other object so as to cause temporary pain and discomfort, a method of punishment which is employed by many local parents, may bring the child within the ambit of s34 of the Protection of Children and Juveniles Ordinance.

However, corporal punishment has now been abolished in schools and other related establishments.[40] In *Cheung Yee-mong v So Kwok-yan*,[41] a primary school teacher exercised disciplinary control over a class by requiring the students to put their hands over their mouths. A student refused and the teacher took the student's hand to cover his mouth which the High Court later found to be an acceptable corrective action, Seagroatt J remarking:

> It did not constitute any assault or any excessive use of force. It was well within the sphere of corrective or disciplinary action delegated by a parent to a school teacher. It did not, nor could it, constitute corporal punishment in any form.[42]

The Right to Administer the Child's Property

S3(1) of the GMO states that mother and father have equal rights and authority in relation to the 'administration of any property belonging to or held in trust for a minor or the application of the income of any such property.' However, the Ordinance does not define the scope of the rights and authority, a position which Bevan summarises thus:

> It is silent on any duty, though there seems to be no doubt that a duty is attributable, which for the majority of parents will be limited at most to

---

[40] See r58 of the Education Regulations. In *R v Wong Tin-kau* (reported in 28 March 1996 *SCMP*) a primary school teacher was convicted of assault causing bodily harm for caning a 10-year-old student twice on the buttocks for not doing his homework. He was sentenced to a conditional discharge for 18 months. Apparently, other forms of disciplinary measures, such as forcing students to stand or run until they are exhausted have, however, been adopted by schools, see *SCMP*, 28 March 1996. Corporal Punishment (Repeal) Ordinance No 72 of 1990; corporal punishment has also been abolished under the Reformatory Schools Ordinance, Training Centre Ordinance, and Detention Centres Ordinance. See also *London Borough of Sutton v Davis* [1994] 1 FLR 437.
[41] [1996] 2 HKC 360.
[42] Ibid., at p. 371.

arranging and administering such minor matters as keeping a savings account on behalf of the child into which gifts to him may be paid.[43]

But he poses an interesting question which may never be litigated in a society like Hong Kong where filial piety is considered an important element of the parent–child relationship. He said:

> Supposing the child continues to live with his parents until the age of 18 and during the previous two years, when he has been working, he has given all his wages to them except for keeping a small percentage of it as "pocket money", with the result that the amount handed over substantially exceeds that required to maintain him. Would he, after attaining majority, be entitled to recover, if not all, the excess over maintenance? Arguably, he could, on the grounds that the parent as natural guardian has a fiduciary duty to account at the end of the guardianship for all property of the child which passed into his hands.[44]

The English Law Reform Commission has studied this matter and observed that very little was known about it.[45] In 1988, in the Report of Child Law: Guardianship and Custody it was said that:

> It might also be helpful to clarify the nature and extent of a parent's powers to administer or deal with a child's property, for the law on this is most obscure ... a particular uncertainty is whether the parents have the same powers as do guardians, for example to receive a legacy on the child's behalf.[46]

Today, s3(2) of the Children Act 1989 provides that 'parental responsibility' includes:

> The rights, powers and duties which a guardian of the child's estate ... would have had in relation to the child and his property.

S3(3) of the same Act provides that this includes:

> The right of the guardian to receive or recover in his own name, for the

---

[43] Hugh K Bevan, *Child Law*, 2nd edition, Butterworths, London, 1989, para 1.54.
[44] Ibid., para 1.54.
[45] English Law Commission Working Paper, No 91, 1985, para 1.10; see n. 2.
[46] English Law Commission Report, No 172, 1988, para 2.8; see n. 4. At common law, an executor could not safely pay to the parent of a minor beneficiary. An executor who did so would be liable to pay again to the legatee when he or she attained full age. See William, Mortimer and Sunnucks, *Executors, Administrators and Probate*, 17th edition, Sweet & Maxwell, London, 1993, p. 1024.

benefit of the child, property of whatever description and wherever situated which the child is entitled to receive or recover.

The Right to Act for the Child in Legal Proceedings

A child can only bring legal proceedings by his 'next friend' and if civil proceedings are brought against him he must be represented by a guardian *ad litem*.[47] A parent or guardian is *prima facie* entitled to act in those capacities unless he has an interest adverse to or in conflict with those of the child.[48] The duty of the next friend is to apply himself conscientiously in the diligent pursuit of the minor's interests, taking all necessary measures for the benefit of the minor in the litigation. Conversely, there appears to be no right to continue proceedings which are not for the benefit of the child.[49]

The Right to Consent to Medical Treatment

The choice of medical treatment, for instance whether a three-year-old should be taken to a doctor or what medicine he should take, is part of a child's day-to-day upbringing. In recent years, however, many controversial cases, such as sterilisation operations, life saving operations, life prolonging operations and contraceptive advice and treatment have been brought before the court. Where problems arise in the context of the parent–child relationship is in the giving of a legally effective consent, or the refusal to give such a consent, to medical treatment.

The importance of a legally effective consent or refusal to consent stems from the common law protection of an individual's right to bodily integrity. Emergency excepted,[50] any invasion of this right amounts to trespass to the person.[51] Minors who are too young to express their views (as to whether to accept a particular medical treatment or procedure) are incompetent to give a valid consent so parents have the power to consent on their behalf. Just as a legally effective consent permits a doctor to embark

---

[47] Rules of the High Court, O80, r2, as amended by the Adaptation of Laws (Courts and Tribunals) Ordinance, 1998.
[48] *Woolf v Pemberton* (1877) 6 Ch D 19; *Re Birchall* (1880) 16 Ch D 41; *Re Taylor's Application* [1972] 2 QB 769.
[49] *Kinnear v DHSS* (1989) 19 Fam Law 146.
[50] *F v West Berkshire Health Authority* [1989] 2 All ER 545.
[51] *Chatterton v Gerson* [1981] 1 QB 432.

on a lawful treatment, a legally effective refusal bars such treatment. Fortunately, parents in consultation with doctors usually agree on the appropriate treatment for the child.

The power of a parent to consent, or withhold consent, on behalf of the child is not absolute. The extent and duration of such power is limited by two important concepts; firstly, the best interests of the child and, secondly, the mature-minor (Gillick-competent minor). The development of both of these concepts has made serious inroads into the notion of parental rights and authority.

Best interests of the child

Advances in medicine and surgery have highlighted the clashes between the interests of the child and the rights of the parents, whose well-meaning decisions have not always been upheld by the courts. Indeed, the courts have shown their willingness to place a restriction on the exercise of such parental discretion, for instance where the treatment infringes the right of the child and thus is not in the child's best interests. In *Re D (a minor) (wardship: sterilisation)*,[52] an 11-year-old girl (D) suffered from a condition called 'Sotos syndrome'. The usual symptoms associated with the condition are accelerated growth during infancy, epilepsy, generalised clumsiness, an unusual facial appearance and behavioural problems, including emotional instability, certain aggressive tendencies, and some impairment of mental function ranging from impaired intelligence to serious mental retardation. D had an IQ of about 80, indicating a level of intelligence below the norm. It was agreed, however, that D had sufficient intelligence to marry in due course. Nonetheless, her mother was convinced that she was seriously mentally retarded and feared that she might be unable to look after children should she have them. She therefore wanted her daughter to be sterilised. An educational psychologist challenged the proposed operation. It was held that the proposed sterilisation operation involved the deprivation of a woman's basic right to reproduce when performed without her consent. The court would not risk irreparable damage being done when there was a strong likelihood that D would understand the implications of the operation when she reached 18. In the circumstances, the operation was not medically indicated and it would not be in the best interest of D.

A very different conclusion was reached in *Re B (a minor) (wardship: sterilisation)*.[53] This case involved a mentally handicapped 17-year-old girl.

---

[52] [1976] 1 All ER 326.
[53] [1987] 2 All ER 206.

Her ability to understand speech was that of a six-year-old and her ability to express herself was that of a two-year-old child but there were signs of sexual awareness. The institution where she lived sought leave for her to undergo a sterilisation operation. Evidence was adduced showing that she could not be placed on any effective contraceptive regime and that she was not capable of knowing the causal connection between intercourse and childbirth. If she were to give birth to a child, she would panic and require heavy sedation during a normal delivery, which carried the risk of injury to the child. Delivery by caesarian section was deemed to be inappropriate owing to the likelihood of B opening up her post-operative wounds. The House of Lords held that a sterilisation operation would be for the welfare of the girl.[54]

Not only have the courts disagreed with parents as to the medical procedures which they have proposed for the child, they have also authorised treatment where parents have refused to do so. The recent case of *Re C (a minor) (wardship: medical treatment)*[55] involved a 15-day-old baby girl who suffered an attack of cyanosis (turning blue due to a lack of oxygen). She was subsequently diagnosed as having an extra pair of rudimentary lungs attached to the oesophagus as well as suffering from other congenital abnormalities. Without surgical intervention, the child would die in a short time. However, as the operation had not been carried out in Hong Kong before, the chance of success was 50/50 although if it was successful, the child would enjoy a relatively normal life. The parents refused to consent to the operation. They worried that if the operation failed, the child would face the prospect of a handicapped life and they preferred to allow the child to die. Kaplan J held that this was not a case of where the child might be a 'cabbage'.[56] Nor was this a case where despite the wonders of modern medicine, nothing could be done to save the child.[57] Although it was a very serious matter to overrule the wishes of caring parents who had carefully weighed up all the factors in refusing to consent to treatment, as there was a real chance that the child might enjoy a normal life, and in the best interest of the child, the court ordered that the child undergo the operation.

A recent case has further highlighted the difficulty of applying the concept of the best interests of the child. The case was unusual and it

---

[54] In *Re B (a minor) (wardship: sterilisation)*, ibid., it was said that non-therapeutic sterilisation falls outside the scope of parental consent, and leave of the court was required.
[55] [1994] 1 HKLR 60; see also *Director of Social Welfare v Tam* [1987] 1 HKLR 66; *Director of Social Welfare v Lam Kwok-wah* [1988] 1 HKLR 206.
[56] *Re B (a minor) (wardship: medical treatment)* [1981] 1 WLR 1421.
[57] See *Re C (a minor) (wardship: medical treatment)* [1989] 3 WLR 240; *Re J (a minor) (wardship: medical treatment)* [1990] 3 All ER 930.

differed from *Re C (a minor) (wardship: medical treatment)* in that death was not imminent. Instead, the medical treatment would give the child a good chance of an extended life and a reasonable quality of life with many years of special care. In *Re T (wardship: medical treatment)*,[58] a one-year-old boy was suffering from a life-threatening liver defect. His parents were both health care professionals experienced in the care of sick children. The unanimous opinion of medical consultants was that the baby should undergo transplant surgery as the prospect of success was good. Without transplantation, on the other hand, the expectation of life was just over two years. The parents refused to consent to the transplant. The father found a job overseas, and against medical advice, the mother travelled with the boy to visit him. The doctor formed the view that the mother was not acting in the best interest of the child. At first instance, the judge found that the mother's refusal to consent to the transplant was unreasonable and directed that she return with the child to the jurisdiction within 21 days. In the Court of Appeal, it was held that there was a strong presumption in favour of a course of action which would prolong life, but to prolong life was not the sole objective of the court, and to require that at the expense of other considerations might not be in the child's best interest. On the facts of the case, it was held that it was not in the best interest of the child to order a course of treatment with which a caring, devoted and well-informed mother did not agree. The best interest of the child required that future treatment be left for the parents to decide. In this case, the court recognised the danger of giving its consent to the operation while passing back to the mother the responsibility of parental care and expecting her to provide the commitment to the child post operation. On the weight to be given to the wishes of the parents, the court remarked:

> It can only be said safely that there is a scale, at one end of which lies the clear case where parental opposition to medical intervention is prompted by scruple or dogma of a kind which is patently irreconcilable with principles of child health and welfare widely accepted by the generality of mankind; and that at the other end lie highly problematic cases where there is genuine scope for a difference of view between parent and judge ... in cases at the latter end of the scale, there must be a likelihood ... that the greater the scope for genuine debate between one view and another the stronger will be the inclination of the court to be influenced by a reflection that in the last analysis the best interests of every child include an expectation that difficult decisions affecting the length and quality of its life will be taken for it by the parent to whom its care has been entrusted by nature.[59]

---

[58] [1997] 1 FLR 502.
[59] Ibid., at p. 514 per Waite LJ.

Mature-minor (or Gillick-competent minor)

Although the age of majority is 18,[60] this does not mean that at common law the giving of a legally effective consent vests in a parent until the child reaches 18. In the landmark decision of the House of Lords in *Gillick v West Norfolk and Wisbech Area Health Authority*,[61] Mrs Gillick sought a declaration that the Department of Health and Social Security's circular which stated that doctors were entitled to give contraceptive advice and treatment to children under 16 without parental consent was unlawful in that it was inconsistent with the rights of Mrs Gillick as a parent to veto any proposed treatment. The House of Lords, by a majority, held that at common law the capacity to consent to medical treatment was not fixed at any specific age. It was a question of fact in each case and depended on the degree of maturity of the minor and the nature of the treatment in question. The test of competence was understanding. As Lord Fraser said, a minor had a capacity to give a valid consent to contraceptive advice, examination and treatment, provided that:

> She has sufficient understanding and intelligence to know what they involve.[62]

Lord Scarman concurred, saying, the question was whether the child had achieved:

> a sufficient understanding and intelligence to enable him or her to understand fully what is proposed.[63]

When that happens,

> parental right to determine whether or not their minor child below the age of 16 will have medical treatment terminates . . .

The test for the level of competence required to give a valid consent appears to be simple, but what in fact is required to show understanding can be onerous. Thus, Lord Scarman said there was much to be understood

---

[60] See the Age of Majority (Related Provisions) Ordinance. The Hong Kong Law Reform Commission, Report on Young Persons: Effects of Age in Civil Law, recommended that a provision similar to the English provision in s8 Family Law Reform Act 1969 which provided a presumption that a child who reached 16 had the ability to give a valid consent be made. They further recommended that instead of 16, the age of 18 be adopted.
[61] [1985] 3 All ER 402.
[62] Ibid., at p. 410.
[63] Ibid., at p. 423.

if the girl was to have the legal capacity to consent to contraceptive advice and treatment:

> It is not enough that she should understand the nature of the advice which is being given: she must also have a sufficient maturity to understand what is involved. There are moral and family questions, especially her relationship with her parents; long-term problems associated with the emotional impact of pregnancy and its termination; and there are the risks to health of sexual intercourse at her age, risks which contraception may diminish but cannot eliminate. It follows that a doctor will have to satisfy himself that she is able to appraise these factors before he can safely proceed on the basis that she has at law capacity to consent to contraceptive treatment.[64]

Where a child has reached a stage of sufficient understanding and intelligence to be capable of making up his own mind, parental right yields to the child's right to make his own decision. Today, the phrase 'Gillick-competence' refers to a child who, although a minor, has reached a sufficient level of understanding and intelligence to be capable to making up his or her own mind on the matter requiring decision. In other words, a Gillick-competent child can override parental objections to a proposed procedure or medical treatment.

However, decisions of the English Court of Appeal in the early 1990s have made clear that a Gillick-competent minor's refusal to consent to medical treatment can be overridden by parental consent. As Brenda Hoggett has remarked, the effect of this is that while the court will start with a preference for respecting the wishes of a child, it will not allow him to die or risk suffering serious harm through lack of treatment, especially if his illness is distorting his judgment. Where a Gillick-competent child refuses medical treatment, a parent or the court may consent. In *Re R (a minor) (wardship: medical treatment)*,[65] a 15-year-old minor had a history of serious mental illness but she refused antipsychotic drugs needed for her treatment. The Court of Appeal held that she did not have the capacity to make decisions about her own medical treatment, but it was said (obiter) that even if she had such capacity, a parent or the court could override her refusal. Again, in *Re W (a minor) (medical treatment)*,[66] a 16-year-old child suffered from anorexia nervosa. She refused treatment and was found to be competent to make such a decision. However, it was held that a parent or a court could authorise treatment in the face of her refusal.[67]

---

[64] Ibid., at p. 424.
[65] [1991] 3 All ER 177.
[66] [1992] 4 All ER 627.
[67] See John Eekelaar, 'White Coats or Flak Jackets? Doctors, Children and the Court — Again' 109 (1993) LQR 182.

This, however, does not mean that with parental consent doctors should simply treat a Gillick-competent minor despite the minor's refusal to consent to treatment. Nolan LJ said:

> I for my part would think it axiomatic, however, in order to avoid the risk of grave breaches of the law that in any case where time permitted, where major surgical or other procedures (such as an abortion) were proposed, and whereby the parents or those in loco parentis were prepared to give consent but the child (having sufficient understanding to make an informed decision) was not, the jurisdiction of the court should always be invoked.[68]

In exercising its discretion, the court would give effect to the child's wishes on the basis that *prima facie* that will be in his or her best interests.[69]

In Hong Kong, the parental right to veto a Gillick-competent child's medical treatment has not been tested, nor has there been a case where a mature-minor has refused medical treatment. It remains to be seen to what extent Gillick represents the law in Hong Kong.

WHO HAS PARENTAL RIGHTS AND AUTHORITY?

Common Law Position

At common law, the father of a legitimate child (under the age of 21) used to have absolute rights over his child to the exclusion of the mother. Furthermore, the father could appoint a testamentary guardian who had the same rights as the father and could remove the child from its mother. The hardship of this common law rule was exemplified in Caroline Norton's case which led to the passage of the Custody of Infants Act 1839 (Talfourd's Act), which enabled the court to grant custody of children aged under seven to the mother and to allow her access to her children between the ages of seven and 21.

An illegitimate child, however, was nobody's child. Neither the mother nor the father had parental rights or authority. It was not until 1883 that this rule was reversed in *R v Nash*.[70] In that case a mother issued a writ of *habeas corpus* to have her illegitimate child, who was in the possession of a third party, delivered up to her, the Court of Appeal holding that the mother had a natural right to custody. This was subsequently confirmed in

---

[68] *Re W (a minor) (medical treatment)* at pp. 648–9.
[69] Balcombe LJ *Re W (a minor) (medical treatment)* [1992] 4 All ER 627 at p. 644.
[70] (1883) 10 QBD 454.

the House of Lords decision in *Barnardo v McHugh*.[71] In that case, one Margaret Roddy bore a child, John, of Mr Jones. John was reared by his natural parents. The mother later married Mr McHugh. John was subsequently found in a destitute condition and was taken to Dr Barnardo's Home. The mother then signed an agreement with the Home to leave the boy there until he was 21 years of age. Two years later, the mother asked for the boy's return and was refused. She sought a writ of *habeas corpus*. On the question of whether the mother of an illegitimate child had the same rights of custody and guardianship as that held by a father of a legitimate child, it was held that the Poor Law imposed a duty on the mother to maintain the child and this gave her a corresponding right to custody.

Married Parents: Equality and Independent Exercise of Parental Rights and Authority

The common law position in relation to a legitimate child has now been changed by s3(a)(ii) of the GMO. The principle today is equality of parental rights and authority. S3(a)(ii) provides that in any proceedings before the court concerning the custody and upbringing of a minor, the court shall not 'take into consideration whether the claim of the father in respect of custody and upbringing is superior to that of the mother,' or vice versa.

3(1)(b) further provides that, in relation to a legitimate child, a mother shall have the same rights and authority as the father, and those rights and authority are exercisable unilaterally. In other words, one parent can, for example, decide which school and Sunday church a child should attend, or which doctor to consult, without consulting the other. This rule is designed to allow each parent, particularly the one who has day-to-day care and upbringing of the child, to exercise responsibility and make decisions without having to consult the other, and the onus is on the objecting parent to raise such an objection in court, but not the other way around.[72]

Resolution of Disagreement

Where a minor's father and mother disagree on any questions affecting his welfare, either of them may apply to the court for its direction[73] and the

---

[71] [1891] AC 388.
[72] English Law Commission Report, No 172, 1988, para 2.10; see n. 4.
[73] S4(2).

court may make such order as it thinks proper. In resolving any disagreement, the welfare of the minor is the first and paramount consideration.[74]

Unmarried Mothers

S3(1)(c) of the GMO states that where a minor is illegitimate, a mother should have all rights and authority.

Unmarried Fathers

Although the Parent and Child Ordinance sweeps away most of the disabilities of an illegitimate child, the position of an unmarried father is not equal to that of a married father, upon whom parental rights and authority are automatically conferred. This rule may yield the following kind of curious result:

> a man who abandoned his wife when she was pregnant, and never saw his child, would have full parental responsibilities and rights, whereas a man who was cohabiting with the mother of his child and playing a full paternal role would have none . . . This may be seen as encouraging irresponsibility in some men. The existing rule also seems to ignore the fact that an unmarried father may be just as motivated to care for and protect his child as a married father, or indeed as the mother of the child. We asked therefore . . . whether the law ought not to be based on the general proposition that a person who brings a child into the world has certain responsibilities towards that child, and certain related rights.[75]

Some may argue that the position of an unmarried father differs from that of a stable partner, a casual liaison or a rape, and that it would be repugnant to any reasonable person's sense of justice to confer automatic parental rights on a casual partner or a rapist.

> . . . the position of the natural father can be infinitely variable; at one end of the spectrum his connection with the child may be only the single act of intercourse . . . which led to conception; at the other end of the spectrum he may have played a full part in the child's life from birth onwards, only the formality of marriage to the mother being absent. Considerable social

---

[74] S3(1)(a).
[75] Scottish Law Commission Report, No 135, 1992, para 2.36; see n. 10.

evils might have resulted if the father at the bottom end of the spectrum had been automatically granted full parental rights . . .[76]

The Scottish Law Reform Commission, however, put forward an interesting argument here.[77] They maintained that in the case of a casual liaison, it is not necessarily inappropriate to give parental responsibilities and rights to such a father; they are conferred not for the benefit of the parents but for the benefit of the child. Further, a mother's parental responsibilities and rights are recognised even if the child resulted from a casual affair. Even though the mother of a child may not wish the father to interfere with her life, it is not the feelings of one parent in a certain type of situation that should determine the law but the general interest of the child and of responsible parents.[78] The Commission said:

> The interests of the child are not necessarily identical to the interests of the parent who has to care for the child. Again, the same dislike of interference is often present after a marriage has broken down but the policy of the law is to encourage involvement by both parents in the child's life, where this is likely to be in the child's interest. The answer to parental involvement which is against the child's welfare is for a court to remove or regulate parental rights. It seems unjustifiable, however, to have what is in effect a presumption that any involvement by an unmarried father is going to be contrary to the child's best interests. Moreover, it is by no means clear that the risk of harassment would be increased by changes in the law of the type we are considering.[79]

Concern has also been expressed in cases where the child is the product of a rape; in which case it would obviously be unacceptable for a rapist to share parental responsibilities and rights with the victim. Although this would appear to be the most convincing argument against conferring automatic parental rights, the Scottish Law Reform Commission argued that the law should not treat some rapists better than others:

> . . . a special exception for rapist fathers would be unprincipled. The nature of the sexual intercourse (whether in or out of marriage) resulting in the conception should not affect the legal relationships arising from the procreation of the child. It is not unknown for rape to be committed by a husband upon his wife, or by a male cohabitant upon his female partner.

---

[76] *Re H (illegitimate children: father: parental rights (No 2))* [1991] 1 FLR 214 at p. 218 per Balcombe LJ.
[77] Although it was not adopted by the Scotland (Children) Act 1995.
[78] Scottish Law Commission Report, No 135, 1992, para 2.40; see n. 10.
[79] Ibid., para 2.41.

> It is not unknown for potentially fertile sexual intercourse to take place only because normal inhibitions of one or both of the parties have been dulled by alcohol. It would, in our view, be wrong to allow such circumstances to affect parental responsibilities and rights which are there for the benefit of the child. . . .[80]

The arguments of the Scottish Law Reform Commission are based on societal values which are quite different from those of Hong Kong. Ultimately, the arguments for and against conferring automatic parental rights concerns the issue of the burden of proof. There are two possible approaches; one is to confer parental rights and authority on a father while giving a mother a right to apply to disenfranchise him of his legal status as a father on the grounds that he is an 'undesirable' or 'irresponsible' parent. This approach would require the law to define the terms 'undesirable' or 'irresponsible'.[81] Another approach would be to empower the court to grant, on an application by the father, such parental rights and authority as appropriate.

Adopting the latter approach, s3(1)(d) of the GMO provides that on application made by an unmarried father, the court may, where it is satisfied that the applicant is the father of a child born out of wedlock, grant him 'some or all the parental rights and authority' he might have had if the minor had been legitimate.[82]

Thus, an unmarried father does not have automatic parental rights and authority but only such as are allowed by a court order.[83] A typical case where a court might make an order would be where the mother and father are living together, the father acknowledges his paternity, plays the role of a father, and the mother agrees to the order being made. An order conferring on him all the parental rights and authority would then put the father in the same position as if he was married to the mother.

In Hong Kong, there has been no decided case on s3(1)(d) of the GMO. English cases concerning 'parental rights orders'[84] and 'parental responsibility orders'[85] suggest that the courts may adopt certain principles in the exercise of its discretion, especially, in cases where the father has no current involvement with the child as a result of the parents' separation.

---

[80] Ibid., para 2.47.
[81] See English Law Reform Commission No 135, 1992; n. 10.
[82] Cf. s4 Family Law Reform Act 1987; s4 Children Act.
[83] English Law Commission Report, Illegitimacy, No 118, HMSO, London, 1982, para 7.29.
[84] S4 Family Law Reform Act 1987.
[85] S4 Children Act 1989.

Firstly, the welfare principle applies.[86] Secondly, where a concerned but absent father has demonstrated a degree of attachment and commitment to his child and his reasons for applying for the order are not demonstrably improper or wrong, it would *prima facie* be for the welfare of a child to grant an order. Further, an order for parental rights and authority is not an order which confers enforceable parental rights; it merely gives to the father a *status qua* father.[87]

Applying these principles, the English courts have shown a general willingness to grant an order conferring legal status on a father. Thus, in *Re S (parental responsibility)*,[88] the parties cohabited for three years and intended at one stage to marry. A child was born to that relationship and was registered in the father's surname. The parties, however, separated twelve months later but the father continued to pay maintenance for the child and had regular contact with her. On his application for a parental responsibility order, it was held that as the father had shown the necessary degree of commitment and attachment to the child, an order would be granted.[89]

However, in *Re T (a minor) (parental responsibility: contact)*,[90] an order for parental responsibility was refused. In that case, the mother and the father separated during the mother's pregnancy. The cause of the separation was a violent assault by the father, so severe that he had to take her to hospital. He was feckless with maintenance and attempts to establish contact dissolved into violence. On one occasion, the father abducted the daughter for a few days without regard for the child's welfare. It was held that the father had no worthwhile part to play in the life of the girl and his application was refused.[91]

Where the father can show some degree of attachment and commitment to his child, an order for parental rights and authority confers a status of parenthood which nature has already ordained. In the case of an absent father, the courts have assumed that the order is declaratory in nature, and such parental rights and authority remain unenforceable. In *Re C (minors) (parental rights)*,[92] the parents cohabited for two years and there were two children. For about twelve months after the parents' separation, the father enjoyed access until the arrangement was terminated by the mother. The

---

[86] See s3(2) GMO; *D v Hereford and Worcester County Council* [1991] 1 FLR 205.
[87] *D v Hereford and Worcester County Council* [1991] 1 FLR 205.
[88] [1995] 2 FLR 648.
[89] This list is not exhaustive, see *Re H (illegitimate children: father: parental rights (No 2))* [1991] 1 FLR 214.
[90] [1993] 2 FLR 450.
[91] *W v Ealing London Borough Council* [1993] 2 FLR 788 order refused because the motive of the father's application was to thwart the making of an adoption order.
[92] [1992] 1 FLR 1.

father then applied for access and a parental rights order. It was held that although the enforceability of a parental rights order was a relevant consideration, it was not an overriding consideration. Where the association between the father and the children had been sufficiently enduring and the father had shown substantial commitment to them, the status of a legitimate father would be granted notwithstanding that circumstances were such that a number of parental rights (including access) were unenforceable. As Waite J said:

> It would be quite wrong, in our view, to assume that just because few or none of the parental rights happen to be enforceable under conditions prevailing at the date of the application, it would necessarily follow as a matter of course that a PRO [parental rights order] would be refused. That can be illustrated by looking ... at the position of a lawful father in analogous circumstances. Conditions may arise (for example in cases of mental illness) where a married father has, regretfully, to be ordered, in effect, to step out of his children's lives altogether. In such a case, his legal status as a parent remains wholly unaffected, and he retains all his rights in law, although none of them may be exercisable in practice. This does not mean that his parental status becomes a dead letter or a mere paper title. It will have real and tangible value, not only as something he can cherish for the sake of his own peace of mind, but also as a status carrying with it rights in waiting, which it may be possible to call into play when circumstances change with the passage of time.'[93]

An absent unmarried father who is granted all parental rights and authority has the following 'rights in waiting'; as he may:
(i) appoint a testamentary guardian,[94]
(ii) act as a surviving guardian,[95]
(iii) veto the child's adoption, and
(iv) consent to the child's marriage.

Thus, in *Re H (a minor) (parental responsibility)*,[96] the mother left the father, taking their child with her. On the mother's remarriage, she refused to allow contact with the child due to the attitude of the child's stepfather. The mother and her husband also expressed a wish to adopt the child. The father's application for contact was refused but his application for parental responsibility was granted. It was held that he was entirely qualified to be

---

[93] Ibid., at p. 3.
[94] S21 GMO.
[95] S21 GMO.
[96] [1993] 1 FLR 484.

granted such an order, especially in light of the possibility that the mother and the stepfather might seek to adopt the child at some time in the future.

An order conferring parental responsibility on an unmarried father would not give him a right to interfere with matters within the day-to-day management of a child's life.[97] Where the parties disagree on a specific issue relating to the child, the court may resolve the conflict or discharge of the order.[98]

AGREEMENT TO TRANSFER PARENTAL RIGHTS

S4(1) of the GMO states that an agreement of a man or woman to give up wholly or partially his or her parental rights regarding any child of his or her shall be unenforceable [except in a separation agreement]. Thus, a surrogacy agreement which purports to transfer parental rights and authority would be unenforceable.[99]

GUARDIANSHIP

As has already been mentioned, guardianship is a concept linked to English feudal landownership and so is of little relevance to Hong Kong today. Although 'guardian' is sometimes used to mean a parent, it more usually denotes a non-parent who has been appointed either by a parent under a deed or will (that is, a testamentary guardian), or a guardian appointed by the court to stand *in loco parentis* to a child.

The GMO does not define the term 'guardian'. S18(1), however, defines the powers of a guardian by reference to two old common-law concepts of 'guardian of the person' and 'guardian of the estate'. Thus, s18(1) of the GMO provides that:

> ... a guardian under this Ordinance, besides being guardian of the person of the minor, shall have all the rights, powers and duties of a guardian of the minor's estate, including in particular the right to receive and recover in his own name for the benefit of the minor property of whatever description and wherever situated which the minor is entitled to receive or recover.

---

[97] *Re P (a minor) (parental responsibility order)* [1994] 1 FLR 578.
[98] S4(2) GMO.
[99] See the Reproductive Technology Bill, 3 January 1997.

The law on guardianship is to be found in Part III of the GMO and it covers all three types of guardianship. Part III deals with the appointment, removal and powers of guardians.

Meaning of Parent: Married and Unmarried Fathers

As we will be examining parents as guardians and parents appointing testamentary guardians, it is worth noting the definition of 'parent' in this context which is 'father or mother'.[100] 'Parent', however, does not include an unmarried father unless:

> (a) he is entitled to the custody of the minor by virtue of an order in force under section 10(1); or
> (b) he enjoys any rights or authority with respect to the minor by virtue of an order in force under s3(1)(d)...[101]

Thus, an unmarried father has no automatic right to act as the guardian of his child on the death of the mother under s5 of the GMO.[102] Any appointment of a testamentary guardian made by him shall be of no effect, unless he is entitled to custody or he has enjoyed any parental rights or authority immediately before his death.[103] For examples:

> F, an unmarried father, and M, the mother, lived together with their child, C, from the time C was born. C is now seven years old. M died recently without appointing a testamentary guardian. On M's death, F has no automatic right to be C's guardian.

> F, an unmarried father, was granted custody of C under s10 of the GMO in 1995. He then appointed G by deed to be C's guardian. Shortly before F died, the custody order was revoked in favour of X. F's appointment would be ineffective.

> F, an unmarried father, appointed G to be C's guardian by deed in 1995. Shortly before F died, he was granted custody of C under s10 of the GMO. F's appointment would be effective.

---

[100] S2.
[101] S21 GMO.
[102] See below.
[103] S21 GMO.

Surviving parents as guardians

S5 of the GMO provides that on the death of a parent of a child, the surviving parent shall be guardian of the minor, either acting alone or jointly with any testamentary guardian appointed by the deceased parent. For instance:

> H and W married and had a child C. H dies without appointing a guardian. W, the surviving parent, becomes the guardian of C.

> H and W married and had a child C. H, by will, appointed X to be the guardian in the event of his death. On the death of H, W and X act jointly as guardians of C.

S5 of the GMO envisages that a surviving parent will act as guardian of his child. This usually creates no difficulty if the surviving parent continues to care for the child. However, in cases where the parents are divorced or separated and the custodial parent dies, this can create problems. For example:

> H and W married and had a child C. Since the divorce of H and W ten years ago, C has been living with W and GM (W's mother), and H has not seen or visited C. W died two years ago and GM has been C's *de facto* carer. W appointed no testamentary guardian. Custody of C reverts to H, the surviving parent and guardian.[104]

Testamentary guardians

Method of appointment

Appointment of a guardian is an exercise of parental rights and authority. S6(1) of the GMO provides that a parent of a minor may by deed or will appoint any person to be guardian of the minor after his death.

When appointment takes effect or is revoked

A guardian so appointed shall act jointly with the surviving parent unless the latter objects to his so acting.[105] It appears that the surviving parent may so object at any time, and where this happens, guardianship terminates. Where the surviving parent objects to the testamentary guardian acting in

---

[104] *Re C* [1978] Fam 105.
[105] S6(2).

that capacity, or where the latter considers the surviving parent unfit to have custody of the child, the guardian may apply to the court, and the court may either:

> (a) refuse to make any order (in which case the surviving parent shall remain sole guardian); or
> (b) make an order that the guardian so appointed–
>   (i) shall act jointly with the surviving parents; or
>   (ii) shall be the sole guardian of the minor.[106]

Where the surviving parent objects, the burden is on the testamentary guardian to bring this matter to the court for determination. Where the court refuses to make any order, the surviving parent remains the sole guardian and the court is not empowered to appoint another guardian.[107] Where the court makes an order that a testamentary guardian shall be the sole guardian to the exclusion of the surviving parent, the court may make orders regarding–

> (a) the custody of the minor; and
> (b) access to the minor of the surviving parent,
> as the court thinks fit having regard to the welfare of the minor.[108]

Court-appointed guardians

Where there is no testamentary guardian, etc.

S5 provides that where, on the death of a parent, no guardian has been appointed or the appointed guardian dies or refuses to act, the court may, if it thinks fit, appoint a guardian to act jointly with the surviving parent.[109] In *Re H (an infant)*,[110] the mother of a ten-year-old girl died shortly after she was granted custody of the girl. The girl had been living with the mother and her adult sister. After the mother's death, the sister applied to be appointed guardian of the infant to act jointly with the father. However, the two were not on speaking terms, and the sister's application was made with a view to obtaining custody.[111] It was held that it was not right to appoint a guardian merely for reasons of convenience. The question was

---

[106] S6(3).
[107] Compare s5.
[108] S11 GMO.
[109] S5(b); *quaere* it is possible for a guardian to resign?
[110] [1959] 3 All ER 746.
[111] See also s12(a) GMO, below.

whether the appointment of a guardian to act jointly with the father would be for the benefit of the infant. The court held that it would not be for her benefit to have as joint guardians persons who were not on speaking terms.

Where a minor has no parent, etc.

S7 provides that where a minor has no parent,[112] no guardian of the person,[113] and no other person having parental rights[114] with respect to him, the court may, on the application of any person appoint the applicant to be the guardian of the minor.

The problems with this provision are twofold and are apparent in the case of *Re N (minors) (parental rights-acquisition)*.[115] Following the death of the father, the mother remarried and her two young daughters lived with her and the stepfather. On the death of the mother, the children's maternal grandmother came to live with them. Disagreement arose between the stepfather and the grandmother regarding the upbringing of the girls and the grandmother left, taking the girls with her. Both the grandmother and the stepfather applied under s5(1) of the English Guardianship of Minors Act 1971 (which is in *pari materia* to s7 of the GMO) to be made a guardian. It was held that the court only had jurisdiction to make a guardianship order, the consequences of which would leave questions of custody and access at large. A guardianship order made in favour of either party would therefore be of little practical utility to the parties. The court advised them to apply for wardship to resolve any disputes between them.[116]

Another practical difficulty with s7 of the GMO is that the jurisdiction of the court can only be invoked if a minor has no parent, no guardian of the person and no other person having parental rights. Where a minor has parents, but they are totally uninterested in the minor's upbringing, leaving the minor in the care of relatives or a child minder on a long-term basis, s7 cannot be invoked.

Power of the High Court to remove or replace guardian

S8 provides that the High Court may, on being satisfied that it is for the welfare of the minor, remove a testamentary guardian or a guardian

---

[112] Not if a parent or the parents cannot be found.
[113] But could have a guardian of the estate.
[114] Any or all parental rights and authority?
[115] [1974] Fam 93.
[116] See Chapter 12.

appointed or acting by virtue of the GMO, and may appoint another guardian to replace the one so removed.[117]

Guardian of the estate

The High Court has power to appoint a guardian of a minor's estate either generally or for a particular purpose.[118] Apart from this power, either the District Court or the High Court may appoint a guardian in the following situations.

Disputes between guardians

Apart from the three types of guardianship, the law also envisages disputes between guardians, and provides methods for their resolution.

Disputes between joint guardians

Where two or more persons acting as joint guardians disagree on any question affecting the welfare of the minor, any of them may apply to the court for its direction, and the court may make such order regarding the matter as it thinks proper.[119]

Disputes between a surviving parent and a guardian

Where a disagreement on any question affecting the welfare of a minor is between a guardian and a surviving parent, the powers to make such order include the power to make an order regarding:

> (i) the custody of the minor; and
> (ii) the right of access to the minor of his surviving parent
> as the court thinks fit having regard to the welfare of the minor.[120]

LAW REFORM

As has been seen, the domain of 'parental rights and authority' covers those legal incidents that attach to parenthood. To reflect the developing

---

[117] *Re McGrath (infants)* [1893] 1 Ch. 143; *F v F* [1902] 1 Ch. 688.
[118] S18(2).
[119] S9.
[120] S12(a).

perception of children as individuals in their own right, as well as the notion that the parent–child relationship is in essence one of responsibility rather than of right, the English Children Act 1989 has shifted to the concept of 'parental responsibility'. This is also one of the recommendations of the Hong Kong Law Reform Commission subgroup on Guardianship and Custody of Minors. The Commission is also of the view that 'custody' and 'access', which carry the notion of proprietary ownership, and 'parental rights' are inconsistent with the concept of 'parental responsibility'. Additionally, 'custody', a term which is often used by the divorce courts, is confusing. Some divorcing parents who obtain sole custody believe that it gives them all parental rights to the exclusion of the non-custodial parents, whereas non-custodial parents think that they are entitled to be consulted on major decisions regarding the child's upbringing.[121] The English law now provides that parents continue to have parental responsibility on divorce and the court's only function is to regulate the child's 'residence' and 'contact' with the non-residential parent. This being so, the court may make orders concerning these two matters, by way of making 'residence' and 'contact' orders. These are also the recommendations of the Hong Kong Law Reform Commission subgroup. The question of allocation of 'parental responsibility' on the divorce of parents will be examined in Chapter 10.

In Hong Kong, working parents often delegate the day-to-day care and upbringing of their children to a relative, a child minder, a domestic helper, or to child care centres, nurseries and schools. However, the law on parental responsibility is at the moment silent on these kinds of arrangement. It is unclear what responsibilities they have *vis-à-vis* a child in their care. S2(9) of the English Children Act 1989 provides that:

> A person who has parental responsibility for a child may not surrender or transfer any part of that responsibility to another but may arrange for some or all of it to be met by one or more persons acting on his behalf.

What a delegate may do in carrying out his or her responsibility depends on the scope of the delegation and may give rise to difficult legal issues which require detailed examination in the future.

Another topic which needs further consideration is the relationship between parents and guardians. This relationship, at the moment, is unsatisfactory. Under the GMO, a parent who has rights and authority is sometimes guardian and sometimes not. This is confusing. Law reform is

---

[121] See English Law Commission Report, No 172, 1988, para 4.3; see n. 4.

needed to rationalise the roles of these people in the care and upbringing of minors.

In England, the law has been reworked by the Children Act 1989. Central to the reform is the concept of parenthood and parental responsibility,[122] and the concept of parental guardianship has been abolished. Today, 'guardians' are restricted to parent-substitutes who take over parental responsibility in caring for a child.[123] A guardian is, in other words, a parent-substitute, and as such, has parental responsibility. As the English Law Commission states:

> The power to control a child's upbringing should go hand in hand with the responsibility to look after him or at least to see that he is properly looked after . . . it is now generally expected that guardians will take over complete responsibility for the care and upbringing of a child if the parents die. If so, it is right that full legal responsibility should also be placed upon them.[124]

Under the Children Act 1989, the distinction between 'guardians of the child's estate' and 'guardians of the child's person' has been abolished. The responsibilities of guardians are now incorporated into the concept of parental responsibility. Parental responsibility embraces all the powers of a guardian of the child's estates, including the powers to give a valid receipt, for example, of legacies.[125]

In order to encourage parents to make arrangements for the care of their children in the event of death, and in light of the general reluctance of especially young parents to utilise testamentary instruments, the method of appointment has been made less formal. Appointment of a testamentary guardian can now be effected if it is in writing, dated and signed.[126]

Under the GMO, the appointment of a testamentary guardian takes effect automatically on the death of a deceased parent. It has been argued that guardianship of a child is a serious responsibility and it is important that it should not be imposed on anyone who is not willing to accept it. Although one may assume that a parent would normally seek the consent of a person before naming him or her as guardian in a will or deed, there is no guarantee that this will happen in all cases. If a formal act of acceptance is not required, the law should at least provide for the possibility of

---

[122] S5(6).
[123] S2(4) of the Children Act 1989 abolished the rule that the father is the natural guardian of his legitimate child.
[124] English Law Commission Report, No 172, 1988, para 2.23; see n. 4.
[125] S3(2)(3).
[126] S5(5); English Law Commission Report, No 172, 1988, para 2.29; see n. 4.

disclaiming guardianship. S6(5) of the Children Act 1989 now provides that a testamentary guardian may disclaim appointment by an instrument in writing signed by him and made within a reasonable time of first knowing the appointment has taken effect.

To prevent conflict between a surviving custodial parent and an appointed guardian, and to avoid a situation where the former caring for the child has to cooperate with the latter, the Children Act 1989 now provides that where a child is living with both parents in a united household, a guardian's appointment shall take effect on the death of the surviving parent (but not immediately upon the death of the appointing parent).[127] As the Law Reform Commission observed:

> Those, comparatively few, children who experience the death of a parent while they are under 18 will usually have been living with both parents at the time. There can be little doubt that those children's interests will generally lie in preserving the stability of their existing home and thus in confirming the continued responsibility of the survivor. There seems little reason why the survivor should share that responsibility with a guardian who almost invariably will not be sharing the household.[128]

Where the parents have separated or divorced, the appointment of a guardian by a deceased custodial parent shall take effect on the death of the custodial parent. In other words, the appointed guardian will share parental responsibility with the non-custodial parent.[129] Where a child has no parent with parental responsibility for him, an appointment shall take effect immediately on the death of a parent.[130]

The parent–child relationship is a difficult and complex area of the law, and one in which major changes can be expected in the near future.

---

[127] S5(8).
[128] English Law Commission Report, No 172, 1988, para 2.27; see n. 4.
[129] S5(7)–(9); see also A Bainham, *Children: The Modern Law*, Family Law, Bristol, 1993, pp. 191–2.
[130] S5(7)(a).

9

Welfare of the Child

INTRODUCTION

The welfare of a minor is the 'first and paramount consideration' is a well established principle of family law. Thus, s3(1) Guardianship of Minors Ordinance (GMO) states that in any proceedings relating to the custody or upbringing of a minor, the court

> (i) shall regard the welfare of the minor as the first and paramount consideration and in having such regard shall give due consideration to–
> (a) the wishes of the minor if, having regard to the age and understanding of the minor and to the circumstances of the case, it is practicable to so; and
> (b) any material information including any report of the Director of Social Welfare available to the court at the hearing . . .

However, such concern for the well-being of a child is only a recent phenomenon. Thus, in the Infants Custody Ordinance (No 48 of 1935), welfare of the infant was only one consideration amongst others in determining the outcome of any dispute concerning a child.[1]

---

[1] S2(1) of the Infants Custody Ordinance (No 48 of 1935) provided that the court might grant custody and access having regard to 'the welfare of the infant, and to the conduct of the parents, and to the wishes as well of the mother as of the father'. For decisions under the Infants Custody Ordinance, see *Lui Yuk-ping v Chow To* [1962] HKLR 515; *Wong Yee-ling v Ng Tung-hoi* [1970] HKLR 183.

The welfare principle has been variously expressed; the best interests of the child, the interest of the child, the welfare of the child and the paramountcy principle, but they all appear to have the same meaning.[2]

MEANING OF FIRST AND PARAMOUNT CONSIDERATION

The notion that the welfare of the minor is the 'first and paramount consideration' means that all considerations, which conflict, or apparently conflict, with such welfare must be subordinated. In the leading case of *J v C*.[3] Lord McDermott stated:

> [These words] must mean more than that the child's welfare is to be treated as the top item in a list of items relevant to the matter in question. I think they connote a process whereby, when all the relevant facts, relationships, claims and wishes of parents, risks, choices and other circumstances are taken into account and weighed, the course to be followed will be that which is most in the interests of the child's welfare as that term, has now to be understood. That is the first consideration because it is of first importance and the paramount consideration because it rules upon or determines the course to be followed.

The balancing exercise of the court is not between serving other people's interests as against the interest of the child. The decision must be one which is in the best interests of a child. *J v C* itself demonstrates how the welfare principle operates. A Spanish boy was sent to live with his English foster parents whilst his natural parents tried to establish themselves economically. During the first ten years of the boy's life, he spent only 18 months with his parents, and the rest of the time with his foster parents, being brought up as an English boy. When his parents claimed for his return to live with them in Spain, the House of Lords held that there was no presumption that the welfare of a minor was best served by allowing him to live with his parents. In this case, the boy hardly knew his parents

---

[2] Mnookin, 'Child Custody Adjudication: Judicial Functions in the Face of Indeterminacy', 39 Law & Contemporary Problems 226 (1975); see also David Chambers; Marygold Melli, 'Towards a Restructuring of Custody Decision-making at Divorce: An Alternative Approach to the Best Interests of the Child', in *Parenthood in Modern Society: Legal and Social Issues for the Twenty-first Century*, ed by John Eekelaar and Petar Sarcevic, Martinus Nijhoff Publishers, London, 1993.
[3] [1969] 1 All ER 788.

and spoke little Spanish. He was well-settled in England, and the parents were ill-equipped to cope with the child's problems in readjusting to a new way of life. The parents' interest in having the boy returned were outweighed by the child's welfare so it was held that care and control should remain with the foster parents. The decision represented a major development in that it required the court to focus on the welfare of the minor independent of parental rights and wishes.[4]

APPLICATION OF THE WELFARE PRINCIPLE

The welfare principle applies in any proceedings relating to the custody and upbringing of a minor. S10(1) of the GMO, however, states that the court may make such order regarding the custody of the minor and the right of access to the minor of either of his parents, 'as the court thinks fit having regard to the welfare of the minor and to the conduct and wishes of the parents'. Despite the difference in wording, it has been held that there is no inconsistency between s10(1) and s3(1) of the GMO.[5]

Notwithstanding the general application of the welfare principle, it is not applicable to an injunction under the Domestic Violence Ordinance or Adoption Ordinance, nor does it apply to all wardship proceedings as discussed below. It is not relevant under s12 or 13 of the Parent and Child Ordinance or s34(1) of the Protection of Children and Juveniles Ordinance.

THE MEANING OF WELFARE: GENERAL CONSIDERATIONS

Although judges often talk about 'welfare', the term encapsulates the widest possible meaning and is incapable of precise definition. Thus, it has been said that:

---

[4] S1 of the Children Act 1989 has dropped the word 'first'. It provides that 'welfare shall be the court's paramount consideration'. This change in wording was not intended to bring about any change to the law.

[5] *Re D (minors) (wardship: jurisdiction)* [1973] 2 All ER 993, at p. 1008 per Bagnall J. See also *Lui Yuk-ping v Chow To* [1962] HKLR 515; *Wong Yee-ling v Ng Tung-hoi* [1970] HKLR 183 but in *Re Lai Kin-fung*, District Court, Civil Jurisdiction, Miscellaneous Proceedings No 401 of 1979 (1980), it was thought that 'welfare', 'conduct' and 'wishes' were of equal importance; *Re Huthart (infants)*, High Court, Miscellaneous Proceedings No 1037 of 1981 (1984).

> The welfare of the child is not to be measured by money only, nor by physical comfort only. The word welfare must be considered in its widest sense. The moral and religious welfare of the child must be considered as well as its physical well-being. Nor can the ties of affection be disregarded.[6]

Further, it has been said that welfare:

> ... must be taken in its large signification as meaning that the welfare of the child as a whole must be considered. It is not merely a question whether the child would be happier in one place than in another, but of her general well-being.[7]

'Welfare' is an evolving concept. In the old English cases, welfare was subsumed under paternal authority. Thus, in *Re Fynn*,[8] a father who had left his children unwashed, ill-clothed and ill-fed, and allowed then to become 'accustomed to using bad language ... and [appeared] to have no idea that they were doing wrong in using these expressions' was able to keep the children. The mother was unable to persuade the court that the father's rights should be suspended, and that it was better for the children to be with the mother. Today, physical well-being, hygiene and a well-mannered upbringing are probably regarded as basic elements of a child's welfare. Some seventy years ago, in *Re Thain*,[9] a widower who, for seven years, left his daughter to be cared for by a married couple, demanded her return. The court found that she would be well cared for in the home of either party. In dealing with the distress which might be caused to the girl being parted from the couple, Eve J said that:

> ... the little girl will be greatly distressed and upset at parting from Mr and Mrs Jones. I can quite understand it may be so, but, at her tender age, one knows from experience how mercifully transient are the effects of partings and other sorrows, and how soon the novelty of fresh surroundings and new associations effaces the recollection of former days and kind friends, and I cannot attach much weight to this aspect of the case.[10]

Forty years later, in *Re W (infants)*,[11] two children had been looked after for four years by a couple who sought to adopt them. Their application was opposed by the father and the question was whether the children

---

[6] *Re McGrath (infants)* [1893] 1 Ch. 143 at p. 148 per Lindley LJ.
[7] *Re Thain* [1926] 1 Ch. 676 at p. 689.
[8] (1848) 2 De G & SM 457.
[9] [1926] 1 Ch. 676.
[10] Ibid., at p. 684.
[11] [1965] 3 All ER 231.

would be harmed if taken away from the couple and returned to the father. The court ordered that the children remain in the care of the couple, the court commenting on the earlier views of Eve J as follows:

On the views of Eve J, it was said that:

> ...the child psychiatrists who give evidence in these cases nowadays, though they do not always agree in detail, all emphasise the risks involved in transferring young children from the care of one person to another... while as to the views of Eve, J., Dr S, when they were put to him, plainly regarded them much as Thomas Huxley would have regarded the suggestion that the world came into being in the manner set out in the first chapter of Genesis.[12]

It would be difficult to isolate all relevant aspects which pertain to the welfare of a minor. Nor would it be possible to produce a scale indicating the relative weight of the factors which have a bearing on the welfare of a child. The elusive nature of the concept of welfare is well summed up by Andrew Bainham:

> ... the "welfare" or "best interests" of children are notoriously indeterminate concepts, so much so that it has been argued that the really crucial issue is not the concept of welfare itself but the choice of decision-makers. What is or is not in children's interests depends largely on who is asked the question. Thus, there are those who assert that the psychological well-being of children following divorce is best protected by "exclusive" custodial arrangements which provide them with the security of one "psychological parent". But, equally, there are others who take the apparently diametrically opposed position that children fare best where contact with both divorcing parents is maximised and maintained. It is, perhaps, inevitable that individual value judgments must intrude to some extent into the determination of a child's best interests.[13]

In order to ensure that the court, in exercising its wide discretion, considers all factors which general experience has shown to be relevant, some jurisdictions have by statute laid down a list of mandatory factors.[14] One example of this approach is s1(3) of the English Children Act 1989

---

[12] Ibid., at p. 249 per Cross J.
[13] See *Children: The Modern Law,* Family Law, Bristol, 1993, p. 43; see Article 9(3) of the UN Convention on the Rights of the Child (hereafter cited as UNC); David Chambers, 'Rethinking the Substantive Rules for Custody Disputes in Divorce' (1984) 83 Mich. LR 477; Mnookin; Stephen Parker, 'The Best Interests of the Child — Principles and Problems', 8 International Journal of Law and the Family (1994) 26.
[14] Children Act 1989, see Australia, Annex I of this chapter, pp. 272–3.

which provides that the court shall have regard to the following matters in determining the welfare of the child, which are:

> (a) the ascertainable wishes and feelings of the child concerned (considered in the light of his age and understanding);
> (b) his physical, emotional and educational needs;
> (c) the likely effect on him of any change in his circumstances;
> (d) his age, sex, background and any characteristics of his which the court considers relevant;
> (e) any harm which he has suffered or is at risk of suffering;
> (f) how capable each of his parents, any other person in relation to whom the court considers the question to be relevant, is of meeting his needs;
> (g) the range of powers available to the court under this Act in the proceedings in question.[15]

The focus of the check-list is on the child and his individual needs, and how those needs could best be met. Dame Margaret Justice Booth, in support of the check-list, remarked:

> By this check-list the statute enjoins the court, in exercising its discretion, to keep in the forefront of its mind the child with which it is concerned. In some instances when difficult findings of fact have to be made, for example, as to the perpetration of sexual abuse, or when adult relationships are complex or personalities are strong, it is easy for the focus of attention to move away from the child whose future is at stake and to become concentrated instead on the adults involved. The provision has the salutory effect of bringing the court back on course.

In some cases, an examination of some or all of the factors may indicate that a child's interests will best be served by being with a particular parent. There are, however, cases where the factors may pull the court in different directions. For instance, an infant's physical and emotional needs may best be served by being with the mother, although his long-term educational needs may be better served if he is with his father. Again, a nine-year-old girl may be adamant that she stays with the father although there may be evidence suggesting that she has been sexually abused by him. Each case, however, depends very much on its own facts, and the weight to be given to any particular factor is a matter of judicial discretion. Precedents, in the strict sense, do not exist.

---

[15] The check-list, however, is not like a list of checks which an airline pilot has to make with his co-pilot, checked aloud to one another before taking off, *H v H (residence order: leave to remove from jurisdiction)* [1995] 1 FLR 529.

MEANING OF WELFARE: SPECIFIC CONSIDERATIONS

The GMO contains no check-list of factors which the court must consider. This, however, does not mean that cases are decided in a vacuum. Analysis of the case law shows that the courts have, for many years, considered the factors (a)–(f) above as important in deciding what is in the best interests of a child. The weight which has been attached to these factors, however, has varied from case to case, and they have to be understood in light of the unique local circumstances and culture. It must be noted that there are no arithmetical point systems or quantitative formulae for assessing any of these factors. The courts are dealing with the lives of human beings, and these cannot be regulated by any rigid prescriptions.[16]

Wishes of the Child

Article 12(1) UN Convention on the Rights of the Child also provides that:

> States Parties shall assure to the child who is capable of forming his or her own views the right to express those views freely in all matters affecting the child, the views of the child being given due weight in accordance with the age and maturity of the child.[17]

S3(1) of the GMO makes specific reference to the wishes of the child. However, there is no uniform method or system for ascertaining a child's wishes although these are normally indicated in the social welfare reports. A number of older cases, however, reveal that it was not uncommon for judges to see a child in chambers.[18] The difficulty with this practice is highlighted in *B v B (minors) (interviews and listing arrangements)*.[19] In that case, the three children were 16, 14 and 11. They were intensely loyal to both parents. When they were interviewed by the judge, they refused to express a preference as to which parent they wished to live with because the judge could not promise them that he would not disclose to their parents what they said to him. As Wall J said:

---

[16] *Re F (an infant)* [1969] 2 Ch. 238.
[17] See also Article (9)(2) UNC.
[18] *Re Y* [1946–1972] HKC 378; *Re Kwok Micah (a minor)*, High Court, Miscellaneous Proceedings No 3040 of 1984 (1985); *Re Chan Heung (an infant)*, High Court, Miscellaneous Proceedings No 349 of 1983 (1983); *L v L* [1970] HKLR 556; *Re Huthart (infants)*, High Court, Miscellaneous Proceedings No 1037 of 1981 (1984); *Wong Yip Yuk-ping v Wong Sze-sang*, Court of Appeal, Civil Appeal Action No 116 of 1985 (1985).
[19] [1994] 2 FLR 489.

> The difficulty ... [was] that there was an inherent contradiction in seeing the children for the purpose of ascertaining their wishes whilst, at the same time, being required to report to their parents anything material which the children said. The children ... are in an impossible dilemma, which can only add to the emotional trauma to which they are already subject. Any expression of a preference for one parent inevitably involves disloyalty to the other.[20]

For the above reasons, it was said in *B v B (minors) (interviews and listing arrangements)*[21] that the discretion to see children should be exercised cautiously and should in no sense be automatic or routine.

Where a child is not caught in this conflict of loyalty, its wishes may be of little value if they reflect an adult's indoctrination, or conflict with the child's long-term interests.[22] The age and understanding of a child is crucial. A six-year-old child's wishes could often be ephemeral, changing from day to day in which case little or no weight should be given to his preferences.[23] Conversely, the wishes of a 15-year-old boy, unless they were plainly contrary to his long-term welfare, could not be ignored lightly.[24] More recently, in *Re S (minors) (access: religious upbringing)*,[25] it was said that children of 13 and 11 years of age were entitled to be treated with respect; they were not packages to be moved around. In *Re Julie Ong*,[26] a nine-year-old girl's strongly held convictions that she wanted to stay in Hong Kong with her stepmother and would throw herself in front of a vehicle if she had to return to the Philippines with her natural mother were considered important. However, in *Wong Chiu Ngar-chi v Wong Hon-wai*,[27] the Court of Appeal held that the wishes of children who were minors of 10 and 6 years old were not to be given too much weight. Similarly in *Seghin v Seghin*,[28] the Court of Appeal refused to take into account the views of children the eldest of whom was 10 years old. On the wishes of children, Ching JA said:

> ... we reject as did the Judge below any submission that reliance should be placed upon the expressed wishes of children as young as these. They are far too young to know what is best for themselves. They, especially a

---

[20] At p. 495.
[21] [1994] 2 FLR 489.
[22] See *Re S (infants)* [1967] 1 All ER 202 at p. 210 per Cross J.
[23] *Re Lee Cheuh-wah (an infant)*, High Court, Miscellaneous Proceedings No 2678 of 1983 (1984).
[24] *C v C*, Court of Appeal, Civil Appeal Action No 44 of 1988 (1988).
[25] [1992] 2 FLR 313, 321 per Butler Sloss LJ.
[26] High Court, Miscellaneous Proceedings No 1895 of 1988 (1989).
[27] [1987] HKLR 179.
[28] Court of Appeal, Civil Appeal Action No 274 of 1995 (1996).

child of the age of Raphael, will know that something is seriously wrong between their parents but they probably will not understand why or what consequences will follow. Their hope will normally be that everything should be as it was in the past and that they should be with both parents. To ask such children with whom they would wish to be is to put them in an intolerable position.

Physical, Emotional and Educational Needs

The different needs of a child vary in their relative importance depending on the child's age and sex.[29] Physical and emotional needs are of paramount importance to an infant, whereas discipline and education can be crucial to a young child. In a number of cases, the education and discipline of a young child and a teenager have been stressed. In *Re Kwok Micah (a minor)*,[30] both parents were blind and the son, the subject of this action, was 12 years old. The father was a shiftless character, insincere and superficial, and had been in financial difficulties for many years. Consequently, the family had moved their home on several occasions to avoid creditors. Additionally, the father's daughter from a previous marriage was not well brought up and she ended up in Tai Tam Gap Correctional Institution. The mother, on the other hand, could provide the child with a stable, affectionate home and the guidance of a sincere mother. It was held that the best interests of the boy lay with the mother who might provide him with the proper character training so that he could mature with a sense of responsibility and discipline. He, however, would not be exposed to these positive influences if he were to live with the father. Again, in *Re Huthart (infants)*,[31] the mother was having difficulties in controlling her older daughter who was 11 years old. Care and control was given to the father who had a sensible appreciation of the need to properly discipline the children. Similarly, in *Mong Ka-hung (a minor)*,[32] the parents of a child were killed in a plane crash and the child was looked after by relatives. Both the paternal grandmother and the uncle (together with his wife) proposed to care for the child. The paternal grandmother and grandfather were aged 66 and 72 respectively, and the latter was in ill-health. The uncle was 27 years old. He had a Bachelor of Science degree and was a qualified Civil Engineer. He earned a reasonable salary and was entitled to acquire Canadian citizenship. It was held that the best interests of the minor would

---

[29] See below, pp. 255–8.
[30] High Court, Miscellaneous Proceedings No 3040 of 1984 (1985).
[31] High Court, Miscellaneous Proceedings No 1037 of 1981 (1984).
[32] High Court, Miscellaneous Proceedings No 1908 of 1982 (1983).

be served if the child was placed in the care of the uncle and his wife. They were of an appropriate age to care for the child, but more importantly, they would be in a financial position to provide for the child's tertiary education should he wish to undertake such.

Status Quo

This means 'the state in which things are' and has become a vital consideration in welfare. Status quo entails continuity of existing relationships, emotional ties and bonds, as well as continuity of environment. A lot more is now known about the effects of a change of care and control on a child's development, and on his mental and physical health. Whereas in the past, judges would dismiss a child's grief in parting with the primary care-giver as transitory,[33] it is now recognised that disruption of the status quo and separation of a child from his psychological parent may be highly detrimental to his mental and physical well-being.[34] It is now accepted that children, particularly in their early years, need continuity of care, which provides a sense of security. Established bonds, thus, are to be preserved if possible, and good reasons need to be adduced to justify transferring a child, even as an interim measure, from his well-established home environment, thereby severing the bonds with his/her psychological parents.[35] Maintenance of the status quo presents a strong argument against a party who has lost contact with a child, or who has never established a bond with a child.[36]

Maintenance of the status quo means that on parents' separation or divorce, the party who continues to look after the children may have an advantage in that the court is likely to confirm existing arrangement, rather than order a transfer of custody. The status quo argument, however, is only useful where existing arrangements are satisfactory. The more satisfactory the arrangement is, the stronger the argument for not interfering with it.[37]

---

[33] *Re Thain* [1926] 1 Ch. 676.
[34] J Goldstein, A Freud, A J Solnit, *Beyond the Best Interests of the Child*, Burnett Books, London, 1979.
[35] *Dicocco v Milne* [1983] 4 FLR 247.
[36] See *B v B (custody of children)* [1985] FLR 166; status quo is not the same as actual possession of the child. See *Edwards v Edwards* [1986] 1 FLR 187; it is not possible for a father to establish status quo in the first three weeks of a newborn's life, *Re W (a minor) (residence order)* [1992] 2 FLR 332.
[37] Cf. Status quo not to be maintained where the father and stepmother were committed scientologists and the children would be gravely at risk if they remained in their care, *Re B and G (minors) (custody)* [1985] FLR 134; *Re B and G (minors) (custody)* [1985] FLR 493.

The courts' reluctance to disrupt the status quo can be seen in *Chow Cheung Suk-king v Chow Yan-piu*[38] where the mother left the matrimonial home and her two boys aged five and 18 months for a period of eight months. The trial judge granted custody to the mother. The Court of Appeal disagreed. It was held that both husband and wife were hardworking, loving and caring parents. The status quo of a loving and caring environment to which the children were accustomed should not be disturbed. The trial judge had underestimated the disruption to the lives of the children in moving to the mother's home and consequently custody of the children should remain with the father. However, where a child is close to both parents and familiar with their home, the importance of the status quo is much reduced. Thus, in *Liu Lau Oi-yuk v Liu Chian-hsiong*,[39] Deputy Judge Saunders said that:

> ... where both parents have maintained very close contact with the child and the child is thoroughly familiar with the surroundings offered by both parents ... the disruption caused as a result of a change in custody will be much less. In this case ... the [boy] is so familiar with both sets of surroundings that if a change were to be made he would cope with it without any adverse effects.

Another example of the court favouring maintaining the status quo can be seen in the case of *Re Lee Cheuh-wah (an infant)*.[40] There the marriage deteriorated and the father took the son and disappeared for almost four years. The boy was subsequently found living with the paternal grandparents. The boy, by then nine-year-old, was well cared for and had developed strong emotional ties with his grandparents. He was happily settled at school, and his academic performance was most satisfactory. Although the court expressed grave disapproval of a parent 'kidnapping' or 'snatching' a child, it was reluctant to disturb the status quo.[41]

Age and Sex of the Children: the Position of Mother Versus Father

The age of a child is relevant in that it relates to his or her needs. These

---

[38] Court of Appeal, Civil Appeal Action No 180 of 1984 (1984); see also *Re Mark Leung*, Miscellaneous Proceedings No 142 of 1985 (1985).
[39] Court of Appeal, Civil Appeal Action No 126 of 1997 (1997).
[40] High Court, Miscellaneous Proceedings No 2678 of 1983 (1984); *Liu Lau Oi-yuk v Liu Chian-hsiong*, Court of Appeal, Civil Appeal Action No 126 of 1997 (1997).
[41] *Re L (minors) (wardship: jurisdiction)* [1974] 1 WLR 250; *W v D* [1980] 1 FLR 393; *Townson v Mahon* [1984] FLR 690; *Re J (a minor) (interim custody: appeal)* [1989] 2 FLR 304.

needs may also point to who is best suited to fulfilling them. In many families, mothers are the primary care-giver to children. This may be so even if the mother works outside the home. As such, she may be placed in an advantageous position, having demonstrated her ability to cater to the children's needs. All things being equal, a child of tender years should be with its mother. One learned judge said:

> "on the whole the best place for a boy of $3\frac{3}{4}$ is with his mother; is there anything to displace that human view?" I entirely agree with that approach. I think there is no doubt — and this is not a proposition of law — that from the point of view of common sense and ordinary humanity, all things being equal, the best place for any small child is with its mother.[42]

In 1992, with regard to a four-week-old baby, Balcombe LJ said:

> Although there is undoubtedly no presumption of law that a child of any given age is better off with one parent or the other ... no court can be ignorant of what would be the natural position if other things were equal. It hardly requires saying that a baby of under four weeks old would normally be with his or her natural mother.[43]

This approach was approved by the Court of Appeal in *Chow Cheung Suk-king v Chow Yan-piu*.[44] The court, however, stressed that this was not a principle, rule, or even presumption, but simply a judicial statement of general experience. In *Wong Yip Yuk-ping v Wong Sze-sang*,[45] it was said that this judicial statement of general experience applied to children of seven and nine years.

> [counsel] suggests that it applies only to children considerably younger than the ones we are concerned with. With respect, I do not think that is so, although naturally the age of the children is relevant. It is a factor that becomes less important as the children grow older, with a caveat perhaps, in the case of young girls approaching puberty. Its importance may perhaps also be less where the circumstances are such that the mother ... has not established such a close bond with the children in their infancy as she might have done. Of course, it is not a rule of law. It is not even indeed a presumption. But it has become so well established that I would expect any judge, when considering custody, to take that as his starting point

---

[42] *H v H* [1969] 1 All ER 262 at p. 263 per Salmon LJ.
[43] *Re W (a minor) (residence order)* [1992] 2 FLR 332 at p. 335; *Re W (a minor) (custody)* [1983] 4 FLR 492.
[44] Court of Appeal, Civil Appeal Action No 180 of 1984 (1984).
[45] Court of Appeal, Civil Appeal Action No 116 of 1985 (1985).

before turning to consider whether in the particular circumstances he should go further.[46]

The judicial statement of general experience that, all things being equal, the best place for any small child is with its mother, however, is to be examined in the light of the facts of each case. In Hong Kong, it is not unusual for both parents to be working full-time outside the home, with children being looked after by domestic helpers, paternal or maternal grandparents. In these cases, the ability of the primary carer to continue to look after the children can be important. This could be the reason why fathers have been successful in obtaining custody in a number of cases.[47]

In 1985, it was said that the fact that a mother was a career woman was detrimental to her obtaining custody. Thus, it was said in *Wong Yip Yuk-ping v Wong Sze-sang* that:[48]

> the wife was a career woman at heart and the judge doubted whether she had a genuine sustainable desire, or the ability, to be a simple housewife ... He relied on [the fact of her] going out to work when, as he found on the evidence ... it was not financially necessary for the sake of the family.

Such an attitude may not be acceptable today; a parent should not be deprived of custody because he or she pursues a career *per se*. Indeed, many fathers may also be well equipped to undertake child-care responsibilities even though they have substantial career responsibilities.[49]

Apart from the age of the child being relevant, there is a related 'principle' that young siblings should, whenever possible, be brought up together in the same household so that they can be of emotional support to each other.[50] If a judge decides against young children being kept together, such decision merits some explanation.[51]

The combined operation of the tender years doctrine and the 'rule' that

---

[46] Per Cons JA; see also *Ng Cheei-fai v Ng Han Lai-wah*, Court of Appeal, Civil Appeal Action No 28 of 1980 (1980).

[47] See *Chow Cheung Suk-king v Chow Yan-piu*, Court of Appeal, Civil Appeal Action No 180 of 1984 (1984); *Wong Yip Yuk-ping v Wong Sze-sang*, Court of Appeal, Civil Appeal Action No 116 of 1985 (1985); *Wong Yee-ling v Ng Tung-hoi* [1970] HKLR 183; *L v L* [1970] HKLR 556.

[48] Court of Appeal, Civil Appeal Action No 116 of 1985 (1985).

[49] *Re S (a minor) (custody)* [1991] 2 FLR 388 at p. 392 per Lord Donaldson.

[50] See *Re Y (minors)* [1984] HKLR 204 concerning two wards aged 8 (female) and $5\frac{1}{2}$ (male) where the court said that children of tender years should not be separated. Cf. *Re P (infants)* [1967] 2 All ER 229.

[51] *C v C (minors: custody)* [1988] 2 FLR 291.

siblings should not be separated can be seen in *Re Ryker (infants)*,⁵² where it was said that:

> I am in no doubt that so far as Elisabeth is concerned she should be placed in the care and control of her mother. She is a three year old child and all other things being equal I am quite satisfied that a girl of that age requires the guidance, advice and companionship that only a mother can give. The position is not as clear with Sarah and [it was said] that she is reaching an age when she is looking more towards her father. However, I consider that even at the age of 9 a daughter requires a mother more than a father. What is very clear is that the two girls should not be separated and that each will in the years to come require and obtain a great deal from the company of each other. I am therefore satisfied that ... [the mother] should be entitled to their care and control.⁵³

Again, in *W v W*,⁵⁴ the court held that young children should not be separated even where the court was faced with a *de facto* separation. It would always examine all the relevant circumstances closely before turning such a situation into a *de jure* one by its order.

Any Harm the Child has Suffered or Is at Risk of Suffering

This is relevant where a parent has neglected or abused (sexually or physically) the child and the court needs to balance the importance of the child maintaining a relationship with that parent against the risk of being harmed by such relationship. A parent who has been found to have sexually abused his child may be denied access. In *Re R (a minor) (child abuse: access)*,⁵⁵ the mother had a casual relationship with the father, and as a result she gave birth to a daughter. The father was 20 years older than the mother, and he continued to live with his wife and children. The court found that the father had sexually abused the daughter and it was held that any benefit to the child of maintaining the relationship with the father (which the court viewed as highly artificial) had no weight as against the risk to her of being further sexually abused. However, in *L v L (child abuse: access)*,⁵⁶ the father was found to have sexually abused his three-

---

[52] High Court, Miscellaneous Proceedings No 1184 of 1980 (1982); see also *Seghin v Seghin* Court of Appeal, Civil Appeal Action No 274 of 1995 (1996).
[53] Per Penlington J.
[54] [1981] HKC 466.
[55] [1988] 1 FLR 206; see also *S v S (child abuse: access)* [1988] 1 FLR 213.
[56] [1989] 2 FLR 16.

year-old daughter. The judge found evidence of a close bond between father and daughter, the girl enjoyed seeing the father and she was socially well adjusted and showed no disturbance after the sexual abuse. It was held that as the daughter had benefited from the access, access should be supervised and the matter be returned for further review and consideration in due course.

The Capacity of Each Parent and Other Person in Meeting the Child's Needs

Where a dispute is between parents, the parent who has established strong emotional ties with a child, appreciates the child's needs and is capable of meeting them, is favoured by the court. In families with working parents, the role of the primary carer is often played by paternal or maternal grandparents, a great-grandmother,[57] or domestic helpers. This sometimes means that the 'real' custody dispute is between the grandmothers or the mother-in-laws.[58] Thus, in *Re Mark Leung*,[59] the parents divorced. The father was not contesting for his 20-month-old boy and the litigation was between the mother and the paternal grandmother. The grandmother had not cared for a baby for over 20 years and would leave the upbringing of the child in the hands of domestic helpers. It was held that the boy should not be deprived of maternal love which the mother was able to provide.[60]

Where a dispute is between parents and a third party, to what extent blood ties are an important consideration is unclear. In *J v C*, the court granted care and control of the child to the foster-parent as opposed to the natural parents, but it was acknowledged that blood ties were not altogether irrelevant.

> ... natural parents have a strong claim to have their wishes considered; first and principally, no doubt, because normally it is part of the paramount consideration of the welfare of the infant that he should be with them, but also because as the natural parents they have themselves a strong claim to have their wishes considered as normally the proper persons to have the upbringing of the child they have brought into the world.[61]

---

[57] *Chow Cheung Suk-king v Chow Yan-piu*.
[58] See e.g. *Re Lai Kin-fung (an infant)*, District Court, Miscellaneous Proceedings No 401 of 1979 (1980).
[59] High Court, Miscellaneous Proceedings No 142 of 1985 (1985).
[60] *Chow Cheung Suk-king v Chow Yan-piu*, Court of Appeal, Civil Appeal Action No 180 of 1984 (1984).
[61] [1969] All ER 788 at p. 832.

Similarly, in *Re Julie Ong*,[62] a five-year-old child was taken by her father from the Philippines to live in Hong Kong. For four years, she settled in Hong Kong with her stepmother, forgot her Tagalog and became fluent in Cantonese. The mother who did not speak Cantonese sought to have the child back. It was held that the status quo should be maintained and the child should remain with her stepmother.[63]

On the other hand, there appears to be a presumption that the welfare of the child is best secured by being with the parents. It matters not whether the parent is wise or foolish, rich or poor, educated or illiterate, provided the child's moral and physical health are not endangered,[64] it being remarked that:

> ... the welfare of the child is indeed the test, but there is a strong supposition, other things being equal, that it is in the interests of the child to be brought up by his natural parents.[65]

In *Re K (a minor) (wardship: adoption)*,[66] a mother, who had two other children of her own, gave birth to a third at a time of difficulty and stress. She left her baby with a couple to look after. The couple were warm and loving and they lavished love and devotion on the child. The mother had properly cared for her other children and genuinely wanted the baby back some seven and a half months later. The judge at first instance asked himself who would provide a better home for the baby. The Court of Appeal held that this was the wrong approach. Butler-Sloss LJ:

> The question was not: where would R get the better home? The question was: was it demonstrated that the welfare of the child positively demanded the displacement of the parental right? ... The mother must be shown to be entirely unsuitable before another family can be considered, otherwise we are in grave danger of slipping into social engineering.[67]

Peculiar to Hong Kong is its crowded living environment and this may be an important consideration in a custody dispute. Thus, in *Chow Cheung Suk-king*, the father lived in a housing unit with his mother, father, and two brothers. The mother lived in a cubicle rented from a principal tenant who lived in another cubicle upon the same premises. The main room of the premises where the mother lived was described as follows:

---

[62] High Court, Miscellaneous Proceedings No 1895 of 1988 (1989).
[63] See also *Trance v Walli*, High Court, Miscellaneous Proceedings No 905 of 1988 (1988).
[64] *Re KD (a minor) (access: principle)* [1988] 2 FLR 139 at p. 141 per Lord Templeman.
[65] *Re W (a minor) (residence order)* [1993] 2 FLR 625 at p. 639 per Waite LJ.
[66] [1991] 1 FLR 57.
[67] Ibid., at pp. 60–2.

[The main room] is used as a workshop by the principal tenant who makes paper envelopes such as *lai see* packets. There is a variable number of employees ranging from [ten-four]. Work continues each week day from nine o'clock in the morning until eight o'clock in the evening. On Sunday the main room is available for use, on a shared basis, as a place to entertain visitors. The kitchen and the lavatory attached to the flat are shared with the principal tenant and, presumably, with her workers while they are on the premises.

The father's accommodation was clearly preferable. However, in *Re Lee Cheuh-wah (an infant)*,[68] the father lived in a 400 sq. ft. flat and the mother resided in a 200 sq. ft. flat. The court rightly took the view that, as far as the physical living conditions were concerned, there did not seem to be anything really to choose between them.

Material well-being is not the same as welfare. Thus, in *Re Mark Leung*, which was discussed previously, the mother came from a middle-class family and the father came from a wealthy family. The mother and paternal grandmother sought care and control of the infant boy. Although the mother's home was not as luxuriously comfortable as that of the father's and she could not provide 'a bevy of servants' for the child, the effect of giving care and control to the paternal grandmother was that:

> The child would be visited by his parents separately and would have to be told why he did not live with either of them. I would venture to add that in such a situation the lack of continued love and affection of both parents might create a feeling of vacuum in the child.[69]

A finely balanced case

Where the welfare plans presented by two loving and devoted parents are both capable of providing a secure and happy home for a child, it is not wrong to give custody to the parent who is able to spend more time with the child. This was the case in *Liu Lau Oi-yuk v Liu Chian-hsiong*.[70] In that case, the father was living with his mother and two sisters. He worked shifts, alternating from week to week with work from 9 am to 5 pm, and then from 2.30 pm to 11 pm. The mother was the primary carer for the child who was aged six. The mother lived with her sister, her brother-in-law and their young baby and she worked part-time from 1.30 pm to 5.30 pm. She would be directly and immediately involved in caring for the

---

[68] High Court, Miscellaneous Proceedings No 2678 of 1983 (1984).
[69] Deputy Judge Henry Wong.
[70] Court of Appeal, Civil Appeal Action No 126 of 1997 (1997).

child. It was found that both mother and father were loving and devoted parents. Deputy Judge Saunders said that:

> When, in all other respects, the ability of either parent to care for a child cannot, by themselves, be criticised, the ability of one parent to give more time to the child will weigh with the court in determining where the child's best interests lie.

The Court of Appeal held that the judge did not place inordinate weight on the time which each parent could give to the boy and the exercise of the judicial discretion did not exceed the generous ambit within which reasonable disagreement is possible.

Irrelevant Considerations

Certain Chinese values have no role to play in the welfare of a child. Thus, it has been held that no weight should be attached to a husband's desire that the child should be brought up in accordance with strict Chiu Chow traditions.[71] Further, it was said that parents trying to avoid court proceedings and yet bargain for what appears to be a fair outcome by dividing the children up one each according to their sex is not a relevant consideration. In other words, where there is one boy and one girl, the desire of the parties to divide them, the girl be given to the mother and the boy to the father, is not a matter which the court would take into account.[72]

Now that the welfare of a minor is the first and paramount consideration, parties' misconduct *vis-à-vis* each other or conduct causing marriage breakdown are no longer relevant.[73] Conduct of a parent is only relevant if it has some bearing on a parent *qua* parent. Thus, in *Re K (minors) (children: care and control)*,[74] the wife formed an adulterous relationship with another man. She left the matrimonial home with the children, a boy aged five and a girl aged two. The father, a clergyman, argued that the spiritual well-being of the children would be affected if the children were given to the mother, as they would be living with an adulterous couple. The court, however, held that this could not override the welfare of

---

[71] *C v C* [1977–1979] HKC 363; *Wong Yee-ling v Ng Tung-hoi* [1970] HKLR 183.
[72] *Re Y (minors)* [1984] HKLR 204.
[73] See *Re Lee Cheuh-wah (an infant)*, High Court, Miscellaneous Proceedings No 2678 of 1983 (1984); *Lui Yuk-ping v Chow To* [1962] HKLR 515; *Re Lai Kin-fung (an infant)*, District Court, Miscellaneous Proceedings No 401 of 1979 (1980); *Re Huthart (infants)*, High Court, Miscellaneous Proceedings No 1037 of 1981 (1984).
[74] [1977] Fam 179.

the children, which could best be served by being with the mother. It has sometimes been said that where the welfare of the child could be equally served by awarding custody to either parent, conduct of the parties may tip the scales.[75] This, it is submitted, may not be right.[76]

The fact that a father has only been able to look after a child successfully by virtue of his being unemployed and could only continue to do so if he remained out of work is not a relevant consideration. In *B v B (custody of children)*,[77] the parents separated and the father continued to look after the child with the help of his parents. The trial judge put into the balance as a determining factor the moral duty of a father to find work and not to take advantage of state benefits, and he granted care and control to the mother. It was held by the Court of Appeal that the judge erred in law in putting that into the balance as a determining factor.

THE BEST INTERESTS OF THE CHILD OR PRESUMPTION IN FAVOUR OF PRIMARY CARER

The best interests of the child is now the central precept in the law relating to children. However, critics have argued that the welfare principle is indeterminate and that indeterminacy encourages litigation. An alternative and better approach, it is suggested, involves a more objective standard, such as a presumption in favour of a primary carer approach. Thus, Mnookin argues that:[78]

> Moreover, whether or not the judge looks to the child for some guidance, there remains the question whether best interests should be viewed from a long-term or a short-term perspective. The conditions that make a person happy at age seven to ten may have adverse consequences at age thirty. Should the judge ask himself what decision will make the child happiest next year? Or at thirty? Or at seventy? Should the judge decide by thinking about what decision the child as an adult looking back, would have wanted made? In this case, the preference-problem is formidable, for how is the

---

[75] See *Re F (an infant)* [1988] 2 Ch. 238.
[76] *Liu Lan Oi-yuk v Liu Chian-hsiong*, see n. 70.
[77] [1985] FLR 166.
[78] Mnookin, 'Child Custody Adjudication: Judicial Functions in the Face of Indeterminacy', 39 Law & Contemporary Problems 226 (1975) 226 at p. 260; see also David Chambers; Marygold Melli, 'Towards a Restructuring of Custody Decision-making at Divorce: An Alternative Approach to the Best Interests of the Child', in *Parenthood in Modern Society: Legal and Social Issues for the Twenty-first Century*, ed by John Eekelaar and Petar Sarcevic, Martinus Nijhoff Publishers, London, 1993.

judge to compare "happiness" at one age with "happiness" at another age.

Deciding what is best for a child poses a question no less ultimate than the purposes and values of life itself. Should the judge be primarily concerned with the child's happiness? Or with the child's spiritual and religious training? Should the judge be concerned with the economic "productivity" of the child when he grows up? Are the primary values of life in warm, interpersonal relationships, or in discipline and self-sacrifice? Is stability and security for a child more desirable than intellectual stimulation? These questions could be elaborated endlessly. And yet, where is the judge to look for the set of values that should inform the choice of what is best for the child? Normally, the custody statutes do not themselves give content or relative weights to the pertinent values. And if the judge looks to society at large, he finds neither a clear consensus as to the best child-rearing strategies nor an appropriate hierarchy of ultimate values.

SOCIAL WELFARE REPORT

In any contested custody hearing, the parties themselves may give evidence and call their own witnesses. However, it is important for the court to have an independent assessment of the facts. In this respect, a social welfare report plays a very important role. S3 of the GMO provides that the court shall have regard to any material information in a social welfare report. R95(1) of the Matrimonial Causes Rules provides that:

> a judge or the registrar may at any time refer to the Director of Social Welfare for investigation and report any matter arising in matrimonial proceedings which concerns the welfare of the child.

R95(2) of the Matrimonial Causes Rules permits a party to request a report from the Director of Social Welfare on any matter arising from the application, and if the registrar is satisfied that the other parties consent and that sufficient information is available to enable the officer to carry out the investigation, the registrar may refer the matter to the Director of Social Welfare for investigation and report before the hearing.[79] This does not mean that the court can appoint anybody other than a court welfare officer to prepare a report without the consent of the other party. In *Cadman v Cadman*,[80] the parties' marriage broke up, and the mother was granted

---

[79] However, it makes no reference to the calling (as a witness) of the reporting social welfare officer, see *Tang Lau Wai-chun v Tang Fung-Fat* [1986] HKLR 907.
[80] [1982] 3 FLR 275.

interim custody of their child. At the custody hearing, the judge had in front of him reports from the court's social welfare officers who recommended that the child should be with the mother. However, at the request of the father, he ordered that an independent social worker be appointed to prepare a report which favoured custody being given to the father. The judge then made an order in his favour. On appeal by the mother, it was held that the appointment of an independent social welfare officer was an unusual step. The judge had no jurisdiction to appoint another officer without the consent of both parties. If one party was not satisfied with the welfare officer's report, he could invite the judge to appoint a different court officer. But, in this case, the father's solicitor procured another welfare officer and recommended her to the court. The father's solicitor had instructed her unilaterally and she had been paid by the father. The case was remitted for a rehearing.

Once appointed, a social welfare officer is expected to investigate the circumstances of the child concerned. He is expected to visit and interview all the parties who play an important role in the child's life.[81] It has been said that without these investigations, the report would be useless.[82] Again, the court is unlikely to be assisted if the social welfare officer has not seen the child with each of the parties and observed the child's relationship with them in their home environment.[83]

Once the social welfare report is obtained, a copy is sent to the parties and their legal advisers. The court may request that the report and its contents be read out in court.[84] If a party to the proceedings objects to anything contained therein, the court shall require the officer who made the statement to give evidence, and any party to the proceedings may call or give evidence with respect to any matters referred to in the report or any evidence given by the officer.[85] It was held in *Tang Lau Wai-chun v Tang Fung-fat*[86] that where a judge had a discretion to call a social welfare officer, he could not ignore it. To avoid a subsequent sense of grievance on the part of 'the losing parent', it would generally be desirable to call for cross-

---

[81] Social Welfare Officer, however, cannot give an undertaking of confidence to his informant, see *Re G (minors) (welfare report: disclosure)* [1993] 2 FLR 293.
[82] *Edwards v Edwards* [1986] 1 FLR 187; *Re W (a minor) (custody)* [1983] 4 FLR 492; *Thompson v Thompson* [1986] 1 FLR 212; *Re H (conciliation: welfare reports)* [1986] 1 FLR 476 where it was said that an officer who has been involved in conciliation should not subsequently investigate and prepare a welfare report and that the functions of conciliation and reporting as welfare officer are distinct, and that the same person should not undertake both functions.
[83] *Edwards v Edwards* [1986] 1 FLR 187.
[84] S17 GMO.
[85] On the question of privilege, see *Re D (minors) (conciliation: privilege)* [1993] 1 FLR 932.
[86] [1986] HKLR 907.

examination of an officer who has expressed an opinion upon facts which are substantially in dispute.[87]

Recommendations in a Social Welfare Report

A social welfare report usually contains the recommendations of the investigating officer. However, they are not binding on the courts as it is the court which is entrusted with the responsibility of making a decision, not the welfare officer. Nonetheless, if the court departs from the recommendations, reasons should be given.[88]

Hearsay in Social Welfare Reports

A social welfare report may contain hearsay evidence. The inclusion of such evidence does not render the report inadmissible. In respect of relatively uncontroversial matters, it is likely to be unobjectionable; but where the matters are acutely controversial, a reporting officer should report his own observations and assessment, and where he is constrained to pass on second-hand information or opinions, he should endeavour to make this explicit, indicating the source and his own reasons, if any, for agreeing or disagreeing with any such information or opinions.[89]

Confidentiality

A social welfare report is a confidential document. It must not be shown to anyone other than the parties and their legal advisers.[90] Could a welfare report be used for subsequent civil proceedings unconnected with the child who was the subject matter of the report? Could it be used for purposes of criminal proceedings? In *Brown v Matthews*,[91] the plaintiff-father brought

---

[87] Applying *Cadman v Cadman* [1982] FLR 275.
[88] *Clark v Clark* (1970) 114 SJ 318; *Re C (a minor)* (1979) Fam Law 50; *Re T (a minor) (welfare report: recommendation)* [1980] 1 FLR 59; *Stephenson v Stephenson* [1985] FLR 1140.
[89] *Thompson v Thompson* [1986] 1 FLR 212.
[90] Practice Direction [1984] 1 All ER 187.
[91] [1990] 2 All ER 155; see also *D v National Society for the Prevention of Cruelty to Children* [1978] AC 171; *Gaskin v Liverpool City Council* [1980] 1 WLR 1549; *Campbell v Tameside Metropolitan BC* [1982] 2 All ER 791; *Re R (MJ) (an infant) (proceedings transcript: publication)* [1975] 2 All ER 749; *Re F (minors) (police investigation)* [1989] Fam 18; *Re X, Y, Z (wardship: disclosure of materials)* (1991) Fam Law 318.

an action against the defendant (his ex-father-in-law) claiming that the defendant bought a house for him and his wife when they married as a gift to him. The plaintiff alleged that the defendant's intention of a gift of the house was recorded in the welfare report and sought to use the report in evidence at the trial. The Court of Appeal held that the report did not fall into the category of documents which could not be disclosed in the public interest except for the purpose for which the document in question came into existence. Leave could be granted for its use if, after evaluating the need for the contents to be put in evidence against confidentiality, the interests of justice required its release for there to be a fair trial.[92]

Other Reports Concerning the Child

Apart from a social welfare report, the court has a discretion to order a medical or psychiatric report concerning the child. In the case of a normal happy child, general evidence of a psychiatric or medical practitioner on the likely outcome, desirable or otherwise, of a particular course of action might be valuable, but it could only support the general knowledge or experience of a judge. Where both parties agree to the preparation of such a report, the court should accede to its preparation. Where there are no unusual features, and one party objects, an order should not be made as there is no reason for subjecting a child to an examination. An order in such a case may suggest that an ordinary case is not properly prepared unless expert evidence has been obtained.[93]

INTERVIEWING THE CHILD IN PRIVATE

A social welfare report usually contains the views of the parties and the child. The court, however, has the discretion to interview the child in private.[94] Where the judge has decided to interview the child in private, it is wrong to promise not to divulge confidences vouchsafed to him.[95]

---

[92] However, statements made by or to a welfare officer for the purposes of preparing a report are absolutely privileged so no action for defamation could arise. See *Gatley on Libel and Slander*, 8th edition, Sweet & Maxwell, London, paras 393–6; see also *Brown v Matthews*, at p. 162.
[93] *Re Huthart (infants)*, High Court, Miscellaneous Proceedings No 1037 of 1981 (1984).
[94] See above, pp. 251–252; see also *D v D (custody of child)* [1981] 2 FLR 74; *Re A (minors) (wardship: children in care)* [1980] 1 FLR 100.
[95] *Elder v Elder* [1986] 1 FLR 610; *H v H (child: judicial interview)* [1974] 1 All ER 1145;

REVIEWING A TRIAL JUDGE'S DECISION

In proceedings concerning custody and welfare of a minor, an appellate court does not overturn a first instance decision simply because it disagrees with its decision,[96] or that it feels that its own view is more appropriate. To overturn a first instance decision, an appellate court has to be satisfied that either the judge has erred as a matter of law, or that he relied upon evidence which he should not have, or ignored evidence which he should have taken into account, or that the decision was so 'plainly wrong'. The last criterion is vague and it allows, to a certain extent, an appellate court to overturn a decision with which it does not agree.

The justification for an appellate court needing to show restraint in intervening with a decision of a first instance court is that in many cases, a trial judge has the benefit of seeing the parties and observing their demeanour. These are important factors which form the basis of the decision of a judge. Furthermore, there is the public policy consideration that it is desirable that litigation should come to an end, and that protracted litigation should not be encouraged in custody disputes where it is often difficult to say that there is a right answer and a wrong answer.

In the House of Lords decision *G v G (minors: custody appeal)*,[97] Lord Fraser had this to say:

> I entirely reject the contention that appeals in custody cases, or in other cases, concerning the welfare of children, are subject to special rules of their own. The jurisdiction in such cases is one of great difficulty as every judge who has had to exercise it must be aware. The main reason is that in most of these cases there is no right answer. All practicable answers are to some extent unsatisfactory and, therefore, to some extent wrong, and the best that can be done is to find an answer that is reasonably satisfactory. It is comparatively seldom that the Court of Appeal, even if it would itself have preferred a different answer, can say that the judge's decision was wrong, and unless it can say so, it will leave his decision undisturbed.

Cumming-Bruce LJ in *Clarke-Hunt v Newcombe*[98] remarked that:

> There was not really a right solution; there were two alternative wrong solutions. The problem of the judge was to appreciate the factors pointing

---

Dickson v Dickson (1983) 13 Fam Law 174; *B v B (minors) (interviews and listing arrangements)* [1994] 2 FLR 489. There is no power to interview the parents separately in private. *C v C* (1981) 11 Fam Law 147.
[96] *G v G (minors: custody appeal)* [1985] FLR 894.
[97] Ibid.
[98] [1983] 4 FLR 482 at p. 486.

in each direction and to decide which of the two bad solutions was the least dangerous, having regard to the long-term interests of the children, and so he decided the matter. Whether I would have decided it the same way if I had been in the position of the trial judge I do not know ... I am sitting in the Court of Appeal deciding a quite different question: has it been shown that the judge to whom Parliament has confided the exercise of discretion, plainly got the wrong answer?

RECENT DEVELOPMENTS: NATURE OF CUSTODY PROCEEDINGS

Given the reluctance of the appellate court in reviewing a trial judge's decision and the indeterminacy of the welfare principle, custody disputes continue to be a contentious area, and the nature of custody proceedings has been the subject of discussions. In 1963, in *Fowler v Fowler*,[99] it was held that the ordinary principles of judicial inquiry must be observed in custody proceedings. Thus, it was thought that a judge in custody proceedings was not entitled to receive confidential information not disclosed to the parties. Justice must be done and must manifestly be seen to be done. Any private conversation, therefore, between a judge and a person concerned with a case, such as a social welfare officer, not disclosed to the parties, involved infraction of that principle. This would be so whether the conversation took place before or after the witnesses were heard, and whether or not it influenced the judge in his decision.[100] This principle was applied in *Ho Lee Kam-wan v Ho Man*.[101] In that case, trial judge, having informed the parties of his intention to contact the social welfare officer, telephoned him instead of writing to him. Having done so, he communicated the answer obtained by way of informing the father's solicitor who appeared before him in another matter, asking the solicitor to inform the other side. On appeal to the Court of Appeal, Cons J. said:

> I would not encourage informal approaches by a judge to a Welfare Officer, even if there are savings apparently to be made as to time or expense. In the present instance the judge did disclose the fact to the parties, both before and afterwards, albeit he did not in the first instance specify the method he had in mind. Later he passed on to the parties what the officer had said. I have no reason to think that anything further was mentioned

---

[99] [1963] P. 311.
[100] *H v H*, (1982) The Times Law Report 1 April.
[101] Court of Appeal, Civil Appeal Action No 78 of 1988 (1988).

which was not disclosed. Subsequently the parties, and the judge, received the written supplemental report. In the circumstances I do not think that we are required to order a rehearing of the question of custody.

In *Re C (a minor) (irregularity of practice)*[102] the Court of Appeal held that the rule in *Official Solicitor v K*[103] applied equally to custody proceedings. Thus, as Lord Devlin said in *Official Solicitor v K*:

> where the judge is not sitting purely, or even primarily, as an arbiter but is charged with the paramount duty of protecting the interests of one outside of the conflict, a rule that is designed for just arbitrament cannot in all circumstances prevail.

The rule in *Official Solicitor v K*,[104] however, is narrowly defined. In all cases concerning the welfare of children, the court has the discretion to direct that materials the disclosure of which may be damaging to the child not be disclosed to a party to the proceedings if:
(i) the court is well satisfied that the confidential information is in truth reliable;
(ii) the court is well satisfied that real harm to the child must ensue from the disclosure of such information; and
(iii) the discretion is only to be exercised in rare and exceptional cases, and for as short a period as possible.[105]

Thus, in rare and exceptional circumstances,[106] it is permissible for a judge in the exercise of his discretion, and acting in the paramount interests of the child, to receive a confidential report or to see a court welfare officer privately in his chambers during a trial. The judge's discretion on these matters could only be challenged on the ground that he was plainly wrong.[107]

In *Re NW (a minor) (medical reports)*,[108] an unmarried father suffering from schizophrenia applied to the court for contact with his three-year-old child. The justices directed medical reports to be filed on the father's

---

[102] [1991] 2 FLR 438.
[103] [1965] AC 201.
[104] Ibid.
[105] *Re C (a minor) (irregularity of practice)* [1991] 2 FLR 438 held that it was wrong for the judge to see the social welfare officer alone in chambers; *Re B (a minor) (disclosure of evidence)* [1993] 1 FLR 191; *Re G (minors) (welfare report: disclosure)* [1993] 2 FLR 293 disclosure ordered in both cases.
[106] *Re C (a minor) (irregularity of practice)* [1991] 2 FLR 438.
[107] See n. 106; *G v G (minors: custody appeal)* [1985] FLR 894.
[108] [1993] 2 FLR 591.

condition and ordered that these were not to be disclosed to any person other than the legal representatives of the parties, court officials and the justices, without leave of the court. The mother's legal representatives applied for the reports to be shown to her, but was refused. It was held that the mother was entitled to see the medical reports in order to be able to properly instruct her legal representatives. Keeping the medical reports confidential would have been inimical to the child's welfare as the mother would have been unable to instruct her legal representatives properly.

The court, in considering the welfare of a child, is entitled to override a legal professional privilege which is set up to preserve or enhance the adversarial position of one of the parties. To that extent custody proceedings are truly 'non-adversarial'. Thus, in *Essex County Council v R*,[109] a consultant psychiatrist was instructed on behalf of the mother. The question arose as to whether the report was subject to discovery, and as to the nature of the mother's advice in relation to the report. It was held that a court considering the welfare of a child was entitled to override a legal professional privilege. The parties to proceedings owed a duty to the court to make full and frank disclosure of any material in their possession relevant to the determination of the future of the child.[110]

---

[109] [1993] 2 FLR 826.
[110] See *Oxfordshire County Council v P* [1995] 1 FLR 552.

Annex I

The Australian Family Law Act 1975 (Cth.) s64(1) provides that:

'In any proceedings in relation to the custody, guardianship or welfare of, or access to, a child–
(b) the court shall consider any wishes expressed by the child ...
(bb) the court shall take the following matters into account:
  (i) the nature of the relationship of the child with each of the parents of the child and with other persons;
  (ii) the effect on the child of any separation from–
    (A) either parent of the child; or
    (B) any child, or other person, with whom the child has been living;
  (iii) the desirability of, and the effect of, any change in the existing arrangements for the care of the child;
  (iv) the attitude to the child, and to the responsibilities and duties of parenthood, demonstrated by each parent of the child;
  (v) the capacity of each parent, or of any other person, to provide adequately for the needs of the child, including the emotional and intellectual needs of the child;
  (vi) the need to protect the child from abuse;
  (vii) any other fact of circumstances (including the education and upbringing of the child) that, in the opinion of the court, the welfare of the child requires to be taken into account.'

This check-list has now been expanded further by s68F in the Family Law Reform Act 1995:

'(1) Subject to subsection (3), in determining what is in the child's best interests, the court must consider the matters set out in subsection (2).
(2) The court must consider:
  (a) any wishes expressed by the child and any factors (such as the child's maturity or level of understanding) that the court thinks are relevant to the weight it should give to the child's wishes;
  (b) the nature of the relationship of the child with each of the child's parents and with other persons;
  (c) the likely effect of any changes in the child's circumstances, including the likely effect on the child of any separation from:
    (i) either of his or her parents; or
    (ii) any other child, or other person, with whom he or she has been living;

(d) the practical difficulty and expense of a child having contact with a parent and whether that difficulty or expense will substantially affect the child's right to maintain personal relations and direct contact with both parents on a regular basis;
(e) the capacity of each parent, or of any other person, to provide for the needs of the child, including emotional and intellectual needs;
(f) the child's maturity, sex and background (including any need to maintain a connection with the lifestyle, culture and traditions of Aboriginal peoples or Torres Strait Islanders) and any other characteristics of the child that the court thinks are relevant;
(g) the need to protect the child from physical or psychological harm caused, or that may be caused, by:
  (i) being subjected or exposed to abuse, ill-treatment, violence or other behaviour; or
  (ii) being directly or indirectly exposed to abuse, ill-treatment, violence or other behaviour that is directed towards, or may affect, another person;
(h) the attitude to the child, and to the responsibilities of the child's parents;
(i) any family violence involving the child or a member of the child's family;
(j) any family violence order that applies to the child or a member of the child's family;
(k) whether it would be preferable to make the order that would be least likely to lead to the institution of further proceedings in relation to the child;
(l) any other fact or circumstance that the court thinks is relevant.
(3) If the court is considering whether to make an order with the consent of all the parties to the proceedings, the court may, but is not required to, have regard to all or any of the matters set out in subsection (2)'.

10

Children on Family Breakdown

INTRODUCTION

Divorce brings a marriage to an end. However, family breakdown is not always evident in divorce. Children are often the innocent victims of family breakdown. If parents separate, arrangements have to be made relating to the children. Parents whose relationship has broken down, or is on the verge of breakdown, often disagree on arrangements for their children. The circumstances in which custody will be dealt with by the court depends on the Ordinance invoked.

There are a number of possible outcomes. In order to understand the effect of the different orders which the court can make, it is useful to remember that married parents have equal parental rights and authority.[1] In the case of unmarried parents, a mother has all parental rights and authority and the father 'shall only have such rights and authority, if any, as may have been ordered by a court'.[2] In many instances, the effect of a court order concerning custody is to divide up and reallocate these parental rights and authority[3] between parents. 'Custody' is dealt with under three different Ordinances, they are: (i) Matrimonial Proceedings and Property Ordinance (MPPO); (ii) Separation and Maintenance Orders Ordinance (SMOO); and (iii) Guardianship of Minors Ordinance (GMO). In this

---
[1] See Chapter 8.
[2] S3 GMO.
[3] See Susan Maidment, 'The Fragmentation of Parental Rights' 40(1981) Camb LR 135.

chapter, the manner in which parental rights and authority under these ordinances are reallocated will be examined.

CUSTODY AND OTHER ORDERS UNDER MATRIMONIAL PROCEEDINGS AND PROPERTY ORDINANCE

Who Can Apply and Jurisdiction of the Court

S19(1) of the Matrimonial Proceedings and Property Ordinance (MPPO) states that the court may make such order as it thinks fit for the custody[4] and education of any child of the family[5] under 18[6] in the following two situations:
(a) in any proceedings for divorce (nullity, or judicial separation), either before, by or after the final decree;
(b) where such proceedings are dismissed after the beginning of the trial, either forwith or within a reasonable period after the dismissal.

Orders Which Can Be Made

Sole custody order

This appears to be the most common order. The spouse who is awarded custody is called the custodial parent. The effect of the order is to transfer most, if not all, parental rights and authority to the custodial parent exclusively. The non-custodial parent, however, retains rights *qua* parent (or guardian), e.g. the right to succeed on the child's intestacy, the right as a guardian on the death of the other parent, the right to appoint a testamentary guardian, and to veto adoption.

Where the court grants custody to one spouse, it is usual for the court to grant access to the non-custodial parent. Access means contact with the child.[7] This can be done in various ways, for instance, by regular meetings and visits, by letters and telephone conversations.[8] In relation to access, different kinds of orders can be made depending on the circumstances of

---

[4] 'Custody' includes access, see s2 MPPO; for access see below, pp. 284–9.
[5] See below, p. 277.
[6] As amended by s26 of the Marriage and Children (Miscellaneous Amendments) Ordinance (No 69 of 1997).
[7] See below, pp. 284–9.
[8] See below the distinction between direct and indirect access, pp. 284–9.

the case. An order for reasonable access leaves the parties to agree on how access is to be arranged.[9] The court may order staying access, that is, the parent with access can have the child staying with him or her during weekends or holidays.[10] Where the parties cannot agree on access arrangements, an order for defined access can be made, detailing access arrangements. Sometimes the court may order that access be supervised (e.g. by the custodial parent or a third party, such as a social welfare officer) or impose conditions on access.

What does a custody order entail? At common law, an order for custody entails the right to exercise full parental rights and authority. Where a sole custody order are made (without any restrictions) parental rights and authority is vested in one to the exclusion of the other. The custodial parent has a duty to ensure, protect and promote the best interests of the child. Apart from day-to-day care, the custodial parent is empowered to make major decisions concerning the child. There is no definition as to what amounts to major decisions, but it probably includes matters such as education, religion, and major medical treatment.

This position was complicated by *Dipper v Dipper*[11] where Ormrod LJ said, obiter, that:

> It used to be considered that the parent having custody had the right to control the children's education, and in the past their religion. This is a misunderstanding. Neither parent has any pre-emptive right over the other ... To suggest that a parent with custody dominates the situation so far as education or any other serious matter is concerned is quite wrong.

Cumming Bruce LJ further said that a non-custodial parent was entitled 'to know and be consulted about the future education of the child and any other major matters.'[12]

How consultation could be enforced is unclear. But in *Lo Chun Wing-yee v Lo Pong-hing*,[13] the High Court dealt with the position of the custodial and non-custodial parents *inter se*. In that case, a consent order for joint custody with the mother having care and control was made. Conflicts then arose between the parties regarding the child's upbringing. The father was content that the mother continued to have care and control, and the question

---

[9] *Wong Chiu Ngar-chi v Wong Hon-wai* [1987] HKLR 179; *Re Ryker (infants)*, High Court, Miscellaneous Proceedings No 1184 of 1980 (1982).
[10] *Lee Wai-chu v Lee Yim-chuen*, High Court, Miscellaneous Proceedings No 2678 of 1983 (1984).
[11] [1980] 2 All ER 722, at p. 731.
[12] Ibid., at p. 733.
[13] [1985] 2 HKC 647 at p. 651; *Jane v Jane* [1983] 4 FLR 712 not cited.

was whether the mother should be given sole custody to the exclusion of the father. It was held that the welfare of the child would best be served by reinstating one single authority in her daily life. However, the court adopted what Cumming Bruce LJ said in *Dipper v Dipper*. Liu J granted sole custody to the mother on condition that she undertook:

> To give a quarterly report to the father under three headings of health, education and activity including the child's out-of-jurisdiction visits, and in such a quarterly report, information under each head should not be less than five sentences.

In *Lo Chun Wing-yee v Lo Pong-hing*, the court was of the view that the sole custody of the mother would not bring about any severance of link between the father and the child. If the father disagreed with a course of action proposed or decided by the mother, he would have a right to resort to the court for guidance.

Parent-child relationships, however, may effectively be ended by the circumstances of the parents.[14] The competing rights of a custodial parent and a parent with access was considered in *Hunt v Hunt*.[15] There the father had custody and the mother was given access to her children. The father, an army officer, was posted to Egypt and intended to take the children with him. The mother sought to restrain the father from doing so on the grounds that the move would frustrate access. It was held that a custodial parent could not be so restrained.[16]

Split order

This is an unusual order[17] and means that custody is given to one party, and care and control to another. This is sometimes called a split order because its effect is to divide up the whole bundle of parental rights and authority between the parties. Of all the parental rights and authority, the mother, for instance, is given those associated with the daily care and control of a child (or custody in its narrow sense). The husband remains the custodial parent without day-to-day care and control of the child.

> An unqualified order giving custody to a parent appears nowadays to be interpreted as having the wide meaning, but if at the same time "care and

---

[14] *Boulter v Boulter* [1977–1979] HKC 282.
[15] (1884) 28 Ch. D 606.
[16] See also *Wong Chiu Nga-chi v Wong Hon-wai* [1987] HKCR 179; *Goertz v Gordon* (2 May 1996), unreported (Supreme Court, Canada).
[17] *Dipper v Dipper* [1980] 2 All ER 722 at p. 733 per Cumming-Bruce LJ.

control" is given to the other parent, then one of the powers, custody in the limited meaning of physical control, is taken out of "custody" in the wide meaning.[18]

This order aims to preserve a role for the absent (but yet custodial) parent on major decisions concerning the child's upbringing. What if, against the wishes of the parent with care and control, the custodial parent wants the child to study at a school which is many hours' bus ride from home? What if the custodial parent wants to send the child to a boarding school which effectively renders care and control meaningless. A split order, therefore, is unworkable where parents cannot agree and cooperate on matters relating to the upbringing of the child. Thus, in *Lo Chun Wing-yee v Lo Pong-hing*,[19] it was said that the court was generally reluctant to grant a split order unless the advantages demonstrably outweighed the inherent disadvantages. In that case, the father had emigrated to Canada, the parents could not cooperate with each other. A split order would only lead to disputes which 'would constantly bring the party back to court'.

A split order can, however, be desirable in some cases. For instance, in *Jane v Jane*,[20] the mother, who was given care and control, was a Jehovah's witness and would refuse to give consent to the daughter's blood transfusion. The father therefore was granted custody of the child so that he could consent to the child's medical treatment.

Joint custody order

This is where custody is given to both, and care and control to one party. This is sometimes called a joint custody order. But again, a joint custody order is almost unknown in Hong Kong.[21] English courts had always been reluctant to grant such an order which is now called a shared-residence order. The fear is that it may create competing homes, causing confusion and stress on the child. However, it appears that a shared residence order may become more common in the future.[22]

The original rationale of a joint custody order is that instead of one party being given the right to decide important matters affecting the upbringing of the child, both parties have that right. Such order symbolises divorced or separated parents playing a joint role in the upbringing of the

---

[18] *Hewer v Bryant* [1970] 1 QB 357 at p. 373.
[19] [1985] 2 HKC 647.
[20] [1984] 4 FLR 712.
[21] *Lo Chun Wing-yee v Lo Pong-hing* [1985] 2 HKC 647, *Boulter v Boulter* [1977–1979] HKC 282.
[22] See *A v A (minors) (shared residence order)* [1994] 1 FLR 669.

child, and neither is excluded. In *Jussa v Jussa*,[23] the father, an Indian Moslem and a teacher by profession married an English Christian. When the parties separated, the court granted custody to the wife with reasonable access to the father. The father appealed against the granting of custody to the mother although he conceded that she should have care and control.

> The joint order for custody with care and control to one of the two parents is, perhaps, of rather more recent origin ... For my part, I recognise that a joint order for custody with care and control to one parent only is an order which should only be made where there is a reasonable prospect that the parties will cooperate. Where you have a case such as the present case, in which the father and the mother are both well qualified to give affection and wise guidance to the children for whom they are responsible, and where they appear to be of such calibre that they are likely to cooperate sensibly over the child for whom both of them feel such affection ... it seems to me that there can be no real objection to an order for joint custody.[24]

Custody to the Director of Social Welfare

Where it appears to the court that there are exceptional circumstances making it impracticable or undesirable for a child to be entrusted to either party of the marriage or any other individual, the court may commit the care of the child to the Director of Social Welfare (DSW).[25] The court shall hear any representation, including any representation as to the making of a financial provision order in favour of the child, from the DSW before making such an order.[26] Whilst the care order is in force, the child continues in the care of the DSW notwithstanding any claim by the parent or another person,[27] the court shall not commit a child to care of DSW if child has attained the age of 18, and the order ceases to have effect when the child attains that age.[28]

Supervision order

Where it appears to the court that there are exceptional circumstances making it desirable that a child should be under the supervision of an independent person, the court may, as respects any period during which

---

[23] [1972] 2 All ER 600.
[24] Ibid., at p. 603 per Wrangham J.
[25] See s48A (1) MCO.
[26] S48A(2) MCO.
[27] S48A(3) MCO.
[28] S48A(4) MCO as amended by s20 of the Marriage and Children (Miscellaneous Amendments) Ordinance (No 69 of 1997).

the child is committed to the custody of any person, order that the child be under the supervision of the DSW.[29]

Ward

The court may, instead of making a custody order, direct that proper proceedings be taken for making the child a ward of court.[30]

Duration of an Order

An order made under s19 shall cease to have effect when the child attains the age of 18.[31]

LEGAL CUSTODY UNDER THE SEPARATION AND MAINTENANCE ORDERS ORDINANCE

Who Can Apply?

Under s5 of the Separation and Maintenance Orders Ordinance (SMOO) the court may grant 'legal custody' of 'any children of the marriage' in favour of a wife or a husband. 'Legal custody' and 'children of the marriage' are not defined,[32] but the former appears to mean custody in the widest sense. However, legal custody could only be made if one of the grounds stated in s3 has been proved. Thus, the order is seen as a 'prize' for a 'winner' applicant as against a 'loser' respondent.

Orders in Favour of Whom

An order for legal custody may be made in favour of either party, but not a third party. It appears that no order for access could be made.[33]

---

[29] S48(1) MCO.
[30] S19(1) MPPO.
[31] S19(7) MPPO.
[32] The same term appeared in s86 of the Children Act 1975 where it means 'as respects a child so much of the parental rights and duties as relate to the person of the child (including the place and manner in which his time is spent); but a person shall not by virtue of having legal custody of a child be entitled to effect or arrange for his emigration from the United Kingdom unless he is a parent or guardian of the child.'
[33] *W (C) v W (R)* [1968] 3 All ER 608.

Bar to a Legal Custody Order

S6(1) of the SMOO precludes a legal custody order being made if it is proved that the applicant has committed 'an act of adultery', provided that the other party has not condoned, or connived at, or by his or her wilful neglect or misconduct conduced to such act of adultery. S6A further provides that adultery should not be deemed to have been condoned by reason only of a continuation or resumption of cohabitation between the parties for one period not exceeding three months, or of anything done during such cohabitation, if it is proved that cohabitation has continued or resumed, as the case may be, with a view to effecting a reconciliation.

Duration of a Legal Custody Order

There is no provision in the SMOO stating the maximum duration of a legal custody order. It seems unlikely that such an order would continue after the child attains the age of 18.

CUSTODY AND RELATED ORDERS UNDER THE GUARDIANSHIP OF MINORS ORDINANCE

Who Can Apply

S10(1) of the Guardianship of Minors Ordinance (GMO) provides that on the application of either parent[34] of a minor[35] or the DSW, the court may make an order regarding:
(a) the custody of the minor; and
(b) access of the minor to either of his parents,

as the court thinks fit, having regard to the 'welfare of the minor and to the conduct and wishes of the parents'.[36]

Under s10(1), only parents and the DSW may apply. Other relatives of a minor, such as a grandparent, aunt or uncle, has no *locus standi*.

---

[34] The GMO provides that parent means 'father or mother', see s2 GMO.
[35] 'Minor' means a person under 18, see Age of Majority (Related Provisions) Ordinance, s6.
[36] There is no conflict between this provision and that in s3 GMO where the interest of the minor is of 'first and paramount consideration', see *Re D (minors) (wardship: jurisdiction)* [1973] 2 All ER 993.

Custody Orders in Favour of Whom

The court may order custody be awarded to a parent or someone other than a parent.[37] Access, however, can only be made in favour of either parent of a minor.

Duration of Custody Order

A custody order can only be made in relation to a minor (i.e. under 18) and it seems unlikely that such an order would extend beyond the age of 18.

Supervision Order

If any person is given custody of a minor under s10(1), but it appears to the court that there are exceptional circumstances, making it desirable that the minor should be under the supervision of an independent person, the court may so order.[38] Where the supervision order is made at a time when the parents of the minor are residing together, the order may direct that it is to cease to have effect if for a period of three months after it is made they continue to reside together. The supervision order may also direct that it is not to operate whilst they are residing together.[39]

Care to the Director of Social Welfare

Where an application under s10(1) relates to custody, the court may commit a minor to the care of the DSW if it appears undesirable or impracticable for the minor to be entrusted to either parent or to any other individual.[40] In such a case, the court may also order either parent to pay to the DSW as the court thinks reasonable having regard to the means of that parent, such lump sum for the immediate and non-recurring needs of the minor, or for the purpose of discharging any liabilities or expenses reasonably incurred in maintaining the child before the making of the order, or both. Additionally, the court may order such periodical payment towards the

---

[37] S10(2) GMO.
[38] S13(1)(a) GMO.
[39] S14(1) as amended by s4 of the Marriage and Children (Miscellaneous Amendments) Ordinance (No 69 of 1997).
[40] S13(1)(b) GMO.

maintenance of the child.[41] Before making an order committing the care of a minor to the DSW, the court shall hear any representations from the DSW.[42]

Social Welfare Report

In dealing with an application under s10 the court may request the DSW to provide the court a welfare report.[43]

ACCESS

On marriage breakdown, a parent may be granted sole custody of a child. The non-custodial parent is sometimes given access. Access is not statutorily defined. But it means contact of a child with a person whether by way of visit by or to that person. In the US, contact is referred to as 'visitation'. In England, access is now know as 'contact'.[44] S8(1) of the Children Act 1989 defines 'contact' to mean an order:

> requiring the person with whom a child lives, or is to live, to allow the child to visit or stay with the person named in the order, or for that person and the child otherwise to have contact with one another.

In this section, the terms 'access' and 'contact' will be used interchangeably. An order for access usually refers to a child visiting or staying with the parent with access for a period of time. This period varies, it may range from one afternoon a week to the whole of a school holiday. An order for access may also refer to a parent visiting the child. These are examples of 'direct' access. To the extent that access impinges upon the control which a custodial parent has in determining who the child should be friends with, it is sometimes described as a 'species of temporary custody'. Recently, forms of 'indirect' access, as a means of enabling a child to maintain contact with a non-custodial parent, such as sending the child cards, presents and telephone calls have also been explored by the English courts.[45]

---

[41] S13(2) GMO.
[42] S15(1) GMO.
[43] S17(1) GMO. (See possible conflict of interest if the DSW is an applicant under s10 and is also requested to provide a welfare report under s17.)
[44] Ss8(1), 11(7) Children Act 1989.
[45] See *Re M (contact: welfare test)* [1995] 1 FLR 274; *Re O (contact: imposition of conditions)* [1995] 2 FLR 124.

In the past it has been said that access is the right of a parent, and a parent should only lose it if he is not a fit and proper person to be brought into contact with the child.[46] At one time, an adulterous wife was not given access to her children. Today, the paradigm has shifted. Access is no longer the right of a parent, but it is the right of a child. Thus, in *M v M (child: access)*:[47]

> It seems to be me ... that the companionship of a parent is in any ordinary circumstances of such immense value to the child that there is a basic right in him to such companionship. I for my part would prefer to call it a basic right in the child rather than a basic right in the parent.[48]

The fundamental principle in determining access is that the welfare of the child is the first and paramount consideration.[49] The court is concerned with interests of a mother and father only in so far as they bear on the welfare of the child.[50] The prevailing judicial view today is that separation of parents involves a loss to a child, and it is desirable that that loss should, so far as is possible, be made good by maintaining contact with the non-custodial parent. This is also reflected in Article 9(3) of the UN Convention on the Rights of a Child:

> States Parties shall respect the right of the child who is separated from one or both parents to maintain personal relations and direct contact with both parents on a regular basis, except if contrary to the child's best interests.

The test to be applied in granting access is not whether any positive advantages are to be gained by access or the resumption of access. Rather, whether there are any cogent reasons why a child should be denied the opportunity of access to the natural parent. The presumption is that access by a non-custodial parent is in the interests of the child unless the contrary is shown.

> ... No court should deprive a child of access to either parent unless it is wholly satisfied that it was in the interests of the child that access should cease, and that was a conclusion at which the court should be extremely slow to arrive ... Save in exceptional cases, to deprive a parent of access is to deprive a child of an important contribution to his emotional and

---

[46] *S v S* [1961] 1 WLR 445; *Re L (an infant)* [1968] P. 119.
[47] [1973] 2 All ER 81 at p. 85 per Wrangham J.
[48] See also *Re KD (a minor) (access: principle)* [1988] 2 FLR 139.
[49] S3 GMO.
[50] *Re O (contact: imposition of conditions)* [1995] 2 FLR 124.

maternal growing up in the long term ... the test to be applied was whether there were any cogent reasons why the children should be denied the opportunity of access to their natural father.[51]

A decision to deprive a child of access to his parent is something at which the court should be slow to arrive. The presumption in favour of access by a non-custodial parent means that the burden is on the custodial parent opposing access to show why access would be contrary to the child's best interests.[52] Introduction or reintroduction of access often results in some upset in the child. Those upsets are usually outweighed by the long-term advantages to the child of keeping in touch with the parent so that they do not become strangers.

> ... where the parents have separated and one has the care of the child, access by the other often results in some upset in the child. Those upsets are usually minor and superficial. They are heavily outweighed by the long-term advantages to the child of keeping in touch with the parent concerned so that they do not become strangers, so that the child later in life does not resent the deprivation and turn against the parent who the child thinks, rightly or wrongly, has deprived him, and so that the deprived parent loses interest in the child and therefore does not make the material and emotional contribution to the child's development which that parent by it companionship and otherwise would make.[53]

Access, however, may be a constant source of difficulties for the parents and the child.[54] Hostility to access may come from parents, and access sometimes is used by the parents to continue their battle and bitterness. Two techniques for using the children are common. The custodial spouse may (1) threaten to withhold access or make access difficult and (2) persuade the child to dislike the other parent. The custodial parent may be adamant that there should be no contact. Such implacable opposition or hostility towards contact is usually accompanied by a declared willingness to defy any court order. The courts are reluctant to allow implacable hostility to deter them from making a contact order where welfare of the child requires.[55]

---

[51] Re H (minors) (access) [1992] 1 FLR 148 at 150; Re W (a minor) (contact) [1994] 2 FLR 441; M v M (child: access) [1973] 2 All ER 81.
[52] However, recently it was held in Re M (contact: welfare test) [1995] 1 FLR 274 that it is for the parent seeking access to show that access is in the best interest of the child.
[53] M v M (child: access) [1973] 2 All ER 81 at p. 88 per Latey J.
[54] Boulter v Boulter [1977–1979] HKC 282.
[55] Re O (contact: imposition of conditions) [1995] 2 FLR 124; Re S (contact: grandparents) [1996] 1 FLR 158; the court has the power to enforce orders for contact, see V-P v V-P (access to child) [1980] 1 FLR 336; imprisonment would be used as the last resort; cf J Goldstein, Freud and Solnit, Beyond the Best Interests of the Child, Burnet Books, London, 1979.

However, implacable hostility of a custodial parent towards access is a factor to be taken into account. Where the custodial parent's attitude towards access is such that the child is at serious risk of major emotional harm if the former is compelled to accept access, access would not be ordered.[56] A serious risk of major emotional harm to the child is to be judged not by what appear likely to be the short-term transient problems of access, but by reference to a medium-term and long-term view of the child's development.[57] Where hostility of stepfather to continuing contact would place the mother's marriage and the child's welfare at risk, contact would be denied:[58]

> Neither parent should be encouraged or permitted to think that the more intransigent, the more unreasonable, the more obdurate and the more unco-operative they are, the more likely they are to get their own way. Courts should remember that in these cases they are dealing with parents who are adults, who must be treated as rational adults, who must be assumed to have the welfare of the child at heart, and who have once been close enough to each other to have produced the child.[59]

With the increasing emphasis of a child's right to know both his biological parents, the court is reluctant to permit a parent opposing contact on the basis that the child believes that the stepfather is his father. Thus, in *Re W (a minor) (contact)*,[60] the parents were divorced and contact between a boy, four years old, and his father had been problematic. When the mother met her second husband (S) she terminated contact. In the meantime, the boy was brought up to believe that S was his father. It was held by the Court of Appeal that despite the obduracy of the mother, contact with a parent was a fundamental right of a child. The mother had no right to deny the child contact with his father. The difficulty as to how to explain to the child that his stepfather was not his biological father was the mother's own making. An order for contact had to be made so that a constructive and sensitive approach could be made for the child to be reintroduced to his father.

In cases where direct contact is not possible, it is highly desirable that there should be indirect contact so that the child grows up knowing of the

---

[56] *Re D (a minor) (contact: mother's hostility)* [1993] 2 FLR 1; see *Re H (a minor) (parental responsibility)* [1993] 1 FLR 484.
[57] *Re O (contact: imposition of conditions)* [1995] 2 FLR 124 at p. 129. *Re B (a minor) (access)* [1984] FLR 648; *Re BC (a minor) (access)* [1985] FLR 639; *Re SM (a minor) (natural father: access)* [1991] 2 FLR 333.
[58] See *Re H (a minor) (parental responsibility)* [1993] 1 FLR 484.
[59] *Re O (contact: imposition of conditions)* [1995] 2 FLR 124 at pp. 129–30.
[60] [1994] 2 FLR 441.

love and interest of the absent parent with whom, in due course, direct contact should be established. Thus, in *Re O (contact: imposition of conditions)*,[61] the parents were never married. The custodial mother was adamant that the boy who was 30 months should have no contact with the father. The father accepted that direct contact would not be possible without the cooperation of the mother, and the court ordered indirect contact requiring the mother to send the father (i) photographs of the child every three months; (ii) copies of all nursery or playgroup reports; (iii) information about any serious illness; and (iv) that the mother accept delivery of cards and presents for the child through the post from the father, and upon acceptance to read and show any such communication, and deliver such presents to the child.[62]

Apart from the above principles, wishes of a mature child or teenagers concerning access will be respected. Thus, children of 11 and 13 are entitled to be treated with respect and no access should be dictated to them if they are adamant that they do not wish to see their father.[63]

There is no principle of law that a father who has been found to have seriously sexually abused his child should not be granted access. Thus, in *H v H (child abuse: access)*,[64] the parties had three children, a daughter and two sons. On divorce, the father was given reasonable access which the mother stopped when it was found the daughter had been a victim of serious sexual abuse by the father. On the application of the father for access, it was found that all the children wanted to see him and there was no sign of serious emotional distress on the part of the daughter. The mother contemplated access in the future. It was held that serious sexual abuse was an extremely important factor to be taken into account when considering access, and each case must be decided on its own particular facts. As the father had had a good relationship with the children whom he wished to see, access should continue with supervision.[65]

The presumption in favour of access applies equally to an unmarried father.[66] Contact by the child with other non-parents such as stepfather or maternal or paternal grandparents, however, is not governed by any

---

[61] [1995] 2 FLR 124.

[62] For problems with enforcement, see Alec Samuels, 'Refusal or Failure to Observe Access Order — The Remedy for the Aggrieved Party'; *Melwani v Melwani*, Court of Appeal, Civil Appeal Action No 39 of 1986 (1986).

[63] *Re S (minors) (access: religious upbringing)* [1992] 2 FLR 313; *Re M (contact: welfare test)* [1995] 1 FLR 274, the views of a nine-year-old child are important.

[64] [1989] 1 FLR 212.

[65] See also *Re R (a minor) (child abuse: access)* [1988] 1 FLR 206; *S v S (child abuse: access)* [1988] 1 FLR 213; *L v L (child abuse: access)* [1989] 2 FLR 16.

[66] See *Re H (a minor) (parental responsibility)* [1993] 1 FLR 484.

presumption. These cases will be decided on the principle that the child's welfare is the first and paramount consideration. In a rather unusual case of *Re H (a minor) (contact)*,[67] the husband and wife separated. After separation, the wife commenced a relationship with and was pregnant by Mr G. Mr G did not want to assume the responsibility of being a father and terminated the relationship. The wife and husband reconciled. The husband attended to the birth of the child, undertook the role of the father and gave a stable environment to the boy for its first six months. The marriage, however, ended in divorce. The husband had regular access to the boy until the mother and Mr G resumed their relationship. The mother sought to terminate access. It was held by the Court of Appeal that there was no presumption that a stepfather should continue a relationship with his stepchild. However, from time to time there were people in the life of a child who could be very important. Although the child's memory of the stepfather was likely to be limited or probably non-existent, the stepfather was a thoroughly good man of generosity, honesty, and would provide some degree of stability to the boy's life, something that might otherwise be missing.[68] Similarly, in *Re A (section 8 order: grandparent application)*,[69] paternal grandmother sought access to a four-and-a-half-year-old child. It was held by the Court of Appeal that there was no presumption in favour of access. A non-parent who sought access had to show grounds for wishing to have contact and the case would be decided on the basis of what would promote the child's best interests.

LAW REFORM

The law governing the reallocation of parental rights and authority (or responsibility) on family breakdown is confusing due to the overlapping and varied jurisdictions involved under different Ordinances. The Hong Kong Law Reform Commission will no doubt deal with how this area of the law may be improved.

---

[67] [1994] 2 FLR 776.
[68] The father of a child born as a result of donor insemination is to be distinguished from a stepfather, see *Re CH (contact: parentage)* [1996] 1 FLR 569.
[69] [1995] 2 FLR 153; see also *Re S (contact: grandparents)* [1996] 1 FLR 158.

11

Adoption

INTRODUCTION

Adoption today is a statutory creation which was first introduced in 1956 by the Adoption Ordinance (AO).[1] It involves the complete severance of the legal relationship between parents and child, and the establishment of a new one between the child and his adoptive parents. The objective is to provide a permanent family environment for a child whose natural parents are unable or unwilling to provide one.

Prior to 1 January 1973, adoption could also be effected under Chinese Customary law. This form of adoption was abolished. However, the status or rights of a person adopted under Chinese Customary law are unaffected.[2]

Adoption is different from foster care which is simply an arrangement whereby a child is looked after by a 'volunteer' on a temporary basis. Such an arrangement does not affect the legal relationship between parent and child, nor does it create any status relationship between the foster-parent and the foster-child.

Although the practice of adoption has undergone significant changes, the law governing it has not been comprehensively reviewed since it was

---

[1] Ordinance No 22 of 1956.
[2] S25 of the Adoption Ordinance; see *Yau Tin-sung v Yan Wan-loi* [1983] 2 HKC 647; *Re Chan Tse-shi* [1954] HKLR 9; *R v Cheung King-po* [1927] HKLR 104; *Chan Yue v Henry Leong Estates Ltd* [1953] HKLR 66; for *kim tiu* adoption, see Chapter 1.

first introduced in 1956. As can be seen in Table 11.1, the majority of the adoptions in Hong Kong are privately arranged. This refers to the placement of a child with the prospective adopters by a person other than through the Director of Social Welfare (DSW). In such cases, the DSW is nonetheless involved when notice is given to the DSW of an intention to apply for an adoption order by the prospective adopters. In all other cases, that is, those adoptions which are not privately arranged, children are placed by the DSW and, prior to such placement, a Home Study Report would be conducted as to the suitability of the prospective adopters.

> An example of private placement might be: Mrs A gives birth to the 7th child, and they feel unable to cope. The child may therefore be placed with Mr and Mrs B whom they have heard are desperate to have a child to raise as their own. The parties meet through an intermediary and the child is placed in the care of Mr and Mrs B. Mr and Mrs B are happy with the child and may want to adopt that child.

The AO provides detailed rules on the jurisdiction of the court, who may adopt, the minimum age of adopters, who may be adopted, residence requirement of adopters, notice to the DSW and period of actual custody of adoptee by adopters. These will be examined below.

Table 11.1 Categories of adoption in Hong Kong between 1989–1997

Category	1989–90	1990–91	1991–92	1992–93	1993–94	1994–95	1995–96	1996–97
No. of abandoned children	5	1	8	9	8	9	11	18
No. of orphans	0	1	0	0	0	0	0	0
No. of illegitimate children	56	73	101	79	97	97	101	98
No. of adoptions by private arrangement	175	200	246	213	212	166	132	126
Total	236	275	355	301	317	272	244	242

Source: Department of Social Welfare, Hong Kong.

JURISDICTION OF THE COURT

S4A(1) of the AO provides that all adoption applications are to be commenced in the District Court. The District Court may on its own motion or at the request of any party to the proceedings transfer the application to the Court of First Instance.[3] Most adoption applications, however, are heard by the District Court, and transfer may occur where consent of the parents is at issue.[4]

Table 11.2 Number of Adoption Orders under the Adoption Ordinance (figures extracted from Hong Kong Annual Reports 1958–70, and A Review of Hong Kong 1970–1997, annual report published by the Hong Kong Government.

1957	93	1986	(9+30) 309
1958	91	1987	(0+322) 322
1959	119	1988	(2+292) 294
1960	173	1989	(3+280) 283
1961	176	1990	(4+290) 294
1962	176	1991	(10+341) 351
1963	139	1992	(8+319) 327
1964	125	1993	(2+332) 334
1965	89	1994	(8+287) 295
1966	160	1995	(3+256) 259
1967	134	1996	(4+253) 257
1968	224	1997	—
1969	292		
1970	271		
1971	320		
1972	398		
1973	364		
1974	411		
1975	450		
1976	392		
1977	415		
1978	347		
1979	409		
1980	412		
1981	398		
1982	400		
1983	(69a+386b) 455c		
1984	(2+437) 439		
1985	(1+0) 1		

a = High Court cases   b = District Court cases   c = a + b

---

[3] S4A(2), s8 of the Hong Kong Reunification Ordinance, amending s3 of the Supreme Court Ordinance.
[4] See Table 11.2.

WHO MAY ADOPT

S4 provides for two categories of applicant who may adopt: (1) adoption by a sole applicant (sometimes also referred to as a 'single' applicant but not necessarily meaning an 'unmarried' applicant as such), and (2) adoption by joint applicants who are married to each other.

Sole Applicant

An adoption order can be made in favour of a sole applicant[5] who may be related or unrelated to the infant. For instance, an applicant may be the natural mother or father of the infant.[6]

There is, however, one restriction on the eligibility of applicants in that the adoption of a female infant is not to be made in favour of a sole male applicant unless the court is satisfied that there are special circumstances justifying it.[7] The fact that the male applicant is the child's putative father does not alone constitute special circumstances. However, in *Re D (an infant)*[8] the mother consented to the daughter's adoption, and in view of the lack of affiliation proceedings at the time, and the putative father's desire to perform his moral obligation, it was held that there were special circumstances warranting adoption. Today, an unmarried father could acknowledge his paternity and obtain an order for parental rights and authority. So adoption of the child would rarely be necessary or desirable.[9]

A single person with homosexual tendencies is not disqualified from adopting. In *Re W (adoption: homosexual adopter)*,[10] a girl (J) was placed with a professional childless woman (L). J settled well and thrived. L had lived with another professional woman (S) in a lesbian relationship for ten years. It was agreed that J should continue to live with L. On her application to adopt J, J's natural mother argued that it was contrary to public policy to make an adoption order in favour of a party living in a homosexual relationship. It was held that the legislation did not exclude, as a matter of

---

[5] S4(1).
[6] S4(3); s2 provides that 'father', in relation to an illegitimate infant, means the natural father. See also pp. 307–310 for the desirability of such adoption.
[7] S5(3).
[8] [1962] HKLR 431.
[9] See Chapter 9.
[10] [1997] 2 FLR 406.

policy, a homosexual cohabiting couple or a single person with homosexual tendencies from applying to adopt a child.[11]

A sole applicant who is a married person can only adopt with the consent of the other spouse,[12] but consent may be dispensed with in any of the following situations:
- the spouse cannot be found;
- the spouse is incapable of giving consent;
- the spouses have lived apart and the separation is likely to be permanent;
- in the opinion of the court the consent ought to be dispensed with in all the circumstances of the case.[13]

Joint Applicants

S4(?) provides that the court may make an adoption order on the application of 'two spouses',[14] authorising them jointly to adopt an infant. No adoption order, however, can be made in favour of an unmarried couple.[15] One or other of the joint applicants may be related to the adoptee. For instance, an adoption order may authorise the adoption of an infant by its mother jointly with her spouse. This happens if a mother is divorced and she and her second husband wish to adopt her child from the first marriage. This is sometimes called 'step-parent' adoption.[16] The effect of such an adoption is to cut off all legal links the child has with the natural father.

Minimum Age of Adopters

Where a parent is the applicant, no minimum age is imposed regardless of whether the parent is a sole applicant, or is applying jointly with a spouse.[17] In the case of a joint application by parties unrelated to the infant, both parties must have attained the age of 25.[18] Where one of the applicants is a relative of the infant, he and his co-applicant must have attained the age of 21.[19] A 'relative' in relation to an infant, means a grandparent, brother,

---

[11] *Re AB (adoption: joint residence)* [1996] 1 FLR 27.
[12] S5(5)(b).
[13] See s6(2).
[14] That is, married to each other, see *Re D (an infant)* [1962] HKLR 431.
[15] S5(4).
[16] S4(3), see also pp. 307–310 for the desirability of such adoption.
[17] S5.
[18] S5.
[19] S5.

sister, uncle[20] or aunt, whether of the full blood, of the half blood or by affinity, and includes:

(a) where an adoption order has been made in respect of the infant or any other person under this Ordinance, any person who would be a relative of the infant within this definition if the adopted person were the child of the adopter born in lawful wedlock;
(b) where the infant is illegitimate, the father of the infant and any person who would be a relative of the infant within the meaning of this definition if the infant were the legitimate child of his mother and father.[21]

WHO MAY BE ADOPTED

The AO defines an 'infant' as any person under the age of 18, but does not include a person who is or has been married.[22]

OTHER REQUIREMENTS

Apart from the above rules governing who may adopt, minimum age of adopters and who may be adopted, the AO specifies a residence requirement in Hong Kong of prospective adopters, prior notice to be given of a pending adoption application to the DSW, and minimum period of actual custody of adoptee by the prospective adopters.

Residence Requirement

S5(6) provides that an adoption order shall not be made in respect of any infant unless the applicant and the infant reside[23] in Hong Kong. 'Residence' requires some degree of permanence of abode so a transient visitor to Hong Kong would not satisfy this requirement. In the case of *Re Adoption*

---

[20] Excluding great-uncle, see *Re C (minors) (wardship: adoption)* [1989] 1 FLR 222.
[21] S2.
[22] S2 as amended by s26 of Law Reform (Miscellaneous Provisions and Minor Amendments) Ordinance (No 80 of 1997).
[23] See *Re NTH (an infant)* [1996] 1 HKC 93. Compare the requirement in English law of the applicant having his 'home' in the UK; see *Re Y (minors) (adoption: jurisdiction)* (1986) 16 Fam Law 26.

Application,[24] an English couple living in Hong Kong wished to adopt the wife's 13-year-old son, who had since the age of 11 been studying in England and had not since returned to Hong Kong. It was held that the child was not residing in Hong Kong. Similarly, a visitor[25] who travelled to Hong Kong with a view to adopting a child could not be said to have satisfied the 'residence' requirement.[26]

Notice to the Director of Social Welfare

An adoption order cannot be made unless the applicant has given notice in writing DSW of his intention to apply for an adoption order six months prior to the date of the order.[27] Further, an adoption order cannot be made unless the applicant has, within four months of the lodging of the notice, applied to the court for an adoption order.

Adoptee in Actual Custody of Adopters

An adoption order cannot be made in respect of any infant unless such an infant has been continuously in the actual custody of the applicant for six consecutive months immediately preceding the date of the order.[28] The period is reduced to 13 weeks if one of the prospective adopters is the natural parent of the child.[29] The continuous actual custody period shall not be regarded as having been broken during the intermission of any period when the infant is an in-patient in a hospital or resides at a boarding school either in or outside Hong Kong.[30]

The Making of an Adoption Order

Apart from the above requirements, the AO provides for consent of the adoptee's parents, and where it is not forthcoming, the court may dispense with such consent. Most importantly, the AO provides that an adoption

---

[24] [1958] HKLR 150.
[25] Ibid. A child who had left Hong Kong and has been studying in England for the previous two years failed to satisfy this requirement.
[26] *Re LYC (an infant)* [1961] HKLR 491.
[27] S5(7)(b). The court may permit a short period of notice, s5(7)(b).
[28] S5(7).
[29] S5(7)(a)(aa).
[30] S5(8), reversing the decision *Re An Infant* [1962] HKLR 167.

order will only be made if it is for the welfare of the infant. Thus, s8(1) of the AO states:

> The Court before making an adoption order shall be satisfied–
> (a) that every person whose consent is necessary under this Ordinance, and whose consent is not dispensed with, has consented to and understands the nature and effect of the adoption order for which application is made, and in particular in the case of any parent understands that the effect of the adoption order will be permanently to deprive him or her of his or her parental rights;
> (b) the order if made will be for the welfare of the infant, due consideration being for this purpose given to the wishes of the infant, having regard to the age and understanding of the infant; and
> (c) that the applicant has not received or agreed to receive, and that no person has made or given or agreed to make or given to the applicant, any payment or other reward in consideration of the adoption except such as the court may sanction.

Consent

S5(5)(a) provides that an adoption order shall not be made in any case except with the consent of every person who is a parent or guardian of the infant or who is liable (by agreement or court order) to contribute to the maintenance of the infant.

'Parent' in relation to a child who is illegitimate means the child's mother, but it does not include the father unless he is entitled to exercise any rights or authority under s3(1)(d) of the Guardian of Minors Ordinance.[31]

In the case of a mother's consent, a document signifying it shall not be admissible unless the child is six weeks old at the date of its execution.[32] The purpose of this mandatory time lapse is to ensure that a mother is given sufficient time after the birth of the child to deliberate on the child's adoption.

Consent is to be given to the DSW by signing the prescribed consent form which can be either general or specific.[33] General consent allows the DSW to select adopters for the child. Specific consent means that the parents consent to make the child available for adoption by specific adopters.[34] Where a child is placed through the DSW, general consent would have been obtained. Specific consent is used in cases of privately arranged adoption.

---

[31] S2 AO.
[32] S7(3).
[33] S5(5A).
[34] See Form 4 and Form 4A, Adoption Rules.

Effect of general consent

Where the consent of a parent is given in the prescribed general form, the parent shall cease to have any 'parental rights, duties, obligations or liabilities in respect of the infant with effect from the execution of the form of consent'.[35] The DSW shall immediately upon the execution of the prescribed general form of consent be the guardian *ad litem* (GAL) of the infant, and may, where the infant does not have a guardian or no guardian can be found, perform such duties of a guardian as may be necessary in the interests of the welfare of the infant.[36]

Revocation of general consent

A parent whose consent has been given in the prescribed general form may revoke it within three months by written notice to the DSW.[37] Furthermore, the parent may at any time after the expiration of three months, and before the making of an adoption order, apply to the court for an order revoking that consent on the ground that he wishes to 'resume parental rights, duties, obligations and liabilities'.[38] In *Re L (an infant)*,[39] a mother gave consent to her child's adoption, and some seven months later she changed her mind. It was held in an application under s5(5D), that the welfare of the child was not the first and paramount consideration. The test to be applied was whether the applicant was genuine and sincere in her application. All the circumstances, from the time of the pregnancy to the date of hearing were relevant in determining sincerity. In this case, the applicant, who was 20 years old and unmarried, had at all times no intention of keeping the child and that attitude was maintained up to the time she gave consent. No steps were taken within three months to revoke that consent, nor was that considered until some nine months after the child was born. The application was dismissed.

Dispensing with consent

Most adoption orders are made with parental consent. However, where an adoption application is made without parental consent, it has been held that the court should first consider whether an adoption order is in all the

---

[35] S5(5B).
[36] S5(5F); see *Mr and Mrs C v Mr D, Guardian ad litem* [1993] 2 HKLR 385.
[37] S5(5C).
[38] S5(5D).
[39] [1989] 1 HKLR 614.

circumstances appropriate, and if so, whether the court should dispense with consent.[40] Thus, in cases where parents adamantly refuse to consent to the adoption of their child, there comes into play a difficult balancing act between the welfare of the infant and the interests of parents in maintaining their legal ties with the child. S6(1) provides that the Court may dispense with consent if it is satisfied:

> (a) in the case of a parent or guardian of the infant, he has abandoned,[41] neglected, or persistently ill-treated the infant;
> (b) in the case of a person liable by virtue of an order or agreement to contribute to the maintenance if the infant, that he has persistently neglected or refused so to contribute;
> (c) in any case, that the person whose consent is required cannot be found[42] or is incapable of giving his consent or that his consent is unreasonably withheld,
> or if it is of opinion that such consent ought, in all the circumstances of the case, to be dispensed with.

Dispensing with consent unreasonably withheld

As can be seen, most of the above grounds for dispensing with consent are fault-based. The court may thus dispense with a parent's consent if the parent has abandoned, neglected or persistently ill-treated the child. Indeed, most of the grounds are of little significance today except dispensing with consent on the basis that it has been unreasonably withheld. This is also the most difficult one. In the leading case of *Re W (an infant)*,[43] the House of Lords held that reasonableness connoted an objective test, and all the circumstances must be examined, as of the time of the hearing.[44]

> ... the test is reasonableness and not anything else. It is not culpability. It is not indifference. It is not failure to discharge parental duties. It is reasonableness, and reasonableness in the context of the totality of the circumstances.

---

[40] *Re B (adoption: child's welfare)* [1995] 1 FLR 895.
[41] Failure of one parent to take advantage of access did not constitute abandonment. Abandonment refers to a parent who has been shown to be thoroughly unsatisfactory, see *Re an infant* [1985] HKLY 512.
[42] This means that all reasonable steps have been taken to find the parent, but without success, *Re F (an infant)* [1970] 1 QB 385. It also includes exceptional circumstances, such as where there are no practicable means of communicating with a parent to obtain his agreement. For instance, where a child had illegally escaped to a country from a totalitarian regime and any attempt to communicate with him there would be very dangerous for him, *Re R (adoption)* [1967] 1 WLR 34.
[43] [1971] AC 682.
[44] Ibid.

Once consent has been given, or once the child has been placed with the adopters, time begins to run against the mother and, as time goes on, it becomes progressively more difficult for her to show that the withdrawal of consent is reasonable.[45] In *Re EL-G (minors) (wardship and adoption)*,[46] the children had repeatedly gone into care because of the mother's illness and she was unable to look after them for a period of four years. There were signs that the children were becoming disturbed when attempts were made to reunite them with the mother. The children settled well with the foster-parents who proposed to adopt them. It was held that it was unreasonable for the mother to object to adoption.

Is consent unreasonably withheld? This is a difficult question. Where the chance of a successful reunification of the child with the mother is low, withholding consent is most likely to be regarded as unreasonable. In theory, the court cannot dispense with consent simply because adoption is conducive to the welfare of the child, but the welfare of the child is relevant, and may even be decisive.

> ... Welfare per se is not the test, the fact that a reasonable parent does pay regard to the welfare of his child must enter into the question of reasonableness as a relevant factor. It is relevant in all cases if, and to the extent that, a reasonable parent would take it into account. It is decisive in those cases where a reasonable parent must so regard it.[47]

How is a reasonable parent to decide whether to consent to adoption, the effect of which is to sever all ties with the child? How much weight should she place on the welfare of the child? How much weight should she place on her own desire to be reunited with the child in the future? Wilberforce LJ attempted a synthesis of these questions by asking how a particular mother in her actual circumstances, endowed with a mind and temperament capable of making a reasonable decision.[48]

These issues surfaced in the case of *Re D (a minor) (adoption: freeing order)*,[49] where the girl (K) was four years old. The mother's relationship with the father ended before K's birth, and the father played no part in K's life. K suffered from unexplained injuries and emotional deprivation. As a result, K was placed in the care of a local authority which then placed her in the care of foster-parents. The mother subsequently gave birth to another child fathered by another man. Rehabilitation of K with her mother proved

---

[45] *Re H (infants) (adoption: parental consent)* [1977] 1 WLR 471 at p. 472 per Ormrod LJ.
[46] [1983] 4 FLR 421.
[47] Ibid., at p. 699 per Lord Hailsham.
[48] *Re D (a minor) (adoption: freeing order)* [1991] 1 FLR 48 at p. 55 per Butler-Sloss LJ.
[49] [1991] 1 FLR 48.

unsuccessful and the child was placed with the prospective adopters. Contact between the mother and K continued, albeit infrequently. The mother agreed to adoption, but then changed her mind, arguing that K enjoyed having contact with her, that she planned to marry and settle down, and desired to reunite the family. On the question of whether a hypothetical reasonable parent in the circumstances of this mother ought reasonably to have given her consent, it was said that:

> Looking at the hypothetical reasonable parent in the circumstances of this mother, we see that the factors in her favour are: she is the mother and the child lived with her for two main periods totalling about 18 months: she now has a settled home with a potential step-father ... she desires to reunite the family; she is continuing to have access and the child on one level enjoys it and is having no ill-effects from it ... The contrary factors are: the efforts at rehabilitation have failed in the past ... there was no present evidence of any close or warm or affective relationship between them or any foundation upon which to recreate it ... but since children cannot wait for ever and will settle where they are, at any time thereafter — consequently the entirely natural aspiration of the mother to have K back and reunite the family are unrealistic; in the absence of eventual rehabilitation and without an adequate existing relationship, the continuance of access in the long term is not likely to be beneficial to the child in any real sense; contact a few times a year without any firm basis of a relationship between the mother and the child of 4 and a half years old would at best be entirely superficial and more for the adult than the child, and at worse, as the child settled with the present family and grew older, might be unsettling and upsetting ...[50]

The Court of Appeal held that there was no real bond between the mother and child apart from a history of interrupted care. The prospect of the child returning to the mother was minimal, and parental consent was dispensed with. Adoption would provide the child with the long-term security of a stable and loving home which the mother could not provide.

The difficulty with an objective test is highlighted in the case of *Re C (a minor) (adoption: parental agreement: contact)*,[51] where the couple were in their forties and the girl was four years old. They loved and wanted to keep her. The mother, however, was of limited intelligence and was not able to cope with the demands of a growing child. The father did not comprehend the effect of this on the child and was not able to provide an acceptable alternative. The local authority was alerted and the child was determined to be suffering from mental, emotional and social deprivation.

---

[50] Ibid., at p. 55 per Butler-Sloss LJ.
[51] [1993] 2 FLR 260.

The girl thrived, however, when she was placed with foster-parents. The unanimous opinion of the experts was that the mother could not cope and that there was to be no rehabilitation. The effect of applying the objective standard was that the judge was to assume:

> the mother was not, as she in fact was, a person of limited intelligence and inadequate grasp of the emotional and other needs of a lively little girl of 4. Instead she had to be assumed to be a woman with a full perception of her own deficiencies and an ability to evaluate dispassionately the evidence and opinions of the expert. She was also endowed with the intelligence and altruism needed to appreciate, if such were the case, that her child's welfare would be so much better served by adoption [and] that her own maternal feelings should take second place.[52]

The conflict between the welfare of the child and the wishes of the parents is the most difficult one to resolve. As Steyn and Hoffmann LJJ have remarked:

> How this conflict of views and interests should be resolved may in some cases strike different minds in different ways. Judges who are all conscientiously trying to make decisions which reflect generally accepted values may in fact be employing somewhat different scales. It is natural, for example, that one judge may give less weight than another to parental interests when they stand in the way of his firmly held views about what the interests of the child require. His "reasonable mother" will be more altruistic, more impressed by expert opinion than her sister in the court of a different judge. Since judges are human, such diversity is inevitable and, within fairly good limits, acceptable.[53]

What this means is that two reasonable parents can come to opposite conclusions on the same set of facts, and still be considered reasonable. Consequently, there is a band of decisions within which the court would not interfere.[54]

Thus, consent of a mother was not dispensed with in *Re V (a minor) (adoption: dispensing with agreement)*.[55] In this case, the boy's parents' marriage broke down, the mother left the matrimonial home with the boy and lived with the applicants. The mother remarried and arranged for the boy to live with the applicants. She at first agreed that the boy could be adopted by the applicants but later changed her mind. By this time, the

---

[52] Ibid., at p. 272 per Steyn and Hoffmann LJJ.
[53] Ibid., at p. 273.
[54] [1971] AC 682 at p. 699 per Lord Hailsham.
[55] [1987] 2 FLR 89.

mother's second marriage ended and she wanted to bring up the child herself together with her two younger children. It was found that the child's long-term welfare dictated that he should remain with the applicants throughout his childhood, but that continued access by the mother was in his interests. The judge made an adoption order dispensing with her agreement on the ground that consent was unreasonably withheld. The Court of Appeal disagreed. It held that a single mother capable of looking after the child could not be said to be harbouring an unreasonable ambition in wishing to do so. This was a consideration which ought to have been carefully weighed in the balance when assessing the reasonableness of her withholding consent. A reasonable parent would also consider whether the child, if adopted, would feel rejected by his mother *vis-à-vis* his siblings with whom he would have frequent contact, and who, unlike him, were not adopted. A reasonable parent would also have in mind the likelihood of the mother communicating to the child her wish to have him back and the consequent unsettling effect that this would have upon both the child and the adopters.

Recently, in *Re MW (adoption: surrogacy)*,[56] consent of a surrogate mother, however, was dispensed with as adoption was in the best interests of the child. In this case, the surrogate mother agreed to a surrogate pregnancy for the applicants who were a married couple. Pursuant to the agreement, the surrogate mother was impregnated by artificial insemination using semen of the husband. The applicants had cared for the boy since birth. Conflict, however, arose regarding contact. The court took the view that the boy had been with the applicants for the last two and a half years and the surrogate mother simply wanted to undo the past. As this was contrary to the welfare of the boy, the surrogate mother's consent was thus dispensed with.

Freeing for adoption

Where consent is likely to be an issue, prospective adopters may be reluctant to accept placement. S5A now provides that where, on an application made by the DSW, the Court is satisfied that any consent required by s5(5)(a) should be dispensed with, it may make an order freeing an infant for adoption. Such an application may only be made where the DSW is the legal guardian of the child or the child is in his care.[57] Before making a freeing order, the court shall notify every person whose consent is to be dispensed with and who can be found, and allow every such person an

---

[56] [1995] 2 FLR 759.
[57] S5A(1).

opportunity to be heard.[58] The effect of a freeing order is that the court can make an adoption order without further evidence of parental consent.[59]

Welfare

So far, we have examined how consent may be given, when it may be revoked and when the court may dispense with a parent's consent when it is unreasonably withheld. Before an adoption order is made, the court also needs to be satisfied that the order will be for the welfare of the infant. The emphasis on welfare is confirmed in Article 21 of the UN Convention on the Rights of the Child which provides that States Parties that recognise the system of adoption shall ensure that 'the best interests of the child shall be the paramount consideration'.

S8(1)(b) AO provides that:

> the court before making an adoption order shall be satisfied ... that the order if made will be for the welfare of the infant, due consideration being for this purpose given to the wishes of the infant, having regard to the age and understanding of the infant.

A similar emphasis on welfare is adopted by s6 of the English Adoption Act 1976. It provides that:

> In reaching any decision relating to the adoption of a child a court ... shall have regard to all the circumstances, first consideration being given to the need to safeguard and promote the welfare of the child throughout his childhood; and shall so far as practicable ascertain the wishes and feelings of the child regarding the decision and give due consideration to them, having regard to his age and understanding.

To borrow Andrew Bainham's terminology, s8(1)(b) expresses a 'diluted welfare principle'.[60] Unlike custody proceedings involving claims of parents, adoption concerns the competing claims between parents, whose ties with the child will be completely severed, and the interests of the child. The court has made it clear that severance of parental ties should not be ordered lightly and without good reason. Thus, it was said that:

---

[58] S5A(3).
[59] S5A(4)(c); *Re G (adoption: freeing order)* [1997] 2 FLR 202; *Re W (adoption: homosexual adopter)* [1997] 2 FLR 406.
[60] See A Bainham, *Children: The Modern Law*, Family Law, Bristol, 1993, p. 223; *Re EL-G (minors) (wardship and adoption)* [1983] 4 FLR 421.

An adoption order is an order of the most serious description. It removes the child once and for all from his natural parents and gives him to the adopted parents as though they were ... his natural parents ... [By] an adoption order the child is removed once and for all and entirely from the parent. That is an extremely serious matter ... once the adoption order is made, the father or the mother can never see their child again unless by permission of the adopting parents.[61]

Where one of the parents wants the child to be adopted but the other refuses and wishes to play the role of a parent, there is a presumption that the child is to be brought up by the natural parent. Thus, in *Re O (a minor) (custody: adoption)*,[62] the natural parents were never married and the child was born as a result of their brief relationship. The mother reconciled with her husband and wanted the child to be adopted but the father wanted custody which the mother opposed. It was held that where the mother could not look after the child, and where the natural father desired to take on parental responsibility for the child, he should be given first consideration as the long-term carer. Provided the child's moral and physical health were not in danger, the best person to bring up a child was the natural parent.[63]

Despite the fact that the welfare of the child is not the overriding consideration in determining whether to make an adoption order, increasing emphasis on the child's welfare means that it may outweigh any other consideration. This can be seen in cases where the parents genuinely desire to be reunited with the child, but this is outweighed by the importance of a child becoming part of a new family and having a new legal status. Thus, in *Re D (a minor) (adoption: freeing order)*[64] which was discussed earlier, it was held that there was no real bond between the mother and child apart from a history of interrupted care, and the prospect of the child returning to the mother was minimal. Adoption would provide the child with the long-term security of a stable and loving home which the mother could not provide. Similarly, in *Re C (a minor) (adoption: parental agreement: contact)*,[65] an adoption order was made. Balcombe LJ expressed a feeling of unease about the outcome of the case in these terms:

---

[61] *Hitchcock v WB* [1952] 2 All ER 119 at 121 per Lord Goddard CJ. The diluted welfare principle means that the welfare is not the overriding consideration; welfare does not outweigh all other considerations, but it does outweigh any single consideration, see *Re B (adoption: child's welfare)* [1995] 1 FLR 895.
[62] [1992] 1 FLR 77.
[63] *Re M (a minor: custody appeal)* [1990] 1 FLR 291.
[64] [1991] 1 FLR 48.
[65] [1993] 2 FLR 260.

In this case ... the only failure on the part of the parents was their inability to give K the standard of parental care necessary for her social and emotional development, which was primarily attributable to the mother's limited intellectual capacity, and the father's inability to comprehend the effect of this or himself to provide an acceptable alternative. If normal social work intervention should prove ineffective, this could well justify K being taken into care and placed during the remainder of her childhood with long-term foster-parents, but I doubt whether Parliament intended that it should be a ground for irrevocably terminating the parents' ... legal relationship with the child. It has the flavour of social engineering.[66]

Apart from permanence and stability, which are important aspects of welfare, the wishes of the infant need to be taken into account, having regard to the child's age and understanding.[67] Thus, in *Re D (minors) (adoption by step-parent)*,[68] the wishes of children aged 13 and $10\frac{1}{2}$ were that they be adopted. It was held that to refuse an adoption order in the face of such wishes would require a clear reason. In *Re W (an infant)*,[69] a married couple wished to adopt the wife's illegitimate son who was $17\frac{1}{2}$ years old. The child was unaware of his status, and the couple was reluctant to disclose it to the child. The court held that the child was of an age and understanding to have an opinion of his own. The court therefore had to ascertain his wishes before declaring itself satisfied that the order was for his welfare. Similarly, in *Re B (a minor) (adoption: parental agreement)*,[70] the wishes of an 11-year-old boy who wished to be adopted was considered to be important.[71]

STEP-PARENT AND RELATIVE ADOPTION

In the past, many proposed adopters would be unrelated to an adoptee. However, with the increase in the number of divorces and remarriages, a custodial spouse who remarries may, together with her new spouse, wish to adopt her children with a view to integrating them into the new family. Yet, the courts may be reluctant to entertain such applications save in

---

[66] Ibid., at p. 269.
[67] S8(1)(b).
[68] [1981] 2 FLR 102.
[69] [1971] HKLR 219.
[70] [1990] 2 FLR 383.
[71] *Re EH and MH (step-parent adoption)* (1993) Fam Law 187.

exceptional cases.[72] The argument against this type of adoption is that where the child is young, adoption effectively severs the child completely from the non-custodial parent and that side of the family.

This restrained approach has been followed in *Re Phillips*,[73] where the wife, who was also the custodial parent of two children (aged 10 and 13) of her previous marriage, together with her new husband applied to adopt them. The father refused to consent. He had been seeing the children regularly once or twice a month and objected to being deprived of the right of access. The High Court refused to grant an adoption order.[74]

However, in *Re D (adoption: parent's consent)*,[75] a practising homosexual father refused to consent to his child's adoption by the mother and her second husband. The House of Lords held that it was better to terminate access now and allow the adoption than to allow access to continue with the likelihood that the child would find out about the father's way of life and meet some of his partners. Again, in the unusual case of *Re D (minors) (adoption by step-parent)*,[76] adoption by a stepfather was allowed. In this case, the prospective adoptees were girls aged 11 and 13. Their parents divorced and the mother remarried. Her second husband had also been divorced and his two children lived with him. The mother and her second husband wished to adopt the mother's two girls prior to emigrating to Australia. The father originally had access to the girls but had ceased to have contact and he consented to their adoption. The girls remembered their own father but they treated the second husband as their 'Dad' and wished to be adopted. At first instance, the judge held that there should be no adoption. The Court of Appeal disagreed. It held that an unusual feature in this case was that the natural father had dropped out of the lives of these children both physically and psychologically. Adoption would clarify their position, allowing the children to emigrate as the adopted children of the family.[77] As regards the reasons for favouring an adoption, Ormrod LJ said:

> I can well understand the adults feeling that it would put their position in their new country much more clearly and explicitly if they go there with these two children as the adopted children of the family . . . . Then it is

---

[72] Such as *Re B (a minor) (adoption: jurisdiction)* [1975] 2 All ER 449.
[73] High Court Adoption Nos 2 & 3 of 1985 (1986).
[74] The acquisition of British citizenship was one possible advantage of an adoption order, but the court would not take that into account, see E Phillips, 'Adoption of Hong Kong Minors by British Citizens' 16 (1986) HKLJ 390.
[75] [1977] AC 602.
[76] [1981] 2 FLR 102.
[77] See also *Re EH and MH (step-parent adoption)* (1993) Fam Law 187.

said that the effect of an adoption order is to cut them off entirely from their father's family — to which, to my mind, the answer is that it may or may not do so. There is no magic in an adoption order. The fact that the child becomes a child of the new family does not, in itself, automatically cut off the children from the natural family.

Adoption may be sought by grandparents or other relatives who have been the children's *de facto* parents.[78] The argument against this type of adoption is that it distorts family relationships. In the case of maternal-grandparents who adopt the mother's daughter, the granddaughter becomes a sibling of the mother.

Although the benefits such adoptions bring are not always clear, there have been a number of cases where such adoptions have been made. In *Re S (a minor) (adoption or custodianship)*,[79] the mother was 18 and she gave birth to a boy after a brief relationship with the father, who disappeared upon learning of the pregnancy. The boy, from birth, was looked after by the mother's father and his second wife (the applicants) who were 52 and 39 respectively. The boy looked upon the applicants as father and mother and was fully integrated into the wider family group. The mother visited the boy regularly and the boy thought she was a member of the applicants' wider family. The mother agreed to the adoption and it was agreed that the welfare of the child would be best secured by his growing up through his minority in the care of the applicants. At first instance, the judge refused to grant an adoption order on the grounds that the change in legal status might confuse the relationship which the child and the applicant already had. The Court of Appeal disagreed and held that the paramount need for the boy's future was to make an adoption order securing his *de facto* relationships so as to minimise the risk of his mother or anyone else seeking to disrupt them. The Court held that in this case, an adoption order would ensure that:

> The legal relationships will then coincide with the actual relationships on which the child is, by now, totally reliant. It seems to me that an adoption order will promote the welfare of the child in another way. When he is tactfully introduced to the true facts about his parentage, the adoption order will have already conferred upon him the legal status of child of the

---

[78] See the Report of the Departmental Committee on the Adoption of Children (Chairman: Sir William Houghton), HMSO, London, 1972; the concept of custodianship created by the Children Act 1975 which represented a halfway house between parental rights and authority and adoption. Now the Children Act 1989 provides that in an adoption application the court may consider other s8 orders.

[79] [1987] 2 FLR 331.

applicants. This is likely to reduce, not increase, the risk of emotional confusion, or the onset of insecurity.[80]

Again, in *Re W (a minor) (adoption by grandparents)*,[81] the maternal grandparents, who were in their mid-sixties, were granted custody of a seven-year-old boy some years earlier when the mother divorced the father. The father was an undesirable person with a bad criminal record, and the mother disappeared from the boy's life and consented to the adoption. It was held by the Court of Appeal that adoption was in the best interests of the child. The grandparents were ageing, and they should be put in a position of control of the child's future. An adoption order would enable them to appoint a testamentary guardian, something which a custody order could not permit them to do.[82]

PROHIBITION OF PAYMENT

Although private placement is not prohibited in Hong Kong, s22 makes it an offence for anyone to make or give, or agree to make or give, or receive or agree to receive any payment for or in connection with the adoption of an infant, save with the sanction of the court.[83] This provision does not apply to payment, renumeration or reward made in consideration of the professional services of a qualified barrister or solicitor within the meaning of the Legal Practitioners Ordinance or payment to the DSW of any fees prescribed by rules.[84] S8(1)(c) provides that prior to the making of an adoption order, the court shall be satisfied that 'the applicant has not received or agreed to receive, and that no person has made or given or agreed to make or give to the applicant, any payment or other reward in consideration of the adoption except such as the court may sanction.' This covers only the situation where the applicant is the recipient of payment or other reward. It would not cover a situation where the applicant makes the payment or reward to the mother.

What is more likely to happen is that payment would be made by the adopters to the mother. In such a case, it has been held that the court may

---

[80] [1987] 2 FLR 331 at p. 338 per Sir Roualeyn Cumming-Bruce.
[81] [1981] 2 FLR 161.
[82] *Re W (a minor) (adoption: custodianship)* (1992) Fam Law 64; *Re W (a minor) (adoption: custodianship: access)* [1988] 1 FLR 175.
[83] Cf parental order in s12 of the Parent and Child Ordinance.
[84] S12; see *Re Adoption Application (non-patrial: breach of procedures)* (1993) Fam Law 275.

authorise payment retrospectively. In *Re Adoption Application (payment for adoption)*,[85] a childless married couple, Mr and Mrs A, made an arrangement to pay Mrs B if she became pregnant following sexual intercourse with Mr A. The agreement further provided that after the birth of the child, Mrs B would hand the child over to Mr and Mrs A to be brought up as their own child. Mr B consented to the arrangement, and the parties agreed that the As would pay a sum of money to cover Mrs B's loss of wages and expenses during pregnancy. A child was conceived and Mrs B was paid the sum of £1000. A further £4000 was paid after the child's birth. Mr and Mrs B having been handed the child, and with the consent of Mrs B, applied to adopt the child. Latey J took the view that there was nothing 'commercial' about the arrangement. The applicants wanted the baby to be brought up as theirs from birth. It was only after the payments had been made and the baby was born that they began to turn their minds to adoption. There was no 'payment' or 'reward' made for the adoption. He said, obiter, that even if payment was made, he would authorise or sanction it retrospectively.[86]

GUARDIAN *AD LITEM*

Appointment

Where the parents give their 'general consent' to the adoption, the DSW shall become the guardian *ad litem* (GAL) of the child.[87] Where the parents give a 'specific consent' — i.e. the parents make the child available for adoption by particular adopters, the prospective adopters may ask the court for the appointment of a person other than the DSW as the GAL.[88]

R9 of the Adoption Rules states that an application to appoint someone other than the DSW as GAL must be supported by an affidavit by the applicant, setting out the facts together with the consent to act in writing of the proposed GAL. Although the discretion to appoint a GAL is vested in a District Court judge, the High Court in *Mr and Mrs C v Mr D, Guardian*

---

[85] [1987] Fam 81.
[86] *Re C (a minor) (adoption application)* [1993] 1 FLR 87; *Re ZHH (adoption application)* [1993] 1 FLR 83; *Re adoption application* [1992] 1 FLR 341. *Re AW (adoption application)* [1993] 1 FLR 62; *Re MW (adoption: surrogacy)* [1995] 2 FLR 759.
[87] S5(5F), r9.
[88] R9.

ad litem[89] has provided the following guidelines on the appointment of a GAL.

(i) Only those with special training in relation to children are fitted to fulfil the duties imposed on a GAL. Social workers, teachers and clinical psychologists are given as examples, but the list is not meant to be exhaustive.

(ii) Rarely will it be appropriate to appoint an individual not backed by the resources of an organisation to assist in pursuing proper investigations into the circumstances of the adoptive parents and children. In practice, it will be appropriate to appoint an organisation rather than an individual as GAL,[90] for instance, the Department of Social Welfare, or voluntary agencies specializing in adoptions.

(iii) Never will it be appropriate to appoint an individual or organization with any material hope or fear at stake in the outcome of adoption investigations.

Thus, it was held in *Mr and Mrs C v Mr D, Guardian ad litem* that appointing someone in the business of acting as a GAL paid by prospective adopters undermined an appearance of independence. Were such a person to make a habit of reporting adversely on the suitability of his paymasters, solicitors would soon lose their enthusiasm for recommending his services as a GAL to their clients. As a GAL with business needs of his own to serve, he was not likely to be, and was certainly not seen to be, independent. There was an inherent conflict between his duty to safeguard the welfare of an adoptive child, and his interest in building up his business.

Duties

In all adoption proceedings, a GAL is appointed. His duty is to safeguard the interests of the child.[91] In performing his duties, he must investigate as fully as possible all circumstances relevant to the proposed adoption, and make a report to the Court for the purposes of safeguarding the interests of the child. In particular, it is his duty to make inquiries as to all matters alleged in the applicant's statement and as to the matters specified in the Second Schedule of the Adoption Rules, and to report to the Court upon them. He shall also interview (either by himself or by an agent appointed by him) every individual being an applicant for the adoption order, or

---

[89] [1993] 2 HKLR 385.
[90] R14.
[91] S12(3).

mentioned in the applicant's statement as a person to whom reference may be made.[92]

Report of Guardian *Ad Litem*

A report is to be supplied to the court alone, and a GAL shall treat as confidential all information obtained in the course of the investigation. It is up to the court to decide who should see the report, and to what extent.[93]

EFFECT OF AN ADOPTION ORDER

S13(1) provides that the effect of an adoption order is the complete severance of legal ties with the birth family and creation of new legal ties with the adoptor's family. Upon the making of an adoption order, all rights, duties, obligations and liabilities of the parents or guardian of the infant in relation to future custody, maintenance and education, including all rights to appoint a guardian and to consent to marriage shall be extinguished. They are now all vested in, and are exercisable by and enforceable against, the adopter as if the infant were a child born to the adopter in lawful wedlock. An illegitimate child, thus, acquires the status of legitimacy.

As regards marriage, an adopted person remains in the same prohibited degrees to his natural parents and other relatives as if he had not been adopted. An adopter and the person whom he adopts are deemed to be within the prohibited degrees and they continue to be so notwithstanding subsequent readoption of the child. Apart from this, there is no prohibition on marriage arising out of adoption.[94]

S15 provides that in relation to intestate succession of any person who dies after the adoption order, property shall devolve as if the adopted person were the child of the adopter, born in lawful wedlock. Any reference to children of the adopter, in any disposition made after the adoption order, shall be construed as including the adopted person.[95] Any reference to the children of the adopted person's natural parents shall be presumed not to be a reference to the adopted person, and any reference to the

---

[92] See r13 and the Second Schedule to the Rules.
[93] R14. See also *Re D (adoption reports: confidentiality)* [1995] 1 FLR 631.
[94] S13(3).
[95] Unless contrary intention appears.

adopted person's relatives shall be presumed to be a reference to him as if he were the child of the adopter born in wedlock and were not the child of any other person.

CONDITIONS IMPOSED IN AN ADOPTION ORDER

In making an adoption order, the court may impose such terms and conditions as it thinks fit.[96] Conditions are rarely imposed without the consent of the prospective adopters. The approach of the court is that the adoption order shall as near as possible put the child in the position of a lawful child of the adoptive parents. It would rarely be appropriate to impose a condition which derogates from this. In *Re S (a minor) (blood transfusion: adoption order condition)*,[97] the adoptive parents were Jehovah's Witnesses. Concern was raised as to whether they would veto blood transfusion for the child. It was held by the Court of Appeal that there was already a satisfactory procedure for dealing with cases of blood transfusion in emergency. It was inappropriate to grant an adoption order with a condition imposed on the adoptive parents that they would not withhold consent to a blood transfusion.

In normal circumstances, it is desirable that adoption effect a complete break between the adoptee and his natural family. Hence, the court will not, except in the most exceptional cases, impose terms or conditions as to access to members of the child's natural family to whom the adoptive parents object. But each case has to be considered on its own particular facts. A complete break is often not a problem in cases of adoption of small babies, who have no knowledge or recollection of their natural parents, grandparents or siblings. Adoption of children who have had their 'own' life which cannot be blotted out, and ought not be blotted out, requires flexibility in the exercise of the court's discretion. In *Re C (a minor) (adoption order: conditions)*,[98] C, the proposed adoptee, aged 13, spent the larger part of her childhood with her older brother (M) in different children's homes. C was very much attached to M. If an adoption order was made, M would technically not be C's brother but that could not alter their affectionate relationship. It was held by the House of Lords that it was in C's best interests to make an adoption order which provided her with the security of a family. Given that the adoptive parents were supportive of

---

[96] S8(2).
[97] [1994] 2 FLR 416.
[98] [1989] AC 1.

access between M and C, the adoption order was made with the condition that there be access between M and C.[99] However, in *Re T (adoption: contact)*,[100] the adoptive child was ten years old and she had been with the adopters for 2½ years. The adoptive mother consented to the child seeing the natural mother once a year. However, the natural mother wished to see the child two or three times a year. The judge ordered that there should be contact not less than once a year. The Court of Appeal held that although the adopters were prepared to continue contact with the natural mother (or what was sometimes termed 'open adoption'), finality of adoption and the importance of letting the new family find its own feet ought not to be threatened by an order.

TRACING NATURAL PARENTS AND RELATIVES

In 1987, in the case of *Re S (a minor) (adoption or custodianship)*,[101] a boy was adopted by his maternal grandfather and his spouse. The boy, who was four years old, thought that his mother was a member of his extended family. On the question as to possible confusion of family relationship, the court was told that the applicants intended to tell the child the truth when it was appropriate to do so.

> ... the prevailing view amongst those concerned with the problem is now that the earlier the process of explanation begins the better, so that this child should not have grown up as long as he has in the belief that the applicants are his natural parents.[102]

The law does not provide for an adopted person the right to know the identity of his own biological parents. S8(1A) only provides that:

> The Court, in making an adoption order shall consider whether it is in the interests of the infant that his true identity should be disclosed to him, having regard to the views of the prospective adopters, the opinion of the Director and also the age and understanding of the infant.

As we have seen, adoption severs a child's link with his biological parents. The adopted child is treated by law as the natural child of the

---

[99] See also *Re J (adoption order: conditions)* [1973] Fam 106 where access by the natural father was imposed as a condition. See also *Re S (a minor) (adoption order: access)* [1976] Fam 1; *Re A (a minor) (adoption: access)* (1991) Fam Law 360.
[100] [1995] 2 FLR 251.
[101] [1987] 2 FLR 331.
[102] Ibid., at p. 336 per Sir Roualeyn Cumming-Bruce.

adopters. Anonymity has always been thought to be necessary in order to protect the parties in the 'adoption triangle'. Indeed, anonymity is given to the adopters, if they so wish,[103] to allow them to start afresh. This, it is believed, shields the adoptive parents from the possible prying of the biological parents who may interfere with their upbringing of the adopted child.

An adopted person is usually given a new name and surname. He will also be re-registered.[104] The Registrar General maintains an Adopted Children Register, and every adoption order contains a direction to the Registrar to make such entries in the Adopted Children Register.[105] Once registered, an adopted child is given a new birth certificate on the basis of the entry in the Adopted Children Register, and it indicates his status as an adopted person. The infant's original birth entry will be marked with the word 'Adopted'.[106] The Registrar keeps other registers and books to make traceable the connection between the original birth entry which has been marked 'Adopted', and the new entry in the Adopted Children Register. These registers and books are not open to public inspection or search. Nor would the Registrar furnish any person with any information contained therein except with a court order[107] and there has been no reported case of any such order being granted.

In other jurisdictions,[108] an adopted person has been given such a right to access to his original birth certificate. For instance, s51 of the English Adoption Act 1976 provides for an adopted person, who has reached the age of 18, to have a copy of the record of his birth, provided that the applicant has been informed of the availability of counselling services.[109]

---

[103] Adoption Rules, r6.
[104] S19.
[105] S18(1).
[106] S19(3). In case of readoption, the entry in the Adopted Children Register shall be marked 'Readopted', see s19(4).
[107] S18(4).
[108] Adoption Act 1984 (Vic); Adoption Act 1991 (ACT); Adoption Information Act 1990 (NSW); Adoption of Children Amendment Act 1990 (NT); Adoption Legislation Amendment Act 1991(Qld); Adoption Act 1988 (SA); Adoption Act 1988 (Tas); Adoption Act 1984 (Vic); Adoption of Children Act 1986–1991(WA); see also Neville Turner, 'Review of the Adoption Information Act 1990 (NSW)', 19 (1993) Monash University Law Review 343.
[109] The right is not absolute. An adopted person who is likely to be a potential menace to his birth parents would not be supplied with a copy of his birth certificate, see *R v Registrar-General, ex parte Smith* [1990] 2 QB 253; s51(2) further provides that an adopted person under 18 intending to marry may apply to the Registrar General who shall inform the applicant whether or not it appears from information contained in the registers that the applicant and the person whom he intends to marry may be within the prohibited degrees of relationship.

S51A of the Adoption Act 1976[110] establishes an Adoption Contact Register. It facilitates the tracing of relatives by an adopted person. The Adoption Contact Register allows for matching between an adopted person who wishes to contact a relative on the one hand, and relatives who would like to contact an adopted person, on the other hand.

The reasons for an adopted person wanting to trace his biological parents are well documented.[111] But a natural relative may want to trace an adopted person for medical reasons. In the rather unusual case of *Re H (adoption: disclosure of information)*,[112] JS was born to the wife as a result of extra-marital affairs. The wife and husband already had a child P. JS was adopted by family friends. After the adoption, this couple, together with P emigrated to Australia. They died some years later and lost contact with the adoptive parents. P, now 45, and on a return visit to England, was told by relations that she had a half-brother. P suffered from a rare form of genetic disease, called Fibrocyn Albeolitis which had destroyed 50% of her lungs. The disease was progressively deteriorative. She sought to establish contact with JS, and made an application, under s50(1) Adoption Act 1976, for an order that the Registrar General furnish her with the information contained in the Adopted Children Register concerning JS. It was held that disclosure of information relating to adoptees was not permissible other than where the adoptee personally sought the information, or under a court order. The court must be persuaded as to the reasonableness of the order sought. On the facts, it appeared to be advisable that the other members of P's family should be screened for the disease. Early detection would open the possibility of treatment that could arrest its development, increasing both life expectancy and quality of life. The order sought was made subject to an undertaking that such information would not be disclosed to P without the express consent of JS.[113]

---

[110] Added to by the Children Act 1989, s88 and Sched. 10 para 21.
[111] Katherine O'Donovan, 'A Right to Know One's Parentage', 2 International Journal of Law and the Family (1988) 27; Erica Haimes, 'Secrecy: What Can Artificial Reproduction Learn from Adoption?' 2 International Journal of Law and the Family (1988) 46; John Triseliotis, *In search of Origins: The Experiences of Adopted People*, Routledge & Kegan Paul, London, 1973; Stephanie Charlesworth, 'Ensuring the Rights of Children in Inter-Country Adoption: Australian Attitudes to Access to Adoption Information', in *Parenthood in Modern Society: Legal and Social Issues for the Twenty-First Century*, ed by John Eekelaar and Petar Sarcevic, Martinus Nijhoff Publishers, London, 1993.
[112] [1995] 1 FLR 236.
[113] *D v Registrar General* [1996] 1 FLR 707.

FUTURE DEVELOPMENTS

The Adoption Ordinance which was first introduced in 1956 needs to be comprehensively reviewed.[114] For instance, on the question of who may adopt, the law should lay down a uniform minimum age criteria on, e.g. 21 although there may be circumstances, rare as they may be, where adoption by a person under 21 may be in the best interests of the child. Selection of suitable adopters for a child depends on the facts of each case and the needs of the child. At the moment, a single (married or not) person can adopt. The rule that the adoption of a female infant is not to be made in favour of a male applicant unless special circumstances justifying is discriminatory. Adoption by a single person, which is and would remain unusual, would in certain circumstances be in a particular child's best interests, for instance, where there exists between them a *de facto* parent–child relationship.

Private placement leaves the selection of a prospective adopter outside the control the DSW. In cases where the placement is thought to be less than desirable, the court, in considering an application for adoption, may nonetheless be confronted with a *fait accompli*. In England, the Adoption Act 1976 has made it an offence for any person other than approved adoption agencies to make arrangements for adoption unless the individual is a relative of the child. Any person who receives a child in contravention of the prohibition also commits an offence.[115]

Adoption, which is based on the idea of a complete legal transplant, raises many difficult issues for the law. Under what circumstances may it be said that a parent's refusal to consent is unreasonable thereby justifying the court in dispensing with parental consent? If the best interests of the child may only be secured by adoption, would withholding of parental consent necessarily be unreasonable? In England, *Adoption — A Service for Children*,[116] recommended removal of all the grounds for dispensing with parental consent, except where the parent cannot be found, or is incapable of giving consent. On the question of parent refusing to consent, the Review proposed a new test:

---

[114] Grace Ko Po-chee, 'Adoptive Parenthood in Hong Kong: Profile, Stresses and Copying', PhD thesis, Department of Social Work and Social Administration, HKU; C O'Brian, 'Transracial Adoption in Hong Kong' LXXXIII, Child Welfare, 4, 319–29; Bagley, Young and Scully, *International and Transracial Adoption: A Mental Health Perspective*, Aldershot, Avebury, 1993.
[115] S16 Adoption Act 1976.
[116] Department of Health & Welsh Office, London, HMSO, 1996.

> ... the court being satisfied that the advantages of a child becoming part of a new family and having a new legal status are so significantly greater than the advantages to the child of any alternative option as to justify overriding the wishes of a parent or guardian.

The rationale for these proposals was to focus on the benefits which adoption may confer on the child, rather than on the faults or shortcomings of parental care.

On the question of step-parent adoption, it would rarely be appropriate. An example where it might be appropriate is where the non-custodial parent has never acted in a parental capacity and the child had never really known any member of that side of the family. In all other cases, the disadvantages of such an adoption outweigh any possible advantages. For example, where the child has some relationship with the parent, or the parent's relatives, it is unlikely to be in the child's interest for their legal relationship to be extinguished. A parent may agree to adoption simply because he has no interest in the child. Where the other parent has died or is no longer interested in the child's upbringing, the possible benefits to the child of retaining a legal relationship with grandparents or other relatives may be overlooked. There may be cases where the prime motivation behind an adoption application is the wish to cement the family unit and put away the past, this may be confusing and lead to identity problems for the child. It is also possible that the step-parent's family has little or no involvement or interest in the adopted child, so that the child loses one family without really gaining another. As divorce has become more common, it is less necessary for families to pursue step-parent adoption in order to avoid embarrassment and difficult explanations.

Adoption: the Future therefore recommended that where step-parent adoption is in a child's interest, the custodial (natural) parent need not adopt the child. A new type of adoption order, available only to step-parents, would not make the natural parent an adoptive parent. However, consent of the spouse to the adoption would still be needed.[117] In the case of adoption by other relatives, it recommended that relatives such as grandparents who were *de facto* carers of children should be offered security and stability by means other than adoption.[118]

---

[117] Para 5.21.
[118] Ibid.

12

Wardship

INTRODUCTION

The High Court in 1984 in *Re Y (minors)*[1] described wardship as a manifestation of the *parens patriae* (literally meaning 'parent of the country') duty of the Crown to protect minors in the following terms:

> The Queen as parens patriae is mother not only of all the children in her Kingdom, but of all the children in all the places scattered all over the globe of which she remains Monarch. That includes Hong Kong ... she is not only a parent of all those children but she also exercises that parental care over any children within Her jurisdiction. That of course is (not) exercised by Her personally, but centuries ago was bestowed upon her Lord Chancellor, and is now delegated to her High Court Judges.[2]

The law relating to wardship is principally common law and it is a form of prerogative powers.[3] It remains unchanged after the resumption of sovereignty on 1 July 1997, although the basis of the jurisdiction is now to be founded in s24(2) of the Hong Kong Reunification Ordinance. It provides that:

---

[1] [1984] HKLR 204.
[2] Ibid., at p. 206.
[3] See Lowe & White, *Wards of Court,* 2nd edition, Barry Rose, London, 1986.

> Those prerogative powers ... exercisable by a public officer immediately before 1 July 1997 ... shall on and after [1 July 1997] continue in existence, vest in the Chief Executive and be exercisable by the corresponding public officer of the HKSAR.

Today, wardship jurisdiction is exercised by a judge of the Court of First Instance of the HKSAR.

Wardship originated as a means of protecting the property of wealthy orphans from exploitation by guardians or relatives, but it has become a unique jurisdiction, exercising its power to safeguard the general welfare of children. A minor on whom the jurisdiction is exercised is known as 'a ward of court'. When exercising its parental power, the courts have, in theory, an unrestricted power to do whatever is necessary for the welfare of the minor.[4]

WHO CAN INVOKE WARDSHIP

Any interested party may invoke wardship. Usually a person who has a personal interest in a child's well-being has sufficient *locus standi*. For instance, a parent, relative or even an educational psychologist who is involved in the development of the child can apply to make the child a ward.[5] In an application to ward a child, the applicant is required to state his relationship with the child, and if it appears that the application is an abuse of the process of the court, it will be dismissed.

WHO CAN BE WARDED

The English court has jurisdiction to make a child who owes allegiance to the Crown a ward of court; a minor owing allegiance has a corresponding right to protection.[6] A British citizen wherever he may be owes a duty of allegiance; however, there appears to be no reported decision on a wardship

---

[4] *Re X (a minor) (wardship: jurisdiction)* [1975] Fam 47.
[5] *Re D (a minor) (wardship: sterilisation)* [1976] All ER 326; *Nguyen Dang Vu v AG*, Miscellaneous Proceedings No 4257 of 1993 (1994); *Trance v Walli*, Miscellaneous Proceedings No 905 of 1988 (1988).
[6] *Re P (GE) (an infant)* [1965] Ch. 568 at p. 587 per Pearson LJ.

order based on allegiance of a child who is neither present nor resident in England.[7]

Apart from allegiance, it has also been held that an alien minor who is physically present in England can be made a ward by the English courts irrespective of his nationality or citizenship. This is because at common law, even an alien owes temporary allegiance whilst present in the jurisdiction.[8] This was the case in *Nguyen Dang Vu v AG*[9] where Kaplan J held that wardship jurisdiction extended over a Vietnamese orphan detained in the refugee camp.

The court also has jurisdiction in respect of an alien minor who is ordinarily resident in England, but is not physically present. In *Re P (GE) (an infant)*,[10] an infant was born in Egypt of Jewish parents. The father was stateless and the mother was Egyptian. They came to England to stay with the mother's relatives. Having stayed for five years, they applied for naturalisation but the process was never completed. The marriage broke down and arrangements were made for the child to live with the mother, and for the father to have access to the child over the weekends. On one access occasion, the father, without the consent of the mother, took the child to Israel. The mother made the child a ward of court. On the question of whether the court had jurisdiction to hear the mother's case, the Court of Appeal held that an alien infant ordinarily resident in England owed an allegiance to the Crown, and had a right to protection from the Crown. The infant was ordinarily resident there, and that could not be changed by kidnapping him.

JURISDICTION OF THE HONG KONG SPECIAL ADMINISTRATIVE REGION

The jurisdiction of HKSAR courts to hear wardship applications is no longer dependent on allegiance to Her Majesty the Queen. To the extent that a ring of care is thrown around a ward by the HKSAR judicial system, it may be more appropriate to consider jurisdiction with reference to ordinary residence or presence within the jurisdiction.

---

[7] Ibid.
[8] Ibid.; see also *Re C (an infant)* (1956) Times, 14 December where it was held that the court had jurisdiction in respect of a child who was en route from the USA to the USSR.
[9] Miscellaneous Proceedings No 4257 of 1993 (1994).
[10] [1965] Ch. 568.

WARDSHIP: PROCEDURES AND EFFECT

The procedure to make a child a ward of court is laid down in s26 of the High Court Ordinance. S26 provides that where application is made for such an order in respect of an infant (i.e. under 18), the infant shall become a ward of court on the making of the application.

Once warded, the ward comes under the guardianship of the court (the whole bundle of parental rights), and a ring of protection is immediately throw around the ward. The wardship judge does not personally exercise 'care and control' over the ward, and this is delegated to a person whom the judge believes will look after the ward to the satisfaction of the court. Having done so, the wardship judge retains to himself the general supervisory functions of the ward. So long as the minor remains a ward, no major decisions affecting the child can be made or taken without the consent of the judge.[11] Although there is no definition of what amounts to a major decision, consent of the court is required for the ward's marriage,[12] adoption,[13] schooling, medical operation,[14] and taking the ward out of the jurisdiction.[15]

A child become a ward immediately on the making of the application. The child ceases to be a ward if an application for an appointment for the hearing is not made within 21 days after the issuing of the summons, or the court refuses to make the child a ward of court on hearing the summons. A wardship judge cannot give up guardianship of a ward until the ward come of age or is de-warded.[16]

NATURE OF WARDSHIP PROCEEDINGS

Unlike ordinary civil proceedings, wardship proceedings are not concerned with the resolution of rights between litigants. In other words, there is no

---

[11] *Re S (infants)* [1967] 1 All ER 202 at p. 209 per Cross J.
[12] Where a marriage of a ward of court takes place without the court's consent, the parties to the marriage commit contempt of court, so does any other person who has helped to bring about the marriage, *Re H's Settlement* [1909] 2 Ch. 260.
[13] The test for deciding whether to grant such leave was whether an application for adoption might reasonably succeed, not whether adoption was in the best interests of the child, *F v S (adoption: ward)* [1973] Fam 203; *So Mei-chu v Wong Wai-anucha*, High Court, Miscellaneous Proceedings No 3360 of 1990 (1991).
[14] *Re D (a minor) (wardship: sterilisation)* [1976] 1 All ER 326.
[15] *Wong Chiu Ngar-chi v Wong Hon-wai* [1987] HKLR 179.
[16] *Re Y (minors)* [1984] HKLR 204.

'lis' between the parties.[17] The applicant-plaintiff is not asserting any rights, he is committing the child to the protection of the court. In exercising wardship jurisdiction, the welfare of the ward is of paramount importance.

> Wardship proceedings are not like ordinary civil proceedings. There is no 'lis' between the parties. The plaintiffs are not asserting any rights; they are committing their child to the protection of the court and asking the court to make such order as it thinks is for [the wards's] benefit.[18]

Again, unlike ordinary civil proceedings, wardship proceedings are not strictly adversarial.[19] It has been various described as 'parental' and 'administrative'.[20]

> But a court in exercising its jurisdiction over its ward should never lose sight of a fundamental feature of the jurisdiction that it was exercising — namely, that it was exercising a wardship not an adversarial jurisdiction. Its duty was not limited to the dispute between the parties: On the contrary, its duty was to act in the way best suited in its judgment to serve the true interest and welfare of the ward.[21]

In safeguarding the interests of the child, it would sometimes be the duty of the court to look beyond the submissions of the parties.[22] The court can order a welfare report and that the ward be separately represented by the Official Solicitor who will act as the ward's guardian *ad litem* (GAL).[23] The tasks of the GAL are to represent the ward's interests and to speak on behalf of the ward.[24] In the course of discharging his functions, he will make inquiries with a view to presenting a detailed report to the court. His views and recommendation will be respected, although not binding.

Where there are both wardship and matrimonial proceedings continuing affecting the same children, the correct procedure is to transfer the matrimonial proceedings in the District Court to the Court of First Instance which will have complete control of both sets of proceedings.[25]

---

[17] Ibid.; *R v Gyngall* (1893) 2 QB 232.
[18] *Re B (JA) (an infant)* [1965] Ch. 1112 at p. 1117 per Cross J.
[19] *Official Solicitor v K* [1965] AC 201.
[20] *Re X (a minor) (wardship: injunction)* [1984] 1 WLR 1422 at p. 1425.
[21] Lord Scarman in *Re E (a minor) (wardship: court's duty)* [1984] 1 WLR 156 at p. 158–9, approved in *Re Y (minors)* [1984] HKLR 204.
[22] *Re E (a minor) (wardship: court's duty)* [1984] 1 WLR 156 at p. 158 per Lord Scarman; see recent developments in the UK on the duty to full and frank disclosure, see *A (minors: disclosure of material)* [1991] 2 FLR 473.
[23] MCR r108, see also the Official Solicitor's Ordinance.
[24] *Re D (a minor) (wardship: sterilisation)* [1976] 1 All ER 326.
[25] *Re Y (minors)* [1984] HKLR 204.

USE OF WARDSHIP TODAY

Wardship jurisdiction is wide and flexible. In theory, there is no limit to its scope. In other words, wardship is not limited by a category of cases in which it has been invoked previously. In the past, wardship had been primarily concerned with protection of a ward's property, or protection of a ward against harmful association.[26] Today, wardship is used to resolve disputes between parents regarding custody, care and control, to prevent a child from being abducted, and to seek the return of an abducted child. Indeed, wardship is the only means for a non-parent, e.g. a grandmother, to bring such matter before the court. Wardship has also been used to effect overseas adoption and control of teenage behaviour. The list is not exhaustive, and wardship has also been used in novel situations such as medical treatment of minors, publication of books and surrogacy agreement. To that extent, it is an extremely versatile jurisdiction capable of resolving issues arising from changing social circumstances.[27]

Wardship proceedings have been used to resolve disputes between parents over custody and access of a minor. Although such disputes can be dealt with in divorce proceedings or under s10 of the Guardianship of Minors Ordinance, wardship may be invoked because of the unique protection it offers.[28] One of the reasons why a parent may invoke wardship is that the general supervisory functions of the court and such supervision may be useful to deter the other parent from taking the child out of the jurisdiction.[29]

Wardship has also been invoked in securing the return of a child already abducted.[30] In such a case the court is not concerned with penalising the 'guilty' party. Conduct of the parties may be a consideration to be taken into account, but whether the court makes a summary order or an order after investigating the merits, the cardinal rule which applies is that the welfare of the ward is the paramount consideration.[31] In *Re V (infants)*,[32]

---

[26] *Iredell v Iredell* (1885) 1 TLR 260 where an injunction was granted against a Catholic priest who tried to induce the ward to adhere to Roman Catholicism against her father's wishes.

[27] See English Law Commission Working Paper, Wards of Court, No 101, HMSO, London, 1987, para 3.53 (hereafter referred to as English Law Commission Working Paper, No 101, 1987).

[28] *Wong Chiu Ngar-chi v Wong Hon-wai* [1987] HKLR 179; *Re Kwok Micah (a minor)*, High Court, Miscellaneous Proceedings No 3040 of 1984 (1985).

[29] English Law Commission Working Paper, No 101, 1987, para 3.8; see n. 27.

[30] *Lee Wai-chu v Lee Yim-chuen*, Miscellaneous Proceedings No 2678 of 1983 (1984); *Chiu Kwai-fun v Lam Hing-keung*, Miscellaneous Proceedings No 968 of 1985 (1985).

[31] *Re L (minors) (wardship: jurisdiction)* [1974] 1 WLR 250; *Re C (minors) (wardship: jurisdiction)* [1977] 3 WLR 561.

[32] Miscellaneous Proceedings No 477 of 1979 (1979).

the mother (a Canadian citizen), without the consent of the father (a Canadian citizen), arrived in Hong Kong with her children (Canadian citizens), leaving their home in Ontario. The father having obtained an interim custody order from the Supreme Court of Ontario, applied to make the children wards of court, and sought an order that they be returned to Ontario. At the time of the hearing, the Supreme Court of Ontario had made a permanent order giving custody to the father with an express reservation of the rights of the mother to make application for the custody of the infants when they were returned. The High Court took the view that the children's main base was in Canada. Their long-term welfare was the first and paramount consideration, and it necessitated that they return to Canada where the courts would be in a much better position to deal with the question of custody. The use of wardship in child abduction cases may be reduced with the introduction of the Child Abduction and Custody Ordinance.[33] However, it will continue to be used to prevent a child from being abducted or to seek for the return of a child from a non-Convention country, e.g. Mainland China.

Wardship can also be used to achieve an object which cannot be achieved under statutes, e.g. a grandparent who otherwise has no standing to seek custody may bring wardship proceedings. For instance, in *Trance v Walli*,[34] the plaintiff maternal grandmother visited Hong Kong with her infant granddaughter. The defendant father who lived in Hong Kong was permitted to take the child out. He failed to return the child and the grandmother made the child a ward. It was held that the plaintiff was to have care and control, with leave to remove the child from the jurisdiction to return home.

There is no procedure permitting a child to leave the jurisdiction to be adopted overseas, and wardship was used to achieve this. Thus, in *Re T.M.H. (an infant) (No 2)*[35] the natural parents of a girl, aged nine, gave her to a couple since birth. The couple left Hong Kong to return to England and wished to take the girl with them so that they could adopt her in England. The girl was then under the statutory guardianship of the Director of Social Welfare. The Director of Social Welfare applied to make the child a ward of court, with the express purpose of seeking leave to send the girl out of the jurisdiction to England so that she could be adopted there. At first instance, Mills-Owen J held that it would be in the best interests of the child to unite with the couple in England, but there was no procedure for

---

[33] See Chapter 13.
[34] High Court, Miscellaneous Proceedings No 905 of 1988 (1988); see also *Re Mark Leung*, High Court, Miscellaneous Proceedings No 142 of 1985 (1985).
[35] [1962] HKLR 316.

sending an infant overseas for adoption. The Court of Appeal disagreed and granted leave for the child to leave the jurisdiction to be adopted in England.

Wardship has also been used to control recalcitrant youngsters. In *Re SW (a minor) (wardship: jurisdiction)*,[36] a recalcitrant 17-year-old girl frequently ran away from home. On many occasions she returned home drunk and showed signs of having indulged in sexual intercourse. She was placed under the care and control of a local authority but soon ran away. On reaching 17, care and control of a local authority ceased. Her parents made her a ward of court. It was held that the child should remain a ward until 18, and care and control be given back to the local authority.

In 1994, wardship has been used by the Director of Social Welfare in cases involving medical treatment of minors. In *Re C (a minor) (wardship: medical treatment)*,[37] it was a life and death operation. The minor was born severely deformed and required an operation without which she would die. The operation had not been performed in Hong Kong before and had a 50/50 chance of success. With a successful operation the baby would live a relatively normal life although there would be some orthopaedic problems which could be treated at a later stage. The parents refused to give their consent and the Director of Social Welfare applied to make the child a ward. It was held that it was the duty of the court to consider what was in the child's best interests. If she had the operation, there was a real chance that she might survive and enjoy a normal life and the court would not condemn her to a certain death without giving the doctors a chance to correct nature's imperfections.

Director of Social Welfare v Tam[38] concerns an operation which would improve quality of life. In that case, a baby was born with spina bifida and developed hydrocephalus and meningitis. A neurosurgeon urged that an operation be performed but the parent refused to consent to the operation. The surgeon's evidence was that the hydrocephalus was not severe and there was no sign of the condition deteriorating. The operation had a 90% chance of success and the child would be able to attend normal school. The Court of Appeal held that there was a real possibility that the child might live a considerable number of years and even reach adulthood without the operation. The court was concerned with the interests of the child, not with the interest of the parents save in so far as the effect on the parents might impinge upon the child itself. In this case, the life of the child was a

---

[36] (1985) 15 Fam Law 322; *Re H's Settlement* [1909] 2 Ch. 260.
[37] [1994] 1 HKLR 60.
[38] [1987] HKLR 66.

very difficult one but it would be even more difficult if the operation was not carried out. The court ordered the operation be performed.

Director of Social Welfare v Lam Kwok-wah[39] concerned a protective medical procedure. Here, an eight-year-old boy suffered a severe head injury after a traffic accident. Four years later, doctors recommended that the skull defect be protected from accidental injury by a procedure known as cranio-plasty. Expert evidence was that the operation itself carried a very small risk. Both parents, lacking faith in Western medicine refused to consent on religious grounds. The Court of Appeal held that the paramount consideration was the best interests of the child. The benefits of the proposed operation far outweighed any risks. The Court ordered the operation be performed.

It can be seen in the above cases that the court in acting as a judicial parent may be compelled in the best interests of the child to substitute its own views to that of the parents. However, in *Re T (wardship: medical treatment)*,[40] the court was unwilling to do so. The facts of the case have been discussed in Chapter 8 but will be repeated here. A one-year-old boy was suffering from a life-threatening liver defect. His parents were both health care professionals experienced in the care of sick children. The unanimous opinion of medical consultants were that the baby should undergo transplant surgery as the prospects of success were good. Without transplantation, the expectation of life was just over two years. The parents refused to consent to the transplant. The father found a job overseas, and against medical advice, the mother travelled with the boy to visit him. The doctor formed the view that the mother was not acting in the best interests of the child. At first instance, the judge found that the mother's refusal to consent to the transplant was unreasonable. The court directed that the mother return with the child to the jurisdiction within 21 days. In the Court of Appeal, it was held that there was a strong presumption in favour of a course of action which would prolong life, but to prolong life was not the sole objective of the court, and to require that at the expense of other considerations might not be in the child's best interests. In this case, the court not only considered the advantages and the disadvantages of the medical procedure, but also the child's post-operative care and development. It was held such care and development would be affected if his day-to-day care depended on the commitment of a mother who had suffered the turmoil of having her child being compelled to undergo a major operation. Consequently, the best interests of the child required that future treatment be left for the parents to decide.

---

[39] [1988] 1 HKLR 206.
[40] [1997] 1 FLR 502.

Wardship has also been used in novel cases concerning surrogacy. In *Re C (a minor) (wardship: surrogacy)*,[41] the plaintiffs (husband and wife) were a foreign couple. They could not have children of their own and through an agency they contacted a surrogate who agreed to bear the husband's child. When the child was due to be born, the plaintiffs came to England to pick up the child. A few hours after the child's birth the surrogate left the child in the hospital to be collected by the couple. The local authority concerned with the child's well-being made a place of safety order. The husband commenced wardship seeking care and control to be committed to him and his wife. It was held that the method by which the child was born raised difficult moral and ethical questions, but they were not relevant to the wardship court. The plaintiffs wanted the child, the surrogate mother did not. They were also excellently equipped to bring up the child. Care and control was granted to them with leave to take the child out of the jurisdiction.

AN INJUNCTION AGAINST THE WORLD AT LARGE

In wardship, the court can do whatever is necessary for the welfare of a ward,[42] and this includes an injunction against the world at large. This can be seen in *Re X (a minor) (wardship: injunction)*.[43] M at the age of 11 achieved notoriety when she was found guilty of the manslaughter of two boys. Upon being released on licence at the age of 27, she gave birth to a daughter. Fearing that newspaper reporting would lead to the identification of M and her two-month-old daughter, the minor was made a ward. It was held that any reporting which identified M or the child or the identity of the father might disturb the fragile stability which M had achieved and harm might result to the ward. The court had the power to make an order restraining, not only the defendant's newspapers, but also the world at large, from publishing any information which might disclose the identity of the mother, ward or father.

---

[41] (1985) 15 Fam Law 191.
[42] See *Re X (a minor) (wardship jurisdiction)* [1975] Fam 47 at p. 61 per Sir John Pennycuick.
[43] [1984] 1 WLR 1422.

SUPERSESSION OF WARDSHIP BY STATUTORY JURISDICTION

The universal nature of wardship and the unfettered powers of the court may bring wardship into conflict with statutory duties and powers. Wardship jurisdiction (which is a manifestation of prerogative powers) is not extinguished by the existence of legislation regarding children.[44] However, the exercise of wardship jurisdiction is circumscribed by statutes which entrust certain functions to public authorities. Thus, in *A v Liverpool City Council*,[45] a mother whose child had been taken into local authority's care had her access reduced. She made the child a ward of court, seeking defined access and care and control. The House of Lords held that the court would decline the exercise of its jurisdiction which would interfere with the day-to-day administration by local authorities of their statutory powers. The same principle has been adopted by the Hong Kong Courts in *Re C (a minor)*.[46] There, Madam Chan entered Hong Kong illegally in 1981 and cohabited with Mr Chan (a Hong Kong resident). A child was born to the parties. When the mother and the minor were arrested, a removal order was made against them under s19(1)(b) of the Immigration Ordinance. Whilst an appeal against the removal order was lodged on behalf of the minor, Mr Chan made the child a ward, seeking care and control of the minor. The High Court struck out the originating summons on the grounds that it was an abuse of the process of the court.

> Wardship proceedings are wholly inconsistent with the statutory powers conferred upon the Director of Immigration for under wardship, the minor cannot be removed from the jurisdiction without the leave of the court. Such proceedings will necessarily amount to a fetter at any stage when the Director of Immigration is required to exercise its statutory powers ... the functions of the Director of Immigration cannot be hamstrung by wardship proceedings which were clearly instituted by the plaintiff in order to thwart those powers that have been specifically given to the legislature to control the vexed policy of immigration and deportation in Hong Kong.[47]

---

[44] *A v Liverpool City Council* [1982] AC 363.
[45] Ibid.
[46] [1989] 2 HKLR 652. See also *Re F (a minor)* [1989] 1 All ER 1155; *A v Liverpool City Council* [1982] AC 363; *Nguyen Dang Vu v AG,* High Court, Miscellaneous Proceedings No 4257 of 1993 (1994).
[47] Per Jones J.

LIMITS OF WARDSHIP JURISDICTION

Wardship, however, is not the same analogy of parental jurisdiction. A parent may be required to pursue a course of action which is in the best interests of a child, but the court in protecting the interests of a ward may need to strike a balance between that and the rights of others. For instance, should the interests of the ward prevail over the public's interests of freedom of publication? In *Re X (a minor) (wardship: jurisdiction)*,[48] the plaintiff stepfather made his stepdaughter, aged 14, a ward of court seeking an injunction to restrain the publication of a book containing passages describing aberrant private activities of the ward's deceased father. Affidavit evidence showed that the ward would suffer grave psychological damage if the offending passages came to her knowledge. The Court of Appeal held that although the court's jurisdiction was in theory unrestricted, on balancing the need for protection of the ward and the right of free publication, an injunction was not granted.

The court does not have jurisdiction to make an unborn child a ward. Thus, in *Re F (in utero)*,[49] an unmarried mother, aged 36, with a history of mental illness, disappeared from her apartment at a time when her child was due for delivery. She told the social worker that her child was a reincarnated spirit. A psychiatrist who attended to her thought her beliefs were close to delusional. The local authority applied to make the unborn a ward of court with the intention that should the mother be found, she be restrained and compelled to give birth in a hospital. The Court of Appeal held that the court had no jurisdiction to make an unborn child a ward.[50]

There are no available statistics on the use of wardship in Hong Kong. The universal character of wardship, its ease of access, the speediness in which the jurisdiction could be invoked, and the almost unfettered powers of the court render wardship a unique jurisdiction which will remain an important jurisdiction for the protection of minors.

---

[48] [1975] Fam 47.
[49] [1988] 2 All ER 193.
[50] See *Paton v British Pregnancy Advisory Service Trustees* [1979] QB 276.

13

International Child Abduction

INTRODUCTION

A parent who snatches a child away from the other parent presents a difficult problem in family law. The child may be snatched and hidden within the jurisdiction, but increasingly such activities have crossed jurisdictional boundaries. Child snatching or abduction happens when parents are at odds with each other, and often, in breach of a court order. Such removal puts the welfare of the child at risk and presents a harrowing experience for the 'innocent' or wronged parent.

The criminal law, however, has a limited role to play. In 1984, the House of Lords in *R v D*,[1] held that the common law offence of kidnapping could be committed by a parent who took or carried away a child under 14 by force or fraud without the child's consent and without lawful excuse. However, it was said that, as a matter of policy, prosecution would be rare unless the parent's conduct was so bad that an ordinary right-thinking person would unhesitatingly regard it as criminal.[2]

As regards international child abduction, prevention requires foresight and anticipation. A parent may on divorce obtain an injunction restraining a child's removal from Hong Kong.[3] Alternatively, wardship proceedings

---

[1] [1984] 1 AC 778.
[2] Ibid., at p. 806 per Lord Brandon.
[3] *Chiu Kwai-fun v Lam Hing-keung*, High Court, Miscellaneous Proceedings No 968 of 1985 (1985).

provide an automatic embargo. Where abduction has taken place, it is difficult for the 'innocent' parent to trace the child and secure its return.

The Hague Convention on the Civil Aspects of International Child Abduction 1980 ('the Convention') heralded an international approach to combat parental child abduction. It was incorporated into Hong Kong law by the Child Abduction and Custody Ordinance (CACO) 1997.[4] The aim of the Convention is to provide a uniform international machinery for tracing abducted children, securing their prompt return and to organise or secure access. The Preamble to the Convention states:

> The states signatory to the present Convention, firmly convinced that the interests of children are of paramount importance in matters relating to their custody, desiring to protect children internationally from the harmful effects of their wrongful removal or retention and to establish procedures to ensure their prompt return to the state of their habitual residence, as well as to secure protection for rights of access, have resolved to conclude a Convention to this effect, and have agreed upon the following provisions.

Under the Convention, a Contracting State is bound to set up an administrative body known as the Central Authority whose tasks are to collate and to send to appropriate agencies information about an abducted child; to initiate steps to trace the child; to seek the child's return or to secure access, and if necessary to initiate judicial proceedings to achieve these goals.

This chapter examines the legal principles governing the treatment of abduction between (i) Convention countries and (ii) non-Convention countries.

ABDUCTION AMONGST HAGUE CONVENTION COUNTRIES

S3 of the CACO provides that the provisions of the Convention as set out in the Schedule shall have the force of law in Hong Kong. For the purposes of the Convention as it has effect under the CACO, the Contracting States shall be those for the time being specified by an order made by the Chief Executive and published in the Gazette under s4.[5] The Convention does

---

[4] The Ordinance mirrors the English Abduction and Custody Act 1985 which came into force on 1 August 1986.
[5] See Annex I of this chapter, pp. 346–8.

not operate with retrospective effect, and it applies as between Hong Kong and a Contracting State only in relation to wrongful removals or retention occurring on or after that date.[6] The function of a Central Authority is to be discharged by the Secretary of Justice.[7] The Court of First Instance has the jurisdiction to hear and determine an application under the Convention.[8]

In *Re F (child abduction: risk if returned)*,[9] Millett LJ said that the Hague Convention was:

> ... an international convention and it is to be hoped that its terms will receive a similar interpretation in all the contracting states. It is to be construed broadly and in accordance with its purpose without attributing to any of its terms a specialist meaning which it may have acquired under domestic law.[10]

Wrongful Removal or Retention in Breach of Rights of Custody

Article 4 provides that the Convention applies to any child under 16 years who has been habitually resident in a Contracting State immediately before any breach of custody or access rights. Article 3 provides that:

> The removal or retention of a child is considered wrongful where–
> (a) it is in breach of rights of custody[11] attributed to a person, an institution or other body, either jointly or alone, under the law of the State in which the child was habitually resident immediately before the removal or retention;[12] and
> (b) at the time of removal or retention those rights were actually exercised, either jointly or alone, or would have been so exercised but for the removal or retention ...

Thus, removal of a child by the mother is not in breach of custody rights of an unmarried father where the law does not recognise him having such rights. In *Re J (a minor) (abduction: custody rights)*,[13] the mother left Western Australia for England with her boy. Under Australian law, an

---

[6] See S4(2)(b) and *Re H (abduction: custody rights)* [1991] 2 FLR 262.
[7] S5.
[8] S6.
[9] [1995] 2 FLR 31.
[10] See also *Re H (abduction: acquiescence)* [1997] 1 FLR 872 at p. 881 per Lord Browne-Wilkinson.
[11] *Re D (a minor) (abduction)* [1989] 1 FLR 403.
[12] *Re R (wardship: child abduction)* [1992] 2 FLR 481.
[13] [1990] 2 AC 562.

unmarried father had no rights of custody or guardianship. The father then obtained an order from the Australian court giving him sole custody and guardianship. The mother, however, failed to return the child and the father applied for his return. The House of Lords held that under Australian law, an unmarried mother alone had custody and guardianship until the order conferring sole guardianship and custody to the father. It followed that the removal of the boy was not wrongful.[14]

Access rights, however, are different from custody rights and cannot be enforced by an order for the return of the child. Thus, in *S v H (abduction: access rights)*,[15] a mother with sole custody took the child from Italy to England. The father with access rights applied to the court for the child's return under Article 3. It was held that provisions of the Convention drew a distinction between rights of custody and rights of access. There was no wrongful removal or retention in terms of Article 3 which only dealt with custody rights which the father did not have.

Removal of a ward of court from the jurisdiction is in breach of the court's rights of custody. Thus, in *Re J (a minor) (abduction)*,[16] an infant was made a ward of court and interim care and control was granted to the mother; the father was granted access. The mother took the child to the USA and remained there. The father conceded that he did not himself have any custodial rights within Article 3, but he relied upon the breach of the rights vested in the court's wardship jurisdiction. It was held that the court came within 'any person, institution or other body', and the removal of the ward from the jurisdiction was a removal in breach of the rights of custody of the court.

Habitual Residence

Removal or retention is only wrongful if it is effected in breach of custody rights enjoyed by a person under the law of the State in which the child is habitually resident immediately before the removal or retention. 'Habitual resident' means residence for a settled purpose continued for an appreciable time. It was a question of fact to be decided by reference to all the circumstances of the case.[17]

---

[14] Compare *Re B (a minor) (abduction)* [1994] 2 FLR 249; see also *Re O (a minor) (abduction: habitual residence)* [1993] 2 FLR 594.
[15] [1997] 1 FLR 971.
[16] [1990] 1 FLR 276.
[17] *Re J (a minor) (abduction: custody rights)* [1990] 2 AC 562; *Re B (minors) (abduction) (No 2)* [1993] 1 FLR 993.

> ... there is a significant difference between a person ceasing to be habitually resident in country A, and his subsequently becoming habitually resident in country B. A person may cease to be habitually resident in country A in a single day if he or she leaves it with a settled intention not to return to it but to take up long-term residence in country B instead. Such a person cannot, however, become habitually resident in B in a single day. An appreciable period of time and a settled intention will be necessary to enable him or her to become so ... where a child ... is in the sole lawful custody of the mother, his situation with regard to habitual residence will necessarily be the same as hers.[18]

A child in the sole lawful custody of the mother will have a habitual residence the same as hers.[19] It has been held that the burden of proving habitual residence is on the person claiming it. In *Re R (wardship: child abduction)*,[20] it was said that Hague Convention applications have to be dealt with expeditiously and time does not allow for more than a quick impression or a panoramic view of the evidence.[21]

REMOVAL OR RETENTION FOR LESS THAN ONE YEAR: SUMMARY RETURN

The object of the Convention is to protect children from the harmful effects of their wrongful removal from their country of habitual residence to another country, or their wrongful retention in some country other than that of their habitual residence.[22] If in the course of seeking the child's return the matter goes to court, the court shall refrain from investigating the merits of the rights to custody, and order the child to return forthwith. This approach is sometimes referred to as summary or pre-emptory return. Article 12 provides that:

> Where a child has been wrongfully removed or retained, and at the date of the commencement of the proceedings before the judicial or administrative authority of the Contracting State where the child is, a period of less than one year has elapsed from the date of the wrongful removal or retention, the authority concerned shall order the return of the child forthwith.

---

[18] *Re J (a minor) (abduction: custody rights)* [1990] 2 AC 562 at pp. 578–9 per Lord Brandon.
[19] Ibid.
[20] [1992] 2 FLR 481.
[21] *Re B (minors) (abduction) (No 2)* [1993] 1 FLR 993.
[22] *Re H (abduction: acquiescence)* [1997] 1 FLR 872 at p. 875 per Lord Browne-Wilkinson.

'Wrongful removal or retention' are events occurring on a specific occasion, and not a continuing state of affairs. They are mutually exclusive concepts. Removal occurs when a child who has previously been in the jurisdiction of his habitual residence is taken beyond the frontier of that jurisdiction. Retention occurs where a child, who has previously been, for a limited period of time, outside the jurisdiction of his habitual residence, is not returned on the expiry of such limited period.[23] Further 'wrongful removal or retention' refers to removal or retention out of the jurisdiction of the courts of the child's habitual residence, not removal or retention out of the care of the parent having the custodial rights.

EXCEPTIONS TO SUMMARY RETURN

The mandatory requirement in Article 12, however, is subjected to three exceptions under Article 13.[24] Article 13 provides that:

> Notwithstanding the provisions of the preceding Article, the judicial or administrative authority of the requested State is not bound to order the return of the child if the person, institution or other body which opposes its return establishes that–
> (a) the person, institution or other body having the care of the person of the child was not actually exercising the custody rights at the time of removal or retention, or had consented to or subsequently acquiesced in the removal or retention; or
> (b) there is a grave risk that his or her return would expose the child to physical or psychological harm or otherwise place the child in an intolerable situation.
>
> The judicial or administrative authority may also refuse to order the return of the child if it finds that the child objects to being returned and has attained an age and degree of maturity at which it is appropriate to take account of its views.

So far, English cases have reflected the purpose of the Convention by ensuring the prompt return of children to the country from which they had been wrongfully removed, and the discretion under Article 13 is exercised only in exceptional cases.[25]

---

[23] *Re H (abduction: custody rights)* [1991] 2 FLR 262.
[24] *S v S (child abduction) (child's view)* [1992] 2 FLR 492.
[25] *Re R (minors: child abduction)* (1994) The Times Law Report 5 December; *S v S (child abduction) (child's view)* [1992] 2 FLR 492.

Consent or Subsequent Acquiescence

If a person had at the time of removal or retention, consented[26] to, or subsequently acquiesced in the removal or detention, the court is not bound to order the child's return. In *Re H (abduction: acquiescence)*,[27] the House of Lords held that whether a wronged parent had acquiesced in the removal or retention of a child depended on his actual state of mind. The subjective intention of the wronged parent was a question of fact, and the burden of proof was on the abducting parent. In reaching a decision, a judge would attach more weight to the contemporaneous words and actions of the wronged parent than to his bare assertions of his intention. Where the words or actions of the wronged parent clearly and unequivocally showed and had led the abducting parent to believe that he was not asserting his right to the summary return of the child, justice required that the wronged parent be held to have acquiesced.

Indeed, the court is reluctant to infer acquiescence from attempts to effect a reconciliation or to reach an agreed voluntary return of the child. Lord Browne-Wilkinson stated:

> Attempts to produce a resolution of problems by negotiation or through religious or other advisers do not, to my mind, normally connote an intention to accept the status quo if those attempts fail.[28]

However, in *AZ (a minor) (abduction: acquiescence)*,[29] the mother took the son to England and left him with an aunt who obtained a residence order. The father did not contest the proceedings, nor did he do anything seeking the child's return. He executed a power of attorney in favour of the aunt to deal with the child's health, welfare and education, and he visited the child on a monthly basis. The Court of Appeal held that the father was an intelligent man capable of seeking advice. He made a clear decision to leave the child where he was, and consequently he had acquiesced in his retention.

Physical or Psychological Harm or Intolerable Situation

Where it is established that there is a grave risk that a child's return would

---

[26] *Re O (abduction: consent and acquiescence)* [1997] 1 FLR 924; *Re HB (abduction: children's objections)* [1997] 1 FLR 392.
[27] [1997] 1 FLR 872.
[28] Ibid., p. 883; see also *Re B (minors) (abduction) (No 2)* [1993] 1 FLR 993.
[29] [1993] 1 FLR 682.

expose him to physical or psychological harm,[30] or otherwise place him in an intolerable position,[31] the court may refuse to order his return. The risk of physical or psychological harm must be substantial and actual.[32] Welfare of the child is an important, but not paramount consideration.[33] There is a difference between a mother refusing to return for her own reasons, and a mother who refuses to return for the sake of the child. Where the grave risk of harm arises not from the return of the child, but from the refusal of the mother to accompany him, it has been held that a parent cannot create the psychological situation and then rely on it.[34] Thus, in *Re L (child abduction) (psychological harm)*,[35] a 19-month-old child was ordered to be returned to his father after the mother had taken him to England despite it having been argued that to separate him from his mother would cause grave psychological harm. More recently, in the unusual case of *Re F (child abduction: risk if returned)*,[36] return was not ordered when it was established that a four-year-old child had been present at acts of violence, and had been the recipient of violence by the father and the father had made threats to kill the mother and the child in his presence.[37]

Child's Objection

If a child objects to being returned and he has attained an age and degree of maturity at which it is appropriate to take account of its views, the court may refuse to order return. In *S v S (child abduction) (child's views)*,[38] the Court of Appeal held that a child's objection to return is separate from a grave risk that a child's return would expose him or her to physical or psychological harm. Further, in *Re R (a minor: abduction)*,[39] it was held

---

[30] *Re C (a minor) (abduction)* [1989] 1 FLR 403; *Re G (a minor) (abduction)* [1989] 2 FLR 475.
[31] *B v B (abduction)* [1993] 1 FLR 238.
[32] *S v S*, High Court, Miscellaneous Proceedings No 364 of 1998 (1998).
[33] *Re A (a minor) (abduction)* [1988] 1 FLR 365; *Re C (a minor) (abduction)* [1989] 1 FLR 403.
[34] *Re C (a minor) (abduction)* [1989] 1 FLR 403.
[35] [1993] 2 FLR 401.
[36] [1995] 2 FLR 31.
[37] See also *N v N (abduction: article 13 defence)* [1995] 1 FLR 107, where there are allegations of sexual abuse by the father but return was ordered; *Re HB (abduction: children's objections)* [1997] 1 FLR 392, where the allegations were of ill-treatment by the stepfather but return was ordered.
[38] [1992] 2 FLR 492.
[39] [1992] 1 FLR 105.

that an objection imports a strength of feeling going far beyond the usual ascertainment of the wishes or preference of a child in a custody dispute.

There is no age below which a child's views will not be taken into account. However, the wishes of a six-year-old child have not been taken into account.[40] Where a child is of an age and maturity at which their views should be taken into account, such views, however, are not decisive. The purpose of the Convention is to ensure the speedy return of children to the country from which they have been wrongfully removed, and the discretion under this heading must be exercised only in exceptional circumstances.[41] Thus, in *Re HB (abduction: children's objections)*,[42] a 13-year-old boy and an 11-year-old girl were returned despite their strong objections.[43]

REMOVAL FOR MORE THAN ONE YEAR

Article 12 provides that:

> The judicial or administrative authority, even where the proceedings have been commenced after the expiration of the period of one year referred to in the preceding paragraph, shall also order the return of the child, unless it is demonstrated that the child is now settled in its new environment.

If it is demonstrated by the abductor that the child is now settled in his new environment, a discretion arises under Article 12 as to whether or not to order return. In *Re N (minors) (abduction)*,[44] it was held that the words 'now settled' referred to the date of the commencement of the proceedings. The onus of proving settlement was on the abducting parent and settlement required more than merely adjusting to the new surroundings. There were two constituents: first, a physical element of being established in a community and an environment, and secondly, the emotional constituent denoting security, as in permanence, and that the present position imported stability when looking into the future. The 'new environment' encompassed

---

[40] *S v S*, High Court, Miscellaneous Proceedings No 364 of 1998 (1998).
[41] *S v S (child abduction) (child's views)* [1992] 2 FLR 492.
[42] [1997] 1 FLR 392.
[43] Compare *B v K (child abduction)* (1993) Fam Law 17, objections of children aged seven and nine were given effect; and *Re K (abduction: child's objections)* [1995] 1 FLR 977 where objection of a child aged seven was not to be given weight; *S v S (child abduction) (child's views)* [1992] 2 FLR 492, a nine-year-old girl's view was taken into account; *Re R (child abduction: acquiescence)* [1995] 1 FLR 716, children aged six and seven order to return made.
[44] [1991] 1 FLR 413.

place, home, school, people, friends, activities and opportunities, but not, *per se*, the relationship with the abducting parent.

ABDUCTION INTO HONG KONG FROM A NON-CONVENTION COUNTRY

Where a child has been brought into Hong Kong from a non-Convention country (e.g. the PRC), return of the child is not governed by the principles laid down in the CACO. Return depends (i) on the voluntary return by the abducting parent or (ii) initiating legal action for the child's return. Wardship proceedings have often been invoked.

The principle which governs the outcome of such a case is the welfare principle. In a number of English cases dealing with abduction of children from non-Convention countries, it has been established that it is proper to apply the general principles of the Convention to non-Convention cases in that it is normally in the interests of children that parents or others should not abduct them, and that any decision relating to custody is best decided in the jurisdiction in which the children have hitherto been habitually resident. In deciding whether to make a summary order for the return of a child, the court has to weigh various factors, always having regard to the welfare of the child as the paramount consideration. In *Re L (minors) (wardship: jurisdiction)*,[45] Buckley LJ said:

> To take a child from his native land, to remove him to another country where, maybe, his native tongue is not spoken, to divorce him from the social customs and contacts to which he has been accustomed, to interrupt his education in his native land and subject him to a foreign system of education, are all acts ... which are likely to be psychologically disturbing to the child, particularly at a time when his family life is also disrupted. If such a case is promptly brought to the attention of a court in this country, the judge may feel that it is in the best interests of the infant that these disturbing factors should be eliminated from his life as speedily as possible. A full investigation of the merits of the case in an English court may be incompatible with achieving this. The judge may well be persuaded that it would be better for the child that those merits should be investigated in a court in his native country than that he should spend in this country the period which must necessarily elapse before all the evidence can be assembled for adjudication here. Anyone who has had experience of the exercise of this delicate jurisdiction knows what complications can result

---

[45] [1974] 1 WLR 250.

from a child developing roots in new soil, and what conflicts this can occasion in the child's own life. Such roots can grow rapidly. An order that the child should be returned forthwith to the country from which he has been removed in the expectation that any dispute about his custody will be satisfactorily resolved in the courts of that country may well be regarded as being in the best interests of the child.[46]

The harm to a child which may arise from not making a summary order must be weighed against the risks to the child of being separated from the mother-carer, of being entrusted to the care of a father whose capabilities and fitness to act as a single parent may be in doubt, in surroundings which may be unfavourable in themselves, and of being subjected to a regime of law under which the protection of their interests may be open to question.[47] Thus, in *G v G (minors) (abduction)*,[48] the father was of dual English and American nationality and the mother was English. They lived in Kenya and the children were born and raised there. The marriage broke down and the mother remained the children's principal carer and the father had regular contact. The mother started proceedings in Kenya for financial relief and custody. She then left Kenya with the children and the father issued wardship proceedings seeking for their return. The Court of Appeal held it had to weigh the danger to the children in being taken away from their home and background, if the order was not made, against the risk of their possible separation from their mother if the order was made, always having regard to their welfare as the paramount consideration. Normally, it was in the interests of the children for custody to be decided in the jurisdiction in which they had hitherto been habitually resident. In this case, there was no reason to believe that a custody hearing in Kenya would not be dealt with on the same principles as in England. From the evidence, it was likely that if the children were ordered to go back, the mother would accompany them and that her financial and housing position would be safeguarded. In all the circumstances, the proper forum to deal with the disputes was the Kenyan court where the proceedings had been initiated and witnesses were available. The children were ordered to be returned.

However, in *Re P (abduction: non-convention country)*,[49] a few months after the birth of a baby girl, the family moved back to India. The mother was unhappy and she returned to England with the girl. The father applied for her return. The Court of Appeal held that the child's habitual residence

---

[46] Ibid., at p. 264.
[47] Ormrod LJ in *Re R (minors) (wardship: jurisdiction)* [1981] 2 FLR 416 at 426.
[48] [1991] 2 FLR 506.
[49] [1997] 1 FLR 780.

was India. Yet, as the girl had no deep roots in India, her father had played no significant role in her life, and her mother's ability to care for her would be impaired were they to return, the welfare of the girl would be best served by refusing to order her return.

Kidnapping is only a factor to be taken into account, and the court is not concerned with penalising a parent for his or her wrongdoing; the child's welfare must always be treated as the paramount consideration.[50] Further, the court has taken the view that it is not bound by a foreign court order and it can make its own independent judgment on the merits of the case.[51]

STAY OF PROCEEDINGS: *FORUM CONVENIENS*

Where the terms of the Convention do not apply or where the case is a non-Convention case, the court may order the child to return and stay proceedings. Thus, in *Re K (abduction: consent: forum conveniens)*,[52] the parents lived in Texas and the child was born there. On divorce, the Texan court granted the father staying contact. The mother being the principal carer remarried, and with the consent of the father, she moved to England with the child. The mother refused to return the child and commenced proceedings in England for an interim residence order, and the father commenced proceedings in Texas seeking for a modification of the original order. The Court of Appeal held that wrongful retention was not established under the Hague Convention. However, on the question of a stay of the English proceedings, the judge erred in attaching excessive weight to the fact that the child had become habitually resident in the UK. In reality, the child was a Texan child with Texan parents who entrusted the validity and future supervision of the agreed custody regime to the Texan court, whose authority the mother had continued to accept. In the case of a child accustomed to travelling between the two countries and to changes of parental care, there was no justification for giving such weight to habitual residence. Texas was the *forum conveniens* and the child's future should be decided there. Waite LJ stated:

---

[50] *Re L (minors) (wardship: jurisdiction)* [1974] 1 WLR 250; *Re T (infants)* [1968] Ch. 704; *Re C (minors) (wardship: jurisdiction)* [1977] 3 WLR 561.
[51] *Mckee v Mckee* [1951] 1 All ER 942; *Re V (infants)*, High Court, Miscellaneous Proceedings No 477 of 1979 (1979).
[52] [1995] 2 FLR 211.

The two systems of law are so similar in approach and in execution that the order which eventually emerges (whether from London or Houston) will lay down a regime for future residence, contact and maintenance that will be expressed (differences of legal terminology apart) and enforced identically in either jurisdiction.

Again, in *H v H (minors) (forum conveniens)*,[53] where it was held that the balance of convenience pointed to England, as against Wisconsin where the mother would be disadvantaged because of the unavailability of legal aid. It was therefore better for the matter to be determined by the English court where the child was also habitually resident.

---

[53] [1993] 1 FLR 958.

Annex I

L.N. 36 of 1998

CHILD ABDUCTION AND CUSTODY (PARTIES TO CONVENTION) ORDER

(Made under section 4 of the Child Abduction and Custody Ordinance (49 of 1997) after consultation with the Executive Council)

1. **Parties to Convention**

    (1) The countries specified in column 1 of the Schedule are the Contracting States to the Convention.

    (2) The territories specified in column 2 of the Schedule are the territories specified in declarations made by the corresponding Contracting States specified in column 1 of the Schedule under Article 39 or 40 of the Convention.

    (3) The date of the coming into force of the Convention as between Hong Kong and any Contracting State or territory specified in the Schedule is 1 September 1997.

SCHEDULE [s. 1]

Column 1	Column 2
Contracting States to the Convention	Territories specified in declarations under Article 39 or 40 of the Convention
Argentina	
Australia	Australian States and Mainland Territories
Austria	
The Bahamas	
Belize	
Bosnia and Herzegovina	
Burkina Faso	
Canada	Ontario New Brunswick British Columbia

Column 1	Column 2
Contracting States to the Convention	Territories specified in declarations under Article 39 or 40 of the Convention
	Manitoba
	Nova Scotia
	Newfoundland
	Prince Edward Island
	Quebec
	Yukon Territory
	Saskatchewan
	Alberta
	Northwest Territories
Chile	
Colombia	
Croatia	
Cyprus	
Denmark (except the Faroe Islands and Greenland)	
Ecuador	
Finland	
France (for the whole of the territory of the French Republic)	
Germany	
Greece	
Honduras	
Hungary	
Iceland	
Israel	
Italy	
Luxembourg	
Mauritius	
Mexico	
Monaco	
Netherlands (for the Kingdom in Europe)	
New Zealand	
Norway	
Panama	
Poland	
Portugal	

Column 1	Column 2
Contracting States to the Convention	Territories specified in declarations under Article 39 or 40 of the Convention
Republic of Macedonia	
Romania	
Saint Kitts and Nevis	
Slovenia	
Spain	
Sweden	
Switzerland	
United Kingdom of Great Britain and Northern Ireland	Isle of Man
United States	
Venezuela	
Zimbabwe	

TUNG Chee-hwa
Chief Executive

12 January 1998

Part III

Financial Provision for Family Members

14

Maintenance Obligations during Marriage

INTRODUCTION

During marriage, intervention of the law may be necessary to provide maintenance for a dependent spouse and children. The law governing maintenance during marriage for a spouse and children is not particularly coherent. Overlapping jurisdictions and varying standards and principles apply depending on the statutory provision invoked. There are three possibilities:

(i) a party to a marriage and 'a child of the marriage' may obtain maintenance under the Separation and Maintenance Orders Ordinance;
(ii) a spouse and 'a child of the family' may obtain maintenance under s8 of the Matrimonial Proceedings and Property Ordinance.
(iii) a spouse and 'a child of the family' may obtain maintenance pending suit under ss3 and 5 of the Matrimonial Proceedings and Property Ordinance;
(iv) on granting a decree of judicial separation, the court is empowered to make financial provision and property adjustment to a party to a marriage and 'a child of the family'. These powers are the same as those on divorce.

The powers of the court under (iv) are the same as those on divorce and they will be examined later.[1] This chapter examines the law governing (i), (ii) and (iii).

---
[1] See Chapters 15 and 16.

SEPARATION AND MAINTENANCE ORDERS ORDINANCE

Provisions in the Separation and Maintenance Orders Ordinance (SMOO) were originally derived from the English Summary Jurisdiction (Married Women) Act 1895. Its long title states: 'to make better provision . . . for the granting by the District Court of separation and maintenance orders'. Although the law has now been substantially amended by the Marriage and Children (Miscellaneous Amendments) Ordinance,[2] some of the restrictions in the SMOO are difficult to reconcile with provisions in the Matrimonial Proceedings and Property Ordinance (MPPO).

Who Can Apply

The Ordinance provides that a 'married person' may apply. S2 of the SMOO states that a 'married person' means a husband or a wife. A husband means 'the husband or partner of a wife or married woman'. Further, a wife and a married woman means the wife or partner of a man by:

- a marriage celebrated or contracted in accordance with the Marriage Ordinance;
- a modern marriage validated by the Marriage Reform Ordinance;
- a customary marriage declared to be valid by the Marriage Reform Ordinance;
- a union of concubinage as defined in s14 of the Legitimacy Ordinance;
- a *kim tiu* marriage entered in accordance with Chinese law and custom applicable thereto in Hong Kong before the appointed day under the Marriage Reform Ordinance; or
- a marriage celebrated or contracted outside Hong Kong in accordance with the law in force at the time and in the place where the marriage was performed.

This definition covers parties to a marriage under the Marriage Ordinance,[3] parties to a validated marriage, parties to a customary marriage and union of concubinage,[4] *kim tiu* marriage[5] and a marriage contracted outside Hong Kong.

---

[2] Marriage and Children (Miscellaneous Amendments) Ordinance (No 69 of 1997).
[3] See Chapter 3.
[4] See Chapter 1.
[5] For the meaning of *kim tiu*, see Chapter 1.

Grounds for Making an Application

S3(1) of the SMOO provides eight grounds under which a person may apply for maintenance.

> Where a married person–
> (a) has been convicted[6] summarily of an assault upon the other party to the marriage which in the opinion of the convicting magistrate is of an aggravated character;
> (b) has been convicted whether on indictment or summarily of an assault upon the other party to a marriage, and sentenced to pay a fine of more than $500 or to a term of imprisonment exceeding 2 months;
> (c) has deserted the other party to the marriage;
> (d) has been guilty of persistent cruelty to the other party to the marriage or that party's children;[7]
> (e) has failed to provide reasonable maintenance for the other party to the marriage or reasonable maintenance and education for that party's children whom the married person is legally liable to maintain;
> (f) has, whilst suffering from a venereal disease, and knowing that he or she was so suffering, insisted on having intercourse with the other party to the marriage;[8]
> (g) has compelled the other party to the marriage to submit to prostitution;[9]
> (h) is a habitual drunkard or a drug addict.[10]
>
> that other party may apply to the district court for an order under this Ordinance.

Subsections (a) and (b) require proof of a criminal conviction. Subsection (c) requires desertion to be proved and this is the same as that required for a petition for divorce except that in case of divorce, the desertion has to be for a continuous period of one year.[11] 'Persistent cruelty' in subsection (d) is an outdated concept in family law and reference could be made to other texts.[12] The grounds in subsections (f), (g) and (h), like the other grounds, consist of serious misconduct on the part of the respondent. Only subsection (e) concerns directly with failure to provide reasonable maintenance.

---

[6] *Cassidy v Cassidy* [1959] 3 All ER 187.
[7] Not 'children of the marriage, cf. S5(b)(d) SMOO. See *Wright v Wright* [1960] P. 85.
[8] See s2 of the Venereal Diseases Ordinance (now repealed). 'Insisted' means something less than compulsion, see *Rigby v Rigby* [1944] P. 33; compare *Browning v Browning* [1911] P. 161.
[9] S3(2).
[10] S2.
[11] See Chapter 4.
[12] See Leonard Pegg, *Family Law in Hong Kong,* 3rd edition, Butterworths Asia, Hong Kong, 1994.

Failure to provide reasonable maintenance

Prior to the Marriage and Children (Miscellaneous Amendments) Ordinance, a husband had an obligation to maintain the wife, but not *vice versa*. The explanatory notes to the Marriage and Children (Miscellaneous Amendments) Bill state that one of the aims of the Bill was to remove existing inequalities between husband and wife.[13] There is now a reciprocal duty to maintain a spouse.

Orders Which Can Be Made

S5(1) of the SMOO provides that on any application under s3, the District Court may make all or any of the following orders:

(a) A non-cohabitation order in favour of either party to the marriage. This relieves the applicant from the duty to cohabit with the respondent. A non-cohabitation order, however, does not exclude a violent respondent from the matrimonial home,[14] but it brings to an end a party's desertion which occurred prior to the order. Thus, an applicant may not rely on that fact as evidencing marriage breakdown for the purposes of divorce or judicial separation.

(b) Legal custody[15] of any children of the marriage be committed to either party. A legal custody order terminates when the child reaches 18.[16]

(c) A party to a marriage to pay to the other party such lump sum or periodical payments, or both, as the court considers reasonable having regard to the means of both parties. A lump sum order may be made for the purpose of enabling any liabilities or expenses reasonably incurred in maintaining such other party before the making of the order.

(d) A party to a marriage to pay the other party such lump sum or periodical payments for the maintenance and education of a child of the marriage committed to such other party's custody that the court considers reasonable having regard to the means of both parties. However, a lump sum order can only be made for the purpose of providing for the immediate and non-recurring needs of a child, or of enabling any

---

[13] This follows the wording of the Domestic Proceedings and Magistrates' Courts Act 1978, s1.
[14] Unlike judicial separation, a non-cohabitation order does not affect intestate estate succession, s4A(2) Intestates' Estates Ordinance.
[15] See Chapter 10 on meaning of 'legal custody'.
[16] S11 of the Marriage and Children (Miscellaneous Amendments) Ordinance (No 69 of 1997).

liabilities or expenses reasonably incurred in maintaining the child before the making of the order, or both.

In making any of the above orders, the court shall have regard primarily to the best interests of the children.[17]

Duration of Child Maintenance Orders

A periodical payments order may begin with the date of the making of an orders or any later date but shall not extend beyond the child attaining the age of 18. However, where a child has not attained the age of 18, an order may extend beyond 18 if it appears:

(a) that child is, or will be, or if such an order or provision were made would be, receiving instruction at an educational establishment or undergoing training for a trade, profession or vocation, whether or not he is also, or will also be, in gainful employment; or
(b) there are special circumstances which justify the making of the order or provisions.[18]

Bar to Relief: Adultery Not Condoned and Connived

S6(1) of the SMOO provides that no order shall be made if it is proved that the applicant has committed an act of adultery provided that the respondent has not condoned or connived at such act of adultery. Condonation and connivance are concepts relating to matrimonial offences which have long been abolished under the Matrimonial Proceedings and Property Ordinance.[19] However, they survive in the SMOO and a brief note on this will suffice.

Condonation refers to the condoning spouse, knowing all the material facts of the offence, forgiving a spouse who has committed a matrimonial offence, and reinstating the offending spouse to his or her matrimonial

---

[17] S5(3).
[18] S12.
[19] Before 1972, the divorce court was entitled to refuse a decree of divorce or judicial separation by what were known as 'absolute' or 'discretionary' bars. The absolute bars were connivance, collusion and condonation, and the discretionary bars included conduct by the petitioner conducing to the offence charged against the respondent, or the commission of a matrimonial offence by the petitioner. All of these bars were abolished by s18A Matrimonial Causes Ordinance.

position. Forgiveness requires the condoning spouse to waive a legal remedy available to him or her.

> Condonation is the reinstatement of a spouse who has committed a matrimonial offence to his or her former matrimonial position in knowledge of all the material facts of that offence with the intention of remitting it, that is to say, with the intention of not enforcing the rights which accrue to the wronged spouse in consequence of the offence.[20]

Condonation bars relief because it would be inequitable to permit a spouse who has forgiven an offence to renege on that. A spouse is not allowed to approbate and reprobate — blowing hot and cold at the same time.[21] Thus, when an innocent spouse knows of the wrong done by the offending spouse, the innocent spouse must either accept the repudiation of the marriage or elect to affirm the relationship. Once affirmed, it is inequitable to allow the innocent spouse to go back on the choice.

Condonation of adultery with one person,[22] of which an innocent spouse is aware, does not mean condonation of adultery with another person of whom the innocent spouse was unaware. Similarly, if an innocent spouse reinstates the offending spouse, believing that he or she has committed adultery once, the innocent spouse will not be held to have condoned three other adulterous occasions which were undisclosed so long as the innocent spouse was unaware of them and would not have reinstated the offending spouse had they been known.[23]

S6A provides that adultery and cruelty shall not be deemed to have been condoned by reason only of continuation of cohabitation or resumption of cohabitation for a period not exceeding three months, or anything done during such cohabitation, if it is proved that cohabitation has continued or resumed with a view to effect reconciliation.

Connivance means that the adultery of one spouse has been caused, or has been knowingly or wilfully or recklessly permitted by the other as an accessory.[24] To establish connivance it is necessary to prove not merely that the plaintiff acted in such a manner as might result in the commission of adultery, but also that it was the plaintiff's intention to promote or encourage either the initiation or the continuation of adultery.[25] A person

---

[20] *Inglis v Inglis* [1967] 2 All ER 71 at pp. 79–80, per Sir Jocelyn Simon P.
[21] Ibid.
[22] *Bernstein v Berstein* [1892] P. 375.
[23] *Inglis v Inglis* [1967] 2 All ER 71; *Wells v Wells* [1954] 3 All ER 491.
[24] *Gipps v Gipps* (1864) 11 HL Cas 1; *Churchman v Churchman* [1945] P. 44; *Woodbury v Woodbury* [1949] P. 154; *Gorst v Gorst* [1952] P. 94.
[25] *Rumbelow v Rumbelow* [1965] P. 207.

may connive at adultery by an express declaration of consent or by conduct. If a plaintiff, with corrupt intention, stands by and permits the adultery to take place, he or she may be guilty of connivance by acquiescence.[26] However, an act done by a plaintiff to keep watch on the other spouse, to see whether or not his or her suspicions of adultery are well founded does not necessarily constitute connivance.[27]

It is often said that once connivance, always connivance. Connivance, therefore, operates to bar all relief in respect of even a subsequent adultery with another person.[28] In *Godfrey v Godfrey*,[29] it was held that this principle was too widely stated. The court, after finding connivance, should investigate all the circumstances in order to determine whether it had spent its force before the subsequent act of adultery. Thus, connivance may be 'spent' if there has been a full and complete reconciliation between the spouses.

Enforceability Whilst Residing Together

S6(2) says that an order under s5 of the SMOO shall be unenforceable and no liability shall accrue under such an order whilst the parties reside together.

Cessation of Orders

An order under s5 of the SMOO shall cease to have effect after three months of the parties continuing residing together.

Attachment of Earnings

Where an order for maintenance is made and the court is satisfied that the maintenance payer has without reasonable excuse failed to make any payment, and there is income capable of being attached payable to the maintenance payer, the court may order the income to be attached, as to the whole or part of the amount payable, and the amount attached to be paid to a designated payee.[30] An attachment order shall be an authority to the person by whom the income is payable to make the payment in

---

[26] *Rogers v Rogers* (1830) 162 ER 1079.
[27] *Douglas v Douglas* [1951] P. 85.
[28] *Gipps v Gipps* (1864) 11 HL Cas 1.
[29] [1965] AC 444.
[30] S9A(1).

accordance with the order, and the receipt of the designated payee shall be a good discharge of that person.[31]

MATRIMONIAL PROCEEDINGS AND PROPERTY ORDINANCE

There is overlapping jurisdiction between the SMOO and s8 of the Matrimonial Proceedings and Property Ordinance (MPPO) as they both deal with maintenance during marriage of dependent spouse and children.

Grounds for Application

S8(1) of the MPPO provides that:

> Either party to a marriage may apply to the court for an order under this section on the ground that the other party to the marriage (in this section referred to as the respondent) has failed–
> (a) to provide reasonable maintenance for the applicant, or
> (b) to provide, or to make a proper contribution towards, reasonable maintenance for any child of the child to whom this section applies.[32]

Prior to the Marriage and Children (Miscellaneous Amendments) Ordinance, the position of husband and wife was different. A wife could apply on the ground that the husband had wilfully neglected to provide reasonable maintenance for her. However, a husband could only obtain maintenance from the wife if he could show that his needs arose by reason of impairment of his earning capacity through age, illness, or disability of mind or body. Now, each spouse has a duty to support the other on a basis of equality.

Jurisdiction of the Court

The court has jurisdiction to hear an application under s8 if it has jurisdiction to entertain proceedings by the applicant for judicial separation.[33]

---

[31] S9A(2).
[32] As amended by s25 of the Marriage and Children (Miscellaneous Amendments) Ordinance (No 69 of 1997).
[33] S8(2), see Chapter 5.

Child of the Family

'Child of the family' is a concept used in the MPPO and is much wider than the concept of 'child of a marriage' in the Separation and Maintenance Orders Ordinance.[34] Where a child is not the child of the respondent, the court will take into account the factors set out in s7(3) of the MPPO.[35]

Orders That Can Be Made

Where the applicant satisfies the court of any ground in s8(1) the court may order one or more of the following orders as it thinks just:[36]

(a) an order that the respondent shall make to the applicant such periodical payments and for such term as may be so specified in the order;
(b) an order that the respondent shall secure to the applicant, to the satisfaction of the court, such periodical payments and for such term as may be so specified;
(c) an order that the respondent shall pay to the applicant such lump sum as may be so specified;
(d) an order that the respondent shall make to such person as may be specified in the order for the benefit of the child to whom the application relates, or to that child, such periodical payments and for such terms as may be so specified;
(e) an order that the respondent shall secure to such person as may be so specified for the benefit of that child, or to that child, to the satisfaction of the court, such periodical payments and for such term as may be so specified;
(f) an order that the respondent shall pay to such person as may be so specified for the benefit of that child, or to that child, such lump sum as may be so specified.

The orders which the court can make are wider in scope than those in s5 of the SMOO. The court can make a secured periodic payments order in favour of an applicant or a child of the family. A lump sum payment may be ordered generally, or may be made for the purpose of enabling any liabilities or expense reasonably incurred in maintaining the applicant or any child before the making of the application.[37] A lump sum order may

---

[34] For definition, see Chapter 16.
[35] See Chapter 16.
[36] S8(6).
[37] S8(7)(a).

provide for its payment to be made by instalments and may require the payment of the instalments to be secured to the satisfaction of the court.[38]

Interim Order

Where it appears to the court that the applicant or a child of the family is in immediate need of financial assistance but it is not yet possible to determine what order, if any, should be made, the court may order the respondent to make to the applicant, until the determination of the application, such periodical payments as the court thinks reasonable.[39]

Duration of a Periodical Payment in Favour of a Child of the Family

Duration of orders is the same as in s12 of the SMOO, that is, an order shall not be made in favour of a child who has attained the age of 18, but where a child has not attained 18, the court may extend the order beyond 18 if it appears:

(a) that child is, or will be, or if such an order or provision were made would be, receiving instruction at an educational establishment or undergoing training for a trade, profession or vocation, whether or not he is also, or will also be, in gainful employment; or
(b) there are special circumstances which justify the making of the order or provisions.[40]

Bar to Maintenance

Unlike the SMOO, there is no bar to an application under s8.

Attachment of Earnings

The orders for maintenance are enforceable by an attachment of earnings order.[41]

---

[38] S8(7)(b).
[39] S8(5).
[40] S10(3).
[41] See pp. 357–8 and ss28 and 28A MPPO.

MAINTENANCE PENDING SUIT: FINANCIAL PROVISION PRE-DECREE

Marriage breakdown often means financial hardship to an economically dependent spouse and to the children. The court is empowered to grant maintenance pending suit to alleviate such hardship from the period beginning with the date of petition (or joint application) for divorce and ending with the granting of a decree absolute. This is called maintenance pending suit.

Nature and Duration of Maintenance Pending Suit

S3 of the Matrimonial Proceedings and Property Ordinance (MPPO) provides that on a petition (or joint application) for divorce, either party may apply to the court for maintenance pending suit. Maintenance pending suit is provided by way of periodical payments from the time of the presentation of the petition (or making of joint application) to the date of decree absolute. The court, however, has no power to order secured periodical payments, lump sum payment or transfer of property. S5 of the MPPO allows maintenance to be ordered for the benefit of a child of the family.[42]

Discretion of the court

The court has the power to determine maintenance pending suit as it thinks reasonable. An order is usually made after the court has an opportunity of hearing both sides. The most important factors to be considered are an applicant's needs, and the respondent's ability to meet those needs. S7(1) of the MPPO does not apply to maintenance pending suit,[43] and it would be inappropriate for the court to make a detailed investigation into the financial position of the parties. In most cases, this means that maintenance pending suit should be such as to enable the wife to live in a fashion she has been accustomed to pending the outcome of the divorce. Thus, in *Leung Yuet-ming v Hui Hon-kit*,[44] the husband's monthly income was HK$15 670. He undertook to pay for rates, utilities, management fees, nursery bus, school fees, and a domestic helper. This came to about HK$7557. His own monthly mortgage payment was HK$7000 which was part of the running expenses

---

[42] See Chapter 16.
[43] See Chapter 15.
[44] Court of Appeal, Civil Appeal Action No 63 of 1994 (1994).

of his company and paid by the firm before profit. The District Court ordered him to pay the wife and three children HK$9000. The husband successfully appealed on the ground that the order exceeded his ability to pay.

In *V v V*,[45] the Court of Appeal held that it would be inappropriate for the court to take a long-term view; potential earning capacity and future capital prospects of the parties should be ignored. Further, the court needed not take into account an expense allowance, unless income might thereby be freed for paying maintenance pending suit. The applicant therefore could not treat such allowance as actual income.[46]

Although it is inappropriate to conduct detailed investigation into all the matters relevant to a final order, there must be some basis upon which an order is sought. To that extent, the court needs to know how much an applicant needs in terms of rental, pocket money, travelling expenses, and expenses for food and clothing, etc. In *Tang Yung Wai-han v Kwing Pui-yung*,[47] the marriage lasted for 11 years and the husband had substantial earnings of HK$1.3m a year. The Court of Appeal held that the needs of the wife were to be equated to her marital standard of living. Allowance therefore was made on items such as housing, pocket money, living expenses, presents and travelling expenses. Adding all the figures under these headings, HK$22 000 was awarded. However, in *F v F (Maintenance Pending Suit)*,[48] the marriage lasted for 5–11 days and the wife's financial position had not been affected by the marriage. It also appeared that the court might at the full hearing make no order or any substantial order in her favour. It was held that it would be inappropriate to make an order for maintenance pending suit.

In granting maintenance pending suit, the court is concerned with an applicant's immediate needs. The order is not intended to affect the final periodical payments order[49] which may be less than that ordered for maintenance pending suit.[50]

---

[45] Court of Appeal, Civil Appeal Action No 200 of 1980 (1981).
[46] *Horton v Horton*, High Court, Divorce Jurisdiction, Action No 19 of 1983 (1984). See also *Heun Sook Jong Miller v Stephen Henry Miller*, High Court, Divorce Jurisdiction, Action No 6 of 1985 (1985); *Agell v Agell*, High Court, Action No 4 of 1977 (1977). The approach in *V v V*, ibid., also applies to an application for interim periodical payment order, see *Wong Che-wa v Wong Chung Yee-fong*, High Court, Divorce Jurisdiction, Action No 64 of 1981 (1983).
[47] Court of Appeal, Civil Appeal Action No 201 of 1985 (1986).
[48] (1982) Fam Law 16.
[49] *V v V*, Court of Appeal, Civil Appeal Action No 200 of 1980 (1981).
[50] See *Cheung Wong Kim-ching v Cheung Chai-kong* [1991] 1 HKLR 698.

15

Money and Property on Divorce

INTRODUCTION

During marriage, the husband and wife (and children) will usually live together as a unit with the properties of the spouses being shared and enjoyed without regard to who owns what. Usually, whatever income is generated by the parties are 'pooled' and used for household expenses. Property and income are thus intermingled in an informal way for the benefit of the family as a whole. When a marriage functions harmoniously, this informal arrangement works well. When it comes to an end, however, it requires to be formalised and money and property need to be clearly separated and disentangled.

Matters concerning money and property on divorce are generally referred to as 'financial provision and property adjustment'. This area is governed by the Matrimonial Proceedings and Property Ordinance (MPPO) which confers wide powers on the court to adjust the financial position of the parties to a marriage. Although these powers are available on the grant of a decree of nullity or judicial separation and exercisable for the benefit of 'a child of the family', the focus of this chapter is on divorce and on the position of the parties to a marriage *inter se*. The position of children, however, is interrelated with that of their parents and *vice versa*. For instance, in *A v A (a minor: financial provision)*,[1] the unmarried father was

---

[1] [1994] 1 FLR 657; *K v W* [1998] 1 HKLRD 402.

a very wealthy person. He and the mother had a child. The father supported the mother during her pregnancy and acquired a home for her and the child. Although the mother could not make a claim against the father because they were never married, she sought a property adjustment order for the benefit of the child (an order no doubt benefitted her indirectly). It was held that the house should be settled in trust for the child until she attained the age of 18 or completed full-time education.

In this chapter, we examine how the discretion of the court is exercised. First we will consider who may apply to the court and what powers the court may exercise. The mechanisms by which the matrimonial home may be dealt with will be considered at the end of the chapter.

WHO MAY APPLY: EQUALITY OF THE SEXES

Either party to a marriage may apply for financial provision and property adjustment post-divorce. This important manifestation of the principle of equality of the sexes was stated in *Calderbank v Calderbank* [1976] Fam 93:

> Husband and wives come to the judgment seat ... upon the basis of complete equality ...[2]

Equality of the sexes, however, does not mean that parties to a marriage are presumed to be, or are to be treated in law, as equal partners in a marriage. For example, in a case where both spouses work, contribute to the finances of the family and participate in raising children, there is no presumption that both are to share equally in the assets acquired and accumulated over the course of the marriage. Alternatively, if both spouses decide that division of labour is beneficial to their marriage, and hence that the wife is to look after the home and children while the husband is the breadwinner, there is no presumption that they are to share equally in the wealth acquired during the marriage. In a Chinese society like Hong Kong, men are still expected to be the breadwinners and women are expected to look after the home and children. Claimants of financial provision or property adjustment on divorce are thus, in most instances, wives, husband-claimants being rare.[3] As a matter of convenience, general reference to claimants will assume them to be female and respondents male, but both genders may, in theory, be applicants.

---

[2] Carman LJ [1976] Fam 93 at 103.
[3] *C v C* [1990] 2 HKLR 183.

POWERS OF THE COURT: ORDERS WHICH CAN BE MADE

Ss4, 6 and 6A of the MPPO provide that where a court grants a decree of divorce, it may make an order for:
(a) periodical payments,
(b) secured periodical payments,
(c) lump sum,
(d) transfer of property,
(e) settlement of property,
(f) variation of settlement of property, and
(g) sale of property.

The term 'financial provision' means money payment, in the form of periodical payments (secured or unsecured), and lump sum payment. 'Property adjustment' refers to the remaining orders which the court can make and these all involve 'property'. Another way of classifying these orders is to consider whether they provide income or capital to the recipient spouse. An important distinction between the two is that a periodical payments order, being an income order, is variable[4] whereas capital orders, that is, orders (c)–(f) are generally not variable.

Periodical Payments Orders

An order for periodical payments provides for the payment of a sum of money at regular (usually monthly) intervals and may be for such term as the court specifies.[5] The maximum duration for an unsecured periodical payments order is for the joint lives of the parties or until remarriage of the payee, whichever is the shorter period.

> For example, the husband is ordered to make periodical payments to his wife at the rate of HK$5000 pm. The maximum duration of the order is until the death of either party. If the wife remarries before the death of the husband, periodical payments end automatically on her remarriage.

---

[4] See Chapter 17.
[5] *Thomson v Thomson*, Court of Appeal, Civil Appeal Action No 82 of 1991 (1991), see below.

Secured Periodical Payments Orders

One of the disadvantages of an unsecured periodical payments order is that where the payer defaults, the payee is required to bring enforcement proceedings,[6] the efficacy of which depends on the husband having sufficient means to pay.[7] The advantage of secured periodical payments is that the payer is required to set aside capital, for instance stocks and shares, or property, which will be charged and resorted to if payments are not made when they fall due. Another advantage of a secure periodical payments order is that its maximum duration is the life of the payee or until remarriage of the payee, whichever is the shorter period.[8] A wife's secured periodical payments are not, therefore, necessarily terminated by the death of the husband.

Various factors are relevant to the decision to order security for periodical payments. In *C v C (financial relief: short marriage)*,[9] the husband lied about his financial position and his relocation to another country. Additionally, there were difficulties in obtaining information as to his means and in him maintaining payments. These were held to be reasons warranting some form of security to protect the payee wife's interest.[10]

Lump Sum Orders

The court may order the payment of a lump sum[11] where, for instance, the husband has substantial assets and is in a position to pay. A lump sum may be ordered to be paid immediately or by instalments.[12] In the latter case, payment by instalments may extend over a period of time where, for instance, the husband's money is tied up in business and it is not possible to provide a lump sum at short notice.[13] Where the court orders that payment

---

[6] See rr86–91 MCR.
[7] *B v C (enforcement: arrears)* [1995] 1 FLR 467; *SN v ST (maintenance order: enforcement)* [1995] 1 FLR 868. The court now has the power to make an attachment of earnings order, see s30 of the Marriage and Children (Miscellaneous Amendments) Ordinance 1997.
[8] S9(1)(2) MPPO.
[9] [1997] 2 FLR 26.
[10] *A v A (a minor): (financial provision)* [1994] 1 FLR 657; *Hill v Hill* [1997] 1 FLR 730.
[11] The court has the power to make more than one lump sum in a single application, see *Coleman v Coleman* [1972] 3 All ER 886, but it does not have the power to make an interim lump sum order, nor could it make an interim lump sum order with a view to varying it later. *Bolsom v Bolsom* [1983] 4 FLR 21.
[12] *Preston v Preston* [1982] Fam 17.
[13] *Murphy v Murphy*, Court of Appeal, Civil Appeal Action No 56 of 1992 (1992).

be made by instalments, it may also require that they be secured to the satisfaction of the court.[14]

Lump sum payment may be ordered generally, or for the purposes of enabling the other spouse to meet any liabilities or expenses reasonably incurred by the payee in maintaining herself, or any child of the family, before making an application for ancillary relief.[15]

Under the MPPO, there is no statutory equivalent to s23(6) of the English Matrimonial Causes Act 1973, which empowers the court to order that instalments will carry interest at such rate as may be specified. Thus, where a lump sum is to be paid by instalments, the court has no power to order interest to be paid.[16] However, where payment of a lump sum is to be paid by instalments over a substantial period of time, the court may take into account the interest component by increasing the total amount of the instalments payable.[17] Once any instalment falls due and remains unpaid, it is a judgment debt on which statutory interest is payable.

Transfer of Property

The court may order one spouse to transfer to the other spouse property to which that spouse is entitled either in possession or reversion. For instance, the court may order a husband who owns the matrimonial home to transfer it to the wife, or order that the matrimonial home which is in the parties' joint names be transferred to the wife. The legal mechanisms by which the court may deal with the matrimonial home will be examined at the end of this chapter. However, at this point, some features of the property market need to be noted.

Public Rental Housing (PRH) and Home Ownership Scheme (HOS)

'Property' is not restricted to property which can be bought and sold or bequeathed by will. A weekly or monthly tenancy is 'property' within s6. In the absence of a contractual or statutory provision which prevents a tenancy from being transferred by the tenant himself, the court can order any transfer which the tenant himself could have made.[18] However, the court would hesitate for a long time before making an order involving a

---

[14] S4(2)(b); see *Keiko Maruko v Yoshio Maruko,* Court of Appeal, Civil Appeal Action No 32 of 1995 (1995).
[15] S4(2)(b) MPPO.
[16] *Murphy v Murphy,* Court of Appeal, Civil Appeal Action No 56 of 1992 (1992).
[17] See *Preston v Preston* [1982] Fam 17 at p. 38 per Brandon LJ.
[18] *Hale v Hale* [1975] 2 All ER 1090.

PRH unit under the Housing Authority. The reason is that the court would not make an order which a third party may lawfully refuse to bring to fruition,[19] and in this case because such an order might conflict with the statutory duty of the Housing Authority. The practice at one time was to 'recommend' a transfer, but in *Chan Wei-yin v Cheong Shun-chiu*,[20] the Court of Appeal held that the court had no jurisdiction to make a 'recommendation', directing the Housing Authority to transfer an existing tenancy to another party.

Properties purchased under the HOS involve special considerations. These are housing units for low-income families sold at less than market value and which carry restrictions on the right to sell. For instance, if sale is within the first ten years of purchase, the property must be sold back to the Housing Authority, subject to payment of a premium calculated in accordance with the Housing Ordinance.[21] Sale after ten years can be on the open market but a premium has to be paid to the Housing Authority representing some of the increased value. Where there is this kind of fetter on alienation, an order of transfer requires the consent of the Housing Authority.[22] Additionally, valuation of such property may be complicated by the restriction on sale. Thus, in *Lai Lai-hing v Lai Kwai-ping*,[23] two valuations were given on the property: one on the basis of a sale back to the Housing Authority, and the other on the basis of sale on the open market which could take place in three and a half years' time. Mortimer JA held that sale on the open market was a factor to be taken into account and it would be unjust to the wife if she was not to participate in some way in the windfall associated with her share of the flat which would arise when it was available for sale on the open market.[24]

Property held by company

A party to a marriage may be entitled to property which is held by a company. Where the company is the alter ego of a husband, the court may order him to transfer the assets held by the company. In other cases, the lifting of the corporate veil would not be appropriate, e.g. where the court

---

[19] *Hale v Hale* [1975] 2 All ER 1090; *Wong Tai-hing v Wong Lau Yuk-ling*, District Court, Divorce Jurisdiction, Action No 776 of 1983 (1984).
[20] [1993] 2 HKLR 485.
[21] See Schedule.
[22] *Ngai Wong Yun-ping v Ngai Yun-lung*, Court of Appeal, Civil Appeal Action No 50 of 1996 (1996).
[23] [1995] 1 HKC 654.
[24] *Kam Leung Kit-yee v Kam Ying-fai*, Court of Appeal, Civil Appeal Action No 194 of 1996 (1997).

could not ignore minority interests which are real. Thus, in *Nicholas v Nicholas*,[25] the wife lived in a property which was owned by a company. The husband had a 71 percent interest whilst the remaining 29 percent was held by his business associates (who were not nominee directors). The property was purchased partly as their matrimonial home and partly for business purposes. The court ordered the husband, who was the major shareholder, to undertake to exercise his controlling rights to procure the sale of the property to the wife. The Court of Appeal, however, held that the lower court did not have the power to order the husband to procure a third party to divest the property, either by exercising his majority voting power or otherwise.

Settlement of Property

The court may order that property to which either party to a marriage is entitled be settled for the benefit of the other party to the marriage, or children of the family, or both. This power is often used to make arrangements concerning the matrimonial home.[26]

Variation of Ante-Nuptial or Post-Nuptial Settlement

'Settlement' refers to a deed vesting property in trustees or creating successive legal or beneficial interests. Further, it includes other documents by which provision is made by one spouse for another.[27] One example is a deed of separation which provides for regular payments to be made by one spouse to another.[28] However, 'settlement' would not cover an outright transfer or gift by one spouse to another.[29] In the past, the courts have held that purchase of a matrimonial home which was then conveyed into the husband's and wife's names upon trust for sale created a 'settlement'.[30] It has also been held that if a conveyance originally constituted a post-nuptial settlement, such nuptial element was not lost by one joint tenant giving a notice of severance after the decree nisi.[31]

---

[25] [1984] FLR 285.
[26] *Hui I-mei v Cheng Yau-shing*, Court of Appeal, Civil Appeal Action No 157 of 1996 (1996).
[27] *Brown v Brown* [1959] P. 86 at p. 89 per Hudson LJ.
[28] Ibid.
[29] Ibid.
[30] Ibid.; *Ulrich v Ulrich* [1968] 1 All ER 67.
[31] *Radziej v Radziej* [1967] 1 All ER 944.

Today, the courts have the power to order transfer or settlement of property, so the power of variation of ante-nuptial or post-nuptial settlement has become somewhat redundant. It has been held that the words 'ante-nuptial settlement' and 'post-nuptial settlement' are to be given a liberal construction, which may cover, for example, a spouse's interest under a life insurance policy,[32] or interest under a pension fund. In *Brooks v Brooks*,[33] the House of Lords held that rights or potential benefits given to the spouse of an employee under a pension fund scheme constituted a post-nuptial settlement which the court had jurisdiction to vary. However, the court would be most unlikely, save in very unusual and exceptional circumstances, to allow the variation power to be used to reduce or disturb the rights of individuals outside the marriage. Where a proposed variation would affect the rights of third parties, the court would confine itself to achieving a compensatory effect under s7(1)(h) of the MPPO.[34]

Sale of Property

Prior to the Marriage and Children (Miscellaneous Amendments) Ordinance,[35] there was no power to order sale[36] under s6 of the MPPO, which was a serious restriction on the power of the court.[37] Now, s6A(1) of the MPPO provides that where the court makes an order under ss4, 5 or 6, then, on making that order or at any time thereafter, the court may make a further order for the sale of such property as may be specified in the order. An order for sale may contain such consequential or supplementary provisions as the court thinks fit.[38] Where a party, not a party to a marriage, has a beneficial interest in any such property, it shall be the duty of the court to give that other person an opportunity to make representations with respect to an order for sale before the court decides whether to make the order.[39]

---

[32] *Lort-Williams v Lort-Williams* [1951] P. 395.
[33] [1995] 2 FLR 13.
[34] See below.
[35] However, see *Chan Cheung-hing v Chan Tang-lan* [1985] 2 HKC 316; *Cheung Wong Kim-ching v Cheung Chai-kong* [1991] 1 HKLR 698. But in *Choy Kin-choy v Choy Chan Lai-ngar*, Court of Appeal, Civil Appeal Action No 47 of 1993 (1993) the matrimonial home was ordered to be sold.
[36] No 69 of 1997.
[37] *Cheung Wong Kim-ching v Cheung Chai-kong, Ngai Wong Yun-ping v Ngai Yun-lung*, Court of Appeal, Civil Appeal Action No 50 of 1996 (1996).
[38] S6A(2).
[39] *Mullard v Mullard* [1982] 3 FLR 330; *Thompson v Thompson* [1985] FLR 863; *Burton v Burton* [1986] 2 FLR 419; *R v Rushmoor Borough Council ex parte Barrett* [1988] 2 FLR 252.

Undertakings

Although the above powers of the court are wide, matters which fall outside the ambit of any of the above orders may need to be settled or agreed. The husband may, for instance, agree with the wife that he will discharge the mortgage repayment, continue to pay children's school fees or maintain premiums payments on a life insurance policy. These could not be brought within the scope of an order but they could be dealt with by way of undertakings.[40]

EXERCISING DISCRETION

Statutory Guidelines

As has been seen, the courts have wide powers to make both financial provision and property adjustment orders under ss 4 and 6 of the MPPO post-divorce. How should such powers be exercised? S7(1) of the MPPO provides that it shall be the duty of the court in deciding whether to exercise its powers, and in determining the manner in which its discretion is exercised, to have regard to 'the conduct of the parties and all the circumstances of the case, including the following, that is to say:

> (a) the income, earning capacity, property and other financial resources which each of the parties to the marriage has or is likely to have in the foreseeable future;
> (b) the financial needs, obligations and responsibilities which each of the parties to the marriage has or is likely to have in the foreseeable future;
> (c) the standard of living enjoyed by the family before the breakdown of the marriage;
> (d) the age of each party to the marriage and the duration of the marriage;
> (e) any physical or mental disability of either of the parties to the marriage;
> (f) the contributions made by each of the parties to the welfare of the family, including any contribution made by looking after the home or caring for the family;
> (g) in the case of proceedings for divorce or nullity of marriage, the value of either of the parties to the marriage of any benefit (for example, a pension) which, by reason of the dissolution or annulment of the marriage, that party will lose the chance of acquiring.

---

[40] Compare orders made in *Ngai Wong Yun-ping v Ngai Yun-lung,* Court of Appeal, Civil Appeal Action No 50 of 1996 (1996); *Choy Kin-choy v Choy Chan Lai-ngar,* Court of Appeal, Civil Appeal Action No 47 of 1993 (1993).

This set of criteria is the same as those set out in s25 of the English Matrimonial Causes Act 1973 before it was amended by the Matrimonial and Family Proceedings Act 1984, except that there is no reference to the minimal loss principle and reference to conduct is in general terms only.[41] The breadth of the court's discretionary power has been well characterised by Lord Denning:

> [the court] takes the rights and obligations of the parties all together and puts the pieces into a mixed bag. Such pieces are the right to occupy the matrimonial home or have a share in it, the obligation to maintain the wife and children, and so forth. The court then takes out the pieces and hands them to the two parties — some to one party and some to the other — so that each can provide for the future with the pieces allotted to him or to her. The court hands them out without paying any too nice a regard to their legal or equitable rights but simply according to what is the fairest provision for the future, for mother and father and the children.[42]

The guidelines in s7(1) delineate the framework within which the discretion of the court is to be exercised. However, it provides little guidance on important questions of principle applicable to the division of capital and maintenance. This can be compared with, for instance, the New Zealand Matrimonial Property Act 1976, which provides for recognition of 'the equal contribution of husband and wife to the marriage partnership and the equal division of certain property on divorce'.[43] Similarly, the Ontario Family Law Act 1986 provides for the equal sharing of the 'net family property'.[44] The purpose of this is:

> to recognise that children, household management and financial provision are the joint responsibilities of the spouses and that inherent in the marital relationship there is equal contribution, whether financial or otherwise, by the spouses to the assumption of these responsibilities, entitling each spouse to the equalisation of the net family properties.

In relation to maintenance, s64(1) of the New Zealand Family Proceedings Act 1980 provides, *inter alia,* that a former spouse shall be liable to maintain the other where the dependent spouse cannot practicably meet his or her reasonable needs because of the effects of child care responsibilities, or because of the need to undergo re-education or training

---

[41] For the possible effect of this, see below.
[42] *Hanlon v Law Society* [1981] AC 124 at 146.
[43] Lord Denning alluded to that possibility in *Wachtel v Wachtel* [1973] Fam 72.
[44] S5(1).

designed to increase the earning capacity diminished as a result of child care responsibilities.

The MPPO provides no specific target which the court should seek to achieve. As was noted by Bagnall J in *Harnett v Harnett*,[45] the legislature did not direct the court to exercise its power so as to achieve a fair or just division of the capital and income resources of the parties. The relative weight to be placed on the various factors in s7(1) is not prescribed and such factors may be interrelated. For example, a wife's physical disability is likely to adversely affect her income or earning capacity. Similarly, the longer a marriage has lasted, the more extensive a wife's contribution in terms of looking after the home and the children is likely to have been. However, the various factors may conflict and pull in different directions but there is no indication as to how such conflicts may be resolved. For example, a marriage may have been short, but the wife might have made a substantial contribution. Again, a marriage may be short and the wife's contribution minimal but she may be elderly and in poor health.

The court's discretion is further complicated by the interplay between financial provision, on the one hand, and property adjustment orders, on the other. As a result, a case may be amenable to more than one outcome. For example, in *Wachtel v Wachtel*, Lord Denning MR said that if the court were only concerned with the capital assets of the family, it would be tempting to divide them 50/50. However, since the wife wanted periodical payments, she could only have one-third of the family assets.

> ... If we were only concerned with the capital assets of the family, and particularly with the matrimonial home, it would be tempting to divide them half and half, as the judge did. That would be fair enough if the wife afterwards went her own way, making no further demands on the husband. It would be simply a division of the assets of the partnership ... But at present few wives are content with a share of the capital assets. Most wives want their former husbands to make periodical payments as well as to support them; because, after the divorce, he will be earning far more than she; and she can only keep up her standard of living with his help. He also has to make payments for the children out of his earnings, even if they are with her. In view of those calls in his future earnings, we do not think she can have both half the capital assets, and half the earnings.[46]

For the reasons given above, there is no clear and simple answer to questions such as 'how will the property of the parties will be divided?' or

---

[45] [1973] 3 WLR 1.
[46] [1973] Fam 72 at p. 95.

'would the wife be entitled to a 50/50 division of the family assets as well as maintenance from the husband?'. The answers depend on the facts of each particular case. The width of judicial discretion allows considerable flexibility in the dispensation of tailor-made justice.

> I appreciate the point [counsel] has made, namely, that it is difficult for practitioners to advise clients in these cases because the rules are not very firm. That is inevitable when the courts are working out the exercise of the wide powers ... It is the essence of such a discretionary situation that the court should preserve, so far as it can, the utmost elasticity to deal with each case on its own facts. Therefore it is a matter of trial and error and imagination on the part of those advising clients. It equally means that the decisions of this court can never be better than guidelines. They are not precedents in the strict sense of the word.[47]

Balcombe LJ summarised the nature of judicial discretion.

> We are here concerned with a judicial discretion, and it is of the essence of such a discretion that on the same evidence two different minds might reach widely different decisions without either being appealable. It is only where the decision exceeds the generous ambit within which reasonable disagreement is possible, and is, in fact, plainly wrong, that an appellate body is entitled to interfere.[48]

The Lack of a 'Target' Provision

As mentioned earlier, the language of s7(1) is almost identical to the former s25 of the English Matrimonial Causes Act 1973 before it was amended in 1984. S25 of the Matrimonial Causes Act 1973 enjoined the court to exercise its discretion in order to:

> place the parties, so far as it is practical and, having regard to their conduct, just to do so, in the financial position in which they would have been if the marriage had not broken down and each had properly discharged his or her financial obligations and responsibilities towards the other.

This is the so-called 'target' provision, or the 'minimal loss principle'. An example where the target is more or less achieved by the divorcing parties themselves would be where both of them remarry and their respective new spouses have the financial attributes of their former partners. For

---

[47] *Martin (BH) v Martin (D)* [1978] Fam 12 at p. 20 per Ormrod LJ.
[48] *Whiting v Whiting* [1988] 1 WLR 565 at p. 575; applied in *Murphy v Murphy*, Court of Appeal, Civil Appeal Action No 56 of 1992 (1992).

instance, in *H v H (financial provision: remarriage)*,[49] the husband remarried and the second wife was in the same financial position as his former wife; similarly, the wife's new husband was a man whose capital assets and income were similar to those of her former husband. In such a case, there was very little that the court needed to do in order to place the parties in the financial position they would have been in if the marriage had not broken down.[50]

In other cases, the target provision is more difficult to achieve. In order to do so, one needs to speculate what the financial position of the parties would have been had the marriage not broken down. The assumption is that a wife is potentially entitled to benefit from all her husband's capital assets at some time and is entitled to be provided for out of his income. For example, where a husband is the breadwinner and the only capital asset is the matrimonial home, assuming that the marriage had not broken down, the wife would have continued to live in the matrimonial home and maintained by the husband.

The 'target' provision has its logical difficulties. The financial position of a couple before and after divorce can be very different and comparison may be impossible except in the crudest terms. In most cases, there is insufficient money for both parties to maintain the same standard of living that they enjoyed during marriage, and it would be, as Griffith LJ put it, 'a sterile exercise to try to get a quart out of a pint pot.'[51] Where a husband is wealthy, such comparison will necessarily be crude. For instance, in *Preston v Preston*, had the marriage continued, the wife would have been a *de facto* joint beneficiary in a very large fund over which she had no control. On divorce, and after the court had made financial provision and property adjustment orders in her favour, there were two separate funds one of which would belong absolutely to the wife and under her sole control.[52]

In light of the above difficulties, the 'target' provision in s25 of the English Matrimonial Causes Act 1973 was removed by the Matrimonial and Family Proceedings Act 1984.

In Hong Kong, the Court of Appeal in *C v C* observed that the omission of the 'target' provision in the MPPO had been deliberate. However, as the intention of the Hong Kong legislature was to follow English examples, the 'target' provision had always been in the background of our law.[53] However, its deliberate omission meant that the MPPO places:

---

[49] [1975] 1 All ER 367.
[50] *Martin (BH) v Martin (D)* [1978] Fam 12.
[51] *Thyssen-Bornemisza v Thyssen-Bornemisza (No 2)* [1985] FLR 1069 at p. 1081.
[52] *Preston v Preston* [1982] Fam 17 at p. 26 per Ormrod LJ.
[53] [1990] 2 HKLR 183 at p. 188.

a lower duty on the court and lowers the significance of this element. It [the omission] may thus diminish a wife's claim and operate marginally in favour of husbands.[54]

But how much diminution is unclear. Yet, it would be wrong for the court to adopt the minimal loss principle in exercising its discretion under s7.[55] It has also been observed that the removal of the 'target' provision in England had not brought about any apparent decline in awards in English cases. To that extent, English cases decided after 1984 will continue to be an important point of reference for Hong Kong.

Clean Break *versus* Continuing Maintenance Obligation

Divorce is the legal mechanism whereby the marital relationship is terminated. So why should a former husband be required to maintain his ex-wife? If such an obligation exists, should it be a lifelong obligation? If not, how long should it last?[56] There is no easy answer to these much debated questions. Thirty years ago, Sir Jocelyn Simon had already recognised the unique or perhaps peculiar nature of the marriage relationship:

> men can only earn their incomes and accumulate capital by virtue of the division of labour between themselves and their wives. The wife spends her youth and early middle age in bearing and rearing children and in tending the home; the husband is thus freed for his economic activities. Unless the wife plays her part the husband cannot play his. The cock bird can feather his nest precisely because he is not required to spend most of his time sitting on it.[57]

---

[54] Ibid., at p. 188.
[55] *Yue Chen Kuei-mei v Yue Kwok-kee,* Court of Appeal, Civil Appeal Action No 19 of 1993 (1993).
[56] Ruth Deech, 'The Principles of Maintenance' (1977) 7 Fam Law 229; Katherine O'Donovan, 'The Principles of Maintenance: An Alternative View' (1978) 8 Fam Law 180; W A Stirling, 'State of the Union' (1982) 45 MLR 425; J Payne, 'Policy Objectives of Private Law Spousal Support Rights and Obligations' in *Contemporary Trends in Family Law: A National Perspective* ed by Katherine Connell-Thouez and Bartha M Knoppers, Carswell Legal Publications, 1984, 55; J Payne, 'Permanent Spousal Support in Divorce Proceedings: Why? How Much? How Long?' (1986) 6 CJFL 384; Katherine Baker, 'Contracting for Security: Paying Married Women What They've Earned' (1988) 55 University of Chicago Law Review 1193; Carol Rogerson, 'The Causal Connection Test in Spousal Support Law' (1989) 8 CFFL 95.
[57] Quoted in Brenda Hoggett and David Pearl, *The Family, Law and Society: Cases and Materials,* 3rd edition, Butterworths, London, 1991, p. 141.

Is marriage more like a partnership in which the husband and wife unite their skills, labour, and resources and then share the benefits? L'Heureux-Dube J of the Supreme Court of Canada eloquently describes marriage as follows:

> Many believe that marriage and the family provide for the emotional, economic, and social well-being of its members. It may be the location of safety and comfort, and may be the place where its members have their most intimate human contact. Marriage and the family act as an emotional and economic support system as well as a forum for intimacy. In this regard, it serves vital personal interests, and may be linked to building a "comprehensive sense of personhood". Marriage and the family are a superb environment for raising and nurturing the young of our society by providing the initial environment for the development of social skills. These institutions also provide a means to pass on the values that we deem to be central to our sense of community.[58]

Despite the advantages that marriage may bring and the common goals that it may enhance, it may ultimately have economic disadvantages:

> ... marriage and the family often require the sacrifice of personal priorities by both parties in the interest of shared goals. All of these elements are of undeniable importance in shaping the overall character of a marriage ... .[59]

> ... in 1988, overall two-thirds of divorced women had total incomes which placed them below the poverty line. When support was excluded, 74% of divorced women fell below the poverty line ... It is apparent that support payments, even assuming they are paid, are making only a marginal contribution to reducing economic hardship among women following divorce.[60]

Where a husband is a wage-earner and the wife looks after the children, this economic division of labour inevitably renders the wife financially dependent on the husband during the marriage. This dependency may continue long after the dissolution of the marriage as the wife may have become too old to work or to be retrained for the work force, or she may have continuing child-rearing commitments. On the other hand, the husband will continue his career unaffected by the breakdown of the marriage. Latey J[61] captured the reality of such a woman.

---

[58] *Moge v Moge* [1992] 2 SCR 813 at p. 848.
[59] Ibid., at p. 848 per L'Heureux-Dube J.
[60] Ibid., at p. 855.
[61] *S v S* [1976] Fam 18 at p. 23.

> This wife like so many wives when there are children has come off worse as the result of the breakdown of the marriage. It is a sad fact of life that, where there are children, both husband and wife suffer on marriage breakdown, but it is the wife who usually suffers more. The husband continues with his career, goes on establishing himself, increasing his experience and qualification for employment — in a word, his security. With children to care for, a wife usually cannot do this. She has not usually embarked on a continuous and progressing career whilst living with her husband caring for her child or children and running the home. If the marriage breaks down she can only start in any useful way after the children are off her hands and then she starts from scratch in middle life while the husband has started in youth.

On divorce, a husband wants to start a new life unencumbered by his previous marriage, and indeed he might have contracted new obligations to his second wife and family. Yet, the need for financial support of an ex-wife whose earning capacity has been seriously impaired could mean that she would need maintenance for the rest of her life, or at least until she has been 'rehabilitated'. The word 'rehabilitated' does not have, of course, the same connotation as in crime; here it means that the wife has undergone training or education as a result of which she has become capable of financial self-sufficiency. However, maintenance for a limited period of time required for her to be retrained to be financially self-dependent may not always be possible. Thus, in *Barrett v Barrett*,[62] the court explored the possibility of financial self-sufficiency of a wife at the age of 45, who was in no way 'work-shy', and who for the past 20 years had raised three children but had no commercial experience other than part-time employment. It was argued by the husband that she should be financially self-sufficient in four years. Butler-Sloss disagreed, saying:

> I ... do not think that a wife in these circumstances at this age, who has not had full-time employment for many years, looking for and willing to find work and indeed prepared to take a course to make her more fit to get employment, and still not finding a job, should be obliged to go back to the court some time shortly before the four years is up and say "I cannot find work; I do not know what to do". It would be far more suitable for the husband to first write to the wife's solicitors and say "Why are you not getting work? What efforts have you made?" and if he is not satisfied, to go back to court and say the time has come ... to have this order brought to an end if she was not making genuine but unsuccessful efforts to get employment.[63]

---

[62] [1988] 2 FLR 516.
[63] Ibid., at p. 521.

So far the courts have adopted three major approaches to the cases. They are: clean break, at the one end of the spectrum, continuing financial provision (or lifelong maintenance) at the other end, and deferred clean break, which represents a mid-point between the two.

Clean break in most cases means a once and for all settlement in the form of capital provision, with no continuing financial provision by way of periodical payments. The alternative to the clean break approach is an order for periodical payments or for a nominal periodical payments order made in favour of a spouse. The purpose of the latter, which may be for an amount as small as $1 per month, is to preserve the right of a claimant to obtain maintenance in the future.[64] An order achieving clean break, on the other hand, terminates the financial obligations of the parties and to that extent, the order is final.

The virtue of clean break was extolled by the House of Lords in *Minton v Minton*:

> The law now encourages spouses to avoid bitterness after family breakdown and to settle their money and property problems. An object of the modern law is to encourage each to put the past behind them and to begin a new life which is not overshadowed by the relationship which has broken down.[65]

The English Matrimonial and Family Proceedings Act 1984, amending s25 of the Matrimonial Causes Act 1973, imposes a duty on the court to consider the possibility of clean break by way of three mechanisms. Firstly, 25A(1) provides that it is the duty of the court to consider whether it would be appropriate for it to exercise its powers so that the financial obligations of each party towards the other will be terminated as soon after the grant of the decree as the court considers just and reasonable. In other words, the court has a duty to consider the possibility of a clean break. Secondly, s25A(2) provides that where the court makes a periodical payments order, it must consider whether it would be appropriate to require those payments to be made only for such term as would be sufficient to enable the recipient to adjust without undue hardship to the termination of his/her financial dependence on the other party. This is sometimes called deferred clean break or rehabilitation. Thirdly, s25A(3) provides that where, on an application for a periodical payments order, the court considers no continuing obligation should be imposed, it must dismiss the application and direct that no further application be made.

---

[64] *L v L* [1962] P. 101 at p. 117 per Willmer.
[65] *Minton v Minton* [1979] 1 All ER 79 at pp. 78–88 per Lord Scarman.

In Hong Kong, the MPPO does not have similar clean break provisions. This, however, does not mean that the court is not free to exercise its powers in such a manner as to achieve clean break. An example of structuring a clean break can be seen in *Attar v Attar (No 2)*,[66] where the wife, an air stewardess, met the husband, who was a wealthy man. They agreed that she should give up her job which secured her a salary of £15 000 p.a. but the marriage lasted only for six months. It was held that as the wife was young she should be allowed two years to re-establish her financial independence. Taking her pre-marital salary as a base figure, she was entitled to a lump sum of £30 000. Although the MPPO does not have a provision similar to s25A(3) above, it was held by the Court of Appeal in *Ngao Tang Yau-lin v Ngao Kai-suen*,[67] that the court had the power to dismiss an application for periodical payments without the consent of the applicant. Additionally, the courts may make periodical payments orders for a specified period. Thus, in *Thomson v Thomson*,[68] the court ordered the husband to make periodical payments to the wife for a limited period of three years.[69]

Clean break is likely to be the approach adopted where parties are wealthy.[70] It has also been favoured in cases where there are no children and both parties are able to earn a living. In *Lai Lai-hing v Lai Kwai-ping*,[71] the marriage lasted only for six years during which time the parties cohabited for four years. Although the parties were of very modest means, they were young, had no children, and were able to be self-supporting. Clean break was achieved by the husband buying out the wife's interest in the matrimonial home. Clean break was also adopted in *Fei Tai-chung v Gloria Fei*,[72] which involved a childless marriage of 13 years. Although the parties were in their 40s, both were well educated professional people and commanded substantial salaries. In *Hamlett v Hamlett*,[73] the marriage lasted for ten years and there were no children. The husband, aged 49, was a flight engineer and the wife, aged 41, was a member of the cabin staff. Their major asset was the matrimonial home, worth HK$6.2m. It was held that a clean break could be achieved by awarding the wife a share of 75 percent of the matrimonial home. Similarly, in *Baillieu v*

---

[66] [1985] FLR 653.
[67] [1984] HKLR 310.
[68] Court of Appeal, Civil Appeal Action No 52 of 1991 (1991).
[69] Such an order, however, will not achieve a clean break or even a deferred clean break in that although the order ends in 3 years, s11 allows the wife to apply for a variation within the three years.
[70] *C v C* [1990] 2 HKLR 183.
[71] [1995] 1 HKC 654.
[72] Court of Appeal, Civil Appeal Action No 170 of 1994 (1995).
[73] [1996] 1 HKC 61.

Baillieu,[74] the parties' marriage lasted for six years and they were in their mid-forties. The wife was described as someone who was 'well able to make her own way in the world'. A lump sum was awarded for her to purchase a home, a car, and for the costs of further study or training which would be required before suitable employment could be found.

Clean break can also be achieved where there are children, provided that adequate provision is made for them. Thus, in *Murphy v Murphy*,[75] the marriage lasted for 18 years and there were four teenage children. Prior to the birth of the first child, the wife had three years' experience as a nurse. Although the wife had never been expected to be entirely self-sufficient during marriage, she started a business with a friend. On divorce, the wife was 40 years old and was granted care and control of the children. The husband assumed the financial obligations in relation to the maintenance and education of the children and the provision of a comfortable life for them. The court, noting the wife's qualification as a trained nurse — a skill which 'seemed to be always and universally in demand' — ordered that there be a clean break by way of a lump sum of HK$2 060 000, which represented 57 percent of the family assets. The court noted that the wife had demonstrated an entrepreneurial potential and had chosen to work when there was no economic necessity for her to do so and when the children were young. She was expected to earn in due course HK$10 000 pm which could cover her non-accommodation needs. Again, in *Hui I-mei v Cheng Yau-shing*,[76] the couple's assets were for the most part in the matrimonial home, which was worth HK$2.6m. The wife was 34 years old, had no educational qualifications, and had custody of two young children. A clean break was achieved by transferring the matrimonial home to her so as to ensure that she and the children were accommodated.

Periodical payments, however, are likely to be provided if there has been a long marriage during which the husband has been the breadwinner and the wife has had little working experience. Thus, in *M v M (financial provision)*,[77] the marriage lasted for 20 years. During this time, the wife did some part-time secretarial work but spent most of her time at home looking after the household and the child. The husband earned a substantial salary as a chartered accountant. At the time of the divorce, she was 47 and her job prospects were not good, her earning capacity being insufficient to provide for her needs. It was held that the husband should be ordered to

---

[74] Court of Appeal, Civil Appeal Action No 149 of 1995 (1995).
[75] Court of Appeal, Civil Appeal Action No 56 of 1992 (1992).
[76] Court of Appeal, Civil Appeal Action No 157 of 1996 (1996).
[77] [1987] 2 FLR 1.

make up for the shortfalls after a long marriage where the wife had been a good mother and homemaker. She was entitled to a decent standard of living and it was unrealistic to suppose that she was likely to become self-sufficient in the foreseeable future. Similarly, in *Boylan v Boylan*,[78] it was said that a wife, at the age of 46, with no training and only modest earning capacity should not be expected to fend for herself with no assistance from her former husband, who was well able to support her. Periodical payments were ordered.[79] Similarly, in *Beynon v Beynon*,[80] the marriage lasted for 24 years during which time the wife had made substantial contribution to looking after a daughter and the family. On divorce the wife had little capital and was too old to work. The husband was ordered to pay her maintenance. Again, in *Moss v Moss*,[81] the marriage lasted for 28 years. The wife was nine years older than the husband. She was in ill-health and could not be expected to be in gainful employment. It was held that maintenance was needed to support her at a standard of living that reflected the resources available to the husband.

Where resources permit, a husband may offer to 'buy out' the wife by providing a lump sum which capitalises his periodical payments obligations.[82] Furthermore, periodical payments are unlikely where the wife has already obtained a fair share of the family assets. For instance, where the parties' major asset is the matrimonial home and this has been transferred to the wife, the court may decide that the generous capital order suffices to relieve the husband of any obligation to make continuing provision for her.[83]

Indeed, a capital order by way of a lump sum is sometimes preferred to periodical payments. Firstly, where a relationship is embittered, periodical payments are to be avoided.[84] Secondly, where evidence indicates that a husband does not have the ability or the intention to discharge his obligations, periodical payments would be inappropriate.[85] Further, it has been said that a lump sum was preferable at times of political uncertainty or economy volatility.[86] Capital order means that the parties' positions

---

[78] [1988] 1 FLR 282.
[79] *Barrett v Barrett* [1988] 2 FLR 516.
[80] District Court, Divorce Jurisdiction, Action No 614 of 1975 (1977).
[81] Court of Appeal, Civil Appeal Action No 145 of 1992 (1993).
[82] *Attar v Attar (No 2)* [1985] FLR 653; *Boylan v Boylan* [1988] 1 FLR 282; *Leadbeater v Leadbeater* [1985] FLR 789.
[83] *Suter v Suter* [1987] 2 All ER 336; *Clutton v Clutton* [1991] 1 FLR 242; *Hamlett v Hamlett* [1996] 1 HKC 61.
[84] See *Page v Page* [1981] 2 FLR 198.
[85] *Chan Chuck-wai v Chan Chan Yin-kwan*, District Court, Divorce Jurisdiction, Action No 245 of 1979 (1981); *Bolsom v Bolsom* [1983] 4 FLR 21.
[86] *Cheung Yuk-lin v Hui Shiu-wing (No 4)* [1970] HKLR 119.

remain unaffected by the economic or other events, for instance, if the wife dies or remarries later, the husband will not be able to seek an order for variation.[87] As periodical payments automatically terminate on remarriage and a wife who has really played a part in the marriage may deserve compensation of a capital nature, capital provision will often be more appropriate. Further consideration is that a periodical payments order for a sizeable amount may be a disincentive to remarriage for a young woman.[88]

A similar approach was adopted in *C v C*,[89] where both parties worked during the marriage and the court said that as periodical payments would automatically terminate on the wife's remarriage, it was right that a lump sum payment be made for her protection. A lump sum order may also serve to provide security to a wife in her middle age despite the fact that she is older than the husband and it is unlikely that the husband will predecease her.[90] A wife who has been provided with a lump sum, however, is not liable to account to her former husband as to how it is used, and she may gamble it all away in one day, spend it on gifts to her boyfriend, or start her own business.[91] However, a capital order would not be made if the payer is not able to pay[92] or if it would deprive the husband of working capital to start a business.[93]

A compromise between lifelong maintenance and clean break is the so-called deferred clean break or rehabilitative maintenance. This refers to maintenance for a limited term. However, it has been held that where a wife has the responsibility of caring for young children and there is real uncertainty as to her future employment, it would be wrong to prohibit her from applying for an extension of the term. Thus, in *Waterman v Waterman*,[94] the marriage lasted for only 17 months but the parties cohabited for 33 months. The wife had custody of a child under five years of age and the court ordered that periodical payments to the wife were to end in five years with no right to apply for an extension. It was held that the wife's employment opportunities were restricted whilst she had the care of the child and that there was real uncertainty as to her future employment. The prohibition to apply for an extension was therefore wrong. Similarly, in *C v C (financial relief: short marriage)*,[95] the parties met while the wife was

---

[87] See Chapter 17.
[88] *O'Donnell v O'Donnell* [1975] 2 All ER 993; *Cumbers v Cumbers* [1975] 1 All ER 1.
[89] [1977–1979] HKC 363.
[90] *Beynon v Beynon*, District Court, Divorce Jurisdiction, Action No 614 of 1975 (1977).
[91] *Gojkovic v Gojkovic* [1990] 1 FLR 140.
[92] *Fei Tai-chung v Gloria Fei*, see n. 72; *Hui I-mei v Cheng Yau-shing*, see n. 26.
[93] *Choy Kin-choy v Choy Chan Lai-ngar*, see n. 35.
[94] [1989] 1 FLR 380.
[95] [1997] 2 FLR 26.

working as a high-class prostitute. The marriage lasted only for ten months and on divorce, at the age of 40 and with the responsibility of caring for a young child of the marriage, her earning capacity was uncertain. It was held that it was inappropriate to impose a term on the periodical payments order as it was always possible for the husband to seek a variation.

QUANTIFICATION

Even if the parties agree on the approach to be adopted, they may disagree on how it will be translated into reality. There are three distinct methods of quantification.

The One-Third Rule

In most cases, meeting the needs of a dependent spouse is a top priority. In *Wachtel v Wachtel*,[96] the court used what has been called the one-third rule as a starting point in quantifying income and capital orders. As regards an income, a 'one-third' order means that a recipient spouse would receive an amount which would bring her income up to one-third of the parties' joint income.

> For instance, if the wife earns $1000 pm and the husband earns $8000, one third of the parties' joint income would be $3000. In order for the wife's income to reach $3000, the court will grant the wife a periodical payments order of $2000 pm.

In *Wachtel v Wachtel*, the marriage lasted for 18 years, and the couple had two children, a boy and a girl. The wife was responsible for looking after the family and also helped as the husband's receptionist in his dental clinic. The parties agreed that the husband and son would stay in the matrimonial home and the wife and daughter would look for alternative accommodation. At first instance, the court ordered the husband to pay to the wife half of his income and half of the capital as represented by the equity in the matrimonial home. However, the Court of Appeal held that these amounts were excessive and reduced the order, giving the wife one-third of their joint-income and one-third of the matrimonial home. The justification for this rule, as Lord Denning MR explained, was (1) a husband

---

[96] [1973] Fam 72.

would have greater expenses post-divorce and (2) a wife would need to be maintained out of her husband's income.

> When a marriage breaks up, there will thenceforward be two households instead of one. The husband will have to go out to work all day and must get some woman to look after the house — either a wife, if he remarried, or a housekeeper, if he does not. He will also have to provide maintenance for the children. The wife will not usually have so much expense. She may go out to work herself, but she will not usually employ a housekeeper. She will do most of the housework herself, perhaps with some help. Or she may remarry, in which case her new husband will provide for her. In any case, when there are two households, the greater expenses will, in most cases, fall on the husband than the wife . . .

The one-third rule is only a rule of thumb or a starting point and is not meant to be an arithmetical approach overshadowing the discretionary power of the court. Although the rule has been criticised,[97] it has been applied in *Hudson v Hudson*,[98] where the parties divorced after 24 years of marriage during which the wife worked intermittently and looked after the children. The court applied the one-third ratio both to periodical payments and to the capital assets to cater for the needs of the wife to have a nest egg to meet any sudden contingencies as her earning capacity diminished with the approach of old age. However, in *Hon To Lai-chu v Hon Wing-chun*,[99] the Court of Appeal held that one-third was the starting point for a lump sum payment even though there were no periodical payments to the wife as envisaged in *Wachtel v Wachtel*.[100] In 1991, in *Cheung Wong Kim-ching v Cheung Chai-kong*,[101] the Court of Appeal held that the one-third rule did not apply to a case where the matrimonial home was jointly owned by the parties but it was used as a starting point for periodical payments.[102]

Where the parties are very wealthy, the one-third rule is not suitable because it gives the wife more than what would be required to meet her reasonable needs.[103] The one-third rule is not suitable where the husband is the applicant.[104]

---

[97] *Stockford v Stockford* [1982] 3 FLR 58; *Furniss v Furniss* [1982] 3 FLR 46; *Slater v Slater* [1982] 3 FLR 364.
[98] District Court, Divorce Jurisdiction, Action No 1223 of 1980 (date of judgment unknown).
[99] [1985] HKLR 490.
[100] See also *C v C* [1977–1979] HKC 363.
[101] [1991] 1 HKLR 698.
[102] *Moss v Moss*, see n. 81; *Hui I-mei v Cheng Yau-shing*, see n. 26.
[103] *C v C* [1990] 2 HKLR 183; *Page v Page* [1981] 2 FLR 198.
[104] *Griffiths v Griffiths* [1974] 1 All ER 932; *Calderbank v Calderbank* [1976] Fam 93; *P v P (financial provision: lump sum)* [1978] 3 All ER 70; *B v B (financial provision)* [1982] 3 FLR 298; *Burgess v Burgess* [1996] 2 FLR 34.

Net Effect Approach

This involves calculating the effect of a proposed order but it does not provide a proposed order as such. The court calculates the parties' available resources and then makes deductions of all items reflecting the parties' needs and liabilities, including liability under the proposed order. The balance of the parties' resources can then be compared, and the hypothetical order adjusted accordingly. In *Cheung Wong Kim-ching v Cheung Chai-kong*,[105] the Court of Appeal emphasised the importance of producing calculations to demonstrate the net effect of any order for financial provision and property adjustment. In Hong Kong, no tax deduction is available for maintenance payable, nor is maintenance treated as taxable in the hands of the recipient.[106]

Taking *Wachtel v Wachtel* as an example, the net effect approach provides a tabular impression of the standard of living of the parties post-divorce. Note that the husband was to have custody of the boy and the wife, the girl.

Husband's financial position			Wife's financial position	
Husband's earnings p.a.		£6000	Wife's income p.a.	£750
Less:			*Add:*	
Wife's maintenance	£1500		Wife's maintenance	£1500
Maintenance	£300		Daughter's maintenance	£300
interest repayment	£450	£2250		
Amount remaining for husband and son		£3750	Amount for wife and daughter	£2250
Husband's accommodation			Wife's accommodation	
Value of the matrimonial home less mortgage £8000			Lump sum of about £6000	

The Duxbury Calculation

In cases where the husband is wealthy and a lump sum payment is envisaged, an appropriate lump sum should be paid to cater for a wife's 'reasonable requirements' and should enable the recipient to expend it by drawing both upon the capital and by relying on the income which it may yield.

---

[105] *Cheung Wong Kim-ching v Cheung Chai-kong* [1991] 1 HKLR 698; *Slater v Slater* [1982] 3 FLR 364; *Stockford v Stockford* [1982] 3 FLR 58.
[106] Inland Revenue Ordinance, s8(2)(i).

The Duxbury calculation is a useful tool in achieving this outcome. It refers to the use of an actuarial exercise for calculating a lump sum which, if invested, would produce enough to meet the recipients needs for life, taking into account factors such as life expectancy, rates of inflation, growth of capital, and return on investment.[107] *Duxbury v Duxbury*[108] was the first case in which this method of computing a lump sum award was used. However, in *Gojkovic v Gojkovic*,[109] it was said that Duxbury was no more than a useful guide and could not be elevated to a rigid mathematical formula for producing a sum to which a wife was entitled.[110]

STATUTORY GUIDELINES

S7(1) of the MPPO provides a list of the matters to which the court should have regard in exercising its powers. They relate to the duration of the marriage, and to the standard of living, financial position, health and contribution (financial or otherwise) of the parties to the marriage. Some of these factors relate to the present, others are retrospective or prospective in nature. The extent to which the court will look to the past and future, however, is a matter of judicial discretion.

Income, Earning Capacity, Property and Other Financial Resources Which Each of the Parties to the Marriage Has or Is Likely to Have in the Foreseeable Future

Affidavit of means

In order for the court to ascertain the parties' income, earning capacity, property and other financial resources, the parties must swear an affidavit of means. A party who refuses to do so will be ordered to file an affidavit containing such particulars.[111] Preparing an affidavit of means can be time-consuming and expensive, particularly where the parties are wealthy and

---

[107] *B v B (financial provision)* [1990] 1 FLR 20 at p. 24 per Ward J.
[108] Trevor Reeve J unreported; [1987] 1 FLR 7.
[109] [1990] 1 FLR 140.
[110] *B v B (financial provision)* [1990] 1 FLR 20; *F v F (Duxbury calculation: rate of return)* [1996] 1 FLR 833.
[111] R73(2) of the Matrimonial Causes Rules.

have assets distributed worldwide. The question of what details of property and income are to be included in the affidavit therefore needs to be approached with common sense and pragmatism.

In *H v H*,[112] the husband stated in his affidavit of means that he had 'net realisable assets of, or in excess of, US$100 million and a commensurate income'. His affidavit stated that he could not particularize his assets but that he possessed sufficient to satisfy any order which the court might reasonably make in favour of the wife. This is the so-called 'millionaire's defence'. The Court of Appeal held that the husband's affidavit failed to provide particulars upon which the court could act under s7(1) of the MPPO. There was not 'one rule for multi-millionaires and another for less wealthy men when it comes to compliance with the rules'.[113] The husband was ordered to file a further affidavit of means.

What counts as sufficient particulars was considered in two Court of Appeal cases. In *Tao Chen Pi-o v Tai Hsiuo-ming*,[114] the husband described himself as a 'merchant' and stated that his total capital assets were worth at least HK$104 million. In a schedule, he set out an estimated valuation of his real properties. He further deposed that he had cash in the bank and two cars worth in total about HK$3.3 million. At the end of his affirmation, he said that he had 'no liquidity problems and could meet any order of the court for the reasonable requirements of the wife and the children'. The Court of Appeal held that the information provided by the husband failed to provide the minimal degree of disclosure required under Rule 73(2) of the Matrimonial Causes Rules, and he was ordered to provide further particulars.

The decision of *Tao Chen Pi-o v Tai Hsiuo-ming* does not mean that a wife is entitled to conduct a microscopic investigation of the husband's financial affairs, which could be highly oppressive and might amount to invasion of privacy (for which an order for costs could not compensate).[115] Where a husband's financial affairs are highly complex, a microscopic investigation is not necessary.

> It is important in these family matters to avoid microscopic investigations and costly valuations which put further strains upon the resources of the parties, heighten the emotional climate and risk indirectly harming the interests of the children.[116]

---

[112] [1981] HKLR 376.
[113] Ibid., p. 383.
[114] Court of Appeal, Civil Appeal Action Nos 37 and 38 of 1993 (1993).
[115] See *Law Lo Shiu-chun v Law Wing-chee*, Court of Appeal, Civil Appeal Action No 130 of 1993 (1994).
[116] *Tao Chen Pi-o v Tai Hsiuo-ming* per Litton, JA.

As Bokhary JA noted in *Tao Chen Pi-o v Tai Hsiuo-ming*:

> Since circumstances vary so greatly from case to case, sufficiency does not readily lend itself to further definition. But, upon a level-headed consideration of the broad circumstances of each case, it should not be too difficult to recognize. If a party does not make sufficient disclosure, the court will, at the instance of the opposite party, compel him to do so. If, on the other hand, he does make sufficient disclosure, the court will protect him from the harassment of any application for further disclosure which the opposite party may make.

Thus, in *Law Lo Shiu-chun v Law Ying-chee*,[117] the husband pleaded the millionaire's defence. At first instance, the court held that the husband failed to provide particulars required by Rule 73(2) of the Matrimonial Causes Rules. The Court of Appeal disagreed. The husband affirmed that he had given HK$22.5 million to his wife, and that he was worth about HK$100 million, amounts that were not disputed by the wife. It was held that no further particulars of the husband's property or income would be necessary for the purposes of s7(1) of the MPPO.[118]

In the recent English case of *Van G v Van G (financial provision: millionaire's defence)*, the husband pleaded the millionaire's defence, provided no information as to his income, and none as to how many properties he owned, where they were, and how much they were worth. It was held that he failed to provide the minimum information required and was ordered, *inter alia,* to provide an estimate as to his income and a summary of all assets worth over £100 000.[119]

Where a party has failed to make full and frank disclosure as to his income, property and any other financial resources, the court is entitled to draw inferences against him[120] and may penalise him in exercising its discretion over costs.

Income and earning capacity

The court will take into account a husband's income and will not make an order which is beyond his means,[121] looking rather at the realities of the

---

[117] Court of Appeal, Civil Appeal Action No 130 of 1993 (1994).
[118] See *Attar v Attar* [1985] FLR 653; *Thyssen-Bornemisza v Thyssen-Bornemisza (No 2)* [1985] FLR 1069; *B v B (discovery: financial provision)* [1990] 2 FLR 180.
[119] [1995] 1 FLR 328; *Dart v Dart* [1996] 2 FLR 286.
[120] *Payne v Payne* [1968] 1 WLR 390; *Ette v Ette* [1964] 1 WLR 1433; *Wong Yiu-lan v Wong Yuen-ting* [1995] 1 HKLR 411.
[121] *Law Shi-ying v Law Kam-tai,* Court of Appeal, Civil Appeal Action No 45 of 1994 (1994). 'Income' which the court takes into account is net of tax.

parties' financial situation. They are not concerned with what a man is shown to have, but what he could have had if he had so chosen. A man who has very little taxable income will be assessed as having what would have been available to him by borrowings secured, for instance, on his properties.[122] Furthermore, a husband's earning capacity would be taken into account if he could have secured employment. Thus, in *McEwan v McEwan*,[123] the husband retired at age 59 and his only income was a pension of £6 per week. The court ordered him to pay that amount to the wife as he could have obtained employment if he had wished.

Where a wife is young and has children to look after, it would be unreasonable to expect her to be financially self-sufficient. However, where a woman does not have child care responsibilities, her husband will not be expected to provide her with 'a meal ticket for life', even if she were to start working in her mid-forties. Thus, in *Baillieu v Baillieu*, the marriage lasted for six years and there were no children. The wife was 44 and had worked as a typist. She suffered from repetitive strain injury and could not work as a typist, but this did not mean that she was unemployable. The court concluded that she could retain employment that would provide a proper income. The reasons given were:

> First, because of the manner in which the [wife] has prepared for and conducted this hearing. Unrepresented and unassisted she has made light of the problems of coping in court, with giving evidence, conducting cross-examination and keeping abreast of many files and documents as they were referred to . . . Second, the [husband] complained that the [wife] . . . did not give him wifely support in relation to his family . . . In response the [wife] was astute to refer to the housework she had done . . . to the cleaning up after and caring for the [husband's] brother and cousin when they stayed for long periods, and to the hundreds of dinner parties and functions she had attended or given since coming to Hong Kong. All that speaks of a lady well able to make her own way in the world.[124]

Similarly, in *Murphy v Murphy*,[125] the marriage lasted for 18 years and there were four teenage children. Prior to the first child being born the wife had had three years' experience as a nurse. Although the wife, 40 years old, had never been expected to be entirely self-sufficient, she started a business with a friend. The court noted her earning capacity as a trained nurse, possessing skills which 'seemed to be always and universally in

---

[122] *J.-P.C. v J.-A.F.* [1955] P. 215.
[123] [1972] 1 WLR 1217.
[124] See n. 74.
[125] Court of Appeal, Civil Appeal Action No 56 of 1992 (1992).

demand', holding that she could be expected to earn $10 000 pm which could cover her non-accommodation needs.

Property and other financial resources they are likely to have in the foreseeable future

This is not restricted to the parties' 'family assets', which means things acquired by either or both of the parties with the intention that there should be continuing provision for them and their children during their joint lives.[126] The phrase 'family assets', however, is sometimes used as a shorthand phrase referring to property which is amenable to s7(1) consideration.

Unlike the meaning of the word in s6 of the MPPO,[127] 'property' is not restricted to assets to which a party to the marriage is entitled either in possession or reversion. It includes property and other financial resources which a party has or is likely to have in the foreseeable future. Thus, it has been held to include damages for personal injuries recovered by one spouse, whether the damages are awarded for loss of future earnings or for pain and suffering.[128] It includes real and personal property, property acquired before the marriage, after the marriage, or inherited by one of the parties.[129] Future interests include an interest under a settlement,[130] a monthly savings-plan scheme, pension entitlement, and accrued surrender value of an insurance policy.[131] All these may be taken into account and, where they are, their inclusion may affect the lump sum which the court may order in favour of the wife. Thus, in *Priest v Priest*,[132] the husband would be eligible for a gratuity in five years' time. The gratuity would be large if he continued to work beyond the five years. The Court of Appeal held that the husband should pay a portion of the cash that he had in hand. Further, taking into account his prospect of receiving his gratuity on retirement, he was also ordered to pay a lump sum amounting to one-third of the gratuity, payment to be made on receipt of such gratuity.[133] In *Wong Sin-yee v Cheung Si-*

---

[126] *Wachtel v Wachtel* [1973] Fam 72.
[127] See above, pp. 367–368.
[128] See *Daubney v Daubney* [1976] 2 All ER 453; *Pritchard v Cobden* [1987] 2 FLR 56; *Wagstaff v Wagstaff* [1992] 1 FLR 333; *C v C (financial provision: personal damages)* [1995] 2 FLR 171.
[129] *Dennis v Dennis* (1976) 6 Fam Law 54.
[130] Settlements under which a spouse is a beneficiary although they are not under his/her absolute control, *B v B (financial provision)* [1982] 3 FLR 298.
[131] *Bennett v Bennett* (1979) 9 Fam Law 19.
[132] [1979] 9 FLR 252.
[133] Cf. *Roberts v Roberts* [1986] 2 All ER 483; *Milne v Milne* [1981] 2 FLR 286.

yan,[134] the Court of Appeal upheld an order that the husband pay the wife 30 percent of his provident fund when it fell due in 15 years' time.[135]

The case of *Schuller v Schuller*[136] serves as a good example of the broad scope of this factor, and, more importantly, how resources acquired after the decree absolute may be taken into account. In that case, the parties parted after 21 years of marriage. The wife then went to work as a housekeeper for an elderly friend. On the death of this friend, the wife inherited a flat and became the residual beneficiary of his estate. The husband remained in the matrimonial home which represented the parties' major asset. On the application by the wife for a lump sum representing 50 percent of the matrimonial home, the court took into account the capital which she had acquired from her friend's estate and reduced her share to 6 percent of the value of the matrimonial home.

Other future contingent interests may include the possibility of future inheritance. However, as the prospect is uncertain as to whether and when an interest under a will may accrue, it may not be possible for such an interest to be taken into account. It has been held that this uncertainty cannot be mitigated by the court compelling a third party to give evidence of his testamentary intentions or to disclose his wealth.[137] In the case of a will, where there is clear evidence that the testator will die in the near future, and he has left a substantial (but uncertain) amount of property to the respondent, and it is highly probable that he will not revoke his will, it would be appropriate to adjourn the application to await the death of the testator.[138] Such a case, however, will be rare. Where it appears that one spouse may acquire a sum of money in the not-too-distant future, instead of the court pressing on to deal with a spouse's application, it may be possible to adjourn some or all of the application to be heard at a later date when the parties' position is clear. For instance, in *MT v MT (financial provision: lump sum)*,[139] the marriage lasted for 20 years and for many years the parties lived beyond their means, a lifestyle which was supported by money from the husband's maternal grandmother. On divorce, the husband had no assets. The husband's father was a man of considerable wealth and was 83 years old. On his death, the husband would automatically be entitled to a share in his estate, although the exact amount was unclear. It was held that the wife's lump sum application would be adjourned since there was a

---

[134] Court of Appeal, Civil Appeal Action No 222 of 1996 (1997).
[135] *Cheung Wong Kim-ching v Cheung Chai-kong* [1991] HKLR 698.
[136] [1990] 2 FLR 193.
[137] *Morgan v Morgan* [1977] 2 All ER 515.
[138] *Michael v Michael* [1986] 2 FLR 389.
[139] [1992] 1 FLR 362.

real possibility of capital from a specific source becoming available in the near future and justice demanded that the wife should receive a share commensurate with her needs and with the amount of capital available. However, in *Lai Lai-hing v Lai Kwai-ping*,[140] adjournment for three and a half years was held to be not necessary in that finality could be achieved so that the parties knew exactly where they stood financially.[141]

Resources of cohabitees and second wife

Income, earning capacity, property and financial resources cover those of the parties to a marriage, not those of a cohabitee or a second wife. Periodical payments can be made out of a husband's income and resources, but not out of the income of his cohabitee or second wife.[142] However, the income of a cohabitee or a second wife is relevant if the husband derives some benefits from them. For example, due to the partner's contribution to living or household expenses, the husband might be relieved of expenditure which he might otherwise have incurred; the husband is thus left with a greater proportion of his income available for payment of the periodical payments order.[143]

In *Suter v Suter*,[144] the wife and children stayed in the matrimonial home. Her boyfriend, a Mr Jones, spent every night there but returned to his mother's home for breakfast. The wife did not ask him for any money and he made no financial contribution for the household. In considering how much the husband should pay the wife by way of periodical payments, it was held that Mr Jones was in a position to contribute for the amenities he enjoyed in the furnished residence. Although the court could not order him to pay for these amenities, a notional value of his contribution was given such that it relieved the husband of his maintenance obligation towards the wife. In *Hamlett v Hamlett*,[145] the husband's new wife was working and was in receipt of a good income, prompting the court to remark that 'no doubt she will make some financial contribution towards expenses.'[146] Again, in *Atkinson v Atkinson*,[147] the parties divorced after 22 years of marriage during which the husband had established a successful business, the parties enjoyed an affluent lifestyle during marriage. On divorce,

---

[140] See n. 71.
[141] *Roberts v Roberts* [1986] 2 All ER 483.
[142] *Macey v Macey* [1982] 3 FLR 7; *Slater v Slater* [1982] 3 FLR 364.
[143] *Macey v Macey*, ibid.
[144] [1987] 2 All ER 336.
[145] [1996] 1 HKC 61.
[146] Ibid., at p. 66; see also *Moss v Moss*, n. 81.
[147] [1988] FLR 353.

generous periodical payments were made to the wife. Five years after divorce, the wife aged 49, and with no prospect of employment, was living with a man on a permanent basis. It was found that the wife's periodical payments income was greater than that of the boyfriend and the couple were mutually dependent on their combined incomes to maintain their lifestyle, the greater contribution coming from the wife. If they were to marry, the wife would lose her periodical payments as an income so their decision not to marry was financially motivated. The husband was in a position to continue periodical payments but he argued that in view of the wife's cohabitation, they should be progressively reduced to a nominal amount. He contended that the law would be seen to be 'an ass' if the couple were permitted to have a 'good life' at the expense of the ex-husband. The Court of Appeal held that the law did not provide that settled cohabitation be equated with remarriage which would disentitle the wife from anything more than nominal maintenance. In this case, because the ex-wife had no means of generating income herself, it would be inappropriate to discontinue maintenance or progressively reduce it to a nominal sum.

As regards capital orders, it has been said that cohabitation and the prospect of remarriage, where such prospect are based purely on guesswork, should not be taken into account. In *Wachtel v Wachtel*, Lord Denning took the view that:

> So far as capital assets are concerned, we see no reason for reducing her share. After all, she has earned a share by her contribution in looking after the home and caring for the family. It should not be taken away from her by the prospect of remarriage.[148]

Thus, in *Duxbury v Duxbury*,[149] a husband appealed against a lump sum and property transfer order. He argued that the judge had failed to consider the wife's cohabitation with another man. The Court of Appeal held that it was right not to take such circumstances into account. The court had to consider what were the reasonable needs of the wife and how she decided to use the money was her business. If she decided to have an impecunious friend or relative to live with her, it would be for her to defray that expense from her income which had been assessed to be appropriate for her needs alone.

But this may not always be the case. In *H v H (financial provision: remarriage)*,[150] the marriage ended after 15 years, during which the wife

---

[148] [1973] Fam 72 at p. 96; see also *Trippas v Trippas* [1973] Fam 134; *Marsden v Marsden* [1973] 2 All ER 851.
[149] [1987] 1 FLR 7.
[150] [1975] 1 All ER 367.

had been a good wife and mother to the four children. On divorce, both parties remarried. The capital position of the wife's new husband was roughly the same as her previous husband's had been, and there was no great disparity between the incomes of the two men. The wife claimed that she was entitled to an equal share in the former matrimonial home. However, the Court of Appeal held that as her second husband had conveyed their new home into their joint names, and she was supported by her second husband, her share in the former matrimonial home was reduced from what would otherwise be one-half to one-third. Reasoning along similar lines, accommodation provided by a new spouse or partner has been taken into account.[151]

Financial Needs, Obligations and Responsibilities Which Each of the Parties to the Marriage Had or Is Likely to Have in the Foreseeable Future

Financial Needs

The financial needs of the parties often relate to the parties' age, health, special needs (if any) and to earning capacity. Where available resources are limited, 'financial needs' refers to those most urgent needs of the parties — a home and day-to-day expenses. Thus, in *Hui I-mei v Cheng Yau-shing*, the paramount concern of the court was to provide the children and the custodial parent with a roof over their heads.[152] Similarly, in *Moss v Moss*, the court's main concern was to provide the wife of 20 years with a home and with sufficient resources to meet her daily needs.[153] In such a case, evidence concerning property prices and mortgage facilities is crucial.[154]

Where the parties are wealthy, 'financial needs' covers not only daily necessities but also 'reasonable requirements'.[155] In *Preston v Preston*, it was said that the wife was entitled to have a home at the top end of the market and probably a second home in the country or abroad, together with a very high spending power.[156] In *Dart v Dart*, it was held that 'reasonable requirements' extend to homes, children and lifestyle.[157] In

---

[151] *Mesher v Mesher* [1980] 1 All ER 126; *Martin (BH) v Martin (D)* [1978] Fam 12.
[152] See n. 114; *Wong Yiu-lan v Wong Yuen-ting* [1995] 1 HKLR 411; *Wong Sin-yee v Cheung Si-yan* Court of Appeal, Civil Appeal Action No 22 of 1996 (1997).
[153] See n. 81.
[154] *Cheung Wong Kim-ching v Cheung Chai-kong* [1991] 1 HKLR 698.
[155] *Page v Page* [1981] 2 FLR 198.
[156] [1982] Fam 17.
[157] [1996] 2 FLR 286.

Cheung Yuk-lin v Hui Shiu-wing (No 4), it was said that this included capital reserves for rainy days.[158]

A party to a marriage is not entitled to apply for a financial provision or property adjustment order if she has remarried.[159] The word 'apply' refers to the initiation of the proceedings, not to the time when the application is to be heard.[160] Where an application has been made before the party remarries, the court has jurisdiction to make an order even after the remarriage has taken place. Special needs may arise out of physical handicap or disability. In *Jones v Jones*,[161] it was held that an order requiring the husband to transfer his interest in the matrimonial home to the wife, stipulating that he was to receive one-fifth of the proceeds of sale when the children became independent, gave insufficient consideration to the wife's disabilities. Similarly, in *S v S*,[162] a child suffering from kidney problems was totally dependent on the wife. It was held that the entire interest in the matrimonial home should be transferred to the wife.

Obligations: moral or legal

'Obligations' refers to obligations of both spouses and means a husband's duty to maintain his wife and *vice versa*.[163] Husband and wife come to the judgment seat in matters of money and property upon a basis of complete equality.[164] Where a husband has remarried, his second wife is presumed to have taken the other partner subject to all existing encumbrances.

'Obligations' is not confined to legally enforceable obligation, and includes moral obligations. A man's obligations to maintain his cohabitees and their children is a relevant factor. However, the claim of a cohabitee on her partner's financial resources would rarely be ranked as superior to that of the ex-wife.[165] In a Chinese society like Hong Kong, it has been said that it is understandable that sons will feel a strong obligation to maintain their parents so the parents' maintenance would be taken into account.[166]

---

[158] [1970] HKLR 119.
[159] S9(4) MPPO.
[160] *Jackson v Jackson* [1973] Fam 99; *Jenkins v Hargood* [1978] 3 All ER 1001.
[161] [1976] Fam 8.
[162] [1976] Fam 18.
[163] See s8 MPPO for a duty by a spouse to maintain the other.
[164] *Calderbank v Calderbank* [1976] Fam 93.
[165] *Roberts v Roberts* [1970] P. 1. It was said that 'all the circumstances' included moral obligations which were not legally enforceable. See also *Blower v Blower* (1986) 16 Fam Law 56.
[166] But they would not be brought into account, see *Cheung Wong Kim-ching v Cheung Chai-kong* [1991] 1 HKLR 698; see also the Maintenance of Parents Ordinance in Singapore which came into effect on 1 June 1996.

Standard of Living Enjoyed by the Family before the Breakdown of the Marriage

In the case of families of moderate means, divorce inevitably brings about a reduction in standard of living as limited income has to be shared by two households. However, where the parties are affluent, divorce need not entail a reduction in the parties' standard of living and,[167] as a general rule, a wife can expect to be maintained post-divorce at the same standard as that to which she has been accustomed during her marriage. But what if a wealthy couple adopts a frugal way of life which is not commensurate with their wealth? Is the wife prejudiced when it comes to financial provision and property adjustment? Can the husband argue that since her standard of living was moderate during marriage, she should be maintained at the same standard post-divorce? In *Preston v Preston*, Ormrod LJ said that it would be anomalous for a wife who accepted a frugal way of life in the hope that the family would benefit, to receive a reduced lump sum.[168] In *Preston v Preston*, the husband left the wife and started living with another woman and it was said that regard should be had to the husband's post-divorce standard of living. In *Cheung Yuk-lin v Hui Shui-wing (No 4)*, the Court of Appeal interpreted 'standard of living' liberally, ruling that 'standard of living' was not limited to 'day-to-day' standard of living. It covered not only the size of the house occupied, the amount of quality food consumed, the size of the car used and jewellery possessed, but also the capital assets and financial security available as a cushion for rainy days.[169] Where a wife had made substantial sacrifices throughout the marriage in the expectation that goods days were coming, she would be entitled to a fair share of the fruits of her frugality.[170]

However, a wife may not be able to maintain her pre-divorce standard of living post-divorce. This may be particularly so when housing is expensive. In *Wong Yiu-lan v Wong Yuen-ting*,[171] the parties were in their forties. After 14 years of marriage, the wife left the matrimonial home with three children and they lived in a flat of 30 square metres. During the marriage, the parties lifestyle had been luxurious, the family having lived in a four-bedroom apartment with domestic helper's quarters. The parties

---

[167] *Calderbank v Calderbank* [1976] Fam 93 where the couple enjoyed a high standard of living supported by the wife's capital resources. The wife was ordered to pay £10 000 (1/8th) of her capital to enable the husband to buy a house suitable to his station in life and to the standard of living the parties had adopted during their marriage.
[168] [1982] Fam 17 at p. 25.
[169] See n. 86.
[170] *Dean v Dean* [1923] P. 172.
[171] [1995] 1 HKLR 411.

wanted a clean break and the husband was ordered to pay the wife a sum of HK$3.8 million. It was argued that the flat was too small for the wife and the children. However, it was said that should the property be too small, the wife would be able to sell it and would have HK$3.8 million with which to buy or rent a larger flat. Compare this outcome with *Fei Tai-chung v Gloria Fei*,[172] in which the matrimonial home was purchased for HK$2.47 million. The wife had made substantial contributions towards its purchase by way of initial deposit and it was almost exclusively she who paid off the mortgage. On divorce, it was agreed that the husband was to stay in the matrimonial home which was now worth HK$14 million. The husband was earning HK$100 000 per month but he had no liquid assets to pay the wife a lump sum. The Court of Appeal held that to require the husband to raise a loan of HK$5.6 million, a lump sum ordered by the lower court, would require him to make a monthly repayment of HK$75 000 and this would significantly reduce his standard of living, placing an unacceptable burden on him. The sum was reduced to HK$4 million.

Age of Each Party to the Marriage and the Duration of the Marriage

There is no hard-and-fast rule as to what constitutes a short or a long marriage, nor is it clear how exactly duration affects the outcome of a case. In the case of a three-year marriage, it was said that:

> I do not think . . . that this can be properly be classed as a short marriage. Of course, it was not a very long marriage. I am not seeking to lay down what is short, what is not very short, what is not very long, and what is long: that would be trying to define the length of a piece of string.[173]

It has been held that a marriage of under five years' duration may not be regarded as a long marriage. Thus, in *Leadbeater v Leadbeater*, a four-and-a-half-year marriage attracted a 25 percent discount on the lump sum, which otherwise was held to be payable.[174] In *Attar v Attar (No 2)*,[175] the marriage lasted for six months. The husband was a millionaire and the wife was an air-hostess. They cohabited only for seven weeks. It was held that where the marriage was short and the parties had no children, one relevant

---

[172] Court of Appeal, Civil Appeal Action No 170 of 1994 (1995).
[173] *Gengler v Gengler* [1976] 2 All ER 81 at p. 82.
[174] [1985] FLR 789.
[175] [1985] FLR 653.

consideration was to put the wife in the position she would have been in had she not married. To that extent, the court needed to consider her reasonable needs and the effect the marriage had upon her. In this case, the wife had given up her job (with a salary of £15 000 pa) at the request of the husband. As she was only 27 years old and was able to work, the court granted her financial support for a duration of two years to rehabilitate herself. Taking into account her pre-marital income, the court ordered a lump sum payment of £30 000 as full and final settlement of her claims against the husband.[176]

In *Baillieu v Baillieu,* duration of the marriage was considered less important. The wife was 44 years old with no children. The marriage lasted for six years and it was argued that it was not a short marriage. The court held that the real issue was not whether the marriage was long or short, but whether

> the wife [was] entitled to relief on the basis that she was a person who could never find employment which would remunerate her at a level which would allow her to live in the style established by the marriage or whether the relief must take into account a capacity, in due course, to "make her own way in the world".[177]

The court adopted the latter approach.

However, in *S v S,*[178] the court looked closely at the effect the marriage had on both the parties. In that case, the parties were in their late fifties at the time of the marriage. Prior to the marriage, the wife had a full-time job and lived in her own house. After marriage, she had worked only part-time and sold her house, giving the bulk of the proceeds to her son. She thus had no capital of her own. Although the marriage lasted for only two years, the Court of Appeal held that but for the marriage, she would have been living in her own house, continuing her full-time employment, earning a larger income and receiving a larger pension. Whilst the court was not attempting to put her in the position she would have been in had there been no marriage, these were all the factors which the court had to bear in mind in making an order which was just in all the circumstances of the case. Again, in the rather unusual case of *C v C (financial relief: short marriage),*[179] the parties met while the wife was working as a high-class prostitute; she was 35 and he was 54. The marriage lasted for only ten

---

[176] *H v H (financial provision: short marriage)* [1981] 2 FLR 392; *C v C (financial relief: short marriage)* [1997] 2 FLR 26.
[177] Court of Appeal, Civil Appeal Action No 149 of 1995 (1995).
[178] [1977] 1 All ER 56.
[179] [1997] 2 FLR 26.

months. On divorce, at the age of 40 and with the responsibility of caring for a young child of the marriage, the wife's earning capacity was uncertain. It was held that the marriage had the effect of causing long-term prejudice to the wife's earning capacity, and it was said that:

> Had the marriage not supervened, the wife would ultimately have been in possession of greater capital and [greater] assets than she was capable of achieving, in the absence of the order I have made.[180]

A relatively generous lump sum of £195 000 and a periodical payment of £19 500 was ordered in light of the uncertainty of the wife's employment position. However, a case with very different facts was *Krystman v Krystman*.[181] The husband and wife cohabited only for a fortnight after a 'shotgun' wedding, but the marriage nevertheless lasted for 26 years. Throughout those years, the wife lived on her own resources. The Court of Appeal held that no financial provision was to be ordered for the wife.[182]

A couple may cohabit for many years before they enter into matrimony which then breaks down after a short time. In many instances, however, a claimant might have contributed extensively to the relationship during the long period of cohabitation. In such a case, 'duration of marriage' would not cover any period of cohabitation prior to marriage. As was said in one case:

> it is the ceremony of marriage and the sanctity of marriage which count; rights and duties and obligations begin on the marriage and not before.[183]

In *Kokosinski v Kokosinski*,[184] the parties were prevented from matrimony for 24 years because the man had not been freed from his first marriage. During the long years of cohabitation, the woman gave the best years of her life to the man and was a faithful, loving and hardworking partner. When the couple finally wed, the marriage broke down after four months. The Court of Appeal held that the wife had earned herself parts of the family business which she had helped to build up. To ignore her contribution during those years of cohabitation would offend a reasonable person's sense of justice.[185]

---

[180] Ibid., at p. 40.
[181] [1973] 1 WLR 927.
[182] See also *Taylor v Taylor* (1974) 119 SJ 30. A very short marriage, the wife earning twice as much as the husband, no financial provision was made for the wife.
[183] *Campbell v Campbell* [1977] 1 All ER 1 at p. 6.
[184] [1980] 1 All ER 1106.
[185] *Campbell v Campbell* [1977] All ER 1; *Foley v Foley* [1981] Fam 160; *Hill v Hill* [1997] 1 FLR 730.

Any Physical or Mental Disability of Either of the Parties to the Marriage

These factors are closely related to the parties' age and needs.

Contributions Made by Each of the Parties to the Welfare of the Family, Including Any Contribution Made by Looking after the Home or Caring for the Family

A spouse's contribution to the welfare of the family includes past, present and future contributions.[186] Contribution includes both financial (e.g. by way of bringing home an income) and non-financial contribution (e.g. by way of looking after the home and the children). In *H v H (financial provision: remarriage)*,[187] the marriage lasted for 15 years and the wife bore four children. When the marriage broke down, she left the matrimonial home for another man. The wife argued that she had, over the years, been a good mother and wife and had earned a share of the matrimonial home. Sir George Baker P said that '. . . if the job is left unfinished you do not earn as much'. Hence, her share in the matrimonial home was reduced from one-third to one-twelfth. This view is no longer adopted. Indeed, Lord Denning had earlier said in *Wachtel v Wachtel*:

> . . . we may take it that Parliament recognised that the wife who looks after the home and family contributes as much to the family assets as the wife who goes out to work. The one contributes in kind. The other in money or money's worth. If the court comes to the conclusion that the home has been acquired and maintained by the joint efforts of both, then, when the marriage breaks down, it should be regarded as the joint property of both of them, no matter in whose name it stands.[188]

Lord Denning appears to suggest that a wife who looks after the home and children makes a contribution equal to that of a husband-breadwinner. He continues:

> Just as the wife who makes substantial money contributions usually gets a share, so should the wife who looks after the home and cares for the family for 20 years.[189]

---

[186] *Ngai Wong Yun-ping v Ngai Yun-lung*, Court of Appeal, Civil Appeal Action No 50 of 1996 (1996).
[187] [1975] 1 All ER 367.
[188] [1973] Fam 72 at pp. 93–4.
[189] Ibid., at p. 94.

How such contribution, whether it be past or future, is to be assessed is unclear.[190] A wife might have made a substantial contribution in the course of a short marriage. Thus, in *C v C*,[191] the parties were young, had been married for three years and had a child. During the marriage both parties worked and the wife contributed financially to the family and its upkeep. It was held that the wife had contributed both financially and non-financially to the family; she was entitled to one-third of the proceeds of the sale of the matrimonial home. Similarly, in *Hui I-mei v Cheng Yau-shing*, the parties had been married for ten years and there were two children. The wife had no qualifications but had worked as a hostess earning three times that which her husband earned. She also contributed substantially to the purchase of the matrimonial home. It was held that she had made substantial financial contribution and she was entitled to two-thirds of the matrimonial home.[192]

In another case, *C v C*,[193] the parties were extremely wealthy, their assets totalling HK$90 million, HK$60 million of which was controlled by the wife and HK$30 million by the husband. The marriage broke down after 29 years. During the marriage, the husband 'pursued a successful career as a solicitor and entrepreneur which had brought him great wealth' and the wife was 'a good wife, mother and hostess'. As most of the husband's wealth was in the wife's name, the husband was the applicant for a lump sum. The Court of Appeal ordered the wife to pay him HK$30 million.

There is, however, a difference between a wife who has made a substantial non-financial contribution to the welfare of the family by looking after the children and the home, on the one hand, and a wife who made both non-financial and financial contribution to the family.[194] When a wife has done more than simply be a good wife and mother by, for instance, making a contribution to the family business, she will have earned an additional share over and above that which is required merely to meet her needs. This additional share represents her entitlement to a share in the success of the family business. In *Preston v Preston*,[195] the marriage lasted for 23 years. At the time of the marriage the wife was 19 and the husband 27. She was a successful model and he was a travel agent. The parties started off with no capital and the wife continued to work for the first ten years of the marriage, making substantial contribution to the household expenses

---

[190] *Burgess v Burgess* [1996] 2 FLR 34.
[191] [1977–1979] HKC 363.
[192] Court of Appeal, Civil Appeal Action No 157 of 1996 (1996).
[193] [1990] 2 HKLR 183.
[194] *Burgess v Burgess* [1996] 2 FLR 34.
[195] [1982] Fam 17.

and to their growing family. The parties had three children and the wife took upon herself all responsibilities for bringing up the children. The husband spent most of his time in business, ploughing the profits back in with the result that it expanded steadily. The marriage broke down when the husband formed an association with the mother of his son's girlfriend. On divorce, the wife had no income and no assets of her own, except a half share of the matrimonial home amounting to £100 000. The husband's assets were £2.3 million and his income was £32 000 pa. The Court of Appeal upheld an award of £600 000 as a lump sum and the transfer of the husband's share of the matrimonial home to the wife. Similarly, in *Gojkovic v Gojkovic*,[196] the parties' marriage lasted for eight years with no children. Both started with very humble backgrounds but established a hotel business with the wife taking on a role as *chatelaine par excellence*. The hotel business prospered and the wife spent her time in the running of the various hotels whilst the husband successfully devoted his skills to property speculation. On divorce, the husband's wealth came to £4 million but the wife had very little. The judge described the wife's contribution as exceptional by ordinary standards, if not exceptional as measured against the husband's contribution. In terms of what was expected of them, it was found that they 'performed equally' and there was a 'quasi-partnership'. The Court of Appeal held that the wife's share was not limited to her needs, which could be met by awarding her the parties' home and £500 000, an amount which was capable of generating sufficient income for her use. As she had made exceptional contribution to the creation of the family assets, she was awarded their home, worth £295 000, together with £1 million as a lump sum, which she could use to start her hotel business.

A recent case which highlights the nature of a wife's contribution is *Smith v Smith*.[197] The parties, of modest means, were married for 33 years. It was not suggested that the contribution of either was greater than the other and together they built up a modest capital position amounting to £107 000 (mainly in the matrimonial home). On divorce the wife was granted a lump sum of £54 000. The wife committed suicide six months later and left the sum to her daughter. The husband appealed out of time seeking from the wife's estate a repayment of the lump sum except for the amount required to pay off the wife's debts and the costs of the estate. This raised the question as to the basis of the order and, if there should be a new order, how it should be reassessed. The husband argued that the order was made predominantly to cater for the wife's needs and that her death meant that they were non-existent. The wife's executors argued that a wife with no

---

[196] [1990] 1 FLR 140.
[197] [1991] 2 All ER 306.

needs was nonetheless entitled to have her contribution recognised. The Court of Appeal held that a significant proportion of the lump sum had been awarded to meet the needs of the wife and that, being deceased, she no longer had any such needs. The husband was thus entitled to have half of that sum repaid. This seems to suggest that the wife's contribution was assessed at most to be half of the husband's.

Any Benefit (e.g. a Pension) Which a Party Will Lose the Chance of Acquiring by Reason of Dissolution of the Marriage

There are a number of benefits which a wife may lose the chance of acquiring by virtue of the dissolution of the marriage. Loss of a chance of benefiting from the husband's pension can be real especially where the parties are near retirement age. In such a case, a pension entitlement may represent a substantial asset of the family. The loss of a pension benefit can be dealt with either here[198] or under s15B Matrimonial Causes Ordinance.[199]

Where the question of pension arises in the context of s7(1)(g), it is necessary to provide evidence of the benefits which any pension scheme may provide. Most pension schemes will provide:
- payment to the widow on death in service and such payments often comprising both a lump sum payment and an annuity;
- payment of a lump sum on retirement; and
- payment of a widow's pension on death after retirement.

The likely benefit a wife may have in a pension depends on the parties' age, health, expectation of life and length of service so the lump sum which may be needed to compensate her loss will vary. For instance, where the parties are 60 years of age on divorce, and retirement age for the husband is 65, the chance of the wife's loss of lump sum benefit for death in service can be calculated with the assistance of an insurance company. The company can provide a quotation for a policy to provide for the anticipated lump sum on death prior to retirement. Where the husband is near the age of retirement, upon which he will receive a lump sum, such a lump sum may be taken into account.

---

[198] See *Cheung Wong Kim-ching v Cheung Chai-kong* [1991] 1 HKLR 698.
[199] See Chapter 4, and see *Parker v Parker* [1972] Fam 116; *Le Marchant v Le Marchant* [1977] 1 WLR 559 where the court ordered the husband to make alternative financial provision for his wife to compensate her for the loss of her rights. See also *K v K (financial relief: widow's pension)* [1997] 1 FLR 35.

So far, the question of a wife's loss of pension or superannuation benefits on divorce has received little attention in Hong Kong. It is unclear whether the court will consider entitlement of pension or superannuation benefits in the future as (i) a factor to be taken into account which goes to the needs of a spouse or, (ii) as a factor to be taken into account in an unspecified manner and in a general sense. In an appropriate case, it is possible for the court to adjourn the application for a lump sum to a later date. With the introduction of the Mandatory Provident Fund Scheme[200] there is a need for the courts to adopt a clear and consistent approach towards pension benefits on divorce.[201]

Conduct of the Parties and All the Circumstances of the Case

There are a number of other factors which the courts take into account but which do not fall within any of the categories in s/(1)(a)–(g) of the MPPO. They include 'conduct of the parties' and 'all the circumstances of the case'. Each case is treated *sui generis*, an approach which allows the court flexibility in dealing with each case on its own facts.

The reference to conduct in s7(1) is general in nature. But the need to examine the conduct of the parties does not mean that the court has to entertain the parties' mutual recriminations as to their respective responsibility for the breakdown of the marriage. Further, in order to properly allocate responsibility for breakdown, a careful assessment of the personalities of the spouses concerned is needed. Thus, in *Wachtel v Wachtel*, it was said that:

> The forensic process is reasonably well adapted to determining in broad terms the share of responsibility of each party for an accident on the road or at work because the issues are relatively confined in scope, but it is much too clumsy a tool for dissecting the complex inter-actions which go on all the time in a family. Shares in responsibility for breakdown cannot be properly assessed without a meticulous examination and understanding of the characters and personalities of the spouses concerned, and the more

---

[200] The Mandatory Provident Fund Schemes Ordinance.
[201] *Cheung Wong Kim-ching v Cheung Chai-kong* [1991] 1 HKLR 698; *Hamlett v Hamlett* [1996] 1 HKC 61. See e.g. The Treatment of Superannuation in Family Law, Discussion paper, Attorney-General's Department, Australia, March 1992; see also Judith Masson, 'Pensions — a Scheme for Divorcing Couples', (1993) Fam Law 479; see also The Cambridge-Tilburg Law Lectures. See also the English Pension Act 1995.

thorough the investigation the more the shares will, in most cases, approach equality.[202]

Since divorce is now granted on the sole ground of irretrievable breakdown of marriage, and neither party needs to prove fault on the part of the other, it would obviously be futile to have a post-mortem after dissolution of a marriage. Such exercise would be costly and time-consuming. Thus, the court is not required to hear mutual recriminations and listen to the parties' petty squabbles for days on end. However, where the conduct of one party is both 'obvious and gross', and to order a party to support the former would be repugnant to anyone's sense of justice,[203] the court remains free to take such conduct into account.

Lord Denning in *Wachtel v Wachtel* took 'obvious and gross' as meaning conduct which it would be repugnant to a reasonable man's sense of justice not to take into account.[204] 'Obvious and gross', however, may not carry with it a connotation of repugnance and moral blameworthiness.[205] 'Gross' has been used to mean conduct which 'is of greatest importance' without any imputation of moral blame.[206] In *Harnett v Harnett*,[207] Bagnall J said that the word 'gross' described the conduct and 'obvious' described the clarity or certainty with which it was seen to be gross. If the conduct of one party was substantially as bad as that of the other, it mattered not how gross that conduct was, they would weigh equally in the balance.[208] Where there is no substantial disparity between the parties' conduct, the court will be reluctant to carry out a detailed investigation into conduct. For instance, in *Harnett v Harnett*, the husband was a perfectionist with a dominating personality and a violent temper which could easily be provoked. The wife had an affair with a man half her age who was staying in the matrimonial home as a result of the couple's hospitality. The wife's conduct was considered not 'obvious and gross' in comparison with that of the husband. Similarly, in *Leadbeater v Leadbeater*,[209] the husband was obsessed with his custody battle concerning the children of his previous marriage and the 16 custody hearings put tremendous stress on the wife. The wife had an alcohol problem and committed adultery. The husband also committed

---

[202] *Wachtel v Wachtel* [1973] Fam 72 at p. 79.
[203] *Wachtel v Wachtel* [1973] Fam 72.
[204] *Robinson v Robinson* [1983] 1 All ER 391.
[205] See also *Armstrong v Armstrong* (1974) 118 SJ 579; *Kokosinski v Kokosinski* [1980] 1 All ER 1106.
[206] *West v West* [1978] Fam 1.
[207] [1973] 3 WLR 1.
[208] [1973] 3 WLR 1 at p. 9.
[209] [1985] FLR 789.

adultery with a woman who was 20 years his junior. The court held that it would not be inequitable to disregard the conduct of both parties.[210]

Kyte v Kyte[211] is an example of when it would be repugnant to a reasonable person's sense of justice for conduct not to be taken into account. The husband was a manic depressive and caused the wife much unhappiness. On two occasions he attempted to commit suicide. On the first occasion, she did nothing to stop him, and on the second occasion the husband telephoned the wife indicating that he again wished to kill himself, asking the wife to bring around to his office some tablets and some alcohol. She did so, but the husband was unable to go through with it. He, phoned the wife and she replied 'I knew you had no guts'. It was held that her conduct in conniving at his suicide attempts with a view to gaining from his death was gross and obvious. The lump sum awarded was reduced accordingly.

'Conduct', however, does not have to relate to the marriage breakdown,[212] nor indeed does it have to be related to the marriage at all. It may include something which happened after the breakdown of the marriage, or after the decree absolute. It is relevant not only for the purposes of cutting down a claim but can also apply so as to increase one. It is particularly relevant where conduct affects the ability of a party's earning capacity. Thus, in *Jones v Jones*,[213] after the decree absolute, the husband attacked the wife and inflicted a number of wounds on her which caused a 75 percent disability in one of her hands, rendering her unemployable. The only asset was the matrimonial home and the court ordered the husband to transfer his interest to the wife, subject to a charge on one-fifth of the share in his favour, enforceable when the youngest child ceased to be dependent. It was held that the husband's attack should be taken into account in deciding what should be the appropriate share of the matrimonial home. When the youngest child ceased to be dependent, the wife would be over 50 years of age and incapable of earning by reason of her injuries. It would be unjust if she were required to sell the home and look for somewhere else to live. The court ordered that the husband transfer the whole of the beneficial interest to the wife. Likewise, in *H v H (financial provision: conduct)*,[214] the husband had been convicted of wounding the wife with intent and with attempted rape for which he had been sentenced to three and a half years' imprisonment. Prior to the attack, the husband had earned

---

[210] S25 Matrimonial Causes Act 1973 as amended by Matrimonial and Family Proceedings Act 1984 provided that conduct was relevant only if it was such that it would in the opinion of the court be inequitable to disregard.
[211] [1987] 3 All ER 1041.
[212] *Martin v Martin* [1976] 3 All ER 625.
[213] [1975] 2 All ER 12.
[214] [1994] 2 FLR 801.

a good living and on release from prison, he hoped to start a business. It was held that although the wife had recovered physically from the attack, nothing could alleviate the extremity and horror of the violence to which she had been subjected. Her material security had been destroyed by the husband's conduct which rendered him unable to continue to support her at the marital standard of living preceding the attack. The husband was ordered to transfer his half share in the matrimonial home, which constituted the major part of the family assets.

'Conduct' may relate to financial misconduct during marriage or after marriage breakdown, either of which has the effect of reducing the funds available post-divorce.[215] For instance, if a party has dissipated the family assets, it would be unfair not to take this into account. A spouse who squandered away family assets by extravagant living or reckless speculation would not be entitled to claim as great a share of what was left as he could have laid claim to if he had behaved reasonably. In *Chan Chuck-wai v Chan Chan Yin-kwan*,[216] the husband was a gambler and squandered large sums of money. This was taken into account.

'All the circumstances of the case' is a catch-all provision which allows the court to take into account any factors which may be regarded as relevant. However, it has been held that the desire of one spouse to make provision by will for adult children who are in no way dependent on their parents is not a relevant factor.[217]

MATRIMONIAL HOME ON DIVORCE

Housing for members of a family (children, wife, husband) is a major problem encountered on divorce. Where a matrimonial home is the only substantial asset, the court has to balance the need of the children and the custodial parent to have a roof over their heads against the claim of the husband who may want to liquidate his interest in the matrimonial home.[218] The powers of the court are extensive, and s6A of the MPPO empowers the court to order the sale of property. S6(1)(a) and (b) of the MPPO allow the court to order a transfer of the matrimonial home from one spouse to

---

[215] *Martin v Martin* [1976] 3 All ER 625.
[216] District Court, Divorce Jurisdiction, Action No 245 of 1979 (1981).
[217] *Page v Page* [1981] 2 FLR 198; *Vicary v Vicary* [1992] 2 FLR 272.
[218] *Hui I-mei v Cheng Yau-shing*, Court of Appeal, Civil Appeal Action No 157 of 1996 (1996).

another, or to order a settlement of property.[219] The choice of any of these options depends on the facts of each case.

Immediate Sale and Division of Proceeds

Where an immediate sale and division of the proceeds provide sufficient money to rehouse the parties, such sale and division would be appropriate.[220] For instance, where the children have come of age and the proceeds of sale are sufficient to rehouse the wife, albeit not at a standard commensurate to that enjoyed during the marriage, the court will order sale. To postpone sale indefinitely would be unfair to the husband as he would be deprived of access to a substantial asset which he may need in time of emergency. Thus, in *Goodfield v Goodfield*,[221] the parties agreed that they should share the matrimonial home equally. The wife had a steady job and reasonable income. The judge ordered that the wife be permitted to remain in the house until her remarriage or death or until the sale of the property, such sale not to take place without her express consent. The Court of Appeal disagreed and held that this was a case where the court should order sale. The wife had a steady job and with half of the equity of the matrimonial home, she could find an alternative home. Postponing sale would deprive the husband of his capital asset for a prolonged or indefinite period, and such hardship could only reasonably be imposed if there were young children of the family.[222] Similarly, an order for sale and division of the proceeds was ordered in *Choy Kin-choy v Choy Chan Kai-ngar*, where the Court of Appeal took the view that it would be unfair to delay the husband access to his capital.[223]

Outright Transfer or a Lump Sum Compensation or a Charge

Where immediate sale and division of the proceeds of sale is inappropriate, for instance where the sale proceeds would not allow one party to be rehoused, and either party could buy out the other's share in the property,

---

[219] The parties to whom the order is directed must take steps to give effect to the order; s26 MPPO.
[220] S6A MPPO.
[221] (1975) 5 Fam Law 197.
[222] See *M v M (sale of property)* [1988] FLR 389.
[223] Court of Appeal, Civil Appeal Action No 47 of 1993 (1993).

an outright transfer may be appropriate. Thus, in *Hanlon v Hanlon*,[224] the wife was living with four children in the matrimonial home and the husband's housing was secured by his employer. During the marriage they had both contributed equally to the family finances in terms of both money and work. At first instance, it was held that the matrimonial home should be held by the parties in equal shares, sale to be postponed until the youngest child had attained the age of 17. The Court of Appeal, however, disagreed and held that as half of the equity would not produce a sum sufficient to enable the wife to rehouse herself, and since she was willing to provide maintenance for the children, the proper order would be for a transfer of the house to the wife absolutely. This was also the case in *Ngai Wong Yun-ping v Ngai Yun-lung*, where the Court of Appeal held that an outright transfer of the matrimonial home to the wife was appropriate because she had shouldered the entire burden of managing the household, paying for all the expenses and raising the children since the breakdown of the marriage.[225]

There may be cases where an absolute transfer of the matrimonial home to one party (e.g. the wife) may result in her obtaining a disproportionate share in it. In such a case, she may be required to compensate the husband by way of a lump sum or a charge representing the husband's interest. This approach has the advantage of crystalising the parties' position and is capable of achieving a clean break. Thus, in *Dunford v Dunford*,[226] the Court of Appeal held that the property be transferred to the wife who would be responsible for the repayment of all the outgoings and the mortgage, and that the house be charged with payment of 25 percent of the net proceeds of sale to the husband when the house was sold or on the wife's death.

The desirability of crystalising the parties' position is that the parties are aware of the status of their interests in the home:

> The wife knows exactly where she stands. The house is vested in her. She has the property in it, and she can keep it going indefinitely ... But if it should happen that she should sell the house (or should die) then the husband is to have one-quarter of the net proceeds.[227]

---

[224] [1978] 2 All ER 889.
[225] Court of Appeal, Civil Appeal Action No 50 of 1996 (1996); *Fung Ling Pui-sim v Fung Ning-sam*, District Court, Divorce Jurisdiction, Action No 69 of 1981 (1982); *Wong Yiu-lan v Wong Yuen-ting* [1995] 1 HKLR 411.
[226] [1980] 1 All ER 122.
[227] Ibid.

For example, in *Lai Lai-hing v Lai Kwai-ping*,[228] the parties were young and had no children. The wife's share in the matrimonial home was assessed at HK$400 000. As the property in question was purchased under the Home Ownership Scheme, it was held that subject to the consent of the Director of the Housing Authority, the flat was to be charged with that amount in favour of the wife. Similarly, in *Fei Tai-chung v Gloria Fei*,[229] the matrimonial home was worth HK$14 million and it was agreed that the husband was to remain in it. The Court of Appeal held that he was to pay the wife HK$4 million, reflecting the need of the husband to have a roof over his head while at the same time acknowledging the legitimate claim of the wife to have a share in equity. Again, in *Hamlett v Hamlett*,[230] the wife obtained the whole beneficial interest in the matrimonial home but was ordered to pay the husband a lump sum in compensation.

One of the advantages of a charge can be seen in *Lau Lap-che v Wong Sut-fan*,[231] where it was held that the matrimonial home was to be transferred to the wife subject to a 15 percent charge in favour of the husband, not be enforced for three years. It was said that as the husband did not need the money at the time, delayed enforcement provided the wife with 'breathing space' and the husband would not have to wait too long for his share either.

A longer period of postponement, however, may be necessary in some cases, which is the Hong Kong version of the Mesher order.[232] For example, in *Wong Sin-yee v Cheung Si-yan*,[233] a wife left the matrimonial home and the husband and children continued to live there. She was given 25 percent of the value of the matrimonial home to be secured by a legal charge, the charge not to be exercised until the youngest child reached 19. Similarly, in *Hui I-mei v Cheng Yau-shing*,[234] the wife had custody of two children of the family. The home was worth HK$2.6 million. The trial judge ordered the husband to transfer his interest to the wife subject to a charge of one-third, enforceable upon the youngest child attaining the age of 18, the wife's remarriage or her cohabitation with another man. The Court of Appeal held that one of the aims of the order was to ensure that the children would have a home at least until the youngest child reached the age of 18. That purpose would be at risk if the charge became enforceable upon the wife's remarriage to someone who could not provide a home or if

---

[228] [1995] 1 HKC 654.
[229] Court of Appeal, Civil Appeal Action No 170 of 1994 (1995).
[230] [1996] 1 HKC 61.
[231] [1996] 1 HKC 165.
[232] *Mesher v Mesher* [1980] All ER 126.
[233] Court of Appeal, Civil Appeal Action No 222 of 1996 (1997).
[234] Court of Appeal, Civil Appeal Action No 157 of 1996 (1996).

she were to cohabit with another man. A new order was made to the effect that the charge was not to be enforceable until the youngest child reached the age of 18 or until both children had ceased full-time education, whichever occurred later. Such an order, however, would be inappropriate if its effect would be to deprive the husband of funds necessary to acquire a flat and working capital for his business. In *Choy Kin-choy v Choy Chan Kai-ngar*,[235] it was held that the inconvenience to the wife of finding and moving to alternative accommodation and the disruption to the children's lives would need to be balanced against the needs of the husband. In this case, it was decided that a seven-year delay was too long.

CONCLUSION

The discretionary powers of the court to adjust the financial position of the parties to a marriage is restricted only by the broadly delineated parameters of s7(1) of the MPPO. But this flexibility in the decision-making process comes at a price of sacrificing predictability of outcomes. In adjusting the financial position of the parties, what goes into determining the parties' financial resources can be controversial. Pensions, for example, have only been recently considered by the courts but they are likely to be of increasing importance.

---

[235] Court of Appeal, Civil Appeal Action No 47 of 1993 (1993).

16

Financial Provision for Children

INTRODUCTION

The District Court has the power to make financial provision for a child. Maintenance during marriage is provided in the Separation and Maintenance Orders Ordinance and s8 of the Matrimonial Proceedings and Property Ordinance.[1] This chapter examines financial provision on divorce, nullity or judicial separation under the Matrimonial Proceedings and Property Ordinance (MPPO) and under the Guardianship of Minors Ordinance (GMO).

JURISDICTION OF THE COURT UNDER MPPO

S5(1) of the MPPO provides that in proceedings for divorce, nullity or judicial separation, the court may order a party to the marriage to make payment for the benefit of a 'child of the family'.

What Orders and When

S5(2) states that the court may order a party to the marriage to make to

---

[1] See Chapter 14.

such person, as the order may specify, for the benefit of a child, or to such a child:

> (a) such periodical payments and for such term as the court may so specify;
> (b) such secured periodical payments and for such term as the court may so specify;
> (c) such lump sum payment as may be so specified.

An order for lump sum payment may be made for the purpose of enabling any liabilities or expenses reasonably incurred by or for the benefit of that child before the making of an application.[2] The lump sum may be paid in instalments for such amount as may be specified in the order, and the order may require the instalments to be secured to the satisfaction of the court.[3] These orders are the same as those in s8 of the MPPO.[4]

S5(1) provides that the court may order a party to a marriage to pay maintenance for the benefit of a child in the following situations:

> (a) before or on the granting of decree of divorce, nullity or judicial separation, or at any time thereafter;
> (b) where any such proceedings are dismissed after the beginning of the trial, either forthwith or within a reasonable period after the dismissal.

Once the court is vested with the power in s5(1)(a), it may make further order 'from time to time'.[5] In other words, 'clean break' does not apply to maintenance of a child.

S6 also empowers the court to make property transfer, property settlement or variation of ante- or post-nuptial settlement for the benefit of any child of the family, but these powers are only exercisable on the granting of decree of divorce, nullity or judicial separation, or at any time thereafter.

'Child of the Family'

S2 of the MPPO defines who is a 'child of the family'. A 'child of the family' in relation to the parties to the marriage, means:

---

[2] S5(3).
[3] S5(4).
[4] See Chapter 13.
[5] S5(5).

FINANCIAL PROVISION FOR CHILDREN

(a) a child of both those parties, and
(b) any other child who has been treated by both those parties as a child of their family.

A 'child', in relation to one or both parties of the marriage, includes an illegitimate child or adopted child of one or both parties. Thus, a 'child of the family' includes not only a biological child of the parties, legitimate or otherwise, it also includes an adopted child, a stepchild living with the parties, or any child who has been treated as a child of the family.

A child must be in existence for it to be 'treated' as a child of the family. In *A v A (family: unborn child)*,[6] the wife was pregnant at the time of the marriage. The husband thought he was the father. He left for Germany before the child was born and the parties never resumed cohabitation. The child had a skin colour indicating that the husband was not the father. The only evidence that the husband had treated the child as his child was that he had married the mother. It was held that whether a child had been treated as a child of the family depended on behaviour towards the child after birth. As the husband had not shown any interest towards the child, the child was not a 'child of the family'. The result probably would be the same if the husband knew all along that he was not the father.[7]

There must be a family unit in which a child was treated as a member. This can happen even if the spouses have lived together for a very short period of time. However, where a child was born after the parties have separated, and the husband acknowledged on social occasions that the child was his, it was held there was no family in which the child could be treated as a member.[8]

The test for 'treatment' is an objective one and it is immaterial that the wife has deceived the husband that he was the father. This, however, is a factor to be taken into account in considering the husband's liability to maintain the child.[9]

Factors Relevant in Exercising Discretion

In exercising its power under ss5 and 6 of the MPPO, the court has a duty to take into account the following considerations when deciding what

---

[6] [1974] 2 WLR 106.
[7] P M Bromley, *Family Law*, 7th edition, Butterworths, London, 1987, p. 293, criticising the decision as over-technical.
[8] *M v M (child of the family)* [1981] 2 FLR 39.
[9] S7(3).

provision to make for a child. The factors include, as stated in s7(2) of the MPPO:

(a) the financial needs of the child;
(b) the income, earning capacity (if any), property and any financial resources of the child;
(c) any physical or mental disability of the child;
(d) the standard of living enjoyed by the family before the breakdown of the marriage;
(e) the manner in which he was being and in which the parties to the marriage expected him to be educated.

'Financial resources' of the child is an important factor. There is a difference in the wordings here and those in s7(2)(a).[10] It has been held that financial resources of the child are not limited to those which the child currently has under his or her absolute control.[11] Thus, where a deceased mother left her estate to trustees who were empowered in their discretion to advance income and capital to the children until they came of age, the trust provided a potential source of income, and the trust fund constituted financial resources which the court must have regard to, even though the children were not absolutely entitled to the fund.[12]

Where the child is not the child of a party to the marriage, the court has to have regard to three factors: firstly, whether that party had assumed any responsibility for the child's maintenance, and if so, to what extent, and upon what basis and for how long; secondly, does that party know that the child is not his; thirdly, his liability to maintain any other child.[13]

Principles of Assessment

With regard to financial provision to children, there is no 'rule of thumb' such as the 'one-third rule'. Cases must be judged on their own merits and the statutory considerations apply. However, it has been said that it was not desirable for children to have their parents living at totally different standards of living.[14]

---

[10] 'The income, earning capacity, property and other financial resources which each of the parties to the marriage has or is likely to have in the foreseeable future.'
[11] *J v J (C intervening)* [1989] 1 FLR 453.
[12] Ibid.
[13] S7(3).
[14] *Camm v Camm* [1983] 4 FLR 577.

According to s7(2), the aim of the court is to place the child, so far as it is practicable, in the financial position in which the child would have been if the marriage had not broken down, and each of the couple had properly discharged his or her financial obligation towards him. However, a rich father is not to be regarded as having the financial responsibility and obligation to provide a settlement making provision for a child during his life when the child is under no disability and his maintenance and education has been secured.[15] Thus, it was held in *Chamberlain v Chamberlain*,[16] that unless special circumstances existed, it would be inappropriate to settle a beneficial interest in the matrimonial home in favour of the children as the capital on the house was acquired by the resources of the parents. Provided that the parents meet their responsibilities to their children, that asset should revert to them.

One instance where it would be appropriate to make capital provision for children is where the father has not provided maintenance for them, and it is unlikely that he would do so in the future. In such a case, the court may make a lump sum order to the wife for the benefit of the children.[17] The danger of awarding a lump sum is that the mother might be tempted to dip into the fund for a purpose unconnected with the children's maintenance and dissipate the whole fund.[18] Another alternative is for the court to order that a lump sum be used to secure periodical payments for children. However, where the lump sum is too small to produce an adequate income, this would not be a viable option.[19]

Duration of an Order

As a general rule, no order shall be made in favour of a child who has attained the age of 18. An order, however, may be made extending beyond the age of 18 if it appears to the court that the child will be receiving instruction at an educational establishment or undergoing training for a trade or profession or vocation or there are special circumstances justifying it.[20]

---

[15] *Lilford (Lord) v Glynn* [1979] 1 WLR 78, applied in *Ho Yiu Chuen-fong v Ho Wei-yiu* [1986] HKLR 99.
[16] [1974] 1 All ER 33.
[17] *Griffiths v Griffiths* [1984] 2 All ER 626.
[18] Ibid.
[19] Ibid.
[20] S10 MPPO as amended by the Marriage and Children (Miscellaneous Amendments) Ordinance.

JURISDICTION OF THE COURT UNDER GUARDIANSHIP OF MINORS ORDINANCE

S10(2) of the Guardianship of Minors Ordinance (GMO) provides that the court may on the application of a person with whom custody of a minor lies at law any one or more the following orders:

Orders Which the Court Can Make

(a) an order requiring payment to the applicant by the parent or either of the parents of the minor of such lump sum (whether in one amount or by instalments) for the immediate and non-recurring needs of the minor or for the purpose of enabling any liabilities or expenses reasonably incurred in maintaining the minor before the making of the order to be met, or for both, as the court thinks reasonable having regard to the means of that parent;

(b) an order requiring payment to the applicant by such parent or either of such parents of such periodical sum towards the maintenance of the minor as the court thinks reasonable having regard to the means of that parent;

(c) an order requiring the securing to the applicant by such parent or either of such parents excluded from having that custody, to the satisfaction of the court, of such periodical sum towards the maintenance of the minor;

(d) an order requiring the transfer to that person for the benefit of the minor, or to the minor, by such parent or either of such parents, of such property, being property to which the parent is entitled (either in possession or reversion), as the court thinks reasonable having regard to the means of that parent;[21]

(e) an order requiring the settlement for the benefit of the minor, to the satisfaction of the court, of such property, being property to which such parent or either of such parents is so entitled, as the court thinks reasonable having regard to the means of that parent.

These orders are much wider than those in the Separation and Maintenance Orders Ordinance.[22] They are also much wider than those in s8 of the MPPO which does not allow for the making of property adjustment orders.[23]

---

[21] 'Benefit' is not confined to benefit of a financial kind, see *K v K (minors: property transfer)* [1992] 2 FLR 220.
[22] See Chapter 14.
[23] See Chapter 14.

Discretion of the Court

The court can grant such order as it thinks 'reasonable having regard to the means of the paying parent'.[24] Unlike s7(2) of the MPPO, there is no reference here that the aim of the court is not to place the child, so far as it is practicable, in the financial position in which the child would have been had the child's parent's marriage not broken down.

It has been said that the obligation of the father is simply to maintain and educate his child.[25] Like s7(2) of the MPPO, a rich father is not regarded to be under any obligations or responsibilities to settle funds for the benefit of the children. Thus, in *T v S (financial provision for children)*,[26] it was held that it was wrong for the court to order that the home be held on trust for sale and that sale be postponed until the children reached the age of majority, and thereafter the benefit passed to the children in equal shares. Similarly, in *A v A (a minor: financial provision)*,[27] the father was a very wealthy person and he had a sexual relationship with the mother but they never cohabited. The mother gave birth to three children, and the father accepted that only A was his child. The father had supported the mother since she was pregnant with A and acquired a property as a home for her and all her children. The mother sought, *inter alia,* an outright transfer of the property either to her for the benefit of A, or to A herself. It was held that property adjustment orders should not ordinarily be made to benefit a child after he or she had attained independence. The right order was to settle the property for the benefit of A, whilst A was under the care of the mother. The mother would have a right to occupy the property to the exclusion of the father, for the purposes of looking after A

In assessing the financial needs of a child, it is acceptable to include the costs of a full-time carer. Where the mother, instead of a hired full-time carer, is looking after the child, she is entitled to an allowance.[28] This was accepted in *K v W*,[29] where Deputy Judge Hartmann said:

> Just as, in my judgment, it would be perfectly proper for the mother to claim the expenses of a maid to look after the child while she was working so I consider it proper for the mother — at this time at least when the

---

[24] S10(2).
[25] S2, which provides that maintenance includes education.
[26] [1994] 2 FLR 883.
[27] [1994] 1 FLR 657.
[28] *Haroutunian v Jennings* [1980] 1 FLR 62; *A v A (a minor: financial provision)* [1994] 1 FLR 657.
[29] [1998] 1 HKLRD 402.

child of such a young age and so very dependent — to claim a remuneration for herself for taking on that duty herself.[30]

The judge acknowledged that it was difficult to assess a proper quantum, but he awarded HK$8000 pm.

Duration of Periodical Payments

Generally a periodical payments order shall not be made in favour of a child who has attained the age of 18, but the court may include a provision for a child who has not attained 18 extending it beyond 18 if it appears to the court:

> (a) that child is, or will be, or if such an order or provision were made would be, receiving instruction at an educational establishment or undergoing training for a trade, profession or vocation, whether or not he is also, or will also be, in gainful employment; or
> (b) there are special circumstances which justify the making of the order or provisions.[31]

Attachment of Earnings

Where an order for maintenance is made under s10(2)(b) and (c) and the court is satisfied that the maintenance payer has without reasonable excuse failed to make any payment, and there is income payable to the maintenance payer capable of being attached, the court may order the income to be attached, as to the whole or part of the amount payable, and the amount attached to be paid to a designated payee.[32] An attachment order shall be an authority to the person by whom the income is payable to make the payment in accordance with the order, and the receipt of the designated payee shall be a good discharge of that person.[33]

---

[30] Ibid., at p. 407.
[31] S12A.
[32] S20 GMO.
[33] S20 GMO.

17

Settlement, Consent Order and Variation

INTRODUCTION

With the increase in the number of divorces, the law encourages spouses to avoid bitterness after family breakdown and to settle their money and property matters amicably.[1] Majority of cases are indeed settled out of court. A settlement, however, rests uneasily with the basic principle that an agreement cannot oust the jurisdiction of the court. In *Hyman v Hyman*,[2] the wife covenanted by a deed of separation not to take proceedings against the husband for an increase in maintenance. On divorce, the wife sought additional maintenance. The House of Lords held that the wife was not precluded from invoking the jurisdiction of the court. The underlying philosophy was that:

> the power of the court to make provision for a wife on the dissolution of her marriage is a necessary incident of the power to decree such a dissolution, conferred not merely in the interests of the wife, but of the public, and that the wife cannot by her own covenant preclude herself from invoking the jurisdiction of the court or preclude the court from the exercise of that jurisdiction.[3]

---

[1] *Minton v Minton* [1979] 1 All ER 79 at p. 87 per Lord Scarman.
[2] [1929] AC 601.
[3] Ibid., at p. 614 per Lord Hailsham LC; *Lau Chu v Lau Tang Su-ping* [1989] 2 HKLR 470.

In many cases, parties negotiate a settlement and agreed terms are made into consent orders. Consent orders, in theory, are no different from orders made after a contested hearing. A judge who is asked to make a consent order cannot be compelled to do so. He is exercising a discretion under s7(1) of the Matrimonial Proceedings and Property Ordinance (MPPO).[4] He is not to rubber stamp an agreement. If he thinks that there are matters of which he needs to be more fully informed before he makes the order, he is entitled to make such inquiries and require such evidence to be put before him.[5] However, he is under no obligation to make inquiries or require evidence. He is entitled to assume that parties of full age and capacity know what is in their own best interests, especially when they are represented by lawyers.

Although the court can only discharge its duty under the MPPO when it is in possession of all the relevant information, there are no statutory provisions or rules of court relating to the making of consent orders. In England, s33(A)(1) of the Matrimonial Causes Act 1973 empowers the court to make a consent order without full investigation and without hearing oral evidence. The problem with this cursory regime for the scrutiny of consent orders was recently described in *B v Miller & Co*[6] where it was said that:

> In practice ... the court's ability to assess the propriety of the proposed consent order was limited, even if detailed and comprehensive affidavits, replies to questionnaires and bundles of documents were before the court. A judge might well refrain from reading them if informed that a consent order had been agreed. Practitioners were aware that judges were unlikely to examine the terms of the settlement closely if both parties were legally represented, and that it was virtually unknown for the court to refuse to approve agreed terms. In any event the court might not be provided with all the material information.[7]

Where a court makes a consent order, the legal effects of the agreed terms no longer stem from the agreement itself, but from the court order.

> Financial arrangements that are agreed upon between the parties ... once they have been made the subject of the court order no longer depend

---

[4] *Livesey v Jenkins* [1985] 1 All ER 106; see *Cho Fok Bo-ying v Cho Chi-biu* [1990] 2 HKC 269 where it was held that a consent order which sought to make one party responsible for the mortgage repayment was void for want of jurisdiction.
[5] *Tommey v Tommey* [1982] 3 All ER 385 at p. 390 per Balcombe J.
[6] [1996] 2 FLR 23.
[7] Ibid., at p. 29; *Pound v Pound* [1994] 1 FLR 775.

upon the agreement of the parties as the source from which their legal effect is derived. Their legal effect is derived from the court order...[8]

The agreement, thus, is no longer a maintenance agreement capable of being varied under s15 of the MPPO.[9] Any variation, therefore, may only be made under s11 of the MPPO. This chapter examines first the effect of a settlement and the possibility of invoking jurisdiction of the court under the MPPO; secondly, under what circumstances may a settlement in the form of a maintenance agreement be varied; thirdly, variation of a court order or an agreement which has been made a consent order, and lastly, the setting aside of an agreement.

SETTLEMENT AND ANCILLARY RELIEF APPLICATION

An agreement enables the parties to resolve their financial matters without the expenses of litigation, thus avoiding bitterness and saving legal fees. Although it cannot oust the jurisdiction of the court, this does not mean that a party can renege on a contract solemnly made. The existence of an agreement will be an important factor which the court takes into account. A formal agreement properly and fairly arrived at with competent legal advice should be given effect, unless grounds are shown that it would be unjust to hold the parties to the terms of the agreement.[10]

The fact that a wife would have done better by going to court, or that one party has a stronger bargaining power is insufficient ground for going behind the agreement. It must be shown that the stronger party has exploited the unequal bargaining power, rendering it unjust to bind the other to the terms. In *Edgar v Edgar*,[11] the wife entered into a separation agreement contrary to legal advice. Under the agreement, she received capital provision and maintenance for herself and the children, and she further agreed not to claim a lump sum or a transfer of property order in subsequent divorce proceedings. On divorce, she applied for a lump sum order. The Court of Appeal held that the existence of an arm's length agreement based on legal

---

[8] *De Lasala v De Lasala* [1980] AC 546 at p. 560 per Lord Diplock.
[9] See below, p. 426.
[10] *Edgar v Edgar* [1980] 3 All ER 887 at p. 893 per Ormrod LJ; *Brockwell v Brockwell* (1976) 6 Fam Law 46.
[11] [1980] 3 All ER 887; *Wright v Wright* [1970] 3 All ER 209.

advice was a factor to be taken into account. In this case, although the husband had superior bargaining power, there was no evidence that he exploited it unfairly so as to induce the wife to act to her disadvantage. The Court of Appeal provided guidance as to the circumstances in which a party might be permitted to renege on an agreement.

> Undue pressure by one side, exploitation of a dominant position to secure an unreasonable advantage, inadequate knowledge, possibly bad legal advice, an important change of circumstances, unforeseen or overlooked at the time of making the agreement, are all relevant to the question of justice between the parties ... There may well be other considerations which affect the injustice of this case; the above list is not intended to be an exclusive catalogue.[12]

Edgar v Edgar, however, was distinguished in *Camm v Camm,*[13] which was said to be a 'truly exceptional case'.[14] In *Camm v Camm,* the wife agreed that the husband was to provide her with a home for herself and three young children, he would also make financial provision for the children, but no maintenance to her. On that basis, both parties agreed not to make any future financial claims. Seven years later, the wife filed an application for periodical payment. The Court of Appeal held that the wife was not bound by the agreement made during the throes of divorce which was 'most disadvantageous' to her. The agreement was concluded when the wife was under extreme pressure and received poor legal advice. The court then ordered maintenance in favour of the wife.[15] More recently, in *Pound v Pound,*[16] it was said that the *Edgar* principles is 'the worst of both worlds' because 'the agreement may be held to be binding, but whether it will can be determined only after litigation.'

VARIATION OF AN MAINTENANCE AGREEMENT

Where an agreement is not made a consent order, it remains an agreement between the parties. S14 of the MPPO provides rules governing the powers of the court to vary, but it is a jurisdiction which is seldom invoked today.

---

[12] Ibid., at p. 893 per Ormrod LJ; *Harris v Manahan* [1997] 1 FLR 205.
[13] [1983] 4 FLR 577.
[14] *Smith v McInerney* [1994] 2 FLR 1077.
[15] *B v B (consent order: variation)* [1995] 1 FLR 9; *Beach v Beach* [1995] 2 FLR 160.
[16] [1994] 1 FLR 775 at p. 791 per Hoffmann LJ.

There are two reasons for this. Firstly, an agreement cannot purport to oust the jurisdiction of the court and consequently a party to an agreement may, if she is not happy with it, make an application to the court. Secondly, most agreements are now made consent orders and variation is under s11 of the MPPO.[17]

Definition

S14 of the MPPO governs a maintenance agreement as defined by s14(2). A 'maintenance agreement' must be in writing and made between the parties to a marriage,[18] being:

> (a) an agreement containing financial arrangements, whether made during the continuance[19] or after the dissolution or annulment of the marriage; or
> (b) a separation agreement which contains no financial arrangements in a case where no other agreement in writing between the same parties contains such arrangements.

'Financial arrangements' means:

> provisions governing the rights and liabilities towards one another when living separately of the parties to a marriage (including a marriage which has been dissolved or annulled) in respect of the making or securing of payments or disposition or use of any property, including such rights and liabilities with respect to the maintenance or education of any child, whether or not a child of the family.[20]

S14(2) does not mention consideration as an essential element of a maintenance agreement. S15(2), however, provides that a provision which has been varied 'shall have effect thereafter as if any alternation made by the order had been made by agreement between the parties and for valuable consideration'.[21] This seems to imply that consideration would be essential.

---

[17] S14(1)(b).
[18] *Young v Young* (1973) 117 SJ 204.
[19] A maintenance agreement may be entered during the marriage or after its termination. The common law rule that spouses cannot in anticipation of separation enter into a valid agreement to provide for their legal rights in case they should separate does not apply. A maintenance agreement need not be made for the purposes of the parties living separately, *Ewart v Ewart* [1959] P. 23.
[20] S14(2).
[21] See below.

Variation during the Parties' Joint Lives

S15(1) of the MPPO provides that:

> (1) Where a maintenance agreement is for the time being subsisting and each of the parties to the agreement is for the time being either domiciled or resident in Hong Kong ... either party may apply to the court for an order under this section.

S15(2) provides:

> If the court to which the application is made is satisfied either–
> (a) that by reason of a change in the circumstances in the light of which any financial arrangements contained in the agreement were made or, as the case may be, financial arrangements were omitted from it (including a change foreseen by the parties when making the agreement),[22] the agreement should be altered so as to make different, or as the case may be, so as to contain, financial arrangements, or
> (b) that the agreement does not contain proper financial arrangements with respect to any child of the family, then, subject to subsections (3), (4) and (5), that court may by order make such alterations in the agreement.
>
> (i) by varying or revoking any financial arrangements contained in it, or
> (ii) by inserting in it financial arrangements for the benefit of one of the parties to the agreement or of a child of the family, as may appear to that court to be just having regard to all the circumstances, including, if relevant, the matters mentioned in s7(3); and the agreement shall have effect thereafter as if any alteration made by the order had been made by agreement between the parties and for valuable consideration.

The language of the subsection is 'far from happily chosen'.[23] There are two questions to be asked:

> (i) whether where was a change in the circumstances in the light of which the agreement was made; and
> (ii) whether by reason of the change of circumstances the court can be satisfied that the agreement is one which should be altered.

'Circumstances in the light of which any financial arrangement were made' has both subjective and objective elements. It includes circumstances which did in fact influence the parties as well as circumstances which a

---

[22] Compare *K v K* [1961] 2 All ER 266.
[23] *Ratcliffe v Ratcliffe* [1962] 3 All ER 993 at p. 996 per Willmer LJ.

reasonable person must have had in mind at the time of the agreement.[24] In *Gorman v Gorman,* it was held that the husband's increased earnings and the wife's ill-health constituted a change of circumstances.

The court, however, is most reluctant to entertain variation of an agreement freely negotiated and with proper legal advice.[25] Further, whether an agreement should be altered depends on whether the agreement has become unjust by reason of a change in the circumstances. Thus, in *Gorman v Gorman*,[26] where the income of the parties had changed (i.e. the wife was no longer self-sufficient, she was plagued by ill-health, and the husband's income increased fourfold), the question was whether the agreement became unjust by reason of the change. The Court of Appeal held that the husband only entered into the agreement on the basis of providing no maintenance to the wife. The changed circumstances affected the fortune of the wife, but it would be most unjust to the husband to insert maintenance for the wife as it would undermine the very foundation of the agreement. Similarly, in *Ratcliffe v Ratcliffe*,[27] it was held that the fact that the husband voluntarily gave up work and undertook a course of study did not render it just that the financial arrangements contained in the agreement be altered. Justice required that he, 'having made his bed, must lie in it'.[28] However, in *Simister v Simister*,[29] the husband and wife entered into an agreement that he pay her one-third of his annual income as maintenance. The husband's business prospered and his income increased dramatically. He sought a variation and it was held that the maintenance agreement, though equitable originally, was now at a rate in excess of the wife's maximum needs. That was a change of circumstances. The agreed maintenance was revoked and a new order made.

The court's power to vary is expressed in very wide terms. It may alter the agreement by varying, revoking any financial arrangements contained therein, or by inserting in it financial arrangements for the benefit of the parties to the agreement or of a child of the family.[30] These powers to vary will only be exercised if it appears to the court that it is 'just' to do so 'having regard to all the circumstances', including the matter mentioned in s7(3).[31] Once a maintenance agreement is varied, it shall have effect thereafter

---

[24] *Gorman v Gorman* [1964] 3 All ER 739 at p. 743.
[25] *Edgar v Edgar* [1980] 3 All ER 887.
[26] [1964] 3 All ER 739.
[27] [1962] 3 All ER 993.
[28] Ibid., at p. 997.
[29] [1987] 1 All ER 233.
[30] S15(2).
[31] See below.

as if any alteration made by the order had been made by agreement between the parties and for valuable consideration.'[32] It was held in *Warden v Warden*,[33] that 'thereafter' should be read as 'then', and it gave the court the power to backdate the variation of a maintenance agreement.

Variation after the Death of Payer

Where a maintenance agreement provides for the continuation of payments after the death of the payer, and he dies domiciled in Hong Kong, the surviving party or the personal representative of the deceased may apply to the court for a variation.[34] Where an application is made, the court shall have the power to direct that the application be deemed to have been accompanied by an application for an order under s4 of the Inheritance (Provision for Family and Dependants) Ordinance.[35] An application shall not be made after the end of the period of six months from the date on which representation in regard to the estate of the deceased is first taken out, except with permission of the court.[36] Where an agreement is altered after the death of a payer, the personal representatives of the deceased shall not be liable for having distributed any part of the estate of the deceased after the expiration of six months on the ground that they ought to have taken into account the possibility that a court might permit an application. This, however, shall not prejudice any power to recover any party of the estate so distributed arising by virtue of the making of an order for variation.

VARIATION OF A COURT ORDER

Periodical payments which were appropriate when ordered might be inappropriate due to inflation or a change of circumstances, such as the reduction of the payer husband's salary or the payer husband's remarriage. In these circumstances, an application to the court to vary or discharge would be necessary. The law governing variation of a court order (whether by consent or after a contested hearing) is governed by s11 of the MPPO. An important distinction is drawn between an income order which is variable

---

[32] S7(2).
[33] [1981] 3 WLR 435.
[34] S16(1).
[35] S20.
[36] S16(2).

SETTLEMENT, CONSENT ORDER AND VARIATION

and a capital order which is not. For instance, in *Jessel v Jessel*,[37] a wife agreed to accept periodical payments in settlement of all her claims and she undertook not to increase the husband's liability. An order was made to that effect. The wife later applied for variation of the periodical payments. It was held that there was a continuing order in force which was capable of variation.

A capital order is final and cannot be varied.[38] Thus, in *Carson v Carson*,[39] the court ordered that the matrimonial home be settled on trust for sale for the husband and wife jointly, sale be postponed until the youngest child attained the age of 18 or completed full-time education. An order was also made in favour of the wife and children for periodical payments. The wife's periodical payments were substantially increased when it was found that the husband had failed to fully disclose his means. The husband deliberately failed to comply with the order and accumulated large arrears. The wife, in financial difficulties, and fearing that half of the proceeds of the sale would not be adequate to purchase a home, applied for the matrimonial home to be transferred to her in lieu of periodical payments. It was held that the court had no jurisdiction to entertain her claim. The order settling the matrimonial home was a final order and the court could not entertain a second application.[40]

Although a capital order is a final order and cannot be varied, there are two minor exceptions. First, where a lump sum payment is to be paid by instalments in favour of a party to the marriage or a child of the family, although the amount cannot be changed, variation is possible to increase or reduce the number of instalments, or to reduce the amount of security after some payments have been made. Second, settlements of property and variation of ante-nuptial and post-nuptial settlements made on or after the granting of a decree of judicial separation are variable[41] in proceedings for the rescission of that decree or for the dissolution of the marriage.[42]

Powers of the Court

The court has the power to 'vary, discharge, suspend any provision of an order temporarily and to revive the operation of any provision so

---

[37] [1979] 3 All ER 645.
[38] *Dinch v Dinch* [1987] 2 FLR 162; *Whitfield v Whitfield* [1985] FLR 955.
[39] [1983] 1 All ER 478; *Norman v Norman* [1983] 1 All ER 486.
[40] Compare *Thompson v Thompson* [1985] FLR 863.
[41] S11(2).
[42] See s11(4); *Whitfield v Whitfield* [1985] 1 FLR 955.

suspended.[43] However, there is no power to remit arrears due under the order in whole or in part. Additionally, there are two major restrictions on the orders which the court can make on an application for.

(i) No order under s6 of the MPPO can be made where the application is made for the variation of periodical payments made in favour of either a party to a marriage or a child of the family.[44]

(ii) No lump sum order can be made on an application for variation of a periodical payments order made in favour of a party to a marriage.

The rationale of these restrictions is to buttress the finality of a capital order. Thus, in *Sandford v Sandford*,[45] an order was made providing for the transfer of the matrimonial home to the wife and periodical payments to her and children. The wife applied for variation of the periodical payments and the court made a lump sum order. The Court of Appeal held that it was not open to the court to make a lump sum order on an application for variation of a periodical payments order.[46]

Restriction (ii) does not apply to an application for variation of a periodical payments order made in favour of a child of the family.[47] This means that a recalcitrant father who has a habit of defaulting on payments which the child needs on a regular basis, e.g. food, clothing and school fees, could be enforced, in a suitable case, by a lump sum order.

Discretion of the Court

In exercising its powers the court shall have regard to all the circumstances of the case, including any change in any of the matters referred to in s7(1) of the MPPO.[48] Where the payer has died, the court needs to take into account the changed circumstances resulting from his or her death.[49] Conduct of a party is also relevant if it would be repugnant to justice to ignore it. Thus, in *J (H.D.) v J (A.M.)*,[50] it was held that the fact that the wife assaulted, harassed and molested the husband was to be taken into account. In that case the wife who sought an increase in periodical payments

---

[43] S11(1) MPPO.
[44] See s11(5) MPPO.
[45] [1986] 1 FLR 412; *Dinch v Dinch* [1987] 2 FLR 162.
[46] *Whitfield v Whitfield* [1985] FLR 955.
[47] *Freeman-Thomas v Freeman-Thomas* [1963] 1 All ER 17.
[48] S11(7).
[49] S11(7)
[50] [1980] 1 WLR 124.

was awarded an amount less than that which she otherwise would have received had she not behaved so badly.

In the case of a consent order, except in unusual circumstances, the courts will uphold agreements freely entered into at arm's length by parties who were properly advised. In *N v N (consent order: variation)*,[51] the wife, against legal advice, agreed that her maintenance was to cease in five years and that she was not to seek further maintenance. The agreement was made a consent order. She then pursued a career as an opera singer but was unsuccessful and commenced a law degree with a view to becoming a barrister. She sought to have an extension of maintenance for another three years. It was held that the existence of the consent order was a most significant factor in the application for variation. Except in unusual circumstances, the courts would uphold agreements freely entered into at arm's length by the parties who were properly advised. The wife's application was rejected.

> It is of great importance not only to the parties but to the community as a whole that contracts of this kind should not be lightly disturbed. Lawyers must be able to advise their clients in respects of their future rights and obligations with some degree of certainty and clients must be able to rely on those agreements and know with some degree of assurance that once [it] is executed their affairs have been settled on a permanent basis. The courts must encourage parties to settle their differences without recourse to litigation. The modern approach in family law is to meditate and conciliate so as to enable the parties to make a fresh start in life on a secure basis.[52]

However, in *Richardson v Richardson (No 2)*,[53] the marriage lasted for 16 years, and the youngest child was to continue full-time education for another five years. The husband, 59 years of age, was a successful surgeon. The wife, 51, was a qualified nurse before the marriage but never worked during marriage. According to the consent order, the husband was to transfer the matrimonial home and pay a lump sum to the wife. He was also to pay for the children's maintenance, and periodical payments to the wife for three years. The intention was that there was to be a clean break in three years' time. At the time of the agreement, the wife was suffering from ill health and was known to be fragile. After the order, she suffered from

---

[51] [1993] 2 FLR 868.
[52] *Pelech v Pelech* [1987] 1 SCR 801 at p. 833 per Wilson J (Supreme Court of Canada); see also Carol Rogerson, 'The Causal Connection Test in Spousal Support Law' [1989] 8 CJFL 95.
[53] [1996] 2 FLR 617.

depression and was not fit to work. She applied for an extension of the periodical payments. It was held that the financial disparity of the parties was largely due to the success the husband had made of his material life and the failure the wife had made of hers since the order. That was not a reason for departing from the principles in *Edgar,* but in this case, the responsibility that the wife undertook since divorce, and still discharging, to care for the children meant that the capital the wife received in the original order was not available for her use. This justified an extension for another five years which would give the wife a more reasonable opportunity to achieve financial independence.

Again, in *B v B (consent order: variation),*[54] the wife was 55 years old and the marriage broke down after three years. A consent order was made providing for a lump sum to be paid to the wife together with periodical payments, diminishing over a period of seven years. The wife sought an extension of the periodical payments order. It was held that it ought to have been manifestly clear to the wife's legal advisers that the wife would be mostly unlikely to survive without periodical payments for the rest of her life. As she had received manifestly bad legal advice, the order was varied.

Once a change of circumstances has been proved, how is the court to vary the original order? Should the court start with the original order, see what changes have taken place since then, and make adjustments roughly in proportion to the changes? Where the husband's salary increased by 10 percent, is the jurisdiction of the court limited to an increased of 10 percent for the maintenance of the wife and children? In *Lewis v Lewis,*[55] it was held that the court had an unfettered discretion to look at the matters as they stood at the time when the case was before it. In other words, the matter of fixing or refixing periodical payments is at large. The court would consider all the circumstances afresh (*de novo*), and make an order which is reasonable in the circumstances.[56]

Variation after Death of the Payer

S11(6) of the MPPO provides that where a person against whom a secured periodical payments order was made has died, an application relating to that order may be made by the person entitled to payments under the

---

[54] [1995] 1 FLR 9.
[55] [1977] 3 All ER 992; *Payne v Payne* [1968] 1 WLR 390; *Garner v Garner* [1992] 1 FLR 573.
[56] *Hill v Hill* [1997] 1 FLR 730.

order, or by the personal representatives of the deceased person. But no application, except with leave of the court, shall be made after six months counting from the date on which representation in regard of the estate of that person is first taken out.[57] Where such an application is made, the court shall have the power to direct that the application be deemed to have been accompanied by an application for an order under s4 of the Inheritance (Provision for Family and Dependants) Ordinance.[58]

SETTING ASIDE

As has been mentioned, a capital order is a final order and no variation is possible. But a difficult question which the law has been confronted with is: what if after the making of a once-and-for-all settlement by way of capital provision, the husband wins the Mark-6 Lottery and comes into possession of a large sum of money? Can the wife seek to have a share of the husband's fortune? Similarly, what if after such an order, the wife remarries or dies? Could the husband seek to claw back payment made? Events occurring after the order may amount to new events justifying it being set aside. This may be done by way of appeal or by way of a fresh action.[59]

In *Barder v Barder (Caluori Intervening)*,[60] the court laid down the requirements for appealing out of time. In *Barder v Barder,* the order required the husband to transfer to the wife his interest in the former matrimonial home within 28 days. Before the order was implemented, the wife killed the two children of the family and committed suicide herself. The wife, by her will, devised her estate to her mother. The husband applied for leave to appeal out of time against the order on the ground that the fundamental basis upon which the order was made had been destroyed (i.e. the wife and the children would continue to live in the matrimonial home for a considerable period of time). The House of Lords held that leave to appeal would be granted to set aside a final order if four conditions could be satisfied:

---

[57] S11(6) of the MPPO.
[58] S20.
[59] For procedure to set aside, see *De Lasala v De Lasala* [1980] AC 546; *Allsop v Allsop* (1981) Fam Law 18; *BT v BT (divorce: procedure)* [1990] 2 FLR 1; *Lui Sik-kuen v Lee Suk-ling* [1992] 2 HKLR 371; *Robinson v Robinson (disclosure)* [1983] 4 FLR 102; *Re C (financial provision: leave to appeal)* [1993] 2 FLR 799; *C v C (financial provision: non-disclosure)* [1994] 2 FLR 272.
[60] [1987] 2 FLR 480.

(i) New events have occurred since the order which invalidated the basis on which the order was made, and if leave were granted to appeal out of time, the appeal would be certain or very likely to succeed.
(ii) The new events happened within a relatively short time of the order.
(iii) The application for leave was made reasonably promptly in the circumstances of the case.
(iv) Granting leave should not prejudice third parties who have acquired, in good faith and for valuable consideration, interest in property which is the subject matter of the relevant order.

Death of the recipient has been held to be a new event. In *Smith v Smith*,[61] the parties married for 33 years and an order was made for the provision of a lump sum in full and final settlement of the wife's claim. The wife committed suicide six months later and left all the money to her daughter. The Court of Appeal held that the death of the wife was a new event which invalidated the basis upon which the order was made. The court had to reconsider the matter afresh in light of the facts, and the estate of the wife was ordered to repay a sum to the husband.[62]

The approach of the court is to restrict the scope of 'new events'.[63] Fluctuation in the value of parties' assets is not a new event. In the recent case of *Cornick v Cornick*,[64] the original order provided to the wife about 51 percent of the parties' total asset. As a result of the increase in the value of the shares which the husband owned, the order represented only about 20 percent of the couple's assets. The wife applied for leave to appeal out of time. The High Court held that where there was no misrepresentation or material non-disclosure, and there was no evidence that there had been a mistake at the trial, it must be shown that there were 'very special and exceptional circumstances' justifying leave being granted. In this case the rise in the share price was nothing more than a fluctuation in the market which was unforeseen and unforeseeable; it did not constitute a 'new event'.

Remarriage of the recipient is not usually a 'new event'. In *Chaudhuri v Chaudhuri*,[65] an order was made that the matrimonial home be transferred to the wife subject to a charge in favour of the husband but that the charge

---

[61] [1991] 2 All ER 306.
[62] *Wells v Wells* [1992] 2 FLR 66.
[63] See *Amey v Amey* [1992] 2 FLR 89; *Chaudhuri v Chaudhuri* [1992] 2 FLR 73; *Cook v Cook* [1988] 1 FLR 521; *Crozier v Crozier* [1994] 1 FLR 126; *Edmonds v Edmonds* [1990] 2 FLR 202; *Hope-Smith v Hope-Smith* [1989] 2 FLR 56; *Penrose v Penrose* [1994] 2 FLR 621; *Thompson v Thompson* [1991] 2 FLR 530; *Worlock v Worlock* [1994] 2 FLR 689; *Ritchie v Ritchie* [1996] 1 FLR 898; *Benson v Benson (deceased)* [1996] 1 FLR 692.
[64] [1994] 2 FLR 530.
[65] [1992] 2 FLR 73.

was not to be enforced until the child ceased full-time education, or until the death or remarriage of the wife or her permanent cohabitation with another man, whichever occurred earlier. Fourteen months after the order, the wife informed the husband of her intention to remarry and move house. The husband sought leave to appeal out of time on the basis of the wife's remarriage. It was held that since the order contemplated the possibility of the wife's remarriage and the sale of the property, it could not be said that there had been a sufficient change in the circumstances underlying the basis of the order. Leave to appeal was refused.

Where the parties continue to live together after divorce, cohabitation does not constitute a new event invalidating the basis upon which the original order was made. Thus, in *Hill v Hill*,[66] the parties divorced and a consent order for financial provision and property adjustment was made in favour of the wife. After the divorce, the parties cohabited for 25 years. When the relationship ended, the wife sought leave to set aside the property adjustment order. Leave, however, to appeal out of time was refused.[67] However, in the rather unique and unusual case of *S v S (financial provision) (post divorce cohabitation)*,[68] the parties cohabited for 13 years after divorce and the wife applied to set aside the consent order which provided for the full and final settlement of the parties' claim for capital provision. The consent order was set aside despite the fact that 15 years had elapsed between the making of the order and the wife's application. The unusual facts were that the parties had lived under the same roof for 29 years but had been married for only eight years. During those years she managed the family home, being a mother to the children, working for a good part of the time and being a loyal 'wife' to a rising and successful businessman.

The court can also set an order aside if at the time the order was made there has been fraud, mistake or material non-disclosure.[69] Where the parties to a marriage wish the court to exercise its discretion under the MPPO, they are under a duty, in both contested and consent proceedings, to make full and frank disclosure of all material facts to the court and the other party, otherwise the court is not equipped to exercise its discretion properly. Thus, in *Livesey v Jenkins*,[70] in consideration of the wife relinquishing her claims for periodical payments, the husband agreed to transfer the

---

[66] [1997] 1 FLR 730.
[67] *Hewitson v Hewitson* [1995] 1 FLR 241.
[68] [1994] 2 FLR 228.
[69] *De Lasala v De Lasala* [1980] AC 546; *Thwaite v Thwaite* [1982] Fam 1; *Livesey v Jenkins* [1985] 1 All ER 106 but not bad legal advice, see *Harris v Manahan* [1997] 1 FLR 205.
[70] [1985] 1 All ER 106.

matrimonial home to her for the purpose of providing a home to her and the children. Six days after the agreement was reached, the wife became engaged to a man. Two days after the consent order was made, the wife remarried. The fact of engagement was not disclosed to the husband or his lawyer. The husband appealed against the consent order. The House of Lords held that the wife's engagement was a material fact, and was directly relevant to the parties' agreement. Her failure to disclose that fact before the agreement was put into effect invalidated the order. The order was thus set aside.[71]

In a recent case of *T v T (consent order: procedure to set aside)*,[72] the parties were married for 11 years. On divorce, financial arrangements were agreed upon and a consent order was made. Two months later, the husband sold his business and received a large sum of money although the agreement was based on an understanding that there was no free market for the business. Six and a half years after the order, the wife applied to set aside the order. It was held that the husband, by his deliberate failure to disclose that active negotiations to acquire his business were being conducted at the relevant time, had acted fraudulently. By reason of the non-disclosure, the wife received substantially less than her just entitlement; the order was set aside.

---

[71] In *Prow v Brown* [1983] 4 FLR 352 the husband applied to set aside the conveyance of the matrimonial home to the wife, which she later conveyed to herself and the man whom she planned to marry. The husband later modified his application to one of ancillary relief against the wife.

[72] [1996] 2 FLR 640.

Part IV

Protection

18

Child Protection

INTRODUCTION

Article 9 of the UN Convention on the Rights of the Child (UNC) provides that:

> ... a child shall not be separated from his or her parents against their will, except when competent authorities subject to judicial review determine, in accordance with applicable law and procedures, that such separation is necessary for the best interests of the child ... all interested parties shall be given an opportunity to participate in the proceedings and make their views known.

The family is assumed to be the best place for a child's upbringing. A child's well-being, however, may suffer at the hands of the parents, childminder, or indeed, anyone who has care and control of the child. Society has a duty to protect its vulnerable citizens, and to do so where necessary, by compulsory intervention in family life. Article 19(1) of the UNC further provides that:

> States parties shall take all appropriate legislative, administrative, social and educational measures to protect the child from all forms of physical or mental violence, injury or abuse, neglect or negligent treatment, maltreatment or exploitation, including sexual abuse, while in the care of parent(s), legal guardian(s) or any other person who has the care of the child.

Protecting children from abuse and neglect has become a major concern of the law in the past decade.[1] The extent of the problem can be seen in the following figures provided by the Department of Social Welfare.

Table 18.1 Number of Active Child Abuse Cases Classified by Type of Abuse

Active Cases as at	Physical	Neglect	Sexual	Psychological	Multiple	Total
31.12.94	293 (65.1%)	26 (5.8%)	77 (17.1%)	15 (3.3%)	39 (8.7%)	450
31.12.95	365 (63.4%)	25 (4.3%)	116 (20.1%)	24 (4.2%)	46 (8%)	576
31.12.96	361 (52.3%)	44 (6.4%)	191 (27.7%)	31 (4.5%)	63 (9.1%)	690
30.6.97	406 (53.2%)	47 (6.2%)	208 (27.3%)	29 (3.8%)	73 (9.5%)	763

Table 18.2 Sex and Age Distribution of Children

Active cases as at 30.6.1997

Age	Male		Female		Total	
0–2	21	6.1%	17	4.1%	38	5.0%
3–5	32	9.3%	62	14.8%	94	12.3%
6–8	63	18.3%	65	15.5%	128	16.8%
9–11	98	28.5%	79	18.9%	177	23.2%
12–14	93	27.0%	94	22.4%	187	24.5%
15–17	37	10.8%	102	24.3%	139	18.2%
Total	344	100%	419	100%	763	100%

---

[1] Conference Proceedings of 1993 and 1995 on Children's Rights in Hong Kong, ed by Nancy Rhind, Hong Kong Committee on Children's Rights and Against Child Abuse, 1997. Report of the Committee on the Evidence of Children in Criminal Proceedings, chaired by Mr I G Cross QC, January 1994, unpublished. Implementing the recommendations of this report, the Evidence (Amendment) Ordinance (No 70 of 1995) (i) removes the disqualification of children under seven years of age from giving evidence in court; (ii) provides that evidence of a child under 14 years of age shall be given unsworn; (iii) removes the requirement that unsworn evidence given by a child of tender years must be corroborated by some other material evidence before a defendant is to be convicted; and (iv) removes the requirement that a jury must be given a warning about the danger of convicting an accused on the uncorroborated evidence of a child.

From Table 18.1, it can be seen that the number of children abused and neglected has increased dramatically. It is unclear if the actual incidence of abuse has increased, or that the figures reflect increasing awareness of the problem, better detection and reporting procedures, or both.

Child abuse is defined as any act or omission that endangers or impairs a child's physical, psychological, or emotional health and development.[2] There are, in broad terms, four types of abuse. 'Physical abuse' includes non-accidental use of force, burning, or poisoning. 'Gross neglect' includes failure to provide a child with adequate food, clothing, shelter, or health care. It also encompasses forcing a child to undertake duties inappropriate to his/her physical strength or age, leaving a child habitually unattended or unreasonably depriving a child of education. 'Sexual abuse' includes exploitation of a child for sexual or erotic gratification, such as incest, exposing a child to other forms of sexual activity such as fondling or pornographic activities. 'Psychological abuse' includes behaviour and the maintenance of attitudes that endanger or impair the emotional or intellectual development of a child.[3]

The criminal law punishes sexual offenders and perpetrators of the crime of incest.[4] Where physical abuse causes death, a charge of murder or manslaughter may be preferred. Injuries of a lesser kind can be dealt with on a charge of ill-treatment or neglect causing bodily harm. S27 of the Offences Against the Person Ordinance provides that if any person over 16 who has the custody, charge or care of any child wilfully assaults, ill-treats, neglects, or abandons a child in a manner likely to cause unnecessary suffering or injury to the child's health shall be guilty of an offence. 'Neglect' means any omission or failure to provide adequately for the child's physical needs. 'Wilful' refers to any situation in which a defendant, after directing his or her mind to the question as to whether the child's health is likely to suffer unless certain action is taken, has come to a conscious decision to refrain from taking that action. Alternatively, it refers to a situation where the defendant does not care whether the child may be in need of care.[5] This subjective test (requiring the defendant to know of his omission or at least to have directed his mind to the child's physical needs) exonerates those parents who due to their own ignorance or lack of intelligence, are genuinely unaware of the risk to the child's health or medical requirements.

---

[2] See Guide to the Identification of Child Abuse, in *Procedure for Handling Child Sexual Abuse Cases,* Working Group On Child Abuse, February 1996, App. 1 (hereafter cited as Guide to the Identification of Child Abuse).
[3] Guide to the Identification of Child Abuse, App. 1, n. 2.
[4] See ss47–51 Crimes Ordinance.
[5] *Li Wang-fat v R* [1982] HKLR 133; *R v Sheppard* [1981] AC 394.

However, a parent may be guilty of manslaughter even if he did not assault the child causing death, but merely condoned the abuser's conduct.[6]

Criminal sanction or punishment operates after injuries have been inflicted and the victim harmed. The duty to investigate alleged child abuse and to protect children rests on the Department of Social Welfare and its Child Protective Services Unit (CPSU), on the police and on other agencies such as Against Child Abuse and Hong Kong Family Welfare Society.

INVESTIGATING CHILD ABUSE AND NEGLECT

In Hong Kong the Director of Social Welfare (DSW) is empowered to initiate proceedings to protect children 'in need of care or protection'.[7] Investigating suspected child abuse and neglect usually begins with referrals.[8] Such referrals usually come from those who are involved with a child's care and development such as teachers, social workers and doctors.[9] The cooperation of all these professional groups is both necessary and important in the detection and investigation of alleged child abuse and neglect. Unlike some jurisdictions,[10] Hong Kong does not have compulsory reporting statutes which impose a duty on any ordinary citizen who knows of the occurrence of child abuse and neglect to report it to the relevant authority. The possibility of introducing such legislation was mooted in connection with the problem of children left unattended at home, but it was thought inappropriate.[11]

Case Conference

Investigation of child abuse often involves the cooperation of teachers, social workers, doctors, and the police in the collation of all available

---

[6] *Chau Ming-cheong v R* [1983] HKLR 187.
[7] See s34(1) of the PCJO later; no action lies for breach of statutory duty or common law negligence, see *X (minors) v Bedfordshire County Council* [1995] 2 FLR 276.
[8] See Guide to the Identification of Child Abuse, n. 2.
[9] *D v National Society for the Prevention of Cruelty to Children* [1978] AC 171.
[10] Douglas Besharov, 'Child Abuse and Neglect Reporting and Investigation: Policy Guidelines for Decision Making' 22 Family Law Quarterly 1988, No 1, 1; Douglas Besharov, 'Combating Child Abuse: Guidelines for Cooperation between Law Enforcement and Child Protective Agencies' 23 Family Law Quarterly, 1990, No 3, 211.
[11] See Consultation Paper on Measures to Prevent Children from Being Left Unattended at Home, Director of Social Welfare, 1991, unpublished.

information about a child. This is done at a case conference to which professionals who are directly concerned with the child's care are invited. The case conference addresses outcome of the investigation, possible action for protecting the victim, therapy and rehabilitation programmes for the victim and the family.

A case conference is not a statutory creation. Its outcome may be that a child is to be placed on the 'at risk' or child protection register (CPR). The decision-making process of a case conference leading to the placing of names on the CPR, however, is unstructured and informal. It is not a judicial process; entry in the register is not a finding of fact, nor a finding of guilt. However, the rules of natural justice apply so there is a duty on those initiating and carrying out a case conference to act fairly. This does not mean that a parent has a right to attend a case conference. However, the proceedings may be regarded as unfair if no proper opportunity is afforded to the suspected person to controvert allegations which may be relevant to the decision. Thus, in *R v London Borough of Harrow ex parte Deal*,[12] the eldest of three children, was found to have serious bruising. The child was examined by a paediatrician who found the injuries consistent with non-accidental injuries. The mother's account was that the bruises were due to the children fighting with each other. A case conference was held. The mother's request to attend was refused but both she and a friend made written representations which were put before the conference. As a result of the conference, all the children were placed on the 'at risk' register, which recorded that injuries had been inflicted on the eldest child by the mother and that child abuse had been substantial. The mother sought judicial review of the decision on the basis that the conclusion of the case conference, and the placing of the mother's and the children's name on the register, was unfair, unreasonable and contrary to natural justice. The Court of Appeal held that the issue was whether the mother was responsible for the injuries inflicted. Natural justice required that she be given an opportunity to account for how those injuries could have occurred. Such opportunity was given to her and she gave her account both orally and in writing. Thus, it could not be said that there had been any breach of the rules of natural justice. A case conference was a part of the protection package for a child believed to have been abused. In balancing adequate protection for a child and fairness to an adult, an adult's interest might have to be placed second to a child's needs.

Where a decision to put a child on an 'at risk' register could be shown

---

[12] (1990) Fam Law 18; see also *R v Devon County Council ex parte L* [1991] 2 FLR 541.

to be unreasonable,[13] judicial review would provide a remedy. However, such remedy is rarely entertained. In *R v Norfolk County Council ex parte X*,[14] the applicant was alleged to have sexually abused a 13-year-old girl. Without notice to, or contact with the applicant, the local authority's social services department convened a case conference. The applicant was then notified of the decision that his and the girl's name had been placed in the child abuse register as abuser and victim. Unbeknown to him, however, his employers were also informed of the decision. On an application for judicial review, it was held that the procedures adopted by the local authority leading to the applicant's registration as an abuser were flawed. There was a failure to draw a distinction between a 'known' and a 'suspected' abuser. Further, the communication with the applicant's employer was obtuse and unfair. The decision of the local authority was quashed.[15]

This can be contrasted with *R v Devon County Council ex parte L*.[16] The applicant, L, and Mrs B lived together as man and wife. Mrs B had two children, one of whom was C. A social worker received a call from C's teacher reporting that C had been showing signs of disturbance at school. During an examination by a consultant paediatrician, C stated that L had been touching her in an inappropriate way. Although there was no physical evidence of abuse, the examination findings were consistent with sexual abuse. C was placed on the 'at risk' register. L denied all allegations and no criminal proceedings were instituted. L started living with Mrs G, who had a child but eventually left Mrs G as a result of a visit by a social worker who told Mrs G that L was alleged to have sexually assaulted a girl, and that if she continued to live with L, consideration would have to be given to placing her child on the 'at risk' register. L thus moved on to live with another woman, Mrs T, who also had two children. After a visit by a social worker, L left Mrs T and lived with Mrs H who again had children. L sought judicial review of the county council's refusal to give him an assurance that it would stop revealing their concern about L's background to mothers of children into whose household L proposed to move. It was held that there was no decision capable of review. The social workers concerned had all acted in good faith and in the honest belief that they had reasonable grounds for concern when they approached Mrs G, Mrs T and Mrs H. Although L had been prejudiced, the need to protect the children's interests prevailed over that of the interests of L.

---

[13] *Associated Provincial Picture Houses Ltd. v Wednesbury Corporation* [1948] 1 KB 223; *Council of Civil Service Unions v Minister of the Civil Service* [1985] AC 374.
[14] [1989] 2 FLR 120.
[15] See also *R v Lewisham London Borough Council ex parte P* [1991] 2 FLR 185.
[16] [1991] 2 FLR 541.

Child Protection Registry

One of the main objectives of the Child Protection Registry (CPR) is to facilitate communication between agencies which handle child abuse and neglect cases. The CPR provides an easy checking mechanism to ascertain whether a case is 'known' to any department or organisation.[17] Entry on the register itself does not offer a child any protection. Indeed, the circumstances under which a child could be so registered are widely defined. It could happen before a case conference is held or pursuant to a decision of a case conference.[18]

ORDERS FACILITATING INVESTIGATION AND PROTECTION

The law governing investigation and protection is to be found in the Protection of Children and Juveniles Ordinance (PCJO) which applies to all children under the age of 18.

Child Assessment Procedure

One important aspect of investigation and protection is the desire to balance a child's need for care or protection on the one hand and family privacy on the other. The balance is a delicate one. If a child dies or suffers serious injury as a result of neglect or abuse, the question will naturally arise as to why the relevant authorities failed to intervene to prevent such a tragedy. On the other hand, where social workers intervene, and on further investigation, a child turns out to have been well-looked after, parents may feel that their parental rights have been unnecessarily violated.

The PCJO provides a procedure which is a halfway house between compulsory intervention and taking no action. S45A(1) provides that where the Director of Social Welfare (DSW) has 'reasonable cause to suspect' that a child 'is, or is likely to be, in need of care or protection',[19] he may require any person having custody or control of the child or juvenile:

---

[17] Guide to the Identification of Child Abuse, n. 2, App. VIII.
[18] Ibid.
[19] For definition, see below s34(2).

(a) to produce the child for an assessment by a medical practitioner, clinical psychologist or an approved social worker,[20] of the state of his health or development or of the way in which he has been treated, or
(b) to allow the DSW to observe the condition of the child.

The person who is required to produce a child shall take reasonable steps to ensure the production of the child at the time and place specified in a notice issued under s45A(1).[21] Where the identity or the whereabouts of the person to be served with a notice cannot be ascertained or where a notice has not been complied with, the DSW can remove the child for the purpose of an assessment.[22] The removed child cannot be detained for more than 12 hours from the time of removal for the purpose of completing the assessment.[23] However, this may be extended to 36 hours in total if the medical practitioner, clinical psychologist, or approved social worker who carries out the assessment is of the opinion that such a further period is necessary to complete the assessment.[24]

In relation to allowing a child to be observed, it is unclear how long an observation may last. S45A(8) provides that the DSW may authorise any officer to enter any premises for the purpose of removing or observing the condition of a child. Entry, however, may not be effected by force unless a warrant is obtained from a magistrate, juvenile court or District Court under s45A(9).[25]

Emergency Protection: Taking a Child to a Place of Refuge

There may be circumstances where speedy and effective measures need to be taken to protect a child from actual danger. S34E(1) of the PCJO provides that a person authorised in writing by the DSW or any police officer of the rank of station sergeant or above may remove a child to a place of refuge, or such other place, as he may consider appropriate where a child appears to be 'in need of care or protection'.[26]

S34E(1) does not require that the relevant person have reasonable cause to believe that a child is 'in need of care or protection'; a subjective test

---

[20] 'Approved social worker' means a 'social worker approved by the DSW as possessing the appropriate qualification and experience to make an assessment pursuant to S45A', s2.
[21] S45A(2).
[22] S45A(4).
[23] S45A(5).
[24] S45A(6).
[25] S8.
[26] For definition, see below.

applies. The power to take a child to a place of refuge applies only in cases where a child appears to 'have been or is being assaulted, ill-treated, neglected or sexually abused' or where the child 'is beyond control, to the extent that harm may be caused to him or others'.

Where a child is 'in need of care or protection' because the child's 'health, development or welfare has been, or is, or appears likely to be neglected or avoidably impaired', the same power to take a child to a place of refuge applies provided that:
(a) the child has within the preceding two weeks been assessed under s45A, or
(b) a notice has been served under s45A(1)(a) within the preceding month but it has not been complied with, or
(c) the DSW is unable to ascertain the identity or whereabouts of any person on whom the notice may be served.

Where a child or juvenile is detained in a place of refuge, the person in charge shall have 'the like control over the child or juvenile as the parent and shall be responsible for his maintenance'.[27] S34F(1)(2) permits a child to be taken to a hospital instead of to a place of refuge. A child who is so taken may be detained for so long as is necessary for the purpose of medical or surgical attention or treatment. Where a child is detained in a hospital, the DSW shall have the like control over, and responsibility for maintenance of that child as if the child is detained in a place of refuge.[28]

A removed child must be brought before a juvenile court within 48 hours and an application must be made under s34(1).[29] However, the court may extend the detention up to 56 hours in total. The DSW has the power of entry; but such entry may not be effected by force unless a warrant has been issued by a magistrate, juvenile court or by the District Court.[30]

PROCEEDINGS FOR CARE AND SUPERVISION

An investigation may reveal that there are grounds for legal intervention, either to remove a child from its parents or to impose some kind of

---

[27] S34E(5).
[28] S34F(4). It is unclear whether the DSW has the power to consent to the child's medical treatment; compare s44 of the English Children Act 1989.
[29] S34E(2).
[30] S34E(6)(7).

supervision on the child's upbringing. Here again, the law needs to balance between family privacy and intervention to safeguard the welfare of children.

S34(1) of the PCJO provides that a juvenile court may, upon being satisfied that a child is 'in need of care or protection', make certain orders.[31]

A Child 'in Need of Care or Protection': The Threshold Conditions

S34(2) of the PCJO defines that a child 'in need of care or protection' as a child or juvenile

(a) who has been or is being assaulted, ill-treated, neglected or sexually abused; or
(b) whose health, development or welfare has been or is being neglected or avoidably impaired; or
(c) whose health, development or welfare appears likely to be neglected or avoidably impaired; or
(d) who is beyond control, to the extent that harm may be caused to him or others, and who requires care or protection.

Assaulted, ill-treated, neglected or sexually abused[32]

The threshold condition in s34(2) is widely drafted. 'Assault' means causing an apprehension of physical violence on the part of the victim.[33] The use of threatening language to a child, which may or may not be accompanied by an aggressive gesture, may suffice. The former is likely to be satisfied if a child is of peculiarly delicate sensibilities or weak disposition. There is no requirement that the assault cause or be likely to cause suffering or injury to health. When an assault is accompanied by actual violence, it amounts to 'ill-treatment'.[34] There is no requirement that ill-treatment be repeated, form a pattern, or be persistent. One instance of assault or ill-treatment

---

[31] See below, pp. 454–5.
[32] S27 Offences Against the Person Ordinance.
[33] Cf. *R v Hatton* [1925] 2 KB 322 ('assault' refers to assault in a manner likely to cause unnecessary suffering; defendant committed acts of indecency in the presence of the child, but not on her, and he placed his hand over her mouth to stop her from screaming. Held: this was not an assault within the meaning of the section).
[34] A slight degree of violence which does not amount to ill-treatment on a normal healthy child may be ill-treatment to a child with brittle bone disease. Here the defendant must have knowledge of the child's peculiar condition, *R v Sheppard* [1981] AC 394.

suffices.[35] 'Neglect' means the failure to provide for the child's physical needs, but it does not include emotional or spiritual needs.[36]

The element of 'sexual abuse' is not defined in s34(2). However, the Guide to the Identification of Child Abuse states that 'sexual abuse' includes exploitation of a child for sexual or erotic gratification, such as incest, or exposing a child to other forms of sexual activity such as fondling or pornographic activities.[37] Another useful definition can be found in Glaser and Frosh.[38]

> Any child below the age of consent may be deemed to have been sexually abused when a sexually mature person has, by design or by neglect of their usual societal or specific responsibilities in relation to the child, engaged or permitted the engagement of that child in any activity of a sexual nature which is intended to lead to the sexual gratification of the sexually mature person. This definition pertains whether or not this activity involves explicit coercion by any means, whether or not initiated by the child, or whether or not there is discernible harmful outcome in the short term.

Thus, a father whose sexual gratification derives from watching pornographic movies with his daughter, or conducting sexual acts with her would be covered by this definition.

Standard of proof: on the balance of probabilities

Care proceedings are civil proceedings so the standard of proof required is on the balance of probabilities. However, where serious allegations are made, amounting to criminal or grossly immoral conduct, the degree of probability must be commensurate with the gravity of the offence alleged.[39] Thus, Lord Nicholls states:[40]

> When assessing the probabilities the court will have in mind a factor ... that the more serious the allegation the less likely it is that the event

---

[35] Thus one slap on the face of a mentally ill patient was held to be ill-treatment, *R v Holmes* [1979] Crim LR 52. However 'is being' or 'has been' seems to denote a state of affairs extending over a period of time, *Re D (a minor)* [1987] 1 AC 317.

[36] See *R v Sheppard* [1981] AC 394.

[37] See n. 2.

[38] Danya Glaser and Stephen Frosh, *Child Sexual Abuse*, 2nd edition, British Association of Social Workers, London, 1993, p. 5.

[39] See *H v H (Kent County Council intervening) (child abuse: evidence)* [1989] 3 All ER 740; *Re H (minors) (sexual abuse: standard of proof)* [1996] 2 WLR 8; cf. Lord Lloyd at p. 15.

[40] *Re H (minors) (sexual abuse: standard of proof)* [1996] 2 WLR 8 at p. 23.

occurred and, hence, the stronger should be the evidence before the court concludes that the allegation is established on the balance of probabilities. A stepfather is usually less likely to have repeatedly raped and had non-consensual oral sex with his under age stepdaughter than on some occasions to have lost his temper and slapped her.

Care proceedings and custody proceedings

Allegations of sexual abuse may arise in custody proceedings, for instance, where a mother alleges that the father had sexually abused the daughter. The appropriate standard of proof as to whether sexual abuse has taken place is on the balance of probabilities. However, a judge, exercising his discretion in deciding whether future access by a father should be permitted, will apply the welfare principle. In doing so, the judge could take into account evidence which, whilst not sufficient to show on the balance of probabilities that the father has abused his child, nevertheless, points to a real possibility or a real risk of abuse in the future.

> [the judge] may have found individual facts, such as inappropriate knowledge or behaviour, which constitute a high degree of concern about the child without being able to say on the test that they amount to actual abuse. They are, however, relevant to the exercise of the discretion. He may have sufficient evidence of concern about the past care of the child to be satisfied that the child was in a potentially abusing situation without having sufficient evidence to be satisfied as to the extent of the abuse in the past or the identity of the abuser. He has to assess the risks, and, if there is a real possibility that the child will be at risk, he will take steps to safeguard the child.[41]

Health, development or welfare

The terms 'development' 'health', and 'welfare' admit of a wide interpretation, but their semantic components overlap to a certain extent and this is apparent from the decisions; they are all continuing concepts,[42] 'development' is not confined to physical but also covers mental and emotional development;[43] 'welfare' overlaps with aspects such as health and development (including physical, intellectual, emotional, psychological, social, and behavioural development).

---

[41] *H v H (Kent County Council intervening) (child abuse: evidence)* [1989] 3 All ER 740 at p. 750 per Butler-Sloss LJ.
[42] *Re D (a minor)* [1987] 1 AC 317.
[43] See *F v Suffolk County Council* [1981] 2 FLR 208.

'Has been', 'is being' or 'appears likely'

Events in the past, present and future are covered by 'has been', 'is being' and 'appears likely'. These phrases provide the court with the widest power to protect children. S34(2) thus covers a child whose health, development or welfare has been avoidably impaired, e.g. when born with drug withdrawal symptoms as a result of the mother's use of narcotics during pregnancy.[44]

'Appears likely' does not mean more probable than not; it suffices if there is a real possibility of the occurrence of an event or a state of affairs:[45]

> ... Parliament cannot have been using likely in the sense of more likely than not. If the word likely were given this meaning, it would have the effect of leaving outside the scope of care and supervision orders cases where the court is satisfied there is a real possibility of significant harm to the child in the future but that possibility falls short of being more likely than not ... In my view, therefore, the context shows that ... likely is being used in the sense of a real possibility that cannot sensibly be ignored having regard to the nature and gravity of the feared harm in the particular case.[46]

Where the allegation is that a child's health appears likely to be neglected, and this arises solely out of alleged misconduct on the part of a parent in the past (for instance, neglect of an older child), the question is whether it is necessary to prove that misconduct has in fact occurred before it could be said that the younger child's health appears likely to be neglected. In a majority decision of the House of Lords in *Re H (minors) (sexual abuse: standard of proof)*,[47] the answer appears to be affirmative. In that case, a mother had four daughters. The eldest daughter, at the age of 13, alleged that she had been sexually abused by her stepfather (R) since she was seven. R was charged with rape, but the jury acquitted him. The local authority proceeded to take the three younger daughters into care, based solely on the alleged sexual abuse of the oldest daughter. The judge refused to make a care order, holding that he was not sure that the girl's allegation was true (on the balance of probabilities); but he had his suspicions that

---

[44] *Re D (a minor)* [1987] 1 AC 317; *Essex County Council v T.L.R. and K.B.R.* (1979) 9 Fam Law 15; see Jonathan Montgomery, 'Mothers and Unborn Children', (1987) 17 Fam Law 227, see also *Re F (in utero)* [1988] 2 All ER 193. Andrew Bainham, *Children, Parents and the State*, p. 83.

[45] See *Re H (minors) (sexual abuse: standard of proof)* [1996] 2 WLR 8; *Newham London Borough Council v AG* [1993] 1 FLR 281.

[46] Ibid., at p. 22 Lord Nicholls.

[47] [1996] 2 WLR 8.

there was a real possibility that her statement and evidence were true. The House of Lords held that the judge had rejected the only evidence giving rise to the care order application. It was not open to him to consider the likelihood of further harm to the children.[48]

Lord Browne-Wilkinson dissenting, disagreed with the need to make a preliminary finding as to the truth of a past allegation before proceeding to make an assessment of future risk:

> ... I agree that the judge can only act on evidence and on facts which, so far as relevant, have been proved. He has to be satisfied by the evidence before him that there is a real possibility of serious harm to the child. Where I part company is in thinking that the facts relevant to an assessment of risks ("is likely to suffer ... harm") are not the same as the facts relevant to a decision that harm is, in fact, being suffered. In order to be satisfied that an event has occurred or is occurring the evidence has to be shown on the balance of probabilities that such an event did occur or is occurring. But in order to be satisfied that there is a risk of such an occurrence, the ambit of the relevant facts is in my view wider. The combined effect of a number of factors which suggest that a state of affairs, though not proved to exist, may well exist is the normal basis for the assessment of future risk. To be satisfied of the existence of a risk does not require proof of the occurrence of past historical events but proof of facts which are relevant to the making of a prognosis.[49]

Lord Lloyd dissenting said that:

> There is nothing [in the subsection] which requires the court to make a finding about anything in the past or present. The finding of future risk must, of course, be based on evidence. It cannot be based on hunch. If there is no evidence to support a finding of risk, the finding will be set aside. But if there is such evidence, then a finding may be made, even though the same evidence is insufficient to support a finding of past event.[50]

Lord Browne-Wilkinson expressed his concern about the need for a preliminary finding:

> My Lords, I am anxious that the decision of the House in this case may establish the law in an unworkable form to the detriment of many children at risk. Child abuse, particularly sex abuse, is notoriously difficult to prove in a court of law. The relevant facts are extremely sensitive and

---

[48] See also *H v H (Kent County Council intervening) (child abuse: evidence)* [1989] 3 All ER 740.
[49] [1996] 2 WLR 8 at p. 11.
[50] Ibid., at p. 18.

emotive. They are often known only to the child and to the alleged abuser. If legal proof of an actual abuse is a prerequisite to a finding that a child is at risk of abuse, the court will be powerless to intervene to protect children in relation to whom there are the gravest suspicions of actual abuse but the necessary evidence legally to prove such abuse is lacking.[51]

The relevant date

The relevant date on which a criterion is or is not satisfied is the date at which the protection procedure is initiated, not the date of the hearing. This was the decision of the House of Lords in *Re M (a minor) (care order: threshold conditions)*.[52] In that case, M was born to unmarried parents. The mother had three other children, all by different fathers. When he was four months old, his father violently killed the mother in the presence of all the children. All his half-siblings went to live with a maternal cousin, Mrs W, but M went into foster-care because Mrs W could not care for all four children. The local authority applied for a care order with a view to placing M for adoption. By the time of the hearing Mrs W was coping well with the half-siblings, and wished to take care of M too. The question which the court had to decide was whether M 'was suffering' from significant harm warranting a care order. It was clear that M had suffered harm, but at the time of the hearing, M was not suffering from significant harm. The House of Lords held that the relevant date the criterion was satisfied was the date at which the local authority initiated the protection procedure, not the date of the hearing. Otherwise, protection would rarely be ordered if protective procedures, once invoked proved to be satisfactory, and the child was no longer at the date of the hearing suffering harm.

Neglected or avoidably impaired

'Development', 'health' or 'welfare' is 'avoidably impaired' if the parent could by an act of will have fostered, promoted, nurtured and enhanced it but failed to do so. Where the harm is a direct consequence of the parent's disability (physical or mental), or if the parent is unaware of (or not cognisant of) any neglect, or of the risk of impairment or the possibility of prevention, the harm could not be said to be 'avoidable' because it was beyond the competence of the parent to have avoided it.[53] 'Neglect', on the other hand, does not have to be 'unavoidable'.

---

[51] Ibid., at p. 12.
[52] [1994] 3 All ER 298.
[53] See S Cretney, *Elements of Family Law,* Sweet & Maxwell, London, 1987, p. 216.

Who is beyond control, to the extent that harm may be caused to him or others

A child may be beyond control and harm may befall him. The degree of 'harm' is unqualified and it appears that any kind of harm is included, no matter how trivial or inconsequential such harm may be. A child who is a victim of verbal abuse by his peers may be said to have been 'harmed'; as has a child who has been taken advantage of in his financial dealings with his friends.

ORDERS WHICH THE COURT CAN MAKE

Where the court is satisfied that a child or juvenile is in need of 'care or protection' under s34(2) of the PCJO, it may make any of the following orders.

Legal Guardianship to Director of Social Welfare

Where a child or juvenile is under the legal guardianship of the DSW, and unless the court orders to the contrary, the DSW may make any order regarding the custody and control of the child or juvenile which he thinks desirable in the interests of the child or juvenile.[54] An order of legal guardianship ceases to have effect when the child or juvenile reaches the age of 21 or marries, whichever is earlier.[55]

Care Committed to Another Person or Institution

S34(4)(a) provides that any person or institution to whose care a child or juvenile is committed shall have the 'like control over the child or juvenile as the parent and shall be responsible for his maintenance'. The child shall continue to be in the care of such person or institution notwithstanding that he is claimed by his parent.

---

[54] S34(5).
[55] S34(6).

Parent's Recognisance

The court can order a parent or guardian to enter into recognisance to exercise proper care and guardianship.

Supervision Order

The court can also make a supervision order. Such an order can be made independently of any of the above orders. Alternatively, it can be made together with a parental recognisance order or the committal to care order.[56] However, a supervision order shall not exceed three years. In the case of a child or juvenile who is a female, she shall be placed under the supervision of a woman.[57]

FUTURE DEVELOPMENTS

The definition of a child 'in need of care or protection' only defines the sort of threshold conditions under which a child may be the subject of the above orders. When should the court make such an order? Article 3(1) UNC provides that:

> in all actions concerning children, whether undertaken by public or private social welfare institutions, courts of law, administrative authorities or legislative bodies, the best interests of the child shall be a primary consideration.

The welfare principle has now become the cornerstone in child law and should be the guiding principle in the PCJO as well. Equally important is the participation of a child in proceedings concerning his or her welfare. Where the child is old enough to express his or her own views, UNC Article 12(1) states that:

> States Parties shall assure to the child who is capable of forming his or her own views the right to express those views freely in all matters affecting the child, the views of the child being given due weight in accordance with the age and maturity of the child. The child shall be provided the opportunity to be heard in any proceedings affecting the child.

---

[56] S34(1)(d).
[57] S34(1AA).

Article 12(2) continues:

> For this purpose, the child shall in particular be provided the opportunity to be heard in any judicial and administrative proceedings affecting the child, either directly, or though a representative . . .

At present, there is no formal structure whereby the views of the children can be heard nor their interests represented. Although the assistance of the Official Solicitor may be sought by the court, this rarely happens.

The importance of inter-agency cooperation has been stressed in the investigation and identification of child abuse and neglect. The kinds of difficulty that can arise were discussed in *Oxfordshire County Council v P*.[58] In that case, care proceedings were initiated with respect to a child following the appearance of unexplained injuries. The mother confided in the guardian *ad litem* (GAL) that she had caused the injuries. The GAL informed the case social worker who then informed the police. The police interviewed the GAL to obtain a witness statement from her for the purposes of criminal proceedings. The mother lost confidence in the GAL and sought to have the GAL replaced. The issue was whether the GAL was at liberty to disclose the mother's admissions to the police? Ward J held that since the report of the GAL was confidential, the information (including the mother's admission) collected by the GAL in preparing the report must also be confidential. Leave of the court, therefore, was required for disclosure to someone who was not a party to the care proceedings. It was wrong for the GAL to make a witness statement to the police, and the police were wrong to seek to rely on it without first obtaining leave of the court.

On the wider question of whether the GAL could pass the information to the social services, Ward J took the view that the GAL could not be criticised for doing so as the social services were also a party to the care proceedings. Yet, the social services were not entitled to pass the information on the police who were not a party to the proceedings.

> [the social services] are not entitled to do so because it was information relating to the proceedings obtained by an officer of the court for the court. Only the court was entitled to allow its use outside the four corners of the proceedings. If that is the strict position, it is not necessarily the sensible position . . . it is a good practice for the police and social services to co-operate in their mutual enquiry. It would be extraordinary if at a child protection conference the police had to be asked to leave the room whilst the conference reviewed the arrangements for the protection of the

---

[58] [1995] 1 FLR 552.

child ... The court is also a partner in this multi-disciplinary approach towards child care and I would be surprised if any court would complain of the disclosure of the information at such a review.[59]

Ward J took the view that practice guidelines are required, permitting the free exchange of information between the social services and the police, particularly on the following matters, on the basis that:[60]
(i) the information is treated by the police as confidential information.
(ii) it may be used by the police to shape the nature and range of inquiries they undertake in the investigation of the alleged criminal offences. They may be permitted to use the information for that investigation but they are not permitted to use it as evidence in any criminal proceedings that may follow.
(iii) if they wish to use as evidence information arising from and in care proceedings, then they must seek leave from the court.

More recently, the question of legal professional privilege was raised in *Re L (police investigation: privileged)*.[61] In that case, a child became seriously ill after ingesting methadone. The child's parents, who were drug addicts, explained that the poisoning was accidental. The local authority obtained an interim care order. On the application of the parents, the court granted an order giving them leave to disclose court papers to a medical expert for the purpose of reporting on the frequency of consumption of methadone by the child, the identity of such expert to be disclosed to the parties. The report, however, cast serious doubts on the mother's account. The police, who were not a party to the care proceedings, heard of the report in a case conference and applied for copies of it for the purpose of investigating criminal offences. The mother argued that the report was protected by legal professional privilege; that its disclosure infringed her privilege against self-incrimination. The House of Lords held by a majority (Lord Mustill and Lord Nicholls dissenting) that there was a distinction between privilege attaching to the solicitor/client relationship and privilege attaching to reports of third parties prepared on the instructions of a client for the purposes of litigation (litigation privilege). The latter was essentially a creature of adversarial procedure. Since care proceedings were non-adversarial in nature, no privilege attached to such a report.

All these are important issues which no doubt will be addressed in the future.

---

[59] Ibid., at p. 562.
[60] Ibid., at p. 562.
[61] [1996] 1 FLR 731.

19

Protection against Domestic Violence

INTRODUCTION

"Battered wives" is a telling phrase. It was invented to call the attention of the public to an evil. Few were aware of it. It arose when a woman suffered serious or repeated physical injury from the man with whom she lived. She might be a wife properly married to her husband: or she might only be a woman ... living with a man in the same household as if she were his wife ....To go back for a few centuries, by the old common law a husband was allowed to beat his wife so long as he did it with a stick no bigger than his thumb. He was able, Blackstone says, to give his wife "moderate correction". But Blackstone goes on to tell us that by his time this power of correction began to be doubted: "Yet the lower rank of people, who were always fond of the old common law, still claim and exert their ancient privilege ... "[1]

Domestic violence can take many forms. In its narrower sense, it means the use or threat of physical force against a victim in the form of an assault or battery. In its wider sense, it covers any form of physical, sexual or psychological molestation or harassment which has a detrimental effect upon the health and well-being of the victim.[2] The majority of the victims

---
[1] *Davis v Johnson* [1979] AC 264 at p. 270.
[2] English Law Reform Commission, Domestic Violence and Occupation of the Family Home, No 207, HMSO, London, 1992, p. 4 (hereafter cited as English Law Reform Commission, No 207).

of domestic violence are women,[3] for instance, wives, cohabitees or girlfriends, but they may also be men, and, for ease of reference, the female pronoun will be used to refer to those who need legal protection.

The extent of domestic violence in Hong Kong is not well-researched,[4] and a battered woman has very few legal options. She may report violence to the police, but they may be reluctant to intervene in domestic or family disputes.[5] Even if the police intervene, violence may be repeated. Criminal proceedings do not offer effective and speedy protection to the victims.[6] Civil action for trespass to the person is inappropriate where emergency protection is needed. An interlocutory injunction restraining the aggressor from assaulting the victim may attract further violence.[7] Divorce proceedings is only appropriate if the victim entertains no hope of saving her marriage.

DOMESTIC VIOLENCE ORDINANCE

In light of the above problems, the Domestic Violence Ordinance (DVO) came into force on 19 December 1986, filling in the gaps of the criminal and private law. Its long title states: 'to provide protection of persons from domestic violence and for matters ancillary thereto'. Based essentially on the English Domestic Violence and Matrimonial Proceedings Act 1976,[8] it gives a victim the right to seek a speedy injunction on a simple application to the District Court,[9] whether or not any other relief is sought in the proceedings.

Who Can Apply: A Party to a Marriage and Cohabitees

The main provision of the DVO is in s3(1). It states that, on an application

---

[3] The Hong Kong Law Reform Commission Privacy Sub-committee, 'Stalking', Consultation Paper, May 1998.
[4] Hong Kong Legislative Council, 9 July 1986, pp. 1439–41; Chan Yuk-chung, 'News Reporting on Family Violence in Hong Kong: A Case Study'. Department of Applied Social Studies, Hong Kong Polytechnic University, Occasional Paper Series No. 2, 1995.
[5] See Annex I of this chapter, p. 476.
[6] On marital rape, see *R v R (rape: marital exemption)* [1991] 2 All ER 257 and the defence of provocation, see *R v Ahluwalia* [1992] 4 All ER 889; *R v Thornton* [1992] 1 All ER 306.
[7] *Patel v Patel* [1988] 2 FLR 179; *Pidduck v Molloy* [1992] 2 FLR 202.
[8] Now repealed by the Family Law Act 1996.
[9] And sometimes the Court of First Instance, see s4.

by a 'party to a marriage', if the District Court[10] is satisfied that 'the applicant or a child living with the applicant has been molested' by the other party to the marriage, it may grant an injunction.

The Ordinance covers 'a party to a marriage', but it does not cover a party to a former marriage.[11] 'A party to a marriage' includes a man and a woman in cohabitation, and references in the Ordinance to 'marriage' and 'matrimonial home' shall be construed accordingly.[12] Lesbian or homosexual couple is not covered, neither is the relationship between a parent and child. Flatmates of opposite sex are excluded if the relationship is non-sexual.

There is no requirement as to how long the parties have to live together to amount to 'cohabitation', However, s6(3) provides that an ouster or entry order shall not be granted unless the court is satisfied that having regard to the permanence of the relationship it is appropriate in all the circumstances to grant such an injunction.[13]

In *Adeoso v Adeoso*,[14] the court gave a liberal interpretation to cohabitation. There, the parties lived together as joint tenants in a very small flat for three years. The relationship broke down and they continued to live together for about one year. They lived in separate rooms, communicated only by notes, and the applicant ceased cooking and washing for the respondent. The Court of Appeal held that on an objective view the parties were a cohabiting couple, and the court had jurisdiction to consider the application.

If a woman leaves the place of violence, could she be said to be cohabiting with the violent party? It has been said that as long as the parties were living together at the time of the incidents relied on, the fact that they are no longer living together at the time of the application matters not. Thus, in *McLean v Nugent*,[15] the respondent man had forced the applicant to admit him to her home, and he stayed there against her will. It was held that the court had jurisdiction to grant an order two months after she was driven out of her home. However, the longer time elapses between the cessation of the relationship and the incident complained of, the more difficult it is for an applicant to obtain remedy under the DVO.[16] In *O'Neill*

---

[10] S4 says that the High Court may exercise the power in s3 in the case of emergency (ex parte).
[11] *White v White* [1983] 4 FLR 696.
[12] S2(2). *Baring v Baring* [1992] HKLY 526, held that a premises where the parties had never cohabited therein could be the matrimonial home.
[13] *Davis v Johnson* [1979] AC 264, at p. 342.
[14] [1981] 1 All ER 107.
[15] [1980] FLR 26.
[16] *McLean v Nugent* [1980] FLR 26 at p. 32; *Harrison v Lewis* [1988] 2 FLR 339.

v Williams,[17] a lapse of six months was held to be too late. In *Harrison v Lewis*,[18] it was held that no complaint could be made concerning behaviour which occurred after the cessation of cohabitation.[19]

Pre-Condition for Granting an Injunction: Molestation

Before granting an order under s3(1), the court must be satisfied that the applicant or a child living with the applicant has been 'molested'. No violence or threat of violence is necessary as 'molestation' covers any conduct which can properly be regarded as such a degree of harassment as to call for the intervention of the court.[20] Viscount Dilhorne said:

> Violence is a form of molestation, but molestation may take place without the threat or use of violence and still be serious and inimical to mental and physical health.[21]

Pestering is the best synonym. In *Vaughan v Vaughan*,[22] the Court of Appeal held that molestation had been made out when a husband called at his wife's house early in the morning, late at night, and at her place of work, making a nuisance of himself to her. In *Horner v Horner*, the defendant-husband's molestation took the form of handing the wife upsetting notes, intercepting her on her way to work. In *Spencer v Camacho*,[23] the molestation involved riffling through the victim's handbag. In *George v George*,[24] the conduct complained consisted of sending abusive letters, shouting obscenities and following the victim around. In *F v F (protection from violence: continuing cohabitation)*,[25] it was said that:

> "Molestation" includes the forcing by the other party of his or her society on the unwilling suffering party, whether the purpose of the molester is seeking to resume affectionate relations or to harm or annoy the suffering party.[26]

---

[17] [1984] FLR 1.
[18] [1988] 2 FLR 339.
[19] See also *Tuck v Nicholls* [1989] 1 FLR 283.
[20] *Horner v Horner* [1982] 2 WLR 914 at p. 916 per Ormrod LJ.
[21] *Davis v Johnson* [1979] AC 264 at p. 334.
[22] [1973] 3 All ER 449.
[23] [1983] 4 FLR 662.
[24] [1986] 2 FLR 347.
[25] [1989] 2 FLR 451.
[26] Ibid., at p. 452 per Judge Fricker QC; see also *Johnson v Walton* [1990] 1 FLR 350 where molestation was held to include the publication in a newspaper of an article about the applicant which included partially nude pictures intended to cause distress to the applicant.

It has been said that deliberate conduct is required.[27] However, in *Wooton v Wooton*,[28] involuntary violence was also included. In the case, the respondent was an epileptic and was violent when having a fit. The Court of Appeal held that the legislation dealt with actual violence and the consequences of it were an important factor to consider.

The victim may be the applicant or a child living with the applicant. A child living with the applicant means a person under the age of 18.[29] Although such a child has no *locus standi* to apply under the DVO, an injunction is available if the court is satisfied that a child living with the applicant has been molested. There is no requirement that the child and the applicant are in any particular relationship, and protection is given to a situation of domestic upheaval.

Orders Which the Court Can Make

Where the court is satisfied that 'the applicant or a child living with the applicant has been molested'[30] by the other party, the court may grant any or all of the following injunctions.

Non-molestation order

This is to restrain the respondent from 'assaulting, molesting, annoying or otherwise interfering with' the applicant, and/or any child living with the applicant. However, a non-molestation order will not be granted to an applicant who is cohabiting with the respondent and intends to continue cohabitation. In *F v F (protection from violence: continuing cohabitation)*,[31] the husband had a drinking problem which caused him to be violent to the wife. The wife intended to continue living with him and continuing with full matrimonial intimacy, but she had not reconciled to his violence and molestation. She sought protection but it was held that a non-molestation order would only be granted to enable the applicant to be free from cohabitation and therefore to keep free from such cohabitation.

---

[27] *F v F (protection from violence: continuing cohabitation)* [1989] 2 FLR 451.
[28] [1984] FLR 871.
[29] As amended by the Marriage and Children (Miscellaneous Amendment) Ordinance (No 69 of 1997).
[30] Threatened molestation is not sufficient.
[31] [1989] 2 FLR 451.

Ouster order/an entry order

An ouster order serves to exclude a party from the matrimonial home, or specified part of the matrimonial home or a specific area. The need to protect a person from domestic violence overrides the proprietary interests of a property owner. In *Davis v Johnson*,[32] the man beat his partner frequently and threatened to kill her and dump her in the river and alternatively to chop her up and put her remains in the freezer. Although they were joint tenant of their flat, the House of Lords held that the legislation was concerned with the evil of domestic violence and a violent person could be excluded from his home which the parties had shared irrespective of his property right. Although an ouster order suspends or restricts the enjoyment of property right, it does not negate property right. Such restriction has no effect on a third party, and the owner may sell, mortgage, or let the property to a third party.[33]

An entry order mandates the respondent to allow the applicant to enter and remain in the matrimonial home or a specific part thereto. This allows a spouse who has been driven out of the home to return safely, and it is normally used in conjunction with an ouster order.

Duration

The aim of DVO is to provide emergency, practical and short-term relief to victims of domestic violence.[34] An exclusion order and a entry order shall be for such period as the court considers necessary, but it shall not exceed three months.[35] Although it may be extended for a further period, but the total period must not exceed six months.[36]

Exercising discretion

According to s3(2) of the DVO, the court, in exercising its jurisdiction in granting an ouster or entry order, shall have regard to:

> the conduct of the parties, both in relation to each other and otherwise, to their respective needs and financial resources, to the needs of any child living with the applicant and to all the circumstances of the case.

---

[32] [1979] AC 264.
[33] Ibid., at p. 343.
[34] *Wooton v Wooton* [1984] FLR 871.
[35] See s6(1) DVO. See also *Davis v Johnson* [1979] AC 264, *Practice Direction (injunction: domestic violence)* [1978] 1 WLR 1123; *Spencer v Camacho* [1983] 4 FLR 662; *Galan v Galan* [1985] FLR 905.
[36] S7.

All these factors are relevant but the weight to be given to each depends on the facts of the case, and none is to be regarded as paramount. In other words, the criteria do not give priority to personal protection.[37]

Conduct

Although violence is not a prerequisite to an ouster order, the conduct of the parties (both in relation to each other and otherwise) is a relevant consideration. In *Richards v Richards*,[38] the wife filed for divorce on the grounds of the husband's unreasonable behaviour. The allegations were flimsy to the extreme. After the petition, she left with two children and went to live in a friend's house in overcrowded conditions and sought an injunction excluding the husband from the matrimonial home. The judge did not accept her allegations that she could not live with the husband, but accepted that her existing accommodation was overcrowded. In the best interests of the children, the judge ordered that the husband be excluded from the matrimonial home. The House of Lords held the court could only exclude the husband where it was just and reasonable to do so, taking into account the statutory criteria. The judge failed to take into account the wife's conduct in refusing to return to the matrimonial home when she had no reasonable grounds for such refusal. It was therefore wrong to grant the ouster order. Similarly, in *Wiseman v Simpson*,[39] the parties were joint tenants living in a council flat. The relationship came to an end. Although there was no violence or threat of violence, both parties agreed that quarrels and tension of the breakup rendered it impractical for them to live under the same roof. The woman changed the lock to prevent the man from returning. The Court of Appeal ruled that there was nothing in the man's conduct justifying her refusal to live in the flat. Her conduct in excluding the man was a serious matter and she ought not gain an advantage.

However, in *Scott v Scott*,[40] the court took a more pragmatic approach and was less concerned with whose conduct was blameworthy. In *Scott v Scott*, the wife obtained a decree nisi, but the husband could not accept that the marriage had come to an end and sought repeatedly, but without using violence, to persuade the wife to effect a reconciliation. The court granted a non-molestation order and on a further application by the wife, an ouster injunction was granted. The Court of Appeal dismissed the husband's appeal and said:

---

[37] *Richards v Richards* [1983] 2 All ER 807.
[38] Ibid.
[39] [1988] 1 FLR 490; see also *G v J (ouster order)* [1993] 1 FLR 1008.
[40] [1992] 1 FLR 529.

The final question is, is this conduct sufficiently serious to justify the making of an ouster order? This had greatly troubled me, because I take the view that it is wrong that ouster injunctions should be used too widely or too commonly, and I think there is a risk that they are. I recognised the force of the previous decisions of this court to the effect that they are only to be used in cases of real necessity. In the end I am persuaded that, knowing as he did all about the history ... the judge was justified in concluding that he had to keep these parties apart if that injunction was not going to be broken in the future, and this was the way in which he could do it. Therefore I cannot say that the judge was wrong to reach the conclusion to which he came.[41]

Needs and financial resources

The parties' needs and financial resources are a relevant consideration. This may relate to the availability of alternative accommodation. An excluded spouse may be made homeless, but if an ouster order is refused, the woman and the children may also be required to live under an intolerable position. However, it is wrong to regard an ouster order as a housing matter.

> The decision which the judge made would appear to most people to be fair and reasonable if the task of the court was to decide who, in fairness, between the man who is going to work and the woman who has the care of the child, should have the flat to live in. As a matter of housing policy the judge's answer may well be right. But the court has no power to decide such a case simply as a matter of housing policy.[42]

Accommodation, however, was an important consideration in the unusual case of *Chan Chun-hon v Chan Lam Lai-bing*.[43] There, the wife, in order to avoid creditors, left the matrimonial home for four years. On the day the wife returned, the husband left the matrimonial home for a fortnight. One month after the wife's return, the husband applied for an ouster order which was followed by divorce proceedings. There was little evidence of actual violence, but the husband complained of the wife's verbal abuse to himself, his family and the daughter. The husband was willing to provide her generous hotel accommodation. In view of the fact that it would be impractical for the wife to remain, an ouster order was made.

---

[41] Ibid., at pp. 536–7.
[42] *G v J (ouster order)* [1993] 1 FLR 1008 at pp. 1015–6 per Purchas LJ.
[43] Court of Appeal, Civil Appeal Action No 43 of 1994 (1994).

The needs of children

The needs of any child living with the applicant are not the first and paramount consideration.[44] However, the need of children to have a secure home with a custodial parent is an important factor. In *Lee v Lee*,[45] as a result of a turbulent relationship, the applicant woman was hospitalised after an overdose. Whilst the applicant was away, the respondent lived with two children, a daughter aged 12 and a boy aged five. The daughter made allegations of indecency against the respondent and a supervision order was made on condition that she stayed with her grandmother until the applicant obtained accommodation. On leaving hospital, the applicant took the boy and lived with a friend in overcrowded conditions, whilst the respondent remained in the three-bedroom flat. On her application for an ouster injunction, the Court of Appeal held that the respondent needed a home for himself, but the applicant needed a home for herself and the children. Taking all these factors into account, the needs of the children to be re-established in the family home carried the greatest weight. An ouster order was granted. Again, in *Chan Chun-hon v Chan Lam Lai-bing*,[46] the Court of Appeal considered that the daughter was mentally very disturbed by the wife's presence in the house and the welfare of the child was an important factor. An ouster order was upheld. However, in *G v J (ouster order)* it was held that where the merits of the case were evenly balanced between the adult parties, it was wrong to consider the interests of the child having decisive weight, tipping the balance in favour of an ouster order.

All the circumstances

'All the circumstances of the case' is a wide 'catch-all' phrase which allows the court to take into account any factor which may be relevant in a particular case. In *Lee v Lee*, the attitude of the local authority that the children should have suitable accommodation with the applicant was taken into account.[47] The criteria in s3(2) of the DVO are identical to those in s1(3) of the English Matrimonial Act 1983 except that the reference to 'just and reasonable' has been omitted. In *Chan Chun-hon v Chan Lam Lai-bing*,[48] Mortimer JA said that the omission should not make any difference.

---

[44] *Richards v Richards* [1983] 2 All ER 807; cf. *Samson v Samson* [1982] 1 WLR 252.
[45] [1984] FLR 243.
[46] Court of Appeal, Civil Appeal Action No 43 of 1994 (1994).
[47] [1984] FLR 243.
[48] Ibid.

Draconian order

Although violence is not a prerequisite to an ouster order,[49] the courts have emphasised that an ouster order is a drastic order and it should only be made in cases of real necessity, not a stepping-stone on the road to divorce.

> ... an ouster order is a very serious order to make ... an order which should only be made in cases of real necessity. It must not be allowed to become a routine stepping-stone on the road to divorce on the ground that the marriage has already broken down and that the atmosphere in the matrimonial home is one of tension.[50]

Ex parte injunction

An ex parte application may be made in an emergency. However, the court has taken the view that such an injunction should be granted rarely and only where the interests of justice, and protection of an applicant or a child clearly demands immediate intervention.[51] If an ex parte injunction is granted, it should be limited to a period required to arrange a preliminary hearing inter parties,[52] and should provide for an application to discharge on giving 24 hours' notice.[53] The injunction should also specify the date on which it expired.[54]

Enforcement: power of arrest

Disobedience of an injunction is brought before the court by way of an application for committal.[55] To ensure speedy and effective remedy for victims of domestic violence, the court may attach a power of arrest to an injunction restraining a respondent from using violence, or excluding him from the matrimonial home, provided that it is satisfied that the respondent

---

[49] *Spindlow v Spindlow* [1978] 3 WLR 777; *Galan v Galan* [1985] FLR 905; *Scott v Scott* [1992] 1 FLR 529; *Brown v Brown* [1994] 1 FLR 233; *Chan Chun-hon v Chan Lam Lai-bing*, Court of Appeal, Civil Appeal Action No 43 of 1994 (1994).
[50] *Burke v Burke* [1987] 2 FLR 71 at p. 73 per Lloyd LJ; *Wiseman v Simpson* [1988] 1 FLR 490; *G v J (ouster order)* [1993] 1 FLR 1008.
[51] *Ansah v Ansah* [1977] 2 All ER 638.
[52] *Loseby v Newman* [1995] 2 FLR 754.
[53] Ibid.
[54] Ibid. The High Court may exercise powers of the District Court in case a case of urgency, see s3 DVO.
[55] An order of committal for contempt must strict comply with Form 85 and would be defective if it fails to specify what acts constituted the contempt complained of, *Re M* [1989] 2 HKLR 117; *Loseby v Newman* [1995] 2 FLR 754.

has caused actual bodily harm to the applicant, or to the child living with the applicant.[56] In the absence of physical injury, there must be clear evidence of real psychological injury. In *Kendricks v Kendricks*,[57] the wife applied to commit her husband for breach of an undertaking not to molest her. She alleged that the husband had used threatening behaviour on a number of occasions and she was too frightened to return home. It was held that in the absence of physical injury, clear evidence that there had been a real change in the psychological condition of the person assaulted was required. The wife was too frightened to return home, but that was insufficient degree of psychological harm to come within the definition of actual bodily harm.

In attaching a power of arrest, it is not necessary to show that the respondent is likely to cause actual bodily harm again.[58] However, it has been said that the power of arrest is not for general and indiscriminate use. It should only be attached in exceptional cases where the respondent has persistently disobeyed an injunction and made a nuisance of himself.[59] As Ormrod LJ said,[60] attaching a power of arrest is a very serious measure; it exposes the husband to immediate arrest; it causes great problems for police officers who have to enforce it; it leads to the husband being kept in custody; anything in this sphere which operates more or less automatically is to be deprecated. Further, if an applicant intends to ask the court to attach a power of arrest to an injunction, notice should be given to the other party to allow him to oppose the imposition of a power of arrest.[61]

Where a power of arrest is attached to an injunction, a police officer may arrest without warrant any person whom he reasonably suspects of being in breach of the injunction.[62] Where a person is arrested, he shall be brought before a court the next day, and shall not be released except on the direction of the court.[63]

---

[56] S5(1) DVO. It seems that a power to arrest cannot be attached to an injunction after divorce or end of cohabitation, see *White v White* [1983] 4 FLR 696.
[57] [1990] 2 FLR 107.
[58] Cf. S2 Domestic Proceedings and Magistrates' Courts Act 1976, see *Horner v Horner* [1982] 2 WLR 914. See also *Carpenter v Carpenter* [1988] 1 FLR 121; *Lewis (AH) v Lewis (RWF)* [1978] 1 All ER 729; *Roberts v Roberts* [1991] 1 FLR 294.
[59] *Lewis (AH) v Lewis (RWF)* [1978] 1 All ER 729.
[60] *Horner v Horner* [1982] 2 WLR 914 at p. 917.
[61] Ibid.
[62] S5(2); r5 Domestic Violence Rules.
[63] S5(3), but the respondent may be released on bail, r6 Domestic Violence Rules.

INJUNCTIONS IN OTHER PROCEEDINGS

DVO provides 'a party to a marriage' or a cohabitee a right to obtain injunctive relief independent of any other relief sought in the proceedings. Where a victim does not fall within the DVO, for example a former spouse or a party to a platonic relationship, s21L(1) of the High Court Ordinance provides that the court may grant an interlocutory or final injunction 'in all cases in which it appears to the court to be just and convenient to do so'. S48(1) of District Court Ordinance confers the court with the same power.[64] These powers are often called the 'inherent' powers of the court, although strictly speaking, they may now be incorporated in these statutory provisions. Thus, in *Richards v Richards*, it was said that the courts' 'inherent' powers are now absorbed under its statutory source.[65]

The power of the court under s21L is wide, and is expressed in very general terms, but it is limited by three general principles relating to granting injunctive relief.

(i) Where there is no action, there is no injunction. In other words, an injunction is ancillary and incidental to some pre-existing cause of action which the applicant proposes to assert by legal proceedings.

(ii) There must be sufficient link between the cause of action and the injunction. For instance, a husband would not be granted an order permitting him to return to the matrimonial home on an application by the wife for maintenance.[66]

(iii) An injunction will only be granted in support of a legal or equitable right. In *Montgomery v Montgomery*,[67] the wife obtained a decree of judicial separation but the parties continued to live in the council flat of which the husband was the sole tenant. The wife sought an injunction restraining him from molesting her and excluding him from the flat. It was held that the court had no jurisdiction to grant an ouster injunction in favour of a person who had no proprietary right in the flat. Similarly, in *Hamlett v Hamlett*,[68] the marriage broke down and the husband moved out of the matrimonial home which was jointly owned by the parties. The wife remained and invited her boyfriend to stay. The husband sought to restrain the wife from permitting the boyfriend into

---

[64] 'The Court, as regards any cause for the time being within its jurisdiction, shall in any proceedings before it — (a) grant such relief ... as ought to be granted or given, in the like case by the Court of First Instance and in as full and ample a manner.'
[65] [1983] 2 All ER 807.
[66] *Des Salles d'Epinoix v Des Salles d'Epinoix* [1967] 1 WLR 553.
[67] [1964] 2 All ER 22; *Robinson v Robinson* [1965] P. 39.
[68] [1996] 1 HKC 61; *Jones v Jones* [1971] 2 All ER 737.

occupation. It was held that the husband had no greater right than a bank mortgagee and therefore he had no right to interfere with the wife's right of possession.

In some cases, the difficulty may be one of identifying the right underpinning the relief sought, especially in post-decree absolute cases. These cases may be explained in terms the special nature of domestic violence in the context of family proceedings.[69]

Non-Molestation/Ouster Order after Decree Absolute

In the case of a former spouse who has a proprietary interest in the matrimonial home, the divorce court has jurisdiction to entertain an application for an injunction excluding the other spouse from the property. In *Lucas v Lucas*,[70] the wife was the sole tenant of a council property. After a decree absolute was granted, and pending ancillary relief proceedings, she sought an injunction excluding the husband from the property. The Court of Appeal held that the court had the jurisdiction to grant injunctive relief if it was ancillary to a claim, and for the purpose of protecting legal or equitable rights. As the wife was the sole tenant, she had an undoubted legal right to possession of the property.[71] However, where the parties are joint tenants, each has an equal right to occupy the property, and neither has a right to occupy to the exclusion of the other.[72] Further, in *Webb v Webb*,[73] the Court of Appeal held that it had the jurisdiction to grant a non-molestation order after decree absolute for the protection of a former spouse.[74]

Welfare of the Children

There are authorities suggesting that the court has the jurisdiction to grant an ouster injunction after decree absolute to protect children. In *Wilde v Wilde*,[75] after the decree absolute the parties were granted joint custody of the children with care and control to the wife with access to the husband.

---

[69] English Law Reform Commission, No 207, 1992, p. 23; see n. 1.
[70] [1992] 2 FLR 53.
[71] See also *Hennie v Hennie* [1993] 2 FLR 351.
[72] *Ainsbury v Millington* [1986] 1 All ER 73; *P v P (ouster)* (1993) Fam Law 283.
[73] [1986] 1 FLR 541.
[74] *Montgomery v Montgomery* [1964] 2 All ER 22; *Robinson v Robinson* [1965] P. 39.
[75] [1988] 2 FLR 83.

Ancillary relief proceedings were pending. Arrangements concerning access broke down and the wife sought to exclude the husband from the matrimonial home save for agreed access. The Court of Appeal held that where children were involved, the court had an inherent jurisdiction to intervene to protect the children's interests by excluding one parent, no matter what the proceedings are.[76]

More recently, in *C v K (inherent powers: exclusion order)*,[77] a grandmother (G) was granted parental responsibility of her grandchild (GC). The mother of the child was in prison and the father played no part in the child's upbringing. The grandmother's ex-cohabitee (C) was a violent person. They were joint-tenant of a flat although they ceased to live together for some years. C returned sporadically and was abusive to G and GC. G sought an injunction preventing C from entering the flat. Wall J held that the court had the inherent power to restrain interference with the exercise of parental responsibility. Such power included ousting a non-parent. It should, however, be exercised with extreme caution and would only be appropriate where there was risk of significant harm to the child.

PRIVATE NUISANCE/*WILKINSON V DOWNTON*

Until recently, the law of tort provided no remedy to a person against harassment by a barrage of pestering and annoying behaviour. For instance, a woman terminates her relationship with her boyfriend, he refuses to accept, he telephones her repeatedly, follow her around, walk in the same direction, try to talk to her, try to attract her attention, shout abusive language at her; none of these constitute an actionable tort.[78] Thus, in *Patel v Patel*,[79] the defendant son-in-law trespassed onto the plaintiff's house and made abusive telephone calls to the plaintiff. The Court of Appeal held that an injunction restraining the defendant from trespassing in the plaintiff's house was correctly granted, but the court had no jurisdiction to restrain the defendant from approaching within 50 yards of the plaintiff's house (i.e. an exclusion zone), as the act of approaching the plaintiff's house was in itself not trespass, and did not confer a cause of action.

---

[76] *Quinn v Quinn* [1983] FLR 394; compare *M v M (custody application)* [1988] 1 FLR 225; *Ainsbury v Millington* [1986] 1 All ER 73; *P v P (ouster)* (1993) Fam Law 283.
[77] [1996] 2 FLR 506.
[78] Bridgeman and Jones, 'Harassing Conduct and Outrageous Acts: A Cause of Action for Intentionally Inflicted Mental Distress?' 14 LS [1994] 180.
[79] [1988] 2 FLR 179.

Private nuisance law attempted to provide a remedy. Thus, in *Khorasandjian v Bush*,[80] an 18-year-old woman became friendly with the defendant but they had never cohabited with one another. When she made it known that she wanted the relationship to end, he pestered her continuously by making calls to her parents' house where she lived. The plaintiff sought an injunction but it was argued that as the plaintiff had no property interest in her parent's house, the alleged private nuisance was not actionable. The Court of Appeal rejected this, and approved an injunction restraining the defendant from 'using violence to, harassing, pestering or communicating with' the plaintiff.

> To my mind, it is ridiculous if in this present age the law is that the making of deliberately harassing and pestering telephone calls to a person is only actionable in the civil courts if the recipient of the calls happens to have the freehold or a leasehold proprietary interest in the premises in which he or she has received the calls.[81]

In 1996, in *Burris v Azadani*,[82] the Court of Appeal extended the protection by granting an exclusion zone order. In that case, the plaintiff formed a social relationship with the defendant when she attended martial arts lessons. After the plaintiff rejected the defendant's advances, he made a number of uninvited visits to her house, often in the middle of the night, and refused to leave. He made nuisance telephone calls to her repeatedly. He threatened to commit suicide and made threats against her. The plaintiff obtained an *ex parte* interlocutory injunction restraining him from assaulting, molesting, or harassing her. The injunction included an exclusion zone order, restraining the defendant from coming or remaining within 250 yards of the plaintiff's home until further order. The defendant breached the order on various occasions, and he was sentenced to three months' imprisonment. He appealed against the exclusion zone order. The Court of Appeal held that the court had the power to impose an exclusion zone when granting a non-molestation order provided that no unnecessary restraint was placed on the defendant. Two competing interests had to be reconciled; on the one hand, the defendant's interest to move freely in public areas, and on the other hand, the plaintiff's interest not to be harassed. In this case it was clear that if the defendant approached the vicinity of the plaintiff's house, he would be tempted to act in a manner distressing to the plaintiff and the court might properly impose a wider measure of restraint called for. Sir Thomas Bingham MR states:

---

[80] [1993] 3 All ER 669; now overruled by *Hunter v Canary Wharf Ltd* [1997] 2 All ER 426.
[81] Ibid., at p. 675; see *R v Ireland* [1997] 1 All ER 112.
[82] [1996] 1 FLR 266.

it would not seem to me to be a valid objection to the making of an exclusion zone order that the conduct to be restrained is not in itself tortious or otherwise unlawful if such an order is reasonably regarded as necessary for the protection of a plaintiff's legitimate interest.[83]

Where the health of the plaintiff has been impaired by such harassment calculated to cause impairment, the tort in the old decisions of *Wilkinson v Downton*[84] and *Janvier v Sweeney*,[85] has also been employed to find a remedy. In these old cases, it was established that lies or threats which the speaker knows are likely to cause physical harm, including shock, are actionable. Thus, in *Burnett v George*,[86] the plaintiff complained of harassment by the defendant when her relationship with the defendant ended. The Court of Appeal held that where the health of the plaintiff was impaired by such harassment calculated to cause impairment, relief would be granted by way of an injunction to avoid that impairment of health. An injunction was granted prohibiting the defendant from 'assaulting, molesting or otherwise interfering with the plaintiff by doing acts calculated to case her harm'. Similarly, in *Pidduck v Molloy*,[87] an injunction was granted to the plaintiff prohibiting the defendant from speaking to 'the plaintiff in an intimidatory, threatening or abusive manner'.

LAW REFORM

There are no comprehensive statistics on domestic violence in Hong Kong.[88] The criminal law at the moment lacks the power to protect the injured party as it focuses mainly on dealing with the aftermath of domestic violence. Protection afforded by the DVO is limited to 'a party to a marriage' and 'cohabitees', but the elderly, parents-in-law, relatives, brothers and sisters are not protected. A child has no *locus standi* to apply. Further, breach of an injunction is not a criminal offence. The power of the court to attach a power of arrest to an injunction is restricted to cases where the respondent has caused actual bodily harm, and there is a general reluctance to invoke such power.

---

[83] Ibid., at 270.
[84] [1897] 2 QB 57.
[85] [1919] 2 KB 316.
[86] [1992] 1 FLR 525.
[87] [1992] 2 FLR 202.
[88] Chang Yuk-chung, 'News Reporting on Family Violence in Hong Kong: A Case Study', Department of Applied Social Studies, Hong Kong Polytechnic University, 1995.

Civil remedy by way of an injunction must be in support of a recognised legal or equitable right, and there is no injunction in respect of conduct which does not amount to a tort or a threatened tort, however distressing or annoying such conduct may be to the victim. Recent development in the law of private nuisance or intentional infliction of emotional distress is uncertain in terms of their scope and requirements.

Consequently, the Hong Kong Law Reform Commission Sub-committee on Stalking[89] recently recommended that harassment be made a criminal offence attracting a penalty of two years' imprisonment. Further, it also recommended that a court sentencing a person convicted of the offence might make an order restraining the defendant from doing anything which amounted to harassment of the victim of the offence or any other person. Breach of an injunction would be made an arrestable offence. The sub-committee further recommended that the law relating to domestic violence be amended to provide better protection to the private life of individuals.

---

[89] See n. 3.

Annex I

DOMESTIC INCIDENT NOTICE

I/N; MRB; CCR; CAR OB No: .... Date .... Formation ....

Mr. ....

    You are hereby notified that an allegation of ....
has been made against you by *(name of complainant)* ....
at *(location)* .... on *(date)* ....
The complainant has not instigated a criminal complaint against you and does not wish at this time for the allegation to be investigated with a view to criminal charges being laid and a prosecution brought.

    Your attention is drawn to the undermentioned legislation, contravention of which may result in a term of imprisonment.

    Offences Against the Person Ordinance Chapter 212 of the Laws of Hong Kong.

    Crimes Ordinance Chapter 200 of the Laws of Hong Kong.

I/N; MRB; CCR; CAR OB No: ....   Date ....

    A Domestic Incident Notice was served on Mr. ....
at *(location)* .... on *(date)* ....
by *(officer, name rank & UI)* ....
of *(formation)* .... with my permission.

                               Signed by complainant ....

                               Signed by issuing officer ....

Index

abduction, see child abduction

access
  defined 276–277
  denial to parent 286
  direct 284
  grandparents, by 288–289
  indirect 284, 287–288
  meaning 211–213, 276–277
  natural mother following adoption, by 314–315
  non-parent, by 288–289
  presumption in favour of 284–289
  right of the child 285
  right of the parent 285
  sexual abuse cases, in 288
  staying 276–277
  unmarried father, by 288–289
  welfare of the child 287–289
  wishes of the child 288

adoption
  access by natural mother as condition of 314–315
  access to birth records, and 315–317
  age of adopted persons 296
  age of adopters 295–318
  Chinese customary law, under 291
  condition imposed in 304, 314–315
  consent unreasonably withheld 300–304
  discrimination against male applicant 294, 318
  dispensing with consent 297, 299–304, 318–319
  effect of 291, 313–314
  foster care, distinguished 291
  freeing for 304–305
  future development 318–319
  general consent, to 298–299
  grandparents, by 309, 315
  guardian ad litem, and 311–313
  guardian, consent by 298
  homosexual adopters 294
  illegitimate children, of 294, 313
  information to court, and 312–313
  joint applicants 294–295
  jurisdiction of the court 292
  marital status of adopters 295
  meaning 291
  natural parents, disclosure of identity of 315–317
  notice of intention, to 297

overseas 326–327
parents, consent by 298
payment, for 310–311
private arrangements, and 292
property rights on 313
relative, by 304–310
residence provisions 296–297
revocation of consent, to 299
secrecy, and 308–9, 315–316
sole applicant 294–295
specific consent, to 298
statistics, of 292, 293
stepchildren, of 295, 307–301, 319
step-parent, by 295, 307–301, 319
succession of adopted child 313–314
total transplant view of 291, 306, 309, 313–314
tracing adopted person by natural relatives, in 315–317
tracing natural relatives, in 315–317
welfare of child 298, 299–304, 305–307
wishes of the child 307

adultery
condonation 355–357
conduct not amounting to 355–357
connivance 355–357
consensual sexual intercourse, as 105–106
continuing cohabitation, effect of 107
co-respondent, adulterer as 108
damages for 107
defences to 104–105, 355–357
intolerability of living with respondent, and 106
irretrievable breakdown of marriage, proof of 105–107
meaning 105–106
standard of proof 106

affinity, see also consanguinity
meaning 145
prohibited degrees 148–149
reforming the law of 150
relaxation of prohibited degrees 147–148

age
marriage-
judicial consent, of 151
parental consent required, for 151
void 151

arrest, power of
effect of 468–469
nature of 468–469

assault, see domestic violence and child abuse

assisted human reproduction
donor insemination 205–210
egg and embryo donation 205–210
in vitro fertilisation 205–210
meaning 205–210
parents, identifying 205–210
status of child 205–210
surrogacy,
meaning 205–210
surrogate born child 205–210
treated as child of the marriage 205–210

attachment of earnings 357–358, 360–361

battery, see domestic violence and child abuse

behaviour
unreasonable, **see unreasonable behaviour**

bigamy
concubine, **see concubinage**
kim tiu marriage, **see customary marriage**
nullity, and 153–154
Ta Tsing Leu Lee, **see customary marriage**

birth
  access to birth records by adopted child   315–317
  illegitimate, **see legitimacy and legitimation**
  registration and presumption of parentage   196–197
  registration of illegitimate child   191–192

blood tests, see also parentage
  power to order   201
  refusal to consent to   204–205
  to determine parentage-
    child's right   203–205
    consent to   201
    discretion of the court, to order   201–205
    husband's right   203–205
    unmarried father's right   203–205
  welfare of the child, and   201–204

care and control, see also custody of child
  custody distinguished from   211–213, 278–279

care or protection proceedings, see child abuse

child
  agreement to give up rights to   235
  child of the family, **see child of the family**
  consent to marriage, of   192, 234
  divorce, arrangements for, **see divorce**
  financial provision, for, **see financial provision and maintenance during marriage**
  guardian, **see guardian**
  legitimacy, **see also illegitimacy**
  parental rights and authority, **see parent**
  property adjustment, for, **see property adjustment**
  rights of, **see Gillick case**
  welfare, **see welfare of child**

child abduction
  abduction amongst Hague Convention countries   334–342
  abduction into Hong Kong from a non-Hague Convention country   342–345
  access right   336
  Central Authority, and   334
  Contracting States   334, 346–348
  criminal sanction   333
  habitual residence, meaning   336–337
  jurisdiction of the court   335
  mandatory return   337–338
  preventing   333–334
  refusal to return   338–342
  rights of custody   335–336
  stay of proceedings   344–345
  wardship proceedings, **see wardship**
  wishes of the child   340–341
  wrongful removal or retention   335–336, 337–338

child abuse
  assault   448
  care committed to non-parent   454
  care or protection proceedings-
    child's view to be heard   455–456
    court orders   454–455
    criterion for discharge from care   454
    custody proceedings, and   450
    grounds, for   448
    legal representation   455–456
    welfare of the child   455
  case conferences   442–444
  child assessment procedure   445–446
  child protection registry   445
  compulsory reporting laws   442
  co-ordination of authorities and agencies   456–457
  criminal law, and   441–442
  definition   440–441

developmental abuse   450–453
Director of Social Welfare as guardian   454
disclosure, and privilege of information   456–457
drug-taking by expectant mother   450–453
emergency protection order   446–447
emotional abuse   450–453
future risk   451–453
grounds for interference by the Director of Social Welfare   445–454
ill-treatment   448–449
in need of care or protection   445–454
institutional care   454
investigation, of   442–445, 456–457
need for intervention, time of assessment   453
neglect   449
parents' self-incrimination   457
place of refuge   446–447
psychological abuse   450–453
recalcitrant teenagers   454
sexual abuse   449
standard of proof   449–450
statistics   440–441
supervision order   455

child assessment procedure, see child abuse

Chinese customary marriage, see customary marriage

Chinese modern marriage, see modern marriage

clean break
application to children, and   414
big money cases   402–403
deferred   379
immediate   379
low-income family   380
periodical payment orders, and   379
power of the court to direct   379
power to impose   379–380
re-opening settlements   433–436
short marriage, after   380
unreliable husband   382–383
wife's earning capacity, and   381–382

concubinage
abolition of   27, 35–37
bigamy   28–31
customary marriage, in   27–37
dissolution of   48
judicial attitudes   32–33
monogamy   28–31, 46–47
polygamy   28–31, 46–47
statistics, of   28
statutory definition   36–37
union of, **see also concubine**

concubine
child, legitimacy of   36, 181
fu ching   32
husband's family, not member of   34
husband's right to take   5, 27–28
meaning   5, 27
mistress, distinguished   27
modern marriage, added to   40, 48
no principal wife, where   37
principal wife, promotion to status of   32
promotion, of   32
requirements for the taking of-
  acceptance by the wife   34–37
  ceremony, yap kung   34–37
  holding out   34–37
  intention of the parties   34–37
  introduction of the husband's family   34–37
  permanence of union   34–37
  public recognition   34–37
rights of children of   35–36, 48
rights of   29, 33–34, 48
second wife, as   26
statistics   28
Ta Tsing Leu Lee   33–35, 46–47

who might have 27
wife, and position of 33–34

conduct
    financial and property adjustment after divorce, and 405–408

consanguinity, see also affinity
    genetic consideration 146
    history 147–148
    meaning 145
    prohibited degrees of 148
    reforming the law of 150
    religion 146
    social policy 146–147

consent order, see maintenance agreement

consummation of marriage, see also voidable marriage
    incapacity, and unwilling distinguished 159
    meaning 158–159
    physical incapacity, refusal to undergo treatment to cure 158–159
    psychiatric condition 159
    wilful refusal 159–160

corporal punishment
    abolition, of 220

criminal law
    bigamy 153–154
    child abuse, and 441–442
    domestic violence, and 459–460
    incest 150

cruelty, persistent, see separation order

custody of child
    access, **see access**
    age of 18, until 281–283
    appeal against decision, and 268–269
    bar, to 282
    care and control, distinguished from 211–213, 278–279
    Director of Social Welfare, to 280, 283–284
    disputes, nature of 269–271
    effect of custody order 276–278
    future of 289
    illegitimate child, and 282
    joint orders for 279–280
    legal custody, and 282
    meaning 211–213, 281, 354
    satisfaction hearings on divorce, and 128–130, 135
    social welfare report 264–267, 284
    sole custody order 276–278
    split orders 278–279
    statutory provisions 275–284
    step parent, and, **see parent**
    strangers, application by 282
    supervision order 280–281, 283
    uncontested cases, court's role in 128–130, 135
    wardship proceedings 281
    welfare and, **see welfare of the child**

customary marriage
    abolition of 15
    betrothal gift 20, 22
    betrothal through go-between 7–9, 11, 20
    by parties to marriage, consent to 7
    Chinese law and custom 5, 13
    Chinese law prevails over custom 23–26
    concubines in 25
    customs-
        contract between parents 7–9, 20–22
        difficulty in ascertaining 11–12, 15
        location variation in 11–12
        of when 17–18
        of where 18
        of whose 18–19
    declaration of subsistence, of 44–45
    dominant features of 11
    evolving customs 10

expert evidence and authoritative writings 11–12, 19
extinction, of 16, 46–48
formal requirements of 12
grounds for dissolution-
  at wife's suit 60
  breaking of the bond 60–61
  Ching law, continuation of 67
  concubine, of 68–69
  husband's unilateral repudiation 56, 58–60
  mutual consent, by 60
  formalities 61
  Marriage Reform Ordinance, under 64–66
  Matrimonial Causes Ordinance, under 67
judicial interpretation of 19–26
kim tiu 46–47
kit fat wife 31
legal basis of 5–6
legitimacy of children 181
maintenance agreements, and 66
meaning 5
minimum age of marriage 7
modern marriage, distinguished from 14
monogamy 16, 28–31
nature of 6–7
origin 6–7
parties to betrothal contract 7–9, 20–22
ping tsai 25, 46–47
polygamy 16, 28–31, 46–47
post-registration of-
  application for 43–45
  provision for 26, 43–45
powers to grant ancillary relief, and 66
preservation of 15–26
prohibition of taking two wives 27
purpose of 6–7
rebuttable presumption of 25–26
registry marriage after 26
seven ousts and three non-ousts 58–59
statistics 3–4,
statutory definition, of 17–19
statutory provisions for dissolution 64–65
Ta Tsing Leu Lee 7, 25–26, 47
three convenants and six rites 7–10
tin fong wife 31
validity of dissolution 65–66
women's position, in 15, 33–34, 56–58

declaratory judgments
power to make 141

desertion
abolition, proposed 116
consensual separation 119–120
consent, absence of 118, 119–120
constructive 121
elements of 117
enforced separation 118
fact of 117–118
intention to live apart permanently 118–119
involuntary separation 118
just or reasonable cause, lack of 120
meaning 117, **see also separation**
period of 119, 122–123
resumption of cohabitation, effect of 123
termination of 122
unreasonable behaviour, as 122

discrimination
father affecting 189–192
illegitimate child, affecting 189–192
single men adopting female child 294, 318

divorce
clean break, **see clean break**
custody of child, **see custody of child**
customary marriage, **see also customary marriage**
decree absolute 123–124, 130–134, 137
decree nisi 123–124, 130–134, 137

defences 130–134
exceptional hardship or depravity 124–127
facts, inquiry into 99–103, 105
fault, importance of 99–103
fault-based facts 99–103, 135–137
finance and property after, see **financial provision and property adjustment**
financial provision, adequacy of 130–131
grave financial or other hardship 132–134
grounds for petitioning-
  adultery, see **adultery**
  desertion, see **desertion**
  facts, proof of 103–104
  irretrievable breakdown of marriage 100–103, 105
  separation, see **separation**
  unreasonable behaviour, see **unreasonable behaviour**
history 99–103
joint application, by 103, 135–137
jurisdiction of the court 104
marriages celebrated in China, and 63–64
modern marriage, see **modern marriage**
mutual consent, by 137
no-fault facts 100–103
notice of intention of 135–137
nullity, distinguished, see **nullity**
objectives of the law 104
one-year discretionary bar 124–126
reconciliation, see **reconciliation**
special procedure 107, 134–135
statistics 102, 116
undefended 107, 134–135
welfare of children, arrangements for 128–130
wrong in the circumstances 134

DNA test, see blood test

domestic violence, see also child abuse
battered wife 459
children, protection of 460, 469
cohabitation, meaning 461
cohabitees, and 460–462
ex parte injunction 460
family members, and 461, 470, 474
harassment, and 472–475
law reform 474–475
molestation-
  meaning 461–463
  precondition to granting order 462–463
nature and extent, of 459–460, 474
non-molestation orders, see **non-molestation order**
ouster orders, see **ouster order**
power of arrest, see **arrest, power of**
private nuisance 473
stalking 472–475

domicile
women's independent 104

duress
fear, threat causing 161–164
life, limb or liberty, threat to 161–164
marriage, vitiating 161–164
party's responsibility for 161–164
reasonably entertained fear 161–164

emergency protection orders, see also child abuse
child assessment procedure, see **child abuse**
supervision order, see **child abuse**

emigration
children born in mainland China 186–188
illegitimate child, and 186–188

exclusion orders, see domestic violence

family assets
adjustment after divorce, see **finance**

provision and property adjustment
   matrimonial home, **see matrimonial home**

father, see also parentage
   assisted human reproduction, in 205–210
   genetic 194–205
   legal 194–205
   non-genetic 205–210
   presumptions-
     from birth registration 196–197
     from marriage 194–196
     rebuttal of 197–198

financial provision
   applicants 364–365
   attachment of earnings 357–358, 360–361
   child of the family, for 414–415, **see also maintenance during marriage**
     age limits 417, 420
     attachment of earnings 420
     discretion, guidelines for exercise of 415–416, 419–420
     duration of orders 417, 420
     orders available 413–414, 418
     property adjustment orders 414, 418
     spouse not child's parent, against 414–415
     spouses, interrelation of orders for 363–364
   clean break 367–384
     appropriate 382–383
     deferred 379, 383–384
     earning capacity, potential increase in 381
     immediate 379
     inappropriate 376–379
     meaning 379
     options available 379
     power to impose 379–380
     specified term, periodical payments order for 380
     statement of principle 379
     supervening events, effect of 433–436
     termination of financial obligations, duty to consider 379
     use of 380–381
     wealthy parties, in case of 380
   discretion of court, exercise of 371–412
     age of parties 398–400
     children's welfare, consideration of 363–364
     conduct, relevant 405–408
     consideration of all circumstances 405–408
     contributions of parties 401–404
     duration of marriage 398–400
     earning capacity, as to 387–395
       disclosure by parties 387–389
       fully exploited, where 389–390
       new partner, of 393–395
       potential as to 390
       reality, considering 389–390
     loss of pension, etc. rights 404–405
     needs of parties 395–396
     obligations and responsibilities of parties 396–397
     physical or mental disability of parties 401
     principles governing 374–376
     standard of living 397–398
     statutory guidelines for 371
     third party's means, evidence of 393–395
   duxbury calculation 386–387
   housing needs, dominance of 408–409, **see also matrimonial home**
   housing orders, factors influencing 408–412, **see also matrimonial home**
   minimal loss principle 374–376
   net effect approach 386
   one-third rule 384–385

order,
- capital 366–370
- categories of 365–370
- children, for 413–420
- income 365–366
- lump sum, see **lump sum order**
- maintenance pending suit 460–461
- periodical payments, see **property adjustment order**
- sale of property, for 370
- settlement of property, see **property adjustment order**
- powers of court 365–367
- principles, flexibility of 371–384
- third parties, powers not affecting 365, 393–395
- variation of orders 428–432
  - discretion of the court 430–32
  - lump sum 429
  - periodical payments 429
  - property adjustment 429

formalities of marriage
- celebrated in the Peoples' Republic of China 77–81
- celebration by an unauthorised person 152
- celebration in an unauthorised place 152
- celebration under a false name 152

fraud
- maintenance agreement 423–424
- mistake, and 165–166

gender
- determining, criteria for 154–157
- gender reassignment operation 154–157

Gillick case
- Gillick competent minors 226–228, 261
- parental rights 216, 226–228
- retreat from 227–228

treatment without parental consent 216, 226–228

grandparents
- access to minors by 288–289
- adoption by 307–310

guardian
- adoption, consent to 298
- appointment-
  - court, by 235, 238, 239–240
  - deed or will, by 235, 237–238
  - revocation of 237–238
- common law, at 211–213
- disputes between 240
- illegitimate child, of 189
- law reform 240–243
- meaning 211–213, 236–237
- minor having no parent, as 239
- non-parent, as 237–240
- parent, as 211–213, 235, 237
- replacement of 239–240
- termination of guardianship 237–238
- testamentary 189, 213, 237–238
- the estate, of 235
- the person, of 235

guardian ad litem 311, 325

hardship
- defence to divorce, as 132–134
- grave financial, or other hardship 132–134

homosexuality
- adoption 298
- marriage 154–157

Housing Authority
- tenancies, orders relating to 367–369

husband and wife, see also parent
- divorced, hardship suffered by wife 132–134, 376–378
- domestic labour, division of 371–374, 401–404

domestic violence, **see domestic violence**
dual worker families 393–395, 401–404
equal partners, as 372–374
interest in money and property, **see financial provision and property adjustment**
matrimonial home, **see matrimonial home**
mutual obligation to support 352, 353–354
    enforcement of 357–358, 360–361

illegitimacy, see also father
    access by unmarried father, **see access**
    adoption of illegitimate child 185
    affiliation proceedings 190
    artificial insemination, child born by 206–207
    birth registration 187, 191–192
    child's right of succession 186–189
    common law, at 198
    consent to marriage 192
    declaration of parentage 198–199
    defined 181
    discrimination, and-
        affecting child 189–192
        affecting unmarried father 189–192
    extramarital conceptions 181–184
    fatal accidents claim 185–186
    financial provision, **see financial provision**
    guardianship, and 189
    in vitro fertilisation 206–207
    intestate succession, and 186
    legitimacy, distinguished 181
    parental rights and authority, and 190
    pension claim, and 185–186
    permanent residence, and 186–188
    proving paternity, **see father**
    provision from deceased's estates 186
    rule of construction 188–189
    subsequent marriage of parents 183–185
    surrogate births 206–207
    unmarried father, rights of 189–192
    void marriage, and 182–183

incest
    child abuse 449
    criminal law 150

injunction, see ouster order and non-molestation order

intestate succession
    adoption, effect of 313–314
    decree of judicial separation, effect of 174
    separation order, effect of 354

judicial separation
    effect of 172–174
    grounds for 173
    history 172
    jurisdiction of the court 173
    obligation to cohabited terminated 172–173
    rescission of decree 174

kindred and affinity, see consanguinity and affinity

legal custody, see custody of child

legitimacy, see also illegitimacy
    artificial insemination by donor child 206–207
    blood tests, **see blood tests**
    concubines, children of 181
    declarations of 198–199
    defined 181
    illegitimacy, distinguished 180
    law reform, effect of 182–192
    lawful unions, children of 181
    presumptions arising from- parents' marriage 194–196

rebuttal on balance of probabilities 197–198
registration of birth 196–197
registration birth 191

legitimation
date of 184
declaration of 198–199
effect of 184–185
legal custody, **see custody of child**
parents subsequent marriage, by 183–184

lump sum order
action to set aside 433–436
appeal against 433–436
child, for 345, 414, 418
instalment 366
interest on 367
power order 366
secured 367
unsecured 367
variation of 433–436

maintenance agreement
binding contract, as 423–424
Chinese modern or customary marriages, in relation to 66
court order, implemented by 421–424
  legal policy 421–422
  powers conferred by law, within 422
  role of court 421–423
  variation of-
    after death of payer 432–433
    capital order 429, 433
    discretion of the court 430–432
    income order 429, 433
    power of the court 429–430
court's jurisdiction, not ousting 421
defined 425
final, whether 423–424, 429
fraud, effect of 423–424

non-material disclosure, effect of 423–424
public policy considerations 421
setting aside 433–436
  appeal out of time 433–434
  change of circumstances 433–436
  new events 433–436
statutory provision 425–428
variation of-
  after death of payer 428
  application of provisions 425–426
  child, maintenance of 426
  court, powers of 426
  during parties joint lives 426–428
  financial arrangements, meaning 425
  periodical payments order 425–428

maintenance during marriage
attachment of earnings 257–258, 360–361
bar to relief 355–357, 360
child, for-
  duration 355, 360
  interim order 360
cohabitation, effect of 357
grounds for application 353
  assault 353
  desertion 353
  drug addiction 353
  failure to provide reasonable maintenance 353, 358
  persistent cruelty 353
  prostitution 353
  venereal disease 353
jurisdiction of the court 258–259
maintenance pending suit-
  discretion of the court 361–362
  duration 361
  nature 361
orders available 354–355, 359
statutory provisions 351

marriage
age at 77, **see also nullity**
arranged marriages 77–79, **see also customary marriage**
Chinese Civil Code, under 78–79
Chinese customary, **see customary marriage**
Christian view of 73–74
compulsory civil preliminaries, need for 74–76
contract, as 73
definition 73–74
duress or lack of consent to 73, **see also nullity**
dying person, of 75
equal partnership, as 372–374
formalities, failure to observe 74, 76–77, **see also formalities of marriage**
modern, **see modern marriage**
monogamous, meaning 73–74
non-consummation of, **see also nullity**
Peoples' Republic of China law, under 79–81
presumptions of-
  essential validity 82–84
  formal validity 71–82
prohibited degrees 77, **see also nullity**
reconciliation, **see reconciliation**
registry-
  celebration, place of 75
  certificate as evidence of 77
  notice of intention 74–75
sexual identity of spouse 77, **see also void marriage**
special licence, by 75–76
statutory provisions 74–77
valid consent, lack of 77, **see also voidable marriage**
void 75, 77, **see void marriage**
voidable, **see voidable marriage**

matrimonial home
adjustment after divorce 367–370, 409–412
charging order on 411–412
home ownership scheme 367–368
ouster order, **see ouster order**
postponing sale 411–412
public rental housing 376–378
sale of 409
transfer of 409–410
undertakings 371
valuation 367–368

matrimonial property
divorce, after, **see financial provision and property adjustment**
matrimonial home, **see matrimonial home**

mediation
information concerning the availability of 127, 139
introduction of 127, 139

modern marriage
Chinese Civil Code, requirements of 38–39
concubines, in 40, 48
customary marriage, distinguished from 14
declaration of subsistence 44–45
dissolution-
  Chinese Civil Code, under 62–64
  Marriage Reform Ordinance, under 64–67
  Matrimonial Causes Ordinance, under 67
  mutual consent, by 62–64
  validation of 63–64
  validity of 62–64
Hong Kong version of 39–40
intention, expression of 42–43
man ming kit fan 37
monogamy 41
open ceremony-
  definition 41–43, 46
  requirement of 40–43
origin 37–38
parties consent to 38–43

parties, contract between   39–43
post registration-
   application for   44–45
   effect of   44–45
   provision for   44–45
powers to grant ancillary relief   66
retrospective validation   39–40
statutory definition, of   40–41
validated marriage   43
witnesses to   40–41

monogamy, see marriage and customary marriage

mother
assisted human reproduction, in   205–210
biological   193
gestational   193–194, 205–210
legal   193
natural conception   194–205
social   193
surrogate   193–194, 205–210

non-molestation order, see also domestic violence
bars to   463
decree absolute, after   471
jurisdiction of the court   470
legal or equitable right, supporting   470
matrimonial proceedings, in   471

nullity
bars to   169–170
canon law of   142
duty of the court   144
grounds for, **see void marriage and voidable marriage**
jurisdiction of the court   144–145
meaning   141
reforming the law of   170–172
void and voidable marriages, distinguished   142–144

official solicitor
wardship proceedings, role in   325

ouster order, see also domestic violence
actual violence not required   466
applicant for   468
children's needs   464
conduct   464–466
decree absolute, after   471
discretion of the court   464–469
draconian   468
duration of   464
financial needs   466–467
matrimonial home, from   462
property rights   464
welfare of the child   471–472

parent
absent   233–235
adjustment after divorce   275–289
child abuse by, **see child abuse**
children's rights   216–217, 226–228
contraception for child   216–217
custody of child, **see custody of child**
declaration of parentage   198–199
foster   291
hostility towards access   287
mature minor, and   216–217, 226–228
meaning, **see father and mother**
rights-
   children's rights and   215–217
   concept of   214–215
rights and authority-
   agreement to transfer   235
   diminishing nature of   215–217
   Gillick case, and   215–217
   married father, of   229
   meaning, of   213–215, 217
   resolving disputes between   229–230
   termination, of   216–217
   unilateral exercise of   229
   unmarried father, of   229–235
   unmarried mother, of   229–235
   welfare of the child, and   215–217, 222–225

wishes of the child, and 216–217, 222–228
step-parents
adoption by 307–310

parentage
blood tests, use of, **see blood tests**
declaration 198–199
donor inseminated child 205–210
posthumous child 208
presumptions arising from-
birth registration 196–197
parents' marriage 194–196
rebutting 197–198
surrogate born child 205–210

pension
loss of on divorce, adjustment for 132–134, 404–405

periodical payments order
appropriate in case of 381–382
clean break, and 379
maintenance pending suit 361–362
nominal 379
secured 366
unsecured 365

polygamy, see also customary marriage

property adjustment order
action to set aside 433–436
appeal against 433–436
discretion of the court, **see financial provision**
duxbury calculation 386–387
matrimonial home, **see matrimonial home**
net effect approach 386
one-third rule 384–385
power of the court 367–371
public rental housing, in respect of 367–368
sale of property 370
settlement of property 369
transfer of property 367–369

home ownership scheme 367–368
public rental housing 367–368
variation of 429
variation of settlements 369–370

reconciliation
certificate of 127
divorce proceeding, in 105
mediation distinguished 127
relevance of 126–128

separation
consent to decree 115
grave financial hardship, wife suffering 132–134
innocent wife, protection of 130–134
living apart, meaning 113
living under one roof, and 113
maintenance, provision of 351–362
marital intercourse, and 113
mental element 115
one year, for 113–115, 123, 135–137
physical separation, insufficient 115
resumption of cohabitation, effect of 123
two years, for 116, 123
wrong to dissolve marriage, where 134

separation order
adultery by applicant, effect of 355
adultery, condoned 355–357
custody or maintenance of children, orders for 354
District Court, jurisdiction of 354
grounds for 354
husband, application by 352–353
intestate succession, effect on 354
married woman, application by 352–353
persistent cruelty 353
provisions of 354
resumption of cohabitation, effect of 354
statutory provisions 352–354

INDEX

sexual abuse, see child abuse

status, see legitimacy and illegitimacy

step-parent, see parent

succession
adopted child 313–314
illegitimacy, effect on 186–189

surrogacy, see assisted human reproduction

tenancy
Housing Authority, property adjustment orders relating to 367–368

unreasonable behaviour
bitterness and hostility, due to allegation of 112
causation 109–110
continuing cohabitation, effect of 112–113
desertion as 110
excessive reaction to 110
incompatibility in personality 109
isolated acts as 110
meaning, of 108
mental or physical illness of respondent, due to 110–112
moral blameworthiness, and 108, 111
negative behaviour 109
objective test 108
petitioner, impact on 108–112
positive behaviour 109
reconciliation after 112–113

variation, see maintenance agreement

void marriage
children of 143
consent obtained by force or fraud 161–165
grounds for 145–157
kindred and affinity, see consanguinity and affinity
lack of consent 161–167
male and female, parties not 154–157
party already married 153–154
sham marriage 164–165
statutory provisions 145
voidable marriage distinguished 142–144

voidable marriage
AIDS 168
bars to 169–170
children of 143
duress 161–164
grounds for 157–169
hepatitis B 168
impotence 158–159
incapacity to consummate 158–159
lack of consent 161–167
mental disorder 167–168
mistake 165–166
pregnancy per alium 168–169
statutory provisions 157
unsoundness of mind 167–168
venereal disease 168
void marriage distinguished 142–144
wilful refusal to consummate 159–160

wardship
alternative jurisdiction, as an 327
effect of 324
guardian ad litem, **see guardian ad litem**
jurisdiction of the court 321–323, 326, 330–332
kidnapping 326, 333
nature of 324–325
overseas adoption 326–327
parens patriae 321
penalising an abductor 344
procedures of 324
recovery of kidnapped child 342–344

use, of 326–330, 332
welfare of the child 325, 326–330, **see also welfare of child**

welfare officer
custody cases, role in 264–267, 284

welfare of child
application 247, 326–330, 342–344
first and paramount consideration, meaning of 215–217, 223–225, 245–247, 247
hearsay in social welfare report 266
long term views 256–258, 253–254, 287
not of paramount consideration 305–307
relevant factors- 250
   age of the child 255–258
   appeal against decision 268–269
   Chinese tradition 262–263
   educational needs of child 253–254
   evolving concept 247–249
   grandparents' role 259–261
   harm or risk of harm to child 258–259
   interviewing the child 267
   material well-being 260–261
   maternal preference 255–258
   natural parents, wishes of 260
   parents, conduct of 262–263
   physical and emotional needs of the child 253–254
   presumption in favour of parents 260
   presumption in favour of primary carer 255–258, 263–264
   quality time 261–262
   sex of the child 255–258
   social welfare report, recommendation in 264–267, 284
   status quo, preserving 254–255
   wishes of child 215–217, 226–228, 251–253, 305, 307
   working parents 259, 261–262
short term view 253–254, 256–258, 287